W9-BUF-603

SUBARU | LEGACY AND FORESTER
2000-2006 REPAIR MANUAL
Deleted

Covers U.S. and Canadian models of Legacy and Forester models

Includes Legacy Outback and Baja models

by Robert Maddox

CHILTON *Automotive Books*

PUBLISHED BY **HAYNES NORTH AMERICA.** Inc.

Manufactured in USA
©2006 Haynes North America, Inc.
ISBN-13: 978-1-56392-623-5
ISBN-10: 1-56392-623-7
Library of Congress Control Number 2006930861

Haynes Publishing Group
Sparkford Nr Yeovil
Somerset BA22 7JJ England

Haynes North America, Inc
861 Lawrence Drive
Newbury Park
California 91320 USA

ABCDE
FGHIJ
KLMNO
PQRST

Chilton is a registered trademark of W.G. Nichols, Inc., and has been licensed to Haynes North America, Inc.

Contents

INTRODUCTORY PAGES

1

TUNE-UP AND ROUTINE MAINTENANCE – 1-1

2

ENGINES – 2A-1
GENERAL ENGINE OVERHAUL PROCEDURES – 2B-1

3

COOLING, HEATING AND AIR CONDITIONING SYSTEMS – 3-1

4

FUEL AND EXHAUST SYSTEMS – 4-1

5

ENGINE ELECTRICAL SYSTEMS – 5-1

6

EMISSIONS AND ENGINE CONTROL SYSTEMS – 6-1

Haynes editorial and sales staff with a 2001 Subaru Legacy

ACKNOWLEDGEMENTS

We are grateful for the help and cooperation of Fuji Heavy Industries, Ltd., for their assistance with technical information and certain illustrations. Technical writers who contributed to this project include Mike Stubblefield, John Wegmann and Joe L. Hamilton. Wiring diagrams provided exclusively for the publisher by Valley Forge Technical Information Services.

All rights reserved. No part of this book may be reproduced or transmitted in any form or by any means, electronic or mechanical, including photocopying, recording or by any information storage or retrieval system, without permission in writing from the copyright holder.

While every attempt is made to ensure that the information in this manual is correct, no liability can be accepted by the authors or publishers for loss, damage or injury caused by any errors in, or omissions from, the information given.

About this manual

ITS PURPOSE

The purpose of this manual is to help you get the best value from your vehicle. It can do so in several ways. It can help you decide what work must be done, even if you choose to have it done by a dealer service department or a repair shop; it provides information and procedures for routine maintenance and servicing; and it offers diagnostic and repair procedures to follow when trouble occurs.

We hope you use the manual to tackle the work yourself. For many simpler jobs, doing it yourself may be quicker than arranging an appointment to get the vehicle into a shop and making the trips to leave it and pick it up. More importantly, a lot of money can be saved by avoiding the expense the shop must pass on to you to cover its labor and overhead costs. An added benefit is the sense of satisfaction and accomplishment that you feel after doing the job yourself.

USING THE MANUAL

The manual is divided into Chapters. Each Chapter is divided into numbered Sections. Each Section consists of consecutively numbered paragraphs.

At the beginning of each numbered Section you will be referred to any illustrations which apply to the procedures in that Section. The reference numbers used in illustration captions pinpoint the pertinent Section and the Step within that Section. That is, illustration 3.2 means the illustration refers to Section 3 and Step (or paragraph) 2 within that Section.

Procedures, once described in the text, are not normally repeated. When it's necessary to refer to another Chapter, the reference will be given as Chapter and Section number. Cross references given without use of the word "Chapter" apply to Sections and/or paragraphs in the same Chapter. For example, "see Section 8" means in the same Chapter.

References to the left or right side of the vehicle assume you are sitting in the driver's seat, facing forward.

Even though we have prepared this manual with extreme care, neither the publisher nor the author can accept responsibility for any errors in, or omissions from, the information given.

➡NOTE

A *Note* provides information necessary to properly complete a procedure or information which will make the procedure easier to understand.

✳ CAUTION

A *Caution* provides a special procedure or special steps which must be taken while completing the procedure where the Caution is found. Not heeding a Caution can result in damage to the assembly being worked on.

✳ WARNING

A *Warning* provides a special procedure or special steps which must be taken while completing the procedure where the Warning is found. Not heeding a Warning can result in personal injury.

Introduction

Legacy and Outback models are available in four-door sedan and wagon body styles. Forester models are available in a four-door SUV body style, and Baja models are available in a four-door sedan/pickup body style.

All models are equipped with a 2.5L SOHC engine or a 2.5L DOHC turbocharged engine. Both engines use 16-valve cylinder heads and are equipped with Multipoint fuel injection systems.

Power from the engine is transferred through a five-speed manual or four-speed automatic transaxle, then through a pair of driveaxles to the front wheels. Power is also transferred through a driveshaft and a rear differential which drives the rear wheels through another pair of driveaxles.

Suspension is fully independent, utilizing MacPherson struts at the front end, steering knuckles bolted to the lower ends of the struts and connected to control arms with a balljoint. A stabilizer bar reduces vehicle roll. The rear suspension on Legacy, Outback and Baja models consists of coil-over shock absorber assemblies, trailing arms with integral knuckles, and located laterally by pair of control arms on each side. A stabilizer bar reduces vehicle roll. Forester models use MacPherson struts at the rear, two lateral links and a trailing arm per side, as well as a stabilizer bar.

The steering gear is a power assisted rack-and-pinion type that is mounted to the bottom of the front crossmember with rubber insulators.

The brakes are disc at the front and disc or drums at the rear, with power assist standard.

Vehicle Identification Numbers

Modifications are a continuing and unpublicized process in vehicle manufacturing. Since spare parts lists and manuals are compiled on a numerical basis, the individual vehicle numbers are necessary to correctly identify the component required.

VEHICLE IDENTIFICATION NUMBER (VIN)

This very important identification number is stamped on a plate

The VIN number is visible through the driver's side window

attached to the dashboard inside the windshield on the driver's side of the vehicle and on the engine compartment firewall (see illustrations). The VIN also appears on the Vehicle Certificate of Title and Registration. It contains information such as where and when the vehicle was manufactured, the model year and the body style.

VIN ENGINE AND MODEL YEAR CODES

Two particularly important pieces of information found in the VIN are the engine code and the model year code. Counting from the left, the engine code letter designation is the 6th digit and the model year code letter designation is the 10th digit.

On the models covered by this manual the engine codes are:

6 .... 2.5L

On the models covered by this manual the model year codes are:

Y	2000
1	2001
2	2002
3	2003
4	2004
5	2005
6	2006

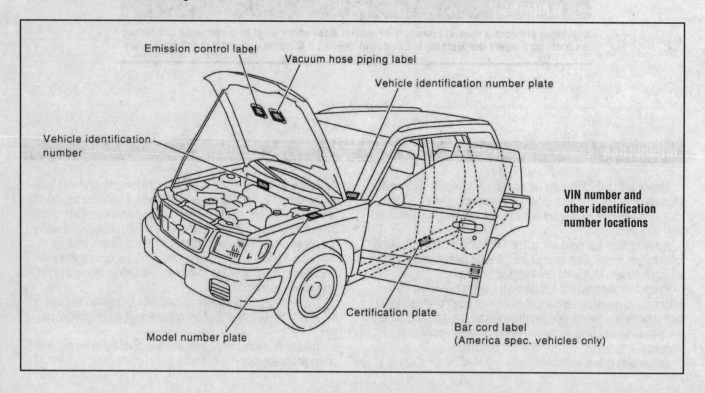

Emission control label

Vacuum hose piping label

Vehicle identification number plate

Vehicle identification number

VIN number and other identification number locations

Model number plate

Certification plate

Bar cord label (America spec. vehicles only)

The vehicle certification label is affixed the to the driver's side door pillar

The engine identification number is located on top of the block, near the transaxle

VEHICLE CERTIFICATION LABEL

The Vehicle Certification Label is attached to the driver's side door pillar (see illustration). Information on this label includes the name of the manufacturer, the month and year of production, and the Vehicle Identification Number.

ENGINE IDENTIFICATION NUMBER

The engine identification number (see illustration) is stamped onto a machined pad on the top of the engine block.

TRANSAXLE IDENTIFICATION NUMBER(S)

The transaxle ID number is located on the top of the bellhousing (see illustration).

REAR DIFFERENTIAL IDENTIFICATION NUMBER

The rear differential ID number is stamped on a tag which is affixed to the differential cover (see illustration).

On automatic and manual transaxles, the transaxle identification number is located on the top of the bellhousing

VEHICLE EMISSIONS CONTROL INFORMATION LABEL

This label is found on the underside of the hood in the engine compartment (see illustration). See Chapter 6 for more information on this label.

The rear differential identification tag is affixed to the differential cover

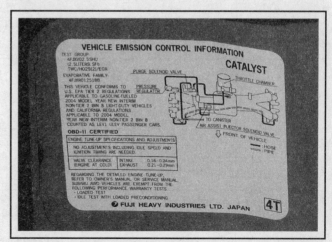

The vehicle emissions label is affixed to the underside of the hood in the engine compartment

Recall information

Vehicle recalls are carried out by the manufacturer in the rare event of a possible safety-related defect. The vehicle's registered owner is contacted at the address on file at the Department of Motor Vehicles and given the details of the recall. Remedial work is carried out free of charge at a dealer service department.

If you are the new owner of a used vehicle which was subject to a recall and you want to be sure that the work has been carried out, it's best to contact a dealer service department and ask about your indi-vidual vehicle - you'll need to furnish them your Vehicle Identification Number (VIN).

The table below is based on information provided by the National Highway Traffic Safety Administration (NHTSA), the body which over-sees vehicle recalls in the United States. The recall database is updated constantly. For the latest information on vehicle recalls, check the NHTSA website at www.nhtsa.gov, or call the NHTSA hotline at 1-888-327-4236.

Recall date	Recall campaign number	Model(s) affected	Concern
Sep 14, 1999	99V249000	2000 Legacy	Sedan L model passenger vehicles. Anti-rust coating was incorrectly applied to the transverse link mounting surface of the vehicle body. Over time the coating shrinks, causing a torque decrease of the bolt that secures the transverse link bracket to the vehicle body.
Mar 23, 2000	00V091000	2000 Legacy	The left-side steering knuckle arm was incorrectly assembled. This condition could result in a loss of steering control.
Nov 21, 2000	00V391000	2001 Legacy	Passenger vehicles. A casting flaw in the right front bearing housing could result in loss of steering if the casting flaw should exist in the tie-rod arm. This casting flaw could cause grease leakage, front wheel bearing failure due to loss of grease, or loss of steering due to tie-rod end separation.
Nov 21, 2000	00V392000	2001 Legacy	Passenger vehicles. Incorrect beige rear center seat belt webbing was installed. the belt length is too short. The seat occupant would not be properly restrained in the event of a crash.
Nov 21, 2000	00V393000	2001 Legacy	Passenger vehicles. Possible fuel leakage of under-hood fuel hoses at low ambient temperatures (-40 degrees c) once the fuel hoses age and become less flexible.
Mar 30, 2001	01V034000	2001 Legacy	Passenger vehicles equipped with manually-adjustable (non-powered) seats. Certain inner front slide rail latch mechanisms may have been improperly welded. If an inner slide rail latch mechanism breaks due to improper welding, forward and rearward seat adjustment will no longer be possible. in the event of a crash, the slide rails could break, exposing the occupant to a risk of injury.
Mar 11, 2002	02V079000	2002 Legacy 2002 Outback	On certain passenger vehicles, the brake master cylinders may not function properly in ambient temperatures below freezing (32-degrees Fahrenheit [0-degrees C] and lower).

Recall date	Recall campaign number	Model(s) affected	Concern
Sep 04, 2002	02V235000	2003 Legacy 2003 Outback	On certain passenger vehicles equipped with 6-cylinder engines, the aluminum wheels may have an off-center diameter. This can result in the eventual loosening of the wheel hub-nuts during vehicle usage, increasing the risk of a crash.
Sep 09, 2002	02V240000	2003 Legacy 2003 Outback 2003 Baja	On certain sport utility and passenger vehicles equipped with 4-cylinder engines, the water pump pulley center hole was improperly machined.
Oct 28, 2002	02V282000	2001, 2002 and 2003 Legacy 2001, 2002 and 2003 Outback 2002 and 2003 Forester 2003 Baja	Certain sport utility and passenger vehicles equipped with automatic transmissions were produced with an improperly manufactured transmission parking rod. When the transmission selector lever is placed in the "P" (park) position, the transmission park mechanism, that is intended to hold your vehicle, may not engage.
Feb 18, 2003	03V047000	2003 Forester	Certain passenger vehicles fail to comply with requirements of Federal Motor Vehicle Safety Standard no. 209, "Seat Belt Assemblies." the left and right front seat belt buckle/latch assemblies were improperly manufactured.
Apr 17, 2003	03V153000	2000, 2001, 2002 and 2003 Legacy 2000, 2001, 2002 and 2003 Outback	Certain rear suspension subframe components were produced with poor paint quality which, after continued exposure to corrosive road salts for a period of several years, could result in rust-out of the component and possible breakage of the subframe.
Aug 19, 2003	03V303000	2004 Legacy 2004 Outback	Certain passenger or sport utility vehicles may have a loose or out of position fuel filler hose clamp. This could result in fuel leakage.
Mar 10, 2004	04V128000	2001, 2002, 2003 and 2004 Legacy 2001, 2002, 2003 and 2004 Outback	On certain passenger sedans, wagons, and sport utility vehicles, the cruise control cable could come out of its track on the cruise control lever and lodge on the control lever tab when the accelerator pedal is released. If this condition occurs, the throttle will not return to the idle position and will remain in an open position.
Jun 04, 2004	04V274000	2005 Legacy 2005 Outback	The left and right side curtain air bags in certain vehicles involved in this campaign may not fully deploy rapidly enough when activated in a side impact collision. During a side impact test conducted by the Insurance Institute for Highway Safety (IIHS), the test results indicated that there was a difference between the IIHS test results and the result of side impact tests conducted by FHI.
Sep 27, 2004	04V473000	2004 Forester 2004 Baja	On certain passenger and sport utility vehicles, the cover bolts for the engine oil control valve may not be sufficiently tightened, allowing oil to leak from around the cover gasket.

Buying parts

Replacement parts are available from many sources, which generally fall into one of two categories - authorized dealer parts departments and independent retail auto parts stores. Our advice concerning these parts is as follows:

Retail auto parts stores: Good auto parts stores will stock frequently needed components which wear out relatively fast, such as clutch components, exhaust systems, brake parts, tune-up parts, etc. These stores often supply new or reconditioned parts on an exchange basis, which can save a considerable amount of money. Discount auto parts stores are often very good places to buy materials and parts needed for general vehicle maintenance such as oil, grease, filters, spark plugs, belts, touch-up paint, bulbs, etc. They also usually sell tools and general accessories, have convenient hours, charge lower prices and can often be found not far from home.

Authorized dealer parts department: This is the best source for parts which are unique to the vehicle and not generally available elsewhere (such as major engine parts, transmission parts, trim pieces, etc.).

Warranty information: If the vehicle is still covered under warranty, be sure that any replacement parts purchased - regardless of the source - do not invalidate the warranty!

To be sure of obtaining the correct parts, have engine and chassis numbers available and, if possible, take the old parts along for positive identification.

Maintenance techniques, tools and working facilities

MAINTENANCE TECHNIQUES

There are a number of techniques involved in maintenance and repair that will be referred to throughout this manual. Application of these techniques will enable the home mechanic to be more efficient, better organized and capable of performing the various tasks properly, which will ensure that the repair job is thorough and complete.

Fasteners

Fasteners are nuts, bolts, studs and screws used to hold two or more parts together. There are a few things to keep in mind when working with fasteners. Almost all of them use a locking device of some type, either a lockwasher, locknut, locking tab or thread adhesive. All threaded fasteners should be clean and straight, with undamaged threads and undamaged corners on the hex head where the wrench fits. Develop the habit of replacing all damaged nuts and bolts with new ones. Special locknuts with nylon or fiber inserts can only be used once. If they are removed, they lose their locking ability and must be replaced with new ones.

Rusted nuts and bolts should be treated with a penetrating fluid to ease removal and prevent breakage. Some mechanics use turpentine in a spout-type oil can, which works quite well. After applying the rust penetrant, let it work for a few minutes before trying to loosen the nut or bolt. Badly rusted fasteners may have to be chiseled or sawed off or removed with a special nut breaker, available at tool stores.

If a bolt or stud breaks off in an assembly, it can be drilled and removed with a special tool commonly available for this purpose. Most automotive machine shops can perform this task, as well as other repair procedures, such as the repair of threaded holes that have been stripped out.

Flat washers and lockwashers, when removed from an assembly, should always be replaced exactly as removed. Replace any damaged washers with new ones. Never use a lockwasher on any soft metal surface (such as aluminum), thin sheet metal or plastic.

Fastener sizes

For a number of reasons, automobile manufacturers are making wider and wider use of metric fasteners. Therefore, it is important to be able to tell the difference between standard (sometimes called U.S.

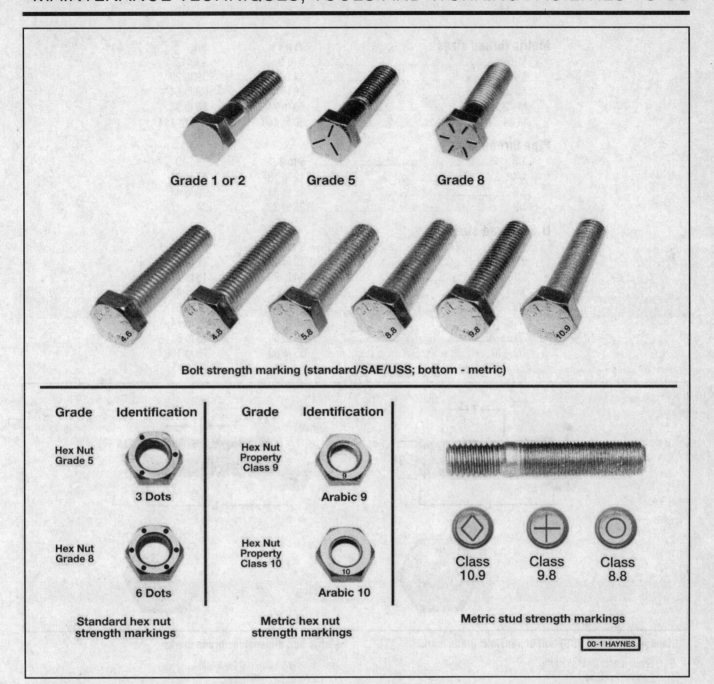

Grade 1 or 2   Grade 5   Grade 8

Bolt strength marking (standard/SAE/USS; bottom - metric)

Grade	Identification	Grade	Identification
Hex Nut Grade 5	3 Dots	Hex Nut Property Class 9	Arabic 9
Hex Nut Grade 8	6 Dots	Hex Nut Property Class 10	Arabic 10

Standard hex nut strength markings

Metric hex nut strength markings

Class 10.9   Class 9.8   Class 8.8

Metric stud strength markings

00-1 HAYNES

or SAE) and metric hardware, since they cannot be interchanged.

All bolts, whether standard or metric, are sized according to diameter, thread pitch and length. For example, a standard 1/2 - 13 x 1 bolt is 1/2 inch in diameter, has 13 threads per inch and is 1 inch long. An M12 - 1.75 x 25 metric bolt is 12 mm in diameter, has a thread pitch of 1.75 mm (the distance between threads) and is 25 mm long. The two bolts are nearly identical, and easily confused, but they are not interchangeable.

In addition to the differences in diameter, thread pitch and length, metric and standard bolts can also be distinguished by examining the bolt heads. To begin with, the distance across the flats on a standard bolt head is measured in inches, while the same dimension on a metric bolt is sized in millimeters (the same is true for nuts). As a result, a standard wrench should not be used on a metric bolt and a metric wrench should not be used on a standard bolt. Also, most standard bolts have

slashes radiating out from the center of the head to denote the grade or strength of the bolt, which is an indication of the amount of torque that can be applied to it. The greater the number of slashes, the greater the strength of the bolt. Grades 0 through 5 are commonly used on automobiles. Metric bolts have a property class (grade) number, rather than a slash, molded into their heads to indicate bolt strength. In this case, the higher the number, the stronger the bolt. Property class numbers 8.8, 9.8 and 10.9 are commonly used on automobiles.

Strength markings can also be used to distinguish standard hex nuts from metric hex nuts. Many standard nuts have dots stamped into one side, while metric nuts are marked with a number. The greater the number of dots, or the higher the number, the greater the strength of the nut.

Metric studs are also marked on their ends according to property class (grade). Larger studs are numbered (the same as metric bolts), while smaller studs carry a geometric code to denote grade.

Metric thread sizes

	Ft-lbs	Nm
M-6	6 to 9	9 to 12
M-8	14 to 21	19 to 28
M-10	28 to 40	38 to 54
M-12	50 to 71	68 to 96
M-14	80 to 140	109 to 154

Pipe thread sizes

	Ft-lbs	Nm
1/8	5 to 8	7 to 10
1/4	12 to 18	17 to 24
3/8	22 to 33	30 to 44
1/2	25 to 35	34 to 47

U.S. thread sizes

	Ft-lbs	Nm
1/4 - 20	6 to 9	9 to 12
5/16 - 18	12 to 18	17 to 24
5/16 - 24	14 to 20	19 to 27
3/8 - 16	22 to 32	30 to 43
3/8 - 24	27 to 38	37 to 51
7/16 - 14	40 to 55	55 to 74
7/16 - 20	40 to 60	55 to 81
1/2 - 13	55 to 80	75 to 108

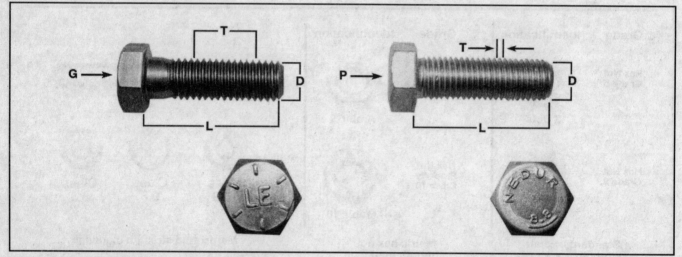

Standard (SAE and USS) bolt dimensions/grade marks

G   Grade marks (bolt strength)
L   Length (in inches)
T   Thread pitch (number of threads per inch)
D   Nominal diameter (in inches)

Metric bolt dimensions/grade marks

P   Property class (bolt strength)
L   Length (in millimeters)
T   Thread pitch (distance between threads in millimeters)
D   Diameter

It should be noted that many fasteners, especially Grades 0 through 2, have no distinguishing marks on them. When such is the case, the only way to determine whether it is standard or metric is to measure the thread pitch or compare it to a known fastener of the same size.

Standard fasteners are often referred to as SAE, as opposed to metric. However, it should be noted that SAE technically refers to a non-metric fine thread fastener only. Coarse thread non-metric fasteners are referred to as USS sizes.

Since fasteners of the same size (both standard and metric) may have different strength ratings, be sure to reinstall any bolts, studs or nuts removed from your vehicle in their original locations. Also, when replacing a fastener with a new one, make sure that the new one has a strength rating equal to or greater than the original.

Tightening sequences and procedures

Most threaded fasteners should be tightened to a specific torque value (torque is the twisting force applied to a threaded component such as a nut or bolt). Overtightening the fastener can weaken it and cause it to break, while undertightening can cause it to eventually come loose. Bolts, screws and studs, depending on the material they are made of and their thread diameters, have specific torque values, many of which are noted in the Specifications at the end of each Chapter. Be sure to follow the torque recommendations closely. For fasteners not assigned a specific torque, a general torque value chart is presented here as a guide. These torque values are for dry (unlubricated) fasteners threaded into steel or cast iron (not aluminum). As was previously mentioned, the size and grade of a fastener determine the amount of torque that can

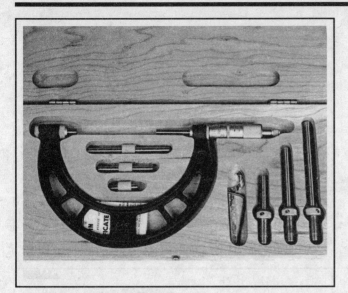

Micrometer set

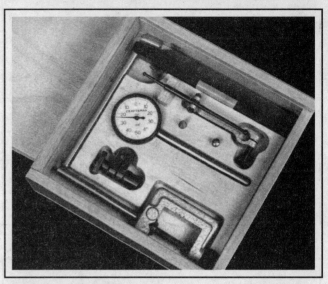

Dial indicator set

safely be applied to it. The figures listed here are approximate for Grade 2 and Grade 3 fasteners. Higher grades can tolerate higher torque values.

Fasteners laid out in a pattern, such as cylinder head bolts, oil pan bolts, differential cover bolts, etc., must be loosened or tightened in sequence to avoid warping the component. This sequence will normally be shown in the appropriate Chapter. If a specific pattern is not given, the following procedures can be used to prevent warping.

Initially, the bolts or nuts should be assembled finger-tight only. Next, they should be tightened one full turn each, in a criss-cross or diagonal pattern. After each one has been tightened one full turn, return to the first one and tighten them all one-half turn, following the same pattern. Finally, tighten each of them one-quarter turn at a time until each fastener has been tightened to the proper torque. To loosen and remove the fasteners, the procedure would be reversed.

Component disassembly

Component disassembly should be done with care and purpose to help ensure that the parts go back together properly. Always keep track of the sequence in which parts are removed. Make note of special characteristics or marks on parts that can be installed more than one way, such as a grooved thrust washer on a shaft. It is a good idea to lay the disassembled parts out on a clean surface in the order that they were removed. It may also be helpful to make sketches or take instant photos of components before removal.

When removing fasteners from a component, keep track of their locations. Sometimes threading a bolt back in a part, or putting the washers and nut back on a stud, can prevent mix-ups later. If nuts and bolts cannot be returned to their original locations, they should be kept in a compartmented box or a series of small boxes. A cupcake or muffin tin is ideal for this purpose, since each cavity can hold the bolts and nuts from a particular area (i.e. oil pan bolts, valve cover bolts, engine mount bolts, etc.). A pan of this type is especially helpful when working on assemblies with very small parts, such as the carburetor, alternator, valve train or interior dash and trim pieces. The cavities can be marked with paint or tape to identify the contents.

Whenever wiring looms, harnesses or connectors are separated, it is a good idea to identify the two halves with numbered pieces of masking tape so they can be easily reconnected.

Gasket sealing surfaces

Throughout any vehicle, gaskets are used to seal the mating surfaces between two parts and keep lubricants, fluids, vacuum or pressure contained in an assembly.

Many times these gaskets are coated with a liquid or paste-type gasket sealing compound before assembly. Age, heat and pressure can sometimes cause the two parts to stick together so tightly that they are very difficult to separate. Often, the assembly can be loosened by striking it with a soft-face hammer near the mating surfaces. A regular hammer can be used if a block of wood is placed between the hammer and the part. Do not hammer on cast parts or parts that could be easily damaged. With any particularly stubborn part, always recheck to make sure that every fastener has been removed.

Avoid using a screwdriver or bar to pry apart an assembly, as they can easily mar the gasket sealing surfaces of the parts, which must remain smooth. If prying is absolutely necessary, use an old broom handle, but keep in mind that extra clean up will be necessary if the wood splinters.

After the parts are separated, the old gasket must be carefully scraped off and the gasket surfaces cleaned. Stubborn gasket material can be soaked with rust penetrant or treated with a special chemical to soften it so it can be easily scraped off.

✳✳ CAUTION:

Never use gasket removal solutions or caustic chemicals on plastic or other composite components.

A scraper can be fashioned from a piece of copper tubing by flattening and sharpening one end. Copper is recommended because it is usually softer than the surfaces to be scraped, which reduces the chance of gouging the part. Some gaskets can be removed with a wire brush, but regardless of the method used, the mating surfaces must be left clean and smooth. If for some reason the gasket surface is gouged, then a gasket sealer thick enough to fill scratches will have to be used during reassembly of the components. For most applications, a non-drying (or semi-drying) gasket sealer should be used.

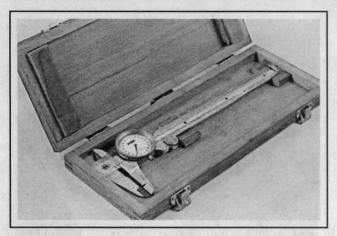

Dial caliper

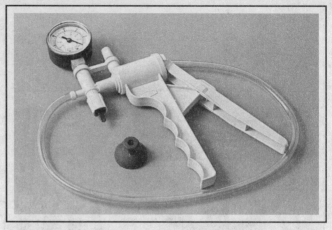

Hand-operated vacuum pump

Timing light

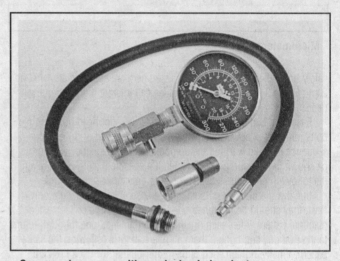

Compression gauge with spark plug hole adapter

Hose removal tips

✳✳ WARNING:

If the vehicle is equipped with air conditioning, do not disconnect any of the A/C hoses without first having the system depressurized by a dealer service department or a service station.

Hose removal precautions closely parallel gasket removal precautions. Avoid scratching or gouging the surface that the hose mates against or the connection may leak. This is especially true for radiator hoses. Because of various chemical reactions, the rubber in hoses can bond itself to the metal spigot that the hose fits over. To remove a hose, first loosen the hose clamps that secure it to the spigot. Then, with slip-joint pliers, grab the hose at the clamp and rotate it around the spigot. Work it back and forth until it is completely free, then pull it off. Silicone or other lubricants will ease removal if they can be applied between the hose and the outside of the spigot. Apply the same lubricant to the inside of the hose and the outside of the spigot to simplify installation.

As a last resort (and if the hose is to be replaced with a new one anyway), the rubber can be slit with a knife and the hose peeled from the spigot. If this must be done, be careful that the metal connection is not damaged.

If a hose clamp is broken or damaged, do not reuse it. Wire-type clamps usually weaken with age, so it is a good idea to replace them with screw-type clamps whenever a hose is removed.

TOOLS

A selection of good tools is a basic requirement for anyone who plans to maintain and repair his or her own vehicle. For the owner who has few tools, the initial investment might seem high, but when compared to the spiraling costs of professional auto maintenance and repair, it is a wise one.

To help the owner decide which tools are needed to perform the tasks detailed in this manual, the following tool lists are offered: *Maintenance and minor repair, Repair/overhaul and Special.*

The newcomer to practical mechanics should start off with the *maintenance and minor repair* tool kit, which is adequate for the simpler jobs performed on a vehicle. Then, as confidence and experience grow, the owner can tackle more difficult tasks, buying additional tools as they are needed. Eventually the basic kit will be expanded into the *repair and overhaul* tool set. Over a period of time, the experienced do-it-yourselfer will assemble a tool set complete enough for most repair and overhaul procedures and will add tools from the special category when it is felt that the expense is justified by the frequency of use.

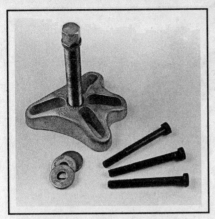

Damper/steering wheel puller

General purpose puller

Hydraulic lifter removal tool

Valve spring compressor

Valve spring compressor

Ridge reamer

Maintenance and minor repair tool kit

The tools in this list should be considered the minimum required for performance of routine maintenance, servicing and minor repair work. We recommend the purchase of combination wrenches (box-end and open-end combined in one wrench). While more expensive than open end wrenches, they offer the advantages of both types of wrench.

Combination wrench set (1/4-inch to 1 inch or 6 mm to 19 mm)
Adjustable wrench, 8 inch
Spark plug wrench with rubber insert
Spark plug gap adjusting tool
Feeler gauge set
Brake bleeder wrench
Standard screwdriver (5/16-inch x 6 inch)
Phillips screwdriver (No. 2 x 6 inch)
Combination pliers - 6 inch
Hacksaw and assortment of blades
Tire pressure gauge
Grease gun
Oil can
Fine emery cloth
Wire brush
Battery post and cable cleaning tool
Oil filter wrench
Funnel (medium size)
Safety goggles
Jackstands (2)
Drain pan

➡**Note: If basic tune-ups are going to be part of routine maintenance, it will be necessary to purchase a good quality stroboscopic timing light and combination tachometer/dwell meter. Although they are included in the list of special tools, it is mentioned here because they are absolutely necessary for tuning most vehicles properly.**

Repair and overhaul tool set

These tools are essential for anyone who plans to perform major repairs and are in addition to those in the maintenance and minor repair tool kit. Included is a comprehensive set of sockets which, though expensive, are invaluable because of their versatility, especially when various extensions and drives are available. We recommend the 1/2-inch drive over the 3/8-inch drive. Although the larger drive is bulky and more expensive, it has the capacity of accepting a very wide range of large sockets. Ideally, however, the mechanic should have a 3/8-inch drive set and a 1/2-inch drive set.

Socket set(s)
Reversible ratchet
Extension - 10 inch
Universal joint
Torque wrench (same size drive as sockets)
Ball peen hammer - 8 ounce
Soft-face hammer (plastic/rubber)
Standard screwdriver (1/4-inch x 6 inch)
Standard screwdriver (stubby - 5/16-inch)
Phillips screwdriver (No. 3 x 8 inch)
Phillips screwdriver (stubby - No. 2)
Pliers - vise grip

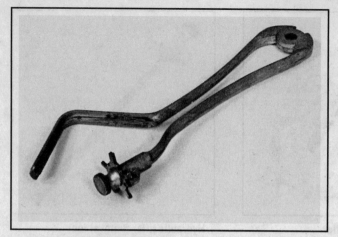

Piston ring groove cleaning tool

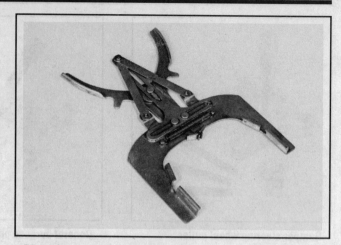

Ring removal/installation tool

Ring compressor

Cylinder hone

Brake hold-down spring tool

Pliers - lineman's
Pliers - needle nose
Pliers - snap-ring (internal and external)
Cold chisel - 1/2-inch
Scribe
Scraper (made from flattened copper tubing)
Centerpunch
Pin punches (1/16, 1/8, 3/16-inch)
Steel rule/straightedge - 12 inch
Allen wrench set (1/8 to 3/8-inch or 4 mm to 10 mm)
A selection of files
Wire brush (large)
Jackstands (second set)
Jack (scissor or hydraulic type)

➡**Note: Another tool which is often useful is an electric drill with a chuck capacity of 3/8-inch and a set of good quality drill bits.**

Special tools

The tools in this list include those which are not used regularly, are expensive to buy, or which need to be used in accordance with their manufacturer's instructions. Unless these tools will be used frequently, it is not very economical to purchase many of them. A consideration would be to split the cost and use between yourself and a friend or friends. In addition, most of these tools can be obtained from a tool rental shop on a temporary basis.

This list primarily contains only those tools and instruments widely available to the public, and not those special tools produced by the vehicle manufacturer for distribution to dealer service depart-

ments. Occasionally, references to the manufacturer's special tools are included in the text of this manual. Generally, an alternative method of doing the job without the special tool is offered. However, sometimes there is no alternative to their use. Where this is the case, and the tool cannot be purchased or borrowed, the work should be turned over to the dealer service department or an automotive repair shop.

Valve spring compressor
Piston ring groove cleaning tool
Piston ring compressor
Piston ring installation tool
Cylinder compression gauge
Cylinder ridge reamer
Cylinder surfacing hone
Cylinder bore gauge
Micrometers and/or dial calipers
Hydraulic lifter removal tool
Balljoint separator
Universal-type puller
Impact screwdriver
Dial indicator set
Stroboscopic timing light (inductive pick-up)
Hand operated vacuum/pressure pump
Tachometer/dwell meter
Universal electrical multimeter
Cable hoist
Brake spring removal and installation tools
Floor jack

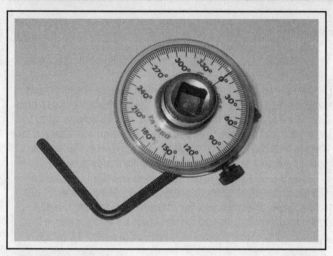

Torque angle gauge

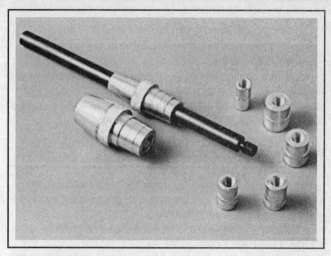

Clutch plate alignment tool

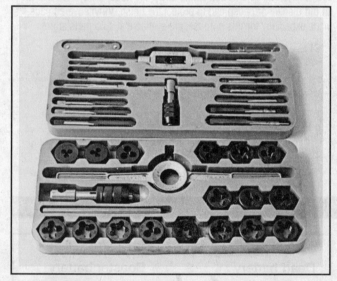

Tap and die set

Buying tools

For the do-it-yourselfer who is just starting to get involved in vehicle maintenance and repair, there are a number of options available when purchasing tools. If maintenance and minor repair is the extent of the work to be done, the purchase of individual tools is satisfactory. If, on the other hand, extensive work is planned, it would be a good idea to purchase a modest tool set from one of the large retail chain stores. A set can usually be bought at a substantial savings over the individual tool prices, and they often come with a tool box. As additional tools are needed, add-on sets, individual tools and a larger tool box can be purchased to expand the tool selection. Building a tool set gradually allows the cost of the tools to be spread over a longer period of time and gives the mechanic the freedom to choose only those tools that will actually be used.

Tool stores will often be the only source of some of the special tools that are needed, but regardless of where tools are bought, try to avoid cheap ones, especially when buying screwdrivers and sockets, because they won't last very long. The expense involved in replacing cheap tools will eventually be greater than the initial cost of quality tools.

Care and maintenance of tools

Good tools are expensive, so it makes sense to treat them with respect. Keep them clean and in usable condition and store them properly when not in use. Always wipe off any dirt, grease or metal chips before putting them away. Never leave tools lying around in the work area. Upon completion of a job, always check closely under the hood for tools that may have been left there so they won't get lost during a test drive.

Some tools, such as screwdrivers, pliers, wrenches and sockets, can be hung on a panel mounted on the garage or workshop wall, while others should be kept in a tool box or tray. Measuring instruments, gauges, meters, etc. must be carefully stored where they cannot be damaged by weather or impact from other tools.

When tools are used with care and stored properly, they will last a very long time. Even with the best of care, though, tools will wear out if used frequently. When a tool is damaged or worn out, replace it. Subsequent jobs will be safer and more enjoyable if you do.

HOW TO REPAIR DAMAGED THREADS

Sometimes, the internal threads of a nut or bolt hole can become stripped, usually from overtightening. Stripping threads is an all-too-common occurrence, especially when working with aluminum parts, because aluminum is so soft that it easily strips out.

Usually, external or internal threads are only partially stripped. After they've been cleaned up with a tap or die, they'll still work. Sometimes, however, threads are badly damaged. When this happens, you've got three choices:

1) *Drill and tap the hole to the next suitable oversize and install a larger diameter bolt, screw or stud.*

2) *Drill and tap the hole to accept a threaded plug, then drill and tap the plug to the original screw size. You can also buy a plug already threaded to the original size. Then you simply drill a hole to the specified size, then run the threaded plug into the hole with a bolt and jam nut. Once the plug is fully seated, remove the jam nut and bolt.*

3) *The third method uses a patented thread repair kit like Heli-Coil or Slimsert. These easy-to-use kits are designed to repair damaged threads in straight-through holes and blind holes. Both are available as kits which can handle a variety of sizes and thread*

patterns. Drill the hole, then tap it with the special included tap. Install the Heli-Coil and the hole is back to its original diameter and thread pitch.

Regardless of which method you use, be sure to proceed calmly and carefully. A little impatience or carelessness during one of these relatively simple procedures can ruin your whole day's work and cost you a bundle if you wreck an expensive part.

WORKING FACILITIES

Not to be overlooked when discussing tools is the workshop. If anything more than routine maintenance is to be carried out, some sort of suitable work area is essential.

It is understood, and appreciated, that many home mechanics do not have a good workshop or garage available, and end up removing an engine or doing major repairs outside. It is recommended, however, that the overhaul or repair be completed under the cover of a roof.

A clean, flat workbench or table of comfortable working height is an absolute necessity. The workbench should be equipped with a vise that has a jaw opening of at least four inches.

As mentioned previously, some clean, dry storage space is also required for tools, as well as the lubricants, fluids, cleaning solvents, etc. which soon become necessary.

Sometimes waste oil and fluids, drained from the engine or cooling system during normal maintenance or repairs, present a disposal problem. To avoid pouring them on the ground or into a sewage system, pour the used fluids into large containers, seal them with caps and take them to an authorized disposal site or recycling center. Plastic jugs, such as old antifreeze containers, are ideal for this purpose.

Always keep a supply of old newspapers and clean rags available. Old towels are excellent for mopping up spills. Many mechanics use rolls of paper towels for most work because they are readily available and disposable. To help keep the area under the vehicle clean, a large cardboard box can be cut open and flattened to protect the garage or shop floor.

Whenever working over a painted surface, such as when leaning over a fender to service something under the hood, always cover it with an old blanket or bedspread to protect the finish. Vinyl covered pads, made especially for this purpose, are available at auto parts stores.

Booster battery (jump) starting

Observe these precautions when using a booster battery to start a vehicle:

a) *Before connecting the booster battery, make sure the ignition switch is in the Off position.*
b) *Turn off the lights, heater and other electrical loads.*
c) *Your eyes should be shielded. Safety goggles are a good idea.*
d) *Make sure the booster battery is the same voltage as the dead one in the vehicle.*
e) *The two vehicles MUST NOT TOUCH each other!*
f) *Make sure the transaxle is in Neutral (manual) or Park (automatic).*
g) *If the booster battery is not a maintenance-free type, remove the vent caps and lay a cloth over the vent holes.*

Connect the red jumper cable to the positive (+) terminals of each battery (see illustration).

Connect one end of the black jumper cable to the negative (-) terminal of the booster battery. The other end of this cable should be connected to a good ground on the vehicle to be started, such as a bolt or bracket on the body.

Start the engine using the booster battery, then, with the engine running at idle speed, disconnect the jumper cables in the reverse order of connection.

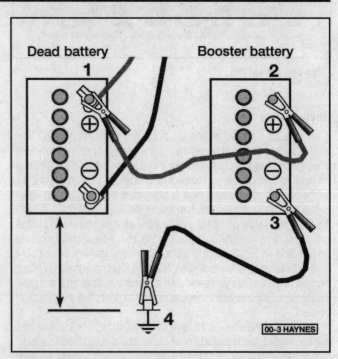

Make the booster battery cable connections in the numerical order shown (note that the negative cable of the booster battery is NOT attached to the negative terminal of the dead battery)

Jacking and towing

JACKING

✳✳ WARNING:

The jack supplied with the vehicle should only be used for changing a tire or placing jackstands under the frame. Never work under the vehicle or start the engine while this jack is being used as the only means of support.

The vehicle should be on level ground. Place the shift lever in Park, if you have an automatic, or Reverse if you have a manual transaxle. Block the wheel diagonally opposite the wheel being changed. Set the parking brake.

Remove the spare tire and jack from stowage. Remove the wheel cover and trim ring (if so equipped) with the tapered end of the lug nut

Front jacking point - place the jack so it engages the notch in the rocker panel (the rear jacking point, which is located just in front of the rear wheels, has a similar notch)

wrench by inserting and twisting the handle and then prying against the back of the wheel cover. Loosen the wheel lug nuts about 1/4-to-1/2 turn each.

Place the scissors-type jack under the side of the vehicle and adjust the jack height until it fits in the notch in the vertical rocker panel flange nearest the wheel to be changed. There is a front and rear jacking point on each side of the vehicle (see illustration).

Turn the jack handle clockwise until the tire clears the ground. Remove the lug nuts and pull the wheel off. Replace it with the spare.

Install the lug nuts with the beveled edges facing in. Tighten them snugly. Don't attempt to tighten them completely until the vehicle is lowered or it could slip off the jack. Turn the jack handle counterclockwise to lower the vehicle. Remove the jack and tighten the lug nuts in a diagonal pattern.

Install the cover (and trim ring, if used) and be sure it's snapped into place all the way around.

Stow the tire, jack and wrench. Unblock the wheels.

TOWING

The vehicle can be towed with all four wheels on the ground, as long as speeds do not exceed 20 mph and the distance is not over six miles.

For distances exceeding six miles, the preferred method for towing these models is on a flat-bed tow truck. Tow trucks that use wheel-lift or sling-type equipment cannot be used.

While towing, the parking brake should be fully released and the transaxle should be in Neutral. The steering must be unlocked (ignition switch in the Off position). Remember that power steering and power brakes will not work with engine off and never use the tie-down tabs to tow another vehicle.

Safety is a major consideration when towing and all applicable state and local laws must be obeyed. A safety chain system must be used at all times. Remember that power steering and power brakes will not work with the engine off.

Automotive chemicals and lubricants

A number of automotive chemicals and lubricants are available for use during vehicle maintenance and repair. They include a wide variety of products ranging from cleaning solvents and degreasers to lubricants and protective sprays for rubber, plastic and vinyl.

CLEANERS

Carburetor cleaner and choke cleaner is a strong solvent for gum, varnish and carbon. Most carburetor cleaners leave a dry-type lubricant film which will not harden or gum up. Because of this film it is not recommended for use on electrical components.

Brake system cleaner is used to remove brake dust, grease and brake fluid from the brake system, where clean surfaces are absolutely necessary. It leaves no residue and often eliminates brake squeal caused by contaminants.

Electrical cleaner removes oxidation, corrosion and carbon deposits from electrical contacts, restoring full current flow. It can also be used to clean spark plugs, carburetor jets, voltage regulators and other parts where an oil-free surface is desired.

Demoisturants remove water and moisture from electrical components such as alternators, voltage regulators, electrical connectors and fuse blocks. They are non-conductive and non-corrosive.

Degreasers are heavy-duty solvents used to remove grease from the outside of the engine and from chassis components. They can be sprayed or brushed on and, depending on the type, are rinsed off either with water or solvent.

LUBRICANTS

Motor oil is the lubricant formulated for use in engines. It normally contains a wide variety of additives to prevent corrosion and reduce foaming and wear. Motor oil comes in various weights (viscosity ratings) from 0 to 50. The recommended weight of the oil depends on the season, temperature and the demands on the engine. Light oil is used in cold climates and under light load conditions. Heavy oil is used in hot climates and where high loads are encountered. Multi-viscosity oils are designed to have characteristics of both light and heavy oils and are available in a number of weights from 5W-20 to 20W-50.

Gear oil is designed to be used in differentials, manual transmissions and other areas where high-temperature lubrication is required.

Chassis and wheel bearing grease is a heavy grease used where increased loads and friction are encountered, such as for wheel bearings, balljoints, tie-rod ends and universal joints.

High-temperature wheel bearing grease is designed to withstand the extreme temperatures encountered by wheel bearings in disc brake equipped vehicles. It usually contains molybdenum disulfide (moly), which is a dry-type lubricant.

White grease is a heavy grease for metal-to-metal applications where water is a problem. White grease stays soft under both low and high temperatures (usually from -100 to +190-degrees F), and will not wash off or dilute in the presence of water.

Assembly lube is a special extreme pressure lubricant, usually containing moly, used to lubricate high-load parts (such as main and rod bearings and cam lobes) for initial start-up of a new engine. The assembly lube lubricates the parts without being squeezed out or washed away until the engine oiling system begins to function.

Silicone lubricants are used to protect rubber, plastic, vinyl and nylon parts.

Graphite lubricants are used where oils cannot be used due to contamination problems, such as in locks. The dry graphite will lubricate metal parts while remaining uncontaminated by dirt, water, oil or acids. It is electrically conductive and will not foul electrical contacts in locks such as the ignition switch.

Moly penetrants loosen and lubricate frozen, rusted and corroded fasteners and prevent future rusting or freezing.

Heat-sink grease is a special electrically non-conductive grease that is used for mounting electronic ignition modules where it is essential that heat is transferred away from the module.

SEALANTS

RTV sealant is one of the most widely used gasket compounds. Made from silicone, RTV is air curing, it seals, bonds, waterproofs, fills surface irregularities, remains flexible, doesn't shrink, is relatively easy to remove, and is used as a supplementary sealer with almost all low and medium temperature gaskets.

Anaerobic sealant is much like RTV in that it can be used either to seal gaskets or to form gaskets by itself. It remains flexible, is solvent resistant and fills surface imperfections. The difference between an anaerobic sealant and an RTV-type sealant is in the curing. RTV cures when exposed to air, while an anaerobic sealant cures only in the absence of air. This means that an anaerobic sealant cures only after the assembly of parts, sealing them together.

Thread and pipe sealant is used for sealing hydraulic and pneumatic fittings and vacuum lines. It is usually made from a Teflon compound, and comes in a spray, a paint-on liquid and as a wrap-around tape.

CHEMICALS

Anti-seize compound prevents seizing, galling, cold welding, rust and corrosion in fasteners. High-temperature anti-seize, usually made with copper and graphite lubricants, is used for exhaust system and exhaust manifold bolts.

Anaerobic locking compounds are used to keep fasteners from vibrating or working loose and cure only after installation, in the absence of air. Medium strength locking compound is used for small nuts, bolts and screws that may be removed later. High-strength locking compound is for large nuts, bolts and studs which aren't removed on a regular basis.

Oil additives range from viscosity index improvers to chemical treatments that claim to reduce internal engine friction. It should be noted that most oil manufacturers caution against using additives with their oils.

Gas additives perform several functions, depending on their chemical makeup. They usually contain solvents that help dissolve gum and varnish that build up on carburetor, fuel injection and intake parts. They also serve to break down carbon deposits that form on the inside surfaces of the combustion chambers. Some additives contain upper cylinder lubricants for valves and piston rings, and others contain chemicals to remove condensation from the gas tank.

MISCELLANEOUS

Brake fluid is specially formulated hydraulic fluid that can withstand the heat and pressure encountered in brake systems. Care must be taken so this fluid does not come in contact with painted surfaces or plastics. An opened container should always be resealed to prevent contamination by water or dirt.

Weatherstrip adhesive is used to bond weatherstripping around doors, windows and trunk lids. It is sometimes used to attach trim pieces.

Undercoating is a petroleum-based, tar-like substance that is designed to protect metal surfaces on the underside of the vehicle from corrosion. It also acts as a sound-deadening agent by insulating the bottom of the vehicle.

Waxes and polishes are used to help protect painted and plated surfaces from the weather. Different types of paint may require the use of different types of wax and polish. Some polishes utilize a chemical or abrasive cleaner to help remove the top layer of oxidized (dull) paint on older vehicles. In recent years many non-wax polishes that contain a wide variety of chemicals such as polymers and silicones have been introduced. These non-wax polishes are usually easier to apply and last longer than conventional waxes and polishes.

CONVERSION FACTORS

LENGTH (distance)

Inches (in)	X 25.4	= Millimeters (mm)	X 0.0394	= Inches (in)
Feet (ft)	X 0.305	= Meters (m)	X 3.281	= Feet (ft)
Miles	X 1.609	= Kilometers (km)	X 0.621	= Miles

VOLUME (capacity)

Cubic inches (cu in; in^3)	X 16.387	= Cubic centimeters (cc; cm^3)	X 0.061	= Cubic inches (cu in; in^3)
Imperial pints (Imp pt)	X 0.568	= Liters (l)	X 1.76	= Imperial pints (Imp pt)
Imperial quarts (Imp qt)	X 1.137	= Liters (l)	X 0.88	= Imperial quarts (Imp qt)
Imperial quarts (Imp qt)	X 1.201	= US quarts (US qt)	X 0.833	= Imperial quarts (Imp qt)
US quarts (US qt)	X 0.946	= Liters (l)	X 1.057	= US quarts (US qt)
Imperial gallons (Imp gal)	X 4.546	= Liters (l)	X 0.22	= Imperial gallons (Imp gal)
Imperial gallons (Imp gal)	X 1.201	= US gallons (US gal)	X 0.833	= Imperial gallons (Imp gal)
US gallons (US gal)	X 3.785	= Liters (l)	X 0.264	= US gallons (US gal)

MASS (weight)

Ounces (oz)	X 28.35	= Grams (g)	X 0.035	= Ounces (oz)
Pounds (lb)	X 0.454	= Kilograms (kg)	X 2.205	= Pounds (lb)

FORCE

Ounces-force (ozf; oz)	X 0.278	= Newtons (N)	X 3.6	= Ounces-force (ozf; oz)
Pounds-force (lbf; lb)	X 4.448	= Newtons (N)	X 0.225	= Pounds-force (lbf; lb)
Newtons (N)	X 0.1	= Kilograms-force (kgf; kg)	X 9.81	= Newtons (N)

PRESSURE

Pounds-force per square inch (psi; lbf/in^2; lb/in^2)	X 0.070	= Kilograms-force per square centimeter (kgf/cm^2; kg/cm^2)	X 14.223	= Pounds-force per square inch (psi; lbf/in^2; lb/in^2)
Pounds-force per square inch (psi; lbf/in^2; lb/in^2)	X 0.068	= Atmospheres (atm)	X 14.696	= Pounds-force per square inch (psi; lbf/in^2; lb/in^2)
Pounds-force per square inch (psi; lbf/in^2; lb/in^2)	X 0.069	= Bars	X 14.5	= Pounds-force per square inch (psi; lbf/in^2; lb/in^2)
Pounds-force per square inch (psi; lbf/in^2; lb/in^2)	X 6.895	= Kilopascals (kPa)	X 0.145	= Pounds-force per square inch (psi; lbf/in^2; lb/in^2)
Kilopascals (kPa)	X 0.01	= Kilograms-force per square centimeter (kgf/cm^2; kg/cm^2)	X 98.1	= Kilopascals (kPa)

TORQUE (moment of force)

Pounds-force inches (lbf in; lb in)	X 1.152	= Kilograms-force centimeter (kgf cm; kg cm)	X 0.868	= Pounds-force inches (lbf in; lb in)
Pounds-force inches (lbf in; lb in)	X 0.113	= Newton meters (Nm)	X 8.85	= Pounds-force inches (lbf in; lb in)
Pounds-force inches (lbf in; lb in)	X 0.083	= Pounds-force feet (lbf ft; lb ft)	X 12	= Pounds-force inches (lbf in; lb in)
Pounds-force feet (lbf ft; lb ft)	X 0.138	= Kilograms-force meters (kgf m; kg m)	X 7.233	= Pounds-force feet (lbf ft; lb ft)
Pounds-force feet (lbf ft; lb ft)	X 1.356	= Newton meters (Nm)	X 0.738	= Pounds-force feet (lbf ft; lb ft)
Newton meters (Nm)	X 0.102	= Kilograms-force meters (kgf m; kg m)	X 9.804	= Newton meters (Nm)

VACUUM

Inches mercury (in. Hg)	X 3.377	= Kilopascals (kPa)	X 0.2961	= Inches mercury
Inches mercury (in. Hg)	X 25.4	= Millimeters mercury (mm Hg)	X 0.0394	= Inches mercury

POWER

Horsepower (hp)	X 745.7	= Watts (W)	X 0.0013	= Horsepower (hp)

VELOCITY (speed)

Miles per hour (miles/hr; mph)	X 1.609	= Kilometers per hour (km/hr; kph)	X 0.621	= Miles per hour (miles/hr; mph)

FUEL CONSUMPTION *

Miles per gallon, Imperial (mpg)	X 0.354	= Kilometers per liter (km/l)	X 2.825	= Miles per gallon, Imperial (mpg)
Miles per gallon, US (mpg)	X 0.425	= Kilometers per liter (km/l)	X 2.352	= Miles per gallon, US (mpg)

TEMPERATURE

Degrees Fahrenheit = (°C x 1.8) + 32   Degrees Celsius (Degrees Centigrade; °C) = (°F - 32) x 0.56

*It is common practice to convert from miles per gallon (mpg) to liters/100 kilometers (l/100km), where mpg (Imperial) x l/100 km = 282 and mpg (US) x l/100 km = 235

FRACTION/DECIMAL/MILLIMETER EQUIVALENTS

DECIMALS to MILLIMETERS

Decimal	mm	Decimal	mm
0.001	0.0254	0.500	12.7000
0.002	0.0508	0.510	12.9540
0.003	0.0762	0.520	13.2080
0.004	0.1016	0.530	13.4620
0.005	0.1270	0.540	13.7160
0.006	0.1524	0.550	13.9700
0.007	0.1778	0.560	14.2240
0.008	0.2032	0.570	14.4780
0.009	0.2286	0.580	14.7320
		0.590	14.9860
0.010	0.2540		
0.020	0.5080		
0.030	0.7620		
0.040	1.0160	0.600	15.2400
0.050	1.2700	0.610	15.4940
0.060	1.5240	0.620	15.7480
0.070	1.7780	0.630	16.0020
0.080	2.0320	0.640	16.2560
0.090	2.2860	0.650	16.5100
		0.660	16.7640
0.100	2.5400	0.670	17.0180
0.110	2.7940	0.680	17.2720
0.120	3.0480	0.690	17.5260
0.130	3.3020		
0.140	3.5560		
0.150	3.8100		
0.160	4.0640	0.700	17.7800
0.170	4.3180	0.710	18.0340
0.180	4.5720	0.720	18.2880
0.190	4.8260	0.730	18.5420
		0.740	18.7960
0.200	5.0800	0.750	19.0500
0.210	5.3340	0.760	19.3040
0.220	5.5880	0.770	19.5580
0.230	5.8420	0.780	19.8120
0.240	6.0960	0.790	20.0660
0.250	6.3500		
0.260	6.6040		
0.270	6.8580	0.800	20.3200
0.280	7.1120	0.810	20.5740
0.290	7.3660	0.820	21.8280
		0.830	21.0820
0.300	7.6200	0.840	21.3360
0.310	7.8740	0.850	21.5900
0.320	8.1280	0.860	21.8440
0.330	8.3820	0.870	22.0980
0.340	8.6360	0.880	22.3520
0.350	8.8900	0.890	22.6060
0.360	9.1440		
0.370	9.3980		
0.380	9.6520		
0.390	9.9060		
		0.900	22.8600
0.400	10.1600	0.910	23.1140
0.410	10.4140	0.920	23.3680
0.420	10.6680	0.930	23.6220
0.430	10.9220	0.940	23.8760
0.440	11.1760	0.950	24.1300
0.450	11.4300	0.960	24.3840
0.460	11.6840	0.970	24.6380
0.470	11.9380	0.980	24.8920
0.480	12.1920	0.990	25.1460
0.490	12.4460	1.000	25.4000

FRACTIONS to DECIMALS to MILLIMETERS

Fraction	Decimal	mm	Fraction	Decimal	mm
1/64	0.0156	0.3969	33/64	0.5156	13.0969
1/32	0.0312	0.7938	17/32	0.5312	13.4938
3/64	0.0469	1.1906	35/64	0.5469	13.8906
1/16	0.0625	1.5875	9/16	0.5625	14.2875
5/64	0.0781	1.9844	37/64	0.5781	14.6844
3/32	0.0938	2.3812	19/32	0.5938	15.0812
7/64	0.1094	2.7781	39/64	0.6094	15.4781
1/8	0.1250	3.1750	5/8	0.6250	15.8750
9/64	0.1406	3.5719	41/64	0.6406	16.2719
5/32	0.1562	3.9688	21/32	0.6562	16.6688
11/64	0.1719	4.3656	43/64	0.6719	17.0656
3/16	0.1875	4.7625	11/16	0.6875	17.4625
13/64	0.2031	5.1594	45/64	0.7031	17.8594
7/32	0.2188	5.5562	23/32	0.7188	18.2562
15/64	0.2344	5.9531	47/64	0.7344	18.6531
1/4	0.2500	6.3500	3/4	0.7500	19.0500
17/64	0.2656	6.7469	49/64	0.7656	19.4469
9/32	0.2812	7.1438	25/32	0.7812	19.8438
19/64	0.2969	7.5406	51/64	0.7969	20.2406
5/16	0.3125	7.9375	13/16	0.8125	20.6375
21/64	0.3281	8.3344	53/64	0.8281	21.0344
11/32	0.3438	8.7312	27/32	0.8438	21.4312
23/64	0.3594	9.1281	55/64	0.8594	21.8281
3/8	0.3750	9.5250	7/8	0.8750	22.2250
25/64	0.3906	9.9219	57/64	0.8906	22.6219
13/32	0.4062	10.3188	29/32	0.9062	23.0188
27/64	0.4219	10.7156	59/64	0.9219	23.4156
7/16	0.4375	11.1125	15/16	0.9375	23.8125
29/64	0.4531	11.5094	61/64	0.9531	24.2094
15/32	0.4688	11.9062	31/32	0.9688	24.6062
31/64	0.4844	12.3031	63/64	0.9844	25.0031
1/2	0.5000	12.7000	1	1.0000	25.4000

Safety first!

Regardless of how enthusiastic you may be about getting on with the job at hand, take the time to ensure that your safety is not jeopardized. A moment's lack of attention can result in an accident, as can failure to observe certain simple safety precautions. The possibility of an accident will always exist, and the following points should not be considered a comprehensive list of all dangers. Rather, they are intended to make you aware of the risks and to encourage a safety conscious approach to all work you carry out on your vehicle.

ESSENTIAL DOS AND DON'TS

DON'T rely on a jack when working under the vehicle. Always use approved jackstands to support the weight of the vehicle and place them under the recommended lift or support points.

DON'T attempt to loosen extremely tight fasteners (i.e. wheel lug nuts) while the vehicle is on a jack - it may fall.

DON'T start the engine without first making sure that the transmission is in Neutral (or Park where applicable) and the parking brake is set.

DON'T remove the radiator cap from a hot cooling system - let it cool or cover it with a cloth and release the pressure gradually.

DON'T attempt to drain the engine oil until you are sure it has cooled to the point that it will not burn you.

DON'T touch any part of the engine or exhaust system until it has cooled sufficiently to avoid burns.

DON'T siphon toxic liquids such as gasoline, antifreeze and brake fluid by mouth, or allow them to remain on your skin.

DON'T inhale brake lining dust - it is potentially hazardous (see *Asbestos* below).

DON'T allow spilled oil or grease to remain on the floor - wipe it up before someone slips on it.

DON'T use loose fitting wrenches or other tools which may slip and cause injury.

DON'T push on wrenches when loosening or tightening nuts or bolts. Always try to pull the wrench toward you. If the situation calls for pushing the wrench away, push with an open hand to avoid scraped knuckles if the wrench should slip.

DON'T attempt to lift a heavy component alone - get someone to help you.

DON'T rush or take unsafe shortcuts to finish a job.

DON'T allow children or animals in or around the vehicle while you are working on it.

DO wear eye protection when using power tools such as a drill, sander, bench grinder, etc. and when working under a vehicle.

DO keep loose clothing and long hair well out of the way of moving parts.

DO make sure that any hoist used has a safe working load rating adequate for the job.

DO get someone to check on you periodically when working alone on a vehicle.

DO carry out work in a logical sequence and make sure that everything is correctly assembled and tightened.

DO keep chemicals and fluids tightly capped and out of the reach of children and pets.

DO remember that your vehicle's safety affects that of yourself and others. If in doubt on any point, get professional advice.

ASBESTOS

Certain friction, insulating, sealing, and other products - such as brake linings, brake bands, clutch linings, torque converters, gaskets, etc. - may contain asbestos. Extreme care must be taken to avoid inhalation of dust from such products, since it is hazardous to health. If in doubt, assume that they do contain asbestos.

FIRE

Remember at all times that gasoline is highly flammable. Never smoke or have any kind of open flame around when working on a vehicle. But the risk does not end there. A spark caused by an electrical short circuit, by two metal surfaces contacting each other, or even by static electricity built up in your body under certain conditions, can ignite gasoline vapors, which in a confined space are highly explosive. Do not, under any circumstances, use gasoline for cleaning parts. Use an approved safety solvent.

Always disconnect the battery ground (-) cable at the battery before working on any part of the fuel system or electrical system. Never risk spilling fuel on a hot engine or exhaust component. It is strongly recommended that a fire extinguisher suitable for use on fuel and electrical fires be kept handy in the garage or workshop at all times. Never try to extinguish a fuel or electrical fire with water.

FUMES

Certain fumes are highly toxic and can quickly cause unconsciousness and even death if inhaled to any extent. Gasoline vapor falls into this category, as do the vapors from some cleaning solvents. Any draining or pouring of such volatile fluids should be done in a well ventilated area.

When using cleaning fluids and solvents, read the instructions on the container carefully. Never use materials from unmarked containers.

Never run the engine in an enclosed space, such as a garage. Exhaust fumes contain carbon monoxide, which is extremely poisonous. If you need to run the engine, always do so in the open air, or at least have the rear of the vehicle outside the work area.

If you are fortunate enough to have the use of an inspection pit, never drain or pour gasoline and never run the engine while the vehicle is over the pit. The fumes, being heavier than air, will concentrate in the pit with possibly lethal results.

THE BATTERY

Never create a spark or allow a bare light bulb near a battery. They normally give off a certain amount of hydrogen gas, which is highly explosive.

Always disconnect the battery ground (-) cable at the battery before working on the fuel or electrical systems.

If possible, loosen the filler caps or cover when charging the battery from an external source (this does not apply to sealed or maintenance-free batteries). Do not charge at an excessive rate or the battery may burst.

Take care when adding water to a non maintenance-free battery and when carrying a battery. The electrolyte, even when diluted, is very corrosive and should not be allowed to contact clothing or skin.

Always wear eye protection when cleaning the battery to prevent the caustic deposits from entering your eyes.

HOUSEHOLD CURRENT

When using an electric power tool, inspection light, etc., which operates on household current, always make sure that the tool is correctly connected to its plug and that, where necessary, it is properly grounded. Do not use such items in damp conditions and, again, do not create a spark or apply excessive heat in the vicinity of fuel or fuel vapor.

SECONDARY IGNITION SYSTEM VOLTAGE

A severe electric shock can result from touching certain parts of the ignition system (such as the spark plug wires) when the engine is running or being cranked, particularly if components are damp or the insulation is defective. In the case of an electronic ignition system, the secondary system voltage is much higher and could prove fatal.

Troubleshooting

CONTENTS

Section Symptom

Engine

1 Engine will not rotate when attempting to start
2 Engine rotates but will not start
3 Engine hard to start when cold
4 Engine hard to start when hot
5 Starter motor noisy or excessively rough in engagement
6 Engine starts but stops immediately
7 Oil puddle under engine
8 Engine lopes while idling or idles erratically
9 Engine misses at idle speed
10 Engine misses throughout driving speed range
11 Engine stumbles on acceleration
12 Engine surges while holding accelerator steady
13 Engine stalls
14 Engine lacks power
15 Engine backfires
16 Pinging or knocking engine sounds during acceleration or uphill
17 Engine runs with oil pressure light on
18 Engine diesels (continues to run) after switching off

Engine electrical system

19 Battery will not hold a charge
20 Alternator light fails to go out
21 Alternator light fails to come on when key is turned on

Fuel system

22 Excessive fuel consumption
23 Fuel leakage and/or fuel odor

Cooling system

24 Overheating
25 Overcooling
26 External coolant leakage
27 Internal coolant leakage
28 Coolant loss
29 Poor coolant circulation

Clutch

30 Fails to release (pedal pressed to the floor-shift lever does not move freely in and out of gear)
31 Clutch slips (engine speed increases with no increase in vehicle speed)
32 Grabbing (chattering) on take-up
33 Squeal or rumble with clutch fully engaged (pedal released)
34 Squeal or rumble with clutch fully disengaged (pedal depressed)
35 Clutch pedal stays on floor when disengaged

Manual transaxle

36 Noisy in Neutral with engine running
37 Noisy in all gears
38 Noisy in one particular gear
39 Slips out of high gear
40 Difficulty in engaging gears
41 Oil leakage

Section Symptom

Automatic transaxle

42 Fluid leakage
43 General shift mechanism problems
44 Transaxle will not downshift with the accelerator pedal pressed to the floor
45 Engine will start in gears other than P (Park) or N (Neutral)
46 Transaxle slips, slips rough, is noisy or his no drivein forward or reverse gears

Driveshaft

47 Leakage of fluid at front of driveshaft
48 Knock or clunk when the transaxle is under initial load (just after transaxle is put into gear)
49 Metallic grating sound consistent with vehicle speed
50 Vibration

Front differential

51 Gear noise when driving
52 Gear noise when coasting
53 Bearing noise
54 Noise when turning

Rear differential

55 Oil leakage
56 Noise when starting or shifting gears
57 Noise when turning

Driveaxles

58 Clicking noise in turns
59 Knock or clunk when accelerating after coasting
60 Shudder or vibration during acceleration

Brakes

61 Vehicle pulls to one side during braking
62 Noise (high-pitched squeal without brake applied)
63 Excessive brake pedal travel
64 Brake pedal feels spongy when depressed
65 Excessive effort required to stop vehicle
66 Pedal travels to floor with little resistance
67 Brake pedal pulsates during brake application
68 Hill-holder fails to hold

Suspension and steering

69 Excessive tire wear (not specific to one area)
70 Excessive tire wear on outside edge
71 Excessive tire wear on inside edge
72 Tire tread worn in one place
73 General vibration at highway speeds
74 Noise whether coasting or in drive
75 Vehicle pulls to one side
76 Shimmy, shake or vibration
77 Excessive pitching and/or rolling around corners or during braking
78 Excessively stiff steering
79 Excessive play in steering
80 Lack of power assistance

ENGINE

1 Engine will not rotate when attempting to start

1 Battery terminal connections loose or corroded (Chapter 1).
2 Battery discharged or faulty (Chapter 1).
3 Automatic transaxle not completely engaged in Park (Chapter 7) or clutch pedal not completely depressed (Chapter 8).
4 Broken, loose or disconnected wiring in the starting circuit (Chapters 5 and 12).
5 Starter motor pinion jammed in flywheel ring gear (Chapter 5).
6 Starter solenoid faulty (Chapter 5).
7 Starter motor faulty (Chapter 5).
8 Ignition switch faulty (Chapter 12).
9 Starter pinion or flywheel teeth worn or broken (Chapter 5).

2 Engine rotates but will not start

1 Fuel tank empty.
2 Battery discharged (engine rotates slowly) (Chapter 5).
3 Battery terminal connections loose or corroded (Chapter 1).
4 Leaking fuel injector(s), faulty fuel pump, pressure regulator, etc. (Chapter 4).
5 Broken or stripped timing belt (Chapter 2).
6 Ignition components damp or damaged (Chapter 5).
7 Worn, faulty or incorrectly gapped spark plugs (Chapter 1).
8 Broken, loose or disconnected wiring in the starting circuit (Chapter 5).
9 Broken, loose or disconnected wires at the ignition coil or faulty coil (Chapter 5).

3 Engine hard to start when cold

1 Battery discharged or low (Chapter 1).
2 Malfunctioning fuel system (Chapter 4).
3 Faulty coolant temperature sensor (Chapter 6).
4 Injector(s) leaking (Chapter 4B).
5 Faulty ignition system (Chapter 5).

4 Engine hard to start when hot

1 Air filter clogged (Chapter 1).
2 Fuel not reaching the fuel injection system (Chapter 4).
3 Corroded battery connections, especially ground (Chapter 1).
4 Faulty coolant temperature sensor (Chapter 6).

5 Starter motor noisy or excessively rough in engagement

1 Pinion or flywheel gear teeth worn or broken (Chapter 5).
2 Starter motor mounting bolts loose or missing (Chapter 5).

6 Engine starts but stops immediately

1 Loose or faulty electrical connections at coil or alternator (Chapter 5).
2 Insufficient fuel reaching the fuel injectors (Chapters 1 and 4).
3 Vacuum leak at the gasket between the intake manifold/plenum (Chapters 1 and 4).

7 Oil puddle under engine

1 Oil pan gasket and/or oil pan drain bolt washer leaking (Chapter 2A).
2 Oil pressure sending unit leaking (Chapter 2B).
3 Valve covers leaking (Chapter 2A).
4 Engine oil seals leaking (Chapter 2A).
5 Oil pump housing leaking (Chapter 2A).

8 Engine lopes while idling or idles erratically

1 Vacuum leakage (Chapters 2 and 4).
2 Leaking EGR valve (Chapter 6).
3 Air filter clogged (Chapter 1).
4 Fuel pump not delivering sufficient fuel to the fuel injection system (Chapter 4).
5 Leaking head gasket (Chapter 2).
6 Timing belt and/or pulleys worn (Chapter 2).
7 Camshaft lobes worn (Chapter 2).

9 Engine misses at idle speed

1 Spark plugs worn or not gapped properly (Chapter 1).
2 Faulty spark plug wires (Chapter 1).
3 Vacuum leaks (Chapter 1).
4 Incorrect ignition timing (Chapter 5).
5 Uneven or low compression (Chapter 2).
6 Problem with the fuel injection system (Chapter 4).

10 Engine misses throughout driving speed range

1 Fuel filter clogged and/or impurities in the fuel system (Chapter 1).
2 Low fuel output at the injectors (Chapter 4).
3 Faulty or incorrectly gapped spark plugs (Chapter 1).
4 Incorrect ignition timing (Chapter 5).
5 Cracked coil (Chapters 1 and 5).
6 Leaking spark plug wires (Chapters 1 or 5).
7 Faulty emission system components (Chapter 6).
8 Low or uneven cylinder compression pressures (Chapter 2).
9 Weak or faulty ignition system (Chapter 5).
10 Vacuum leak in fuel injection system, intake manifold or vacuum hoses (Chapter 4).

11 Engine stumbles on acceleration

1 Spark plugs fouled (Chapter 1).
2 Problem with fuel injection system (Chapter 4).
3 Fuel filter clogged (Chapters 1 and 4).
4 Incorrect ignition timing (Chapter 5).
5 Intake manifold air leak (Chapters 2 and 4).
6 Problem with the emissions control system (Chapter 6).

12 Engine surges while holding accelerator steady

1 Intake air leak (Chapter 4).
2 Fuel pump or fuel pressure regulator faulty (Chapter 4).
3 Problem with fuel injection system (Chapter 4).
4 Problem with the emissions control system (Chapter 6).

13 Engine stalls

1 Fuel filter clogged and/or water and impurities in the fuel system (Chapters 1 and 4).
2 Ignition components damp or damaged (Chapter 5).
3 Faulty emissions system components (Chapter 6).
4 Faulty or incorrectly gapped spark plugs (Chapter 1).
5 Faulty spark plug wires (Chapter 1).
6 Vacuum leak in the fuel injection system, intake manifold or vacuum hoses (Chapters 2 and 4).
7 Valve clearances incorrectly set (Chapter 2).

14 Engine lacks power

1 Faulty spark plug wires or coil (Chapters 1 and 5).
2 Faulty or incorrectly gapped spark plugs (Chapter 1).
3 Problem with the fuel injection system (Chapter 4).
4 Plugged air filter (Chapter 1).
5 Brakes binding (Chapter 9).
6 Automatic transaxle fluid level incorrect (Chapter 1).
7 Clutch slipping (Chapter 8).
8 Fuel filter clogged and/or impurities in the fuel system (Chapters 1 and 4).
9 Emission control system not functioning properly (Chapter 6).
10 Low or uneven cylinder compression pressures (Chapter 2).
11 Obstructed exhaust system (Chapter 4).

15 Engine backfires

1 Emission control system not functioning properly (Chapter 6).
2 Faulty secondary ignition system (cracked spark plug insulator, faulty plug wires) (Chapters 1 and 5).
3 Problem with the fuel injection system (Chapter 4).
4 Vacuum leak at fuel injector(s), intake manifold or vacuum hoses (Chapters 2 and 4).
5 Valve clearances incorrectly set and/or valves sticking (Chapter 2).

16 Pinging or knocking engine sounds during acceleration or uphill

1 Incorrect grade of fuel.
2 Fuel injection system faulty (Chapter 4).
3 Improper or damaged spark plugs or wires (Chapter 1).
4 Knock sensor defective (Chapter 6).
5 EGR valve not functioning (Chapter 6).
6 Vacuum leak (Chapters 2 and 4).

17 Engine runs with oil pressure light on

1 Low oil level (Chapter 1).
2 Idle rpm below specification (Chapter 1).
3 Short in wiring circuit (Chapter 12).
4 Faulty oil pressure sender (Chapter 2).
5 Worn engine bearings and/or oil pump (Chapter 2).

18 Engine diesels (continues to run) after switching off

Excessive engine operating temperature (Chapter 3).

ENGINE ELECTRICAL SYSTEM

19 Battery will not hold a charge

1 Alternator drivebelt defective or not adjusted properly (Chapter 1).
2 Battery electrolyte level low (Chapter 1).
3 Battery terminals loose or corroded (Chapter 1).
4 Alternator not charging properly (Chapter 5).
5 Loose, broken or faulty wiring in the charging circuit (Chapter 5).
6 Short in vehicle wiring (Chapter 12).
7 Internally defective battery (Chapters 1 and 5).

20 Alternator light fails to go out

1 Faulty alternator or charging circuit (Chapter 5).
2 Alternator drivebelt defective or out of adjustment (Chapter 1).
3 Alternator voltage regulator inoperative (Chapter 5).

21 Alternator light fails to come on when key is turned on

1 Warning light bulb defective (Chapter 12).
2 Fault in the printed circuit, dash wiring or bulb holder (Chapter 12).

FUEL SYSTEM

22 Excessive fuel consumption

1 Dirty or clogged air filter element (Chapter 1).
2 Emissions system not functioning properly (Chapter 6).
3 Fuel injection system not functioning properly (Chapter 4).
4 Low tire pressure or incorrect tire size (Chapter 1).

23 Fuel leakage and/or fuel odor

1 Leaking fuel feed or return line (Chapters 1 and 4).
2 Tank overfilled.
3 Evaporative canister filter clogged (Chapter 6).
4 Problem with fuel injection system (Chapter 4).

COOLING SYSTEM

24 Overheating

1 Insufficient coolant in system (Chapter 1).
2 Water pump defective (Chapter 3).
3 Radiator core blocked or grille restricted (Chapter 3).
4 Thermostat faulty (Chapter 3).
5 Electric coolant fan inoperative or blades broken (Chapter 3).
6 Radiator cap not maintaining proper pressure (Chapter 3).

25 Overcooling

1 Faulty thermostat (Chapter 3).
2 Inaccurate temperature gauge sending unit (Chapter 3).
3 Cooling fan runs continuously.

26 External coolant leakage

1 Deteriorated/damaged hoses; loose clamps (Chapters 1 and 3).
2 Water pump defective (Chapter 3).
3 Leakage from radiator core or coolant reservoir bottle (Chapter 3).
4 Engine drain or water jacket core plugs leaking (Chapter 2).

27 Internal coolant leakage

1 Leaking cylinder head gasket (Chapter 2).
2 Cracked cylinder bore or cylinder head (Chapter 2).

28 Coolant loss

1 Too much coolant in system (Chapter 1).
2 Coolant boiling away because of overheating (Chapter 3).
3 Internal or external leakage (Chapter 3).
4 Faulty radiator cap (Chapter 3).

29 Poor coolant circulation

1 Inoperative water pump (Chapter 3).
2 Restriction in cooling system (Chapters 1 and 3).
3 Water pump drivebelt defective/out of adjustment (Chapter 1).
4 Thermostat sticking (Chapter 3).

CLUTCH

→ Note: All clutch related service information is located in Chapter 8, unless otherwise noted.

30 Fails to release (pedal pressed to the floor-shift lever does not move freely in and out of gear)

1 Freeplay incorrectly adjusted.
2 Clutch contaminated with oil. Remove clutch disc and inspect.
3 Clutch disc warped, distorted or otherwise damaged.
4 Diaphragm spring fatigued. Remove clutch cover/pressure plate assembly and inspect.
5 Leakage of fluid from clutch hydraulic system. Inspect master cylinder, operating cylinder and connecting lines.
6 Air in clutch hydraulic system. Bleed the system.
7 Insufficient pedal stroke. Check and adjust as necessary.
8 Piston seal in master or release cylinder deformed or damaged.
9 Lack of grease on pilot bearing.

31 Clutch slips (engine speed increase with no increase in vehicle speed)

1 Worn or oil-soaked clutch disc.
2 Clutch disc not broken in. It may take 30 or 40 starts for a new clutch to seat.
3 Diaphragm spring weak or damaged. Remove clutch cover/pressure plate assembly and inspect.
4 Debris in master cylinder preventing the piston from returning to its normal position.
5 Clutch hydraulic line damaged internally (not allowing fluid to return to the clutch master cylinder).
6 Binding in the release mechanism.

32 Grabbing (chattering) as clutch is engaged

1 Oil on clutch disc. Remove and inspect. Repair any leaks.
2 Worn or loose engine or transaxle mounts. These units may move slightly when clutch is released. Inspect mounts and bolts.
3 Worn splines on clutch disc. Remove clutch components and inspect.
4 Warped pressure plate or flywheel. Remove clutch components and inspect.
5 Diaphragm spring fatigued. Remove clutch cover/pressure plate assembly and inspect.
6 Clutch linings hardened or warped.
7 Clutch lining rivets loose.

33 Squeal or rumble with clutch fully engaged (pedal released)

1 Improper pedal adjustment. Adjust pedal freeplay.
2 Release bearing binding on transaxle input shaft. Remove clutch components and check bearing. Remove any burrs or nicks, clean and relubricate before reinstallation.
3 Pilot bearing worn or damaged.
4 Clutch rivets loose.
5 Clutch disc cracked.
6 Fatigued clutch disc torsion springs. Replace clutch disc.
7 Weak pedal return spring. Replace the spring.

34 Squeal or rumble with clutch fully disengaged (pedal depressed)

1 Worn, faulty or broken release bearing.
2 Worn or broken pressure plate diaphragm fingers.

35 Clutch pedal stays on floor when disengaged

1 Bind in cable or release bearing. Inspect cable or remove clutch components as necessary.
2 Clutch pressure plate weak or broken. Remove and inspect clutch pressure plate.

MANUAL TRANSAXLE

→ Note: All manual transaxle service information is located in Chapter 7A, unless otherwise noted.

36 Noisy in Neutral with engine running

1 Mainshaft bearing worn.
2 Damaged pinion shaft bearing.
3 Insufficient transaxle lubricant.
4 Transaxle lubricant in poor condition. Drain and fill with proper grade (Chapter 1). Inspect old lubricant for water and debris.

37 Noisy in all gears

1 Mainshaft bearing worn.
2 Damaged pinion shaft bearing.
3 Insufficient lubricant (see checking procedures in Chapter 1).

38 Noisy in one particular gear

1 Worn, damaged or chipped gear teeth for that particular gear.
2 Worn or damaged synchronizer for that particular gear.

39 Slips out of high gear

1 Transaxle mounting bolts loose.
2 Shift mechanism not working freely.
3 Damaged pilot bearing.
4 Worn or improperly adjusted linkage.

40 Difficulty in engaging gears

1 Clutch not releasing (Chapter 8).
2 Loose, damaged or misadjusted shift linkage. Make a thorough inspection, replacing parts as necessary. Adjust as described in Chapter 8.

41 Oil leakage

1 Excessive amount of lubricant in transaxle (see Chapter 1 for correct checking procedures). Drain lubricant as required.
2 Driveaxle oil seals defective.
3 Extension housing seal or speedometer driven-gear O-ring defective.

AUTOMATIC TRANSAXLE

➡**Note: Due to the complexity of the automatic transaxle, it is difficult for the home mechanic to properly diagnose and service this component. For problems other than the following, the vehicle should be taken to a reputable mechanic.**

42 Fluid leakage

1 Automatic transaxle fluid is a deep red color and fluid leaks should not be confused with engine oil which can easily be blown by air flow to the transaxle.
2 To pinpoint a leak, first remove all built-up dirt and grime from around the transaxle. Degreasing agents and/or steam cleaning will achieve this. With the underside clean, drive the vehicle at low speeds so that air flow will not blow the leak far from its source. Raise the vehicle and determine where the leak is coming from. Common areas of leakage are:

a) *Fluid pan: tighten mounting bolts and/or replace pan gasket as necessary (Chapter 1)*
b) *Extension housing seal: replace seal as necessary (Chapter 7B)*
c) *Vent pipe: transaxle over-filled and/or water in fluid (see checking procedures, Chapter 1)*
d) *Speedometer driven gear: O-ring defective.*

43 General shift mechanism problems

Chapter 7 deals with checking and adjusting the shift linkage on automatic transaxles. Common problems which may be attributed to out-of-adjustment linkage are:

a) *Engine starts in gears other than P (Park) or N (Neutral)*
b) *Gear position indicator points to a gear other than the one the transaxle is actually in*
c) *Vehicle will not hold firm when in P (Park) position*

44 Transaxle will not downshift with the accelerator pedal pressed to the floor

Faulty electronics in transaxle control system. Take the vehicle to a dealer or other qualified repair shop.

45 Engine will start in gears other than P (Park) or N (Neutral)

Check the Transmission Range (TR) sensor (see Chapter 6).

46 Transaxle slips, shifts rough, is noisy or has no drive in forward or reverse gears

1 There are many probable causes for the above problems, but the home mechanic should concern himself only with one possibility: fluid level.
2 Before taking the vehicle to a repair shop, check the level of the fluid and condition of the fluid as described in Chapter 1. Correct fluid level as necessary or change the fluid and filter if needed. If problem persists, have a professional diagnose the probable cause.

DRIVESHAFT

47 Leakage of fluid at front of driveshaft

Defective extension housing seal (Chapter 7). Also, inspect the splined yoke for burrs or a rough condition which may be damaging the seal. If found, these can be dressed with crocus cloth or a fine whetstone.

48 Knock or clunk when the transaxle is under initial load (just after transaxle is put into gear)

1 Loose or disconnected rear suspension components. Check all mounting bolts and bushings (Chapters 1 and 10).
2 Loose driveshaft bolts. Inspect all bolts and nuts and tighten to the specified torque.
3 Worn or damaged universal joint bearings. Replace the driveshaft (Chapter 8).
4 Worn sleeve yoke and mainshaft splines (Chapter 8).

49 Metallic grating sound consistent with vehicle speed

Pronounced wear in the universal joint bearings. Replace the driveshaft (Chapter 8).

50 Vibration

➡**Note: Before it can be assumed that the driveshaft is at fault, make sure the tires are perfectly balanced and perform the following test.**

1 Install a tachometer inside the vehicle to monitor engine speed as it is driven. Drive the vehicle and note the engine speed at which the vibration (roughness) is most pronounced. Now shift the transaxle to a different gear and bring the engine speed to the same point.
2 If the vibration occurs at the same engine speed (rpm) regardless of which gear the transaxle is in, the driveshaft is NOT at fault since the driveshaft speed varies.

3 If the vibration decreases or is eliminated when the transaxle is in a different gear at the same engine speed, refer to the following probable causes.

4 Bent or dented driveshaft. Inspect and replace as necessary (Chapter 8).

5 Undercoating or built-up dirt, etc. on the driveshaft. Clean the shaft thoroughly and test.

6 Worn universal joint bearings (Chapter 8).

FRONT DIFFERENTIAL

51 Gear noise when driving

If noise increases as vehicle speed increases, it may be due to insufficient gear oil (Chapter 1), incorrect gear engagement or damaged gears. Remove the transaxle/differential unit and have it checked and repaired by a Subaru dealer service department or other qualified repair shop.

52 Gear noise when coasting

Damaged gears caused by bearings and shims that are worn or out of adjustment.

53 Bearing noise

Usually caused by cracked, broken or otherwise damaged bearings (see Section 48).

54 Noise when turning

Damaged or worn differential side gear, pinion gear or pinion shaft (see Section 51).

REAR DIFFERENTIAL

55 Oil leakage

1 Worn or incorrectly installed pinion seal or axleshaft oil seal.
2 Scored or excessively worn sliding surface of companion flange.
3 Clogged air vent.
4 Loose rear cover attaching bolts or damaged gasket.
5 Loose oil fill or drain plug.

56 Noise when starting or shifting gears

1 Excessive gear backlash.
2 Insufficient bearing preload.
3 Loose drive pinion nut.

57 Noise when turning

1 Damaged or worn side gears or bearings.
2 Broken or seized spider gear shaft.
3 Excessively worn side gear thrust washer.
4 Broken teeth on differential hypoid gears.

DRIVEAXLES

➡**Note: All driveaxle service procedures are in Chapter 8.**

58 Clicking noise in turns

Worn or damaged outer CV joint. Check for cut or damaged boots. Repair as necessary.

59 Knock or clunk when accelerating after coasting

Worn or damaged inner CV joint. Check for cut or damaged boots. Repair as necessary.

60 Shudder or vibration during acceleration

1 Excessive joint angle. Check and correct as necessary.
2 Worn or damaged inner or outer CV joints. Repair or replace as necessary.
3 Sticking inner CV joint assembly. Correct or replace as necessary.

BRAKES

➡**Note: Before assuming that a brake problem exists, make sure that the tires are in good condition and inflated properly (see Chapter 1), the wheel alignment is correct (see Chapter 10) and that the vehicle is not loaded with weight in an unequal manner. All service procedures for the brakes are included in Chapter 9, unless otherwise noted.**

61 Vehicle pulls to one side during braking

1 Defective, damaged or oil-contaminated disc pad on one side. Inspect as described in Chapter 1. Replace as necessary.
2 Excessive wear of brake pad material or disc on one side. Inspect and correct as necessary.
3 Loose or disconnected front suspension components. Inspect and tighten all bolts to the torque listed in the Chapter 10 Specifications.
4 Defective caliper assembly. Remove caliper and inspect for stuck piston or damage.

62 Noise (high-pitched squeal without brake applied)

Front brake pads worn out. This noise comes from the wear sensor or pad backing plate rubbing against the disc. Replace pads with new ones immediately.

63 Excessive brake pedal travel

1 Partial brake system failure. Inspect entire system (Chapter 1) and correct as required.
2 Insufficient fluid in master cylinder. Check (Chapter 1), add fluid and bleed system if necessary.
3 Rear brakes not adjusting properly (models with rear drum brakes). Make a series of starts and stops while the vehicle is in Reverse. If this does not correct the situation, remove rear drums and inspect self-adjusters.

64 Brake pedal feels spongy when depressed

1   Air in hydraulic lines. Bleed the brake system.
2   Faulty flexible hoses. Inspect all system hoses and lines. Replace parts as necessary.
3   Master cylinder mount loose. Inspect master cylinder bolts (nuts) and tighten to the torque listed in the Chapter 9 Specifications.
4   Master cylinder faulty.

65 Excessive effort required to stop vehicle

1   Power brake booster not operating properly.
2   Excessively worn linings or pads. Inspect (Chapter 1) and replace if necessary.
3   One or more caliper pistons or wheel cylinders seized. Inspect and replace as required.
4   Brake linings or pads contaminated with oil or grease. Inspect and replace as required (Chapter 1).
5   New pads or linings installed and not yet seated. It will take a while for the new material to seat against the drum (or disc).

66 Pedal travels to floor with little resistance

Little or no fluid in the master cylinder reservoir (caused by leaking wheel cylinder(s), leaking caliper piston(s), loose, damaged or disconnected brake lines). Inspect entire system and correct as necessary.

67 Brake pedal pulsates during brake application

1   Wheel bearings not adjusted properly or in need of replacement (Chapter 1).
2   Caliper not sliding properly due to improper installation or obstructions. Remove and inspect.
3   Disc not within specifications. Remove the disc and check for excessive lateral run-out and parallelism. Have the disc machined or replace it with a new one.
4   Out-of-round rear brake drums. Remove the drums and have them machined, or replace them.

68 Hill-holder fails to hold

1   Incline of hill may be too gentle to activate holder.
2   Pressure holder valve in need of adjustment.

SUSPENSION AND STEERING

➡Note: All service procedures related to suspension and steering are located in Chapter 10, unless otherwise noted.

69 Excessive tire wear (not specific to one area)

1   Incorrect tire pressures (Chapter 1).
2   Tires out of balance. Have professionally balanced.
3   Wheel damaged. Inspect and replace as necessary.
4   Suspension or steering components excessively worn (Chapter 1).

70 Excessive tire wear on outside edge

1   Inflation pressures not correct (Chapter 1).
2   Excessive speed on turns.
3   Front end alignment incorrect (excessive toe-in). Have professionally aligned.
4   Suspension arm bent or twisted.

71 Excessive tire wear on inside edge

1   Inflation pressures incorrect (Chapter 1).
2   Front or rear toe incorrect. Have wheels aligned.
3   Loose or damaged steering components (Chapter 1).

72 Tire tread worn in one place

1   Tires out of balance. Balance tires professionally.
2   Damaged or buckled wheel. Inspect and replace if necessary.
3   Defective tire.

73 General vibration at highway speeds

1   Out-of-balance front wheels or tires. Have them professionally balanced.
2   Front or rear wheel bearings loose or worn. Check and replace as necessary.
3   Defective tire or wheel. Have them checked and replaced if necessary.

74 Noise whether coasting or in drive

1   Road noise. No corrective procedures available.
2   Tire noise. Inspect tires and tire pressures (Chapter 1).
3   Front wheel bearings loose, worn or damaged. Check (Chapter 1) and replace if necessary.
4   Damaged shock absorbers or mounts (Chapter 1).
5   Loose road wheel lug nuts. Check and tighten as necessary (Chapter 1).

75 Vehicle pulls to one side

1   Tire pressures uneven (Chapter 1).
2   Defective tire (Chapter 1).
3   Excessive wear in suspension or steering components (Chapter 1).
4   Front end in need of alignment.
5   Front brakes dragging. Inspect brakes as described in Chapter 1.

76 Shimmy, shake or vibration

1   Tire or wheel out of balance or out of round. Have professionally balanced.
2   Loose or worn wheel bearings. Replace as necessary.
3   Struts and/or suspension components worn or damaged.

77 Excessive pitching and/or rolling around corners or during braking

1   Defective struts. Replace as a set.
2   Broken or weak coil springs and/or suspension components. Inspect as described in Chapter 11.

78 Excessively stiff steering

1   Lack of fluid in power steering fluid reservoir (Chapter 1).
2   Incorrect tire pressures (Chapter 1).
3   Lack of lubrication at balljoints (Chapter 1).
4   Front end out of alignment.

79 Excessive play in steering

1   Loose wheel bearings (Chapter 1).
2   Excessive wear in suspension or steering components.

80 Lack of power assistance

1   Steering pump drivebelt faulty, broken or not adjusted properly (Chapter 1).
2   Fluid level low (Chapter 1).
3   Hoses or lines restricting the flow. Inspect and replace parts as necessary.
4   Air in power steering system. Bleed system.

Notes

Section

Reference to other Chapters

CHECK ENGINE light on - See Chapter 6

1

TUNE-UP AND ROUTINE MAINTENANCE

Typical engine compartment component locations - non-turbo engine

1	Air filter housing	5	Battery	9	Automatic transaxle fluid dipstick
2	Brake fluid reservoir	6	Coolant reservoir	10	Radiator cap
3	Windshield washer fluid reservoir	7	Engine oil filler cap	11	Power steering fluid reservoir
4	Underhood fuse/relay block	8	Engine oil dipstick		

Typical engine compartment component locations - turbo engine

1 Brake fluid reservoir	5 Engine coolant reservoir	9 Coolant filler tank cap
2 Underhood fuse/relay block	6 Radiator cap	10 Air filter housing
3 Battery	7 Engine oil filler cap	11 Power steering fluid reservoir
4 Windshield washer fluid reservoir	8 Engine oil dipstick	

Typical engine compartment underside component locations

1	Oil filter	3	Driveaxle boot	5	Exhaust pipe
2	Lower radio hose	4	Automatic transaxle drain plug	6	Engine oil drain plug

Typical rear underside component locations

1	*Muffler*	*2*	*Disc brake caliper*	*3*	*Rear driveaxle*	*4*	*Rear differential*

1   Maintenance schedule

The following maintenance intervals are based on the assumption that the vehicle owner will be doing the maintenance or service work, as opposed to having a dealer service department do the work. Although the time/mileage intervals are loosely based on factory recommendations, most have been shortened to ensure, for example, that such items as lubricants and fluids are checked/changed at intervals that promote maximum engine/driveline service life. Also, subject to the preference of the individual owner interested in keeping his or her vehicle in peak condition at all times, and with the vehicle's ultimate resale in mind, many of the maintenance procedures may be performed more often than recommended in the following schedule. We encourage such owner initiative.

When the vehicle is new it should be serviced initially by a factory authorized dealer service department to protect the factory warranty. In many cases the initial maintenance check is done at no cost to the owner (check with your dealer service department for more information).

EVERY 250 MILES OR WEEKLY, WHICHEVER COMES FIRST

Check the engine oil level (Section 4)
Check the engine coolant level (Section 4)
Check the brake and clutch fluid level (Section 4)
Check the windshield washer fluid level (Section 4)
Check the power steering fluid level (Section 4)
Check the automatic transaxle fluid level (Section 4)
Check the tires and tire pressures (Section 5)

EVERY 3000 MILES OR 3 MONTHS, WHICHEVER COMES FIRST

All items listed above, plus . . .
Change the engine oil and filter (Section 6)

EVERY 7500 MILES OR 6 MONTHS, WHICHEVER COMES FIRST

All items listed above, plus . . .
Check and service the battery (Section 7)
Rotate the tires (Section 8)
Inspect and replace, if necessary, the windshield wiper blades (Section 9)
Inspect the exhaust system (Section 10)
Check the seat belts (Section 11)
Inspect and replace, if necessary, all underhood hoses (Section 12)
Check the cooling system (Section 13)

EVERY 15,000 MILES OR 12 MONTHS, WHICHEVER COMES FIRST

All items listed above, plus . . .
Inspect the fuel system (Section 14)

Check the brakes (Section 15)
Inspect the suspension and steering components (Section 16)
Inspect and replace, if necessary, the air filter (Section 17)
Check the clutch pedal height (see Chapter 8)
Check the brake pedal height and hill holder adjustment (see Chapter 9)

EVERY 30,000 MILES OR 30 MONTHS, WHICHEVER COMES FIRST

All items listed above, plus . . .
Change the brake fluid (Section 18)
Check the engine drivebelts (Section 19)
Replace the fuel filter (Section 20)
Service the cooling system (drain, flush and refill) (Section 21)
Replace the spark plugs (non-platinum type plugs) (Section 22)
Inspect the ignition coils (turbo engines) (Section 23)
Inspect the spark plug wires (non-turbo engines) (Section 24)
Change the automatic transaxle fluid (Section 25)**
Change the manual transaxle lubricant (Section 26)
Change the differential lubricant (Section 27)
Inspect the timing belt (Chapter 2A)
Replace the air filter (Section 17)*

EVERY 60,000 MILES OR 48 MONTHS, WHICHEVER COMES FIRST

All items listed above, plus . . .
Replace the spark plugs (platinum-type plugs) (Section 22)
Inspect the front and rear wheel bearings (Section 28)

EVERY 105,000 MILES OR 105 MONTHS, WHICHEVER COMES FIRST

Replace the engine drivebelts (Section 19)
Replace the timing belt (Chapter 2A)

*This item is affected by "severe" operating conditions, as described below. If the vehicle is operated under severe conditions, perform all maintenance indicated with an asterisk (*) at 7500 mile/six-month intervals. Severe conditions exist if you mainly operate the vehicle . . .

in dusty areas
towing a trailer
idling for extended periods and/or driving at low speeds when outside temperatures remain below freezing and most trips are less than four miles long

**If operated under one or more of the following conditions, change the automatic transaxle fluid every 15,000 miles:

in heavy city traffic where the outside temperature regularly reaches 90-degrees F or higher
in hilly or mountainous terrain
frequent trailer pulling

2 Introduction

This Chapter is designed to help the home mechanic maintain the Subaru for peak performance, economy, safety and long life.

On the following pages is a master maintenance schedule, followed by Sections dealing specifically with each item on the schedule. Visual checks, adjustments, component replacement and other helpful items are included. Refer to the accompanying illustrations of the engine compartment and the underside of the vehicle for the location of various components.

Servicing your Subaru in accordance with the mileage/time maintenance schedule and the following Sections will provide it with a planned maintenance program that should result in a long and reliable service life. This is a comprehensive plan, so maintaining some items but not others at the specified service intervals will not produce the same results.

As you service your vehicle, you will discover that many of the procedures can, and should, be grouped together because of the nature of the particular procedure you're performing or because of the close proximity of two otherwise unrelated components to one another.

For example, if the vehicle is raised for any reason, you should inspect the exhaust, suspension, steering and fuel systems while you're under the vehicle. When you're rotating the tires, it makes good sense to check the brakes and wheel bearings since the wheels are already removed.

Finally, let's suppose you have to borrow or rent a torque wrench. Even if you only need to tighten the spark plugs, you might as well check the torque of as many critical fasteners as time allows.

The first step of this maintenance program is to prepare yourself before the actual work begins. Read through all Sections pertinent to the procedures you're planning to do, then make a list of and gather together all the parts and tools you will need to do the job. If it looks as if you might run into problems during a particular segment of some procedure, seek advice from your local parts man or dealer service department.

OWNER'S MANUAL AND VECI LABEL INFORMATION

Your vehicle owner's manual was written for your year and model and contains very specific information on component locations, specifications, fuse ratings, part numbers, etc. The Owner's Manual is an important resource for the do-it-yourselfer to have; if one was not supplied with your vehicle, it can generally be ordered from a dealer parts department.

Among other important information, the Vehicle Emissions Control Information (VECI) label contains specifications and procedures for applicable tune-up adjustments and, in some instances, spark plugs (see Chapter 6 for more information on the VECI label). The information on this label is the exact maintenance data recommended by the manufacturer. This data often varies by intended operating altitude, local emissions regulations, month of manufacture, etc.

This Chapter contains procedural details, safety information and more ambitious maintenance intervals than you might find in manufacturer's literature. However, you may also find procedures or specifications in your Owner's Manual or VECI label that differ with what's printed here. In these cases, the Owner's Manual or VECI label can be considered correct, since it is specific to your particular vehicle.

3 Tune-up general information

The term tune-up is used in this manual to represent a combination of individual operations rather than one specific procedure.

If, from the time the vehicle is new, the routine maintenance schedule is followed closely and frequent checks are made of fluid levels and high wear items, as suggested throughout this manual, the engine will be kept in relatively good running condition and the need for additional work will be minimized.

More likely than not, however, there will be times when the engine is running poorly due to lack of regular maintenance. This is even more likely if a used vehicle, which has not received regular and frequent maintenance checks, is purchased. In such cases, an engine tune-up will be needed outside of the regular routine maintenance intervals.

The first step in any tune-up or diagnostic procedure to help correct a poor running engine is a cylinder compression check. A compression check (see Chapter 2B) will help determine the condition of internal engine components and should be used as a guide for tune-up and repair procedures. If, for instance, the compression check indicates serious internal engine wear, a conventional tune-up won't improve the performance of the engine and would be a waste of time and money. Because of its importance, the compression check should be done by someone with the right equipment and the knowledge to use it properly.

The following procedures are those most often needed to bring a generally poor running engine back into a proper state of tune.

MINOR TUNE-UP

Check all engine related fluids (Section 4)
Clean, inspect and test the battery (Section 7)
Check the cooling system (Section 13)
Check all underhood hoses (Section 12)
Check and adjust the drivebelts (Section 19)
Inspect the spark plug wires (Section 24)
Replace the spark plugs (Section 22)
Check the air filter (Section 17)

MAJOR TUNE-UP

All items listed under Minor tune-up, plus . . .

Check the fuel system (Section 14)
Replace the fuel filter (Section 20)
Replace the spark plug wires (Section 22)
Replace the air filter (Section 17)
Check the charging system (Chapter 5)

4 Fluid level checks (every 250 miles or weekly)

➥Note: The following are fluid level checks to be done on a 250 mile or weekly basis. Additional fluid level checks can be found in specific maintenance procedures which follow. Regardless of intervals, be alert to fluid leaks under the vehicle which would indicate a fault to be corrected immediately.

1   Fluids are an essential part of the lubrication, cooling, brake and windshield washer systems. Because the fluids gradually become depleted and/or contaminated during normal operation of the vehicle, they must be periodically replenished. See *Recommended lubricants and fluids* at the end of this Chapter before adding fluid to any of the following components.

➥Note: The vehicle must be on level ground when fluid levels are checked.

ENGINE OIL

▶ **Refer to illustrations 4.2 and 4.4**

2   The engine oil level is checked with a dipstick that extends through a tube and into the oil pan at the bottom of the engine (see illustration). The oil dipstick is located on the left side of the engine compartment near the battery.

3   The oil level should be checked before the vehicle has been driven, or about 5 minutes after the engine has been shut off. If the oil is checked immediately after driving the vehicle, some of the oil will remain in the upper engine components, resulting in an inaccurate reading on the dipstick.

4   Pull the dipstick out of the tube and wipe all the oil from the end with a clean rag or paper towel. Insert the clean dipstick all the way back into the tube, then pull it out again. Note the oil at the end of the dipstick. Add oil as necessary to keep the level between the ADD and FULL marks on the dipstick (see illustration).

5   Do not overfill the engine by adding too much oil since this may result in oil-fouled spark plugs, oil leaks or oil seal failures.

6   Oil is added to the engine after removing the threaded cap from the oil filler tube (see illustration 4.2). A funnel may help to reduce spills.

7   Checking the oil level is an important preventive maintenance step. A consistently low oil level indicates oil leakage through damaged seals, defective gaskets or past worn rings or valve guides. If the oil looks milky or has water droplets in it, the cylinder head gasket(s) may be blown or the head(s) or block may be cracked. The engine should be checked immediately. The condition of the oil should also be checked. Whenever you check the oil level, slide your thumb and index finger up the dipstick before wiping off the oil. If you see small dirt or metal particles clinging to the dipstick, the oil should be changed (see Section 6).

ENGINE COOLANT

▶ **Refer to illustration 4.8**

✱✱ WARNING 1:

Do not allow antifreeze to come in contact with your skin or painted surfaces of the vehicle. Flush contaminated areas immediately with plenty of water. Don't store new coolant or leave old coolant lying around where it's accessible to children or pets - they're attracted by its sweet smell. Ingestion of even a small amount of coolant can be fatal! Wipe up garage floor and drip pan spills immediately. Keep antifreeze containers covered and repair cooling system leaks as soon as they're noticed.

✱✱ WARNING 2:

DO NOT remove the radiator cap or the coolant reservoir cap while the cooling system is hot, as escaping steam could cause serious injury.

4.2 The engine oil dipstick is located on the left side of the engine near the oil filler cap

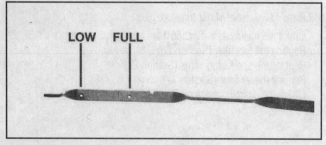

4.4 The oil level must be maintained between the marks at all times

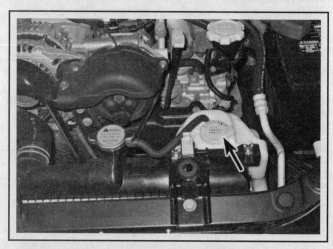

4.8 Coolant can be added to the cooling system after removing the cap from the coolant reservoir

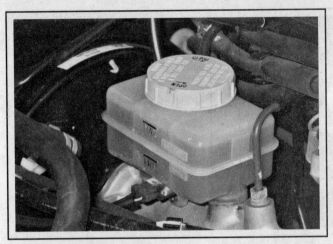

4.16a The fluid level inside the brake reservoir can easily be checked by observing the level from the outside

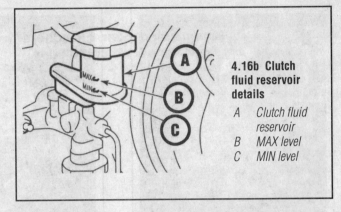

4.16b Clutch fluid reservoir details

A   Clutch fluid reservoir
B   MAX level
C   MIN level

8   These models are equipped with a pressurized coolant recovery system. A white coolant reservoir, which is located by the radiator in the engine compartment, is connected by a hose to the base of the radiator cap (see illustration). If the coolant gets too hot during engine operation, coolant can escape from the radiator through a pressurized filler cap, then through a connecting hose into the reservoir. As the engine cools, the coolant is automatically drawn back into the cooling system to maintain the correct level.

9   The coolant level should be checked regularly. The coolant level should be between the FULL and LOW lines on the reservoir tank. The level will vary with the temperature of the engine. When the engine is cold, the coolant level should be at or slightly above the LOW mark on the tank. Once the engine has warmed up, the level should be at or near the FULL mark. If it isn't, allow the fluid in the tank to cool, then remove the cap from the reservoir and add coolant to bring the level up to the FULL line.

10   Use only ethylene-glycol type coolant and water in the mixture ratio recommended by your owner's manual. Do not use supplemental inhibitor additives. If only a small amount of coolant is required to bring the system up to the proper level, water can be used. However, repeated additions of water will dilute the recommended antifreeze and water solution. In order to maintain the proper ratio of antifreeze and water, it is advisable to top up the coolant level with the correct mixture. Refer to your owners' manual for the recommended ratio.

11   If the coolant level drops within a short time after replenishment, there may be a leak in the system. Inspect the radiator, hoses, engine coolant filler cap, drain plugs and water pump. If no leak is evident, have the radiator cap pressure tested by your dealer.

❊❊ WARNING:

Never remove the radiator cap or the coolant recovery reservoir cap when the engine is running or has just been shut down, because the cooling system is hot. Escaping steam and scalding liquid could cause serious injury.

12   If it is necessary to open the radiator cap, wait until the system has cooled completely, then wrap a thick cloth around the cap and turn it to the first stop. If any steam escapes, wait until the system has cooled further, then remove the cap.

13   When checking the coolant level, always note its condition. It should be relatively clear. If it is brown or rust colored, the system should be drained, flushed and refilled. Even if the coolant appears to be normal, the corrosion inhibitors wear out with use, so it must be replaced at the specified intervals.

14   Do not allow antifreeze to come in contact with your skin or painted surfaces of the vehicle. Flush contacted areas immediately with plenty of water.

BRAKE AND CLUTCH FLUID

▶ **Refer to illustrations 4.16a and 4.16b**

15   The brake and clutch fluid level is checked by looking through the plastic reservoir mounted on the master cylinder. The brake master cylinder is mounted on the front of the power booster unit in the driver's side rear corner of the engine compartment and the clutch master cylinder is mounted near the firewall.

16   The fluid level should be between the MAX and MIN lines on the side of the reservoir (see illustrations).

17   If the fluid level is low, wipe the top of the reservoir and the cap with a clean rag to prevent contamination of the system as the cap is unscrewed.

18   Add only the specified brake fluid to the reservoir (refer to *Recommended lubricants and fluids* at the end of this Chapter or your owner's manual). Mixing different types of brake fluid can damage the system. Fill the reservoir to the MAX line.

❊❊ WARNING:

Brake fluid can harm your eyes and damage painted surfaces, so use extreme caution when handling or pouring it. Do not use brake fluid that has been standing open or is more than one year old. Brake fluid absorbs moisture from the air, which can cause a dangerous loss of braking effectiveness.

19   While the reservoir cap is off, check the master cylinder reservoir for contamination. If rust deposits, dirt particles or water droplets are present, the system should be bled repeatedly until clean brake fluid emerges from the bleeder valves (see Section 18).

20   After filling the reservoir to the proper level, make sure the cap is seated to prevent fluid leakage and/or contamination.

21   The fluid level in the master cylinder will drop slightly as the brake shoes or pads at each wheel wear down during normal operation. If the brake fluid level drops consistently, check the entire system for leaks immediately. Examine all brake lines, hoses and connections, along with the calipers and master cylinder (see Section 15).

22   When checking the fluid level, if you discover one or both res-

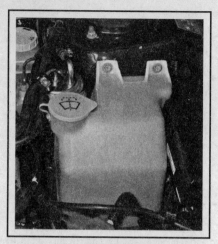

4.23 The windshield washer fluid reservoir is located at the left front of the engine compartment

4.26 The power steering fluid reservoir is located at the front of the engine compartment - turn the cap counterclockwise to remove it

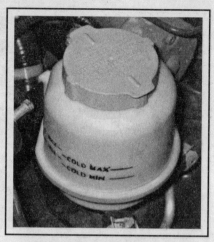

4.30 At normal operating temperature, the power steering fluid level should be between the MAX and MIN marks

ervoirs empty or nearly empty, the brake system should be bled (see Chapter 9).

WINDSHIELD WASHER FLUID

▶ **Refer to illustration 4.23**

23 Fluid for the windshield washer system is stored in a plastic reservoir located on the left side of the engine compartment (see illustration).

24 In milder climates, plain water can be used in the reservoir, but it should be kept no more than 2/3 full to allow for expansion if the water freezes. In colder climates, use windshield washer system antifreeze, available at any auto parts store, to lower the freezing point of the fluid. Mix the antifreeze with water in accordance with the manufacturer's directions on the container.

❋❖❋ **CAUTION:**

Do not use cooling system antifreeze - it will damage the vehicle's paint.

POWER STEERING FLUID

▶ **Refer to illustrations 4.26 and 4.30**

25 Check the power steering fluid level periodically to avoid steering system problems, such as damage to the pump.

❋❖❋ **CAUTION:**

DO NOT hold the steering wheel against either stop (extreme left or right turn) for more than five seconds. If you do, the power steering pump could be damaged.

26 The power steering reservoir, located at the right side of the engine compartment (see illustration), has MIN and MAX fluid level marks on the side. The fluid level can be seen without removing the reservoir cap.

27 Park the vehicle on level ground and apply the parking brake.

28 Run the engine until it has reached normal operating temperature. With the engine at idle, turn the steering wheel back and forth about 10 times to get any air out of the steering system.

29 Shut the engine off with the wheels in the straight-ahead position.

30 Note the fluid level on the side of the reservoir. It should be between the two marks (see illustration).

31 Add small amounts of fluid until the level is correct.

❋❖❋ **CAUTION:**

Do not overfill the reservoir. If too much fluid is added, remove the excess with a clean syringe or suction pump.

32 Check the power steering hoses and connections for leaks and wear.

AUTOMATIC TRANSAXLE FLUID

▶ **Refer to illustrations 4.36 and 4.38**

33 The level of the automatic transaxle fluid should be carefully maintained. Low fluid level can lead to slipping or loss of drive, while overfilling can cause foaming, loss of fluid and transaxle damage.

34 The transaxle fluid level should only be checked when the transaxle is hot (at its normal operating temperature). If the vehicle has just been driven over 10 miles (15 miles in a frigid climate), and the fluid temperature is 160 to 175-degrees F, the transaxle is hot.

❋❖❋ **CAUTION:**

If the vehicle has just been driven for a long time at high speed or in city traffic in hot weather, or if it has been pulling a trailer, an accurate fluid level reading cannot be obtained. Allow the fluid to cool down for about 30 minutes.

35 If the vehicle has not been driven, park the vehicle on level ground, set the parking brake, then start the engine and bring it to operating temperature. While the engine is idling, depress the brake pedal

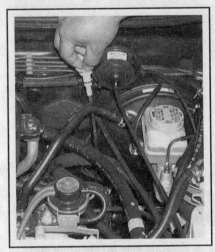

4.36 On some models the automatic transaxle fluid dipstick is located at the left rear of the engine compartment; on others, it's near the center of the engine

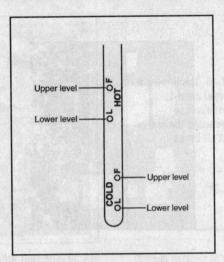

4.38 The automatic transaxle fluid level must be maintained between the UPPER LEVEL mark and the LOWER LEVEL mark at the indicated operating temperature (Cold or Hot)

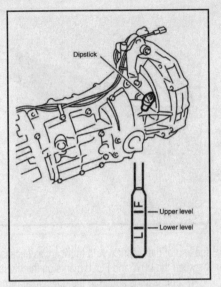

4.41 The manual transaxle/front differential dipstick is located on the right side of the engine compartment

and move the selector lever through all the gear ranges, beginning and ending in Park.

36 With the engine still idling, remove the dipstick from its tube (see illustration). Check the level of the fluid on the dipstick and note its condition.

37 Wipe the fluid from the dipstick with a clean rag and reinsert it back into the filler tube until the cap seats.

38 Pull the dipstick out again and note the fluid level. If the transaxle is cold, the level should be in the COLD or COOL range on the dipstick. If it is hot, the fluid level should be in the HOT range. If the level is at the low side of either range, add the specified automatic transaxle fluid through the dipstick tube with a funnel (see illustration).

39 Add just enough of the recommended fluid to fill the transaxle to the proper level. It takes about one pint to raise the level from the low mark to the high mark when the fluid is hot, so add the fluid a little at a time and keep checking the level until it is correct.

40 The condition of the fluid should also be checked along with the level. If the fluid at the end of the dipstick is black or a dark reddish brown color, or if it emits a burned smell, the fluid should be changed (see Section 25). If you are in doubt about the condition of the fluid, purchase some new fluid and compare the two for color and smell.

MANUAL TRANSAXLE/FRONT DIFFERENTIAL LUBRICANT

♦ Refer to illustration 4.41

➡ Note: Vehicles equipped with a manual transaxle have an integral front differential (meaning they share the same lubricant). Vehicles equipped with an automatic transaxle have a non-integral front differential (meaning they DO NOT share the same lubricant). The dipstick for the manual transaxle and the front differential on automatic transaxle equipped vehicles is approximately in the same position in the engine compartment and the lubricant level checking procedure is the same.

41 The manual transaxle has a dipstick that extends through a tube and into the transaxle (see illustration).

42 Pull the dipstick out of the tube and wipe all the lubricant from

4.45 The front differential dipstick (automatic transaxle) is located on the right side near the firewall

the end with a clean rag or paper towel. Insert the clean dipstick all the way back into the tube, then pull it out again. Note the lubricant at the end of the dipstick. Add lubricant as necessary to keep the level between the ADD and FULL marks on the dipstick.

43 Lubricant is added to the transaxle through the dipstick tube. A funnel may help to reduce spills. Do not overfill the transaxle since this may result in lubricant leaks or lubricant seal failures.

44 Reinstall the dipstick and close the hood.

FRONT DIFFERENTIAL LUBRICANT (AUTOMATIC TRANSAXLE VEHICLES)

♦ Refer to illustrations 4.45 and 4.46

45 The front differential has a dipstick that extends through a tube and into the differential (see illustration).

46 Pull the dipstick out of the tube and wipe all the lubricant from the end with a clean rag or paper towel. Insert the clean dipstick all the way back into the tube, then pull it out again. Note the lubricant at

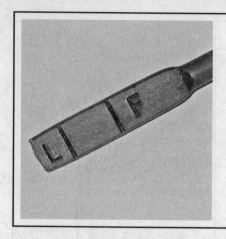

4.46 The lubricant level must be maintained between the marks at all times

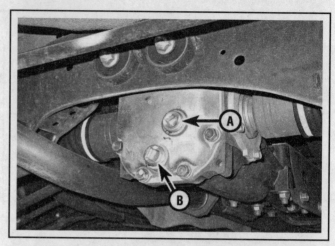

4.50 The rear differential check/fill plug (A) and drain plug (B) are located on the differential cover - use your finger as a dipstick to check the lubricant level

the end of the dipstick. Add lubricant as necessary to keep the level between the LOW and FULL marks on the dipstick (see illustration).

47 Lubricant is added to the differential through the dipstick tube. A funnel may help to reduce spills. Do not overfill the differential since this may result in lubricant leaks or lubricant seal failures.

48 Reinstall the dipstick and close the hood.

REAR DIFFERENTIAL LUBRICANT LEVEL CHECK

▶ Refer to illustration 4.50

49 The rear differential has a check/fill plug which must be removed to check the lubricant level. If the vehicle must be raised to gain access

to the plug, be sure to support it safely on jackstands - DO NOT crawl under the vehicle when it's supported only by the jack.

50 Remove the check/fill plug from the back of the rear differential (see illustration).

51 Use a finger to reach inside the housing to determine the lubricant level. The lubricant level should be at the bottom of the plug opening. If it isn't, use a hand pump (available at auto parts stores) to add the specified lubricant until it just starts to run out of the opening.

52 Install the plug and tighten it securely.

5 Tire and tire pressure checks (every 250 miles or weekly)

▶ Refer to illustrations 5.2, 5.3, 5.4a, 5.4b and 5.8

1 Periodic inspection of the tires may spare you the inconvenience of being stranded with a flat tire. It can also provide you with vital information regarding possible problems in the steering and suspension systems before major damage occurs.

2 The original tires on this vehicle are equipped with 1/2-inch wide wear bands that will appear when tread depth reaches 1/16-inch,

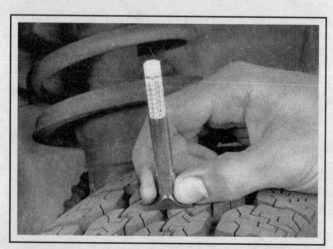

5.2 A tire tread depth indicator should be used to monitor tire wear - they are available at auto parts stores and service stations and cost very little

at which time the tires can be considered worn out. Tread wear can be monitored with a simple, inexpensive device known as a tread depth indicator (see illustration).

3 Note any abnormal tread wear (see illustration). Tread pattern irregularities such as cupping, flat spots and more wear on one side than the other are indications of front end alignment and/or balance problems. If any of these conditions are noted, take the vehicle to a tire shop or service station to correct the problem.

4 Look closely for cuts, punctures and embedded nails or tacks. Sometimes a tire will hold air pressure for a short time or leak down very slowly after a nail has embedded itself in the tread. If a slow leak persists, check the valve stem core to make sure it's tight (see illustration). Examine the tread for an object that may have embedded itself in the tire or for a "plug" that may have begun to leak (radial tire punctures are repaired with a rubber plug that's installed in the hole). If a puncture is suspected, it can be easily verified by spraying a solution of soapy water onto the puncture area (see illustration). The soapy solution will bubble if there's a leak. Unless the puncture is unusually large, a tire shop or service station can usually repair the tire.

5 Carefully inspect the inner sidewall of each tire for evidence of brake fluid leakage. If you see any, inspect the brakes immediately.

6 Correct air pressure adds miles to the lifespan of the tires, improves mileage and enhances overall ride quality. Tire pressure cannot be accurately estimated by looking at a tire, especially if it's a radial. A tire pressure gauge is essential. Keep an accurate gauge in the vehicle. The pressure gauges attached to the nozzles of air hoses at gas stations are often inaccurate.

7 Always check tire pressure when the tires are cold. Cold, in this

UNDERINFLATION

CUPPING

Cupping may be caused by:
- Underinflation and/or mechanical irregularities such as out-of-balance condition of wheel and/or tire, and bent or damaged wheel.
- Loose or worn steering tie-rod or steering idler arm.
- Loose, damaged or worn front suspension parts.

OVERINFLATION

INCORRECT TOE-IN OR EXTREME CAMBER

FEATHERING DUE TO MISALIGNMENT

5.3 This chart will help you determine the condition of your tires, the probable cause(s) of abnormal wear and the corrective action necessary

case, means the vehicle has not been driven over a mile in the three hours preceding a tire pressure check. A pressure rise of four to eight pounds is not uncommon once the tires are warm.

8   Unscrew the valve cap protruding from the wheel or hubcap and push the gauge firmly onto the valve stem (see illustration). Note the reading on the gauge and compare the figure to the recommended tire pressure shown on the placard on the driver's side door pillar. Be sure

to reinstall the valve cap to keep dirt and moisture out of the valve stem mechanism. Check all four tires and, if necessary, add enough air to bring them up to the recommended pressure.

9   Don't forget to keep the spare tire inflated to the specified pressure (consult your owner's manual). Note that the air pressure specified for the compact spare is significantly higher than the pressure of the regular tires.

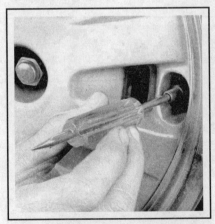

5.4a If a tire loses air on a steady basis, check the valve core first to make sure it's snug (special inexpensive wrenches are commonly available at auto parts stores)

5.4b If the valve core is tight, raise the corner of the vehicle with the low tire and spray a soapy water solution onto the tread as the tire is turned slowly - slow leaks will cause small bubbles to appear

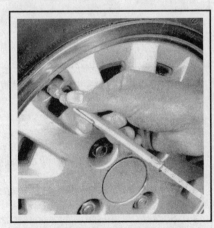

5.8 To extend the life of your tires, check the air pressure at least once a week with an accurate gauge (don't forget the spare!)

6 Engine oil and filter change (every 3000 miles or 3 months)

▶ **Refer to illustrations 6.2, 6.4, 6.7, 6.12 and 6.14**

1   Frequent oil changes are the best preventive maintenance the home mechanic can give the engine, because aging oil becomes diluted and contaminated, which leads to premature engine wear.

2   Make sure that you have all the necessary tools before you begin this procedure (see illustration). You should also have plenty of rags or newspapers handy for mopping up any spills.

3   Access to the underside of the vehicle is greatly improved if the vehicle can be lifted on a hoist, driven onto ramps or supported by jackstands.

4   If this is your first oil change, get under the vehicle and familiarize yourself with the location of the oil drain plug (see illustration). The engine and exhaust components will be warm during the actual work, so try to anticipate any potential problems before the engine and accessories are hot.

5   Park the vehicle on a level spot. Start the engine and allow it to reach its normal operating temperature (the needle on the temperature gauge should be at least above the bottom mark). Warm oil and contaminants will flow out more easily. Turn off the engine when it's warmed up. Remove the filler cap in the valve cover.

6   Raise the vehicle and support it securely on jackstands,

✳✳ WARNING:

To avoid personal injury, never get beneath the vehicle when it is supported by only by a jack. The jack provided with your vehicle is designed solely for raising the vehicle to remove and install the wheels. Always use jackstands to support the vehicle when it becomes necessary to place your body underneath the vehicle.

7   Being careful not to touch the hot exhaust components, place the drain pan under the drain plug in the bottom of the pan and remove the plug (see illustration). You may want to wear gloves while unscrewing the plug the final few turns if the engine is really hot.

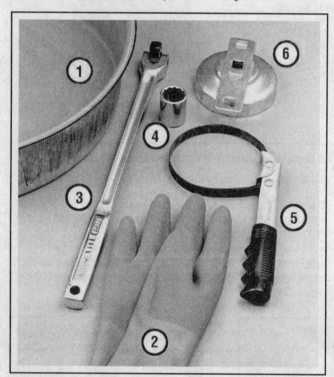

6.2 These tools are required when changing the engine oil and filter

*1   **Drain pan** - It should be fairly shallow in depth, but wide in order to prevent spills*

*2   **Rubber gloves** - When removing the drain plug and filter, it is inevitable that you will get oil on your hands (the gloves will prevent burns)*

*3   **Breaker bar** - Sometimes the oil drain plug is pretty tight and a long breaker bar is needed to loosen it*

*4   **Socket** - To be used with the breaker bar or a ratchet (must be the correct size to fit the drain plug)*

*5   **Filter wrench** - This is a metal band-type wrench, which requires clearance around the filter to be effective*

*6   **Filter wrench** - This type fits on the bottom of the filter and can be turned with a ratchet or beaker bar (different size wrenches are available for different types of filters)*

6.4 Remove the clips securing the service hole cover, then rotate the cover to access the engine oil drain plug and oil filter

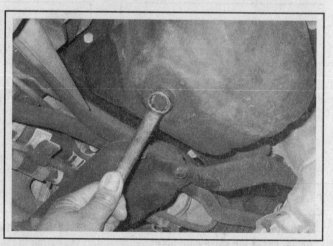

6.7 The engine oil drain plug is located on the bottom of the oil pan - it is usually very tight, so use the proper size box end wrench or socket to avoid rounding it off (engine cover removed for clarity)

8 Allow the old oil to drain into the pan. It may be necessary to move the pan farther under the engine as the oil flow slows to a trickle. Inspect the old oil for the presence of metal shavings and chips.

9 After all the oil has drained, wipe off the drain plug with a clean rag. Even minute metal particles clinging to the plug would immediately contaminate the new oil.

10 Clean the area around the drain plug opening, reinstall the plug and tighten it securely, but do not strip the threads.

11 Move the drain pan into position under the oil filter.

12 Loosen the oil filter (see illustration) by turning it counterclockwise with the filter wrench. Any standard filter wrench should work. Once the filter is loose, use your hands to unscrew it from the block.

✳✳ WARNING:

The exhaust pipes may still be hot, so be careful.

13 With a clean rag, wipe off the mounting surface on the block. If a residue of old oil is allowed to remain, it will smoke when the block is heated up. It will also prevent the new filter from seating properly. Also make sure that the none of the old gasket remains stuck to the mounting surface. It can be removed with a scraper if necessary.

14 Compare the old filter with the new one to make sure they are the same type. Smear some engine oil on the rubber gasket of the new filter and screw it into place (see illustration). Because over-tightening the filter will damage the gasket, do not use a filter wrench to tighten the filter. Tighten it by hand until the gasket contacts the seating surface. Then seat the filter by giving it an additional 3/4-turn.

15 Remove all tools, rags, etc. from under the vehicle, being careful not to spill the oil in the drain pan, then lower the vehicle.

16 Add new oil to the engine through the oil filler cap in the valve cover. Use a spout or funnel to prevent oil from spilling onto the top of the engine. Pour three quarts of fresh oil into the engine. Wait a few minutes to allow the oil to drain into the pan, then check the level on the oil dipstick (see Section 4 if necessary). If the oil level is at or near the H mark, install the filler cap hand tight, start the engine and allow the new oil to circulate.

17 Allow the engine to run for about a minute. While the engine is running, look under the vehicle and check for leaks at the oil pan drain plug and around the oil filter. If either is leaking, stop the engine and tighten the plug or filter slightly.

18 Wait a few minutes to allow the oil to trickle down into the pan, then recheck the level on the dipstick and, if necessary, add enough oil to bring the level to the H mark.

19 During the first few trips after an oil change, make it a point to check frequently for leaks and proper oil level.

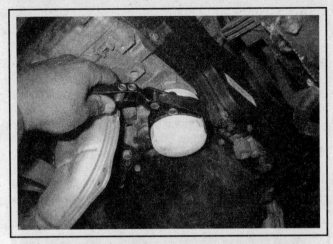

6.12 The oil filter is usually on very tight and will require a special wrench for removal - DO NOT use the wrench to tighten the new filter! (engine cover removed for clarity)

6.14 Lubricate the oil filter gasket with clean engine oil before installing the filter on the engine

20 The old oil drained from the engine cannot be reused in its present state and should be discarded. Check with your local refuse disposal company, disposal facility or environmental agency to see if they will accept the oil for recycling. Don't pour used oil into drains or on the ground. After the oil has cooled, it can be drained into a suitable container (capped plastic jugs, topped bottles, milk cartons, etc.) for transport to one of these disposal sites.

7 Battery check, maintenance and charging (every 7500 miles or 6 months)

▸ Refer to illustrations 7.1, 7.6a, 7.6b, 7.7a and 7.7b

✳✳ WARNING:

Certain precautions must be followed when checking and servicing the battery. Hydrogen gas, which is highly flammable, is always present in the battery cells, so keep lighted tobacco and all other open flames and sparks away from the battery. The electrolyte inside the battery is actually dilute sulfuric acid, which will cause injury if splashed on your skin or in your eyes. It will also ruin clothes and painted surfaces. When removing the battery cables, always detach the negative cable first and hook it up last!

MAINTENANCE

1   A routine preventive maintenance program for the battery in your vehicle is the only way to ensure quick and reliable starts. But before performing any battery maintenance, make sure that you have the proper equipment necessary to work safely around the battery (see illustration).

2   There are also several precautions that should be taken whenever battery maintenance is performed. Before servicing the battery, always turn the engine and all accessories off and disconnect the cable from the negative terminal of the battery.

3   The battery produces hydrogen gas, which is both flammable and explosive. Never create a spark, smoke or light a match around the battery. Always charge the battery in a ventilated area.

4   Electrolyte contains poisonous and corrosive sulfuric acid. Do not allow it to get in your eyes, on your skin on your clothes. Never ingest it. Wear protective safety glasses when working near the battery. Keep children away from the battery.

5   Note the external condition of the battery. If the positive terminal and cable clamp on your vehicle's battery is equipped with a rubber protector, make sure that it's not torn or damaged. It should completely cover the terminal. Look for any corroded or loose connections, cracks in the case or cover or loose hold-down clamps. Also check the entire length of each cable for cracks and frayed conductors.

6   If corrosion, which looks like white, fluffy deposits (see illustration) is evident, particularly around the terminals, the battery should be removed for cleaning. Loosen the cable clamp bolts with a wrench, being careful to remove the ground cable first, and slide them off the terminals (see illustration). Then disconnect the hold-down clamp bolt and nut, remove the clamp and lift the battery from the engine compartment.

7   Clean the cable clamps thoroughly with a battery brush or a

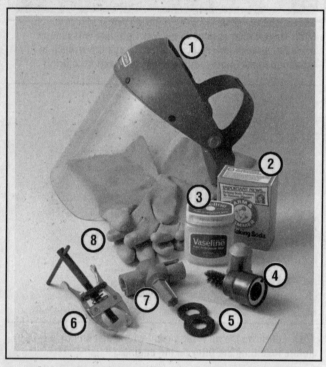

7.1 Tools and materials required for battery maintenance

1   *Face shield/safety goggles* - When removing corrosion with a brush, the acidic particles can easily fly up into your eyes

2   *Baking soda* - A solution of baking soda and water can be used to neutralize corrosion

3   *Petroleum jelly* - A layer of this on the battery posts will help prevent corrosion

4   *Battery post/cable cleaner* - This wire brush cleaning tool will remove all traces of corrosion from the battery posts and cable clamps

5   *Treated felt washers* - Placing one of these on each post, directly under the cable clamps, will help prevent corrosion

6   *Puller* - Sometimes the cable clamps are very difficult to pull off the posts, even after the nut/bolt has been completely loosened. This tool pulls the clamp straight up and off the post without damage

7   *Battery post/cable cleaner* - Here is another cleaning tool which is a slightly different version of number 4 above, but it does the same thing

8   *Rubber gloves* - Another safety item to consider when servicing the battery; remember that's acid inside the battery

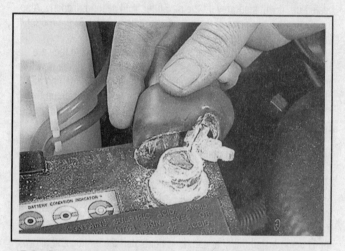

7.6a Battery terminal corrosion usually appears as light, fluffy powder

7.6b Removing a cable from the battery post with a wrench - sometimes a pair of special battery pliers are required for this procedure if corrosion has caused deterioration of the nut hex (always remove the ground (-) cable first and hook it up last!)

7.7a When cleaning the cable clamps, all corrosion must be removed (the inside of the clamp is tapered to match the taper on the post, so don't remove too much material)

7.7b Regardless of the type of tool used to clean the battery posts, a clean, shiny surface should be the result

terminal cleaner and a solution of warm water and baking soda (see illustration). Wash the terminals and the top of the battery case with the same solution but make sure that the solution doesn't get into the battery. When cleaning the cables, terminals and battery top, wear safety goggles and rubber gloves to prevent any solution from coming in contact with your eyes or hands. Wear old clothes too - even diluted, sulfuric acid splashed onto clothes will burn holes in them. If the terminals have been extensively corroded, clean them up with a terminal cleaner (see illustration). Thoroughly wash all cleaned areas with plain water.

8   Make sure that the battery tray is in good condition and the hold-down clamp bolts are tight. If the battery is removed from the tray, make sure no parts remain in the bottom of the tray when the battery is reinstalled. When reinstalling the hold-down clamp bolts, do not over-tighten them.

9   Any metal parts of the vehicle damaged by corrosion should be covered with a zinc-based primer, then painted.

10   Information on removing and installing the battery can be found in Chapter 5. Information on jump starting can be found at the front of this manual.

CHARGING

✳✳ WARNING:

When batteries are being charged, hydrogen gas, which is very explosive and flammable, is produced. Do not smoke or allow open flames near a battery. Wear eye protection when near the battery during charging. Also, make sure the charger is unplugged before connecting or disconnecting the battery from the charger.

➡**Note: The manufacturer recommends the battery be removed from the vehicle for charging because the gas that escapes during this procedure can damage the paint. Fast charging with the battery cables connected can result in damage to the electrical system.**

11   Slow-rate charging is the best way to restore a battery that's discharged to the point where it will not start the engine. It's also a good way to maintain the battery charge in a vehicle that's only driven a few miles between starts. Maintaining the battery charge is particularly important in the winter when the battery must work harder to start the

engine and electrical accessories that drain the battery are in greater use.

12   It's best to use a one or two-amp battery charger (sometimes called a "trickle" charger). They are the safest and put the least strain on the battery. They are also the least expensive. For a faster charge, you can use a higher amperage charger, but don't use one rated more than 1/10th the amp/hour rating of the battery. Rapid boost charges that claim to restore the power of the battery in one to two hours are hardest on the battery and can damage batteries not in good condition. This type of charging should only be used in emergency situations.

13   The average time necessary to charge a battery should be listed in the instructions that come with the charger. As a general rule, a trickle charger will charge a battery in 12 to 16 hours.

14   Remove all the cell caps (if equipped) and cover the holes with a clean cloth to prevent spattering electrolyte. Disconnect the negative battery cable and hook the battery charger cable clamps up to the battery posts (positive to positive, negative to negative), then plug in the charger. Make sure it is set at 12-volts if it has a selector switch.

15   If you're using a charger with a rate higher than two amps, check the battery regularly during charging to make sure it doesn't overheat. If you're using a trickle charger, you can safely let the battery charge overnight after you've checked it regularly for the first couple of hours.

16   If the battery has removable cell caps, measure the specific gravity with a hydrometer every hour during the last few hours of the charging cycle. Hydrometers are available inexpensively from auto parts stores - follow the instructions that come with the hydrometer. Consider the battery charged when there's no change in the specific gravity reading for two hours and the electrolyte in the cells is gassing (bubbling) freely. The specific gravity reading from each cell should be very close to the others. If not, the battery probably has a bad cell(s).

17   Some batteries with sealed tops have built-in hydrometers on the top that indicate the state of charge by the color displayed in the hydrometer window. Normally, a bright-colored hydrometer indicates a full charge and a dark hydrometer indicates the battery still needs charging.

18   If the battery has a sealed top and no built-in hydrometer, you can hook up a voltmeter across the battery terminals to check the charge. A fully charged battery should read 12.6 volts or higher after the surface charge has been removed.

19   Further information on the battery and jump starting can be found in Chapter 5 and at the front of this manual.

8 Tire rotation (every 7500 miles or 6 months)

▸ **Refer to illustration 8.2**

1 The tires should be rotated at the specified intervals and whenever uneven wear is noticed. Since the vehicle will be raised and the tires removed anyway, check the brakes (see Section 15) at this time.

2 Radial tires must be rotated in a specific pattern (see illustration).

3 Refer to the information in *Jacking and towing* at the front of this manual for the proper procedures to follow when raising the vehicle and changing a tire. If the brakes are to be checked, do not apply the parking brake as stated. Make sure the tires are blocked to prevent the vehicle from rolling.

4 Preferably, the entire vehicle should be raised at the same time. This can be done on a hoist or by jacking up each corner and then lowering the vehicle onto jackstands placed under the frame rails. Always use four jackstands and make sure the vehicle is firmly supported.

5 After rotation, check and adjust the tire pressures as necessary and be sure to check the lug nut tightness.

6 For further information on the wheels and tires, refer to Chapter 10.

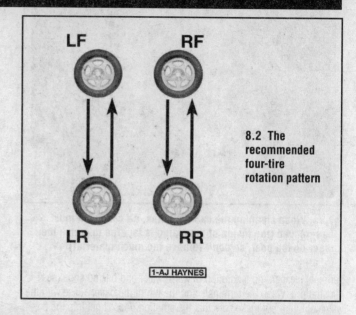

8.2 The recommended four-tire rotation pattern

9 Windshield wiper blade inspection and replacement (every 7500 miles or 6 months)

▸ **Refer to illustrations 9.5a and 9.5b**

1 The windshield wiper and blade assembly should be inspected periodically for damage, loose components and cracked or worn blade elements.

2 Road film can build up on the wiper blades and affect their efficiency, so they should be washed regularly with a mild detergent solution.

3 The action of the wiping mechanism can loosen bolts, nuts and fasteners, so they should be checked and tightened, as necessary, at the same time the wiper blades are checked.

4 If the wiper blade elements are cracked, worn or warped, or no longer clean adequately, they should be replaced with new ones.

5 Lift the arm assembly away from the glass for clearance, press the release lever, then slide the wiper blade assembly out of the hook at the end of the arm (see illustrations).

6 Attach the new wiper to the arm. Connection can be confirmed by an audible click.

9.5a Depress the release lever . . .

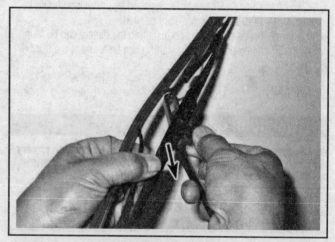

9.5b . . . and slide the wiper assembly down the wiper arm and out of the hook in the end of the arm

10 Exhaust system check (every 7500 miles or 6 months)

▸ **Refer to illustrations 10.2a and 10.2b**

1 With the engine cold (at least three hours after the vehicle has been driven), check the complete exhaust system from the cylinder head to the end of the tailpipe. Be careful around the catalytic converter (if equipped), which may be hot even after three hours. The inspection should be done with the vehicle on a hoist to permit unrestricted access. If a hoist isn't available, raise the vehicle and support it securely on jackstands.

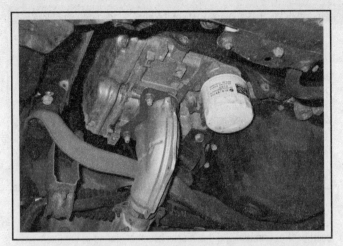

10.2a Check the exhaust pipes and connections for signs of leakage and corrosion

10.2b Check the exhaust system rubber hangers for cracks and damage

2 Check the exhaust pipes and connections for signs of leakage and/or corrosion indicating a potential failure. Make sure that all brackets and hangers are in good condition and tight (see illustrations).

3 Inspect the underside of the body for holes, corrosion, open seams, etc. which may allow exhaust gasses to enter the passenger compartment. Seal all body openings with silicone sealant or body putty.

4 Rattles and other noises can often be traced to the exhaust system, especially the hangers, mounts and heat shields. Try to move the pipes, mufflers and catalytic converter. If the components can come in contact with the body or suspension parts, secure the exhaust system with new brackets and hangers.

11 Seat belt check (every 7500 miles or 6 months)

1 Check seat belts, buckles, latch plates and guide loops for obvious damage and signs of wear.

2 Where the seat belt receptacle bolts to the floor of the vehicle, check that the bolts are secure.

3 See if the seat belt reminder light comes on when the key is turned to the Run or Start position.

12 Underhood hose check and replacement (every 7500 miles or 6 months)

GENERAL

> **⁂ CAUTION:**
>
> **Replacement of air conditioning hoses must be left to a dealer service department or air conditioning shop that has the equipment to depressurize the system safely and recover the refrigerant. Never remove air conditioning components or hoses until the system has been depressurized.**

1 High temperatures in the engine compartment can cause the deterioration of the rubber and plastic hoses used for engine, accessory and emission systems operation. Periodic inspection should be made for cracks, loose clamps, material hardening and leaks. Information specific to the cooling system hoses can be found in Section 13.

2 Some, but not all, hoses are secured to their fittings with clamps. Where clamps are used, check to be sure they haven't lost their tension, allowing the hose to leak. If clamps aren't used, make sure the hose has not expanded and/or hardened where it slips over the fitting, allowing it to leak.

VACUUM HOSES

3 It's quite common for vacuum hoses, especially those in the emissions system, to be color-coded or identified by colored stripes molded into them. Various systems require hoses with different wall thickness, collapse resistance and temperature resistance. When replacing hoses, be sure the new ones are made of the same material.

4 Often the only effective way to check a hose is to remove it completely from the vehicle. If more than one hose is removed, be sure to label the hoses and fittings to ensure correct installation.

5 When checking vacuum hoses, be sure to include any plastic T-fittings in the check. Inspect the fittings for cracks and the hose where it fits over the fitting for distortion, which could cause leakage.

6 A small piece of vacuum hose (1/4-inch inside diameter) can be used as a stethoscope to detect vacuum leaks. Hold one end of the

hose to your ear and probe around vacuum hoses and fittings, listening for the "hissing" sound characteristic of a vacuum leak.

> ❊❊ **WARNING:**
>
> **When probing with the vacuum hose stethoscope, be very careful not to come into contact with moving engine components such as the drivebelt, cooling fan, etc.**

FUEL HOSE

> ❊❊ **WARNING:**
>
> **There are certain precautions that must be taken when inspecting or servicing fuel system components. Work in a well-ventilated area and do not allow open flames (cigarettes, appliances, etc.) or bare light bulbs near the work area. Mop up any spills immediately and do not store fuel soaked rags where they could ignite. The fuel system is under high pressure, so if any fuel lines are to be disconnected, the pressure in the system must be relieved first (see Chapter 4 for more information).**

7   Check all rubber fuel lines for deterioration and chafing. Check especially for cracks in areas where the hose bends and just before fittings, such as where a hose attaches to the fuel filter.

8   High quality fuel line, made specifically for high-pressure fuel injection systems, must be used for fuel line replacement. Never, under any circumstances, use unreinforced vacuum line, clear plastic tubing or water hose for fuel lines.

9   Spring-type clamps are commonly used on fuel lines. These clamps often lose their tension over a period of time, and can be "sprung" during removal. Replace all spring-type clamps with screw clamps whenever a hose is replaced.

METAL LINES

10 Sections of metal line are routed along the frame, between the fuel tank and the engine. Check carefully to be sure the line has not been bent or crimped and that cracks have not started in the line.

11 If a section of metal fuel line must be replaced, only seamless steel tubing should be used, since copper and aluminum tubing don't have the strength necessary to withstand normal engine vibration.

12 Check the metal brake lines where they enter the master cylinder and brake proportioning unit for cracks in the lines or loose fittings. Any sign of brake fluid leakage calls for an immediate and thorough inspection of the brake system.

13 Cooling system check (every 7500 miles or 6 months)

♦ **Refer to illustration 13.4**

1   Many major engine failures can be attributed to a faulty cooling system. If the vehicle is equipped with an automatic transmission, the cooling system also cools the transaxle fluid and thus plays an important role in prolonging transaxle life.

2   The cooling system should be checked with the engine cold. Do this before the vehicle is driven for the day or after it has been shut off for at least three hours.

3   Remove the cooling system pressure cap and thoroughly clean the cap, inside and out, with clean water. Also clean the filler neck on the radiator. All traces of corrosion should be removed. The coolant inside the radiator should be relatively transparent. If it is rust-colored, the system should be drained, flushed and refilled (see Section 21). If the coolant level is not up to the top, add additional antifreeze/coolant mixture (see Section 4).

4   Carefully check the large upper and lower radiator hoses along with the smaller diameter heater hoses that run from the engine to the firewall. Inspect each hose along its entire length, replacing any hose that is cracked, swollen or shows signs of deterioration. Cracks may become more apparent if the hose is squeezed (see illustration). Regardless of condition, it's a good idea to replace hoses with new ones every two years.

5   Make sure all hose connections are tight. A leak in the cooling system will usually show up as white or rust-colored deposits on the areas adjoining the leak. If wire-type clamps are used at the ends of the hoses, it may be a good idea to replace them with more secure screw-type clamps.

6   Use compressed air or a soft brush to remove bugs, leaves, etc. from the front of the radiator or air conditioning condenser. Be careful not to damage the delicate cooling fins or cut yourself on them.

7   Every other inspection, or at the first indication of cooling system problems, have the cap and system pressure tested. If you don't have a pressure tester, most repair shops will do this for a minimal charge.

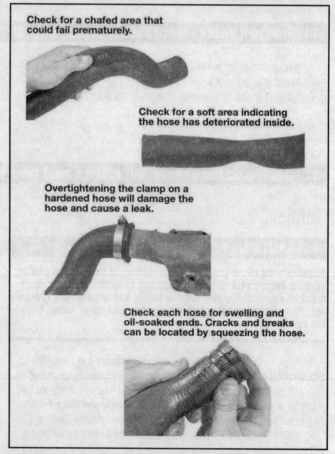

Check for a chafed area that could fail prematurely.

Check for a soft area indicating the hose has deteriorated inside.

Overtightening the clamp on a hardened hose will damage the hose and cause a leak.

Check each hose for swelling and oil-soaked ends. Cracks and breaks can be located by squeezing the hose.

13.4 Hoses, like drivebelts, have a habit of failing at the worst possible time - to prevent the inconvenience of a blown radiator or heater hose, inspect them carefully as shown here

14 Fuel system check (every 15,000 miles or 12 months)

❊ WARNING:

Gasoline is flammable, so take extra precautions when you work on any part of the fuel system. Don't smoke or allow open flames or bare light bulbs near the work area, and don't work in a garage where a gas-type appliance (such as a water heater or clothes dryer) is present. Since fuel is carcinogenic, wear fuel-resistant gloves when there's a possibility of being exposed to fuel, and, if you spill any fuel on your skin, rinse it off immediately with soap and water. Mop up any spills immediately and do not store fuel-soaked rags where they could ignite. When you perform any kind of work on the fuel system, wear safety glasses and have a Class B type fire extinguisher on hand. The fuel system is under constant pressure, so, before any lines are disconnected, the fuel system pressure must be relieved (see Chapter 4).

1 If you smell fuel while driving or after the vehicle has been sitting in the sun, inspect the fuel system immediately.

2 Remove the fuel filler cap and inspect it for damage and corrosion. The gasket should have an unbroken sealing imprint. If the gasket is damaged or corroded, install a new cap.

3 Inspect the fuel feed line for cracks. Make sure that the connections between the fuel lines and the fuel injection system and between the fuel lines and the in-line fuel filter are tight.

❊ WARNING:

Your vehicle is fuel injected, so you must relieve the fuel system pressure before servicing fuel system components.

The fuel system pressure relief procedure is outlined in Chapter 4.

4 Since some components of the fuel system - the fuel tank and part of the fuel feed and return lines, for example - are underneath the vehicle, they can be inspected more easily with the vehicle raised on a hoist. If that's not possible, raise the vehicle and support it on jackstands.

5 With the vehicle raised and safely supported, inspect the fuel tank and filler neck for punctures, cracks and other damage. The connection between the filler neck and the tank is particularly critical. Sometimes a rubber filler neck will leak because of loose clamps or deteriorated rubber. Inspect all fuel tank mounting brackets and straps to be sure that the tank is securely attached to the vehicle.

❊ WARNING:

Do not, under any circumstances, try to repair a fuel tank (except rubber components). A welding torch or any open flame can easily cause fuel vapors inside the tank to explode.

6 Carefully check all rubber hoses and metal lines leading away from the fuel tank. Check for loose connections, deteriorated hoses, crimped lines and other damage. Repair or replace damaged sections as necessary (see Chapter 4).

15 Brake system check (every 15,000 miles or 12 months)

❊ WARNING:

The dust created by the brake system is harmful to your health. Never blow it out with compressed air and don't inhale any of it. An approved filtering mask should be worn when working on the brakes. Do not, under any circumstances, use petroleum-based solvents to clean brake parts. Use brake system cleaner only!

➡ **Note: For detailed photographs of the brake system, refer to Chapter 9.**

15.7a With the wheel off, check the thickness of the inner pad through the inspection hole (front brake shown, rear disc brake similar)

1 In addition to the specified intervals, the brakes should be inspected every time the wheels are removed or whenever a defect is suspected.

2 Any of the following symptoms could indicate a potential brake system defect: The vehicle pulls to one side when the brake pedal is depressed; the brakes make squealing or dragging noises when applied; brake pedal travel is excessive; the pedal pulsates; or brake fluid leaks, usually onto the inside of the tire or wheel.

3 Loosen the wheel lug nuts.

4 Raise the vehicle and place it securely on jackstands.

5 Remove the wheels (see *Jacking and towing* at the front of this book, or your owner's manual, if necessary).

DISC BRAKES

▸ **Refer to illustrations 15.7a, 15.7b and 15.9**

6 There are two pads (an outer and an inner) in each caliper. The pads are visible with the wheels removed.

7 Check the pad thickness by looking at each end of the caliper and through the inspection window in the caliper body (see illustrations). If the lining material is less than the thickness listed in this Chapter's Specifications, replace the pads.

➡ **Note: Keep in mind that the lining material is riveted or bonded to a metal backing plate and the metal portion is not included in this measurement.**

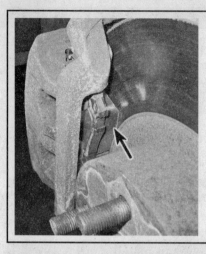

15.7b The outer pad is more easily checked at the edge of the caliper

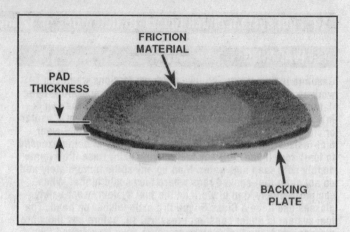

15.9 If a more precise measurement of pad thickness is necessary, remove the pads and measure the remaining friction material

8   If it is difficult to determine the exact thickness of the remaining pad material by the above method, or if you are at all concerned about the condition of the pads, remove the caliper(s), then remove the pads from the calipers for further inspection (see Chapter 9).

9   Once the pads are removed from the calipers, clean them with brake cleaner and re-measure them with a ruler or a vernier caliper (see illustration).

10 Measure the disc thickness with a micrometer to make sure that it still has service life remaining. If any disc is thinner than the specified minimum thickness, replace it (refer to Chapter 9). Even if the disc has service life remaining, check its condition. Look for scoring, gouging and burned spots. If these conditions exist, remove the disc and have it resurfaced (see Chapter 9).

11 Before installing the wheels, check all brake lines and hoses for damage, wear, deformation, cracks, corrosion, leakage, bends and twists, particularly in the vicinity of the rubber hoses at the calipers. Check the clamps for tightness and the connections for leakage. Make sure that all hoses and lines are clear of sharp edges, moving parts and the exhaust system. If any of the above conditions are noted, repair, reroute or replace the lines and/or fittings as necessary (see Chapter 9).

DRUM BRAKES

▶ **Refer to illustration 15.15**

12 On models with rear drum brakes, make sure the parking brake is off then tap on the outside of the drum with a rubber mallet to loosen it.

13 Remove the brake drums. If the drum still won't come off, refer to Chapter 9

14 With the drums removed, carefully clean the brake assembly with brake system cleaner.

❋❋ WARNING:

Don't blow the dust out with compressed air and don't inhale any of it (it is harmful to your health).

15 Note the thickness of the lining material on both front and rear brake shoes (see illustration). Compare the measurement with the limit given in this Chapter's Specifications; if any lining thickness is less than specified, then all of the brake shoes must be replaced (see Chapter 9). The shoes should also be replaced if they're cracked, glazed (shiny areas), or covered with brake fluid.

16 Make sure all the brake assembly springs are connected and in good condition.

17 Check the brake components for signs of fluid leakage. With your finger or a small screwdriver, carefully pry back the rubber cups on the wheel cylinder located at the top of the brake shoes. Any leakage here is an indication that the wheel cylinders should be replaced immediately (see Chapter 9). Also, check all hoses and connections for signs of leakage.

18 Wipe the inside of the drum with a clean rag and denatured alcohol or brake cleaner. Again, be careful not to breathe the dangerous brake dust.

19 Check the inside of the drum for cracks, score marks, deep scratches and "hard spots" which will appear as small discolored areas. If imperfections cannot be removed with fine emery cloth, the drum must be taken to an automotive machine shop for resurfacing.

20 Repeat the procedure for the remaining wheel. If the inspection reveals that all parts are in good condition, reinstall the brake drums, install the wheels and lower the vehicle to the ground.

BRAKE BOOSTER CHECK

21 Sit in the driver's seat and perform the following sequence of tests.

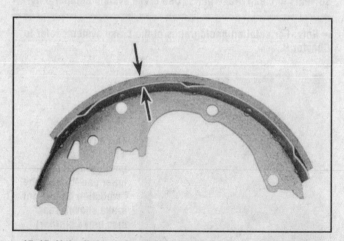

15.15 If the lining is bonded to the brake shoe, measure the lining thickness from the outer surface to the metal shoe. If the lining is riveted, measure from the lining outer surface to the rivet head

22 With the brake fully depressed, start the engine - the pedal should move down a little when the engine starts.

23 With the engine running, depress the brake pedal several times - the travel distance should not change.

24 Depress the brake, stop the engine and hold the pedal in for about 30 seconds - the pedal should neither sink nor rise.

25 Restart the engine, run it for about a minute and turn it off. Then firmly depress the brake several times - the pedal travel should decrease with each application.

26 If your brakes do not operate as described, the brake booster has failed. Refer to Chapter 9 for the replacement procedure.

PARKING BRAKE

27 One method of checking the parking brake is to park the vehicle on a steep hill with the parking brake set and the transaxle in Neutral (be sure to stay in the vehicle for this check!). If the parking brake cannot prevent the vehicle from rolling, it's in need of adjustment (see Chapter 9).

16 Suspension, steering and driveaxle boot check (every 15,000 miles or 12 months)

➡ Note: The steering linkage and suspension components should be checked periodically. Worn or damaged suspension and steering linkage components can result in excessive and abnormal tire wear, poor ride quality and vehicle handling and reduced fuel economy. For detailed illustrations of the steering and suspension components, refer to Chapter 10.

SHOCK ABSORBER CHECK

◆ Refer to illustration 16.6

1 Park the vehicle on level ground, turn the engine off and set the parking brake. Check the tire pressures.

2 Push down at one corner of the vehicle, then release it while noting the movement of the body. It should stop moving and come to rest in a level position within one or two bounces.

3 If the vehicle continues to move up-and-down or if it fails to return to its original position, a worn or weak shock absorber is probably the reason.

4 Repeat the above check at each of the three remaining corners of the vehicle.

5 Raise the vehicle and support it securely on jackstands.

6 Check the shock absorbers for evidence of fluid leakage (see illustration). A light film of fluid is no cause for concern. Make sure that any fluid noted is from the shocks and not from some other source. If leakage is noted, replace the shocks as a set.

7 Check the shocks to be sure that they are securely mounted and undamaged. Check the upper mounts for damage and wear. If damage or wear is noted, replace the shocks as a set (front or rear).

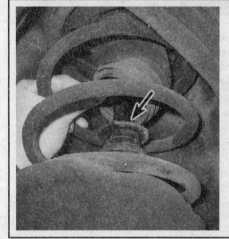

16.6 Check for signs of fluid leakage at this point on shock absorbers

8 If the shocks must be replaced, refer to Chapter 10 for the procedure.

STEERING AND SUSPENSION CHECK

◆ Refer to illustrations 16.9a, 16.9b and 16.11

9 Visually inspect the steering and suspension components (front and rear) for damage and distortion. Look for damaged seals, bushings and leaks of any kind. Examine the bushings where the control arms meet the chassis (see illustrations).

16.9a Examine the mounting points for the control arms . . .

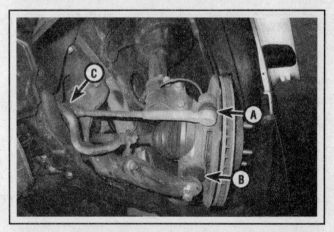

16.9b . . . the tie-rod ends (A), the balljoints (B), and the steering gear boots (C)

16.11 With the steering wheel in the locked position and the vehicle raised, grasp the front tire as shown and try to move it back-and-forth - if any play is noted, check the steering gear mounts and tie-rod ends for looseness

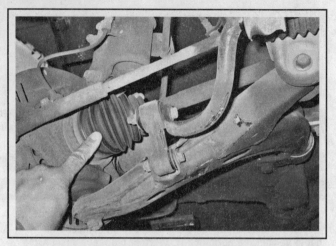

16.14 Inspect the inner and outer driveaxle boots for loose clamps, cracks or signs of leaking lubricant

10 Clean the lower end of the steering knuckle. Have an assistant grasp the lower edge of the tire and move the wheel in-and-out while you look for movement at the steering knuckle-to-control arm balljoint. If there is any movement the suspension balljoint(s) must be replaced.

11 Grasp each front tire at the front and rear edges, push in at the front, pull out at the rear and feel for play in the steering system components. If any freeplay is noted, check the idler arm and the tie-rod ends for looseness (see illustration).

12 Additional steering and suspension system information and illustrations can be found in Chapter 10.

DRIVEAXLE BOOT CHECK

▶ **Refer to illustration 16.14**

13 The driveaxle boots are very important because they prevent dirt, water and foreign material from entering and damaging the constant velocity (CV) joints. Oil and grease can cause the boot material to deteriorate prematurely, so it's a good idea to wash the boots with soap and water. Because it constantly pivots back and forth following the steering action of the front hub, the outer CV boot wears out sooner and should be inspected regularly.

14 Inspect the boots for tears and cracks as well as loose clamps (see illustration). If there is any evidence of cracks or leaking lubricant, they must be replaced as described in Chapter 8.

17 Air filter check and replacement (every 15,000 miles or 12 months)

▶ **Refer to illustrations 17.1a and 17.1b**

1 The air filter is located inside a housing in the engine compartment. Separate the cover halves and remove the air filter element (see illustrations).

2 Inspect the outer surface of the filter element. If it is dirty, replace it. If it is only moderately dusty, it can be reused by blowing it clean from the back to the front surface with compressed air. Because it is a pleated paper type filter, it cannot be washed or oiled. If it cannot be cleaned satisfactorily with compressed air, discard and replace it. While the cover is off, be careful not to drop anything down into the housing.

17.1a Release the spring clips to access the filter element (early models)

17.1b Loosen the intake hose clamp (A), then unlatch the clips (B) to get to the air filter element (late models)

※※ CAUTION:

Never drive the vehicle with the air cleaner removed. Excessive engine wear could result.

3   Wipe out the inside of the air cleaner housing.
4   Place the new filter into the air cleaner housing, making sure it seats properly.
5   Installation of the housing is the reverse of removal.

18 Brake fluid change (every 30,000 miles or 30 months)

※※ WARNING:

Brake fluid can harm your eyes and damage painted surfaces, so use extreme caution when handling or pouring it. Do not use brake fluid that has been standing open or is more than one year old. Brake fluid absorbs moisture from the air. Excess moisture can cause a dangerous loss of braking effectiveness.

1   At the specified intervals, the brake fluid should be drained and replaced. Since the brake fluid may drip or splash when pouring it, place plenty of rags around the master cylinder to protect any surrounding painted surfaces.
2   Before beginning work, purchase the specified brake fluid (see *Recommended lubricants and fluids* at the end of this Chapter).
3   Remove the cap from the master cylinder reservoir.
4   Using a hand suction pump or similar device, withdraw the fluid from the master cylinder reservoir.

5   Add new fluid to the master cylinder until it rises to the base of the filler neck.
6   Bleed the brake system as described in Chapter 9 at all four brakes until new and uncontaminated fluid is expelled from the bleeder screw. Be sure to maintain the fluid level in the master cylinder as you perform the bleeding process. If you allow the master cylinder to run dry, air will enter the system.
7   Refill the master cylinder with fluid and check the operation of the brakes. The pedal should feel solid when depressed, with no sponginess.

※※ WARNING:

Do not operate the vehicle if you are in doubt about the effectiveness of the brake system.

19 Drivebelt check, adjustment and replacement (every 30,000 miles or 30 months)

CHECK

▶ **Refer to illustrations 19.3 and 19.4**

1   The drivebelts are located at the front of the engine and play an important role in the overall operation of the vehicle and its components. Due to their function and material make-up, the belts are prone to failure after a period of time and should be inspected and adjusted periodically to prevent major engine damage.

2   The number of belts used on a particular vehicle depends on the accessories installed. Drivebelts are used to turn the alternator, power steering pump and air conditioning compressor.
3   With the engine off, open the hood and locate the belts at the front of the engine. Using your fingers (and a flashlight, if necessary), move along the belts checking for cracks and separation of the belt plies. Also check for fraying and glazing, which gives the belt a shiny appearance. Check the ribs on the underside of the belt. They should all be the same depth, with none of the surface uneven (see illustration).

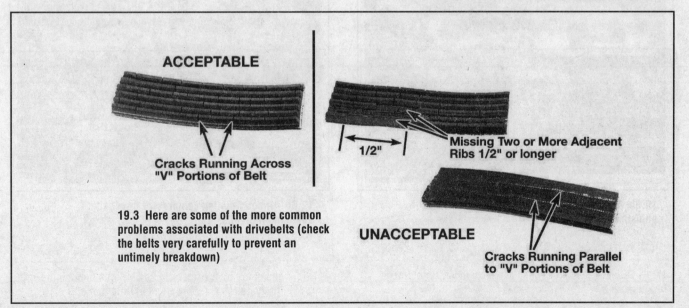

ACCEPTABLE

Cracks Running Across "V" Portions of Belt

19.3 Here are some of the more common problems associated with drivebelts (check the belts very carefully to prevent an untimely breakdown)

1/2"

Missing Two or More Adjacent Ribs 1/2" or longer

UNACCEPTABLE

Cracks Running Parallel to "V" Portions of Belt

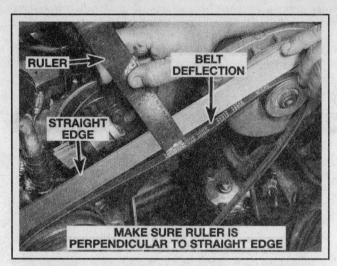

19.4 Measuring drivebelt deflection with a straightedge and ruler

4   The tension of each belt is checked by pushing on the belt at a distance halfway between the pulleys. Push firmly with your thumb and see how much the belt moves (deflects) (see illustration). As rule of thumb, the belt should deflect approximately 1/4-inch.

ADJUSTMENT

♦ **Refer to illustration 19.6a, 19.6b and 19.6c**

5   If it is necessary to adjust the belt tension, either to make the belt tighter or looser, it is done by either of two adjusting assemblies mounted on the front of the engine.

6   For each belt on the engine there will be one adjusting assembly with a slider bolt and a lock bolt. The lock bolts must be loosened slightly to enable you to move the assembly (see illustrations) while the slider bolt is rotated to loosen or tighten the belt tension.

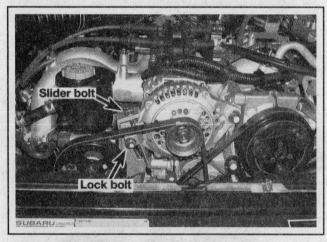

19.6b Alternator/power steering pump drivebelt adjustment details

19.6a Remove the drivebelt cover bolts

7   After the lock bolt has been loosened, turn the slider bolt to loosen or tighten the drivebelt. Hold the accessory in position and check the belt tension. If it is correct, tighten the lock bolt until just snug, then recheck the tension. If the tension is alright, tighten the bolts.

8   Do not use a prybar to move the assembly while the belt is being adjusted. Be sure the drivebelt is correctly aligned within each pulley before applying complete tension to the drivebelt.

REPLACEMENT

9   To replace a belt, follow the above procedures for drivebelt adjustment but slip the belt off the pulleys and remove it. Since belts tend to wear out more or less at the same time, it's a good idea to replace all of them at the same time. Mark each belt and the corresponding pulley grooves so the replacement belts can be installed properly.

10 Take the old belts with you when purchasing new ones in order to make a direct comparison for length, width and design.

11 Adjust the belts as described earlier in this Section.

19.6c Air conditioning compressor drivebelt adjustment details

20 Fuel filter replacement (every 30,000 miles or 30 months)

▶ Refer to illustration 20.2

❊❊ WARNING 1:

Gasoline is extremely flammable, so take extra precautions when you work on any part of the fuel system. Don't smoke or allow open flames or bare light bulbs near the work area, and don't work in a garage where a gas-type appliance (such as a water heater or clothes dryer) is present. Since gasoline is carcinogenic, wear fuel-resistant gloves when there's a possibility of being exposed to fuel, and, if you spill any fuel on your skin, rinse it off immediately with soap and water. Mop up any spills immediately and do not store fuel-soaked rags where they could ignite. The fuel system is under constant pressure, so, if any fuel lines are to be disconnected, the fuel pressure in the system must be relieved first (see Chapter 4 for more information). When you perform any kind of work on the fuel system, wear safety glasses and have a Class B type fire extinguisher on hand.

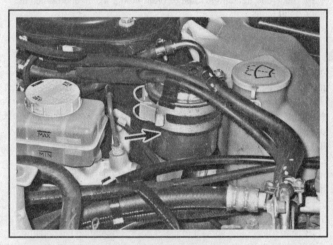

20.2 The fuel filter is located in the left side of the engine compartment, near the brake master cylinder

❊❊ WARNING 2:

Refer to Chapter 4 and depressurize the fuel system before removing the filter!

➡ Note 1: This procedure applies to 2000 through 2003 non-turbocharged Legacy and Outback models, and 2000 through 2004 non-turbocharged Forester models with an external fuel filter in the engine compartment. These models also use another filter, which is an integral part of the fuel pump/fuel level sending unit assembly. You must change the external fuel filter in the engine compartment at the interval specified. There is no specified maintenance interval for the in-tank filter on these models, but you should inspect it, clean it and replace it, if necessary, whenever you have to remove the fuel pump/fuel level sending unit (see Chapter 4).

➡ Note 2: On all other models there is no external fuel filter in the engine compartment. Instead, these models rely on the filter that's an integral part of the fuel pump/fuel level sending unit. On these models, the specified maintenance interval is also 30,000 miles or 30 months, whichever comes first. See Chapter 4, Section 2 for the replacement procedure.

1 This job should be done with the engine cold (after sitting at least three hours). Place rags or newspapers under the filter to catch spilled fuel.

2 The fuel filter is located in the engine compartment on the left side (see illustration).

3 To replace the filter, loosen the clamps and slide them down the hoses, past the fittings on the filter.

4 Carefully twist and pull on the hoses to separate them from the filter. If the hoses are in bad shape, now would be a good time to replace them with new ones.

5 Unclip the filter bracket, pull the filter out of the bracket and install the new one, then hook up the hoses and reposition the clamps, tightening them securely. Make sure the hose from the fuel tank connects to the fitting marked IN. Start the engine and check carefully for leaks at the filter hose connections.

21 Cooling system servicing (draining, flushing and refilling) (every 30,000 miles or 30 months)

▶ Refer to illustrations 21.3 and 21.4

❊❊ WARNING:

Do not allow antifreeze to come in contact with your skin or painted surfaces of the vehicle. Rinse off spills immediately with plenty of water. Antifreeze is highly toxic if ingested. Never leave antifreeze lying around in an open container or in puddles on the floor; children and pets are attracted by it's sweet smell and may drink it. Check with local authorities about disposing of used anti-freeze. Many communities have collection centers which will see that antifreeze is disposed of safely.

1 Periodically, the cooling system should be drained, flushed and refilled to replenish the antifreeze mixture and prevent formation of rust and corrosion, which can impair the performance of the cooling system and cause engine damage. When the cooling system is serviced, all hoses and the radiator cap should be checked and replaced if necessary.

2 Apply the parking brake and block the wheels.

❊❊ WARNING:

If the vehicle has just been driven, wait several hours to allow the engine to cool down before beginning this procedure.

21.3 Radiator drain location

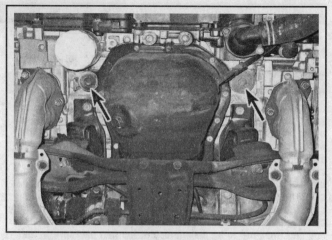

21.4 Engine block drain plug locations

3   Move a large container under the radiator drain to catch the coolant. The radiator drain plug is located at the lower right corner of the radiator (see illustration). Attach a hose to the drain fitting (if possible) to direct the coolant into the container, then unscrew the drain fitting.

4   Remove the radiator cap and allow the radiator to drain, then, move the container under the engine block. Remove the engine block drain plugs and allow the coolant in the block to drain (see illustration).

5   While the coolant is draining, check the condition of the radiator hoses, heater hoses and clamps (refer to Section 13 if necessary).

6   Replace any damaged clamps or hoses.

7   Once the system is completely drained, flush the radiator with fresh water from a garden hose until it runs clear at the drain. The flushing action of the water will remove sediments from the radiator but will not remove rust and scale from the engine and cooling tube surfaces.

8   These deposits can be removed with a chemical cleaner. Follow the procedure outlined in the manufacturer's instructions. If the radiator is severely corroded, damaged or leaking, it should be removed (see Chapter 3) and taken to a radiator repair shop.

9   Remove the cap and the overflow hose from the coolant reservoir

and flush the reservoir with clean water, then reconnect the hose.

10 Close and tighten the radiator drain fitting. Install and tighten the block drain plugs.

11 Place the heater temperature control in the maximum heat position.

12 Slowly add new coolant (a 50/50 mixture of water and antifreeze) to the radiator (non-turbo models) or coolant filler tank (turbo models) until it's full. Add coolant to the reservoir up to the lower mark.

13 Install the radiator cap and, on turbo models the coolant filler tank cap, and run the engine in a well-ventilated area until the thermostat opens (coolant will begin flowing through the radiator and the upper radiator hose will become hot).

14 Turn the engine off and let it cool. Add more coolant mixture to bring the level back up to the lip on the radiator filler neck or coolant filler tank neck.

15 Squeeze the upper radiator hose to expel air, then add more coolant mixture if necessary. Reinstall the radiator cap.

16 Start the engine, allow it to reach normal operating temperature and check for leaks.

22   Spark plug replacement (every 30,000 miles or 30 months)

⬧ **Refer to illustrations 22.1, 22.4a, 22.4b, 22.7, 22.9, 22.10, 22.11a and 22.11b**

1   In most cases, the tools necessary for spark plug replacement include a spark plug socket which fits onto a ratchet (spark plug sockets are padded inside to prevent damage to the porcelain insulators on the new plugs), various extensions and a gap gauge to check and adjust the gaps on the new plugs (see illustration). A torque wrench should be used to tighten the new plugs.

2   The best approach when replacing the spark plugs is to purchase the new ones in advance, adjust them to the proper gap and replace the plugs one at a time. When buying the new spark plugs, be sure to obtain the correct plug type for your particular engine. This information can be found in the *Specifications* Section at the end of this Chapter or in your owner's manual.

3   Allow the engine to cool completely before attempting to remove any of the plugs. These engines are equipped with aluminum cylinder heads, which can be damaged if the spark plugs are removed when the engine is hot. While you are waiting for the engine to cool, check the

new plugs for defects and adjust the gaps.

4   The gap is checked by inserting the proper-thickness gauge between the electrodes at the tip of the plug (see illustration). The gap between the electrodes should be the same as the one specified on the Emissions Control Information label or in this Chapter's Specifications. The gauge should just slide between the electrodes with a slight amount of drag. If the gap is incorrect, use the adjuster on the gauge body to bend the curved side electrode slightly until the proper gap is obtained (see illustration). If the side electrode is not exactly over the center electrode, bend it with the adjuster until it is. Check for cracks in the porcelain insulator (if any are found, the plug should not be used).

✳✳ CAUTION:

When checking the gap on platinum or iridium-tipped plugs, don't force the gauge between the electrodes; doing so could scrape the thin coating from the electrodes and greatly reduce the spark plug's life.

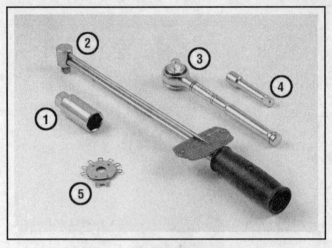

22.1 Tools required for changing spark plugs

1 **Spark plug socket** - This will have special padding inside to protect the spark plug's porcelain insulator
2 **Torque wrench** - Although not mandatory, using this tool is the best way to ensure the plugs are tightened properly
3 **Ratchet** - Standard hand tool to fit the spark plug socket
4 **Extension** - Depending on model and accessories, you may need special extensions and universal joints to reach one or more of the plugs
5 **Spark plug gap gauge** - This gauge for checking the gap comes in a variety of styles. Make sure the gap for your engine is included

5   On turbo engines, remove the battery and battery tray (see Chapter 5).

6   If equipped, remove the engine cover, then remove the air intake duct and, on models where it would interfere with access to the spark plugs, the resonator and/or the air filter housing (see Chapter 4).

7   Turbo engines are equipped with individual ignition coils which must be removed first to access the spark plugs (see illustration). On non-turbo engines, remove the spark plug wire from one spark plug. Pull only on the boot at the end of the wire - do not pull on the wire. A plug wire removal tool should be used if available.

8   If compressed air is available, use it to blow any dirt or foreign material away from the spark plug hole. The idea here is to eliminate the possibility of debris falling into the cylinder as the spark plug is removed.

9   Place the spark plug socket over the plug and remove it from the engine by turning it in a counterclockwise direction (see illustration).

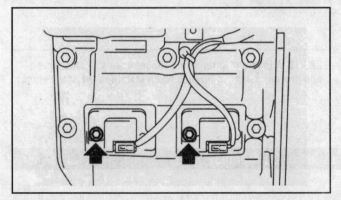

22.7 Remove the mounting bolts securing the ignition coils

22.4a Spark plug manufacturers recommend using a wire type gauge when checking the gap - if the wire does not slide between the electrodes with a slight drag, adjustment is required

22.4b To change the gap, bend the side electrode only, as indicated by the arrows, and be very careful not to crack or chip the porcelain insulator surrounding the center electrode

22.9 Use a socket and extension to unscrew the spark plugs

A normally worn spark plug should have light tan or gray deposits on the firing tip.

A carbon fouled plug, identified by soft, sooty, black deposits, may indicate an improperly tuned vehicle. Check the air cleaner, ignition components and engine control system.

An oil fouled spark plug indicates an engine with worn piston rings and/or bad valve seals allowing excessive oil to enter the chamber.

This spark plug has been left in the engine too long, as evidenced by the extreme gap- Plugs with such an extreme gap can cause misfiring and stumbling accompanied by a noticeable lack of power.

A physically damaged spark plug may be evidence of severe detonation in that cylinder. Watch that cylinder carefully between services, as a continued detonation will not only damage the plug, but could also damage the engine.

A bridged or almost bridged spark plug, identified by a build-up between the electrodes caused by excessive carbon or oil build-up on the plug.

22.10 Inspect the spark plug to determine engine running conditions

10 Compare the spark plug with this chart (see illustration) to get an indication of the general running condition of the engine.

11 Apply a small amount of anti-seize compound to the spark plug threads (see illustration). Install one of the new plugs into the hole until you can no longer turn it with your fingers, then tighten it with a torque wrench (if available) or the ratchet. It is a good idea to slip a short length of rubber hose over the end of the plug to use as a tool to thread it into place (see illustration). The hose will grip the plug well enough to turn it, but will start to slip if the plug begins to cross-thread in the hole - this will prevent damaged threads and the accompanying repair costs.

12 On turbo engines, before pushing the ignition coil onto the end of the plug, inspect the ignition coil following the procedures outlined in Section 23. On non-turbo engines, inspect the plug wire following the procedures outlined in Section 24.

13 Repeat the procedure for the remaining spark plugs.

22.11a Apply a thin coat of anti-seize compound to the spark plug threads

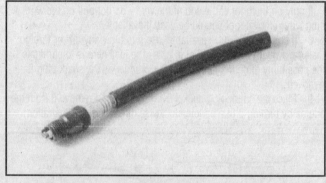
22.11b A length of snug-fitting rubber hose will save time and prevent damaged threads when installing the spark plugs

23 Ignition coil check (turbo engines) (every 30,000 miles or 30 months)

1 Remove the ignition coils (see illustration 22.7). Clean the coil(s) with a dampened cloth and dry them thoroughly.

2 Inspect each coil, for cracks, damage and carbon tracking. If damage exists, replace the coil.

24 Spark plug wire check and replacement (non-turbo engines) (every 30,000 miles or 30 months)

1 The spark plug wires should be checked at the recommended intervals or whenever new spark plugs are installed.

2 Begin this procedure by making a visual check of the spark plug wires while the engine is running. In a darkened garage (make sure there is adequate ventilation) or at night while using a flashlight, start the engine and observe each plug wire. Be careful not to come into contact with any moving engine parts. If possible, use an insulated or non-conductive object to wiggle each wire. If there is a break in the wire, you will see arcing or a small blue spark coming from the damaged area. Secondary ignition voltage increases with engine speed and sometimes a damaged wire will not produce an arc at idle speed. Have an assistant press the accelerator pedal to raise the engine speed to approximately 2000 rpm. Check the spark plug wires for arcing as stated previously. If arcing is noticed, replace all spark plug wires.

3 Perform the following checks with the engine OFF. The wires should be inspected one at a time to prevent mixing up the order that is essential for proper engine operation.

4 With the engine cool, disconnect the spark plug wire from the ignition coil pack. Pull only on the boot at the end of the wire; don't pull on the wire itself. Use a twisting motion to free the boot/wire from the coil. Disconnect the same spark plug wire from the spark plug, using the same twisting method while pulling on the boot. Disconnect the spark plug wire from any retaining clips as necessary and remove it from the engine.

5 Check inside the boot for corrosion, which will look like a white, crusty powder (don't mistake the white dielectric grease used on some plug wire boots for corrosion protection).

6 Now push the wire and boot back onto the end of the spark plug. It should be a tight fit on the plug end. If not, remove the wire and use a pair of pliers to carefully crimp the metal connector inside the wire boot until the fit is snug.

7 Now push the wire and boot back into the end of the ignition coil terminal. It should be a tight fit in the terminal. If not, remove the wire and use a pair of pliers to carefully crimp the metal connector inside the wire boot until the fit is snug.

8 Now, using a cloth, clean each wire along its entire length. Remove all built-up dirt and grease. As this is done, inspect for burned areas, cracks and any other form of damage. Bend the wires in several places to ensure that the conductive material inside hasn't hardened. Repeat the procedure for the remaining wires.

9 If new spark plug wires are required, purchase a complete set for your particular engine. The terminals and rubber boots should already be installed on the wires. Replace the wires one at a time to avoid mixing up the firing order and make sure the terminals are securely seated on the coil pack and the spark plugs.

10 Attach the plug wire to the new spark plug and to the ignition coil pack using a twisting motion on the boot until it is firmly seated. Attach the spark plug wire to any retaining clips to keep the wires in their proper location on the valve cover.

25 Automatic transaxle fluid change (every 30,000 miles or 30 months)

▶ **Refer to illustration 25.7**

1 At the specified time intervals, the automatic transaxle fluid should be drained and replaced.

2 Before beginning work, purchase the specified transmission fluid (see *Recommended fluids and lubricants* and *Capacities* at the end of this Chapter).

3 Other tools necessary for this job include jackstands to support the vehicle in a raised position, a wrench, a drain pan capable of holding at least eight quarts, newspapers and clean rags.

4 The fluid should be drained after the vehicle has been driven and brought to operating temperature. Hot fluid is more effective than cold fluid at removing built up sediment.

❊❊ WARNING:

Fluid temperature can exceed 350-degrees F in a hot transaxle. Wear protective gloves.

5 Raise the vehicle and place it on jackstands.

6 Move the necessary equipment under the vehicle, being careful not to touch any of the hot exhaust components.

7 Place the drain pan under the drain plug in the transaxle housing or fluid pan and remove the drain plug (see illustration). Be sure the drain pan is in position, as fluid will come out with some force. Once the fluid is drained, reinstall the drain plug securely.

8 Lower the vehicle.

9 With the engine off, add new fluid to the transaxle through the dipstick tube. Use a funnel to prevent spills. It is best to add a little fluid at a time, continually checking the level with the dipstick (see Section 4). Allow the fluid time to drain into the pan.

10 Start the engine and shift the selector into all positions from Park through Low then shift into Park and apply the parking brake.

11 With the engine idling, check the fluid level. Add fluid up to the lower level on the dipstick.

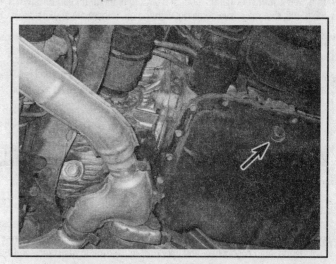

25.7 Location of the automatic transmission fluid drain plug

26 Manual transaxle lubricant change (every 30,000 miles or 30 months)

▶ Refer to illustration 26.3

1   Drive the vehicle to warm the lubricant, then raise the vehicle and support it securely on jackstands.

2   Move a drain pan, rags, newspapers and wrenches under the transaxle.

3   Remove the transaxle drain plug at the bottom of the case and allow the lubricant to drain into the pan (see illustration).

4   After the lubricant has drained completely, reinstall the plug and tighten it securely.

5   Fill the transaxle with the recommended lubricant as described in Section 4.

6   Lower the vehicle.

7   Drive the vehicle for a short distance, then check the drain plug for leakage.

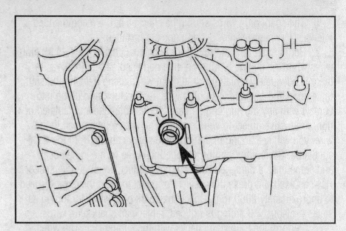

26.3 On manual transaxles, the drain plug is located on the bottom of the transaxle case

27 Differential lubricant change (every 30,000 miles or 30 months)

▶ Refer to illustration 27.3

➡Note: The following procedure is used for the rear differential as well as the front differential on vehicles equipped with automatic transaxles.

1   Drive the vehicle for several miles to warm up the differential oil, then raise the vehicle and support it securely on jackstands.

2   Move a drain pan, rags, newspapers and the proper tools under the vehicle.

3   With the drain pan under the differential, use a socket and ratchet to loosen the drain plug on the rear differential (see illustration 4.50). On automatic transaxle models, also drain the front differential (see illustration).

4   Once the plug is loosened, carefully unscrew it with your fingers until you can remove it from the case.

5   Allow all of the oil to drain into the pan, then replace the drain plug and tighten it securely.

6   Feel with your hands along the bottom of the drain pan for any metal bits that may have come out with the oil. If there are any, it's a sign of excessive wear, indicating that the internal components should be carefully inspected in the near future.

7   Remove the rear differential check/fill plug (see Section 4). Using a hand pump, syringe or funnel, fill the differential with the correct amount and grade of oil (see the Specifications) until the level is just at

the bottom of the plug hole.

8   Reinstall the plug and tighten it securely.

9   On vehicles equipped automatic transaxles, fill the front differential with the recommended lubricant as described in Section 4.

10 Lower the vehicle. Check for leaks at the drain plug after the first few miles of driving.

27.3 Front differential drain plug (automatic transaxle)

28 Wheel bearing check (every 60,000 miles or 48 months)

1   These models are equipped with sealed bearings in the front and rear hub assemblies. In most cases the wheel bearings will not need servicing. However, the bearings should be checked whenever the vehicle is raised for any reason. With the vehicle securely supported on jackstands, spin each wheel and check for noise, rolling resistance and freeplay.

2   Grasp the top of each tire with one hand and the bottom with the other. Move the wheel in and out on the spindle. If there's any noticeable movement, remove the front wheel and check the freeplay using a dial indicator. Refer to the Specifications listed in this Chapter.

3   Replace the bearing assembly if excess freeplay and bearing noise exists (refer to Chapter 10).

Specifications

Recommended lubricants and fluids

➡Note: Listed here are manufacturer recommendations at the time this manual was written. Manufacturers occasionally upgrade their fluid and lubricant specifications, so check with your auto parts store for current recommendations.

Engine oil
    Type   API "Certified for gasoline engines"
    Viscosity   See accompanying chart

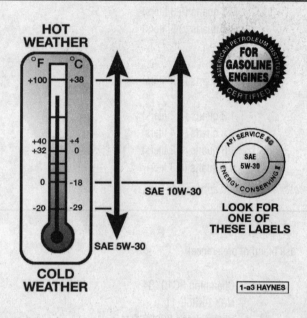

Engine oil viscosity chart - for best fuel economy and cold starting, select the lowest SAE viscosity grade for the expected temperature range

1-a3 HAYNES

Coolant	Genuine Subaru coolant or equivalent anti-corrosive, ethylene glycol-based anti-freeze
Brake fluid	DOT 3 or DOT 4
Clutch fluid	DOT 3 or DOT 4
Power steering fluid	DEXRON III ATF
Automatic transaxle fluid	
Legacy and Outback models	
2004 and earlier	DEXRON III ATF
2005 and later	Subaru ATF (or equivalent)
Forester models	
2005 and earlier	DEXRON III ATF
2006	Subaru ATF (or equivalent)
Manual transaxle lubricant	API GL-5 SAE 75W-90 gear oil
Differential lubricant	
Front differential (automatic transaxle)	
2003 and earlier models	API GL-5 SAE 80W-90 gear oil
2004 and later models	API GL-5 SAE 75W-90 gear oil
Rear differential	API GL-5 SAE 75W-90 gear oil

Capacities*

Engine oil (with filter change)	4.2 quarts (4.0 liters)
Cooling system	
Automatic transaxle	
Legacy and Outback	
2004 and earlier models	9.8 quarts (9.3 liters)
2005 and later	
Non-turbo models	9.8 quarts (9.3 liters)
Turbo models	10.4 quarts (9.8 liters)
Forester models	9.8 quarts (9.3 liters)
Manual transaxle	3.7 quarts (3.5 liters)
Automatic transaxle front differential	
Legacy and Outback	
2004 and earlier models	1.3 quarts (1.2 liters)
2005 and later	
Non-turbo models	1.3 quarts (1.2 liters)
Turbo models	1.5 quarts (1.4 liters)
Forester	1.3 quarts (1.2 liters)
Rear differential	0.8 quarts (0.8 liter)

All capacities approximate. Add as necessary to bring to appropriate level.

Ignition system

Spark plug type (types are equivalents - use brand of preference)	
2001 and earlier engines	
Type I	Champion RC10YC4
Type II	NGK BKR6E-11
Type III	Nippondenso K20PR-U11
2002 and 2003 engines	
Type I	Champion RC10YC4
Type II	NGK BKR6E-11
Type III	NGK BKR5E-11
2004 models	
Non-turbo engine	
Type I	Champion RC10YC4
Type II	NGK BKR6E-11
Type III	NGK BKR5E-11
(California spec model only)	NGK FR5AP-11
Turbo engine	NGK ILFR6B
2005 and later models	
Non-turbo engine	NGK FR5AP-11
Turbo engine	NGK ILFR6B
Spark plug gap	
Non-turbo engine	0.039 to 0.043 inch (1.0 to 1.1 mm)
Turbo engine	0.028 to 0.031 inch (0.7 to 0.8 mm)
Firing order	1-3-2-4

Brakes

Disc brake pad lining thickness (minimum)	1/16 inch (1.5 mm)
Brake pedal freeplay	
Legacy and Outback	
2004 and earlier models	0.04 to 0.12 inch (1 to 3 mm)
2005 and later models	0.02 to 0.08 inch (0.5 to 2.0 mm)
Forester	
2002 and earlier models	0.04 to 0.12 inch (1 to 3 mm)
2003 and later models	0.02 to 0.08 inch (0.5 to 2.0 mm)
Wheel bearing freeplay limit	0.002 inch (0.05 mm)

Torque specifications	Ft-lbs	Nm
Automatic transaxle drain plug		
Legacy and Outback		
2004 and earlier models	18	25
2005 and later models		
4AT	18	25
5AT	20	14.5
Forester	25	18.4
Manual transaxle drain plug		
Legacy and Outback		
2004 and earlier models	32.5	44
2005 and later models	50.6	69
Forester		
2003 and earlier models	32.5	44
2004 and later models	51.6	70
Front differential drain plug (automatic transaxle)		
Legacy and Outback		
2003 and earlier models	32.5	44
2004 and 2005 models	51.6	70
2006 models		
Aluminum gasket	32.5	44
Copper gasket	51.6	70
Forester		
2004 and earlier models	32.5	44
2005 and later models		
Aluminum gasket	32.5	44
Copper gasket	51.6	70
Engine oil drain plug	33	44
Spark plugs	15.5	21
Wheel lug nuts		
Legacy and Outback		
2004 and earlier models	65	88
2005 and later models	81	110
Forester	66	90

Notes

Section

Reference to other Chapters

2A

ENGINES

1 General information

The engines in these vehicles are of the horizontally opposed, four-cylinder configuration. The crankcase is made of aluminum and is vertically split. The cylinder heads are also aluminum, while the crankshaft is made of steel and supported by five main bearings. The aluminum pistons have two compression rings and one combination-type oil control ring. Each cylinder is equipped with two intake valves and two exhaust valves, for a total of 16 valves.

The non-turbocharged engine is a single overhead-cam (SOHC) design. The camshafts (one mounted in each cylinder head) operate the valves with rocker arms. The valves are adjusted with threaded adjuster screws on the rocker arms.

Some models with the non-turbocharged engine are designated with an Ultra Low Emission Vehicle (ULEV) rating for their lower emissions output. These ULEV models are available in certain states and will be marked as such on the Vehicle Emission Control Information (VECI) label under the hood. Refer to the introductory pages of this manual for information on the VECI label.

A turbocharged engine is available as an option in certain models. It's a double overhead-cam (DOHC) design with four camshafts, two mounted on each cylinder head. The camshafts operate the valves by depressing bucket-type valve lifters. Valve adjustment is carried out by replacing lifters with ones of different head thickness.

2006 non-turbocharged engines and all turbocharged engines are equipped with Variable Valve Timing and Lift systems. Turbocharged models are equipped with a variable valve timing system that adjusts the phase angle (advance or retard) of the intake camshafts. 2006 non-turbocharged models are equipped with a variable valve lift system that alters valve lift by actuating the valves through an additional set of cam lobes of a different profile. Both systems are hydraulically actuated.

The camshafts are driven by the crankshaft with a single timing belt. Timing belt tension is maintained by a tensioner mounted between the cylinder banks. The tensioner incorporates a compression spring that acts against a main spring and oil chamber to keep the tensioner balanced. The water pump is also driven by the timing belt. The timing belt is scheduled for replacement at prescribed service intervals (see Chapter 1).

The engine oil pump is driven by the crankshaft and it is mounted directly in the center of the engine behind the timing belt and covers.

2 Repair operations possible with the engine in the vehicle

Some major repair operations can be accomplished without removing the engine from the vehicle.

Clean the engine compartment and the exterior of the engine with some type of degreaser before any work is done. It will make the job easier and help keep dirt out of the internal areas of the engine.

Depending on the components involved, it may be helpful to remove the hood to improve access to the engine as repairs are performed (refer to Chapter 11 if necessary). Cover the fenders to prevent damage to the paint. Special pads are available, but an old bedspread or blanket will also work.

If vacuum, exhaust, oil or coolant leaks develop, indicating a need for gasket or seal replacement, the repairs can generally be made with the engine in the vehicle. The intake and exhaust gaskets, oil pan gasket, crankshaft oil seals and cylinder head gasket are all accessible with the engine in place. However, cylinder head gasket replacement is easier with the engine out of the chassis.

Exterior engine components, such as the intake and exhaust, the oil pan (and the oil pump), the water pump, the starter motor, the alternator, the ignition system and fuel system components can be removed for repair with the engine in place.

Since the cylinder heads can be removed without pulling the engine (although this is difficult), valve component servicing can also be accomplished with the engine in the vehicle. Replacement of the camshafts, rockers and lifters can be accomplished with the engine in the chassis.

3 Top Dead Center (TDC) for number one piston - locating

▶ **Refer to illustration 3.7**

1 Top Dead Center (TDC) is the highest point in the cylinder that each piston reaches as it travels up the cylinder bore. Each piston reaches TDC on the compression stroke and again on the exhaust stroke, but TDC generally refers to piston position on the compression stroke.

2 Positioning the piston(s) at TDC is an essential part of procedures such as valve adjustment, camshaft and timing belt/sprocket removal.

3 Before beginning this procedure, be sure to place the transaxle in Neutral and apply the parking brake or block the rear wheels. Also, disable the ignition system by disconnecting the harness connector from the ignition coil (see Chapter 5). Disable the fuel pump (see Chapter 4, Section 2). Remove the spark plugs (see Chapter 1).

4 In order to bring any piston to TDC, the crankshaft must be turned using one of the methods outlined below. When looking at the front of the engine, normal crankshaft rotation is clockwise.

a) *The preferred method is to turn the crankshaft with a socket and ratchet attached to the bolt threaded into the front of the crankshaft. Turn the bolt in a clockwise direction only. Never turn the bolt counterclockwise.*

b) *A remote starter switch, which may save some time, can also be used. Follow the instructions included with the switch. Once the piston is close to TDC, use a socket and ratchet as described in the previous paragraph.*

c) *If an assistant is available to turn the ignition switch to the Start position in short bursts, you can get the piston close to TDC without a remote starter switch. Make sure your assistant is out of the vehicle, away from the ignition switch, then use a socket and ratchet as described in Paragraph (a) to complete the procedure.*

5   To find TDC on the compression stroke for the number one cylinder, install a compression gauge in the number one spark plug hole (see Chapter 2B).

6   Rotate the crankshaft using a socket and breaker bar on the crankshaft pulley while observing the compression gauge. When the compression stroke of number one cylinder is reached, compression pressure will begin to build and register on the gauge.

7   Continue rotating the crankshaft until the notch in the crankshaft pulley aligns with the "0" on the timing scale (see illustration). If you go past the marks, release the gauge pressure and rotate the crankshaft two revolutions.

3.7 TDC mark on the crankshaft pulley aligned with zero mark on the timing scale

4   Valve covers - removal and installation

REMOVAL

1   Disconnect the cable from the negative terminal of the battery (see Chapter 5).

Right side (passenger's side) valve cover

2   Remove the air intake ducts, the resonator and the air filter housing (see Chapter 4).

➡**Note: Depending on the year and model of the vehicle, the air filter housing may not need to be removed.**

3   Disconnect the breather hose from the valve cover.

Turbocharged models

4   Remove the coolant filler tank (see Chapter 3).

5   Disconnect the oil line and remove the Variable Valve Timing (VVT) oil flow control solenoid from the valve cover (see Chapter 6).

All models

♦ **Refer to illustration 4.7**

6   Disconnect the spark plug wires (see Chapter 1) or the ignition coils (see Chapter 5) from each cylinder.

7   Remove the bolts from the valve cover (see illustration) and separate the cover from the cylinder head. Depending on the tools you

are using, it may be easier to remove the lower valve cover bolts from under the vehicle. If this is the case, raise the vehicle and support it securely on jackstands.

Left side (driver's side) valve cover

8   Remove the battery and the battery tray from the engine compartment (see Chapter 5).

9   Remove the windshield washer fluid reservoir from the engine compartment.

10 Disconnect the breather hose from the valve cover.

11 Remove the oil filler pipe.

➡**Note: On some models it may not be necessary to remove the oil filler pipe. However, most models will require the extra clearance for valve cover removal.**

12 Disconnect the spark plug wires (see Chapter 1) or the ignition coils (see Chapter 5) from each cylinder.

13 Remove the bolts from the valve cover (see illustration 4.7) and separate the cover from the cylinder head. Depending on the tools you are using, it may be easier to remove the lower valve cover bolts from under the vehicle. If this is the case, raise the vehicle and support it securely on jackstands.

All models

♦ **Refer to illustrations 4.14a, 4.14b, 4.15, 4.16a and 4.16b**

14 Installation is the reverse of removal. Be sure to install a new

4.7 Remove the bolts from the valve cover (non-turbocharged model shown)

4.14a When replacing the valve cover gasket, make sure it seats in its groove properly

4.14b Replace the spark plug seals before installing the valve cover

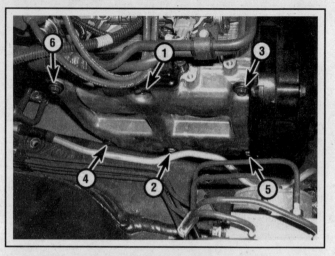

4.15 Valve cover bolt tightening sequence on 2006 non-turbocharged models

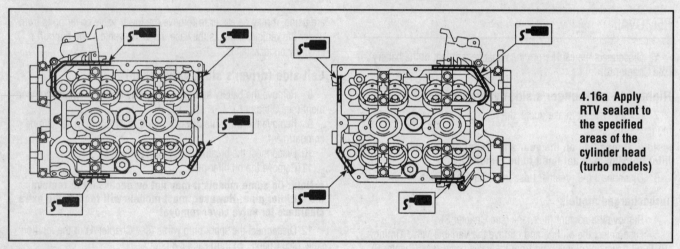

4.16a Apply RTV sealant to the specified areas of the cylinder head (turbo models)

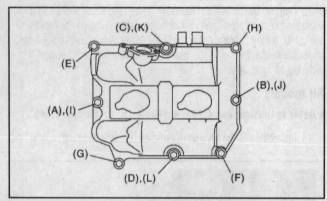

4.16b Valve cover bolt tightening sequence on turbocharged models

valve cover gasket (see illustrations) and tighten the bolts to the torque listed in this Chapter's Specifications.

15 On 2006 non-turbocharged models, use the correct bolt tightening sequence (see illustration).

16 On all turbocharged models, first apply RTV sealant to the specified areas of the cylinder head (see illustration), then install the valve cover and tighten the bolts in the correct sequence (see illustration).

5 Intake manifold - removal and installation

✳✳ WARNING:

ait until the engine is completely cool before beginning this procedure.

REMOVAL

▸ **Refer to illustrations 5.3 and 5.6**

1 Relieve the fuel pressure (see Chapter 4).

5.3 Remove the engine cover fasteners and engine cover - 2006 Outback turbocharged model shown

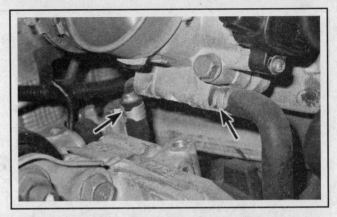

5.6 Location of the coolant hoses on the throttle body (2001 non-turbocharged model shown)

2   Disconnect the cable from the negative terminal of the battery (see Chapter 5).

3   Remove the engine cover, if equipped (see illustration).

4   Remove the air filter housing, the resonator and air intake ducts, as necessary, for access to the intake manifold (see Chapter 4).

➡Note: Depending on the year and model of the vehicle, the air filter housing and/or resonator may not need to be removed.

5   On non-turbo models, detach the spark plug wires from the ignition coil.

6   Clamp-off and disconnect the coolant hoses from the throttle body (see illustration). Place a rag under the connections to catch any coolant left in the hoses and throttle body.

7   Disconnect the electrical connectors from the fuel injectors, the CKP, CMP. ECT, knock sensors, oxygen sensors, etc. (see Chapters 4

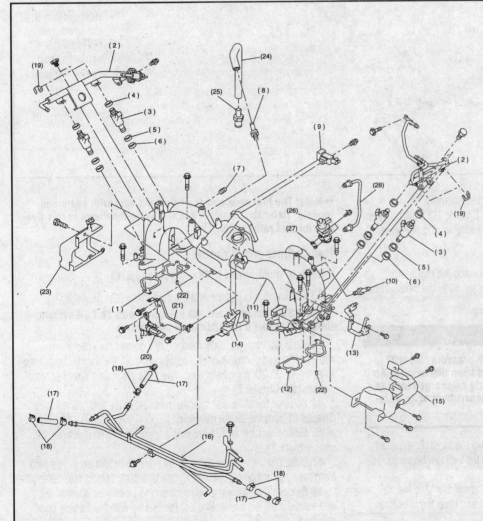

5.13a Exploded view of the intake manifold and related components - 2000 through 2004 non-turbocharged, non-ULEV models

1   Intake manifold gasket
2   Fuel injector rail
3   Fuel injector
4   O-ring
5   O-ring
6   O-ring
7   Plug
8   Nipple
9   Purge control solenoid valve
10   Nipple
11   Intake manifold
12   Intake manifold gasket (left side)
13   Plug cord holder (left side)
14   Accelerator cable bracket
15   Fuel rail protector (left side)
16   Fuel rail assembly
17   Fuel hose
18   Clip
19   Clip
20   Air assist injector solenoid valve
21   Air assist injector solenoid valve bracket
22   Guide pin
23   Fuel rail protector (right side)
24   PCV hose
25   PCV valve
26   EGR valve
27   EGR valve gasket
28   EGR pipe

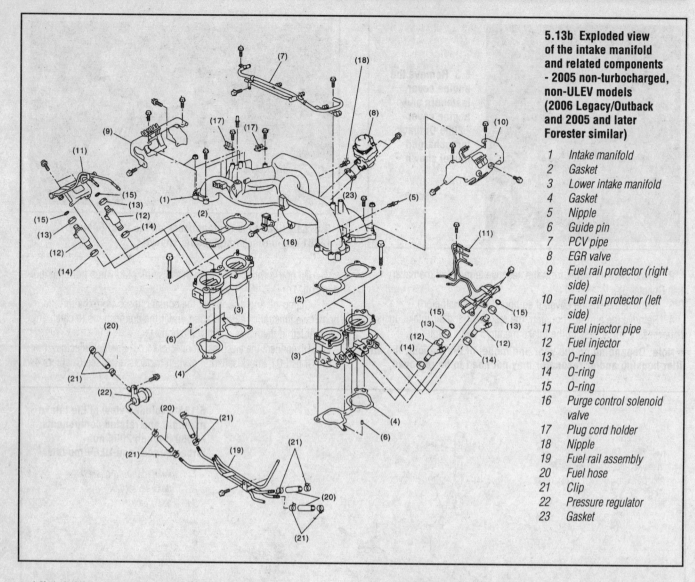

5.13b Exploded view of the intake manifold and related components - 2005 non-turbocharged, non-ULEV models (2006 Legacy/Outback and 2005 and later Forester similar)

1   Intake manifold
2   Gasket
3   Lower intake manifold
4   Gasket
5   Nipple
6   Guide pin
7   PCV pipe
8   EGR valve
9   Fuel rail protector (right side)
10   Fuel rail protector (left side)
11   Fuel injector pipe
12   Fuel injector
13   O-ring
14   O-ring
15   O-ring
16   Purge control solenoid valve
17   Plug cord holder
18   Nipple
19   Fuel rail assembly
20   Fuel hose
21   Clip
22   Pressure regulator
23   Gasket

and 6). Label the connectors to insure correct reassembly.

8   Remove the power steering pump (see Chapter 10). Position the power steering pump off to the side without disconnecting the power steering fluid lines.

9   Remove the alternator (see Chapter 5).

10   Remove the air conditioning compressor and the mounting bracket (see Chapter 3). Position the compressor off to the side without disconnecting the refrigerant lines.

✷✷ WARNING:

The air conditioning system is under high pressure. DO NOT loosen any fittings unless the system has been discharged. Air conditioning refrigerant should be properly discharged into an approved container at a dealer service department or an automotive air conditioning repair facility.

11   Disconnect the PCV hose from the intake manifold. Remove all vacuum lines from the intake manifold. Label the vacuum hoses to insure correct reassembly.

12   Disconnect the fuel delivery and return hoses from the fuel rail. Remove the fuel rails from each cylinder head and keep the injectors attached to the fuel rail (see Chapter 4).

➡Note: The fuel rails and their designs vary with years and models. Refer to Chapter 4 and the exploded views in this Section for fuel rail details.

Non-turbocharged models

▸ **Refer to illustrations 5.13a, 5.13b and 5.18**

13   Remove the EGR pipe and the EGR valve (see illustrations).

➡Note: Some models are not equipped with an EGR system. Refer to Chapter 6 for additional information.

14   On 2000 through 2005 models, disconnect the accelerator cable and cruise control cable, if equipped, from the throttle body (see Chapter 4). On 2006 models, disconnect the electronic throttle control system (see Chapter 6).

15   Remove the air assist injector solenoid valve and bracket (see Chapter 6) from the intake manifold.

16   Disconnect the air filter housing brace and remove it from the engine block.

17   Disconnect the vacuum hose, the vent hose and the purge hose from the evaporation pipe. Label all the hoses for correct reassembly.

18   Remove the intake manifold mounting bolts (see illustration) and carefully lift the manifold off of the engine with the throttle body attached.

→Note: 2004 and 2005 Legacy/Outback models are equipped with a lower intake manifold assembly that contains the tumble generator valves (see Chapter 6). Continue with the procedure if the lower intake manifold assemblies (one on each cylinder head) must be removed.

Lower intake manifold (2004 and 2005 Legacy/Outback models)

19 Disconnect the connectors from the tumble generator valve position sensor and the tumble generator valve actuator (see Chapter 6).

20 Remove the lower intake manifold mounting bolts (see illustration 5.12b) and carefully separate the lower intake manifold from the cylinder heads.

Ultra Low Emissions Vehicle (ULEV) models

▶ Refer to illustration 5.22

→Note: The intake manifold on ULEV engines is a three-piece unit; two manifold runner assemblies and a central plenum which includes the tumble generator valve system (see Chapter 6). If the tumble generator valve system must be replaced, it will be necessary to disassemble the intake manifold. If the intake manifold must be removed for cylinder head servicing, unbolt the manifold at the cylinder head.

21 Disconnect the electrical connector from the throttle body (see Chapter 4).

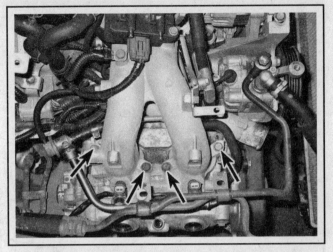

5.18 Location of the intake manifold mounting bolts on the right cylinder head of a non-turbocharged model

22 Remove the EGR pipe and the EGR valve (see illustration).

23 Disconnect the air filter housing brace and remove it from the engine block.

24 Disconnect the vacuum hose, the vent hose and purge hose from

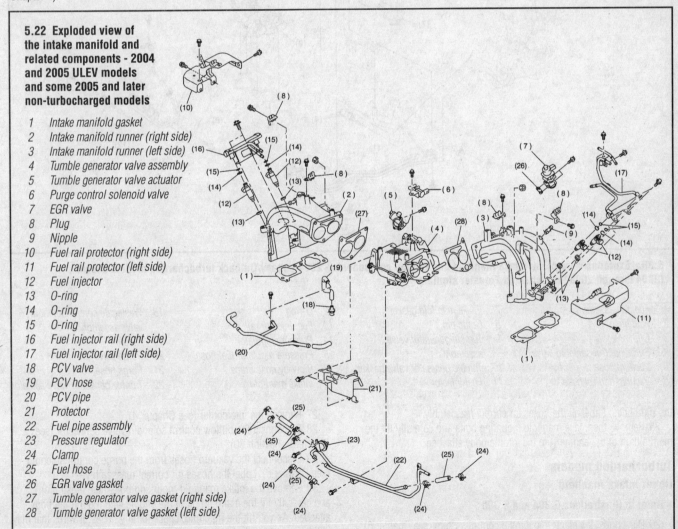

5.22 Exploded view of the intake manifold and related components - 2004 and 2005 ULEV models and some 2005 and later non-turbocharged models

1   Intake manifold gasket
2   Intake manifold runner (right side)
3   Intake manifold runner (left side)
4   Tumble generator valve assembly
5   Tumble generator valve actuator
6   Purge control solenoid valve
7   EGR valve
8   Plug
9   Nipple
10 Fuel rail protector (right side)
11 Fuel rail protector (left side)
12 Fuel injector
13 O-ring
14 O-ring
15 O-ring
16 Fuel injector rail (right side)
17 Fuel injector rail (left side)
18 PCV valve
19 PCV hose
20 PCV pipe
21 Protector
22 Fuel pipe assembly
23 Pressure regulator
24 Clamp
25 Fuel hose
26 EGR valve gasket
27 Tumble generator valve gasket (right side)
28 Tumble generator valve gasket (left side)

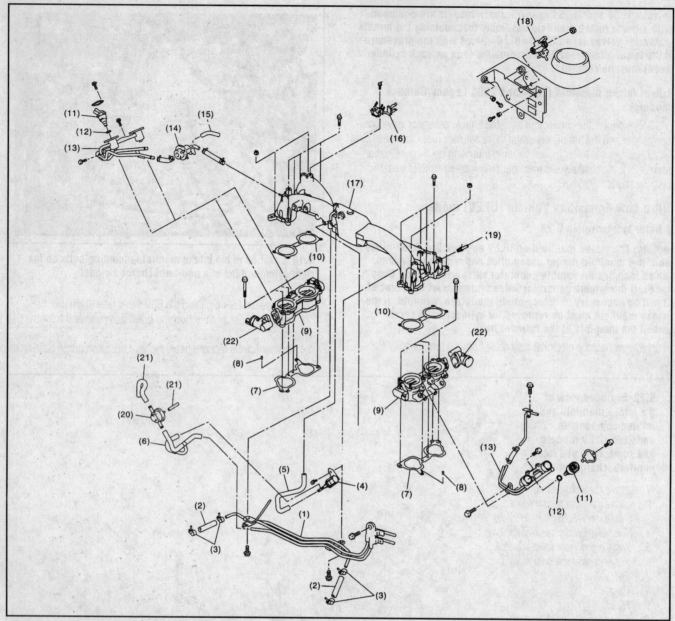

5.30a Exploded view of the intake manifold and related components - 2004 Legacy/Outback turbocharged models shown (2004 through 2006 turbocharged Forester similar)

1	Fuel rail assembly	7	Intake manifold gasket	12	O-ring	18	Wastegate control solenoid
2	Fuel hose	8	Guide pin	13	Fuel injector rail		valve assembly
3	Clip	9	Tumble generator valve	14	Pressure regulator	19	Nipple
4	Purge control solenoid valve		assembly	15	Pressure regulator fuel hose	20	Purge valve
5	Vacuum hose	10	Tumble generator valve gasket	16	Blow-by hose brace	21	Purge hose
6	Vacuum control hose	11	Fuel injector	17	Intake manifold	22	Tumble generator valve actuator

the rigid lines. Label all the hoses for correct reassembly.

25 Remove the intake manifold mounting bolts and carefully lift the manifold off of the engine with the throttle body attached.

Turbocharged models

Upper intake manifold

▶ **Refer to illustrations 5.30a and 5.30b**

26 Disconnect the electronic throttle control system (see Chapter 6).

27 Remove the intercooler (see Chapter 4).

28 Disconnect the oilflow control solenoid valve connector (see Chapter 6, Section 30).

29 Disconnect the vacuum hoses from the purge control solenoid (see Chapter 6). Label the hoses for correct reassembly.

30 Remove the intake manifold mounting bolts (see illustration) and carefully lift the manifold off of the engine with the throttle body attached. As you lift the manifold, check for any hoses or wires that may still be connected.

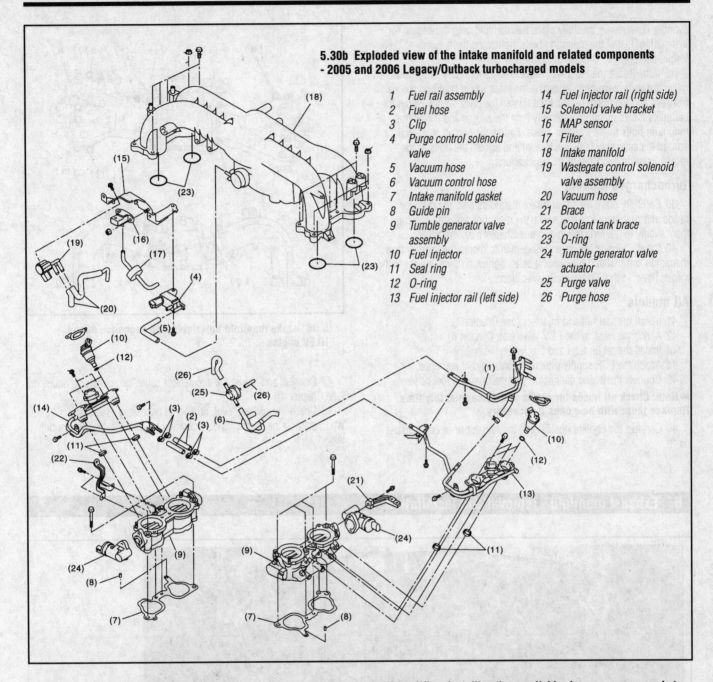

5.30b Exploded view of the intake manifold and related components - 2005 and 2006 Legacy/Outback turbocharged models

1	Fuel rail assembly	14	Fuel injector rail (right side)
2	Fuel hose	15	Solenoid valve bracket
3	Clip	16	MAP sensor
4	Purge control solenoid valve	17	Filter
5	Vacuum hose	18	Intake manifold
6	Vacuum control hose	19	Wastegate control solenoid valve assembly
7	Intake manifold gasket	20	Vacuum hose
8	Guide pin	21	Brace
9	Tumble generator valve assembly	22	Coolant tank brace
10	Fuel injector	23	O-ring
11	Seal ring	24	Tumble generator valve actuator
12	O-ring	25	Purge valve
13	Fuel injector rail (left side)	26	Purge hose

Lower intake manifold

31 Disconnect the connectors from the tumble generator valve position sensor and the tumble generator valve actuator (see Chapter 6).

32 Remove the fuel injector rail (see Chapter 4) from the lower intake manifold. Remove the coolant reservoir brace if it's in the way of the left side lower manifold.

33 Remove the lower intake manifold mounting bolts (see illustrations 5.30a and 5.30b) and carefully separate the lower intake manifold from the cylinder heads.

INSTALLATION

34 Scrape away any traces of sealant or old gasket materials from the intake manifold mounting surfaces and clean the gasket surface with a rag and lacquer thinner.

➡**Note: When installing the manifold, always use new gaskets or O-rings, and do not use sealant on the gaskets. Clean the threads of the bolts with a wire brush before installation.**

Non-turbocharged models

35 Carefully place the lower intake manifold (2004 and 2005 Legacy/Outback models) onto each cylinder head and install the mounting bolts, tightening them evenly to the torque listed in this Chapter's Specifications.

36 Carefully place the intake manifold onto the engine or the lower intake manifolds (2004 and 2005 Legacy/Outback models) and install the mounting bolts, tightening them evenly to the torque listed in this Chapter's Specifications.

Ultra Low Emission Vehicles (ULEV)

▶ **Refer to illustration 5.38**

37 If the intake manifold was removed as one complete unit for

cylinder head repair, carefully place the manifold onto the engine for installation. Install the mounting bolts, tightening them evenly to the torque listed in this Chapter's Specifications.

38 If the intake manifold was disassembled for repair of the tumble generator valve assembly, assemble the three intake manifold pieces (runners and tumble generator) but tighten the bolts lightly. Install the complete intake manifold assembly onto the engine and install the mounting bolts to the cylinder heads. Follow the correct sequence around the assembly (see illustration) and tighten the bolts to the torque listed in this Chapter's Specifications.

Turbocharged models

39 Carefully place the lower intake manifolds onto the cylinder heads and bolt them into place with the mounting bolts, tightening them evenly to the torque listed in this Chapter's Specifications.

40 Carefully place the upper intake manifold onto the lower intake manifolds and install the mounting bolts, tightening them evenly to the torque listed in this Chapter's Specifications.

All models

41 Install the fuel rail and injectors (see Chapter 4).
42 Attach the hose to the PCV valve (see Chapter 6).
43 Install the oil fill tube and bracket on the engine.
44 Attach the EGR supply pipe to the manifold, if equipped.
45 Connect the wiring connectors and vacuum and fuel hoses.
➡Note: Check all hoses for cracks and damage at this time. Replace them with new ones if necessary.

46 Connect the coolant hose(s) and the radiator hose (see Chapter 3).

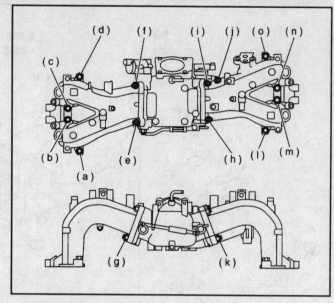

5.38 Intake manifold bolt tightening sequence on the ULEV engine

47 Connect and adjust the accelerator cable, on models so equipped (see Chapter 4).

48 Check the coolant level, adding as necessary (see Chapter 1). When starting the engine, check carefully for coolant, fuel or vacuum leaks.

6 Exhaust manifold - removal and installation

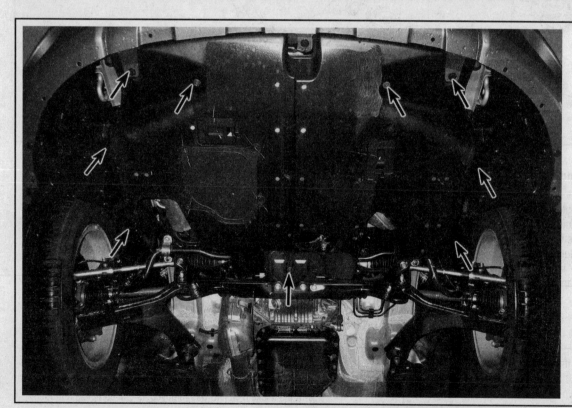

6.3 Location of the engine splash shield fasteners - 2006 Outback shown

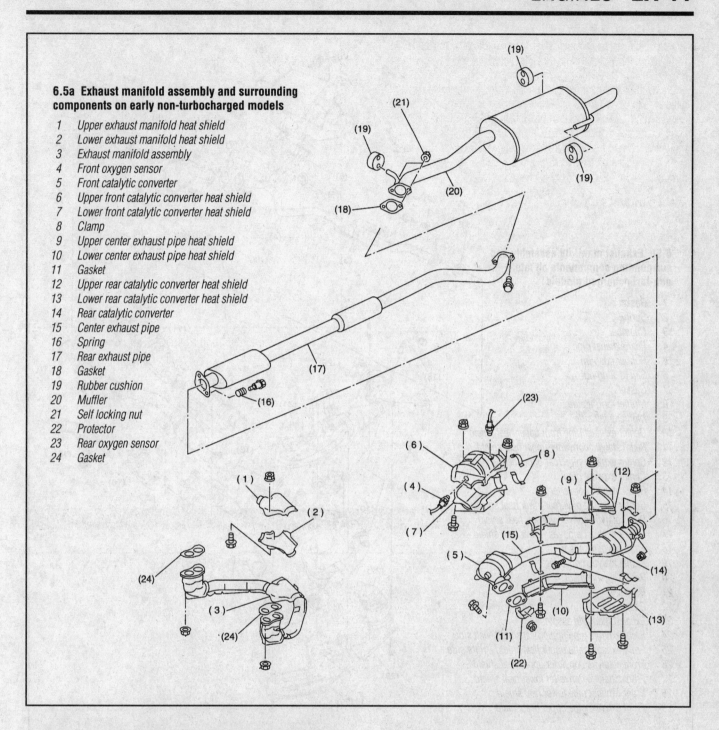

6.5a Exhaust manifold assembly and surrounding components on early non-turbocharged models

1   Upper exhaust manifold heat shield
2   Lower exhaust manifold heat shield
3   Exhaust manifold assembly
4   Front oxygen sensor
5   Front catalytic converter
6   Upper front catalytic converter heat shield
7   Lower front catalytic converter heat shield
8   Clamp
9   Upper center exhaust pipe heat shield
10   Lower center exhaust pipe heat shield
11   Gasket
12   Upper rear catalytic converter heat shield
13   Lower rear catalytic converter heat shield
14   Rear catalytic converter
15   Center exhaust pipe
16   Spring
17   Rear exhaust pipe
18   Gasket
19   Rubber cushion
20   Muffler
21   Self locking nut
22   Protector
23   Rear oxygen sensor
24   Gasket

☀☀ WARNING:

The engine must be completely cool before beginning this procedure.

REMOVAL

♦ Refer to illustration 6.3

1   Disconnect the cable from the negative terminal of the battery (see Chapter 5).
2   Raise the vehicle and support it securely on jackstands.

3   Remove the engine splash shield (see illustration).
4   Disconnect the front and rear oxygen sensor connectors (see Chapter 6).

Non-turbocharged models

♦ Refer to illustrations 6.5a, 6.5b, 6.7a and 6.7b

5   Remove the heat shields from the exhaust pipes and the exhaust manifold (see illustrations).

➡Note: Be sure to spray penetrating lubricant on the bolts and studs to prevent thread stripping.

6   Remove the bolts from the exhaust manifold connector at the center exhaust pipe.

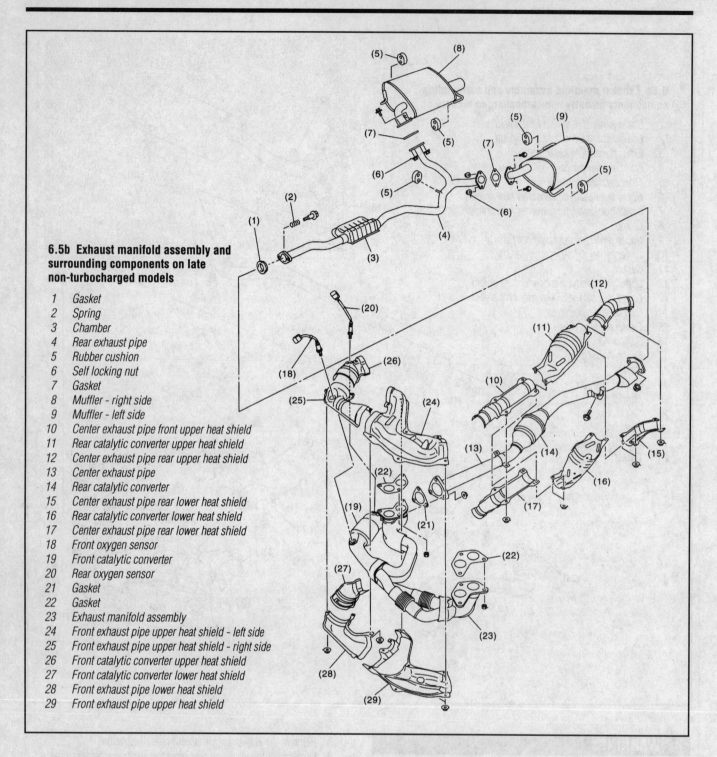

6.5b Exhaust manifold assembly and surrounding components on late non-turbocharged models

1 Gasket
2 Spring
3 Chamber
4 Rear exhaust pipe
5 Rubber cushion
6 Self locking nut
7 Gasket
8 Muffler - right side
9 Muffler - left side
10 Center exhaust pipe front upper heat shield
11 Rear catalytic converter upper heat shield
12 Center exhaust pipe rear upper heat shield
13 Center exhaust pipe
14 Rear catalytic converter
15 Center exhaust pipe rear lower heat shield
16 Rear catalytic converter lower heat shield
17 Center exhaust pipe rear lower heat shield
18 Front oxygen sensor
19 Front catalytic converter
20 Rear oxygen sensor
21 Gasket
22 Gasket
23 Exhaust manifold assembly
24 Front exhaust pipe upper heat shield - left side
25 Front exhaust pipe upper heat shield - right side
26 Front catalytic converter upper heat shield
27 Front catalytic converter lower heat shield
28 Front exhaust pipe lower heat shield
29 Front exhaust pipe upper heat shield

7   Remove the nuts from the exhaust manifold on both cylinder heads (see illustrations).

8   Remove the exhaust manifold.

Turbocharged models

♦ Refer to illustration 6.9

9   Remove the heat shields from the exhaust pipes and the exhaust manifold(s) (see illustration).

➡Note: Be sure to spray penetrating lubricant on the bolts and studs to prevent thread stripping.

10   Working on the right side exhaust manifold, remove the bolts from the turbocharger joint pipe.

11   Remove the nuts from the exhaust manifold on both cylinder heads. Remove the center exhaust pipe and separate it from the left and right exhaust manifolds if the entire assembly is difficult to remove.

INSTALLATION

12   Using a scraper, thoroughly clean the mating surfaces on the cylinder heads, manifold(s) and exhaust pipe. Remove the residue with a solvent such as acetone or lacquer thinner.

13   Check that the mating surfaces are perfectly flat and not damaged

6.7a Location of the exhaust manifold nuts on the right-side cylinder head

6.7b Location of the exhaust manifold nuts on the left-side cylinder head

in any way. Warped or damaged manifolds will require replacement. Install the new gaskets to the cylinder head and place the manifold on the cylinder heads. Tighten the bolts evenly to the torque listed in this Chapter's Specifications.

14 Connect the center pipe (non-turbocharged models) or turbo-

charger joint pipe (turbocharged models) to the manifold and tighten the nuts evenly to the torque listed in this Chapter's Specifications.

15 The remainder of installation is the reverse of the removal steps.

16 Reconnect the battery (see Chapter 5).

17 Run the engine and check for exhaust leaks.

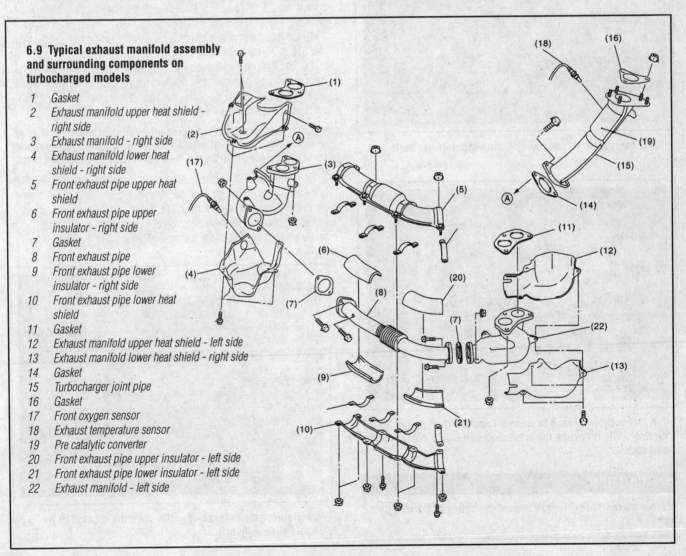

6.9 Typical exhaust manifold assembly and surrounding components on turbocharged models

1   Gasket
2   Exhaust manifold upper heat shield - right side
3   Exhaust manifold - right side
4   Exhaust manifold lower heat shield - right side
5   Front exhaust pipe upper heat shield
6   Front exhaust pipe upper insulator - right side
7   Gasket
8   Front exhaust pipe
9   Front exhaust pipe lower insulator - right side
10 Front exhaust pipe lower heat shield
11 Gasket
12 Exhaust manifold upper heat shield - left side
13 Exhaust manifold lower heat shield - right side
14 Gasket
15 Turbocharger joint pipe
16 Gasket
17 Front oxygen sensor
18 Exhaust temperature sensor
19 Pre catalytic converter
20 Front exhaust pipe upper insulator - left side
21 Front exhaust pipe lower insulator - left side
22 Exhaust manifold - left side

7 Timing belt and sprockets - removal, inspection and installation

REMOVAL

▶ **Refer to illustrations 7.5, 7.7 and 7.8**

1 Position the engine at TDC for cylinder number 1 (see Section 3).
2 Disconnect the cable from the negative terminal of the battery (see Chapter 5).
3 Remove the drivebelts (see Chapter 1).
4 Remove the air filter housing, the resonator and the air intake ducts (see Chapter 4).

➡**Note: Depending on the year and model of the vehicle, the air filter housing may not need to be removed.**

5 Remove the air conditioning drivebelt tensioner adjuster (see illustration), if equipped, and the main drivebelt tensioner (see Chapter 1).
6 Remove the engine cooling fan(s) and shroud (see Chapter 3).
7 Use a breaker bar and socket to remove the bolt from the crankshaft pulley. Use a chain wrench to hold the pulley while loosening the bolt (see illustration).

✳ CAUTION:

Do not use power tools to remove the crankshaft pulley bolt. The pulley and/or crankshaft bolt may become damaged.

8 Remove the crankshaft pulley. The crankshaft pulley should come off by hand (see illustration), if not, use a screwdriver on either side of it to lever it off evenly.

Non-turbocharged engines

▶ **Refer to illustrations 7.9a, 7.9b, 7.9c, 7.11a, 7.11b, 7.11c, 7.13, 7.14 and 7.16**

9 Remove the outer belt covers (see illustrations). There are two covers; one larger cover that extends over the camshaft and the crankshaft sprocket and another smaller cover.
10 On manual transaxle models, remove the timing belt guide (see illustration 7.21a).
11 Turn the crankshaft and align the marks on the crankshaft sprocket, the left camshaft sprocket and the right camshaft sprocket with the notches on the oil pump, the inner timing belt cover and the cylinder head seam (see illustrations).

➡**Note: The right camshaft sprocket alignment notch must align with the mark on the cylinder head seam. Only the left camshaft sprocket uses the rear timing belt cover for the alignment mark.**

12 Use white paint to clearly mark these alignment marks in relation to the engine block (center) and the inner belt cover (left) or the cylinder head (right) (see illustration 7.11a, 7.11b and 7.11c).
13 Use paint to mark the direction of belt rotation if the arrow has faded (see illustration). If the original timing belt marks (yellow

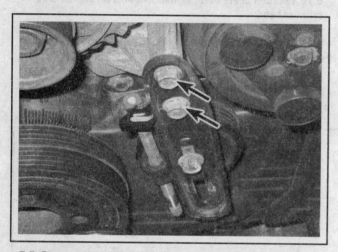

7.5 Remove the air conditioning drivebelt adjuster bolts

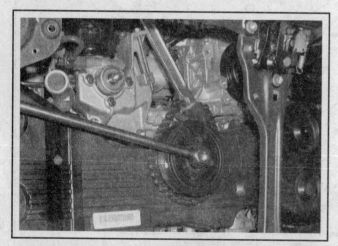

7.7 Use a chain wrench to prevent the crankshaft pulley from turning while removing the crankshaft bolt with a breaker bar and socket.

✳ CAUTION:

Wrap a piece of old drivebelt around the pulley to prevent damage to it

7.8 Remove the crankshaft pulley from the crankshaft (it should slide right off)

7.9a Exploded view of the timing belt and related components - non-turbocharged engine

1   Drivebelt protector bracket
2   Timing belt guide (manual transaxle models)
3   Crankshaft sprocket
4   Inner timing belt cover - left side
5   Camshaft sprocket - right cylinder head
6   Upper timing belt idler pulley
7   Tensioner bracket
8   Timing belt idler pulley number 12
9   Tensioner
10 Timing belt idler sprocket number 2
11 Camshaft sprocket - left cylinder head
12 Timing belt
13 Front timing belt cover - right side
14 Front timing belt cover - left side
15 Crankshaft pulley

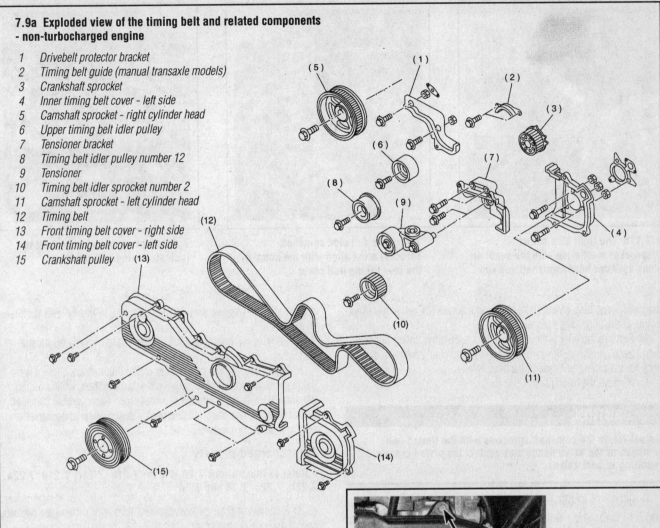

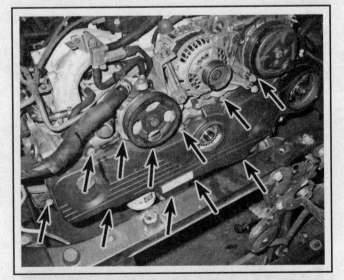

7.9b Location of the front right timing belt cover mounting bolts

7.9c Location of the front left timing belt cover mounting bolts

7.11a The crankshaft sprocket alignment notches (two) must align with the notch in the oil pump flange - non-turbocharged model shown

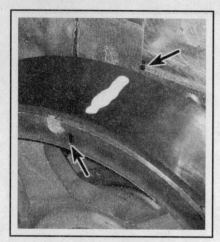

7.11b The right side camshaft sprocket must align with the seam on the cylinder head/camshaft end cap

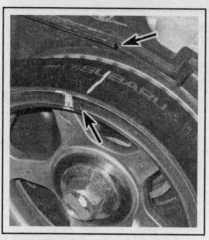

7.11c The left side camshaft sprocket must align with the notch in the rear timing belt cover

7.13 Paint an arrow on the belt to indicate timing belt rotation

diagonal lines) have faded, paint new marks across the belt at the exact points of the alignment notches.

14 Remove the idler pulley number 1 to release the timing belt tension (see illustration). Remove idler sprocket number 2 to make clearance for the timing belt (see illustration 7.9a).

15 Remove the timing belt.

✳✳ CAUTION:

Do not rotate the camshaft sprockets with the timing belt removed or the valve heads may contact the piston crowns, resulting in bent valves.

16 If only the timing belt is to be replaced, proceed to the *Inspection* and *Installation* Steps. If the sprockets are to be replaced, continue with the following Steps.

17 Remove the crankshaft pulley sprocket from the crankshaft. If it

doesn't slip off, use two screwdrivers behind it to evenly lever it off (see illustration).

18 Remove the bolt(s) and the timing belt tensioner (see illustration 7.9a).

19 While keeping the camshaft sprocket timing mark aligned with the mark on the inner cover, remove the sprocket bolt, while holding the sprocket with a pin wrench or similar tool. Remove both camshaft sprockets and mark them left and right. Do not interchange the left and right camshaft sprockets.

Turbocharged models

◆ **Refer to illustrations 7.20, 7.21a, 7.21b, 7.21c, 7.21d, 7.22a, 7.22b, 7.22c, 7.28 and 7.30**

20 Remove the outer belt covers (see illustration). There are two side covers and one central cover.

21 On manual transaxle models, remove the timing belt guides (see illustrations).

22 Turn the crankshaft and align the marks on the crankshaft and left and right camshaft sprockets with the notches on the rear timing belt cover and the cylinder head (see illustrations).

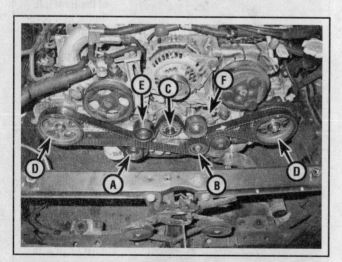

7.14 Timing belt details on the non-turbocharged engine

A	Idler pulley number 1	D	Camshaft sprocket
B	Idler sprocket number 2	E	Idler pulley
C	Crankshaft sprocket	F	Tensioner

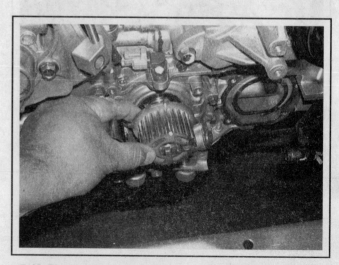

7.16 Remove the crankshaft sprocket from the crankshaft

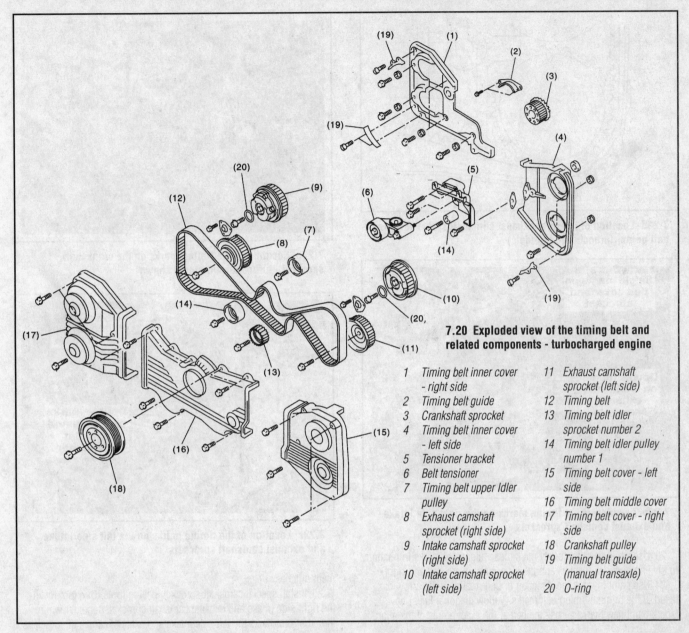

7.20 Exploded view of the timing belt and related components - turbocharged engine

1 Timing belt inner cover - right side
2 Timing belt guide
3 Crankshaft sprocket
4 Timing belt inner cover - left side
5 Tensioner bracket
6 Belt tensioner
7 Timing belt upper Idler pulley
8 Exhaust camshaft sprocket (right side)
9 Intake camshaft sprocket (right side)
10 Intake camshaft sprocket (left side)
11 Exhaust camshaft sprocket (left side)
12 Timing belt
13 Timing belt idler sprocket number 2
14 Timing belt idler pulley number 1
15 Timing belt cover - left side
16 Timing belt middle cover
17 Timing belt cover - right side
18 Crankshaft pulley
19 Timing belt guide (manual transaxle)
20 O-ring

7.21a Remove the crankshaft sprocket timing belt guide

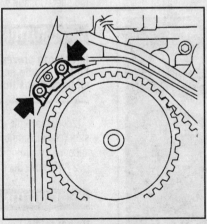

7.21b Location of the right intake camshaft sprocket timing belt guide (turbocharged models)

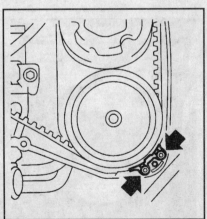

7.21c Location of the left exhaust camshaft sprocket timing belt guide (turbocharged models)

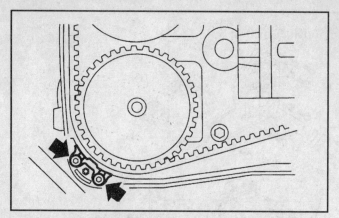

7.21d Location of the right exhaust camshaft sprocket timing belt guide (turbocharged models)

7.22a Location of the timing marks on the crankshaft sprocket - turbocharged model shown

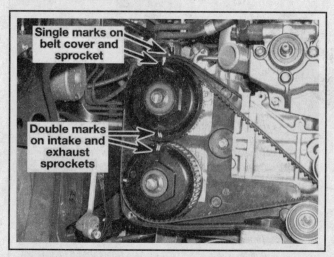

7.22b Location of the timing marks on the right side intake and exhaust camshaft sprockets

23 Use white paint to clearly mark these alignment marks in relation to the engine block (center) and the inner belt covers (left and right).

24 Use paint to mark the direction of belt rotation if the arrow has faded. If the original timing belt marks (yellow diagonal lines) have faded, paint new marks across the belt at the exact points of the align-

7.22c Location of the timing marks on the left side intake and exhaust camshaft sprockets

ment notches.

25 Install special camshaft sprocket locking tools. One tool locks the right side intake and exhaust camshaft sprockets together while the other tool locks the left side intake and exhaust camshaft sprockets together. Consult with a special tool distributor.

❊❊ CAUTION:

In order to prevent any valve contact when removing the timing belt, it will be necessary to lock the camshaft sprockets in a stationary position.

26 Remove the idler pulley number 1 to release the timing belt tension (see illustration). Remove idler sprocket number 2 to make clearance for the timing belt (see illustration 7.20).

27 Remove the timing belt.

❊❊ CAUTION:

Do not rotate the camshaft sprockets with the timing belt removed or the valve heads may contact each other resulting in bent valves.

7.26 Remove idler pulley number 1 to release the timing belt tension

7.30 Location of the tensioner on a turbocharged engine

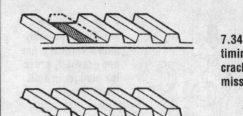

7.34 Check the timing belt for cracked and missing teeth

7.36 Wear on one side of the belt indicates sprocket misalignment problems

28 If only the timing belt is to be replaced, proceed to the *Inspection* and *Installation* Steps. If the sprockets are to be replaced, continue with the following Steps.

29 Remove the crankshaft sprocket from the crankshaft. If it doesn't slip off, use two screwdrivers behind it to evenly lever it off (see illustration 7.16).

30 Remove the bolt and the timing belt tensioner (see illustration).

31 While keeping the camshaft sprocket timing mark aligned with the mark on the inner cover, remove the sprocket bolts, while holding the sprocket with a pin wrench or similar tool. Remove both camshaft sprockets and mark them left and right.

INSPECTION

◗ Refer to illustrations 7.34 and 7.36

> ✳✳ **CAUTION:**

Do not bend, twist or turn the timing belt inside out. Do not allow it to come in contact with oil, coolant or fuel. Do not use timing belt tension to keep the camshaft or crankshaft from turning when installing the sprocket bolt(s). Do not turn the crankshaft or camshaft more than a few degrees (necessary for tooth alignment) while the timing belt is removed.

32 Rotate the tensioner pulley and idler pulley by hand and move it side-to-side to detect roughness and excessive play. Replace them if they don't turn smoothly or if play is noted.

33 If the timing belt was broken during engine operation, the belt may have been fouled by debris or may have been damaged by a defective component in the area of the timing belt; check for belt material in the teeth of the sprockets. Any defective parts or debris in the sprockets must be cleaned out of all the sprockets before installing the new belt or the belt will not mesh properly when installed.

➡ **Note: If one of the sprockets is damaged or worn, replace the sprockets as a set.**

34 If the belt teeth are cracked or pulled off (see illustration), the oil pump or camshaft(s) may have seized.

35 If there is noticeable wear or cracks in the belt, check to see if there are nicks or burrs on the sprockets.

36 If there is wear or damage on only one side of the belt (see illustration), check the belt guide and the alignment of all sprockets. Also

7.39 Right side timing belt inner cover mounting bolts on turbocharged models

check the oil seals at the front of the engine and replace them if they are leaking.

37 Replace the timing belt with a new one if obvious wear or damage is noted or if it is the least bit questionable. Correct any problems which contributed to belt failure prior to belt installation.

➡ **Note: We recommend replacing the belt whenever it is removed, since belt failure will almost certainly lead to expensive engine damage.**

INSTALLATION

◗ Refer to illustrations 7.39, 7.43a and 7.43b

➡ **Note: If the inner timing belt covers were removed from the engine (only necessary if the cylinder heads had been removed or the engine was to be overhauled), continue as below. If the inner covers were not removed, proceed to Step 42.**

38 If removed as part of the camshaft sprocket and tensioner removal, install the tensioner bracket on the cylinder block.

39 Attach the seals and inner timing belt cover mounts to the left inner timing belt cover and the right inner timing belt cover (see illustration), then install the assembly on the cylinder head and block.

40 Install the camshaft sprockets. Tighten the bolts to the torque

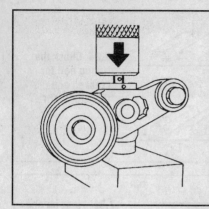

7.43a Place the tensioner assembly onto a vertical press and gradually press the plunger in until the holes align - press the plunger in very slowly, taking at least three minutes to complete the procedure

7.43b Insert a stopper pin through the holes - DO NOT force the adjuster rod past this point or damage to the tensioner assembly will occur

listed in this Chapter's Specifications.

41 Install the crankshaft sprocket onto the crankshaft. Make sure the crankshaft and camshaft sprocket timing marks are still aligned (see illustrations 7.11a, 7.11b and 7.11c for the non-turbocharged engines and 7.22a, 7.22b and 7.22c for the turbocharged engines). If necessary, rotate the sprockets slightly to align the timing marks.

42 Install idler sprocket number 2 and torque the bolt to the Specifications listed in this Chapter.

43 Reinstall the tensioner. Make sure the tensioner plunger is locked in place with a stopper pin (see illustrations). Install the assembly onto the engine. Tighten the bolt to the torque listed in this Chapter's Specifications.

Non-turbocharged models

▸ **Refer to illustrations 7.46 and 7.47**

44 Install the timing belt onto the sprockets and pulleys (see illustrations 7.11a, 7.11b and 7.11c) making sure that all the timing marks align with the marks on the engine and the arrow indicates the correct direction of rotation. Be careful to allow for belt correction at the tensioner when the timing belt tensioner is released and the left camshaft sprocket rotates slightly.

45 Install the idler pulley number 1. Torque the bolt to the Specifications listed in this Chapter.

46 Remove the stopper pin from the tensioner adjuster (see illustration). Double-check all the timing marks for correct alignment.

47 Install the timing belt guide, if equipped, maintaining the proper clearance between the guide and timing belt (see illustration). Refer to the Specifications listed in this Chapter.

Turbocharged models

48 Install the timing belt onto the sprockets and pulleys (see illustrations 7.22a, 7.22b and 7.22c) making sure that all the timing marks align with the marks on the engine and the arrow indicates the correct direction of rotation. Be careful to allow for belt correction at the tensioner when the timing belt tensioner is released and the left intake camshaft sprocket rotates slightly.

➡**Note: The exhaust camshaft sprockets on turbocharged models are also equipped with separate timing notches offset 90 degrees to the main timing marks. These secondary alignment timing notches should align with the notch in each of the inner timing belt covers.**

49 Install the idler pulley number 1. Torque the bolt to the Specifications listed in this Chapter.

50 Remove the stopper pin from the tensioner adjuster (see illustration 7.46). Double-check all the timing marks for correct alignment.

51 Install the timing belt guide, if equipped, maintaining the proper clearance between the guide and timing belt (see illustration 7.47).

52 Remove the special camshaft sprocket locking tools. Check the valve clearances and install the correct valve lifter(s) on cylinders that have incorrect clearance (see Section 12).

All models

53 Install the timing belt covers and crankshaft pulley.

54 The remainder of installation is the reverse of the removal procedure.

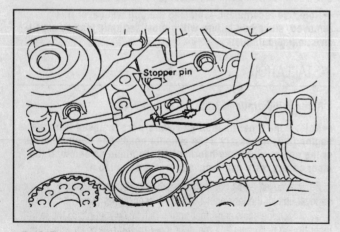

7.46 To release the tensioner and apply tension onto the timing belt, remove the stopper pin

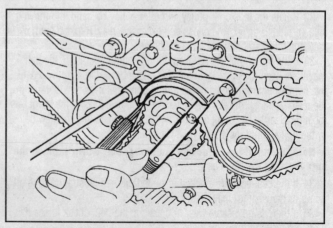

7.47 Check the clearance using a feeler gauge - it should be between 0.019 to 0.059 inch

8   Variable Valve Timing and Lift systems

Refer to Chapter 6 for information on these systems.

9   Crankshaft front oil seal - replacement

▶ **Refer to illustration 9.5**

1   Disconnect the cable from the negative terminal of the battery (see Chapter 5).

2   Remove the timing belt and crankshaft sprocket (see Section 7).

3   Carefully pry the seal out of the cover with a seal puller or a large screwdriver.

✳✳ CAUTION:

Be careful not to scratch, gouge or distort the area that the seal fits into or an oil leak will develop.

➡**Note: An alternative method is to drill two 1/8-inch holes in the seal, being careful not to hit the seal housing or crankshaft. Screw two self-tapping screws into the holes and pull on them, alternating side to side, with a slide-hammer or self-locking pliers on the screws.**

4   Clean the bore to remove any old seal material and corrosion. Position the new seal in the bore with the seal lip (usually the side with the spring) facing IN (toward the engine). A small amount of oil applied to the outer edge of the new seal will make installation easier - but don't overdo it!

5   Drive the seal into the bore with a large socket and hammer until it's completely seated (see illustration). Select a socket that's the same

9.5 Drive the new seal in with a hammer and a deep socket

outside diameter as the seal and make sure the new seal is pressed into place until it bottoms against the cover flange, to the same depth as the original seal.

6   Refer to Section 7 for installation of the sprockets and timing belts.

7   The remainder of installation is the reverse of the removal process.

10 Camshaft oil seals - replacement

1   Refer to Section 7 and remove the timing belt and camshaft sprocket(s).

2   Unbolt the inner timing belt covers to access the camshaft seals (see illustrations 7.9a and 7.20).

3   Pull the camshaft oil seal from the engine. Use a seal puller to pry the old seal from the cylinder head.

4   Install the new seal by gently tapping the seal into the cylinder head recess using a deep socket and hammer.

➡**Note: Drive the seal in squarely and only to the same depth as the original seal was installed.**

5   The remainder of the procedure is the reverse of the disassembly process.

11 Camshafts and valve actuating components - removal, inspection and installation

REMOVAL

1   Remove the timing belt, crankshaft and camshaft sprockets (see Section 7).

2   Remove the inner timing belt covers (see illustrations 7.9a and 7.20).

3   Remove the valve covers (see Section 4).

4   Remove the camshaft position sensor (CMP) (see Chapter 6).

2000 through 2005 non-turbocharged models

5   Working in the reverse order of the tightening sequence (see illustration 11.30c), gradually loosen the rocker arm bolts and remove the rocker arm assembly.

6   Store all the components in an organized manner (see illustration 11.22).

7   Remove the timing belt tensioner and the tensioner bracket (see Section 7).

8   Unbolt the oil dipstick tube from the left cylinder head.

9   Remove the camshaft end cap assembly. Follow the reverse of the tightening sequence (see illustration 11.30a).

✳✳ CAUTION:

Remove the camshaft carefully from the cylinder head, so that the lobes do not nick the journal bores. Remove the camshaft oil seal and the end plug from the camshaft end cap assembly.

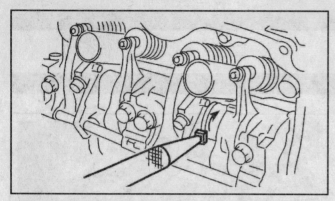

11.10a Use a special spring installer tool to rotate the spring stopper

2006 non-turbocharged models

▶ Refer to Illustrations 11.10a, 11.10b and 11.11

10 Use a special spring installer tool to rotate the spring stopper (see illustrations) to remove it from the adjuster pin.

11 Working from the outer bolts to the center bolts in the reverse order of installation (see illustration 11.30d), gradually loosen the rocker arm bolts. Install special tools onto the intake rocker arm assembly to lock it in position before lifting the assembly from the cylinder head (see illustration).

12 Store all the components in an organized manner (see illustration 11.22).

13 Remove the timing belt tensioner and the tensioner bracket (see Section 7).

14 Remove the oil dipstick tube.

15 Remove the camshaft end cap assembly. Follow the reverse of the tightening sequence (see illustration 11.30b).

⁂ CAUTION:

Remove the camshaft carefully from the cylinder head, so that the lobes do not nick the journal bores. Remove the camshaft oil seal and the end plug from the camshaft end cap assembly.

Turbocharged models

16 Check the valve clearances (see Section 13). Write down all of your measurements.

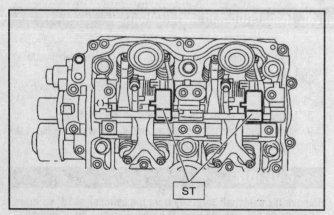

11.11 Use the special tool to lock the intake rocker arms in position before lifting the assembly from the cylinder head

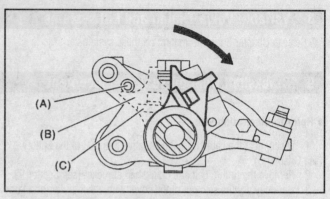

11.10b Rotate the spring stopper in the direction of the arrow to remove it from the adjuster pin

A   Adjuster pin   B   Spring stopper   C   Spring

17 Disconnect the VVT oil flow control solenoid connectors from each cylinder head (see Chapter 6).

18 Remove the timing belt tensioner and the tensioner bracket (see Section 7). Remove the oil dipstick tube.

19 Remove the oil pipe from the VVT oil flow control solenoid and the cylinder head (see Chapter 6).

20 Working from the outer bolts to the center bolts, gradually loosen the intake camshaft cap bolts. Lift the intake camshaft cap assembly from the cylinder head.

21 Working from the outer bolts to the center bolts, gradually loosen the exhaust camshaft cap bolts. Lift the exhaust camshaft cap assembly from the cylinder head.

22 Store all the components in an organized manner so they won't get mixed up.

23 Remove the valve lifters if the valve clearance must be adjusted.

INSPECTION

▶ Refer to illustrations 11.24, .11.27a, 11.27b and 11.27c

24 On turbocharged models, remove the lifters from the cylinder heads. Keep the lifters organized so they can be returned to their original locations.

⁂ CAUTION:

Do not use pliers to remove the lifters. If they are varnished and can't be removed easily, spray some carburetor cleaner around their bores and let it soak.

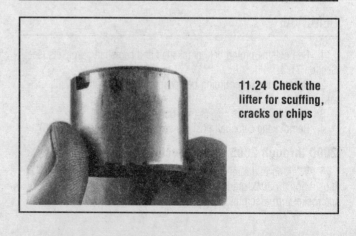

11.24 Check the lifter for scuffing, cracks or chips

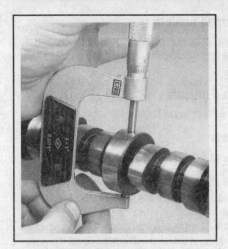

11.27a Measure the camshaft bearing journal diameter

11.27b Measure the camshaft lobe at its greatest dimension . . .

11.27c . . . and subtract the camshaft lobe diameter at its smallest dimension to obtain the lobe lift specification

The lifters should come out by hand. Check each lifter for signs of wear (see illustration). Measure the lifter outer diameter. Check the Specifications listed in this Chapter. Measure the inside diameter of the lifter bore in the cylinder head. If the distance between the outer diameter and the inner diameter (bore) exceeds the correct Specifications, replace the cylinder head.

25 Check the pivot seat in each rocker arm and the pivot faces. Look for galling, stress cracks and unusual wear patterns. If the rocker arms are worn or damaged, replace them with new ones.

26 Visually examine the camshaft lobes, journals, bearing caps, pivot points and metal-to-metal contact areas. Check for score marks, pitting and evidence of overheating (blue, discolored areas). If wear is excessive or damage is evident, the component will have to be replaced. Also check the front of the camshaft for wear where the seal rides.

27 Using a micrometer, measure camshaft journal diameter and lobe height (see illustrations), and compare your measurements to this Chapter's Specifications. If the lobe height is less than the minimum allowable, the camshaft is worn and must be replaced.

28 On non-turbocharged engines, measure the inside diameter of each camshaft journal bore. If the oil clearance (bore diameter minus the camshaft journal diameter) is greater than the Specifications, the cylinder head, camshaft and camshaft end cap must be replaced (the clearance can also be checked with Plastigage). On turbocharged

engines install the camshafts onto the cylinder head (with the lifters removed) and use Plastigage to determine the oil clearance.

INSTALLATION

29 Lubricate the camshaft journals and lobes with camshaft installation lubricant.

2000 through 2005 non-turbocharged models

▸ **Refer to illustrations 11.30a, 11.30b, 11.30c and 11.30d**

30 Prepare the camshaft end cap assembly for installation. Apply a bead of anaerobic sealant approximately 0.12 inch (3 mm) wide onto the outer edge of the end cap assembly and allow the RTV sealant to set-up (approximately 20 minutes). Install the camshafts carefully onto the cylinder heads. Use camshaft installation lubricant applied to the camshaft lobes. Install the end cap assembly and tighten the bolts to the torque listed in this Chapter's Specifications in the correct sequence (see illustration). Next, install the rocker arm assembly and tighten the bolts to the torque listed in this Chapter's Specifications in the correct sequence (see illustrations). Install a new camshaft oil seal (see Section 10) and the end plug.

➡**Note 1: The end plug must be installed with a special tool. Be sure the end plug is installed even with the outer edge of the cylinder head and the end cap assembly.**

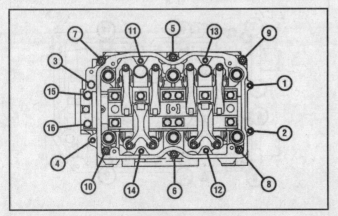

11.30a Camshaft end cap tightening sequence - non-turbocharged models

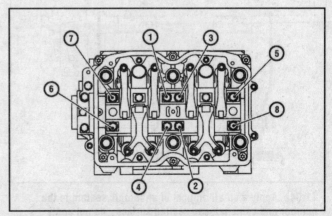

11.30b Rocker arm bolt tightening sequence on 2000 through 2005 non-turbocharged models

Note 2: If only the rocker arms were removed from the cylinder head, follow the correct torque sequence in illustrations 11.30b and 11.30c for installation.

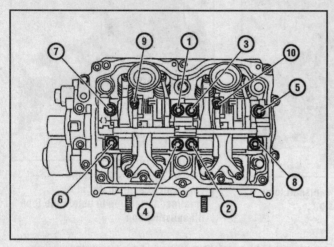

11.30c Rocker arm bolt tightening sequence on 2006 non-turbocharged models

2006 non-turbocharged models

31 Use a special spring installer tool to rotate the spring stopper in the direction of the arrow (see illustrations 11.10a and 11.10b) to lock the adjuster pin.

All non-turbocharged models

32 Adjust the valve clearances (see Section 13).

Turbocharged models

▶ **Refer to illustrations 11.33, 11.34a and 11.34b**

33 Lubricate the valve lifters with camshaft installation lubricant and install them in their original locations. If any valve clearance was out of specification, calculate the proper-thickness of lifter to install. Use camshaft installation lubricant applied to the camshaft lobes. Install the camshafts with the base circle of the camshaft lobes nearest the valve lifters (see illustration).

34 Apply a small amount of anaerobic sealant to each number one cap sealing surface (see illustration). Lubricate the bearing surface of the camshaft caps with camshaft installation lubricant and install them in their original locations. Tighten the camshaft bearing cap bolts in the recommended sequence to the torque listed in this Chapter's Specifications (see illustration). Install new camshaft oil seals (see Section 10).

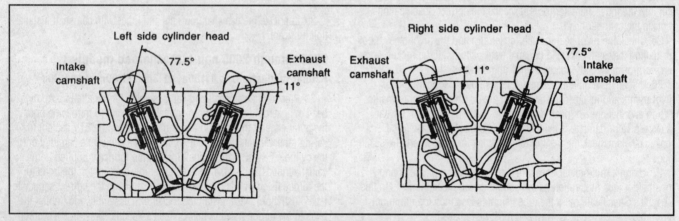

11.33 On turbocharged engines, it is important to install the camshaft at the correct angle to avoid damaging the valves during installation. The right side cylinder head camshafts do not have to be rotated after installation to align the timing marks. Only the left side intake camshaft will have to be rotated 80-degrees clockwise and the left side exhaust camshaft will have to be rotated 45-degrees counterclockwise after the camshafts have been installed

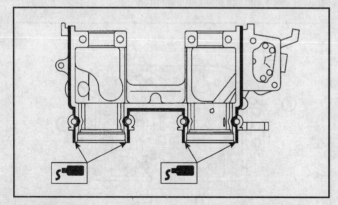

11.34a Apply a small amount of anaerobic sealant to the number one camshaft cap sealing surface - do not apply excessive sealant or it may flow into the oil seal area and oil leaks may develop

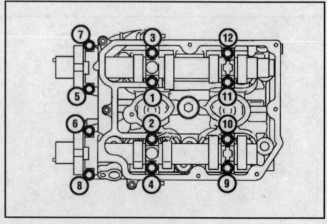

11.34b Camshaft bearing cap tightening sequence - turbocharged engine

35 Check and, if necessary, adjust the valve clearances (see Section 13).

36 Connect the VVT oil flow control solenoid connectors on each cylinder head (see Chapter 6).

All models

37 Install the camshaft sprockets and timing belt (see Section 7).

38 Install the valve covers (see Section 4).

39 The remainder of the installation is the reverse of the disassembly process.

➡**Note: Be sure to use new gaskets on the valve covers.**

40 Start the engine, listen for unusual valve train noises and check for oil leaks at the valve cover gaskets.

12 Cylinder heads - removal and installation

REMOVAL

1 Relieve the fuel pressure (see Chapter 4)

2 Disconnect the cable from the negative terminal of the battery (see Chapter 5).

3 Drain the cooling system and remove the spark plugs (see Chapter 1).

4 Remove the timing belt, camshaft sprockets and inner timing belt covers (see Section 7).

✷✷ CAUTION:

On turbocharged models, remove the rocker arm assemblies before the timing belt is removed.

5 Remove the camshafts (see Section 11).

6 Disconnect the exhaust manifold from the cylinder heads (see Section 6).

➡**Note: Apply penetrating oil to the fasteners before beginning the procedure, and allow it to soak-in for awhile.**

7 Remove the intake manifold (see Section 5). Remove any hoses or brackets bolted to the cylinder heads, and on models equipped with air conditioning, remove the air conditioning compressor bracket from the left cylinder head.

8 Loosen the cylinder head bolts in the reverse of the tightening sequence (see illustration 12.13).

9 Remove the cylinder heads and the old gaskets.

➡**Note: The block and cylinder heads are aluminum. Do not pry between the cylinder heads and the crankcase, as damage to the gasket sealing surfaces may result. Instead use a soft-faced hammer to tap the cylinder heads and break the gasket seal.**

10 Cylinder head disassembly and inspection procedures should be performed by a qualified automotive machine shop.

INSTALLATION

▶ **Refer to Illustrations 12.11, 12.12 and 12.13**

11 Clean the gasket mating surfaces of the cylinder heads and crankcase (see illustration) with lacquer thinner or acetone. They must be clean and oil-free.

12 Install the cylinder head gasket onto the cylinder head locating dowels on the engine block (see illustration).

13 Install the cylinder head(s). Lubricate the bolt threads and washers with engine oil, then install them hand-tight. Tighten the bolts in the recommended sequence to the torque listed in this Chapter's Specifications (see illustration).

12.11 Be careful not to gouge the aluminum surfaces of the cylinder head or block when removing the old gasket material

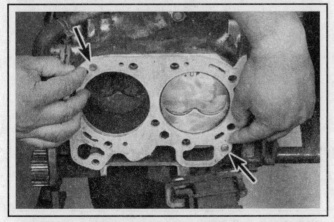

12.12 Place the new head gasket over the dowels in the block - look for markings on the gaskets to indicate TOP or FRONT

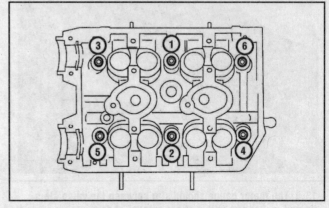

12.13 Cylinder head bolt tightening sequence

✳✳ CAUTION:

The cylinder head bolt tightening procedure must be followed exactly.

Follow the steps as listed in this Chapter's Specifications and use a torque-angle meter (available at most automotive parts stores) or mark the bolt heads with white paint and tighten the bolts the required angle on the designated Steps of the torque sequence.

14 The remainder of installation is the reverse of removal.

13 Valve clearance check and adjustment

➥**Note: The valve clearances are checked with the engine cold.**

1 Remove the air filter housing and the resonator (see Chapter 4). Remove the battery and the battery tray (see Chapter 5).

2 Remove the valve covers (see Section 4).

NON-TURBOCHARGED MODELS

◆ **Refer to illustrations 13.4, 13.5, 13.7 and 13.8**

3 Remove the timing belt cover from the left side (driver's) cylinder head (see Section 7). It is only necessary to see the timing marks on the left side sprocket for valve adjustment.

13.4 Align the arrow on the left camshaft sprocket with the notch in the inner timing belt cover

4 Use the timing mark (arrow) on the camshaft sprocket (see illustration) to position the number one piston at TDC (see Section 3).

5 With the number one piston at TDC, measure the clearance of the intake and exhaust valves on the number one cylinder (see illustration). Insert a feeler gauge of the specified thickness (see this Chapter's Specifications) between the valve stem tip and the rocker arm. The feeler gauge should slip between the valve stem tip and rocker arm with a slight amount of drag.

6 If the clearance is incorrect (too loose or too tight), loosen the locknut and turn the adjusting screw slowly until you can feel a slight drag on the feeler gauge as you withdraw it from between the valve stem tip and the rocker arm.

7 Once the clearance is adjusted, hold the adjusting screw with a screwdriver (to keep it from turning) and tighten the locknut (see illustration). Recheck the clearance to make sure it hasn't changed after tightening the locknut.

8 The valves in the remaining cylinders can now be checked. It is essential to adjust cylinder 3 next, followed by 2 and finally 4 (follow the firing order sequence). Before checking clearances, bring each cylinder (in firing order) to TDC by turning the crankshaft 180 degrees in a clockwise direction (the camshaft sprocket will rotate 90-degrees for each 180-degree turn of the crankshaft). Verify TDC by checking the position of the arrow on the camshaft sprocket (see illustration). With the number 1 cylinder at TDC, the arrow should be pointing straight UP. Be sure the valves are closed at each adjustment position.

9 If necessary, repeat the adjustment procedure described in Steps 5, 6 and 7 until all the valves are adjusted to specifications.

10 Install the valve covers (use new gaskets) (see Section 4).

11 Install the spark plug wires and the various hoses and vacuum lines (if removed).

12 Start the engine and check for oil leakage between the valve covers and the cylinder heads.

13.5 The feeler gauge should slip between the valve stem tip and rocker arm with a slight amount of drag

13.7 Hold the adjusting screw with a screwdriver and tighten the locknut

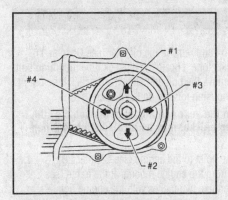

13.8 Rotate the crankshaft 180-degrees until the arrow on the camshaft sprocket indicates another valve clearance checking/adjusting position

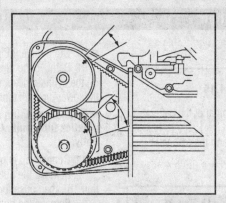

13.14 With the camshaft sprocket arrow mark at the 2:30 clock position, measure the number 1 intake valve and the number 3 exhaust valve clearances

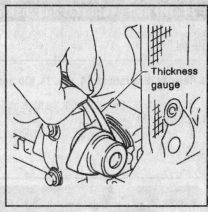

13.15 Measure the clearance using a feeler gauge

TURBOCHARGED MODELS

▶ **Refer to illustrations 13.14, 13.15, 13.16, 13.17 and 13.18**

13 Remove the timing belt cover from the right side camshaft assembly to expose the timing belt sprocket (see Section 7).

14 Turn the crankshaft pulley clockwise until the arrow mark on the camshaft sprocket is set approximately at the 2:30 clock position (see illustration). Measure the number 1 intake valve and the number 3 exhaust valve clearances.

15 Measure the clearances of the number 1 and number 3 valves with feeler gauges (see illustration). Refer to the Specifications listed in this Chapter. Record the measurements that are out of specification. They will be used later to determine the required replacement lifters.

16 Turn the crankshaft until the timing marks on the sprocket are at approximately the 4:30 clock position (see illustration). Measure the number 2 exhaust valve and the number 3 intake valve clearances.

17 Turn the crankshaft until the timing marks on the sprocket are at approximately the 7:30 clock position (see illustration). Measure the number 2 intake valve and the number 4 exhaust valve clearances.

18 Turn the crankshaft until the timing marks on the sprocket are at approximately the 10:30 clock position (see illustration). Measure the number 1 exhaust valve and the number 4 intake valve clearances.

19 After all the valve clearances are checked and recorded, replace the lifter on any valve assembly that is out of specification. Remove the camshaft(s) from the necessary cylinder head(s) (see Section 11).

20 Measure the thickness of the lifter with a micrometer. To calculate the correct thickness of a replacement lifter that will place the valve clearance within the specified value, use the following formula:

Intake valve $S = (V + T) - 0.008$ inch (0.20 mm)
Exhaust valve $S = (V + T) - 0.010$ inch (0.35 mm)
T = thickness of the old lifter
V = valve clearance measured
S = thickness of the new lifter

21 Select a lifter with a thickness as close as possible to the thickness calculated. Lifters are available in sizes in increments of 0.0004 inch (0.01 mm). Consult with a dealer parts department or other qualified automotive parts department for availability and parts numbers for each lifter.

22 Remove the camshafts from the cylinder head on the out-of-adjustment valves (see Section 11).

23 Repeat this procedure until all the valves which are out of clearance have been corrected.

24 Installation of the spark plugs, valve cover, spark plug wires and boots, etc. is the reverse of removal.

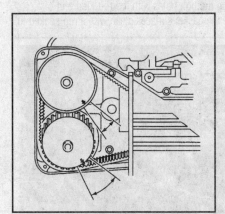

13.16 With the camshaft sprocket arrow mark in the 4:30 clock position, measure the number 2 exhaust valve and the number 3 intake valve clearances

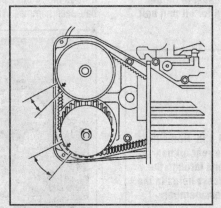

13.17 With the camshaft sprocket arrow mark in the 7:30 clock position, measure the number 2 intake valve and the number 4 exhaust valve clearances

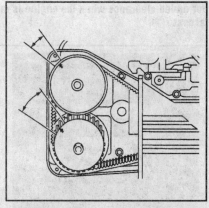

13.18 With the camshaft sprocket arrow mark in the 10:30 clock position, measure the number 1 exhaust valve and the number 4 intake valve clearances

14 Oil pan - removal and installation

REMOVAL

♦ **Refer to illustrations 14.13a, 14.13b and 14.15**

1   Disconnect the cable from the negative terminal of the battery (see Chapter 5).

2   Remove the air filter housing, intake ducts and the resonator (see Chapter 4).

14.13a Remove the oil pan bolts (not all bolts are visible in this view)

➥**Note: Depending on the year and model of the vehicle, the air filter housing may not need to be removed.**

3   On turbocharged models, remove the intercooler (see Chapter 4).

4   Remove the engine support brace (see Section 18).

5   Remove the radiator support brackets (see Chapter 3).

6   Raise the vehicle and support it securely on jackstands. Remove the front wheels and tires.

7   Remove the engine splash shield (see Section 6).

8   On non-turbocharged models, remove the exhaust manifold (see Section 6).

➥**Note: It will be necessary to remove the exhaust manifold for added clearance when the engine is raised for oil pan bolt access.**

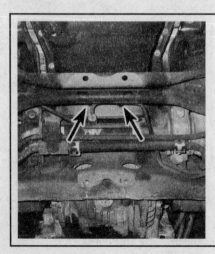

14.13b Remove the rear oil pan bolts through the access holes in the crossmember

9   Drain the engine oil and remove the oil filter (see Chapter 1).

10   Remove the dipstick tube. Locate the dipstick tube mounting bolt on the cylinder head, remove the bolt and slide the dipstick tube out of the lower dipstick tube housing located on the oil pan.

➥**Note: Depending on the year and model of the vehicle, the dipstick tube mounting bracket may be located slightly differently.**

11   Connect an engine hoist to the engine (see Chapter 2B).

12   Remove the nuts from the engine mounts at the frame (see Section 18), then raise the engine two inches with the engine hoist.

13   Remove the bolts securing the oil pan to the engine (see illustration).

➥**Note: There are two oil pan bolt access holes in the center crossmember, if necessary (see illustration).**

14   Tap on the pan with a soft-faced hammer to break the gasket seal, then lower the oil pan from the engine. A thin putty knife can be inserted between the pan and the block to break the gasket seal, but the block is aluminum, so do not use screwdriver or other sharp tool at the pan/block interface.

✳✳ CAUTION:

Before using force on the oil pan, be sure all the bolts have been removed.

15   If the oil pump pickup tube interferes with oil pan removal, remove the pickup tube bolts and remove the oil pan and pickup tube from the vehicle (see illustration).

INSTALLATION

16   Using a gasket scraper, scrape off all traces of the old gasket from the engine block and the oil pan. Be especially careful not to nick or gouge the gasket sealing surfaces of the crankcases (they are made of aluminum and are quite soft).

17   Clean the oil pan with solvent and dry it thoroughly. Check the gasket sealing surfaces for distortion. If the oil pan is distorted at the bolt hole areas, straighten the flange by supporting it from below on a wood block and tapping the bolt holes with the rounded end of a ball-peen hammer. Wipe the gasket surfaces clean with a rag soaked in

14.15 Remove the oil pump pickup tube bolts and remove the pickup tube with the oil pan

lacquer thinner or acetone.

18 Install a new O-ring on the pickup tube and place it in the oil pan.

19 Apply a thin coat of gasket sealant to the new oil pan gasket and place it carefully on the oil pan.

20 Raise the oil pan in position and install the pickup tube. Be careful not to disturb the gasket. Install the oil pan to the engine block and tighten the bolts hand-tight. Working from the center of the pan out to the ends, tighten the bolts to the torque listed in this Chapter's Specifications. Do not overtighten the bolts or oil leaks may occur.

21 The remainder of installation is the reverse of the removal process. After refilling with fresh oil and installing a new filter, start the engine and check for oil leaks.

15 Oil pump - removal, inspection and installation

✷✷ WARNING:

Wait until the engine is completely cool before beginning this procedure.

REMOVAL

1 Drain the engine oil (see Chapter 1). Remove the oil filter.

2 Raise the front of the vehicle and place it on jackstands.

3 Remove the timing belt, the tensioner and crankshaft sprocket (see Section 7).

4 Remove the upper timing belt idler pulley, the idler pulley number 1 and idler sprocket number 2 (see Section 7).

Turbocharged models

5 Drain the coolant (see Chapter 1).

6 Remove the coolant pipes from the oil cooler at the front of the engine (see Chapter 3).

7 Remove the water pump (see Chapter 3).

8 Remove the radiator (see Chapter 3).

All models

▸ **Refer to illustration 15.10**

9 Remove the crankshaft position sensor (CKP) (see Chapter 6).

10 Remove the mounting bolts and the oil pump (see illustration). Place a drain pan under the oil pump to catch the oil that will be spilled as the pump is removed.

INSPECTION

▸ **Refer to illustrations 15.11, 15.18a, 15.18b and 15.18c**

11 Remove the pump cover from the back of the oil pump assembly (see illustration).

12 Apply alignment marks to the inner and outer rotors so they can be installed in their original relationship to each other. Withdraw the rotors from the pump housing. Remove the relief valve plug, washer, spring and relief valve from the pump housing.

13 Clean the components with solvent, dry them thoroughly and inspect for any obvious damage.

14 Carefully check the interior surface of the pump housing and the exterior surfaces of the rotors for score marks and damage.

15 Check the relief valve and spring for damage.

16 Check the pump housing for clogged oil passages, case cracks and damage.

17 If there is damage to any of the components, replace the oil pump assembly.

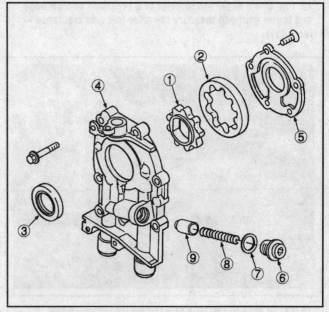

15.11 Exploded view of the oil pump assembly

1	Inner rotor	6	Plug
2	Outer rotor	7	Washer
3	Oil seal	8	Relief valve spring
4	Oil pump housing	9	Relief valve
5	Oil pump cover		

15.10 Remove the oil pump mounting bolts

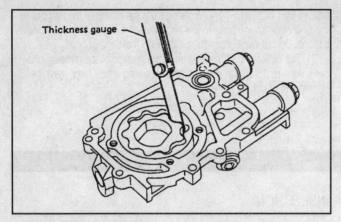

15.18a Using a feeler gauge, measure the clearance between the rotor tips

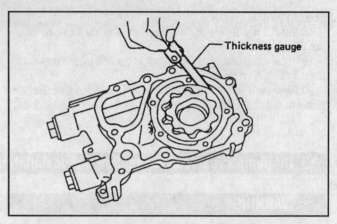

15.18b Measure the clearance between the outer rotor and the housing

18 Install the rotors in the pump housing and measure the rotor tip clearance; the outer rotor-to-oil pump housing clearance; and the rotor-to-cover clearance (endplay) (see illustrations). If any clearance exceeds the limit listed in this Chapter's Specifications, replace the oil pump assembly.

INSTALLATION

▶ **Refer to illustrations 15.21 and 15.22**

19 Lubricate the relief valve with clean engine oil and install the relief valve, spring, washer and plug.

20 Lubricate the rotors with clean engine oil and install the rotors into the pump housing, aligning the matchmarks made previously. Install the rotor cover.

21 Be sure to replace the oil pump housing-to-engine block O-ring and install a new crankshaft oil seal (see illustration).

22 Apply a bead of anaerobic sealant to the oil pump housing sealing surface (see illustration). Install the oil pump onto the engine block and tighten the bolts to the torque listed in this Chapter's Specifications.

23 The remainder of installation is the reverse of the removal procedure. Refill the engine with fresh oil and install a new filter (see Chapter 1). On turbo models, refill the cooling system (see Chapter 1). Start the engine and check for proper oil pressure and oil leaks.

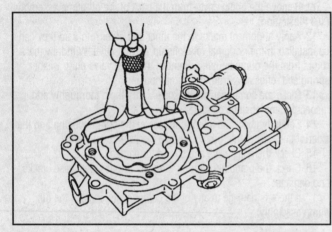

15.18c Use a depth micrometer or a precision straightedge and feeler gauge to measure the rotor-to-cover clearance (endplay)

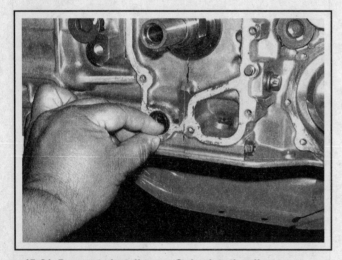

15.21 Be sure to install a new O-ring into the oil pump housing or engine block

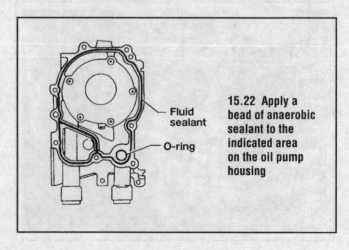

Fluid sealant

O-ring

15.22 Apply a bead of anaerobic sealant to the indicated area on the oil pump housing

16 Flywheel/driveplate - removal and installation

REMOVAL

1 Remove the transaxle (see Chapter 7). If equipped with a manual transaxle, remove the clutch disc and pressure plate (see Chapter 8).

2 Remove the attaching bolts and separate the flywheel/driveplate from the crankshaft.

INSTALLATION

3 Apply thread locking compound to the bolt threads. On automatic transaxle models, align the small hole in the driveplate with the mark on the backplate. Hold the flywheel/driveplate in position and install the bolts.

➡**Note: The flywheel/driveplate can only be installed in one position, since the bolt holes are not equally spaced. If the bolt holes do not align, rotate the flywheel/driveplate relative to the crankshaft until they all are in exact alignment.**

4 Hold the flywheel/driveplate so that it doesn't turn with an appropriate tool and tighten the bolts (using a crisscross pattern) to the torque listed in this Chapter's Specifications.

5 Install the clutch disc and clutch cover assembly as described in Chapter 8, if equipped.

6 Install the transaxle (see Chapter 7).

17 Rear main oil seal - replacement

1 Refer to Chapters 7 and 8 for removal of the transaxle and clutch assembly.

2 Remove the flywheel or driveplate (see Section 16).

3 Pry the rear main oil seal from the back of the block with a seal-removal tool. Be very careful not to nick the crankshaft seal surface with the tool.

4 Clean the seal bore and make sure the seal mounting surface is free of burrs.

5 Lubricate the new seal's inner lip with multi-purpose grease, and the outer diameter with clean engine oil.

6 Drive the new seal in place squarely with a seal driver, large socket, or section of pipe that's the same diameter as the outer diameter of the seal. Drive the seal to the original depth.

7 Install the flywheel/driveplate, clutch assembly (if equipped) and transaxle.

18 Engine mounts - check and replacement

CHECK

1 Engine mounts seldom require attention, but broken or deteriorated mounts should be replaced immediately or the added strain placed on the driveline components may cause damage.

2 During the check, the engine must be raised slightly to remove the weight from the mounts. Disconnect the cable from the negative terminal of the battery (see Chapter 5).

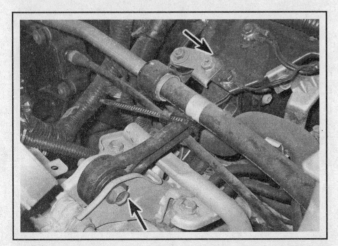

18.9 Location of the upper engine mount bolts

3 Raise the vehicle and support it securely on jackstands, then position the jack under the engine oil pan. Place a wood block between the jack head and the oil pan, then carefully raise the engine just enough to take the weight off the mounts.

4 Check the mounts to see if the rubber is cracked, hardened or separated from the metal plates. Sometimes the rubber will split right down the center. Rubber preservative may be applied to the mounts to slow deterioration.

5 Check for relative movement between the mount plates and the engine or frame (use a large screwdriver or pry bar to attempt to move the mounts). If movement is noted, lower the engine and tighten the mount fasteners.

REPLACEMENT

6 Disconnect the cable from the negative terminal of the battery (see Chapter 5).

Upper engine mount

▶ **Refer to illustration 18.9**

7 On non-turbocharged models, remove the air filter housing (see Chapter 4).

8 On turbocharged models, remove the intercooler (see Chapter 4).

9 Remove the upper engine mount brace mounting bolts (see illustration) and remove it from the engine compartment.

10 Installation is the reverse of removal.

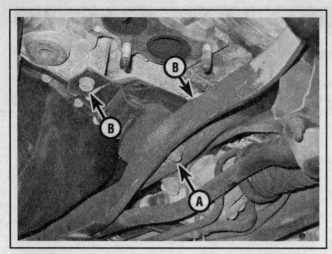

18.15a Working on the right side engine mount, first remove the lock nut (A) and the engine mount bolts (B) (one bolt hidden from view)

18.15b Working on the left side mount, first remove the lock nut (A) and the engine mount bolts (B) (one bolt hidden from view)

Lower engine mounts

▶ **Refer to illustrations 18.15a and 18.15b**

11 Remove the radiator support brackets, the engine cooling fans and the radiator (see Chapter 3).

➡**Note: It will be necessary to remove components that will interfere with the engine when it is raised.**

12 Install an engine hoist onto the engine lifting brackets (see Chapter 2A).

13 Raise the vehicle and support it securely on jackstands. Remove the front wheels and tires.

14 Remove the engine splash shield (see Section 6).

15 Remove the engine mount locknut from the stud projecting through the crossmember (see illustrations).

16 Raise the front of the engine high enough for the mount stud to clear the crossmember, but do not force the engine up too high. If anything interferes before the mounts are free, remove the component for clearance. Block the engine in this position with wood blocks.

17 Remove the two bolts securing the mount to the engine block and remove the mount.

18 Slip the new engine mount between the crossmember and the engine. Install the bolts into the engine block and tighten them securely.

19 Lower the engine slowly, making sure that both lower studs go through their respective holes in the crossmember. Remove the wood blocks and lower the engine to its original height and tighten the nuts securely.

Specifications

General

Firing order   1-3-2-4

Cylinder head gasket surface warpage limit

     2006 turbocharged models   0.0014 inch (0.035 mm)

     All other models   0.0020 inch (0.050 mm)

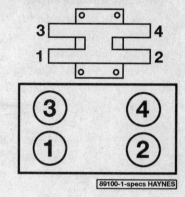

Engine cylinder numbering and coil pack terminal locations

89100-1-specs HAYNES

Camshaft

Non-turbocharged engine

Lobe height

     2000 through 2003

         Intake   1.5545 to 1.5585 inches (39.485 to 39.585 mm)

         Exhaust   1.5455 to 1.5495 inches (39.257 to 39.357 mm)

         Wear limit

             Intake   1.5506 inches (39.385 mm)

             Exhaust   1.5416 inches (39.157 mm)

     2004

         Ultra Low Emissions Vehicle (ULEV)

             Intake   1.5545 to 1.5585 inches (39.485 to 39.585 mm)

             Exhaust   1.5686 to 1.5726 inches (39.843 to 39.943 mm)

             Wear limit

                 Intake   1.5506 inches (39.385 mm)

                 Exhaust   1.5647 inches (39.743 mm)

         non-ULEV

             Intake   1.5545 to 1.5585 inches (39.485 to 39.585 mm)

             Exhaust   1.5455 to 1.5495 inches (39.257 to 39.357 mm)

             Wear limit

                 Intak   1.5506 inches (39.385 mm)

                 Exhaust   1.5416 inches (39.157 mm)

     2005

         Ultra Low Emissions Vehicle (ULEV)

             Intake   1.5545 to 1.5585 inches (39.485 to 39.585 mm)

             Exhaust   1.5686 to 1.5726 inches (39.843 to 39.943 mm)

         non-ULEV

             Legacy/Outback

                 Intake   1.5545 to 1.5585 inches (39.485 to 39.585 mm)

                 Exhaust   1.5638 to 1.5677 inches (39.720 to 39.820 mm)

             Forester

                 Intake   1.5545 to 1.5585 inches (39.485 to 39.585 mm)

                 Exhaust   1.5491 to 1.5530 inches (39.720 to 39.820 mm)

Camshaft (continued)

Non-turbocharged engine
Lobe height (continued)
    2006
        Intake

Constant	1.5778 to 1.5817 inches (40.075 to 40.175 mm)
Low speed	1.3851 to 1.3891 inches (35.182 to 35.282 mm)
High speed	1.5872 to 1.5911 inches (40.315 to 40.415 mm)
Exhaust	
Legacy/Outback	1.5783 to 1.5822 inches (40.088 to 4.0188 mm)
Forester	1.5807 to 1.5846 inches (40.149 to 4.0249 mm)
Journal diameter	1.2570 to 1.2577 inches (31.928 to 31.945 mm)
Journal bore	1.2598 to 1.2605 inches (32.000 to 32.018 mm)
Journal oil clearance	
Standard	0.0022 to 0.0035 inch (0.055 to 0.090 mm)
Limit	0.0039 inch (0.10 mm)
Thrust clearance (endplay)	
Standard	0.0012 to 0.0035 inch (0.030 to 0.090 mm)
Limit	0.0039 inch (0.10 mm)

Turbocharged engine

Lobe height	
Intake	1.8330 to 1.8370 inches (46.55 to 46.65 mm)
Exhaust	1.8410 to 1.8440 inches (46.75 to 46.85 mm)
Wear limit	
Intake	1.8290 inches (46.45 mm)
Exhaust	1.8370 inches (46.65 mm)
Journal diameter	
Front	1.4939 to 1.4946 inches (37.946 to 37.963 mm)
Center and Rear	1.1790 to 1.1796 inches (29.946 to 29.963 mm)
Journal bore	Not available
Journal oil clearance	
Standard	0.0015 to 0.0028 inch (0.037 to 0.072 mm)
Limit	0.0039 inch (0.10 mm)
Thrust clearance (endplay)	
Standard	0.0027 to 0.0046 inch (0.068 to 0.116 mm)
Limit	0.0055 inch (0.14 mm)

Valve lifters on turbocharged engines

Outer diameter	1.3763 to 1.3770 inch (34.959 to 34.975 mm)
Lifter bore diameter	1.3777 to 1.3786 inch (34.994 to 35.016 mm)
Lifter-to-bore clearance	
Standard	0.0007 to 0.0022 inch (0.019 to 0.057 mm)
Service limit	0.0039 inch (0.100 mm)

Valve clearances

Non-turbocharged engine
    2000 through 2005 models

Intake	0.007 to 0.009 inch (0.18 to 0.22 mm)
Exhaust	0.009 to 0.011 inch (0.23 to 0.27 mm)

Non-turbocharged engine
   2006 models
      Intake   0.006 to 0.010 inch (0.16 to 0.24 mm)
      Exhaust   0.008 to 0.012 inch (0.21 to 0.29 mm)
Turbocharged engine
   2004 models (includes 2005 Legacy/Outback models)
      Intake   0.006 to 0.010 inch (0.14 to 0.24 mm)
      Exhaust   0.012 to 0.016 inch (0.30 to 0.40 mm)
   2005 and 2006 models (excludes 2005 Legacy/Outback models)
      Intake   0.007 to 0.009 inch (0.18 to 0.22 mm)
      Exhaust   0.013 to 0.015 inch (0.33 to 0.37 mm)

Oil pump

Inner and outer rotor tip clearance
   Standard   0.0016 to 0.0055 inch (0.04 to 0.14 mm)
   Limit   0.0071 inch (0.18 mm)
Outer rotor-to-pump housing clearance
   Standard   0.0039 to 0.0069 inch (0.100 to 0.175 mm)
   Limit   0.0079 inch (0.20 mm)
Rotor-to-cover clearance (endplay)
   Standard   0.0008 to 0.0028 inch (0.02 to 0.07 mm)
   Limit   0.0047 inch (0.12 mm)

Timing belt guide clearance

All models   0.019 to 0.059 inch (0.5 to 1.5 mm)

Torque specifications	Ft-lbs (unless otherwise indicated)	Nm
Camshaft sprocket bolts		
Non-turbocharged models	58	78
Turbocharged models		
Intake sprocket bolt		
Step 1	22	30
Step 2	Tighten an additional 45 degrees	
Exhaust sprocket bolt		
2004 models	72	98
2005 and later models		
Step 1	22	30
Step 2	Tighten an additional 45 degrees	
Crankshaft pulley bolt		
Non-turbocharged models		
2000 through 2004 models	130	177
2005 and later models	133	180
Turbocharged models	133	180
Camshaft cap bolts (turbocharged models) (see illustration 11.34b)		
Bolts 1 through 4	180 in-lbs	20
Bolts 5 through 8	86 in-lbs	10
Bolts 9 through 12	180 in-lbs	20

Torque specifications	Ft-lbs (unless otherwise indicated)	Nm
Camshaft end cap assembly mounting bolts (non-turbocharged models)		
2000 through 2005 (see illustration 11.30a)		
Step 1 Bolts 1 through 4	Tighten lightly	
Step 2 rocker arm bolts	Refer to rocker arm torque specifications	
Step 3 Bolts 5 through 10	13	18
Step 4 Bolts 11 through 14 then 1 through 4	86 in-lbs	10
Step 5 Bolts 15 and 16	86 in-lbs	10
2006 (see illustration 11.30b)		
Step 1 Bolts 1 through 4	Tighten lightly	
Step 2 rocker arm bolts	Refer to rocker arm torque specifications	
Step 3 Bolts 5 through 10	13	18
Step 4 Bolts 11 through 14 then 1 through 4	86 in-lbs	10
Step 5 Bolts 15 and 16	86 in-lbs	10
Cylinder head bolts (see illustration 12.13)		
Non-turbocharged models		
2000 through 2004 models		
Step 1	22	29
Step 2	51	69
Step 3	Loosen all bolts 180-degrees (reverse order of tightening)	
Step 4	Loosen all bolts an additional 180 degrees	
Step 5 Bolts 1 and 2 only	25	34
Step 6 Bolts 3, 4, 5 and 6	132 in-lbs	15
Step 7	Tighten all bolts an additional 80 to 90 degrees	
Step 8	Tighten all bolts an additional 80 to 90 degrees	
2005 and 2006 models		
Step 1	22	29
Step 2	51	69
Step 3	Loosen all bolts 180-degrees (reverse order of tightening)	
Step 4	Loosen all bolts an additional 180-degrees	
Step 5	31	42
Step 6	Tighten all bolts an additional 80 to 90 degrees	
Step 7	Tighten all bolts an additional 40 to 45 degrees	
Step 8 Bolts 1 and 2	Tighten bolts an additional 40 to 45 degrees	
Turbocharged models		
Step 1	22	29
Step 2	51	69
Step 3	Loosen all bolts 180-degrees (reverse order of tightening)	
Step 4	Loosen all bolts an additional 180 degrees	
Step 5	36	49
Step 6	Tighten all bolts an additional 80 to 90-degrees	
Step 7	Tighten all bolts an additional 40 to 45-degrees	
Step 8 Bolts 1 and 2	Tighten bolts an additional 40 to 45 degrees	
Exhaust manifold-to-cylinder head bolts	22	30
Flywheel/driveplate-to-crankshaft bolts	53	72
Fuel rail protector mounting bolts	14	19

Torque specifications	Ft-lbs (unless otherwise indicated)	Nm
Intake manifold bolts		
Non-turbocharged, non-ULEV models		
2000 through 2004	18	25
2005		
Forester	18	25
Legacy/Outback		
Upper intake manifold-to-lower intake manifold bolts	74 in-lbs	10
Lower intake manifold-to-cylinder head bolts	18	25
2006	18	25
Non-turbocharged ULEV models	18	25
Non-turbocharged ULEV models (complete assembly) (see illustration 5.38)		
Step 1 Bolts A through O	Tighten lightly	
Step 2 Bolts E through K	48 in-lbs	5
Step 3 Bolts A through D and L through O	84 in-lbs	11
Step 4 Bolts E through G	18	25
Step 5 Bolts H through K	18	25
Step 6 Bolts A through D and L through O	18	25
Turbocharged models		
Upper intake manifold-to-lower intake manifold bolts	74-in lbs	10
Lower intake manifold-to-cylinder head bolts	18	25
Oil pan bolts	44 in-lbs	5
Oil pressure sending unit	18	25
Oil pump housing mounting bolts	56 in-lbs	6
Oil pump cover mounting screws	44 in-lbs	5
Oil strainer mounting bolts	74 in-lbs	10
Rocker arm assembly bolts (non-turbocharged models)		
2000 through 2005 (see illustration 11.30c)	18	25
2006 (see illustration 11.30d)		
Step 1 Bolts 1 through 8	18	25
Step 2 Bolts 9 and 10	68 in-lbs	8
Timing belt cover bolts	44 in-lbs	5
Timing belt upper idler pulley	29	39
Timing belt idler pulley number 1 bolt	29	39
Timing belt idler sprocket number 2 bolt	29	39
Timing belt tensioner mounting bolt	29	39
Timing belt tensioner bracket bolts	18	25
Timing belt guide (crankshaft sprocket) bolts	84 in-lbs	10
Timing belt guide (right intake sprocket) bolts (turbocharged models)	54 in-lbs	6
Timing belt guide (right exhaust sprocket) bolts (turbocharged models)	54 in-lbs	6
Timing belt guide (left exhaust sprocket) bolts (turbocharged models)	54 in-lbs	6

Torque specifications	Ft-lbs (unless otherwise indicated)	Nm
Valve cover bolts		
Non-turbocharged models		
2000 through 2005	44 in-lbs	5
2006 (see illustration 4.15)		
Step 1	54 in-lbs	6
Step 2	54 in-lbs	6
Turbocharged models (see illustration 4.16b)	54 in-lbs	6

Section

Reference to other Chapters

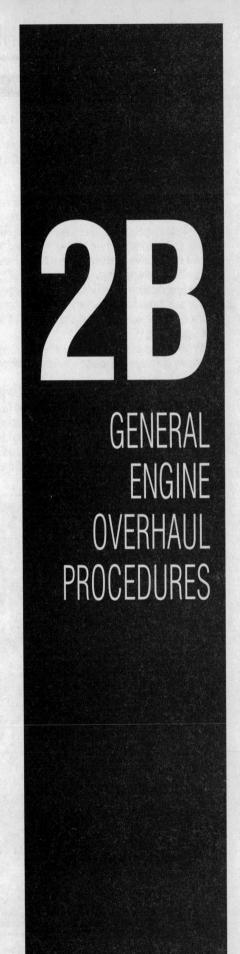

2B

GENERAL ENGINE OVERHAUL PROCEDURES

1 General information - engine overhaul

▶ **Refer to illustrations 1.1, 1.2, 1.3, 1.4, 1.5 and 1.6**

Included in this portion of Chapter 2 are general information and diagnostic testing procedures for determining the overall mechanical condition of your engine.

The information ranges from advice concerning preparation for an overhaul and the purchase of replacement parts and/or components to detailed, step-by-step procedures covering removal and installation.

The following Sections have been written to help you determine whether your engine needs to be overhauled and how to remove and install it once you've determined it needs to be rebuilt. For information concerning in-vehicle engine repair, see Chapter 2A.

The Specifications included in this Part are general in nature and include only those necessary for testing the oil pressure and checking the engine compression. Refer to Chapter 2A for additional engine Specifications.

It's not always easy to determine when, or if, an engine should be completely overhauled, because a number of factors must be considered.

High mileage is not necessarily an indication that an overhaul is needed, while low mileage doesn't preclude the need for an overhaul. Frequency of servicing is probably the most important consideration. An engine that's had regular and frequent oil and filter changes, as well as other required maintenance, will most likely give many thousands of miles of reliable service. Conversely, a neglected engine may require an overhaul very early in its service life.

Excessive oil consumption is an indication that piston rings, valve seals and/or valve guides are in need of attention. Make sure that oil leaks aren't responsible before deciding that the rings and/or guides are bad. Perform a cylinder compression check to determine the extent of the work required (see Section 3). Also check the vacuum readings under various conditions (see Section 4).

Check the oil pressure with a gauge installed in place of the oil pressure sending unit and compare it to this Chapter's Specifications (see Section 2). If it's extremely low, the bearings and/or oil pump are probably worn out.

Loss of power, rough running, knocking or metallic engine noises, excessive valve train noise and high fuel consumption rates may also point to the need for an overhaul, especially if they're all present at the same time. If a complete tune-up doesn't remedy the situation, major mechanical work is the only solution.

An engine overhaul involves restoring the internal parts to the specifications of a new engine. During an overhaul, the piston rings are replaced and the cylinder walls are reconditioned (rebored and/or honed) (see illustrations 1.1 and 1.2). If a rebore is done by an automotive machine shop, new oversize pistons will also be installed. The main bearings and connecting rod bearings are generally replaced with new ones and, if necessary, the crankshaft may be reground to restore the journals (see illustration 1.3). Generally, the valves are serviced as well, since they're usually in less-than-perfect condition at this point.

1.1 An engine block being bored. An engine rebuilder will use special machinery to recondition the cylinder bores

1.2 If the cylinders are bored, the machine shop will normally hone the engine on a machine like this

1.3 A crankshaft having a main bearing journal ground

1.4 A machinist checks for a bent connecting rod, using specialized equipment

While the engine is being overhauled, other components, such as the starter and alternator, can be rebuilt as well. The end result should be similar to a new engine that will give many trouble free miles.

➡Note: Critical cooling system components such as the hoses, drivebelts, thermostat and water pump should be replaced with new parts when an engine is overhauled. The radiator should be checked carefully to ensure that it isn't clogged or leaking (see Chapter 3). If you purchase a rebuilt engine or short block, some rebuilders will not warranty their engines unless the radiator has been professionally flushed. Also, we don't recommend overhauling the oil pump - always install a new one when an engine is rebuilt.

Overhauling the internal components on today's engines is a difficult and time-consuming task which requires a significant amount of specialty tools and is best left to a professional engine rebuilder

(see illustrations 1.4, 1.5 and 1.6). A competent engine rebuilder will handle the inspection of your old parts and offer advice concerning the reconditioning or replacement of the original engine, never purchase parts or have machine work done on other components until the block has been thoroughly inspected by a professional machine shop. As a general rule, time is the primary cost of an overhaul, especially since the vehicle may be tied up for a minimum of two weeks or more. Be aware that some engine builders only have the capability to rebuild the engine you bring them while other rebuilders have a large inventory of rebuilt exchange engines in stock. Also be aware that many machine shops could take as much as two weeks time to completely rebuild your engine depending on shop workload. Sometimes it makes more sense to simply exchange your engine for another engine that's already rebuilt to save time.

1.5 A bore gauge being used to check the main bearing bore

1.6 Uneven piston wear like this indicates a bent connecting rod

2 Oil pressure check

♦ **Refer to illustrations 2.2 and 2.3**

1   Low engine oil pressure can be a sign of an engine in need of rebuilding. A low oil pressure indicator (often called an idiot light) is not a test of the oiling system. Such indicators only come on when the oil pressure is dangerously low. Even a factory oil pressure gauge in the instrument panel is only a relative indication, although much better for driver information than a warning light. A better test is with a mechanical (not electrical) oil pressure gauge.

2   Locate the oil pressure indicator sending unit on the engine block (see illustration).

3   Unscrew and remove the oil pressure sending unit and then screw in the hose for your oil pressure gauge (see illustration). If necessary, install an adapter fitting. Use Teflon tape or thread sealant on the threads of the adapter and/or the fitting on the end of your gauge's hose.

4   Connect an accurate tachometer to the engine, according to the tachometer manufacturer's instructions.

5   Check the oil pressure with the engine running (normal operating temperature) at the specified engine speed, and compare it to this Chapter's Specifications. If it's extremely low, the bearings and/or oil pump are probably worn out.

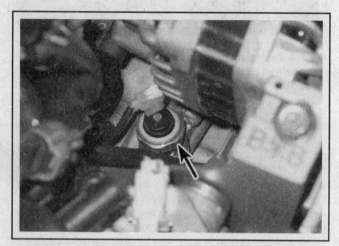

2.2 The oil pressure sending unit is located on top of the engine block near the alternator

2.3 Remove the alternator and the oil pressure sending unit and attach an oil pressure gauge - be sure the fittings you use have the same thread as the sending unit

3 Cylinder compression check

3.6 A compression gauge with a threaded fitting for the spark plug hole is preferred over the type that requires hand pressure to maintain the seal - be sure to open the throttle valve as far as possible during the compression check

♦ **Refer to illustration 3.6**

1   A compression check will tell you what mechanical condition the upper end of your engine (pistons, rings, valves, head gaskets) is in. Specifically, it can tell you if the compression is down due to leakage caused by worn piston rings, defective valves and seats or a blown head gasket.

➡**Note: The engine must be at normal operating temperature and the battery must be fully charged for this check.**

2   Begin by cleaning the area around the spark plugs before you remove them (compressed air should be used, if available). The idea is to prevent dirt from getting into the cylinders as the compression check is being done.

3   Remove all of the spark plugs from the engine (see Chapter 1).

4   Block the throttle wide open.

5   Disable the ignition system by unplugging the wiring harness from the ignition coil pack or by disconnecting each ignition coil (see Chapter 5). Disable the fuel system by removing the fuel pump relay (see Chapter 4, Section 2).

➡**Note: Follow the Fuel Pressure Relief procedure in Chapter 4 for disabling the fuel system.**

6   Install a compression gauge in the spark plug hole (see illustration).

7   Crank the engine over at least seven compression strokes and watch the gauge. The compression should build up quickly in a healthy engine. Low compression on the first stroke, followed by gradually increasing pressure on successive strokes, indicates worn piston rings. A low compression reading on the first stroke, which doesn't build up during successive strokes, indicates leaking valves or a blown head gasket (a cracked head could also be the cause). Deposits on the undersides of the valve heads can also cause low compression. Record the highest gauge reading obtained.

8   Repeat the procedure for the remaining cylinders and compare the results to this Chapter's Specifications.

9   Add some engine oil (about three squirts from a plunger-type oil can) to each cylinder, through the spark plug hole, and repeat the test.

10   If the compression increases after the oil is added, the piston rings are definitely worn. If the compression doesn't increase significantly, the leakage is occurring at the valves or head gasket. Leakage past the valves may be caused by burned valve seats and/or faces or warped, cracked or bent valves.

11   If two adjacent cylinders have equally low compression, there's a strong possibility that the head gasket between them is blown. The appearance of coolant in the combustion chambers or the crankcase would verify this condition.

12   If one cylinder is slightly lower than the others, and the engine has a slightly rough idle, a worn lobe on the camshaft could be the cause.

13   If the compression is unusually high, the combustion chambers are probably coated with carbon deposits. If that's the case, the cylinder head(s) should be removed and decarbonized.

14   If compression is way down or varies greatly between cylinders, it would be a good idea to have a leak-down test performed by an automotive repair shop. This test will pinpoint exactly where the leakage is occurring and how severe it is.

4   Vacuum gauge diagnostic checks

♦ **Refer to illustrations 4.4 and 4.6**

A vacuum gauge provides inexpensive but valuable information about what is going on in the engine. You can check for worn rings or cylinder walls, leaking head or intake manifold gaskets, restricted exhaust, stuck or burned valves, weak valve springs, improper ignition or valve timing and ignition problems.

Unfortunately, vacuum gauge readings are easy to misinterpret, so they should be used in conjunction with other tests to confirm the diagnosis.

Both the absolute readings and the rate of needle movement are important for accurate interpretation. Most gauges measure vacuum in inches of mercury (in-Hg). The following references to vacuum assume the diagnosis is being performed at sea level. As elevation increases (or atmospheric pressure decreases), the reading will decrease. For every 1,000 foot increase in elevation above approximately 2,000 feet, the gauge readings will decrease about one inch of mercury.

Connect the vacuum gauge directly to the intake manifold vacuum, not to ported (throttle body) vacuum (see illustration on next page). Be sure no hoses are left disconnected during the test or false readings will result.

Before you begin the test, allow the engine to warm up completely. Block the wheels and set the parking brake. With the transaxle in Park, start the engine and allow it to run at normal idle speed.

❋❋ WARNING:

Keep your hands and the vacuum gauge clear of the fans.

Read the vacuum gauge; an average, healthy engine should normally produce about 17 to 22 in-Hg with a fairly steady needle (see illustration). Refer to the following vacuum gauge readings and what they indicate about the engine's condition:

1   A low, steady reading usually indicates a leaking gasket between the intake manifold and cylinder head(s) or throttle body, a leaky vacuum hose, late ignition timing or incorrect camshaft timing. Check ignition timing with a timing light and eliminate all other possible causes, utilizing the tests provided in this Chapter before you remove the timing belt cover to check the timing marks.

4.4 An inexpensive vacuum gauge can tell a lot about the tune and general condition of an engine - test engine vacuum before beginning an overhaul

2   If the reading is three to eight inches below normal and it fluctuates at that low reading, suspect an intake manifold gasket leak at an intake port or a faulty fuel injector.

3   If the needle has regular drops of about two-to-four inches at a steady rate, the valves are probably leaking. Perform a compression check or leak-down test to confirm this.

4   An irregular drop or down-flick of the needle can be caused by a sticking valve or an ignition misfire. Perform a compression check or leak-down test and read the spark plugs.

5   A rapid vibration of about four in-Hg vibration at idle combined with exhaust smoke indicates worn valve guides. Perform a leak-down test to confirm this. If the rapid vibration occurs with an increase in engine speed, check for a leaking intake manifold gasket or head gasket, weak valve springs, burned valves or ignition misfire.

6   A slight fluctuation, say one inch up and down, may mean ignition problems. Check all the usual tune-up items and, if necessary, run the engine on an ignition analyzer.

7   If there is a large fluctuation, perform a compression or leak-down test to look for a weak or dead cylinder or a blown head gasket.

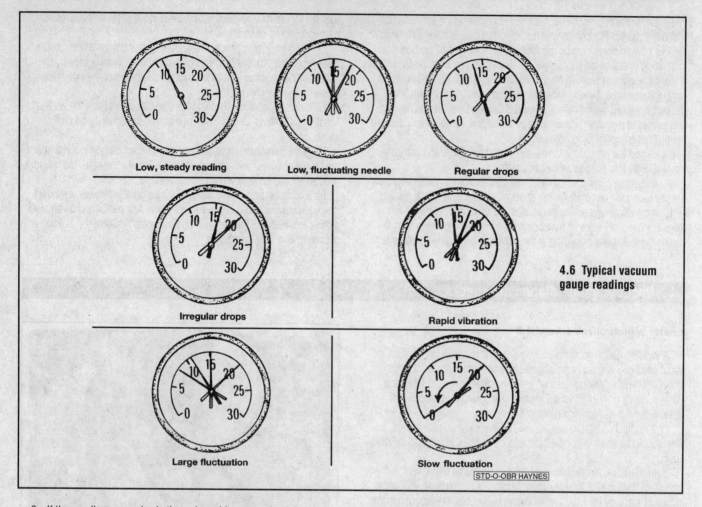

Low, steady reading

Low, fluctuating needle

Regular drops

Irregular drops

Rapid vibration

Large fluctuation

Slow fluctuation

4.6 Typical vacuum gauge readings

STD-O-OBR HAYNES

8 If the needle moves slowly through a wide range, check for a clogged PCV system, incorrect idle fuel mixture, throttle body or intake manifold gasket leaks.

9 Check for a slow return after revving the engine by quickly snapping the throttle open until the engine reaches about 2,500 rpm and let it shut. Normally the reading should drop to near zero, rise above normal idle reading (about 5 in-Hg over) and then return to the previous idle reading. If the vacuum returns slowly and doesn't peak when the throttle is snapped shut, the rings may be worn. If there is a long delay, look for a restricted exhaust system (often the muffler or catalytic converter). An easy way to check this is to temporarily disconnect the exhaust ahead of the suspected part and redo the test.

5 Engine rebuilding alternatives

The do-it-yourselfer is faced with a number of options when purchasing a rebuilt engine. The major considerations are cost, warranty, parts availability and the time required for the rebuilder to complete the project. The decision to replace the engine block, piston/connecting rod assemblies and crankshaft depends on the final inspection results of your engine. Only then can you make a cost effective decision whether to have your engine overhauled or simply purchase an exchange engine for your vehicle.

Some of the rebuilding alternatives include:

Individual parts - If the inspection procedures reveal that the engine block and most engine components are in reusable condition, purchasing individual parts and having a rebuilder rebuild your engine may be the most economical alternative. The block, crankshaft and piston/connecting rod assemblies should all be inspected carefully by a machine shop first.

Long block - A long block consists of an engine block plus an oil pump, oil pan, cylinder heads, valve cover, camshaft and valve train components, timing sprockets and chain or gears and timing cover. All components are installed with new bearings, seals and gaskets incorporated throughout. The installation of manifolds and external parts is all that's necessary.

Low mileage used engines - Some companies now offer low mileage used engines which is a very cost effective way to get your vehicle up and running again. These engines often come from vehicles which have been totaled in accidents or come from other countries which have a higher vehicle turn over rate. A low mileage used engine also usually has a similar warranty like the newly remanufactured engines.

Give careful thought to which alternative is best for you and discuss the situation with local automotive machine shops, auto parts dealers and experienced rebuilders before ordering or purchasing replacement parts.

6 Engine removal - methods and precautions

▶ **Refer to illustrations 6.1, 6.2, and 6.3**

If you've decided that an engine must be removed for overhaul or major repair work, several preliminary steps should be taken. Read all removal and installation procedures carefully prior to committing to this job.

Locating a suitable place to work is extremely important. Adequate work space, along with storage space for the vehicle, will be needed. If a shop or garage isn't available, at the very least a flat, level, clean work surface made of concrete or asphalt is required.

Cleaning the engine compartment and engine before beginning the removal procedure will help keep tools clean and organized (see illustrations 6.1 and 6.2).

An engine hoist will also be necessary. Make sure the hoist is rated in excess of the weight of the engine. Safety is of primary importance, considering the potential hazards involved in removing the engine from the vehicle.

If you're a novice at engine removal, get at least one helper. One person cannot easily do all the things you need to do to remove an engine from the engine compartment. Also helpful is to seek advice and assistance from someone who's experienced in engine removal.

Plan the operation ahead of time. Arrange for or obtain all of the tools and equipment you'll need prior to beginning the job (see illustration 6.3). Some of the equipment necessary to perform engine removal and installation safely and with relative ease are (in addition to an engine hoist) a heavy duty floor jack (preferably fitted with a transaxle jack head adapter), complete sets of wrenches and sockets as described in the front of this manual, wooden blocks, plenty of rags and cleaning solvent for mopping up spilled oil, coolant and gasoline.

Plan for the vehicle to be out of use for quite a while. A machine

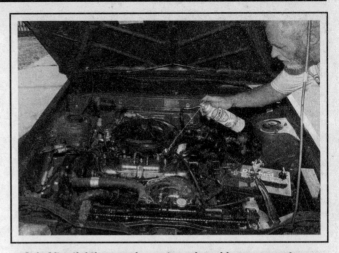

6.1 After tightly wrapping water-vulnerable components, use a spray cleaner on everything, with particular concentration on the greasiest areas, usually around the valve cover and lower edges of the block. If one section dries out, apply more cleaner

shop can do the work that is beyond the scope of the home mechanic. Machine shops often have a busy schedule, so before removing the engine, consult the shop for an estimate of how long it will take to rebuild or repair the components that may need work.

6.2 Depending on how dirty the engine is, let the cleaner soak in according to the directions and then hose off the grime and cleaner. Get the rinse water down into every area you can get at; then dry important components with a hair dryer or paper towels

6.3 Get an engine stand sturdy enough to firmly support the engine while you're working on it. Stay away from three-wheeled models; they have a tendency to tip over more easily, so get a four-wheeled unit.

7 Engine - removal and installation

※※ WARNING 1:

Gasoline is extremely flammable, so take extra precautions when you work on any part of the fuel system. Don't smoke or allow open flames or bare light bulbs near the work area, and don't work in a garage where a gas-type appliance (such as a water heater or clothes dryer) is present. Since gasoline is carcinogenic, wear fuel-resistant gloves when there's a possibility of being exposed to fuel, and, if you spill any fuel on your skin, rinse it off immediately with soap and water. Mop up any spills immediately and do not store fuel-soaked rags where they could ignite. The fuel system is under constant pressure, so, if any fuel lines are to be disconnected, the fuel pressure in the system must be relieved first (see Chapter 4 for more information). When you perform any kind of work on the fuel system, wear safety glasses and have a Class B type fire extinguisher on hand.

※※ WARNING 2:

The air conditioning system is under high pressure. DO NOT loosen any fittings or remove any components until after the system has been discharged. Air conditioning refrigerant should be properly discharged into an EPA-approved container at a dealer service department or an automotive air conditioning repair facility. Always wear eye protection when disconnecting air conditioning system fittings.

※※ WARNING 3:

The engine must be completely cool before beginning this procedure.

REMOVAL

◆ **Refer to illustrations 7.12, 7.18a, 7.18b, 7.19, 7.27a, 7.27b and 7.27c**

1   Have the air conditioning system discharged by an automotive air conditioning technician.

2   Place protective covers on the fenders and cowl and remove the hood (see Chapter 11).

3   Relieve the fuel system pressure (see Chapter 4).

4   Disconnect the cable from the negative terminal of the battery (see Chapter 5).

5   Remove the engine cover, if equipped, and the engine splash shield (see Chapter 2A).

6   Remove the air filter housing, the resonator and the air intake ducts (see Chapter 4).

7   Drain the cooling system and remove the drivebelts (see Chapter 1).

8   Remove the fan shrouds, the engine cooling fans and the radiator (see Chapter 3).

9   Disconnect the heater hoses (see Chapter 3).

10 On turbocharged models, remove the intercooler (see Chapter 4) and the coolant filler tank (see Chapter 3).

11 On 2006 Forester turbocharged models, remove the Secondary Air pump (see Chapter 6).

12 Clearly label and disconnect all vacuum lines, emissions hoses, wiring harness connectors, ground straps and fuel lines. Masking tape and/or a touch up paint applicator work well for marking items (see illustration). Take instant photos or sketch the locations of components and brackets.

13 Remove the battery and the battery tray (see Chapter 5).

14 Detach the ground cable from the engine ground terminal in the engine compartment.

15 Disconnect the air conditioning lines from the air conditioning compressor (see Chapter 3).

16 Remove the power steering pump and brackets without disconnecting the power steering fluid hoses and tie the assembly out of the way (see Chapter 10).

17 Disconnect the accelerator cable (see Chapter 4) or the electronic throttle control system (see Chapter 6) and the cruise control system, if equipped.

18 On automatic transaxle models, remove the rubber service plug (see illustration) and remove the torque converter-to-driveplate bolts (see illustration).

19 Remove the upper engine brace (see Chapter 2A). Remove the air filter housing upper and side mounting brackets from the engine compartment (see illustration).

20 Disconnect the wires from the starter solenoid and remove the starter (see Chapter 5).

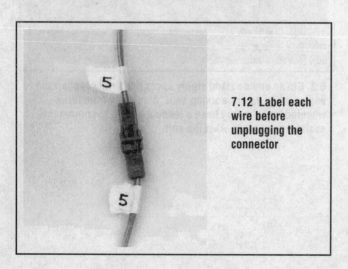

7.12 Label each wire before unplugging the connector

7.18a Location of the rubber service plug on the engine bellhousing (located directly behind the throttle body)

7.18b Remove the torque converter bolts through the service hole

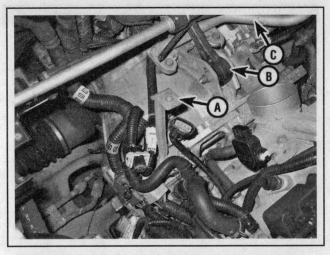

7.19 Location of the air filter housing side bracket (A), the upper transaxle brace (B) and the air filter housing upper bracket (C)

21 Disconnect the fuel lines from the fuel rail (see Chapter 4) and plug the lines to prevent fuel loss.

22 Raise the front of the vehicle and support it on jackstands. Block the rear wheels to keep the vehicle from rolling.

23 Remove the exhaust manifold (see Chapter 2A).

24 Remove the engine-to-transaxle lower mounting nuts and bolts.

25 Drain the engine oil (see Chapter 1).

26 Remove the engine oil cooler lines and brackets, if equipped (see Chapter 3).

27 Support the engine from above with a hoist. Attach the hoist chain to the engine lifting brackets (see illustrations). If no brackets are present, you will have to fasten the chains to a substantial part of the engine - one that is strong enough to take the weight, but in a location that will provide good balance. If you're attaching a chain to the stud on the engine, or are using a bolt passing through the chain and into a threaded hole, place a washer between the nut or bolt head and the chain and tighten the nut or bolt securely.

28 Support the transaxle with a floor jack.

29 Remove the transaxle-to-engine bolts (see Chapter 7).

30 Use the hoist to take the weight off the engine mounts, then remove the engine mount stud nuts (see Chapter 2A).

31 Check to make sure everything is disconnected, then slowly lift the engine out of the vehicle. The engine will probably need to be tilted and/or maneuvered as it's lifted out, so have an assistant handy.

7.27a Attach the chain to the engine lift bracket located on the rear of the engine and . . .

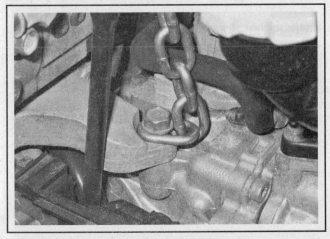

7.27b . . . to a solid mounting point on the front of the engine block (if no lifting bracket is present)

7.27c Raise the engine with the hoist and carefully guide it out of the engine compartment

✷✷ WARNING:

Do not place any part of your body under the engine when it is supported only by a hoist or other lifting device.

32 Remove the flywheel/driveplate and mount the engine on an engine stand or set the engine on the floor and support it so it doesn't tip over. Then disconnect the engine hoist.

INSTALLATION

33 Check the engine mounts. If they're worn or damaged, replace them (see Chapter 2A).

34 Inspect the converter seal and bushing.

35 Attach the hoist to the engine, remove the engine from the engine stand and install the flywheel/driveplate (see Chapter 2A).

36 Carefully guide the engine into place, lowering it slowly and moving it back into the engine compartment until the engine mounts can be secured.

37 With the engine still supported by the hoist, use the floor jack under the transaxle, if necessary, to adjust of the angle of the transaxle to bring it into alignment with the engine.

38 Install and tighten all the transaxle-to-engine bolts and the nuts on the engine mounts, then remove the hoist and jack.

39 Reinstall the remaining components in the reverse order of removal.

40 Add coolant, oil, power steering and transaxle fluid as needed (see Chapter 1).

41 Run the engine and check for proper operation and leaks. Shut off the engine and recheck the fluid levels.

42 Have the air conditioning system evacuated, charged and leak tested by the shop that discharged it.

8   Engine overhaul - disassembly sequence

1   It's much easier to remove the external components if it's mounted on a portable engine stand. A stand can often be rented quite cheaply from an equipment rental yard. Before the engine is mounted on a stand, the flywheel/driveplate should be removed from the engine.

2   If a stand isn't available, it's possible to remove the external engine components with it blocked up on the floor. Be extra careful not to tip or drop the engine when working without a stand.

3   If you're going to obtain a rebuilt engine (long block), all external components must come off first, to be transferred to the replacement engine. These components include:

Flywheel/driveplate
Ignition system components
Emissions-related components
Engine mounts and mount brackets
Intake manifold
Fuel injection components
Oil filter/oil cooler
Spark plug wires and spark plugs

Thermostat and housing assembly
Coolant crossover pipe
Water pump
Oil separator cover

➡**Note: When removing the external components from the engine, pay close attention to details that may be helpful or important during installation. Note the installed position of gaskets, seals, spacers, pins, brackets, washers, bolts and other small items.**

4   If you're going to rebuild the engine, disassemble the engine in the following order. See *Engine rebuilding alternatives* for additional information regarding the different possibilities to be considered.

Remove the external components listed above
Remove the cylinder heads
Remove the pistons
Separate the crankcase halves
Remove the crankshaft and connecting rods

9   Pistons - removal

9.1 Before you try to remove the pistons, use a ridge reamer to remove the raised material (ridge) from the top of the cylinders

▶ **Refer to illustrations 9.1, 9.2, 9.3a, 9.3b, 9.3c, 9.4a and 9.4b**

1   Temporarily install the crankshaft pulley bolt in the crankshaft front end so you can turn the crankshaft. Check for the presence of a wear ridge at the top of each cylinder. If a ridge has formed, it must be machined out before the pistons are removed (see illustration).

2 Remove the plugs from the four service holes with an Allen wrench for access to the piston pin circlips (see illustration).

➡Note: These plugs may be difficult to remove. Soak them first with penetrating oil. If you have to hit the Allen wrench with a hammer, make sure the wrench is fully into the plug to avoid rounding off the hexagonal opening.

3 To remove the piston pin circlips from a piston, position that piston at bottom dead center by turning the crankshaft, then insert needle-nose pliers through the service holes and remove the circlips (see illustrations).

➡Note: Use a small flashlight to see that the circlip is positioned directly at the access hole. You may have to make small movements of the crankshaft to align the piston just right.

9.2 Remove the four access plugs (arrow indicates one) that allow piston pin removal

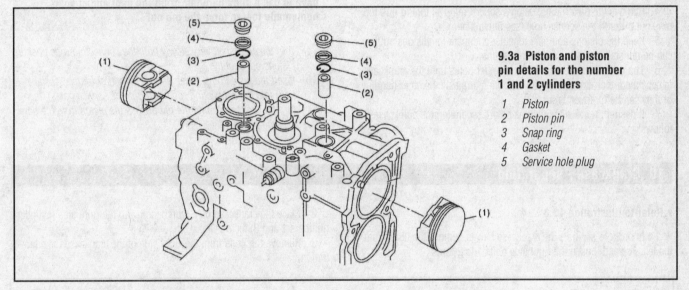

9.3a Piston and piston pin details for the number 1 and 2 cylinders

1 Piston
2 Piston pin
3 Snap ring
4 Gasket
5 Service hole plug

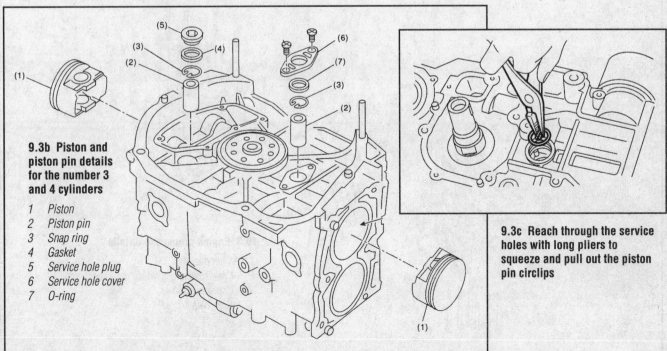

9.3b Piston and piston pin details for the number 3 and 4 cylinders

1 Piston
2 Piston pin
3 Snap ring
4 Gasket
5 Service hole plug
6 Service hole cover
7 O-ring

9.3c Reach through the service holes with long pliers to squeeze and pull out the piston pin circlips

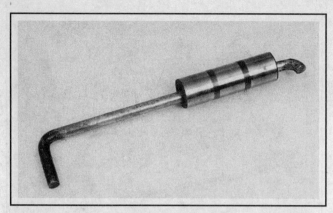

9.4a A special removal tool is needed to remove the piston pins - one can be fabricated from steel rod; bend the end to grab the rear edge and extract the pin

4   Remove the piston pins, using a special removal tool to pull the pins out through the service hole (see illustrations).

5   Keep the pistons and pins together and mark the pistons so they can be reinstalled in their original locations.

6   The pistons can remain in the cylinder bores until the crankcase is separated, then driven out with a wooden or plastic hammer handle, or they can be removed first.

7   If desired, remove the pistons before separating the crankcase as follows:

9.4b If the pins are varnished from high mileage, you may have to use a slide hammer or hit the bent end of your homemade tool to force the pin out

a) Turn the crankshaft very slowly until the connecting rods push the pistons out slightly.
b) Insert the piston pins (clean and oil them first for easy installation) into the connecting rods (through the service holes), then turn the crankshaft until the pin pushes the piston from the bore.
c) Pull the pistons out.

10 Crankcase - separation

♦ **Refer to illustration 10.3**

1   In order to separate the crankcase halves, remove the bolts from the left side and loosen the right side bolts 1 to 2 turns.

2   Place the crankcase on a workbench with the right side (cylinder numbers 1 and 3) facing UP.

3   Remove the bolts from the right side of the crankcase (see illustration).

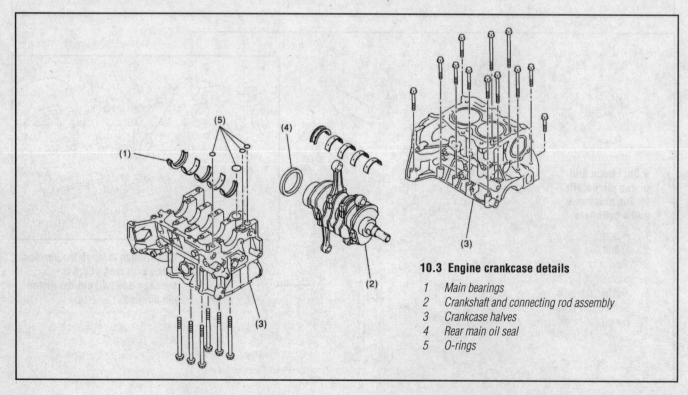

10.3 Engine crankcase details

1   Main bearings
2   Crankshaft and connecting rod assembly
3   Crankcase halves
4   Rear main oil seal
5   O-rings

4   Pull straight up on the right crankcase half to separate the two sections. You may have to tap the right crankcase section with a soft-faced hammer to break the gasket seal. Be careful when separating the halves, do not allow the connecting rods to fall and damage the crankcase. The crankshaft and connecting rod assembly will remain in the left half.

11   Crankshaft and connecting rods - removal

▶ **Refer to illustration 11.2**

1   Separate the crankcase (see Section 10) and remove the crankshaft rear oil seal.

2   Before lifting out the crankshaft/connecting rod assembly, check the crankshaft endplay. Gently pry or push the crankshaft all the way to the rear of the engine. Slip feeler gauges between the crankshaft and the thrust face of the center main bearing to determine the clearance (which is equivalent to crankshaft endplay) (see illustration). A typical crankshaft endplay will fall between 0.003 to 0.010 inch (0.076 to 0.254 mm). If it is greater than that, check the crankshaft thrust surfaces for wear after it's removed. If no wear is evident, new main bearings should correct the endplay.

3   Carefully lift out the crankshaft and store it where it will not fall or get damaged.

4   Remove the main bearings from the case halves and store them in a clearly marked container so they can be reinstalled in their original locations (if they are reused).

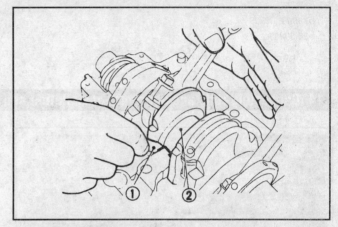

11.2 Position the feeler gauge (1) between the crankshaft (2) and the thrust bearing

12   Connecting rods and bearings - removal

▶ **Refer to illustrations 12.1 and 12.2**

1   Before removing the connecting rods from the crankshaft, check the endplay (side clearance) with a feeler gauge (see illustration). Slide the feeler gauge between the first connecting rod and the crankshaft throw until the play is removed (see illustration). Repeat this procedure for each connecting rod. The endplay is equal to the thickness of the feeler gauge(s). Check with an automotive machine shop for the endplay service limit (a typical end play limit should measure between 0.005 to 0.015 inch [0.127 to 0.369 mm]). If the play exceeds the service limit, new connecting rods will be required. If new rods (or a new crankshaft) are installed, the endplay may fall under the minimum allowable. If it does, the rods will have to be machined to restore it. If necessary, consult an automotive machine shop for advice.

2   If the rods and caps are not numbered, carefully mark the connecting rods and caps so they can be reinstalled in the same position on the same crankshaft journal (see illustration). Mark the connecting rod and cap at the front of the crankshaft with one dot, the second connecting rod and cap with two dots and so on (both the rods and caps must be marked since they are going to be separated). Loosen the cap nuts or bolts on one connecting rod in three steps, carefully lift off the cap and bearing insert, then carefully remove the connecting rod and remaining bearing insert from the crankshaft journal. Temporarily reassemble the connecting rod, the bearing and the cap to prevent mixing up parts.

3   Repeat the procedure for the remaining connecting rods. Be very careful not to nick or scratch the crankshaft journals with the connecting rod bolts.

4   Without mixing them up, clean the parts with solvent and dry them thoroughly. Make sure the oil holes are clear.

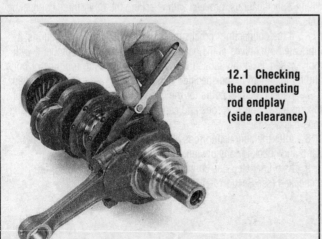

12.1 Checking the connecting rod endplay (side clearance)

12.2 If the connecting rods or caps are not marked, use permanent ink or paint to mark the caps to the rods by cylinder number (for example, this would be number 4 cylinder connecting rod)

13 Engine overhaul - reassembly sequence

To assemble the engine, install the following items in the order given:

Crankshaft and connecting rods
Join the crankcase halves
Pistons
Cylinder heads
Camshafts

Rocker arm assembly (non-turbo models)
Oil pump
Timing belt and sprockets
Valve covers
Oil strainer/pick-up tube
Oil pan
Flywheel/driveplate and housing
Engine external components

14 Connecting rods and bearings - installation and oil clearance check

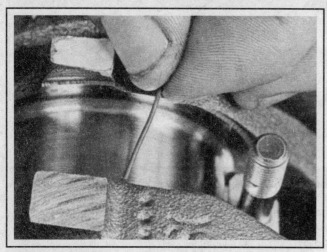

14.4 Place Plastigage on each connecting rod bearing journal parallel to the crankshaft centerline

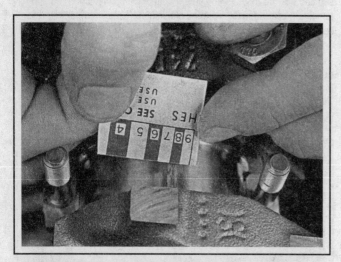

14.5 Use the scale on the Plastigage package to determine the bearing oil clearance - be sure to measure the widest part of the Plastigage and use the correct scale; it comes with both standard and metric scales

◆ **Refer to illustrations 14.4 and 14.5**

1   Once the crankshaft and connecting rods have been cleaned and inspected and the decision has been made concerning bearing replacement, the connecting rods can be reinstalled on the crankshaft.

➡**Note: If new bearings are being used, check the oil clearances before final installation of the connecting rods. If the clearances are within the specified limits, proceed with the installation. Never assume that the clearances are correct even though new bearings are involved.**

2   Make sure the bearing faces and backs are perfectly clean, then fit them to the connecting rod and cap. The tab on each bearing must be engaged in the recess in the cap or connecting rod.

3   Clean the number one connecting rod journal on the crankshaft, then slip the number one connecting rod into place. Make sure the mark on the side of the connecting rod is facing the front of the crankshaft.

4   Apply a length of Plastigage to the crankshaft journal, just off center (see illustration). Gently install the connecting rod cap in place, without turning the connecting rod on the journal. Make sure the mating mark on the cap is on the same side as the mark on the connecting rod. Lubricate the threads of the connecting rod nuts or bolts and tighten them to the torque listed in this Chapter's Specifications.

5   Remove the connecting rod nuts or bolts without allowing the connecting rod to turn on the journal, then remove the cap. Examine the Plastigage and compare its width to the scale on the Plastigage package (see illustration). The connecting rod oil clearance is usually about 0.001 to 0.002 inch. Consult an automotive machine shop for the clearance specified for the rod bearings on your engine. If the clearance is within Specifications, proceed with checking the other three connecting rods.

6   If the connecting rod clearances are all within Specifications, lubricate both halves of the bearings of connecting rod number 1 with moly-based assembly lube, and install the connecting rod nuts or bolts and tighten them to the specified torque, working up to it in three steps.

7   Repeat the procedure for the remaining connecting rods: do not mix up the connecting rods and caps and do not install the connecting rods backwards.

8   After the connecting rods have been installed, rotate them by hand and check for any obvious binding.

9   As a final step, the connecting rod side clearance must be rechecked (see Section 12).

15 Crankshaft and main bearings - installation and oil clearance check

▶ **Refer to illustrations 15.12 and 15.13**

1   Before installation of the crankshaft, the main bearing oil clearance must be checked.

2   Position the left crankcase section on a workbench with the bearing saddles facing up. Wipe the main bearing surfaces of the crankcase with a clean lint-free cloth. They must be kept spotlessly clean.

3   Clean the back sides of the main bearing inserts and lay one bearing half in each main bearing saddle in the crankcase on the workbench and the other bearing half from each set in the corresponding location in the remaining crankcase section. Make sure the tab on the bearing insert fits into the recess in the crankcase. Do not hammer the bearings into place and do not nick or gouge the bearing faces. No lubrication should be used at this time.

4   Clean the faces of the bearings in the crankcase and the crankshaft main bearing journals with a clean, lint-free cloth. Once you are certain that the crankshaft is clean, carefully lay it in position in the (left) crankcase section on the workbench.

5   Trim three pieces of Plastigage so that they are slightly shorter than the width of the main bearings and place one piece on each crankshaft main bearing journal, parallel with the journal axis (see illustration 14.4).

6   Clean the faces of the bearings in the right crankcase, then carefully lay it in position. Do not disturb the Plastigage.

7   Install the crankcase bolts and tighten them as described in Section 14. Do not rotate the crankshaft at any time during this operation.

8   Remove the bolts and carefully lift off the right crankcase section. Do not disturb the Plastigage or rotate the crankshaft.

9   Compare the width of the crushed Plastigage on each journal to the scale printed on the Plastigage container to obtain the main bearing oil clearances (see illustration 14.5). A typical main bearing oil clearance should fall between 0.0015 to 0.0023 inch (0.038 to 0.058 mm). Check with an automotive machine shop for the crankshaft main bearing oil clearance limits for your engine.

10 If the clearance is not correct. double-check to make sure that you have the right size bearing inserts. Also, recheck the crankshaft main bearing journal diameters and make sure that no dirt or oil was between the bearing inserts and the main bearing caps or the block when the clearance was measured.

11 Be sure to remove all traces of the Plastigage from the bearing faces and/or journals. To prevent damage to the bearing surfaces, use a wood or plastic tool.

12 Carefully lift the crankshaft out of the crankcase. Clean the bearing faces, then apply a thin layer of engine assembly lube to each of the bearing faces in both crankcase halves (see illustration). Be sure to coat the thrust bearing faces as well.

13 Carefully lay the crankshaft in the left crankcase section. Make sure the connecting rods are directed into the cylinder bores (see illustration).

14 Refer to Section 16 and rejoin the two crankcase halves.

15.12 Apply engine assembly lubricant to the main bearing inserts before final assembly

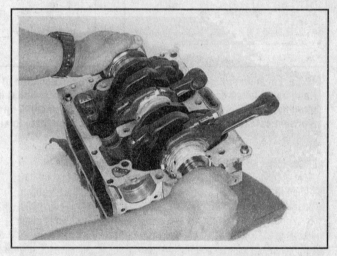

15.13 Install the crankshaft/connecting rod assembly onto the bearings in the left crankcase

16 Crankcase - reassembly

▶ **Refer to illustrations 16.3a, 16.3b, 16.5a, 16.5b, 16.5c, 16.5d and 16.5e**

1   Clean the block mating surfaces with lacquer thinner or acetone (they must be clean and oil-free).

2   Install the O-rings in the left crankcase section (see illustration 10.3).

3   Apply a thin layer of anaerobic sealant to the crankcase mating

16.3a Apply a bead of anaerobic sealant to the face of the left crankcase

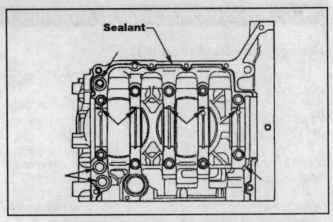

16.3b Run the bead to the inside of the bolt holes to ensure proper sealing of the crankcase - DO NOT allow the sealant to flow into the O-ring grooves, oil passages or bearing grooves when the case is joined together!

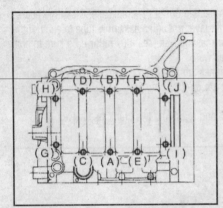

16.5a Location of Bolts A through J (long bolts) in left case half on 2000 through 2002 models (tighten them in alphabetical order)

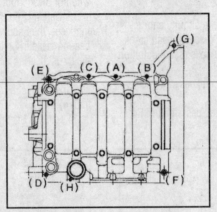

16.5b Location of Bolts A through G (perimeter bolts) in right case half and Bolt H on 2000 through 2002 models (tighten them in alphabetical order)

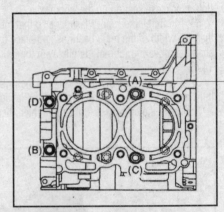

16.5c Location of Bolts A through D (long bolts) in left case half on 2003 and later models (tighten them in alphabetical order)

surfaces (see illustrations).

4   Carefully lower the right crankcase section into position on the left crankcase and install the right-side bolts, tightening them lightly. Reposition the engine block horizontally and install the left-side bolts.

5   Follow the correct torque sequence (see illustration) and tighten the bolts to the torque listed in this Chapter's Specifications. Follow the tightening sequence carefully to allow the crankcase halves to mate evenly and uniformly.

6   Install a new rear main oil seal into the crankcase (see Chapter 2A). Apply a thin bead of RTV sealant to the perimeter of the oil separator cover and install the cover.

7   Install the pistons (see Section 10).

8   Be sure to install a new front oil seal in the oil pump housing (see Chapter 2A).

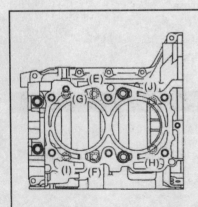

16.5d Location of Bolts E through J (long bolts) in right case half on 2003 and later models (tighten them in alphabetical order)

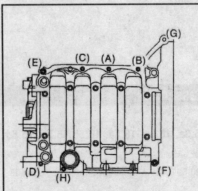

16.5e Location of Bolts A through G (perimeter bolts) and Bolt H on 2003 and later models (tighten them in alphabetical order)

17 Piston rings - installation

▶ **Refer to illustration 17.2, 17.4, 17.5, 17.6, 17.10a, 17.10b, 17.10c and 17.13**

1   Lay out the pistons and the new ring sets so the ring sets will be matched with the same piston and cylinder during the side clearance check, end gap measurement and engine assembly.

2   Before installing the rings on the pistons, the piston ring side clearance must be checked by laying a new ring in each groove and slipping a feeler gauge in beside it (see illustration). Check the clearance at three or four locations around each groove. Be sure to use the correct ring for each groove - they are different. A typical ring groove clearance for compression rings would be around 0.0015 to 0.004-inch (0.038 mm to 0.101 mm). Check with an automotive machine shop for the clearance for your particular engine. If the side clearance is excessive new pistons will have to be used.

3   The ring end gaps must also be checked. It's assumed that the piston ring side clearance has been checked and verified correct.

4   Insert the top (number one) ring into the first cylinder and square it up with the cylinder walls by pushing it in with the top of the piston (see illustration). The ring should be near the bottom of the cylinder, at the lower limit of ring travel.

5   To measure the end gap, slip feeler gauges between the ends of the ring until a gauge equal to the gap width is found (see illustration). The feeler gauge should slide between the ring ends with a slight amount of drag. A typical ring gap should fall between 0.010 and 0.020 inch (0.25 to 0.50 mm) for compression rings and up to 0.030 inch (0.76 mm) for the oil ring steel rails. If the gap is larger or smaller than specified, double-check to make sure you have the correct rings before proceeding.

6   If the gap is too small, it must be enlarged or the ring ends may come in contact with each other during engine operation, which can cause serious damage to the engine. If necessary, increase the end gaps by filing the ring ends very carefully with a fine file. Mount the file in a vise equipped with soft jaws, slip the ring over the file with the ends contacting the file face and slowly move the ring to remove material from the ends. When performing this operation, file only by pushing the ring from the outside end of the file towards the vise

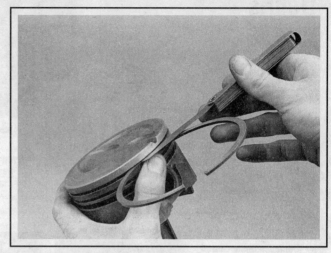

17.2 Check the ring side clearance with a feeler gauge at several points around the piston

(see illustration).

7   Excess end gap isn't critical unless it's greater than 0.040 inch (1.01 mm). Again, double-check to make sure you have the correct ring type.

8   Repeat the procedure for each ring that will be installed in the first cylinder and for each ring in the remaining cylinders. Remember to keep rings, pistons and cylinders matched up.

9   Once the ring end gaps have been checked/corrected, the rings can be installed on the pistons.

10 The oil control ring (lowest one on the piston) is usually installed first. It's composed of three separate components. Slip the spacer/expander into the groove (see illustration). Next, install the upper side rail in the same manner (see illustration). Don't use a piston ring installation tool on the oil ring side rails, as they may be damaged. Instead, place one end of the side rail into the groove between the spacer/expander and the ring land, hold it firmly in place and slide a finger

17.4 Install the piston ring into the cylinder then push it down into position using a piston so the ring will be square in the cylinder

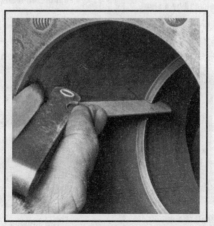

17.5 With the ring square in the cylinder, measure the ring end gap with a feeler gauge

17.6 If the ring end gap is too small, clamp a file in a vise as shown and file the piston ring ends - be sure to remove all raised material

ENGINE BEARING ANALYSIS

Debris

Babbitt bearing embedded with debris from machinings

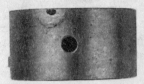

Microscopic detail of debris

Microscopic detail of gouges

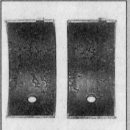

Overplated copper alloy bearing gouged by cast iron debris

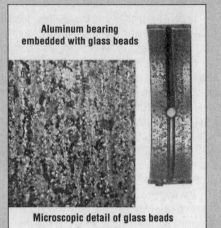

Aluminum bearing embedded with glass beads

Microscopic detail of glass beads

Damaged lining caused by dirt left on the bearing back

Misassembly

Result of a lower half assembled as an upper - blocking the oil flow

Excessive oil clearance is indicated by a short contact arc

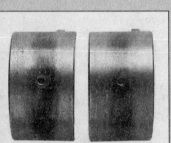

Polished and oil-stained backs are a result of a poor fit in the housing bore

Result of a wrong, reversed, or shifted cap

Overloading

Damage from excessive idling which resulted in an oil film unable to support the load imposed

Damaged upper connecting rod bearings caused by engine lugging; the lower main bearings (not shown) were similarly affected

The damage shown in these upper and lower connecting rod bearings was caused by engine operation at a higher-than-rated speed under load

Misalignment

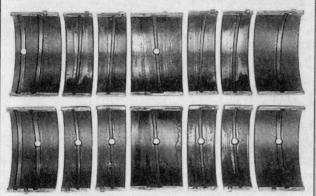

A warped crankshaft caused this pattern of severe wear in the center, diminishing toward the ends

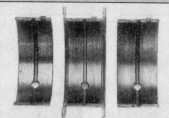

A poorly finished crankshaft caused the equally spaced scoring shown

A tapered housing bore caused the damage along one edge of this pair

A bent connecting rod led to the damage in the "V" pattern

Lubrication

Result of dry start: The bearings on the left, farthest from the oil pump, show more damage

Result of a low oil supply or oil starvation

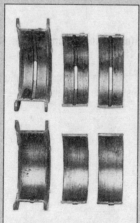

Severe wear as a result of inadequate oil clearance

Corrosion

Microscopic detail of corrosion

Corrosion is an acid attack on the bearing lining generally caused by inadequate maintenance, extremely hot or cold operation, or interior oils or fuels

Microscopic detail of cavitation

Example of cavitation - a surface erosion caused by pressure changes in the oil film

Damage from excessive thrust or insufficient axial clearance

Bearing affected by oil dilution caused by excessive blow-by or a rich mixture

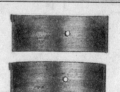

© 1986 Federal-Mogul Corporation
Copy and photographs courtesy of Federal Mogul Corporation

17.10a Installing the spacer/ expander in the oil ring groove

17.10b DO NOT use a piston ring installation tool when installing the oil control side rails

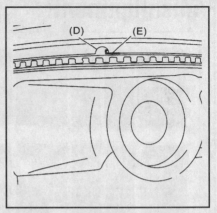

17.10c Make sure the upper rail spin stopper (E) is aligned with the side-hole in the piston (D)

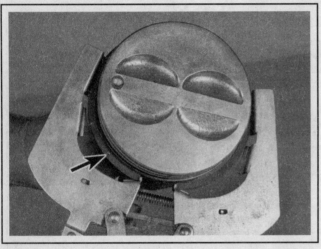

17.13 Use a piston ring installation tool to install the number 2 and the number 1 (top) rings - be sure the directional mark on the piston ring(s) is facing toward the top of the piston

around the piston while pushing the rail into the groove. Finally, install the lower side rail. Make sure the upper rail spin stopper is aligned with the side-hole in the piston (see illustration).

11 After the three oil ring components have been installed, check to make sure that both the upper and lower side rails can be rotated smoothly inside the ring grooves.

12 The number two (middle) ring is installed next. It's usually stamped with a mark which must face up, toward the top of the piston. Do not mix up the top and middle rings, as they have different cross-sections.

➡ **Note: Always follow the instructions printed on the ring package or box - different manufacturers may require different approaches.**

13 Use a piston ring installation tool and make sure the identification mark is facing the top of the piston, then slip the ring into the middle groove on the piston (see illustration). Don't expand the ring any more than necessary to slide it over the piston.

14 Install the number one (top) ring in the same manner. Make sure the mark is facing up. Be careful not to confuse the number one and number two rings.

15 Repeat the procedure for the remaining pistons and rings.

18 Pistons - installation

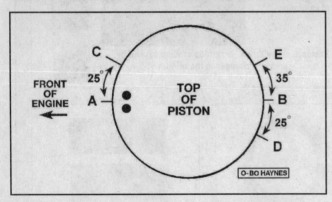

18.1a Position of the piston ring end gaps on 2000 and 2001 models (includes 2002 Forester models) and all turbocharged models

▸ **Refer to illustrations 18.1a, 18.1b, 18.1c, 18.1d, 18.2, 18.6 and 18.7**

1 Position the piston ring end gaps at the correct intervals around the piston (see illustrations).

A Top compression ring gap	C Upper oil ring gap
B Second compression ring gap	D Expander ring gap
	E Lower oil ring gap

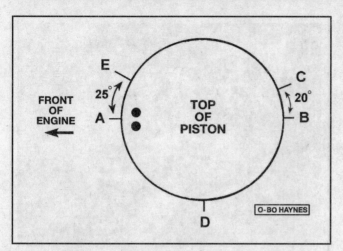

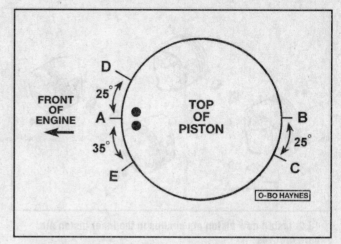

18.1b Position of the piston ring end gaps on 2002 through 2004 models (excludes 2002 Forester models, ULEV models, and turbocharged models)

A	Top compression ring gap	C	Upper oil ring gap
B	Second compression ring gap	D	Expander ring gap
		E	Lower oil ring gap

18.1c Position of the piston ring end gaps on 2005 models (excludes ULEV and turbocharged models)

A	Top compression ring gap	C	Upper oil ring gap
B	Second compression ring gap	D	Expander ring gap
		E	Lower oil ring gap

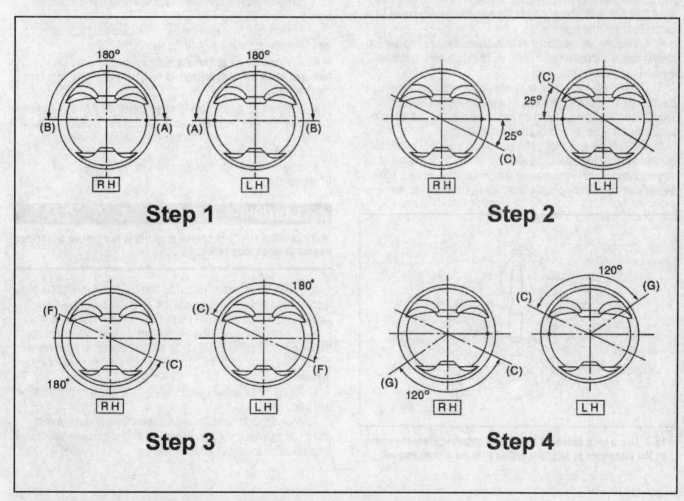

18.1d Position of the piston ring end gaps on 2006 non-turbocharged and ULEV models

A	Top compression ring gap	C	Upper oil ring gap	G	Lower oil ring gap
B	Second compression ring gap	F	Expander ring gap		

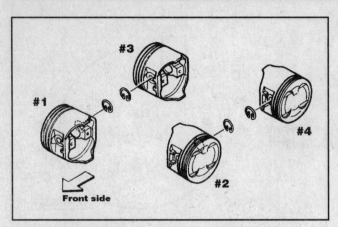

18.2 Install new piston pin circlips in the inner piston pin bore grooves

2   Install new piston pin circlips in the inner piston pin bore groove of each piston (see illustration). Make sure the piston is positioned correctly and the circlip is installed in the groove opposite the crankcase service hole when the piston is installed.

3   Lubricate the skirt and rings with clean engine oil. Install a piston ring compressor on the number one piston. Leave the skirt protruding about 1-inch to guide the piston into the cylinder. The rings must be compressed as far as possible.

4   Carefully rotate the crankshaft until the number one and two connecting rods are at bottom dead center. Align the connecting rods with the center of the cylinder.

5   Gently guide the number one piston into the cylinder. Make sure the mark on the piston crown faces the front (timing belt end) of the engine. Tap the exposed edge of the ring compressor so that it is contacting the crankcase around its entire circumference.

6   Carefully tap on the top of the piston with a wood or plastic hammer handle (see illustration). The piston rings may try to pop out of the ring compressor just before entering the cylinder bore, so keep some pressure on the ring compressor. Work slowly, and if any resistance is

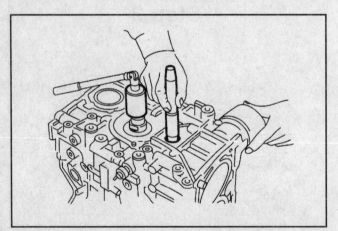

18.7 Use a long drift with a diameter approximately the same as the piston pin to align the piston with the connecting rod

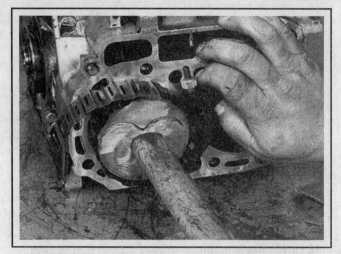

18.6 Use a plastic or wooden hammer handle to push the piston into the cylinder

felt as the piston rings enter the cylinder, stop immediately. Find out what is hanging up and fix it before proceeding. Do not, for any reason, force the piston into the cylinder, as you will break a ring and/or the piston.

7   Push the piston in until the piston pin bore and the small end of the connecting rod are aligned in the service hole.

➡**Note: Fabricate an alignment tool to insert into the service hole and align the connecting rod with the piston pin bore (see illustration).**

8   Lubricate the piston pin with clean engine oil, then slip it through the service hole into the piston and connecting rod. If resistance is felt, do not force the pin. Instead, check to make sure the pin bore and connecting rod are aligned.

9   Install the new outer circlip in the piston pin bore groove (see illustration 9.3c).

✳✳ CAUTION:

Make sure the circlip is seated properly in the groove or serious engine damage may result.

10   Repeat the procedure for the number two piston. Apply RTV sealant to the service hole plug gaskets and install the gaskets and plugs. Tighten the plugs to the torque listed in this Chapter's Specifications.

11   Turn the engine over (crankshaft snout facing down) and rotate the crankshaft until the number three and four connecting rods are at bottom dead center. Align the connecting rods with the center of the cylinder.

12   Repeat the piston and pin installation procedure for pistons three and four.

13   Apply RTV sealant to the service hole plug and cover gaskets and install the plug and cover. Tighten the plug and cover screws to the torque listed in this Chapter's Specifications.

19 Initial start-up and break-in after overhaul

❋❋ **WARNING:**

Have a fire extinguisher handy when starting the engine for the first time.

1 Once the engine has been installed in the vehicle, double-check the engine oil and coolant levels.

2 With the spark plugs out of the engine and the ignition system and fuel pump disabled, crank the engine until oil pressure registers on the gauge or the light goes out.

3 Install the spark plugs, hook up the plug wires (non-turbo models) or install the ignition coils (turbo models) and restore the ignition system and fuel pump functions.

4 Start the engine. It may take a few moments for the fuel system to build up pressure, but the engine should start without a great deal of effort.

5 After the engine starts, it should be allowed to warm up to normal operating temperature. While the engine is warming up, make a thorough check for fuel, oil and coolant leaks.

6 Shut the engine off and recheck the engine oil and coolant levels.

7 Drive the vehicle to an area with minimum traffic, accelerate from 30 to 50 mph, then allow the vehicle to slow to 30 mph with the throttle closed. Repeat the procedure 10 or 12 times. This will load the piston rings and cause them to seat properly against the cylinder walls. Check again for oil and coolant leaks.

8 Drive the vehicle gently for the first 500 miles (no sustained high speeds) and keep a constant check on the oil level. It is not unusual for an engine to use oil during the break-in period.

9 At approximately 500 to 600 miles, change the oil and filter.

10 For the next few hundred miles, drive the vehicle normally. Do not pamper it or abuse it.

11 After 2000 miles, change the oil and filter again and consider the engine broken in.

GLOSSARY

B

Backlash - The amount of play between two parts. Usually refers to how much one gear can be moved back and forth without moving gear with which it's meshed.

Bearing Caps - The caps held in place by nuts or bolts which, in turn, hold the bearing surface. This space is for lubricating oil to enter.

Bearing clearance - The amount of space left between shaft and bearing surface. This space is for lubricating oil to enter.

Bearing crush - The additional height which is purposely manufactured into each bearing half to ensure complete contact of the bearing back with the housing bore when the engine is assembled.

Bearing knock - The noise created by movement of a part in a loose or worn bearing.

Blueprinting - Dismantling an engine and reassembling it to EXACT specifications.

Bore - An engine cylinder, or any cylindrical hole; also used to describe the process of enlarging or accurately refinishing a hole with a cutting tool, as to bore an engine cylinder. The bore size is the diameter of the hole.

Boring - Renewing the cylinders by cutting them out to a specified size. A boring bar is used to make the cut.

Bottom end - A term which refers collectively to the engine block, crankshaft, main bearings and the big ends of the connecting rods.

Break-in - The period of operation between installation of new or rebuilt parts and time in which parts are worn to the correct fit. Driving at reduced and varying speed for a specified mileage to permit parts to wear to the correct fit.

Bushing - A one-piece sleeve placed in a bore to serve as a bearing surface for shaft, piston pin, etc. Usually replaceable.

C

Camshaft - The shaft in the engine, on which a series of lobes are located for operating the valve mechanisms. The camshaft is driven by gears or sprockets and a timing chain. Usually referred to simply as the cam.

Carbon - Hard, or soft, black deposits found in combustion chamber, on plugs, under rings, on and under valve heads.

Cast iron - An alloy of iron and more than two percent carbon, used for engine blocks and heads because it's relatively inexpensive and easy to mold into complex shapes.

Chamfer - To bevel across (or a bevel on) the sharp edge of an object.

Chase - To repair damaged threads with a tap or die.

Combustion chamber - The space between the piston and the cylinder head, with the piston at top dead center, in which air-fuel mixture is burned.

Compression ratio - The relationship between cylinder volume (clearance volume) when the piston is at top dead center and cylinder volume when the piston is at bottom dead center.

Connecting rod - The rod that connects the crank on the crankshaft with the piston. Sometimes called a con rod.

Connecting rod cap - The part of the connecting rod assembly that attaches the rod to the crankpin.

Core plug - Soft metal plug used to plug the casting holes for the coolant passages in the block.

Crankcase - The lower part of the engine in which the crankshaft rotates; includes the lower section of the cylinder block and the oil pan.

Crank kit - A reground or reconditioned crankshaft and new main and connecting rod bearings.

Crankpin - The part of a crankshaft to which a connecting rod is attached.

Crankshaft - The main rotating member, or shaft, running the length of the crankcase, with offset throws to which the connecting rods are attached; changes the reciprocating motion of the pistons into rotating motion.

Cylinder sleeve - A replaceable sleeve, or liner, pressed into the cylinder block to form the cylinder bore.

D

Deburring - Removing the burrs (rough edges or areas) from a bearing.

Deglazer - A tool, rotated by an electric motor, used to remove glaze from cylinder walls so a new set of rings will seat.

E

Endplay - The amount of lengthwise movement between two parts. As applied to a crankshaft, the distance that the crankshaft can move forward and back in the cylinder block.

F

Face - A machinist's term that refers to removing metal from the end of a shaft or the face of a larger part, such as a flywheel.

Fatigue - A breakdown of material through a large number of loading and unloading cycles. The first signs are cracks followed shortly by breaks.

Feeler gauge - A thin strip of hardened steel, ground to an exact thickness, used to check clearances between parts.

Free height - The unloaded length or height of a spring.

Freeplay - The looseness in a linkage, or an assembly of parts, between the initial application of force and actual movement. Usually perceived as slop or slight delay.

Freeze plug - See Core plug.

G

Gallery - A large passage in the block that forms a reservoir for engine oil pressure.

Glaze - The very smooth, glassy finish that develops on cylinder walls while an engine is in service.

H

Heli-Coil - A rethreading device used when threads are worn or damaged. The device is installed in a retapped hole to reduce the thread size to the original size.

I

Installed height - The spring's measured length or height, as installed on the cylinder head. Installed height is measured from the spring seat to the underside of the spring retainer.

J

Journal - The surface of a rotating shaft which turns in a bearing.

K

Keeper - The split lock that holds the valve spring retainer in position on the valve stem.

Key - A small piece of metal inserted into matching grooves machined into two parts fitted together - such as a gear pressed onto a shaft - which prevents slippage between the two parts.

Knock - The heavy metallic engine sound, produced in the combustion chamber as a result of abnormal combustion - usually detonation. Knock is usually caused by a loose or worn bearing. Also referred to as detonation, pinging and spark knock. Connecting rod or main bearing knocks are created by too much oil clearance or insufficient lubrication.

L

Lands - The portions of metal between the piston ring grooves.

Lapping the valves - Grinding a valve face and its seat together with lapping compound.

Lash - The amount of free motion in a gear train, between gears, or in a mechanical assembly, that occurs before movement can begin. Usually refers to the lash in a valve train.

Lifter - The part that rides against the cam to transfer motion to the rest of the valve train.

M

Machining - The process of using a machine to remove metal from a metal part.

Main bearings - The plain, or babbitt, bearings that support the crankshaft.

Main bearing caps - The cast iron caps, bolted to the bottom of the block, that support the main bearings.

O

O.D. - Outside diameter.

Oil gallery - A pipe or drilled passageway in the engine used to carry engine oil from one area to another.

Oil ring - The lower ring, or rings, of a piston; designed to prevent excessive amounts of oil from working up the cylinder walls and into the combustion chamber. Also called an oil-control ring.

Oil seal - A seal which keeps oil from leaking out of a compartment. Usually refers to a dynamic seal around a rotating shaft or other moving part.

O-ring - A type of sealing ring made of a special rubberlike material; in use, the O-ring is compressed into a groove to provide the sealing action.

Overhaul - To completely disassemble a unit, clean and inspect all parts, reassemble it with the original or new parts and make all adjustments necessary for proper operation.

P

Pilot bearing - A small bearing installed in the center of the flywheel (or the rear end of the crankshaft) to support the front end of the input shaft of the transmission.

Pip mark - A little dot or indentation which indicates the top side of a compression ring.

Piston - The cylindrical part, attached to the connecting rod, that moves up and down in the cylinder as the crankshaft rotates. When the fuel charge is fired, the piston transfers the force of the explosion to the connecting rod, then to the crankshaft.

Piston pin (or wrist pin) - The cylindrical and usually hollow steel pin that passes through the piston. The piston pin fastens the piston to the upper end of the connecting rod.

Piston ring - The split ring fitted to the groove in a piston. The ring contacts the sides of the ring groove and also rubs against the cylinder wall, thus sealing space between piston and wall. There are two types of rings: Compression rings seal the compression pressure in the combustion chamber; oil rings scrape excessive oil off the cylinder wall.

Piston ring groove - The slots or grooves cut in piston heads to hold piston rings in position.

Piston skirt - The portion of the piston below the rings and the piston pin hole.

Plastigage - A thin strip of plastic thread, available in different sizes, used for measuring clearances. For example, a strip of plastigage is laid across a bearing journal and mashed as parts are assembled. Then parts are disassembled and the width of the strip is measured to determine clearance between journal and bearing. Commonly used to measure crankshaft main-bearing and connecting rod bearing clearances.

Press-fit - A tight fit between two parts that requires pressure to force the parts together. Also referred to as drive, or force, fit.

Prussian blue - A blue pigment; in solution, useful in determining the area of contact between two surfaces. Prussian blue is commonly used to determine the width and location of the contact area between the valve face and the valve seat.

R

Race (bearing) - The inner or outer ring that provides a contact surface for balls or rollers in bearing.

Ream - To size, enlarge or smooth a hole by using a round cutting tool with fluted edges.

Ring job - The process of reconditioning the cylinders and installing new rings.

Runout - Wobble. The amount a shaft rotates out-of-true.

S

Saddle - The upper main bearing seat.

Scored - Scratched or grooved, as a cylinder wall may be scored by abrasive particles moved up and down by the piston rings.

Scuffing - A type of wear in which there's a transfer of material between parts moving against each other; shows up as pits or grooves in the mating surfaces.

Seat - The surface upon which another part rests or seats. For example, the valve seat is the matched surface upon which the valve face rests. Also used to refer to wearing into a good fit; for example, piston rings seat after a few miles of driving.

Short block - An engine block complete with crankshaft and piston and, usually, camshaft assemblies.

Static balance - The balance of an object while it's stationary.

Step - The wear on the lower portion of a ring land caused by excessive side and back-clearance. The height of the step indicates the ring's extra side clearance and the length of the step projecting from the back wall of the groove represents the ring's back clearance.

Stroke - The distance the piston moves when traveling from top dead center to bottom dead center, or from bottom dead center to top dead center.

Stud - A metal rod with threads on both ends.

T

Tang - A lip on the end of a plain bearing used to align the bearing during assembly.

Tap - To cut threads in a hole. Also refers to the fluted tool used to cut threads.

Taper - A gradual reduction in the width of a shaft or hole; in an engine cylinder, taper usually takes the form of uneven wear, more pronounced at the top than at the bottom.

Throws - The offset portions of the crankshaft to which the connecting rods are affixed.

Thrust bearing - The main bearing that has thrust faces to prevent excessive end-play, or forward and backward movement of the crankshaft.

Thrust washer - A bronze or hardened steel washer placed between two moving parts. The washer prevents longitudinal movement and provides a bearing surface for thrust surfaces of parts.

Tolerance - The amount of variation permitted from an exact size of measurement. Actual amount from smallest acceptable dimension to largest acceptable dimension.

U

Umbrella - An oil deflector placed near the valve tip to throw oil from the valve stem area.

Undercut - A machined groove below the normal surface.

Undersize bearings - Smaller diameter bearings used with re-ground crankshaft journals.

V

Valve grinding - Refacing a valve in a valve-refacing machine.

Valve train - The valve-operating mechanism of an engine; includes all components from the camshaft to the valve.

Vibration damper - A cylindrical weight attached to the front of the crankshaft to minimize torsional vibration (the twist-untwist actions of the crankshaft caused by the cylinder firing impulses). Also called a harmonic balancer.

W

Water jacket - The spaces around the cylinders, between the inner and outer shells of the cylinder block or head, through which coolant circulates.

Web - A supporting structure across a cavity.

Woodruff key - A key with a radiused backside (viewed from the side).

Specifications

General

Bore and stroke	3.92 x 3.11 inches (99.5 x 79 mm)
Displacement	150 cubic inches (2.5 liters)
Cylinder compression pressure	
Non-turbocharged engine	
2000 through 2004	156 to 185 psi (1,079 to 1,275 kPa)
2005 and 2006	148 to 185 psi (1,020 to 1,275 kPa)
Turbocharged engine	142 to 171 psi (981 to 1,177 kPa)
Oil pressure	
@ 600 rpm	14 psi (98 kPa)
@ 5,000 rpm	43 psi (294 kPa)

Valves

Valve clearance	See Chapter 2A

Crankcase

Mating surface warpage limit	0.001 inch (0.025 mm)
Surface grinding limit	0.004 inch (0.100 mm)

Torque specifications	Ft-lbs (unless otherwise indicated)	Nm
Engine-to-transaxle bolts	37	50
Connecting rod cap bolts/nuts		
Non-turbocharged models	33	45
Turbocharged models*	38	52
Crankcase halves mounting bolts		
2000 through 2002 (see illustrations 11.16a and 11.16b)		
Step 1 Bolts A through J (long bolts in left case half)	35	47
Step 2 Bolts A through G (perimeter bolts in right case half)	18	25
Step 3 Bolt H	54 in-lbs	6
2003 and 2004 non-turbocharged models (see illustrations 11.16c, 11.16d and 11.16e)		
Step 1 Bolts A through D (long bolts in left case half)	132 in-lbs	15
Step 2 Bolts E through J (long bolts in right case half)	132 in-lbs	15
Step 3 Bolts A through D (long bolts in left case half)	Tighten bolts an additional 90-degrees	
Step 4 Bolts E through J (long bolts in right case half)	Tighten bolts an additional 90-degrees	
Step 5 Bolts A through G (perimeter bolts)	18	25
Step 6 Bolt H	54 in-lbs	6
2004 turbocharged models (see illustrations 11.16c, 11.16d and 11.16e)		
Step 1 Bolts A through D (long bolts in left case half)	86 in-lbs	10
Step 2 Bolts E through J (long bolts in right case half)	86 in-lbs	10
Step 3		
Bolts A and C (long bolts in left case half)	15	20
Bolts B and D (long bolts in left case half)	132 in-lbs	15
Step 4 Bolts		
Bolts E, F, G and I (long bolts in right case half)	15	20
Bolts H and J (long bolts in right case half)	156 in-lbs	18

Torque specifications	Ft-lbs (unless otherwise indicated)	Nm
2004 turbocharged models (see illustrations 11.16c, 11.16d and 11.16e) (continued)		
Step 5 Bolts A through D (long bolts in left case half)	Tighten bolts an additional 90-degrees	
Step 6 Bolts E through J (long bolts in right case half)	Tighten bolts an additional 90-degrees	
Step 7 Bolts A through G (perimeter bolts)	18	25
Step 8 Bolt H	54 in-lbs	6
2005 and later non-turbocharged and turbocharged models (see illustrations 11.16c, 11.16d and 11.16e)		
Step 1 Bolts A through D (long bolts in left case half)	86 in-lbs	10
Step 2 Bolts E through J (long bolts in right case half)	86 in-lbs	10
Step 3 Bolts A through D (long bolts in left case half)	13	18
Step 4 Bolts E through J (long bolts in right case half)	13	18
Step 5		
Bolts A and C (long bolts in left case half)	Tighten bolts an additional 90-degrees	
Bolts B and D (long bolts in left case half)	30	40
Step 6 Bolts E through J (long bolts in right case half)	Tighten bolts an additional 90-degrees	
Step 7 Bolts A through G (perimeter bolts)	18	25
Step 8 Bolt H	54 in-lbs	6
Crankcase service hole plugs		
Plugs	51	70
Cover screws (left rear)	54 in-lbs	6
Torque converter bolts	See Chapter 7B	

*Use new connecting rod cap bolts

Notes

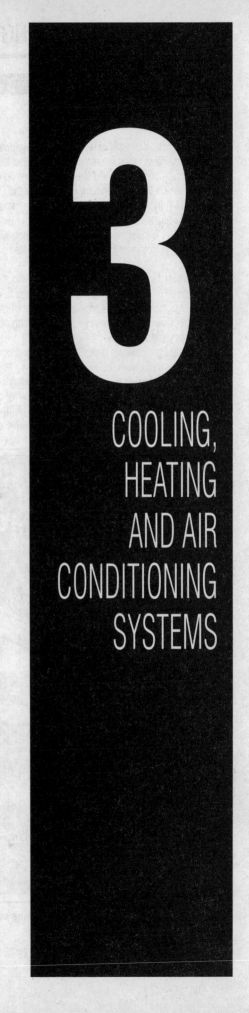

3

COOLING, HEATING AND AIR CONDITIONING SYSTEMS

Section

Reference to other Chapters

1 General information

▶ **Refer to illustration 1.1**

On all models, a cross-flow type radiator equipped with two electric-motor-driven fans is employed (see illustration). With this system, cooling ability at idling speed and warm-up characteristics, are improved. The electric fans are activated by the Powertrain Control Module (PCM) in response to the temperature changes of the coolant in the engine block relayed by the engine coolant temperature (ECT) sensor. The ECT sensor also works in conjunction with the Electronic Fuel Injection system and Emission Control systems (see Chapters 4 and 6).

The radiator fans are mounted in individual housings/shrouds at the engine side of the radiator. They are designed to come on when the engine reaches a certain temperature, and shut off again when the engine cools down some, thereby keeping the engine in the desired operating temperature range.

The coolant temperature gauge on the dash is controlled by the PCM based on input from the ECT sensor.

The system is sealed by a spring-loaded radiator cap, which, by maintaining pressure, increases the boiling point of the coolant. If the coolant temperature goes above this increased boiling point, the extra pressure in the system forces the radiator cap valve off its seat and exposes the overflow pipe or hose. The overflow pipe/hose leads to a coolant recovery system. This consists of a plastic reservoir, mounted to the left side of the radiator, into which the coolant that normally escapes due to expansion is retained. When the engine cools, the excess coolant is drawn back into the radiator by the vacuum created as the system cools, maintaining the system at full capacity. This is a continuous process and provided the level in the reservoir is correctly maintained, it is not necessary to add coolant to the radiator.

On models equipped with an automatic transaxle, an oil cooler is built into the radiator to cool the automatic transmission fluid. Heated transmission fluid is circulated through the oil cooler and is cooled by the coolant, thus maintaining the fluid at an adequate temperature.

The heating system works by directing air through the heater core, which is like a small radiator mounted behind the dash. Hot engine coolant heats the core, over which air passes to the interior of the vehicle by a system of ducts. Temperature is controlled by mixing heated air with fresh air, using a system of flapper doors in the ducts, and a heater blower motor.

The air conditioning system consists of an evaporator core located under the dash, a condenser in front of the radiator, an accumulator/drier in the engine compartment and a belt-driven compressor mounted at the front of the engine.

1.1 Underhood cooling and air conditioning components (non-turbo model shown)

1 Radiator	4 Air conditioning service port (low side)	6 Upper radiator hose
2 Radiator cap	5 Receiver/drier	7 Air conditioning compressor
3 Coolant reservoir		

2   Antifreeze - general information

▶ **Refer to illustration 2.4**

❄❄ WARNING:

Do not allow antifreeze to come in contact with your skin or painted surfaces of the vehicle. Rinse off spills immediately with plenty of water. Antifreeze is highly toxic if ingested. Never leave antifreeze lying around in an open container or in puddles on the floor; children and pets are attracted by it's sweet smell and may drink it. Check with local authorities about disposing of used anti-freeze. Many communities have collection centers which will see that antifreeze is disposed of safely. Never dump used antifreeze on the ground or pour it into drains.

1   The cooling system should be filled with a water/ethylene glycol based antifreeze solution which will prevent freezing down to at least -20-degrees F (even lower in cold climates). It also provides protection against corrosion and increases the coolant boiling point. The engines in the vehicles covered by this manual have an aluminum block and heads. The manufacturer recommends that only coolant designated as safe for aluminum engine components be used.

2   The cooling system should be drained, flushed and refilled at least every other year (see Chapter 1). The use of antifreeze solutions for periods of longer than two years is likely to cause damage and encourage the formation of rust and scale in the system.

3   Before adding antifreeze to the system, check all hose connections. Antifreeze can leak through very minute openings.

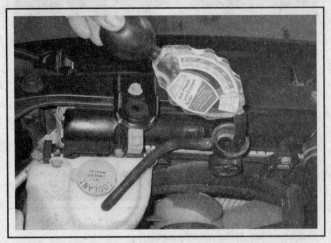

2.4 Use an antifreeze hydrometer (available at most auto parts stores) to test the condition of your coolant

4   The exact mixture of antifreeze to water which you should use depends on the relative weather conditions. The mixture should contain at least 50-percent antifreeze, but should never contain more than 70-percent antifreeze. Consult the mixture ratio chart on the container before adding coolant. Hydrometers are available at most auto parts stores to test the coolant (see illustration). Use antifreeze which meets specifications for engines with aluminum heads and blocks.

3   Thermostat - check and replacement

1   The thermostat is located at the front of the engine, bolted to the bottom of the water pump (see illustrations 7.15a and 7.15b). The thermostat allows for quicker warm-ups and governs the normal operating temperature of the engine.

CHECK

2   If the thermostat is functioning properly, the temperature gauge should rise to the normal operating temperature quickly and then-stay there, only rising above the normal position occasionally when the engine gets unusually warm. If the engine does not rise to normal operating temperature quickly, or if it overheats, the thermostat should be removed and checked or replaced.

3   Before condemning the thermostat, check the coolant level, cooling fans and temperature gauge (or light) operation.

4   If the engine takes a long time to warm up, the thermostat is probably stuck open. Replace the thermostat.

5   If the engine runs hot, check the temperature of the upper radiator hose. If the hose isn't hot, the thermostat is probably stuck shut. Replace the thermostat.

6   If the upper radiator hose is hot, it means the coolant is circulating and the thermostat is open. Refer to the *Troubleshooting* section at the front of this manual for the cause of overheating.

7   If an engine has been overheated, you may find damage such as leaking head gaskets, scuffed pistons and warped or cracked cylinder heads.

REPLACEMENT

▶ **Refer to illustrations 3.11 and 3.12**

❄❄ WARNING:

Wait until the engine is completely cool before starting this procedure.

8   Raise the front of the vehicle and support it securely on jackstands.

9   Drain the cooling system (see Chapter 1).

10 Place the drain pan under the thermostat housing.

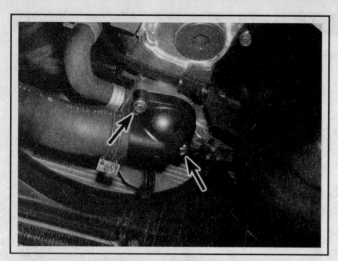

3.11 Remove the thermostat housing cover bolts (non-turbo engine shown, turbo models similar)

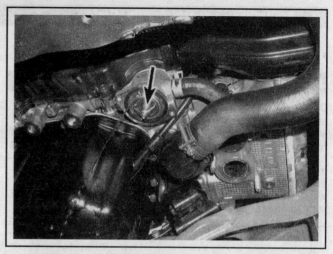

3.12 Note the installed direction of the thermostat and remove it from the housing

➡Note: If the lower radiator hose is old, you may want to remove it from the thermostat housing cover and replace it. Otherwise, the cover can be removed with the radiator hose still attached.

11 Remove the bolts and lift off the housing cover. You may have to tap the cover with a soft-faced hammer to break the gasket seal (see illustration).

12 After the cover has been removed, note how the thermostat is installed and pull it out (see illustration).

13 Clean the mating surfaces of the thermostat housing and cover. Do not nick or gouge the sealing surfaces.

14 Install a new seal on the thermostat, then place the thermostat into the housing with the proper end facing out (see illustrations 7.15a and 7.15b). Make sure that the thermostat flange is properly seated in the recessed area of the housing.

15 Carefully position the housing cover, install the bolts and tighten them to the torque listed in this Chapter's Specifications.

16 Place the radiator hose onto the housing cover (if removed), install the hose clamp and tighten it securely.

17 Refill the radiator with coolant (see Chapter 1). Start the engine and check for leaks around the thermostat housing and the lower radiator hose.

4 Cooling fan and relay - check, removal and installation

CHECK

▶ Refer to illustrations 4.1, 4.2 and 4.5

1 All models are equipped with electric cooling fans (see illustration). The cooling fans are actuated by a series of relays controlled by the Powertrain Control Module (PCM). The PCM receives information from the engine coolant temperature (ECT) sensor (mounted on the engine block), and uses this information to determine when to operate the cooling fans. The air conditioning system affects the use of the cooling fans as well. If the engine overheats because the cooling fans fail to operate, check the motor and relays as described in this Section.

2 First check the fan fuse (see Chapter 12). If the fuse is good, check the fan motor for proper operation. Unplug the electrical connector for the fan motor and attach jumper wires to the two terminals in the connector (on the fan side of the harness) (see illustration).

❋❋ **CAUTION:**

Make sure the jumper wires are not contacting each other.

➡Note: If necessary, remove the bottom engine splash shield for access to the fan electrical connectors (see Chapter 2A).

3 Connect the ends of the jumper wires to battery voltage and see if the fan operates.

❋❋ **CAUTION:**

Keep your hands and the wires away from the cooling fan.

4 If the fan fails to operate when connected directly to battery power, replace the fan motor.

5 If the fan motor tested good in the previous steps but does not operate under normal conditions, disconnect the connector and check for battery voltage at the connector with the engine hot. If battery voltage is not present at the connector, check the fan relays mounted in the engine compartment fuse/relay box (see Chapter 12) (see illustration). If the relay does not perform as described, replace it with a new part.

➡Note: Be sure to check both relays when diagnosing fan circuit problems.

6 If the relays tested good, check the wiring in the circuit (see

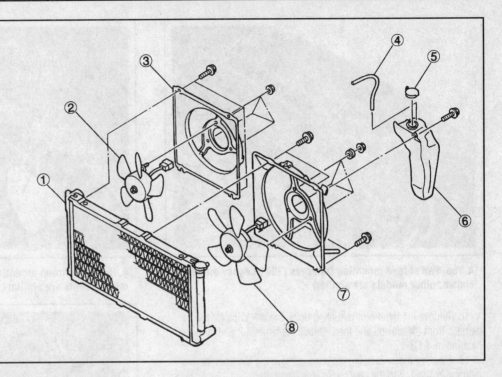

4.1 Typical radiator cooling fan details:

1   Radiator
2   Radiator sub-fan and motor
3   Radiator sub-fan shroud
4   Overflow hose
5   Reservoir tank cap
6   Coolant reservoir
7   Radiator main fan shroud
8   Radiator main fan and motor

Chapter 12). Any further checking should be directed to a qualified repair facility.

REMOVAL AND INSTALLATION

▶ **Refer to illustrations 4.15a, 4.15b and 4.17**

➡**Note: The 2003 and later Forester models have both cooling fans mounted in a single shroud assembly.**

7   On 2005 and later turbo Legacy models, and 2003 and later Forester models, drain the cooling system. (see Chapter 1).

8   Remove the engine splash shield from the bottom of the engine compartment (see Chapter 2A).

9   Remove the air intake duct from above the radiator, if applicable (see Chapter 4).

10 Remove the coolant reservoir (see Section 5).

➡**Note: This step may not be necessary for removing individual fan assemblies on the passenger's side.**

11 On 2005 and later turbo Legacy models with an automatic transmission, remove the heat-shield from the bottom of the radiator.

12 On 2004 and later turbo Forester models, remove the cover attached to the lower portion of the radiator.

13 Disconnect the fan motor electrical connectors (see illustration 4.2).

14 On 2005 and later Legacy turbo models and 2003 and later Forester models, detach the upper radiator hose from the radiator.

15 Remove anything else that might be attached to the fan shroud (except the motor) and then remove it from the radiator (see illustrations).

➡**Note: Remove passenger side fan shrouds from underneath the vehicle and driver's side fan shrouds from the above. On 2003 and later Forester models, remove the shroud assembly from above.**

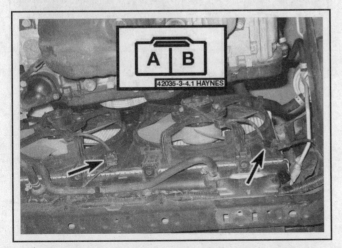

4.2 Disconnect the harness connector and apply battery voltage to the connector leading to the fan

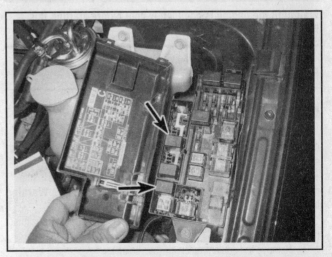

4.5 The cooling fan relays are located in the underhood fuse and relay box - refer to the inside of the fuse/relay box cover to locate the correct relays for your particular model

4.15a Fan shroud mounting fasteners (2001 Legacy model shown, other models are similar)

4.15b Fan shroud mounting fasteners (2004 Forester shown, other models are similar)

16 Remove the fan motor mounting bolts and any clips for the harness from the shroud and then remove the fan motor and fan (see illustration 4.1).

17 If the fan motor is being replaced, remove the fan from the old motor and attach it to the new motor (see illustration).

18 Installation is the reverse of removal. Refill the cooling system (see Chapter 1). Start the engine and allow it to reach normal operating temperature, then verify proper fan operation.

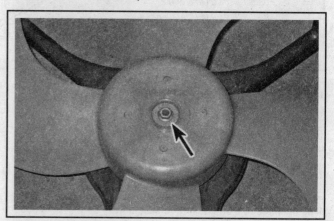

4.17 Fan blade fastener

5 Radiator, coolant reservoir and coolant filler tank - removal and installation

❄ **WARNING:**

Wait until the engine is completely cool before starting this procedure.

RADIATOR

▶ Refer to illustrations 5.8a, 5.8b, 5.9, 5.11 and 5.16

1 Set the parking brake and block the rear wheels. Raise the front of the vehicle and support it securely on jackstands. Remove the splash shield beneath the radiator (see Chapter 2A).

2 Drain the cooling system (see Chapter 1). If the coolant is relatively new or in good condition, save it and reuse it. Read the **Warning** in Section 2.

3 Remove the air intake duct from above the radiator, if applicable (see Chapter 4).

4 Remove the coolant reservoir (see below).

5 On 2005 and later turbo Legacy models with an automatic transmission, remove the heat-shield from the bottom of the radiator.

6 On 2004 and later turbo Forester models, remove the cover

5.8a Upper radiator hose and clamps (2001 Legacy model shown, other models are similar)

attached to the lower portion of the radiator.

7 On Forester models, remove the drivebelt covers (see Chapter 1).

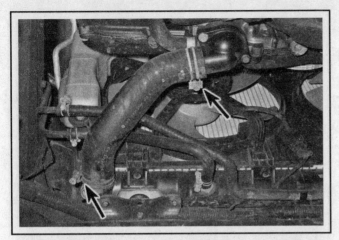

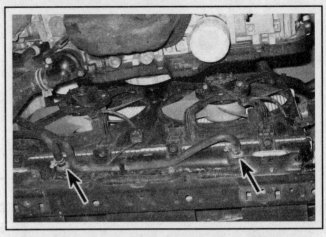

5.8b Lower radiator hose and clamps (2001 Legacy model shown, other models are similar)

5.9 Automatic transmission fluid cooler line connections (2001 Legacy model shown, other models are similar)

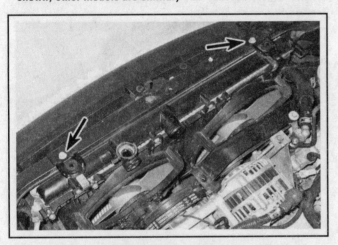

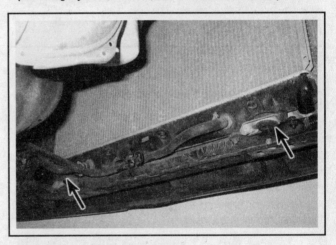

5.11 Radiator mounting brackets and fasteners

5.16 Radiator lower rubber mounts

8   Disconnect the upper and lower radiator hoses from the radiator by loosening the hose clamps (see illustrations).

9   On automatic transaxle models, disconnect the fluid cooler lines from the radiator (see illustration).

➡**Note: Plug the ends of the transaxle cooling lines to minimize fluid loss and contamination.**

10   Disconnect the fan electrical connectors (see Section 4).

11   Remove the radiator mounting brackets (see illustration). Remove any clips, brackets, harnesses or hoses that may be attached to the radiator or fan shroud.

12   Carefully lift out the radiator along with the cooling fans. Don't spill coolant on the vehicle or scratch the paint.

13   Remove the cooling fans and shroud from the radiator (see Section 4).

14   Inspect the radiator for leaks and damage. If it needs repair, have a radiator shop or dealer service department perform the work as special techniques are required.

15   Bugs and dirt can be removed from the radiator by spraying it with a garden hose nozzle from the back side. The radiator should be flushed out with a garden hose before reinstallation.

16   Check the radiator mounts for deterioration and replace them if necessary (see illustration).

17   Installation is the reverse of the removal procedure. Guide the radiator into the mounts until it seats completely.

18   Tighten the radiator bracket bolts to the torque listed in this Chapter's Specifications.

19   After installation, fill the cooling system with the proper coolant (see Chapter 1).

20   Start the engine and allow it to reach normal operating temperature while checking for leaks. Recheck the coolant level and add more if required.

21   Check and add transaxle fluid as needed (see Chapter 1).

COOLANT RESERVOIR

◗ **Refer to illustrations 5.22a and 5.22b**

22   Remove the mounting bolts from the coolant reservoir, detach the hose to the radiator and then remove the reservoir (see illustration). Some later models have a retaining tab securing the reservoir (see illustration).

23   Pull the reservoir straight up and out of its bracket near the radiator. Be careful not to spill any coolant on the paint.

24   Prior to installation make sure the reservoir is clean and free of debris which could be drawn into the radiator (wash inside it with soapy water and a long brush if necessary). It will be easier to read the coolant level if the tank is cleaned.

25   Installation is the reverse of removal. Fill the cooling system with the proper coolant (see Chapter 1).

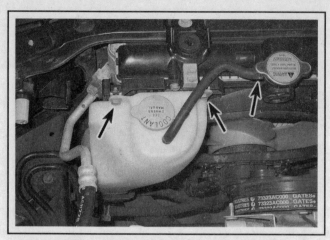

5.22a Reservoir mounting fasteners and hose connection (2001 Legacy model shown, other models are similar)

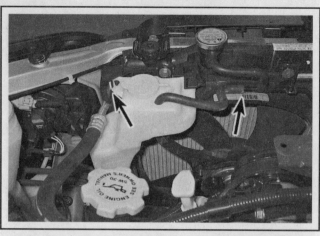

5.22b Reservoir plastic retaining clip and hose connection (2006 Legacy Outback model shown)

COOLANT FILLER TANK

◆ **Refer to illustration 5.28**

➥**Note: Only turbocharged models are equipped with a coolant filler tank.**

26 Drain about 3.5 quarts from the cooling system (see Chapter 1).
27 Remove the top engine cover (see Chapter 2A).
28 Remove the hoses to the tank and the mounting fastener and then remove the tank (see illustration).

➥**Note: Some models have three mounting fasteners.**

29 Installation is the reverse of removal. Fill the cooling system with the proper coolant (see Chapter 1).

5.28 Coolant filler tank hose connections and mounting fastener (fastener hidden from view - vicinity given) (2006 Legacy Outback shown, other models are similar)

6 Water pump - check

1 A failure in the water pump can cause serious engine damage due to overheating. If the pump is defective, it must be replaced with a new or rebuilt unit.
2 The two most common signs of water pump failure are coolant leakage and/or a howling or screeching sound. Don't mistake drivebelt slippage, which causes a squealing sound, for water pump bearing failure. If a squealing sound is heard, check the drivebelt tension and condition.
3 The water pump is driven by the timing belt and is located at the front of the engine. If you notice a puddle of coolant under the front of the vehicle, emanating from the timing belt cover, chances are that the water pump seal has failed. Water pumps are equipped with weep holes; if the seal fails, coolant will leak from them. To verify this, the timing belt cover must be removed (see Chapter 2A).
4 If the water pump is making noise, the impeller shaft bearing has worn out. This can sometimes be confirmed by wiggling the water pump drive pulley (again, to check this the timing belt cover must be removed).

7 Water pump - replacement

◆ **Refer to illustration 7.2**

❄❄ **WARNING:**

Wait until the engine is completely cool before starting this procedure.

1 Drain the cooling system (see Chapter 1).
2 Disconnect the radiator hose and the bypass hose(s) from the water pump (see illustration).

➥**Note: The 2002 and earlier Forester models have an additional hose attached to the thermostat housing cover that must be removed.**

3 Remove both cooling fans from the radiator (see Section 4).
4 Remove the drivebelt cover and drivebelts (see Chapter 1).
5 Remove the timing belt (see Chapter 2A).

NON-TURBO ENGINES

6 Remove the timing belt tensioner and the idler pulley located below the water pump (see Chapter 2A).
7 Remove the sprocket from the left side camshaft (see Chapter 2A).
8 Remove the left side rear timing belt cover (see Chapter 2A).
9 Remove the mounting bracket for the belt tensioner (see Chapter 2A).

TURBOCHARGED ENGINES

10 Remove the timing belt tensioner and the idler pulleys located above and below the water pump (see Chapter 2A).
11 Remove the camshaft position sensor (see Chapter 6).
12 Remove the sprockets from the left side camshafts (see Chapter 2A).
13 Remove the left side rear timing belt cover (see Chapter 2A).
14 Remove the mounting bracket for the belt tensioner (see Chapter 2A).

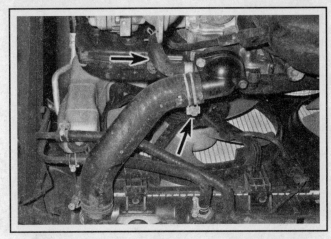

7.2 Remove the lower radiator hose and bypass hose from the water pump

ALL ENGINES

▶ **Refer to illustrations 7.15a and 7.15b**

15 Loosen the bolts to the water pump (see illustrations), then separate the water pump and gasket from the engine. You may have to tap

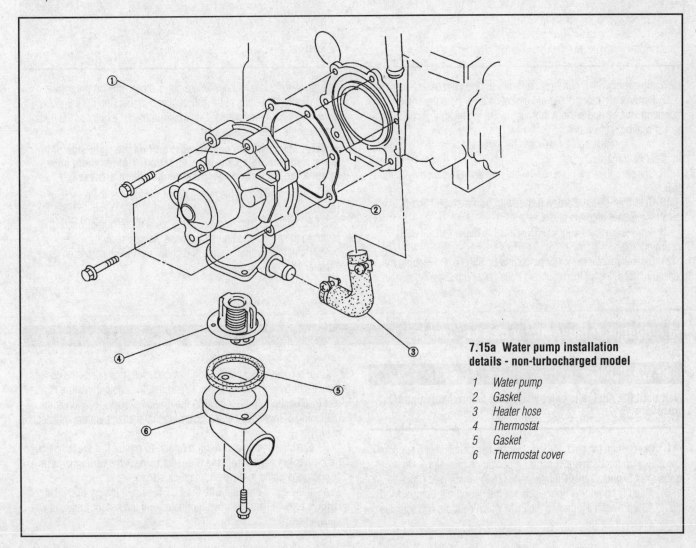

7.15a Water pump installation details - non-turbocharged model

1 Water pump
2 Gasket
3 Heater hose
4 Thermostat
5 Gasket
6 Thermostat cover

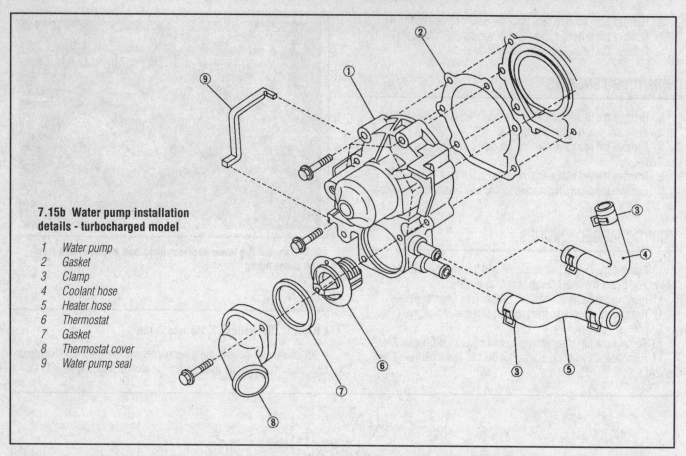

7.15b Water pump installation details - turbocharged model

1. Water pump
2. Gasket
3. Clamp
4. Coolant hose
5. Heater hose
6. Thermostat
7. Gasket
8. Thermostat cover
9. Water pump seal

the pump gently with a soft-faced hammer to break the gasket seal.

16 Remove all traces of the old gasket material from the engine mounting surface and clean it thoroughly. Do not nick or gouge the gasket sealing surfaces.

17 Make sure the bolt threads and the threaded holes in the engine are clear of corrosion.

18 Compare the new pump to the old one to make sure they're identical.

19 Coat both sides of a new gasket with gasket sealant and then install the gasket onto the pump.

20 Apply a small amount of RTV sealant to the threads of each mounting bolt.

21 Carefully move the water pump into position while keeping the gasket in place. Install the mounting bolts finger tight making certain

that the water pump and gasket are aligned correctly on the engine.

22 Tighten the bolts to the torque listed in this Chapter's Specifications in 1/4-turn increments. Don't over-tighten the bolts or the pump may become distorted and leak.

➡**Note: Start with the center-most bolt on the right side of the pump and work in a clockwise direction. Tighten them once again after the torque specification has been achieved.**

23 The remainder of the installation procedure is the reverse of removal.

24 Reinstall all parts removed for access to the pump. Attach the hoses to the pump and tighten the hose clamps securely.

25 Refill the cooling system and check the drivebelt tension (see Chapter 1).

8 Coolant temperature indicator - check

✳✳ WARNING:

Wait until the engine is completely cool before beginning this procedure.

1 The coolant temperature indicator system consists of a temperature gauge on the dash and a sensor mounted on the engine. On all models, an Engine Coolant Temperature (ECT) sensor (see Chapter 6), which is an information sensor for the Powertrain Control Module (PCM), provides a signal to the PCM which controls and actuates the temperature gauge.

2 If an overheating indication has occurred, first check the coolant level in the system (see Chapter 1) and that the coolant mixture is correct (see Section 2). Also, refer to the *Troubleshooting* section at the beginning of this book before assuming that the temperature indicator is faulty.

3 Start the engine and warm it up for 10 minutes. If the temperature gauge has not moved from the C position, check the wiring harness connections going to the instrument cluster.

4 If there is a problem with the ECT sensor, it is very likely that the CHECK ENGINE lamp will be illuminated and the sensor or circuit will need repair (see Chapter 6).

9   Blower motor resistor and blower motor - replacement

▶ Refer to illustration 9.2

✳✳ WARNING:

The models covered by this manual are equipped with Supplemental Restraint systems (SRS), more commonly known as airbags. Always disable the airbag system before working in the vicinity of any airbag system component to avoid the possibility of accidental deployment of the airbag, which could cause personal injury (see Chapter 12).

➥Note: Models that have the automatic climate control feature are equipped with a Power transistor instead of a blower motor resistor.

1   Remove the glove box (see Chapter 11).
2   Remove the glove box panel (see illustration).

➥Note: 2005 and later Legacy models are not equipped with a glove box panel.

9.2 Glove box panel mounting fasteners

BLOWER MOTOR RESISTOR

▶ Refer to illustration 9.3

3   Disconnect the electrical connector from the blower motor resistor or power transistor (see illustration).

4   Remove the blower motor resistor mounting screws and then remove the resistor.

5   Installation is the reverse of removal.

BLOWER MOTOR

▶ Refer to illustration 9.8

6   Disconnect the electrical connector from the blower motor (see illustration 9.3).

7   Remove the blower motor mounting screws and then remove the blower motor assembly.

8   Remove the fan from the motor (see illustration).

9   Installation is the reverse of removal.

9.3 Blower motor resistor and blower motor details (2001 Legacy model shown, other models similar):

1)   *Blower motor resistor screws*
2)   *Blower motor resistor electrical connector*
3)   *Blower motor screws (one hidden from view)*
4)   *Blower motor electrical connector*

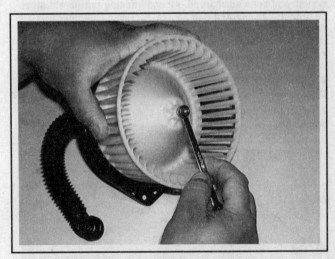

9.8 Remove the fastener that retains the blower fan to the motor

10 Heater core - removal and installation

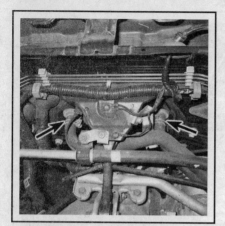

10.4a Heater hoses on a 2001 Legacy model (other models are similar)

10.4b Heater hoses on a 2004 Forester model (other models are similar)

10.5 Typical refrigerant line connection at firewall

✻✻ WARNING 1:

The models covered by this manual are equipped with Supplemental Restraint systems (SRS), more commonly known as airbags. Always disable the airbag system before working in the vicinity of any airbag system component to avoid the possibility of accidental deployment of the airbag, which could cause personal injury (see Chapter 12).

✻✻ WARNING 2:

The air conditioning system is under high pressure. DO NOT loosen any fittings or remove any components until after the system has been discharged. Air conditioning refrigerant must be properly discharged into an EPA-approved container at a dealer service department or an automotive air conditioning repair facility. Always wear eye protection when disconnecting air conditioning system fittings.

✻✻ WARNING 3:

Wait until the engine is completely cool before beginning this procedure.

10.7 Location of the airbag control module

REMOVAL

▶ Refer to illustrations 10.4a, 10.4b, 10.5 and 10.7, 10.8, 10.9, 10.10 and 10.11a through 10.11d

1 Have the refrigerant discharged and recovered by an air conditioning technician.

2 Disconnect the cable from the negative battery terminal (see Chapter 5, Section 1).

3 Drain the cooling system (see Chapter 1).

4 Disconnect the heater hoses from the firewall (see illustrations).

5 Disconnect the line fittings for the air conditioning evaporator (see illustration).

6 Disconnect the temperature control cable from the heater unit (see illustration 11.5b).

➡Note: Models equipped with the automatic temperature control feature do not have a temperature control cable.

7 Remove the center console, the instrument panel and the support beam from behind the instrument panel (see Chapter 11).

➡Note: On 2001 through 2004 Legacy models, remove the airbag control module. It is located directly below the ashtray (see illustration).

8 Remove the blower motor housing (see illustration).

9 Remove the fasteners for the heater housing and then lift it from the vehicle (see illustration).

➡Note: Keep some shop towels on the vehicle's floor to protect the carpeting from spilled coolant. If the coolant spills on any painted surfaces, wash it off immediately with cold water.

10 On 2005 and later Legacy models, remove the screws for the heater core cover on the heater housing (see illustration). Pull the heater core straight out of the housing.

11 For all other models, the heater housing must be separated to remove the heater core. Remove the fasteners from the housing and separate the two halves to remove the heater core (see illustrations).

INSTALLATION

12 Slide the new heater core into the housing, making sure that the sealing foam is in place and secure the heater core cover (if applicable).

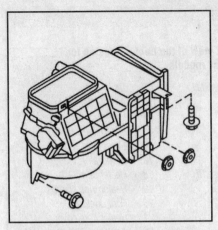

10.8 Typical blower motor housing and mounting fasteners

10.9 Typical heater housing and mounting fasteners

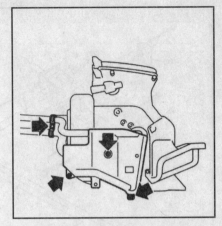

10.10 Remove the heater core cover to remove the heater core

10.11a An exploded view of the heater housing for 2004 and earlier Legacy models

1	Vent door actuator	8	Foot duct
2	Side link	9	Foot door
3	Vent door lever	10	Case D
4	Case A	11	Mix door
5	Defrost door	12	Case C
6	Vent door	13	Heater core
7	Case B	14	Foot door lever

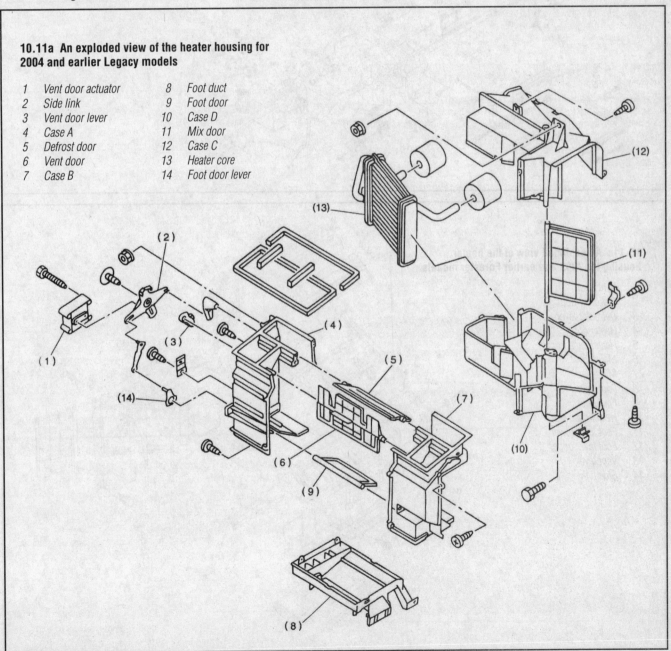

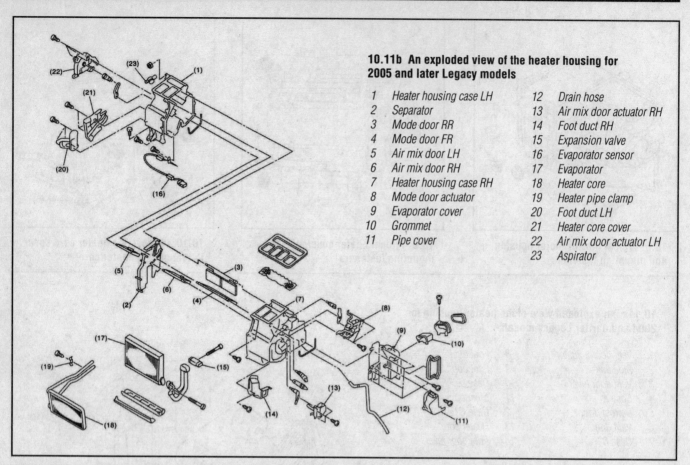

10.11b An exploded view of the heater housing for 2005 and later Legacy models

1	Heater housing case LH	12	Drain hose
2	Separator	13	Air mix door actuator RH
3	Mode door RR	14	Foot duct RH
4	Mode door FR	15	Expansion valve
5	Air mix door LH	16	Evaporator sensor
6	Air mix door RH	17	Evaporator
7	Heater housing case RH	18	Heater core
8	Mode door actuator	19	Heater pipe clamp
9	Evaporator cover	20	Foot duct LH
10	Grommet	21	Heater core cover
11	Pipe cover	22	Air mix door actuator LH
		23	Aspirator

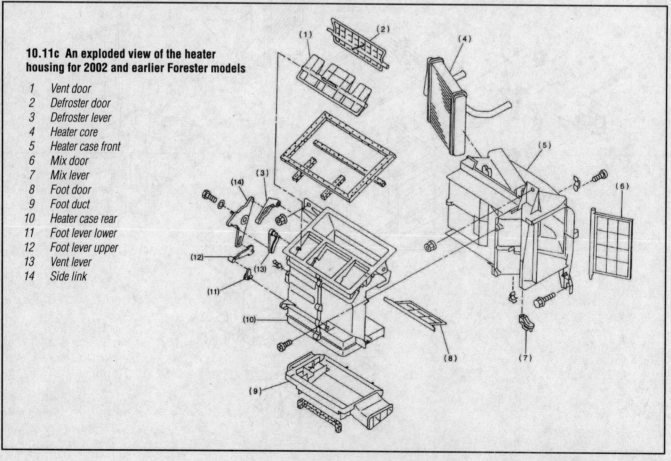

10.11c An exploded view of the heater housing for 2002 and earlier Forester models

1 Vent door
2 Defroster door
3 Defroster lever
4 Heater core
5 Heater case front
6 Mix door
7 Mix lever
8 Foot door
9 Foot duct
10 Heater case rear
11 Foot lever lower
12 Foot lever upper
13 Vent lever
14 Side link

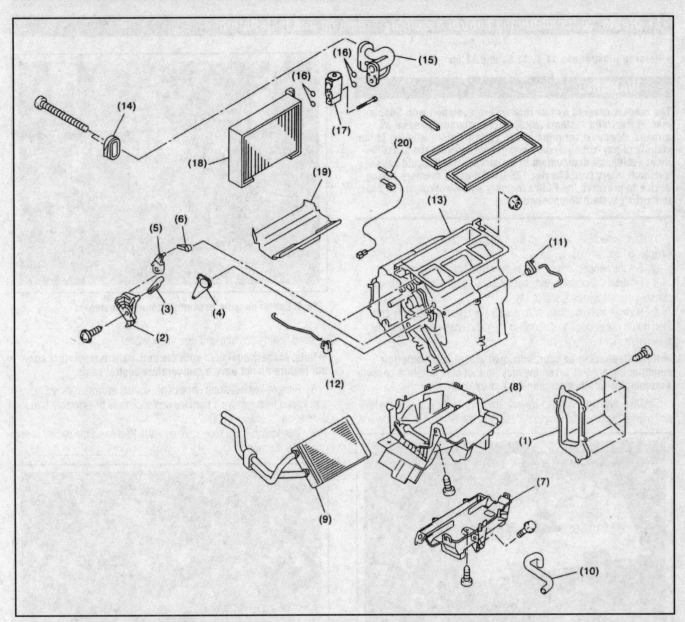

10.11d An exploded view of the heater housing for 2003 and later Forester models

1	Evaporator cover	6	Defroster lever	11	Mix actuator lever
2	Mode main lever	7	Foot duct	12	Foot door lever
3	Vent door lever	8	Lower case	13	Upper case
4	Foot door lever	9	Heater core	14	Gasket
5	Mode actuator link	10	Drain hose	15	Cooling unit pipe

16	O-ring
17	Expansion valve
18	Evaporator
19	Evaporator lining
20	Evaporator sensor

Reassemble the heater core housing (if applicable).

13 Install the heater unit in the vehicle.

14 Install any heater ducts which may have been removed or separated.

15 Install the support beam, the instrument panel and the center console. Install the air bag control module (if removed).

16 Install the temperature control cable.

17 Connect the heater hoses and the refrigerant lines at the firewall. If the hoses are hardened or split at the end, replace them with new ones.

18 Fill the radiator with coolant (see Chapter 1) and reconnect the battery (see Chapter 5, Section 1).

19 Start the vehicle and operate the heater controls. Check for any leakage around the hose connections.

11 Heater/air conditioning control assembly - removal and installation

◆ Refer to illustrations 11.4, 11.5a and 11.5b

❋ WARNING:

The models covered by this manual are equipped with Supplemental Restraint systems (SRS), more commonly known as airbags. Always disarm the airbag system before working in the vicinity of any airbag system component to avoid the possibility of accidental deployment of the airbag, which could cause personal injury (see Chapter 12). Do not use a memory saving device to preserve the PCM's memory when working on or near the airbag system components.

1 Disconnect the cable from the negative battery terminal (see Chapter 5, Section 1).

2 Set the temperature control to the FULL hot position.

3 Remove the center trim panel (or bezel) from around the center console assembly (see Chapter 11).

4 Remove the mounting fasteners for the console assembly and then pull it out enough to disconnect the radio antenna, if necessary (see illustration).

➡Note: Depending on your individual model, the heater/air conditioning control assembly may be mounted within a console assembly (with other components) or by itself.

5 Disconnect the connectors from the back of the control assembly and then disconnect the temperature control cable from the heating and

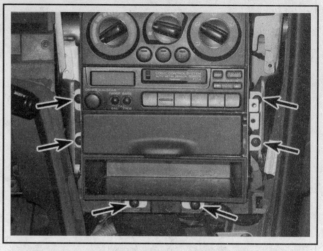

11.4 Center console assembly mounting fasteners

air conditioning housing unit (see illustrations).

➡Note: Models equipped with the automatic temperature control feature do not have a temperature control cable.

6 Remove the heater/air conditioner control assembly mounting screws and then remove it from the center console or assembly (see illustration 11.5a).

7 Installation is the reverse of removal. Reconnect the battery (see Chapter 5, Section 1).

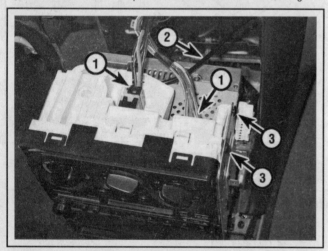

11.5a Control assembly details (2001 Legacy model shown, other models similar):

1 *Electrical connectors*   3 *Mounting fasteners*
2 *Temperature control cable*

11.5b Disconnect the temperature control cable from the heater and air conditioning housing unit

12 Air conditioning and heating system - check and maintenance

♦ Refer to illustration 12.1

❋❋ WARNING:

The air conditioning system is under high pressure. Do not loosen any hose fittings or remove any components until after the system has been discharged by a dealer service department or service station. Always wear eye protection when disconnecting air conditioning system fittings.

1   The following maintenance checks should be performed on a regular basis to ensure the air conditioner continues to operate at peak efficiency.

   a) *Check the compressor drivebelt. If it's worn or deteriorated, replace it (see Chapter 1).*

   b) *Check the drivebelt tension and, if necessary, adjust it (see Chapter 1).*

   c) *Check the system hoses. Look for cracks, bubbles, hard spots and deterioration. Inspect the hoses and all fittings for oil bubbles and seepage. If there's any evidence of wear, damage or leaks, replace the hose(s).*

   d) *Inspect the condenser fins for leaves, bugs and other debris. Use a fin comb or compressed air to clean the condenser.*

   e) *Make sure the system has the correct refrigerant charge.*

   f) *Check the evaporator housing drain tube (see illustration) for blockage.*

2   It's a good idea to operate the system for about 10 minutes at least once a month, particularly during the winter. Long term non-use can cause hardening, and subsequent failure, of the seals.

3   Because of the complexity of the air conditioning system and the special equipment necessary to service it, in-depth troubleshooting and repairs are not included in this manual. However, simple checks and component replacement procedures are provided in this Chapter.

4   The most common cause of poor cooling is simply a low system refrigerant charge. If a noticeable drop in cool air output occurs, the following quick check will help you determine if the refrigerant level is low.

CHECKING THE REFRIGERANT CHARGE

5   Warm the engine up to normal operating temperature.

6   Place the air conditioning temperature selector at the coldest setting and the blower at the highest setting. Open the vehicle doors (to make sure the air conditioning system doesn't cycle off as soon as it cools the passenger compartment).

7   With the compressor engaged - the clutch will make an audible click and the center of the clutch will rotate - feel the pipes going to and from the evaporator at the firewall. If the compressor discharge line (the small-diameter pipe) feels warm and the compressor inlet pipe (the large-diameter pipe) feels cool, the system is properly charged.

8   Place a thermometer in the dashboard vent nearest the evaporator and operate the system until the indicated temperature is around 40 to 45-degrees F. If the ambient (outside) air temperature is very high, say 110 degrees F, the duct air temperature may be as high as 60-degrees F, but generally the air conditioning is 30 to 40 degrees F cooler than the ambient air.

➡Note: Humidity of the ambient air also affects the cooling capacity of the system. Higher ambient humidity lowers the effectiveness of the air conditioning system.

12.1 Evaporator drain tube location (2001 Legacy model shown, others similar)

ADDING REFRIGERANT

♦ Refer to illustrations 12.9, 12.12 and 12.15

9   Buy an automotive air conditioning system charging kit at an auto parts store. A charging kit includes a can of refrigerant, a tap valve and a short section of hose that can be attached between the tap valve and the system low side service valve (see illustration). Because one can of refrigerant may not be sufficient to bring the system charge up to the proper level, it's a good idea to buy an additional can. Make sure that one of the cans contains red refrigerant dye. If the system is leaking, the red dye will leak out with the refrigerant and help you pinpoint the location of the leak.

❋❋ CAUTION:

There are two types of refrigerant used in automotive systems; R-12 - which has been widely used on earlier models and the more environmentally-friendly R-134a used in all models

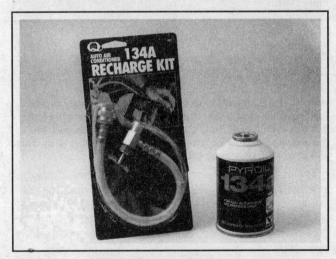

12.9 A basic charging kit for R-134a systems is available at most auto parts stores - it must say R-134a (not R-12) and so should the can of refrigerant

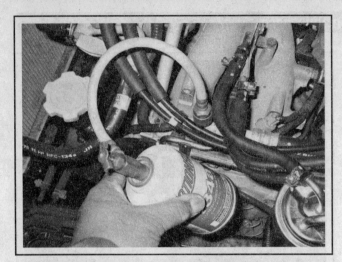

12.12 Add refrigerant to the low-side port only

covered by this manual. These two refrigerants (and their appropriate refrigerant oils) are not compatible and must never be mixed or components will be damaged. Use only R-134a refrigerant in the models covered by this manual.

10 Hook up the charging kit by following the manufacturer's instructions.

> **※※ WARNING:**
>
> DO NOT attempt to hook the charging kit hose to the system high side! The fittings on the charging kit are designed to fit only on the low side of the system.

11 Back off the valve handle on the charging kit and screw the kit onto the refrigerant can, making sure first that the O-ring or rubber seal inside the threaded portion of the kit is in place.

> **※※ WARNING:**
>
> Wear protective eyewear when dealing with pressurized refrigerant cans.

12 Remove the dust cap from the low-side charging connection and attach the quick-connect fitting on the kit hose (see illustration).

13 Warm up the engine and turn on the air conditioner. Keep the charging kit hose away from the fan and other moving parts.

➡ **Note: The charging process requires the compressor to be running. Your compressor may cycle off if the pressure is low due to a low charge. If the clutch cycles off, you can pull the low-pressure cycling switch plug and attach a jumper wire. This will keep the compressor ON.**

14 Turn the valve handle on the kit until the stem pierces the can, then back the handle out to release the refrigerant. You should be able to hear the rush of gas. Add refrigerant until the compressor discharge line (the small-diameter pipe) feels warm and the compressor inlet pipe (the large-diameter pipe) feels cool. Allow stabilization time between each addition.

15 If you have an accurate thermometer, place it in the center air conditioning vent (see illustration) and note the temperature of the air coming out of the vent. A fully-charged system which is working cor-

12.15 Insert a thermometer into the center vent, turn on the air conditioning system and wait for it to cool down; depending on the humidity, the output air should be 30 to 40-degrees cooler than the ambient temperature

rectly should cool down to about 40 degrees F. Generally, an air conditioning system will put out air that is 30 to 40-degrees F cooler than the ambient air. For example, if the ambient (outside) air temperature is very high (over 100 degrees F), the temperature of air coming out of the registers should be 60 to 70-degrees F.

16 When the can is empty, turn the valve handle to the closed position and release the connection from the low-side port. Replace the dust cap.

> **※※ WARNING:**
>
> Never add more than two cans of refrigerant to the system.

17 Remove the charging kit from the can and store the kit for future use with the piercing valve in the UP position, to prevent inadvertently piercing the can on the next use.

HEATING SYSTEMS

18 If the carpet under the heater core is damp, or if antifreeze vapor or steam is coming through the vents, the heater core is leaking. Remove it (see Section 10) and install a new unit (most radiator shops will not repair a leaking heater core).

19 If the air coming out of the heater vents isn't hot, the problem could stem from any of the following causes:

a) *The thermostat is stuck open, preventing the engine coolant from warming up enough to carry heat to the heater core. Replace the thermostat (see Section 3).*

b) *There is a blockage in the system, preventing the flow of coolant through the heater core. Feel both heater hoses at the firewall. They should be hot. If one of them is cold, there is an obstruction in one of the hoses or in the heater core, or the heater control valve is shut. Detach the hoses and back flush the heater core with a water hose. If the heater core is clear but circulation is impeded, remove the two hoses and flush them out with a water hose.*

c) *If flushing fails to remove the blockage from the heater core, the core must be replaced (see Section 10).*

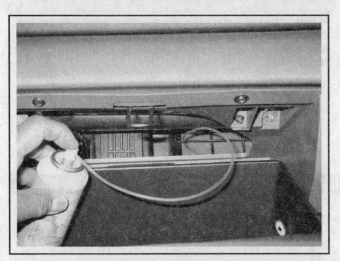

12.23 Open the glovebox and place the disinfectant nozzle into the evaporator housing through the edge of the cabin recirculation door

ELIMINATING AIR CONDITIONING ODORS

▶ **Refer to illustration 12.23**

20 Unpleasant odors that often develop in air conditioning systems are caused by the growth of a fungus, usually on the surface of the evaporator core. The warm, humid environment there is a perfect breeding ground for mildew to develop.

21 The evaporator core on most vehicles is difficult to access, and dealership service departments have a lengthy, expensive process for eliminating the fungus by opening up the evaporator case and using a powerful disinfectant and rinse on the core until the fungus is gone. You can service your own system at home, but it takes something much stronger than basic household germ-killers or deodorizers.

22 Aerosol disinfectants for automotive air conditioning systems are available in most auto parts stores, but remember when shopping for them that the most effective treatments are also the most expensive. The basic procedure for using these sprays is to start by running the system in the RECIRC mode for ten minutes with the blower on its highest speed. Use the highest heat mode to dry out the system and keep the compressor from engaging by disconnecting the wiring connector at the compressor (see Section 14).

23 Make sure that the disinfectant can comes with a long spray hose. Point the nozzle through the air recirculation door; just above the blower motor section of the housing (see illustration), and spray according to the manufacturer's recommendations. Follow the manufacturer's recommendations for the length of spray and waiting time between applications.

❋❋ CAUTION:

Be careful not to let the spray hose get caught in the blower motor fan.

24 Once the evaporator has been cleaned, the best way to prevent the mildew from coming back again is to make sure your evaporator housing drain tube is clear (see illustration 12.1).

13 Air conditioning receiver-drier - removal and installation

▶ **Refer to illustration 13.3**

❋❋ WARNING:

The air conditioning system is under high pressure. Do not loosen any hose fittings or remove any components until after the system has been discharged. Air conditioning refrigerant must be properly discharged into an EPA-approved recovery/recycling unit at a dealer service department or an automotive air conditioning repair facility. Always wear eye protection when disconnecting air conditioning system fittings.

❋❋ CAUTION:

When replacing entire components, additional refrigerant oil should be added equal to the amount that is removed with the component being replaced. Be sure to read the label on the container before adding any oil to the system to confirm that it is compatible with the R-134a system.

➡ **Note: On 2003 and later Forester models and 2005 and later Legacy models, the receiver-drier is integrated with the condenser and not serviceable separately.**

1 Have the refrigerant discharged and recovered by an air conditioning technician.

2 Disconnect the cable from the negative battery terminal (see Chapter 5, Section 1).

13.3 Air conditioning receiver-drier details (2001 model shown, others are similar):

1 Refrigerant line fittings	3 Bracket bolt
2 A/C pressure switch	

3 Remove the refrigerant lines from the receiver-drier and cap them immediately to prevent the entry of dirt or moisture into the system (see illustration). Discard the O-ring seals.

4 Disconnect the electrical connector for the pressure switch (see illustration 13.3).

5 Remove the bracket bolt that secures the receiver-drier and remove the unit from its bracket (see illustration 13.3).

6 Installation is the reverse of removal. Be sure to install new O-rings onto the line fittings and lightly coat them with refrigerant oil. Tighten the line fittings to the torque listed in this Chapter's Specifications.

➡**Note: Only use O-rings that are designed specifically for A/C system applications. If you are replacing the receiver-drier with a new unit, add 0.3-ounce (10 ml) of refrigerant oil to the replacement.**

7 Reconnect the battery. Refer to Chapter 5, Section 1.

8 Have the system evacuated, charged and leak tested by the shop that discharged it.

14 Air conditioning compressor - removal and installation

✳✳ WARNING:

The air conditioning system is under high pressure. Do not loosen any hose fittings or remove any components until after the system has been discharged. Air conditioning refrigerant must be properly discharged into an EPA-approved recovery/recycling unit at a dealer service department or an automotive air conditioning repair facility. Always wear eye protection when disconnecting air conditioning system fittings.

✳✳ CAUTION:

When replacing entire components, additional refrigerant oil should be added equal to the amount that is removed with the component being replaced. Be sure to read the label on the container before adding any oil to the system to confirm that it is compatible with the R-134a system.

REMOVAL

◗ **Refer to illustrations 14.5, 14.7a, 14.7b and 14.7c**

1 Have the refrigerant discharged and recovered by an air conditioning technician.

2 Disconnect the cable from the negative battery terminal (see Chapter 5, Section 1).

3 Remove the A/C compressor drivebelt (see Chapter 1).

4 On 2002 and earlier Legacy models and 2001 and earlier Forester models, remove the electrical harness from the alternator. On 2003 and later Legacy models and 2002 and later Forester models, remove the alternator (see Chapter 5)

5 Disconnect the refrigerant lines from the compressor (see illustration). Plug the open fittings immediately to prevent entry of dirt and moisture

6 Disconnect the air conditioning compressor clutch electrical connector.

7 Remove the compressor mounting bolts attaching the compressor to the brackets and then remove the compressor (see illustration 14.5 and the accompanying illustrations).

INSTALLATION

8 If a new compressor is being installed, follow the accompanying directions on draining the excess oil from it prior to installation.

9 The clutch may have to be transferred from the old compressor to the new unit.

10 Installation is the reverse of removal. Use new O-rings (lightly coated with fresh refrigerant oil) at the line fittings. Tighten the compressor mounting bolts and line fittings to the torque listed in this Chapter's Specifications.

➡**Note: Only use O-rings that are designed specifically for A/C system applications.**

11 Reconnect the battery (see Chapter 5, Section 1).

12 Have the system evacuated, recharged and leak tested by an air conditioning technician.

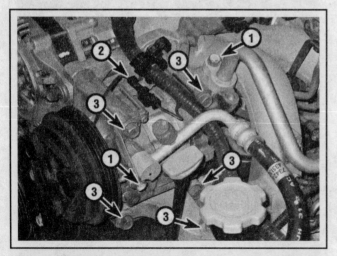

14.5 Air conditioning compressor mounting details (2001 Legacy model shown, other models similar):

1 *Refrigerant line fittings*
2 *Compressor clutch electrical connector*
3 *Bracket and compressor mounting bolts*

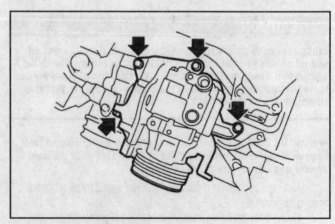

14.7a 2003 and later Legacy compressor mounting bolts

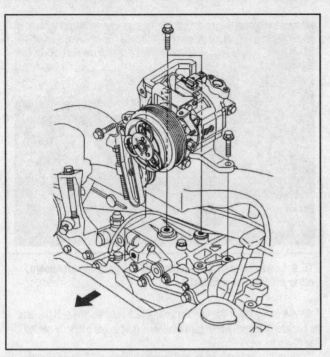

14.7b 2003 and later Forester model compressor mounting bolts

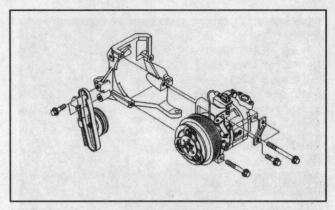

14.7c Remove the compressor mounting bolts

15 Air conditioning condenser - removal and installation

⚹⚹ WARNING:

The air conditioning system is under high pressure. Do not loosen any hose fittings or remove any components until after the system has been discharged. Air conditioning refrigerant must be properly discharged into an EPA-approved recovery/recycling unit at a dealer service department or an automotive air conditioning repair facility. Always wear eye protection when disconnecting air conditioning system fittings.

⚹⚹ CAUTION:

When replacing entire components, additional refrigerant oil should be added equal to the amount that is removed with the component being replaced. Be sure to read the label on the container before adding any oil to the system to confirm that it is compatible with the R-134a system.

➡Note: On 2003 and later Forester models and 2005 and later Legacy models, the receiver-drier is integrated with the condenser.

REMOVAL

▶ **Refer to illustrations 15.6 and 15.7**

1   Have the refrigerant discharged and recovered by an air conditioning technician.

2   Disconnect the cable from the negative battery terminal (see Chapter 5, Section 1).

3   Remove the air intake duct from above the radiator, if necessary, (see Chapter 4).

4   Remove the radiator brackets (see Section 5). On 2005 and later Legacy models, remove the hood bracket (next to the hood latch) above the radiator.

5   On 2005 and later Legacy models, and 2001 and earlier Forester models, remove the front grill (see Chapter 11).

6   Disconnect the refrigerant lines from the condenser and plug or cap all openings immediately to prevent dirt or moisture from enter the system (see illustration).

➡Note: Depending on what model and year you're working on, the line fittings can be found on either one or both sides of the condenser.

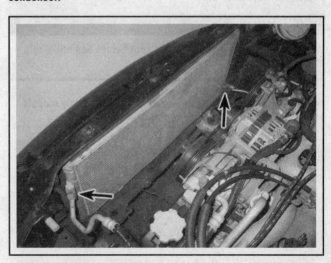

15.6 Condenser line fittings (2001 Legacy model shown, other models are similar)

15.7 Condenser mounting bolts (2001 Legacy model shown, other models are similar)

15.9 Lower condenser mounts (2001 Legacy model shown, other models are similar)

7   Remove the condenser mounting bolts (see illustration). Lean the radiator back and use the gap to carefully lift the condenser from its lower mounts and remove it.

INSTALLATION

▶ **Refer to illustration 15.9**

➡**Note: When a new condenser is installed, a new receiver/drier should also be installed.**

8   When installing a new condenser, drain the oil from the old condenser into a measured container. Install that amount of fresh refrigerant oil into the new condenser.

9   Carefully lower the condenser in place between the radiator and the radiator support. Make sure the lower guides are properly seated (see illustration).

10   Installation is the reverse of removal. Use new O-rings (lightly coated with fresh refrigerant oil) at the line fittings. Tighten the compressor mounting bolts and line fittings to the torque listed in this Chapter's Specifications.

➡**Note: Only use O-rings that are designed specifically for A/C system applications.**

11   Reconnect the battery (see Chapter 5, Section 1).

12   Have the system evacuated, recharged and leak tested by an air conditioning technician.

16 Engine coolant passage - removal and installation

▶ **Refer to illustration 16.6**

✳✳ **WARNING:**

Wait until the engine is completely cool before beginning this procedure.

➡**Note: Non-turbocharged engine models are the only models equipped with this particular engine coolant passage.**

1   Drain the cooling system (see Chapter 1)

2   Relieve the fuel pressure in the fuel system (see Chapter 4), then disconnect the cable from the negative terminal of the battery (see Chapter 5).

3   Remove the intake manifold (see Chapter 2A)

4   Disconnect the electrical connector for the engine coolant temperature sensor (see Chapter 6).

5   Disconnect the radiator and heater hoses from the coolant passage.

6   Remove the mounting fasteners and then remove the coolant passage (see illustration).

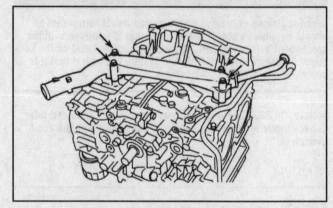

16.6 Coolant passage mounting fasteners

7   Installation is the reverse of removal. Use new O-ring seals and tighten the mounting fasteners to the torque listed in this Chapter's Specifications.

8   Refill the cooling system (see Chapter 1).

Specifications

General

Coolant type and capacity	See Chapter 1
Thermostat rating	
Opening temperature range	169 to 176-degrees F (76 to 80 degrees C)
Fully open temperature	196 degrees F (91 degrees C)
Radiator pressure cap	
Specified cap pressure	14 to 18 psi
Refrigerant capacity	
R134a systems	Refer to HVAC specification tag

Torque specifications

	Ft-lbs (unless otherwise indicated)	Nm
Air conditioning lines-to-compressor	130 in-lbs	15
Air conditioning lines-to-condenser	130 in-lbs	15
Air conditioning lines-to-receiver-drier	65 in-lbs	7
Compressor bracket-to-engine mounting bolts	26	35
Compressor-to-bracket mounting bolts	21	29
Condenser mounting bolts	65 in-lbs	7
Engine coolant passage	60 in-lbs	6
Radiator bracket mounting bolts	108 in-lbs	12
Thermostat housing bolts	60 in-lbs	7
Water pump-to-engine mounting bolts	108 in-lbs	12

Notes

Section

Reference to other Chapters

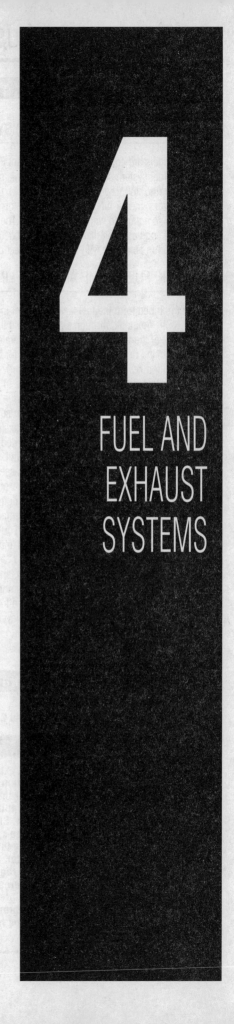

4

FUEL AND
EXHAUST
SYSTEMS

1 General information

MULTIPOINT FUEL INJECTION (MFI) SYSTEM

These models are equipped with a Multipoint Fuel Injection (MFI) system. The fuel system consists of the fuel tank, an electric fuel pump/fuel level sending unit (mounted in the fuel tank), the fuel pump relay, the fuel injectors, the air filter housing and the throttle body unit. Some models are also equipped with a turbocharger. The fuel system for turbocharged engines is similar to the non-turbocharged models. For more information about the MFI system, see Section 12.

FUEL TANK, FUEL PUMP AND FUEL LINES

Fuel is pumped from the fuel tank to the fuel injection system, and back to the fuel tank, through a pair of metal lines running along the underside of the vehicle. The fuel pump operates anytime that the engine is cranking or running. It also operates for two or three seconds when the ignition key is turned to ON, to pressurize the system, but shuts off after that unless the key is then turned to START.

The fuel tank is equipped with a fuel pump/fuel level sending unit and a second fuel level sending unit. The pump/sending unit assembly consists of the fuel inlet strainer, an integral filter (on 2004 and later non-turbocharged models and on all turbocharged models), the pump itself, the jet pump and the fuel level sending unit. You can separate the fuel level sending unit from the fuel pump assembly, but no further disassembly is possible. In other words, if you want to replace the fuel level sending unit, you can remove it from the pump assembly and install a new sending unit. But if you need to replace the pump itself, you can swap the old sending unit onto it, but you must replace the inlet strainer, pump, integral filter (if equipped) and jet pump as a single assembly.

All models are equipped with a divided fuel tank to distribute the weight of the fuel inside the tank in an even fashion, and to make room for the driveshaft and rear differential. There is a fuel level sending unit in each compartment of the fuel tank. The fuel level sending unit in the right fuel tank compartment is part of the fuel pump/fuel level sending unit assembly. The other sending unit is located in the left compartment. Both the fuel pump/fuel level sending unit and the stand-alone fuel level sending unit can be removed without dropping the fuel tank. The rear seat must be removed to access either unit.

The fuel tank is another matter. To remove the fuel tank on these vehicles, you must disconnect the rear brake calipers and the parking brake cables, then you must lower the rear suspension assembly. You should never have to remove the fuel tank unless dirt somehow gets into it, but it you do, be aware that this is a major job.

The fuel tank is equipped with a jet pump that circulates fuel from the left compartment to the right compartment to keep the fuel evenly distributed so that the weight of the fuel is evenly distributed between the two compartments. The jet pump utilizes the velocity of the fuel returning from the engine via the return line to produce negative pressure, which produces a siphoning effect. The jet pump is an integral component of the fuel pump/fuel level sending unit assembly.

EXHAUST SYSTEM

The exhaust system consists of the exhaust manifold, the catalytic converters, the resonator, the muffler and the exhaust pipes connecting these components together. The exhaust manifold is a one-piece assembly that comes together at a flange behind the engine. Heat shields are riveted on the exhaust manifold to protect the underside of the engine from excessive heat. You must remove the entire exhaust manifold, even to replace just one manifold gasket.

There are two oxygen sensors and two catalysts. The catalysts are located right behind the exhaust manifold flange. The upstream catalyst is the first catalyst, followed by a short pipe and the downstream catalyst. The upstream and downstream catalysts and the short pipe between them are welded together into a single assembly. If either catalyst must be replaced, you must replace both catalysts. For more information about the catalytic converters, refer to Chapter 6.

2 Fuel pressure relief procedure

▶ **Refer to illustrations 2.2a, 2.2b, 2.2c and 2.2d**

※ WARNING:

Gasoline is extremely flammable, so take extra precautions when you work on any part of the fuel system. Don't smoke or allow open flames or bare light bulbs near the work area, and don't work in a garage where a gas-type appliance (such as a water heater or a clothes dryer) is present. Since gasoline is carcinogenic, wear latex gloves when there's a possibility of being exposed to fuel, and, if you spill any fuel on your skin, rinse it off immediately with soap and water. Mop up any spills immediately and do not store fuel-soaked rags where they could ignite. The fuel system is under constant pressure, so, if any fuel lines are to be disconnected, the fuel pressure in the system must be relieved first. When you perform any kind of work on the fuel system, wear safety glasses and have a Class B type fire extinguisher on hand.

1 Remove the fuel filler cap to release any pressure that has built up in the tank.

2 Remove the fuel pump relay from the fuel pump circuit:

On 2000 through 2004 Legacy and Outback models - the fuel pump relay (see illustrations) is located on the right end of the passenger compartment fuse and relay box. This fuse and relay box is located at the left end of the dash, ahead of the coin tray (2000 through 2003 models) or ahead of the fuse panel cover (2004 models). It's not actually necessary to remove the knee bolster to disconnect the electrical connector from the fuel pump relay. Instead, using a flashlight, locate the connector on the back of the relay (see illustration) and disconnect it.

On 2005 and 2006 Legacy and Outback models - the fuel pump relay is located behind the right kick panel. Remove the right kick panel (see Chapter 11), then pull out the fuel pump relay

On 2000 through 2002 Forester models - the fuel pump relay

2.2a Fuel pump relay (2000 through 2004 Legacy and Outback models) (knee bolster removed for clarity)

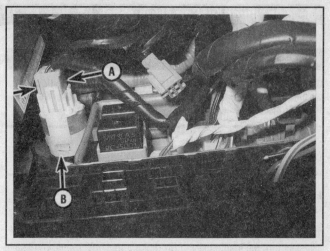

2.2b This is how the fuel pump relay looks when you're lying on the floor and looking straight up at the backside of the relay. To disconnect the electrical connector (A) from the fuel pump relay (B) on a 2000 through 2004 Legacy or Outback, depress the release tab (left upper arrow)

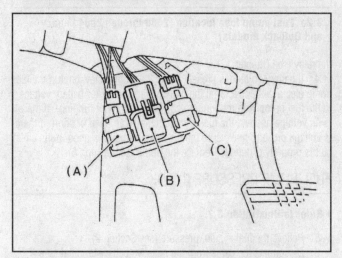

2.2c To open the fuel pump circuit on 2000 through 2002 Forester models, disconnect the electrical connector from the fuel pump relay

A   Blower fan motor relay   C   Fuel pump relay
B   Main relay

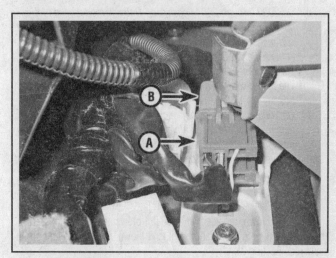

2.2d To open the fuel pump circuit on 2003 and later Forester models, disconnect the electrical connector (A) from the fuel pump relay (B)

(see illustration) is located on a small bracket mounted under the left end of the dash.

On 2003 and later Forester models - the fuel pump relay (see illustration) is located behind the right kick panel. Remove the right kick panel (see Chapter 11), then disconnect the electrical connector from the fuel pump relay.

3   Start the engine and allow it to run until it stops.

4   Disconnect the cable from the negative battery terminal (see Chapter 5) before working on the fuel system.

5   The fuel system pressure is now relieved.

◆ **Note: Even after the fuel pressure has been relieved. it's a good idea to lay a shop towel over any fuel connection to be disassembled, to absorb the residual fuel that may leak out when servicing the fuel system.**

6   When you're finished working on the fuel system, simply reconnect the fuel pump/sending unit harness connector and connect the negative cable to the battery.

3 Fuel pump/fuel pressure check

✳✳ WARNING:

Gasoline is extremely flammable, so take extra precautions when you work on any part of the fuel system. See the Warning in Section 2.

PRELIMINARY INSPECTION

▶ **Refer to illustrations 3.2a, 3.2b and 3.2c**

1   Should the fuel system fail to deliver sufficient fuel, or any fuel at all, inspect it as follows. First, remove the fuel filler cap. Have an assistant turn the ignition key to ON (but not to START) while you listen at the fuel filler opening. You should hear a whirring sound for two or three seconds. If you do, this indicates that the pump is operating, and has just pressurized the system, then turned off.

2   If you don't hear the pump priming the system, check the fuel pump fuse.

    a) On 2000 through 2004 Legacy and Outback models, the fuel pump fuse is the No. 13 fuse in the passenger compartment fuse and relay box (see illustration). This fuse and relay box is located at the left end of the dash, ahead of the coin tray (2000 through 2003 models) or ahead of the fuse panel cover (2004 models). The fuse box cover indicates the location of all fuses in the fuse box.

    b) On 2005 and 2006 Legacy and Outback models, the fuel pump fuse in the No. 11 fuse in the engine compartment fuse and relay box (see illustration), which is located on the left side of the engine compartment. The fuse box cover indicates the location of all fuses in the fuse box.

    c) On Forester models, the fuel pump fuse is the No.11 fuse in the passenger compartment fuse and relay box (see illustration).

If the fuse is blown, replace it and see if it blows again. If it does, trace the fuel pump circuit for a short. If it isn't blown, remove the fuel pump relay (see Section 2).

3   After removing the fuel pump relay, check for battery voltage to the fuel pump relay connector. If there is battery voltage present, test

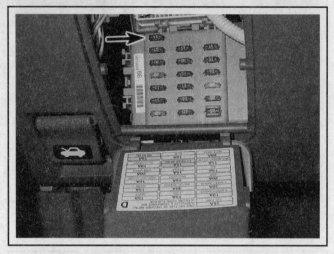

3.2a Fuel pump fuse location (2000 through 2004 Legacy and Outback models)

the relay (see Chapter 12).

4   If battery voltage is present at the fuel pump relay, unplug the fuel pump electrical connector at the fuel tank and check for battery voltage to the fuel pump with the ignition key ON (engine not running). If there is no voltage, inspect the fuel pump circuit for an open or short. If there is voltage present, make sure the fuel pump ground is good. If the circuit is properly grounded, replace the pump (see Section 6).

FUEL PUMP PRESSURE CHECK

▶ **Refer to illustration 3.7**

5   Relieve the fuel system pressure (see Section 2).

6   Disconnect the cable from the negative battery terminal (see Chapter 5).

7   In addition to a fuel pressure gauge capable of reading fuel pressure up to 50 psi, you'll need a hose and an adapter suitable for tee-ing into the fuel system at the quick-connect fitting between the fuel delivery hose and the fuel rail (see illustration).

3.2b Fuel pump fuse location (2005 and 2006 Legacy and Outback models)

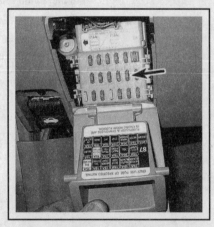

3.2c Fuel pump fuse location on Forester models

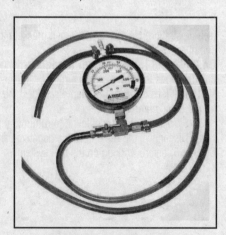

3.7 A typical fuel pressure gauge, with hoses suitable for tee-ing into the fuel system between the fuel delivery line and the fuel rail

3.8 On 2000 through 2003 Legacy and Outback models, loosen the hose clamp and disconnect the fuel inlet hose from the fuel filter

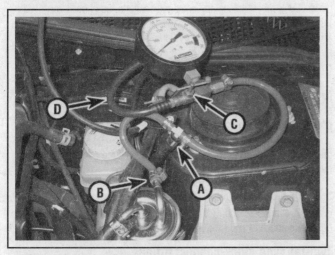

3.9 Here's how the gauge looks when hooked up to the fuel system on the inlet side of the fuel filter (if your vehicle doesn't have a fuel filter in the engine compartment, tee-in the gauge between the fuel supply hose and the inlet pipe on the left fuel rail):

A   Insert the tee-fitting into the end of the fuel supply hose
B   Clamp the end of the hose that's not on same side of the gauge as the bleeder valve to the fuel inlet pipe
C   Some fuel pressure gauges are equipped with a bleeder valve (which is not necessary for measuring fuel pressure, but handy for draining off residual pressure)
D   Bleeder valve hose (again, not necessary for measuring fuel pressure, but handy for routing residual fuel into an approved container)

2000 through 2003 Legacy and Outback models and 2000 through 2004 Forester models

▶ **Refer to illustrations 3.8 and 3.9**

8   Disconnect the fuel supply inlet hose from the fuel filter inlet pipe (see illustration).

9   Tee-in the fuel pressure gauge between the fuel supply hose and the fuel filter inlet pipe (see illustration).

2004 through 2006 Legacy and Outback models and 2005 and 2006 Forester models

10   These models don't have a fuel filter in the engine compartment (it's an integral part of the fuel pump/fuel level sending unit in the fuel tank). But the hook-up procedure is essentially the same. Instead of disconnecting the fuel supply hose from the fuel filter, disconnect the fuel supply hose from the left fuel rail and tee your fuel pressure gauge into the system between the fuel supply hose and the fuel rail inlet pipe.

ALL MODELS

11   Start the engine and allow it to idle. Compare the pressure reading with the engine running value listed in this Chapter's Specifications. Disconnect and plug the vacuum hose from the fuel pressure regulator (see Section 15) - the pressure should increase immediately by approximately 3 to 10 psi (see the values listed in this Chapter's Specifications). If the pressure readings are correct, the system is operating properly.

12   If the fuel pressure is not within specifications, check the following:

a)   *If the pressure is higher than specified, check for vacuum at the hose to the fuel pressure regulator. Vacuum must fluctuate with the increase or decrease in the engine rpm. If vacuum is present, check for a pinched or clogged fuel return hose or pipe. If the return line is not obstructed, replace the fuel pressure regulator.*

b)   *If the pressure is lower than specified, check for a restriction in the fuel filter or fuel line. If the fuel filter and lines are OK, start the engine (if possible) and slowly pinch the return hose shut. If the pressure rises to normal or above, replace the fuel pressure regulator (see Section 15).*

❊❊ WARNING:

Don't allow the fuel pressure to exceed 50 psi. If the pressure is still low, replace the fuel pump (see Section 6).

▶ **Note: A leaking fuel injector could also cause lower-than-normal fuel pressure, but would most likely set a diagnostic trouble code.**

13   After the testing is complete, relieve the fuel pressure (see Section 2), remove the fuel pressure gauge and reconnect the fuel delivery line to the fuel filter or fuel rail.

4 Fuel lines and fittings - replacement

✳ WARNING:

Gasoline is extremely flammable, so take extra precautions when you work on any part of the fuel system. See the Warning in Section 2.

1 Always relieve the system fuel pressure before servicing fuel lines or fittings (see Section 2).

2 The fuel supply and return lines extend from the fuel tank to the engine compartment. The EVAP purge line extends from the EVAP canister, which is located behind the fuel tank, up to the purge valve, which is located in the engine compartment.

3 Anytime you raise the vehicle for underbody service, inspect the lines underneath the vehicle for leaks, kinks and dents.

STEEL TUBING

4 If it's necessary to replace a fuel line or EVAP line, use steel tubing that complies with the manufacturer's specifications, or its equivalent.

5 Don't use copper or aluminum tubing to replace steel tubing. These materials cannot withstand normal vehicle vibration.

6 Because steel fuel lines are under high pressure when the engine is running, they require special consideration:

 a) *Inspect all O-rings for cuts, cracks and deterioration. If an O-ring is torn, cracked, hardened or otherwise damaged, replace it.*

 b) *If the lines are replaced, always use original equipment parts, or parts that meet the original equipment standards specified in this Section.*

 c) *Never allow metal lines to chafe against the frame. Maintain a minimum of 1/4-inch clearance around a line to prevent contact with the frame.*

7 If you find dirt in the system during disassembly, disconnect the fuel supply line and then blow it out with compressed air. And be sure to inspect the fuel filter (see Chapter 1) and the fuel pump inlet strainer for contamination (see Section 6).

FLEXIBLE HOSES

✳ CAUTION:

Use only original equipment replacement hoses or their equivalent. Unapproved hoses might fail when subjected to the fuel pressure at which this system operates.

8 Don't route fuel hose within four inches of any part of the exhaust system or within ten inches of the catalytic converter. Never allow rubber hoses to chafe against the frame. Maintain a minimum of 1/4-inch clearance around a hose to prevent contact with the frame.

9 If a hose is equipped with quick-connect fittings, the quick-connect fittings cannot be serviced separately. If the fitting the hose is damaged, replace the entire fuel hose assembly. Do not attempt to service fuel hoses.

REPLACING FUEL LINES AND HOSES AND EVAP LINES

10 If a fuel line or hose or an EVAP line is damaged, replace it with factory replacement parts. Do not substitute fuel lines or hoses or EVAP lines of inferior quality. They might not be suitable for, and might fail when subjected to, the operating pressure of this system.

11 Always relieve the fuel system pressure before replacing fuel or EVAP lines (see Section 2).

12 Always disconnect the cable from the negative terminal of the battery (see Chapter 5) before replacing fuel or EVAP lines.

13 Remove all clips that secure the fuel or EVAP line to the vehicle body. Pay close attention to all clips; they not only secure the fuel line and hoses, they also route them correctly. The hoses and line must be reattached to their respective clips when reassembled.

14 Be sure to use the correct tool and the correct procedure when disconnecting any fuel or EVAP couplings or fittings (see below).

DISCONNECTING AND CONNECTING FUEL LINE AND EVAP LINE FITTINGS

15 If you must replace any damaged sections, use hoses approved for use in fuel systems or tubing made from steel only (it's best to use an original-type pipe that's already flared and pre-bent). Do not install substitutes constructed from inferior or inappropriate material, as this could result in a fuel leak and a fire.

16 Always, before disconnecting or disassembling any part of the fuel system, note the routing of all hoses and pipes and the orientation of all clamps and clips to assure that replacement sections are installed in exactly the same manner.

17 Before detaching any part of the fuel system, be sure to relieve the fuel pressure (see Section 2) and disconnect the cable from the negative terminal of the battery.

18 Always use new hose clamps after loosening or removing them.

19 While you're under the vehicle, it's a good idea to inspect the evaporative emission control (EVAP) system. Verify that all of the EVAP hoses are attached and in good condition (see Chapter 6).

Two-tab type quick-connect fittings

▶ **Refer to illustrations 4.21a, 4.21b, 4.22, 4.23 and 4.24**

➡ **Note 1: This type of fitting can be distinguished by the two white tabs that protrude from the female end. The retainer for a two-tab type quick-connect fitting can be replaced separately, but not the O-rings and spacers. So if this type of fitting is damaged, it cannot be repaired. Instead, you must replace the fitting, and the fuel line to which it's permanently connected, as a single assembly.**

➡ **Note 2: The two-tab quick-connect fitting depicted here is located on top of the fuel pump/fuel level sending unit assembly, which is located in the upper part of the right fuel tank compartment. You might also find the same fittings elsewhere on the fuel or EVAP systems, but the one we show you how to disconnect here is typical of this type of fitting.**

20 Always disconnect the cable from the negative battery terminal before servicing a fuel line quick-connect fitting (see Chapter 5).

21 Squeeze the plastic retainer tabs into the fitting with a pair of needle-nose pliers, then pull the female side of the fitting off the male side (see illustrations). The plastic retainer remains on the fuel line or pipe (the male side of the fitting). The O-rings and spacer remain inside the quick-connect fitting connector body (the female side of the fitting).

22 Wipe off both halves of the quick-connect fitting with a clean

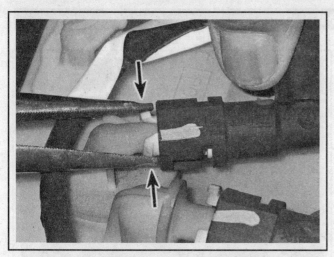

4.21a Squeeze the two plastic retainer tabs together . . .

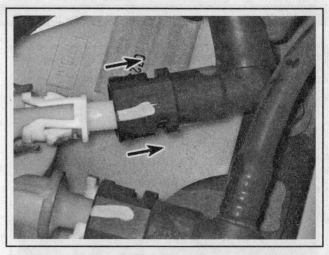

4.21b . . . then pull off the female side of the fitting. Note the retainer, which remains on the male side of the fitting

shop rag, then inspect the condition of the fitting body (the female side) and inspect the condition of the O-ring inside the fitting (see illustration). If anything is damaged or worn, replace the fitting and the fuel line to which it's attached. Neither the fitting body nor the O-ring is available separately.

23 Remove the retainer from the fuel line or pipe (see illustration) and inspect it carefully for damage and wear. Subaru doesn't specifically say that you must replace the retainer every time that you disconnect a quick-connect fitting, but it's a good idea to do so because an old retainer is more likely to disengage and cause a fuel leak. We therefore recommend replacing the retainer EVERY time that you disconnect a quick-connect fitting.

24 Lubricate the fuel line with clean engine oil and push the quick-connect fitting onto the fuel line until you feel/hear an audible click, which indicates that the retainer has seated (see illustration). Verify that the two halves are locked together by trying to pull them apart.

25 Reconnect the negative battery cable, then start the engine and check the quick-connect fitting for leaks.

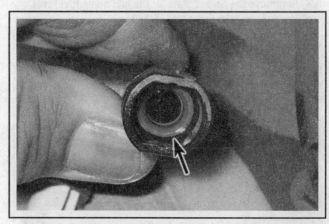

4.22 Inspect the condition of the O-ring inside the female side of the fitting. If it's damaged or worn, replace the fitting and the fuel line to which it's attached

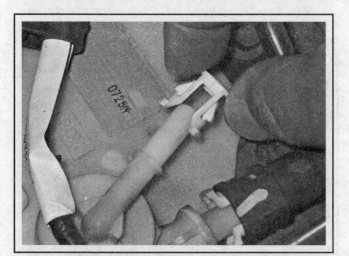

4.23 At the very least, remove the old retainer from the fuel line or pipe and inspect it carefully for damage. If it's still in good shape you can re-use it. However, to be on the safe side, we recommend replacing the retainer EVERY time that you disconnect a quick-connect fitting

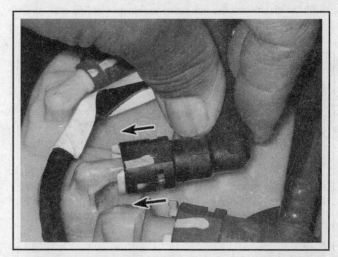

4.24 When reconnecting a quick-connect fitting, lubricate the fuel line or pipe with clean engine oil, then push the fitting on to the line or pipe until you feel/hear a click. Verify that the two sides of the fitting are locked together by trying to pull them apart

5 Fuel pump/fuel level sending unit - removal and installation

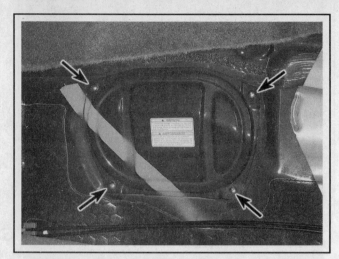

5.4 To remove the access plate for the fuel pump/fuel level sending unit, remove these four screws

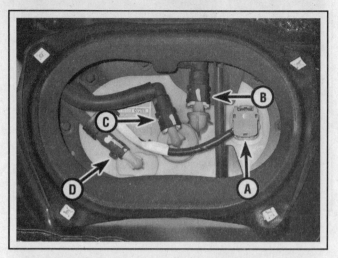

5.5a Typical fuel pump/fuel level sending unit electrical and fuel connections:

A *Fuel pump/fuel level sending unit electrical connector*
B *Fuel supply hose quick-connect fitting (see Section 4)*
C *Fuel return hose quick-connect fitting (see Section 4)*
D *Jet pump hose*

▶ **Refer to illustrations 5.4, 5.5a, 5.5b, 5.7, 5.8, 5.9a and 5.9b**

※※ **WARNING:**

Gasoline is extremely flammable, so take extra precautions when you work on any part of the fuel system. See the Warning in Section 2.

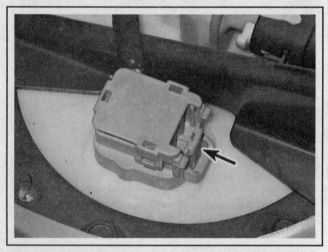

5.5b To disconnect the fuel pump/fuel level sending unit electrical connector, depress this release tab and pull the connector straight up

1 Relieve the fuel system pressure (see Section 2).
2 Disconnect the cable from the negative battery terminal (see Chapter 5).
3 Remove the rear seat and the rear floor mat (see Chapter 11).
4 There are two access plates. The right (passenger side) plate (see illustration) is the one you want to remove for this procedure. Remove the access plate screws and lift the plate from the body floorpan.

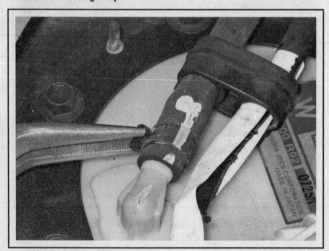

5.7 To disconnect the jet pump hose, squeeze this hose clamp, slide it back, then pull off the hose

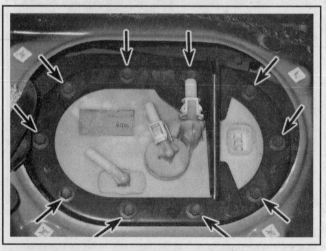

5.8 To detach the fuel pump/fuel level sending unit assembly from the fuel tank, remove these bolts

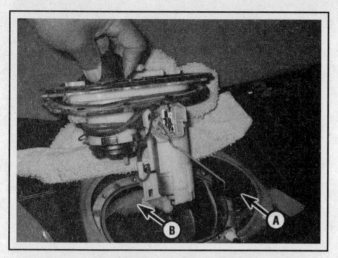

5.9a Carefully lift the fuel pump/fuel level sending unit assembly from the fuel tank. Angle the pump/sending unit as necessary to protect the sending unit float arm (A) and the fuel pump inlet strainer (B) from damage

5   Disconnect the fuel pump/sending unit electrical connector (see illustrations).

6   Disconnect the quick-connect fittings for the fuel supply hose and the fuel return hose (see Section 4 if you're unfamiliar with quick-connect fittings).

7   Loosen the hose clamp (see illustration) and disconnect the jet pump hose.

8   Remove the fuel pump/fuel level sending unit mounting bolts (see illustration).

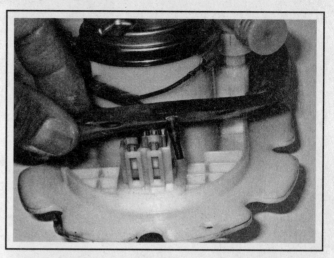

5.9b Remove the old gasket from the fuel pump/fuel level sending unit assembly. Always use a new gasket when installing the pump/sending unit

9   Lift the fuel pump/fuel level sending unit assembly from the fuel tank (see illustration). Carefully angle the pump/sending unit as necessary to protect the float arm from damage. Remove the old pump gaskets (see illustration).

10   Be sure to clean the pump inlet strainer before installing the pump.

11   Be sure to use a new gasket when installing the pump.

12   Installation is otherwise the reverse of removal.

13   When you're done, run the engine and check for leaks.

6   Fuel pump/fuel level sending unit/fuel filter - replacement

※※ WARNING:

Gasoline is extremely flammable, so take extra precautions when you work on any part of the fuel system. See the Warning in Section 2.

➡Note: The fuel pump/fuel level sending unit assembly consists of the pump, the fuel level sending unit, an integral filter, the jet pump and the pump holder to which everything is attached. You can replace the pump, the sending unit or the integral filter separately. Or you can replace the entire assembly. However, you cannot replace the holder or the jet pump separately.

1   Relieve the fuel system pressure (see Section 2). Disconnect the negative battery cable.

2   Remove the fuel pump/fuel level sending unit assembly from the fuel tank (see Section 5) and place it on a clean workbench.

FUEL PUMP

▶ Refer to illustrations 6.3a, 6.3b, 6.3c and 6.4

3   Separate the fuel pump and pump holder (the small plastic cap on the end of the pump) from the fuel pump/fuel level sending unit mounting assembly (see illustrations), then disconnect the electrical

6.3a Using a pair of screwdrivers, disengage the locking pawls on the fuel pump holder from their corresponding slots in the fuel pump mounting assembly . . .

connector from the fuel pump (see illustration) and remove the pump.

4   Remove the pump from the pump holder and disconnect the inlet strainer tube from the pump (see illustration).

5   Installation is the reverse of removal.

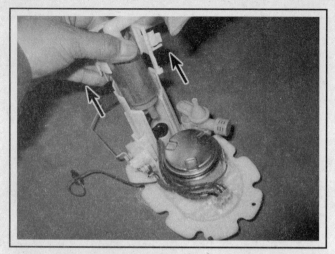

6.3b . . . pull up the fuel pump . . .

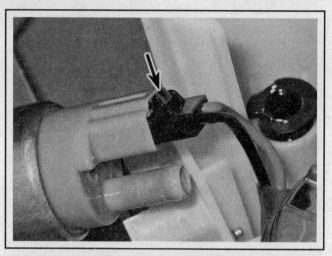

6.3c . . . depress this release tab and disconnect the electrical connector from the fuel pump

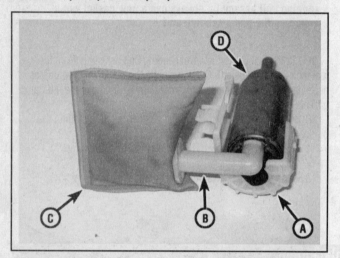

6.4 After removing the pump from the mounting assembly, remove the pump holder (A), then pull off the inlet strainer tube (B) from the pump (D). The inlet strainer (C) and the strainer tube are a one-piece assembly. If you're unable to clean the strainer, replace the strainer and tube as a single assembly

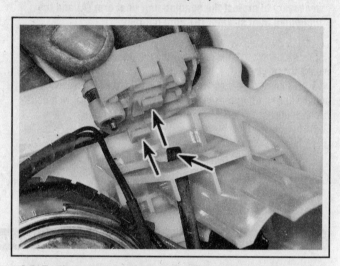

6.6 To disengage the fuel level sending unit from the fuel pump mounting assembly, use a screwdriver to disengage these two locking lugs from their corresponding mounting holes

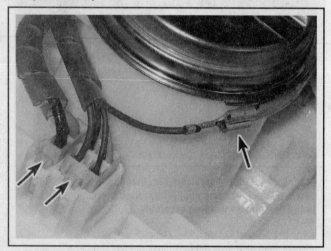

6.7 Disconnect the ground wire, depress the release tabs and disconnect the two electrical connectors, then remove the fuel level sending unit

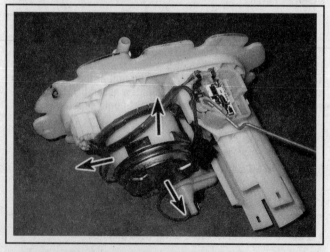

6.9 To disengage the fuel filter from the fuel pump/fuel level sending unit assembly, pry the plastic tabs away from the filter, then pull out the filter

FUEL LEVEL SENDING UNIT

▶ **Refer to illustrations 6.6 and 6.7**

6   Using a screwdriver, release the locking pawls (see illustration) and remove the fuel level sending unit from the fuel pump/fuel level sending unit mounting assembly.

7   Disconnect the fuel level sending unit ground wire and electrical connectors (see illustration) and remove the fuel level sending unit.

8   Installation is the reverse of removal.

FUEL FILTER

▶ **Refer to illustration 6.9**

9   To remove the fuel filter from the fuel pump/fuel level sending unit mounting assembly, pry the plastic tabs (see illustration) away from the filter and pull out the filter.

10   Installation is the reverse of removal. Make sure that the fuel filter snaps into place.

---

7   Sub-compartment fuel level sending unit - removal and installation

▶ **Refer to illustrations 7.4, 7.5, 7.6, 7.8 and 7.9**

✳✳ WARNING:

Gasoline is extremely flammable, so take extra precautions when you work on any part of the fuel system. See the Warning in Section 2.

➡Note: The fuel pump/fuel level sending unit assembly consists of the pump, the fuel level sending unit, an integral filter, the jet pump and the pump holder to which everything is attached. You can replace the pump, the sending unit or the integral filter separately. Or you can replace the entire assembly. However, you cannot replace the holder or the jet pump separately.

1   Relieve the fuel system pressure (see Section 2).

2   Disconnect the cable from the negative battery terminal (see Chapter 5).

3   Remove the rear seat and the rear floor mat (see Chapter 11).

4   There are two access plates. The left (driver's side) plate (see illustration) is the one you want to remove for this procedure. Remove the access plate screws and remove the plate from the body floor pan.

5   Disconnect the quick-connect fittings for the fuel supply and return hoses (see illustration). If you're unfamiliar with quick-connect fittings, refer to Section 4.

6   Disconnect the electrical connector for the sub-compartment fuel

7.4 To remove the access plate for the sub-compartment fuel level sending unit, remove these screws

level sending unit (see illustration).

7   Disconnect the jet pump hose (see illustration 7.6).

8   Remove the sub-compartment fuel level sending unit mounting bolts (see illustration).

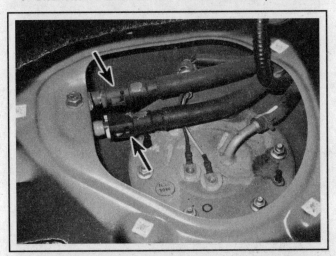

7.5 Disconnect the quick-connect fittings for the supply and return hoses, plug the hoses and set them aside (if you're unfamiliar with quick-connect fittings, refer to Section 4)

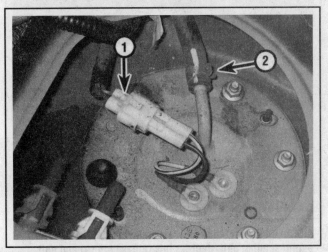

7.6 To disconnect the electrical connector for the sub-compartment fuel level sending unit, depress this release tab (1) and pull off the connector. To disconnect the jet pump hose, loosen this hose clamp (2) and pull off the hose

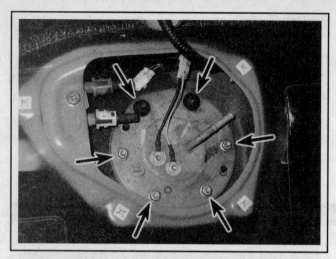

7.8 To detach the sub-compartment fuel level sending unit from the fuel tank, remove these bolts

9 Lift the sub-compartment fuel level sending unit out of the fuel tank (see illustration). Carefully angle the sending unit as necessary to protect the float arm from damage.

10 After removing the sending unit, remove the old gasket and inspect it for cracks, tears and deterioration. If the gasket is cracked,

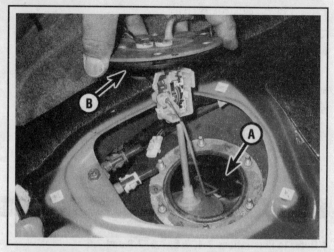

7.9 Carefully lift the sub-compartment fuel level sending unit from the fuel tank. Angle the sending unit as necessary to protect the float (A) from damage. After removing the sending unit, remove the old gasket (B) and inspect it for cracks, tears and deterioration

torn or deteriorated, replace it.

11 Installation is the reverse of removal.

8 Fuel tank - removal and installation

▶ Refer to illustrations 8.5, 8.6, 8.10, 8.11a, 8.11b, 8.13a, 8.13b, 8.14, 8.23, 8.25, 8.26, 8.27 and 8.29

✳✳ WARNING:

Gasoline is extremely flammable, so take extra precautions when you work on any part of the fuel system. See the Warning in Section 2.

➡Note: The following procedure is much easier to perform if the fuel tank is empty.

1 Remove the fuel tank filler cap to relieve fuel tank pressure.
2 Relieve the fuel system pressure (see Section 2).
3 Disconnect the cable from the negative battery terminal (see Chapter 5).
4 Remove the rear seat and floor mat (see Chapter 11).
5 Disconnect the electrical connector for the fuel pump/fuel level sending unit harness (see illustration).
6 Push the sealing grommet for the fuel pump/fuel level sending

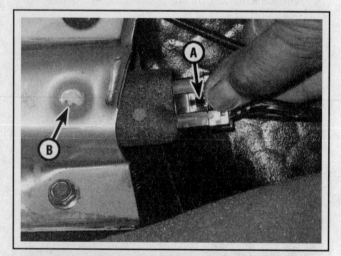

8.5 To disconnect the electrical connector for the fuel pump/ sending unit, depress this release tab (A) and pull off the connector. If you have difficulty, disengage the clip (B) and pull the harness out from the bracket. This will give you some slack so that you can grasp the other side of the connector while disconnecting it

8.6 Push the sealing grommet for the fuel pump/fuel level sending unit harness through the pump/sending unit access plate

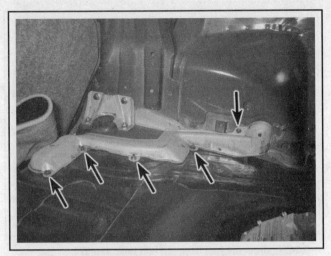

8.10 After removing the trim from the right side of the trunk (sedan models) or the rear quarter lower trim (wagon models), remove these fasteners and remove the protector for the EVAP line that's routed through the right front corner of the trunk (sedans) or luggage compartment (wagons)

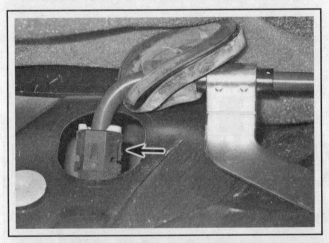

8.11b . . . and disconnect this EVAP line quick-connect fitting (if you're unfamiliar with quick-connect fittings, refer to Section 4)

8.11a Pull this grommet from the floor pan . . .

unit harness through the access plate for the sub-compartment fuel level sending unit (see illustration).

7   Remove the access plate for the sub-compartment fuel level sending unit (see illustration 7.4) and disconnect the quick-connect fittings for the fuel supply and return hoses (see illustration 7.5). If you're unfamiliar with quick-connect fittings, refer to Section 4.

8   Remove the center console (see Chapter 11) and disconnect the parking brake cable from the equalizer (see Chapter 9).

9   Remove the trim carpeting from the right side of the trunk (sedan models) or the rear quarter lower trim (wagon models) (see Chapter 11).

10 Remove the EVAP line protector (see illustration).

11 Remove the grommet and disconnect the EVAP line quick-connect fitting (see illustrations) for the EVAP line that runs through the right front corner of the trunk (sedan models) or the luggage compartment (wagon models). If you're unfamiliar with quick-connect fittings, refer to Section 4.

12 Loosen the rear wheel lug nuts. Raise the vehicle and support it securely on jackstands. Remove the rear wheels.

13 Remove the left and right covers from the front of the fuel tank (see illustrations).

14 Remove the drain plug (see illustration) and drain the fuel from

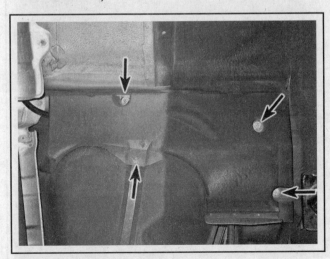

8.13a To detach the left forward fuel tank cover, remove these four screws

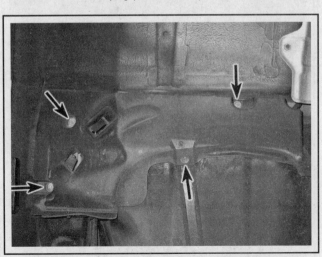

8.13b To detach the right forward fuel tank cover, remove these four screws

the right side of the fuel tank into an approved fuel container. To drain the left (driver's) side of the fuel tank, remove the sub-compartment fuel level sending unit (see Section 7) and siphon the fuel into an approved fuel container.

✳✳ WARNING:

Don't start the siphoning action by mouth; use a siphoning kit (available at most auto parts stores).

15 Remove the rear exhaust pipe and muffler (see Section 21).

16 Remove the driveshaft (see Chapter 8).

17 Disconnect the electrical connector from the ABS sensor (see Chapter 9).

18 Remove the parking brake cable assembly (see Chapter 9).

19 On models with rear drum brakes, disconnect the metal brake lines from the wheel cylinders (see Chapter 9). Be sure to plug the brake lines to prevent excess fluid leakage and the entry of contaminants.

20 On models with rear disc brakes, remove the bolts that attach the rear brake hose clips, then remove the rear brake calipers and suspend them out of the way with a couple of coat hangers or some other suitable wire (see Chapter 9).

21 Support the rear differential with a floor jack. Put a piece of plywood between the jack head the differential to protect the differential housing.

22 Disconnect the lower ends of the rear shock absorbers from the rear knuckles (see Chapter 10).

23 Remove the bolts that attach the rear suspension assembly to the body (see illustration).

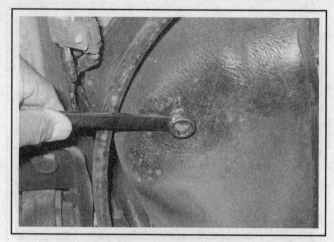

8.14 To drain the fuel from the fuel tank, remove the drain plug

24 Carefully lower the rear suspension assembly.

25 Remove the rear fuel tank covers (see illustration).

26 Disconnect the fuel filler neck hose and the fuel tank pressure sensor hose (see illustration).

27 Disconnect the air vent hose from the EVAP pipe assembly and disconnect the EVAP hose from the pressure control solenoid valve (see illustration).

28 Support the fuel tank.

29 Remove the fuel tank strap bolts (see illustration), then carefully lower the fuel tank.

30 Installation is the reverse of removal.

8.23 To detach the rear suspension assembly from the vehicle body, remove these bolts

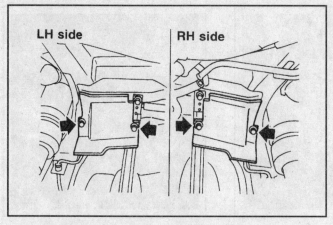

8.25 To detach the rear fuel tank covers, remove these bolts

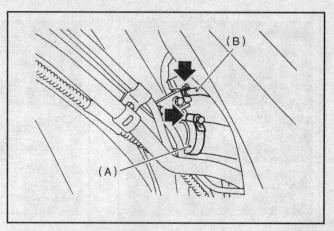

8.26 Loosen the screw type hose clamp and disconnect the fuel tank filler neck hose (A), then loosen the spring type clamp and disconnect the fuel tank pressure sensor hose (B)

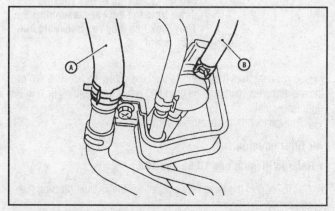

8.27 Loosen the spring type hose clamp and disconnect the air vent hose (A), then loosen the spring type clamp and disconnect the EVAP line (B)

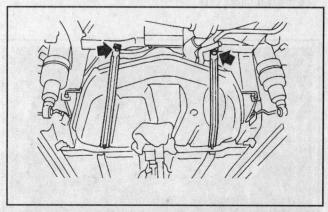

8.29 To detach the fuel tank from the vehicle, remove these fuel tank strap bolts

9   Fuel tank cleaning and repair - general information

1   All repairs to the fuel tank or filler neck must be carried out by a professional who has experience in this critical and potentially dangerous work. Even after cleaning and flushing of the fuel system, explosive fumes can remain and ignite during repair of the tank.

2   If the fuel tank is removed from the vehicle, it should not be placed in an area where sparks or open flames could ignite the fumes coming out of the tank. Be especially careful inside garages where a gas-type appliance is located, because it could cause an explosion.

10   Air filter housing - removal and installation

NON-TURBOCHARGED MODELS

2000 through 2003 Legacy and Outback models and 2004 non-ULEV Legacy and Outback models

Air intake ducts and resonator assembly

♦ Refer to illustrations 10.1, 10.2a, 10.2b and 10.4

1   To remove the front air intake duct, remove the two bolts that attach the duct to the radiator crossmember (see illustration), then pull it off the rear intake duct.

2   To remove the rear air intake duct, remove the single bolt that attaches it to the right strut tower (see illustrations), then pull it off the air filter housing. Note the two resonators attached to the underside of the duct. These resonators are not removable (even though they look like they might be). If either of them is damaged, replace the rear duct assembly.

3   Inspect the condition of the accordion pleat section that connects the two parts of the rear intake duct assembly. If it's cracked, torn or deteriorated, replace it. To replace it, simply loosen the hose clamps and separate it from the two parts of the rear intake duct.

4   There is a third, larger, resonator (see illustration) that is a sepa-

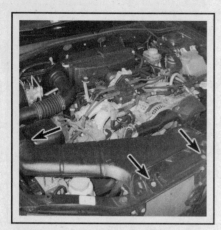

10.1 To detach the front air intake duct from the radiator crossmember, remove these two bolts, then pull it off the rear intake duct

10.2a To detach the rear air intake duct from the right strut tower, remove this bolt . . .

10.2b . . . then pull the duct off the air filter housing and lift it out. Those two funny looking things sticking down from the duct are resonators. They look like they're removable but they're not

10.4 To detach the big resonator from the engine compartment, remove this bolt (1) and pull the resonator insulator grommet (2) out of its mounting hole in the right fender wall

rate component from the air intake duct assembly. To detach it, remove the mounting bolt and pull the grommet out of its mounting hole in the right fender wall.

5   Installation is the reverse of removal.

Air filter housing

▶ **Refer to illustrations 10.6a and 10.6b**

6   Disconnect the three PCV hoses from the air filter housing (see illustrations).

7   Loosen the hose clamp that secures the air filter housing to the throttle body (see illustration 10.6b).

8   Remove the air filter housing mounting bolts (see illustration 10.6b) and remove the air filter housing.

9   Installation is the reverse of removal.

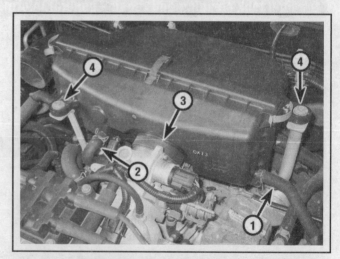

10.6b . . . disconnect the left-side PCV hose (1), disconnect the crankcase PCV hose (2), loosen the screw for the hose clamp (3) that secures the filter housing to the throttle body, then remove the two air filter housing mounting bolts (4) and remove the housing (2000 through 2004 Legacy and Outback models)

10.6a To remove the air filter housing, disconnect the right-side PCV hose . . .

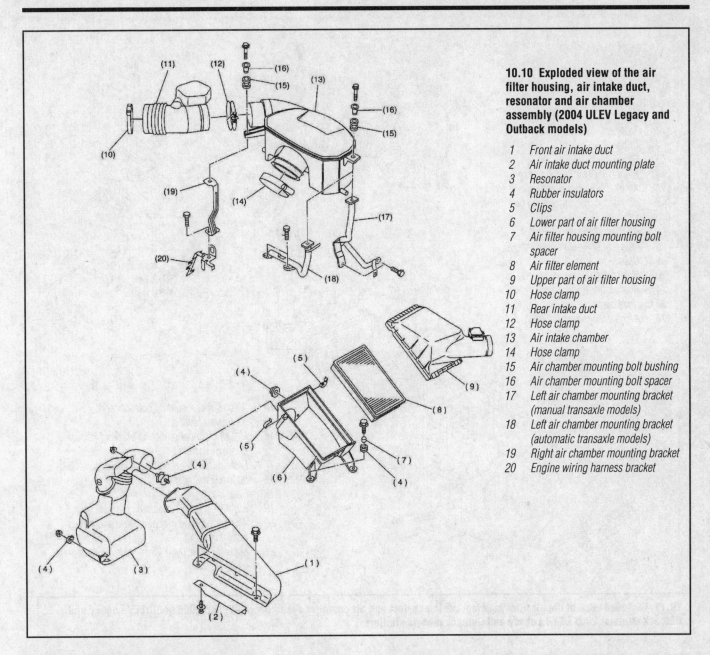

10.10 Exploded view of the air filter housing, air intake duct, resonator and air chamber assembly (2004 ULEV Legacy and Outback models)

1 Front air intake duct
2 Air intake duct mounting plate
3 Resonator
4 Rubber insulators
5 Clips
6 Lower part of air filter housing
7 Air filter housing mounting bolt spacer
8 Air filter element
9 Upper part of air filter housing
10 Hose clamp
11 Rear intake duct
12 Hose clamp
13 Air intake chamber
14 Hose clamp
15 Air chamber mounting bolt bushing
16 Air chamber mounting bolt spacer
17 Left air chamber mounting bracket (manual transaxle models)
18 Left air chamber mounting bracket (automatic transaxle models)
19 Right air chamber mounting bracket
20 Engine wiring harness bracket

2004 ULEV Legacy and Outback models

▶ Refer to illustration 10.10

10 On these models, the air filter housing (see illustration) is not located at the throttle body. It's located between the front air intake duct and the rear intake duct, which is connected to an air chamber, which looks like the air filter housing on earlier non-ULEV models, but is empty. The air chamber is connected to the throttle body. The resonator is also shaped differently and is connected to the air filter housing instead of the rear air intake duct. If you need to remove some or all of the induction assembly on one of these models, disassemble it in the sequence indicated in the caption for the accompanying illustration.

2005 ULEV and 2005 and later non-ULEV models

▶ Refer to illustration 10.11

11 On these models, the air filter housing (see illustration) is also

located between the front air intake duct and the rear intake duct, but it's split vertically, instead of horizontally like 2004 ULEV models. And there is no large resonator assembly on these models. If you need to remove some or all of the induction assembly on one of these models, disassemble it in the sequence indicated in the caption for the accompanying illustration.

2000 through 2002 Forester models

▶ Refer to illustration 10.12

12 On these models, the air filter housing (see illustration) is behind the throttle body and the air intake duct and resonator are located on the right side of the engine compartment. If you need to remove some or all of the induction assembly on one of these models, disassemble it in the sequence indicated in the caption for the accompanying illustration.

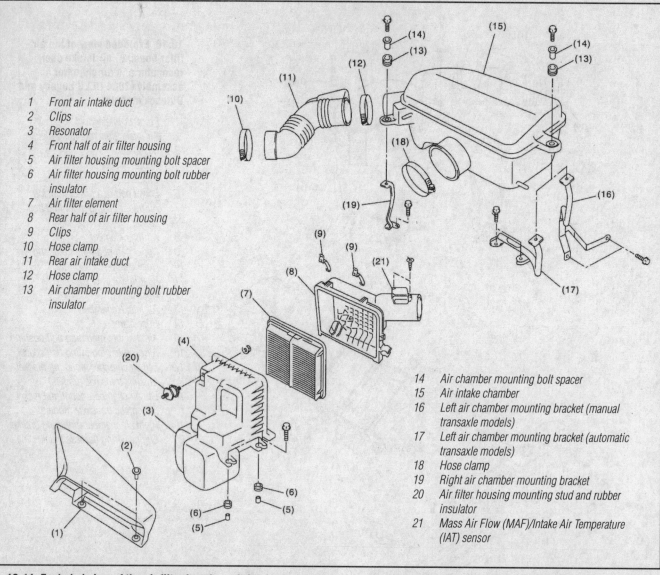

1   Front air intake duct
2   Clips
3   Resonator
4   Front half of air filter housing
5   Air filter housing mounting bolt spacer
6   Air filter housing mounting bolt rubber insulator
7   Air filter element
8   Rear half of air filter housing
9   Clips
10 Hose clamp
11 Rear air intake duct
12 Hose clamp
13 Air chamber mounting bolt rubber insulator

14 Air chamber mounting bolt spacer
15 Air intake chamber
16 Left air chamber mounting bracket (manual transaxle models)
17 Left air chamber mounting bracket (automatic transaxle models)
18 Hose clamp
19 Right air chamber mounting bracket
20 Air filter housing mounting stud and rubber insulator
21 Mass Air Flow (MAF)/Intake Air Temperature (IAT) sensor

10.11 Exploded view of the air filter housing, air intake duct and air chamber assembly (2005 and 2006 non-ULEV Legacy and Outback models, 2005 ULEV Legacy and Outback models similar)

2003 through 2005 Forester models

Air intake duct and resonator assembly

▶ **Refer to illustration 10.13**

13 To remove the front air intake duct, remove the bolt that attaches the duct to the radiator crossmember and the clip that attaches the duct to the resonator (see illustration), then pull the duct off the resonator.

14 To remove the resonator, remove the resonator mounting bolts, then pull the resonator off the rear intake duct.

15 To remove the rear intake duct (see illustration 10.13), simply pull it off the air filter housing.

Air filter housing

▶ **Refer to illustration 10.16**

16 Disconnect the electrical connector from the Intake Air Temperature (IAT) sensor (see illustration).

17 Loosen the hose clamp screw (see illustration 10.16) on the hose clamp that secures the air filter housing to the throttle body.

18 Remove the air filter housing mounting bolts (see illustration 10.16).

19 Pull up the air filter housing and disconnect the PCV hoses from the housing (see illustration 10.16).

20 Installation is the reverse of removal.

2006 Forester models

▶ **Refer to illustration 10.21**

21 On these models, the air filter housing (see illustration), which is located at the right front corner of the engine compartment, is connected to the air intake chamber by the rear air intake duct. A resonator, which is connected to and located below the front air intake duct, connects the front air intake duct to the air filter housing. If you need to remove some or all of the induction assembly on one of these models, disassemble it in the sequence indicated in the caption for the accompanying illustration.

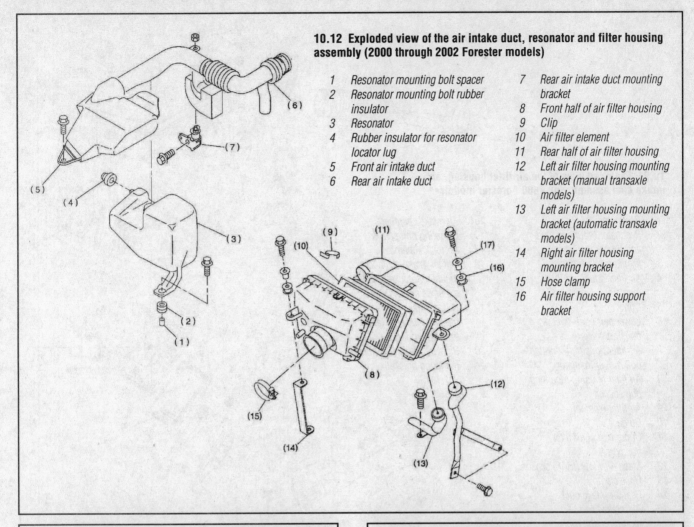

10.12 Exploded view of the air intake duct, resonator and filter housing assembly (2000 through 2002 Forester models)

1 Resonator mounting bolt spacer
2 Resonator mounting bolt rubber insulator
3 Resonator
4 Rubber insulator for resonator locator lug
5 Front air intake duct
6 Rear air intake duct
7 Rear air intake duct mounting bracket
8 Front half of air filter housing
9 Clip
10 Air filter element
11 Rear half of air filter housing
12 Left air filter housing mounting bracket (manual transaxle models)
13 Left air filter housing mounting bracket (automatic transaxle models)
14 Right air filter housing mounting bracket
15 Hose clamp
16 Air filter housing support bracket

10.13 To remove the front air intake duct (A) from the resonator (B), remove the duct retaining bolt (1) and clip (2) and pull the duct off the resonator. To remove the resonator (B), remove the two mounting bolts (3 and 4). To remove the rear intake duct (C), simply pull it off the air filter housing (2000 through 2004 Forester models)

10.16 To remove the air filter housing on a 2000 through 2004 Forester model:

1 Disconnect the electrical connector from the Intake Air Temperature (IAT) sensor
2 Loosen the hose clamp screw to release the air filter housing from the throttle body
3 Remove the air filter housing mountain bolts
4 Loosen and slide back the spring-type clamps and disconnect the Positive Crankcase Ventilation (PCV) hoses from the air filter housing

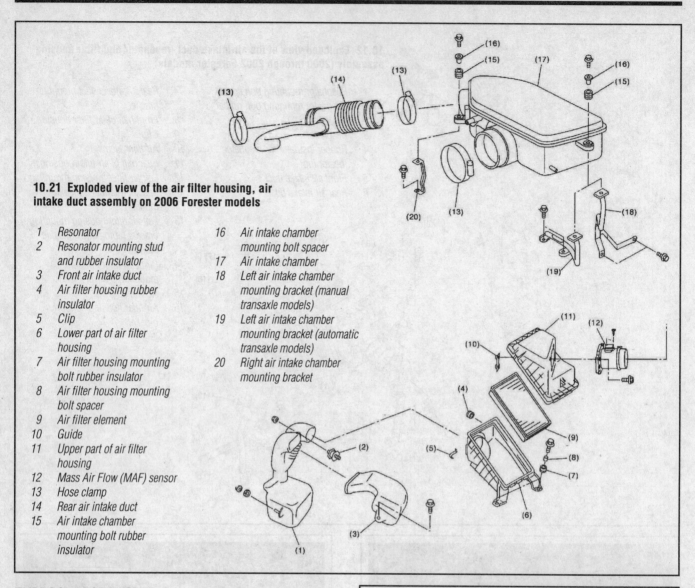

10.21 Exploded view of the air filter housing, air intake duct assembly on 2006 Forester models

1   Resonator
2   Resonator mounting stud and rubber insulator
3   Front air intake duct
4   Air filter housing rubber insulator
5   Clip
6   Lower part of air filter housing
7   Air filter housing mounting bolt rubber insulator
8   Air filter housing mounting bolt spacer
9   Air filter element
10   Guide
11   Upper part of air filter housing
12   Mass Air Flow (MAF) sensor
13   Hose clamp
14   Rear air intake duct
15   Air intake chamber mounting bolt rubber insulator
16   Air intake chamber mounting bolt spacer
17   Air intake chamber
18   Left air intake chamber mounting bracket (manual transaxle models)
19   Left air intake chamber mounting bracket (automatic transaxle models)
20   Right air intake chamber mounting bracket

TURBOCHARGED MODELS

2004 Legacy and Outback models and 2004 and later Forester models

▶ **Refer to illustration 10.22**

22 On these models, the air filter housing (see illustration) is located at the right front corner of the engine compartment. It uses a large resonator, which is connected directly to the air filter housing. If you need to remove some or all of the induction assembly on one of these models, disassemble it in the sequence indicated in the caption for the accompanying illustration.

2005 and later Legacy and Outback models

▶ **Refer to illustrations 10.23a and 10.23b**

23 On these models, the air filter housing (see illustrations) is located at the right front corner of the engine compartment. If you need to remove some or all of the induction assembly on one of these models, disassemble it in the sequence indicated in the caption for the accompanying illustration.

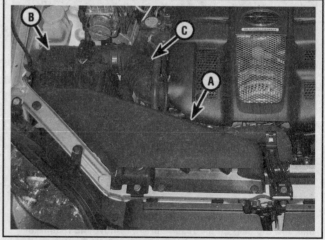

10.23a The induction assembly on turbocharged 2005 and 2006 Legacy and Outback models

A   Front air intake duct
B   Air filter housing
C   Rear air intake duct (air intake boot)

10.22 Exploded view of the air intake duct, resonator and air filter housing (2004 turbocharged Legacy and Outback models; 2004 through 2006 turbocharged Forester models similar)

1   Mass Air Flow (MAF)/Intake Air Temperature (IAT) sensor
2   Upper part of air filter housing
3   Air filter element
4   Air filter housing mounting bolt spacer
5   Air filter housing mounting bolt rubber insulator
6   Clip
7   Lower part of air filter housing
8   Rubber insulator for air filter housing mounting lug
9   Front air intake duct
10 Resonator
11 Resonator mounting stud rubber insulator
12 Hose clamp
13 Air intake boot
14 Resonator mounting stud and rubber insulator
15 Front air intake duct mounting plate

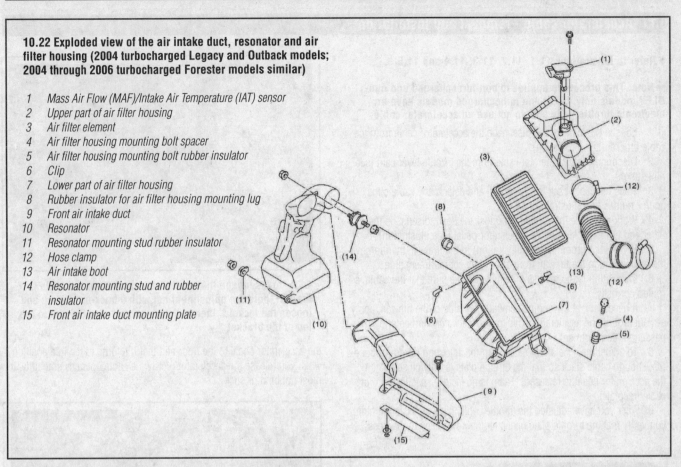

1   Mass Air Flow (MAF)/Intake Air Temperature (IAT) sensor
2   Rear part of air filter housing
3   Clips
4   Rear air intake duct (air intake boot)
5   Hose clamp
6   Air filter element
7   Front part of air filter housing
8   Front air intake duct
9   Front air intake duct mounting fasteners
10 Resonator
11 Air filter housing mounting bolt rubber insulator
12 Air filter housing mounting bolt spacer
13 Air filter housing mounting stud and rubber insulator

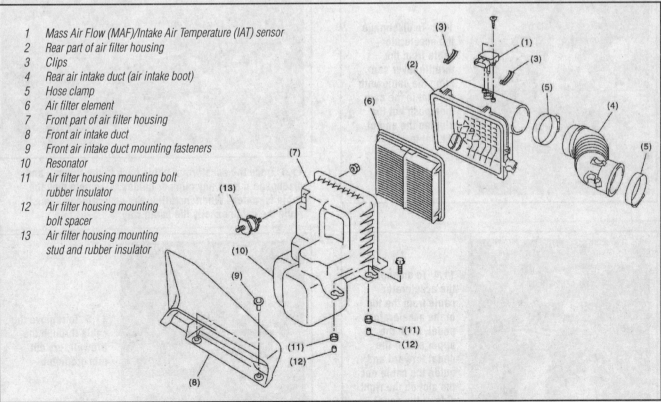

10.23b An exploded view of the air intake ducts and air filter housing assembly on 2005 and 2006 turbocharged Legacy and Outback models

11 Accelerator cable - removal and installation

▶ Refer to illustrations 11.1, 11.2, 11.3, 11.4 and 11.5

➡Note: This procedure applies to non-turbocharged and non-ULEV models only. ULEV and turbocharged models have an electronic throttle body and do not use an accelerator cable.

1   Loosen the locknut and disengage the accelerator cable from the cable bracket (see illustration).

2   Disconnect the accelerator cable from the throttle lever cam (see illustration).

3   Trace the cable back to the firewall and detach any cable clips and/or guides (see illustration).

4   Working inside the vehicle, up under the dash, disengage the other end of the cable from the accelerator pedal (see illustration).

5   Pry out the grommet (see illustration) in the firewall, then remove the cable through the firewall from the engine compartment side.

6   Installation is the reverse of removal. Make sure that the cable is routed correctly.

7   If necessary, at the engine compartment side of the firewall, apply sealant around the accelerator cable to prevent water from entering the passenger compartment.

8   To adjust the accelerator cable, turn the adjusting nut to produce just enough cable slack so that the throttle plate is fully closed when the accelerator pedal is released. (There is no factory specification for cable freeplay.)

9   After you have adjusted the throttle cable, have an assistant help you verify that the throttle plate opens all the way when you depress

11.1 To disengage the accelerator cable from the cable bracket, hold the adjustment nut with a back-up wrench and loosen the locknut, then slide the cable out of the slot in the top of the bracket

the accelerator pedal to the floor and that it returns to the idle position when you release the accelerator. Verify the cable operates smoothly. It must not bind or stick.

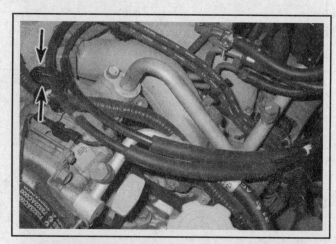

11.3 Trace the accelerator cable back to the firewall and disengage it from any clips or guides. Also note how the cable is routed. When installing the new cable you must route the cable exactly the same way

11.2 To disengage the accelerator cable from the throttle lever cam, align the cable with the slot in the cam, then push out the plug on the end of the cable

11.4 To disengage the accelerator cable from the top of the accelerator pedal, push the upper end of the pedal forward and guide the cable out the slot on the right side of the pedal assembly

11.5 To remove the cable through the firewall, pry out this grommet

12 Multipoint Fuel Injection (MFI) system - general information

MFI SYSTEM

These models are equipped with a Multipoint Fuel Injection (MFI) system. The fuel system consists of the fuel tank, an electric fuel pump/fuel level sending unit (mounted in the fuel tank), the fuel pump relay, the fuel injectors, the air filter housing and the throttle body unit. Some models are also equipped with a turbocharger. The fuel system for turbocharged engines is similar to the non-turbocharged models.

The MFI system uses timed impulses, in firing order sequence, to inject fuel directly into the intake port of each cylinder. The injectors are controlled by the Powertrain Control Module (PCM). The PCM uses an array of information sensors to monitor various engine operating conditions and delivers the correct air/fuel mixture into the intake ports by controlling the pulse width (open time) of each injector.

FUEL DELIVERY SYSTEM

An electric fuel pump located inside the fuel tank supplies fuel under constant pressure to the fuel rail, which distributes fuel evenly to all injectors. From the fuel rail, fuel is injected into the intake ports, just above the intake valves, by the fuel injectors. The Powertrain Control Module (PCM) precisely controls the amount of fuel supplied by the injectors. A pressure regulator controls system pressure in relation to intake manifold vacuum. The injectors are protected from contamination by one or two fuel filters located between the fuel pump and the fuel rail.

On 2000 through 2003 non-turbocharged Legacy and Outback models and on 2000 through 2004 non-turbocharged Forester models there is an external fuel filter in the engine compartment. These models also use another filter, which is an integral part of the fuel pump/fuel level sending unit assembly. You must change the external fuel filter in the engine compartment at the interval specified in Chapter 1. There is no specified maintenance interval for the in-tank filter on these models, but you should inspect it, clean it and replace it, if necessary, anytime that you have to remove the fuel pump/fuel level sending unit (see Section 6).

On all other models there is no external fuel filter in the engine compartment. Instead, these models rely on the filter that's an integral part of the fuel pump/fuel level sending unit. On these models, the specified maintenance interval is 30 months or 30,000 miles, whichever comes first (see Chapter 1).

AIR INDUCTION SYSTEM

The air induction system consists of the air intake duct, the air filter housing and the throttle body. Various numbers and configurations of resonators are used on different models, which help quiet down induction noise. Smaller resonators are an integral part of the air intake duct; these resonators are permanently attached to the air intake duct. Larger resonators are actually separate components that are attached to the air intake duct and are secured to the vehicle body. These larger resonators can be left in place when removing the air intake duct.

The throttle body controls the amount of air entering the intake manifold. All Non-turbocharged models, except Ultra Low Emission Vehicles (ULEVs), are equipped with a conventional throttle body that uses an accelerator cable to open and close the throttle plate. On these models, idle speed is regulated by the idle air control solenoid valve, which in turn is controlled by the PCM.

All ULEV and turbocharged models are equipped with an electronic control throttle system, which consists of an accelerator pedal position sensor, which is located at the top of the accelerator pedal, and a throttle position sensor and throttle motor, both of which are located on the electronic throttle body. Models with an electronic control throttle system do not use an accelerator cable. On these models, there is no idle air control solenoid valve; the PCM controls the idle speed by adjusting the angle of the throttle plate.

ELECTRONIC CONTROL SYSTEM

The Powertrain Control Module (PCM) controls the MFI system by processing incoming data from a wide array of information sensors, such as intake air temperature, throttle plate angle, coolant temperature, engine rpm, vehicle speed and exhaust oxygen content. The PCM compares this constantly changing data input to its map (program), then alters the operation of the engine through a series of output actuators. Typical output actuators include the ignition coil(s), the throttle plate (on models equipped with an electronic throttle body), the fuel injectors, the idle air control valve, the EVAP purge control valve, etc. For example, certain data inputs help the PCM determine what it needs to do to maintain a stoichiometric (optimum) air/fuel ratio of 14.7:1, which it maintains by altering the injector pulse width (duration of time during which each injector is open, measured in milliseconds). For further information regarding the PCM and its relationship to the engine fuel, ignition and emission control systems, see Chapter 6.

13 Fuel injection system - general check

✳✳ WARNING:

Gasoline is extremely flammable, so take extra precautions when you work on any part of the fuel system. See the Warning in Section 2.

➡**Note: The following procedure is based on the assumption that the fuel pump is working and the fuel pressure is adequate (see Section 3).**

PRELIMINARY CHECKS

1   Inspect all electrical connectors that are part of the MFI system. Loose electrical connectors and poor grounds can cause many problems that resemble more serious malfunctions.

2   Verify that the battery is fully charged. The Powertrain Control Module (PCM), the information sensors and the output actuators must receive adequate and stable voltage to function correctly.

3   Inspect the condition of the air filter element. A dirty or partially

blocked filter will severely degrade performance and fuel economy (see Chapter 1).

4   Check the fuses that are related to the MFI system. If you find a blown fuse, replace it and note whether it blows again. If it does, look for a grounded or shorted wire in the harness for the relevant circuit (fuel pump, fuel injectors, etc.). (For more information on fuses, refer to Chapter 12. For a complete guide to the fuses on your vehicle, refer to your owner's manual.)

5   Inspect the condition of all vacuum hoses connected to the intake manifold and to the throttle body. A loose, disconnected, cracked or torn vacuum hose can cause an air leak, which will cause rough running at idle or a "wandering" idle as the PCM tries to correct for the extra air entering the manifold, which leans out the air/fuel mixture.

SYSTEM CHECK

▶ **Refer to illustration 13.7**

6   Remove the air intake duct and filter housing (non-turbocharged models) or the intercooler (turbocharged models) and inspect the bore of the throttle body for dirt, carbon or other residue build-up, particularly around the throttle plate.

7   With the engine running, place an automotive stethoscope against each injector, one at a time, and listen for a clicking sound, indicating operation (see illustration). If you don't have a stethoscope, you can place the tip of a long screwdriver against the injector and listen through the handle.

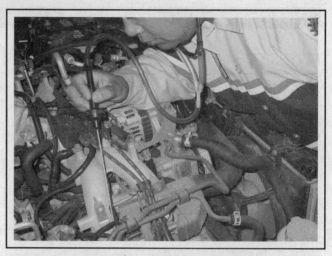

13.7 Using a stethoscope, listen to each fuel injector and verify that it's making a clicking sound when the engine is running

8   If an injector isn't operating (i.e. not clicking), inspect the condition of the injector wiring harness. Make sure that the wiring is in good shape and that the injector electrical connector is securely connected.

9   Any further diagnosis of the fuel injection system should be delegated to a dealer service department.

14 Throttle body - removal and installation

❊❊ WARNING:

Gasoline is extremely flammable, so take extra precautions when you work on any part of the fuel system. See the Warning in Section 2.

NON-TURBOCHARGED MODELS

1   Disconnect the cable from the negative battery terminal (see Chapter 5).

2   Remove the air filter housing (see Section 10).

Non-ULEV models

▶ **Refer to illustration 14.5, 14.7, 14.8, 14.9 and 14.11**

❊❊ WARNING:

Wait until the engine is completely cool before beginning this procedure.

3   Disconnect the accelerator cable from the throttle body (see Section 11).

4   If the vehicle is equipped with cruise control, disconnect the cruise control cable from the throttle body (removal is similar to that of an accelerator cable - see Section 11).

5   Disconnect the air bypass hose (for the air assist injector solenoid valve) from the throttle body (see illustration).

14.5 Disconnect the air bypass hose (1) from the throttle body, depress the release tab (2) and disconnect the electrical connector from the Idle Air Control (IAC) solenoid valve and depress the release tab (3) and disconnect the electrical connector from the Throttle Position (TP) sensor (non-ULEV models)

6   Disconnect the electrical connectors from the Idle Air Control (IAC) solenoid valve and from the Throttle Position (TP) sensor (see illustration 14.5).

7   Carefully mark and remove the coolant hoses (see illustration) from the throttle body. Clamp-off or plug the coolant hoses to prevent leakage.

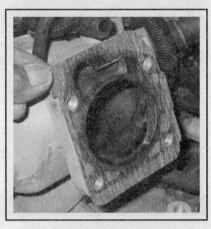

14.7 Loosen these two spring-type hose clamps and disconnect both of the coolant hoses from the underside of the throttle body (non-ULEV models)

14.8 To detach the throttle body from the intake manifold, remove these four bolts (non-ULEV models)

14.9 Remove and discard the old throttle body gasket (non-ULEV models)

8 Remove the four throttle body mounting bolts (see illustration) and remove the throttle body from the intake manifold.

9 Remove the throttle body gasket (see illustration) and discard it. Use a new gasket when installing the throttle body.

10 Thoroughly clean the gasket mating surfaces. If scraping is necessary, be careful not to damage the gasket surfaces or allow material to drop into the manifold.

11 While the throttle body is removed, inspect the bore (see illustration) for carbon deposits and/or a build-up of residue. If it's dirty, clean it out with aerosol carburetor cleaner. Make sure that the aerosol can of cleaner states specifically that it's safe for use with oxygen sensors and catalytic converters.

12 Installation is the reverse of removal. Be sure to tighten the throttle body mounting bolts to the torque listed in this Chapter's Specifications.

13 If a significant amount of coolant was lost when the hoses were disconnected, check the coolant level and top it off as necessary (see Chapter 1).

14.11 Inspect the bore of the throttle body for carbon deposits and/or a buildup of residue. If it's dirty, clean it out with aerosol carburetor cleaner (non-ULEV models)

ULEV models

14 Disconnect the electrical connectors from the Throttle Position (TP) sensor and from the Manifold Absolute Pressure (MAP) sensor.

15 Disconnect the coolant hoses from the throttle body.

16 Remove the four throttle body mounting bolts and remove the throttle body from the intake manifold.

17 Remove the old throttle body gasket and discard it. Thoroughly clean the gasket mating surfaces. If scraping is necessary, be careful not to damage the gasket surfaces or allow material to drop into the manifold.

18 While the throttle body is removed, inspect the bore for carbon deposits and/or a build-up of residue. If it's dirty, clean it out with aerosol carburetor cleaner. Make sure that the aerosol can of cleaner states specifically that it's safe for use with oxygen sensors and catalytic converters.

19 Installation is the reverse of removal. Be sure to tighten the throttle body mounting bolts to the torque listed in this Chapter's Specifications.

20 If a significant amount of coolant was lost when the hoses were disconnected, check the coolant level and top it off as necessary (see Chapter 1).

TURBOCHARGED MODELS

21 Remove the engine cover (see *Intake manifold - removal and installation* in Chapter 2A).

22 Disconnect the cable from the negative battery terminal (see Chapter 5).

23 Remove the intercooler (see Section 19).

24 Disconnect the electrical connector from the Throttle Position (TP) sensor.

25 Disconnect the coolant hoses from the throttle body.

26 Remove the throttle body mounting bolts and remove the throttle body.

27 Remove the throttle body gasket.

28 Thoroughly clean the gasket mating surfaces. If scraping is necessary, be careful not to damage the gasket surfaces or allow material to drop into the manifold.

29 While the throttle body is removed, inspect the bore (see illustration) for carbon deposits and/or a build-up of residue. If it's dirty, clean it out with aerosol carburetor cleaner. Make sure that the aerosol can of cleaner states specifically that it's safe for use with oxygen sensors and catalytic converters.

30 Installation is the reverse of removal. Be sure to tighten the throttle body mounting bolts to the torque listed in this Chapter's Specifications.

31 If a significant amount of coolant was lost when the hoses were disconnected, check the coolant level and top it off as necessary (see Chapter 1).

15 Fuel pressure regulator - removal and installation

NON-TURBOCHARGED MODELS

1 Relieve the fuel system pressure (see Section 2).
2 Disconnect the cable from the negative battery terminal (see Chapter 5).

15.4 Disconnect the vacuum hose (A) from the fuel pressure regulator, then loosen this hose clamp screw (B) and disconnect the fuel hose from the regulator

2000 through 2004 models

▶ Refer to illustrations 15.4, 15.6 and 15.7

➡Note: On these models, the fuel pressure regulator is located at the rear end of the right fuel rail.

3 Remove the air intake duct (see Section 10).
4 Disconnect the vacuum hose from the fuel pressure regulator (see illustration).
5 Disconnect the fuel hose from the fuel pressure regulator.
6 Remove the two fuel pressure regulator mounting screws (see illustration) and remove the regulator from the fuel rail.
7 Remove the old O-ring from the fuel pressure regulator (see illustration) and discard it.
8 Install new O-ring on the fuel pressure regulator. Apply a light coat of clean engine oil to the new O-ring to protect it during installation.
9 Installation is the reverse of removal. Tighten the pressure regulator mounting screws and the hose clamp securely.
10 When you're done, start the engine and check for leaks.

2005 models

▶ Refer to illustrations 15.11 and 15.12

➡Note: On these models, the fuel pressure regulator is located on top of the engine, underneath the left front intake manifold runner.

15.6 To detach the fuel pressure regulator from the right fuel rail, remove these two Phillips screws (fuel rail removed for clarity)

15.7 Remove and discard the old fuel pressure regulator O-ring. Always use a new O-ring when installing the regulator

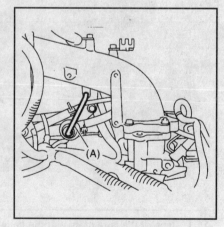

15.11 Disconnect the vacuum hose from the fuel pressure regulator (2005 non-turbocharged models)

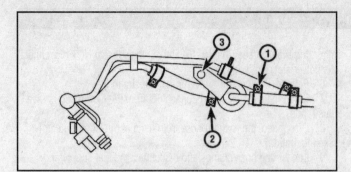

15.12 Loosen the hose clamps (1 and 2), pull back the clamps and disconnect the fuel hoses from the fuel pressure regulator, then remove the pressure regulator mounting bracket bolt (3) to detach the regulator from the intake manifold

11 Disconnect the vacuum hose from the fuel pressure regulator (see illustration).

12 Loosen the hose clamps and disconnect the fuel hoses from the fuel pressure regulator (see illustration).

13 Remove the bolt that attaches the fuel pressure regulator mounting bracket to the intake manifold.

14 Installation is the reverse of removal.

2004 and 2005 ULEV models

➡Note: On these models, the fuel pressure regulator is located at the right end of, and is an integral part of, the metal fuel pipe assembly that connects the left and right fuel rails together.

15 Remove the fuel pressure regulator protector (see illustration 5.22 in Chapter 2A).

16 Disconnect the vacuum hose from the fuel pressure regulator.

17 Loosen the hose clamp screws, pull back the hose clamps and disconnect all fuel hoses from the fuel pipe assembly (see illustration 5.22 in Chapter 2A).

18 Unbolt the fuel pipe assembly from the tumble generator valve assembly (see illustration 5.22 in Chapter 2A).

19 Remove the fuel pipe and fuel pressure regulator assembly.

20 Installation is the reverse of removal.

TURBOCHARGED MODELS

2004 models

➡Note: The fuel pressure regulator is located at the rear end of the right fuel rail.

21 Remove the engine cover (see *Intake manifold - removal and installation* in Chapter 2A).

22 Disconnect the vacuum hose from the fuel pressure regulator

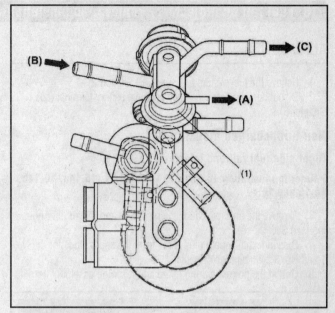

15.27 Fuel pressure regulator (2005 and 2006 turbocharged models)

1 Pressure regulator
A Vacuum hose to intake manifold
B Fuel supply hose from fuel pump
C Fuel return hose to fuel tank

(see illustration 5.30a in Chapter 2A).

23 Loosen the hose clamp screws, pull back the clamps and disconnect the hoses from the pressure regulator (see illustration 5.30a in Chapter 2A).

24 Remove the fuel pressure regulator.

25 Installation is the reverse of removal.

2005 and 2006 models

▶ Refer to illustration 15.27

➡Note: The fuel pressure regulator is located at the junction between the fuel supply and return hoses.

26 Remove the engine cover (see *Intake manifold - removal and installation* in Chapter 2A).

27 Disconnect the vacuum hose from the fuel pressure regulator (see illustration).

28 Loosen the hose clamp screws, pull back the clamps and disconnect the hoses from the pressure regulator.

29 Remove the fuel pressure regulator.

30 Installation is the reverse of removal.

16 Fuel rail and injectors - removal and installation

ALL MODELS

1 Relieve the fuel system pressure (see Section 2).

2 Disconnect the cable from the negative battery terminal (see Chapter 5).

Non-turbocharged models

Right-side fuel rail and injectors

⬧ **Refer to illustration 16.6, 16.7, 16.8, 16.11, 16.14a, 16.14b, 16.15 and 16.17**

3 Remove the air intake duct, the resonator and the air filter housing (see Section 10).

4 Disconnect the spark plug wires from the spark plugs for the No. 1 and No. 3 cylinders (see Chapter 1).

5 Unbolt the power steering pump and reservoir assembly from its mounting bracket (see Chapter 10) and set it aside. Do NOT disconnect the power steering fluid hoses.

6 Remove the fuel rail protector (see illustration).

7 Disconnect the electrical connectors from the fuel injectors (see illustration).

8 Disconnect the vacuum hose from the fuel pressure regulator (see illustration).

9 Loosen the hose clamps and disconnect the fuel supply and return hoses from the fuel rail.

⬧ **Note: On some models it's easier to disconnect the hoses when the fuel rail is being removed.**

10 Remove the fuel rail mounting bolts.

11 Remove the fuel rail and injectors from the intake manifold as a single assembly (see illustration).

12 Plug the injector holes in the intake manifold with clean shop rags to prevent debris from entering the combustion chambers.

13 Place the fuel rail/injector assembly on a clean workbench.

14 Remove the fuel injectors from the fuel rail (see illustrations).

15 Remove the old O-rings from each injector (see illustration) and discard them.

16 Install new O-rings on each injector. Apply a light coat of engine oil to each new O-ring to protect it when installing the injector into the fuel rail and the intake manifold.

17 Carefully install the injectors into the fuel rail, then secure them with the injector retainers (see illustration).

18 Install the fuel rail and injectors as a single assembly. Carefully work each injector into its mounting hole in the intake manifold until it's fully seated. Be careful not to damage the injector O-rings.

19 Install the fuel rail mounting bolts and tighten them to the torque listed in this Chapter's Specifications.

20 The remainder of installation is the reverse of removal.

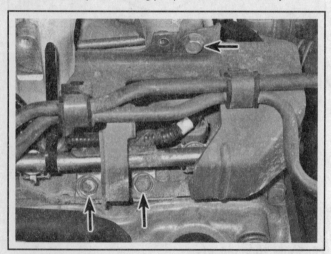

16.6 To detach the protector for the right fuel rail on 2000 through 2002 Legacy and Outback models, remove these three bolts; other models have four or five bolts securing the cover (except Forester models, which have no protective cover)

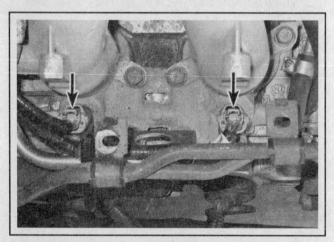

16.7 To disconnect the electrical connectors from the fuel injectors, depress these release tabs and pull off the connectors (right-side fuel rail shown)

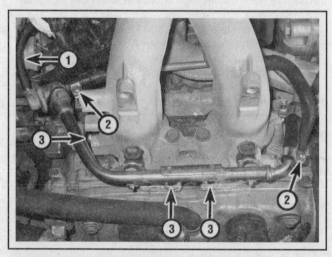

16.8 To detach the right-side fuel rail from the intake manifold:

1 Disconnect the vacuum hose from the fuel pressure regulator (it's not necessary to remove the regulator from the fuel rail to remove the fuel rail)

2 Loosen these two hose clamp screws

3 Remove the fuel rail mounting bolts (on these models, the two bolts in the middle of the fuel rail also secure the protector, so they're already removed)

16.11 To remove the fuel rail and the injectors from the intake manifold, grasp the rail firmly and pull. If either injector is difficult to dislodge from its mounting hole in the intake manifold, wiggle the injector(s) from side-to-side while simultaneously pulling on the fuel rail (right fuel rail)

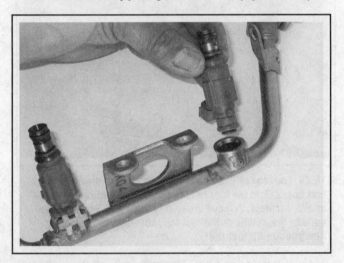

16.14b . . . and pull the injector out of the fuel rail

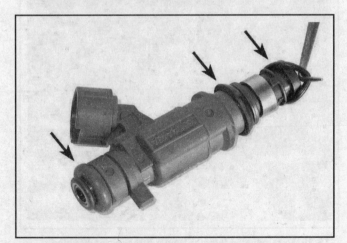

16.15 Remove the old O-rings from the fuel injector and replace them with new ones. Apply a light coat of clean engine oil to the new O-rings to protect them when installing the injector into the fuel rail and the intake manifold

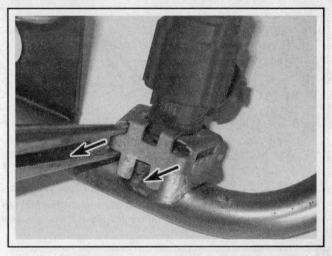

16.14a To remove each fuel injector from the fuel rail, pull off the retainer with a pair of needle-nose pliers . . .

Left fuel rail and injectors

◆ **Refer to illustration 16.24a, 16.24b, 16.24c, 16.24d, 16.25, 16.26 and 16.28**

21 On 2000 through 2004 models, remove the two bolts that secure the windshield washer fluid reservoir to the left strut tower, lift up the reservoir and disconnect the electrical connectors from the front windshield washer motor and, on wagons, from the rear window washer motor. Disconnect the rear window washer hose from the washer motor and plug the hose. Set the windshield washer reservoir assembly aside.

22 Disconnect the spark plug wires from the spark plugs for the No. 2 and No. 4 cylinders (see Chapter 1).

23 Disconnect the PCV hose from the pipe on the left valve cover (see Chapter 6).

24 Remove the fuel rail protector(s) (see illustrations).

25 Cut or remove the cable tie that secures the injector harness to the fuel rail, then disconnect the electrical connectors from the fuel injectors (see illustration).

26 Loosen the hose clamp screws and disconnect the two fuel hoses from the fuel rail (see illustration).

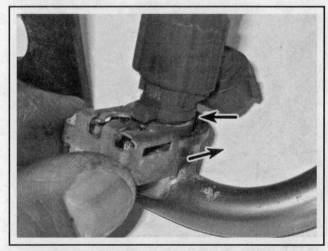

16.17 When securing each injector with its retainer, make sure that the inner edge of the retainer is aligned with the groove in the injector body, then push the retainer into place

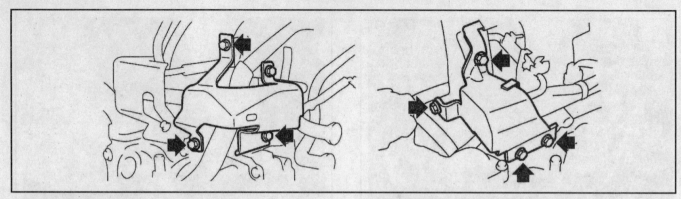

16.24 To remove the front and rear protectors for the left fuel rail on 2000 through 2002 Legacy and Outback models, remove these bolts; other models have one-piece protectors, secured by four or five bolts (except Forester models, which have no protective covers)

16.25 Cut or remove the cable tie (1) that secures the injector harness to the fuel rail, then depress the release tabs (2) and disconnect the electrical connectors from the fuel injectors. To detach the fuel rail from the intake manifold, remove these two bolts (3) and the rear bolt, shown in the next illustration (left fuel rail)

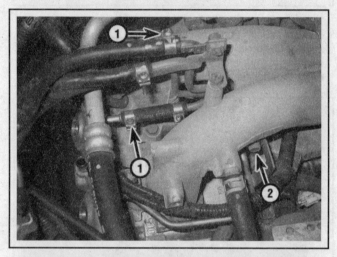

16.26 Loosen the hose clamp screws (1) and disconnect the fuel hoses from the fuel rail. To detach the fuel rail from the intake manifold, remove the rear bolt (2) and the other two bolts in the middle of the fuel rail, shown in the previous illustration (left fuel rail)

16.28 To remove the fuel rail and the injectors from the intake manifold, grasp the rail firmly and pull. If either injector is difficult to dislodge from its mounting hole in the intake manifold, wiggle the injector(s) from side-to-side while simultaneously pulling on the fuel rail (left fuel rail)

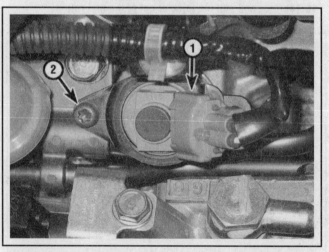

16.36 To remove an injector from a turbocharged engine, disconnect the electrical connector (1) and remove the injector retaining screw (2), then pull the injector straight up

27 Remove the three fuel rail mounting bolts (see illustrations 16.25 and 16.26).

28 Remove the fuel rail and injectors from the intake manifold as a single assembly (see illustration). The rear fuel rail pipe snakes around the backside of the intake manifold and emerges between the two intake runners, so be careful when removing the fuel rail

29 To remove the injectors from the fuel rail and replace the O-rings, refer to Steps 14 through 18.

30 The remainder of installation is the reverse of removal.

Turbocharged models

▶ **Refer to illustration 16.36**

31 Relieve the fuel system pressure (see Section 2).

32 On 2005 and 2006 models, remove the engine cover (see *Intake manifold - removal and installation* in Chapter 2A).

33 Disconnect the cable from the negative battery terminal (see Chapter 5).

34 If you're going to remove an injector from the right cylinder head (cylinder No.1 and cylinder No. 3), remove the air intake duct (see Section 10).

35 If you're going to remove an injector from the right cylinder head, remove the engine coolant reservoir (see Chapter 3).

36 Disconnect the electrical connector from the fuel injector (see illustration).

37 Remove the fuel injector retaining screw and remove the fuel injector.

38 Remove and discard the old injector O-ring and discard it.

39 Install a new O-ring on the injector and apply a light coat of engine oil to the O-ring to protect it during installation of the injector.

40 Installation is the reverse of removal.

17 Turbocharger - description and inspection

DESCRIPTION

▶ **Refer to illustration 17.2**

1 A turbocharger system increases engine horsepower by means of an exhaust gas-driven turbine that turns an impeller, or compressor, which in turn pressurizes the air entering the intake manifold. The faster the engine speed, the higher the speed of the exhaust gases and the speed of the exhaust gas-driven turbine. And the faster the exhaust gases, the faster the compressor spins, which pumps even more air into the intake manifold. As the amount of air being pumped into the intake manifold increases, so does the pressure of the air entering the manifold. This pressurized air is known as boost. The amount of boost (or intake manifold pressure) is controlled by the wastegate, a pop-off valve that's controlled by the Powertrain Control Module (PCM).

2 The turbocharger system (see illustration) consists of the turbocharger assembly, the PCM and an array of information sensors, the wastegate controller solenoid valve, the wastegate controller, the

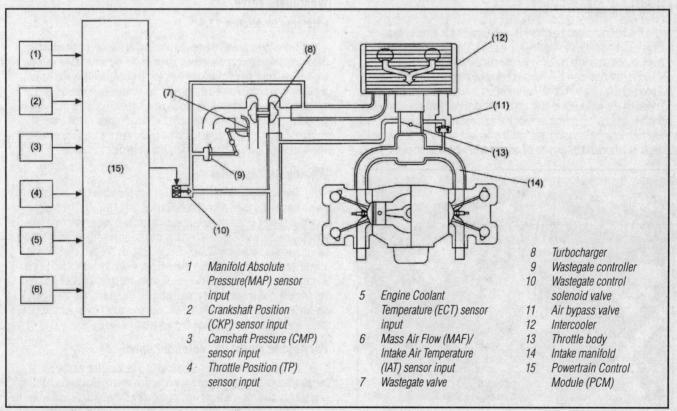

1 Manifold Absolute Pressure(MAP) sensor input
2 Crankshaft Position (CKP) sensor input
3 Camshaft Pressure (CMP) sensor input
4 Throttle Position (TP) sensor input
5 Engine Coolant Temperature (ECT) sensor input
6 Mass Air Flow (MAF)/ Intake Air Temperature (IAT) sensor input
7 Wastegate valve
8 Turbocharger
9 Wastegate controller
10 Wastegate control solenoid valve
11 Air bypass valve
12 Intercooler
13 Throttle body
14 Intake manifold
15 Powertrain Control Module (PCM)

17.2 Schematic of the turbocharger system on 2004 Legacy and Outback models and on 2004 through 2006 Forester models (others similar)

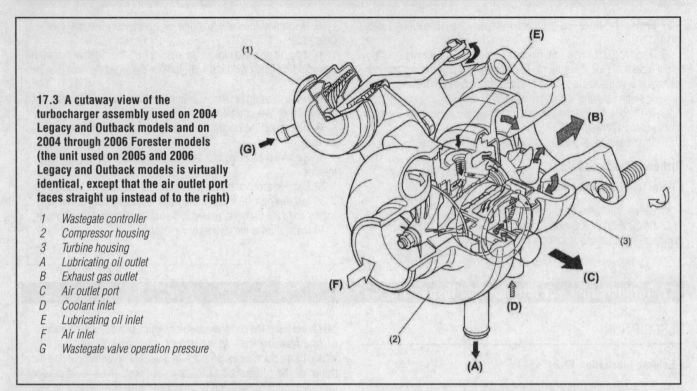

17.3 A cutaway view of the turbocharger assembly used on 2004 Legacy and Outback models and on 2004 through 2006 Forester models (the unit used on 2005 and 2006 Legacy and Outback models is virtually identical, except that the air outlet port faces straight up instead of to the right)

1 Wastegate controller
2 Compressor housing
3 Turbine housing
A Lubricating oil outlet
B Exhaust gas outlet
C Air outlet port
D Coolant inlet
E Lubricating oil inlet
F Air inlet
G Wastegate valve operation pressure

wastegate valve, the air bypass valve and the intercooler. The rest of the system - the throttle body and the intake manifold - isn't that much different from the components used on a normally-aspirated engine.

Turbocharger assembly

▶ **Refer to illustration 17.3**

3   The turbocharger assembly (see illustration) is actually two lightweight, thin-wall, heat resistant castings. The housing for the turbine is cast iron; the housing for the compressor is aluminum. A common shaft riding on full-floating bearings connects the turbine and the compressor. The turbocharger assembly is water-cooled. Coolant is pumped by the water pump through a line from the right cylinder head, then through cooling passages near the turbine shaft bearings, then out of the turbocharger housing and into the coolant reservoir. The turbocharger is lubricated by engine oil pumped through the turbocharger

17.4 A typical wastegate valve (2006 turbocharged Outback model shown, other models similar)

housing by the engine oil pump. The lubrication system also helps to cool the bearings for the turbine shaft by carrying away some of the heat generated by the exhaust gases moving through the turbine housing.

Wastegate valve

▶ **Refer to illustration 17.4**

4   The wastegate valve (see illustration) is designed to restrict the maximum boost level by allowing some of the exhaust gases to bypass the turbine when boost pressure gets too high. As long as the boost is below the predetermined threshold, the wastegate is closed, and all exhaust gases are directed through to the turbine housing. But when the boost pressure exceeds the specified level, some of the exhaust gases are diverted to the exhaust pipe by way of the wastegate valve. The wastegate valve is controlled by the wastegate controller.

Wastegate controller

5   The wastegate controller housing has two chambers inside it. One chamber contains atmospheric pressure (14.7 psi). The other chamber is connected to the output side of the compressor by a hose, and the pressure inside this chamber can be anywhere between atmospheric and the predetermined boost threshold. The two chambers are divided by a spring-loaded diaphragm, which is connected to the wastegate valve. As long as the boost pressure on the output side of the compressor is below the predetermined threshold, the wastegate controller is inactive. But when the boost pressure hits or exceeds the threshold, the controller opens the wastegate valve.

Wastegate controller solenoid valve

6   As the vehicle is driven into higher altitudes, the air thins and the atmospheric pressure goes down, which means that turbocharging pressure is also diminished. The wastegate controller solenoid valve, which is controlled by the PCM, keeps the wastegate controller closed to optimize the pressure on the outlet side of the compressor.

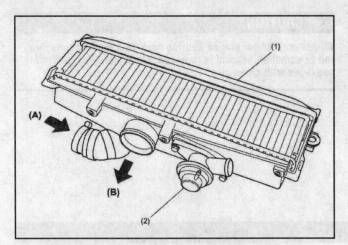

17.7a The intercooler assembly used on 2004 Legacy and Outback models and on 2004 through 2006 Forester models

1   Intercooler assembly
2   Air bypass valve
A   Pressurized hot air from turbocharger enters intercooler
B   Pressurized cooler air exits intercooler and enters throttle body

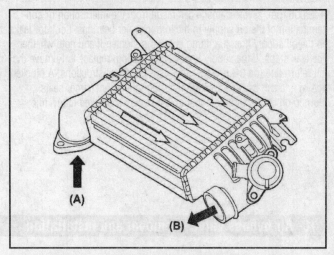

17.7b The intercooler assembly used on 2005 and 2006 Legacy and Outback models

A   Pressurized hot air from turbocharger enters intercooler
B   Pressurized cooler air exits intercooler and enters throttle body

Intercooler

▶ **Refer to illustrations 17.7a and 17.7b**

7   Have you ever noticed how your vehicle's engine seems to make more power under a load (accelerating, passing, going uphill, etc.) on a cool morning than it does later in the day when the ambient air temperature is higher? That's because the cooler morning air is denser, i.e. has more oxygen in it, which means that it can produce more power when mixed with fuel and burned. The intake air that's compressed by a turbocharger is very hot. And because hot air expands, it results in lower effective supercharging efficiency because hot air is not as dense as cold air, which means that it has less oxygen in it, which means that it will make less power when mixed with fuel and burned in the combustion chambers. But as this hot intake air passes through the air-cooled intercooler, it cools down significantly, which makes it denser again and therefore able to provide more oxygen for the combustion process.

Air bypass valve

8   When the throttle plate is snapped shut during deceleration, a sudden rise in air pressure inside the passage between the turbocharger outlet and the throttle body occurs. If not for the air bypass valve, this would cause a braking effect on the turbocharger. The air bypass valve reduces this effect by routing the excess air back to the turbocharger inlet duct. Here's how it works: The air bypass valve is mounted on the intercooler. A diaphragm housing on the bypass valve is connected to the intake manifold by a vacuum hose. When you lift your foot off the accelerator pedal, the throttle plate closes, intake manifold vacuum goes up and pulls the diaphragm up into its housing. The diaphragm is connected to a valve that opens and allows air from the intercooler to be directed through a passage back to the turbocharger inlet duct. When you accelerate again, intake manifold vacuum goes down, the spring-loaded diaphragm closes the valve and all air is once again directed from the intercooler through throttle body and into the intake manifold.

PCM and information sensors

9   For explanations of what the PCM and the various sensors do, refer to Chapter 6.

INSPECTION

Turbocharger

10   Though it's a relatively simple device, the turbocharger is a precision component. Special tools are needed to disassemble and overhaul a turbocharger, so servicing should be left to a dealer service department. However, you can inspect some things yourself, such as a cracked turbo mounting flange, a blocked or restricted oil supply line, a worn out or overheated turbine/compressor shaft bearing or a defective wastegate actuator.

11   A turbocharger has its own distinctive sound, so a change in the quality or the quantity of noise can be a sign of potential problems. But before assuming that a funny sound is caused by a defective turbocharger, inspect the exhaust manifold for cracks and loose connections. For example, a high-pitched or whistling sound might indicate an intake air or exhaust gas leak. Inspect the turbocharger mounting flange at the exhaust manifold and make sure that the hose clamp that attaches the air intake duct to the turbocharger is tight.

12   If an unusual sound is coming from the turbocharger, turn the engine off and allow it to cool completely, then remove the intake duct between the air cleaner housing and the turbocharger. Reach inside the housing and turn the compressor wheel to make sure it spins freely. If it doesn't, it's possible the turbo lubricating oil has sludged or coked up from overheating. Push in on the turbine wheel and check for binding. The turbine should rotate freely with no binding or rubbing on the housing. If it does the turbine or compressor shaft bearing is worn out.

❊❊ WARNING:

Inspect the turbocharger with the engine off and cool to the touch. Touching or reaching inside a hot and/or operating turbocharger can cause serious injury.

13   The turbocharger is lubricated by engine oil. Oil is delivered to the turbocharger by a supply line that's tapped into the right cylinder head. Oil travels to the turbocharger, where it lubricates the shaft and bearings. A return pipe routes the heated oil back to the crankcase. Because the turbine and compressor wheels spin at speeds up to

140,000 rpm, severe damage can result from the interruption or contamination of the oil supply to the turbocharger bearings. Look for leaks in the oil supply line. If a fitting is leaking, tighten it and note whether the leak stops. If the supply line itself is leaking, replace it. Remove the oil return line (on the bottom) and inspect it for obstructions. A blocked return line can cause a loss of oil through the turbocharger seals. Burned oil on the turbine housing is a sign of a blocked return line.

> **✳✳ CAUTION:**
>
> **Whenever a major engine bearing such as a main, connecting rod or camshaft bearing is replaced, flush the turbocharger oil passages with clean oil.**

18 Air bypass valve - removal and installation

2004 LEGACY AND OUTBACK MODELS AND 2004 THROUGH 2006 FORESTER MODELS

▶ **Refer to illustrations 18.2 and 18.3**

1   On 2006 Forester models, remove the engine cover (see *Intake manifold - removal and installation* in Chapter 2A).
2   On 2004 Legacy and Outback and on 2004 and 2005 Forester

models, disconnect the turbocharger inlet duct and the vacuum hose from the air bypass valve, then remove the air bypass valve mounting bolts (see illustration). Remove the valve.
3   On 2006 Forester models, remove the air bypass valve mounting bolts (see illustration), lift up the bypass valve, disconnect the vacuum hose and the turbocharger inlet duct and remove the valve.
4   Installation is the reverse of removal.

2005 AND 2006 LEGACY AND OUTBACK MODELS

▶ **Refer to illustration 18.6**

5   Remove the engine cover (see *Intake manifold - removal and installation* in Chapter 2A).
6   Disconnect the vacuum hose and air bypass hose from the air bypass valve (see illustration).
7   Remove the air bypass valve mounting bolts.
8   Remove the air bypass valve
9   Installation is the reverse of removal.

18.2 To detach the air bypass valve from the intercooler on 2004 Legacy and Outback and on 2004 and 2005 Forester models, remove these two bolts

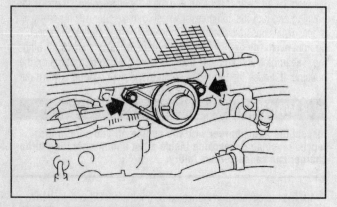

18.3 To detach the air bypass valve from the intercooler on 2006 Forester models, remove these two bolts, then lift up the valve and disconnect the vacuum hose and turbocharger inlet duct from the valve

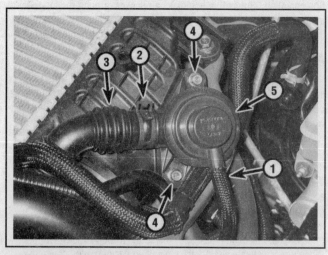

18.6 Air bypass valve assembly (2005 and 2006 Legacy and Outback models):

1   *Disconnect the vacuum hose*
2   *Loosen the spring-type hose clamp*
3   *Disconnect the air bypass hose*
4   *Remove the mounting bolts*
5   *Remove the air bypass valve*

19 Intercooler - removal and installation

2004 LEGACY AND OUTBACK MODELS AND 2004 THROUGH 2006 FORESTER MODELS

▶ **Refer to illustration 19.2**

1   On 2006 Forester models, remove the engine cover (see Intake manifold - removal and installation in Chapter 2A).

2   Disconnect the PCV hoses from the PCV metal lines and disconnect the PCV metal lines from the intercooler (see illustrations).

3   Disconnect the turbocharger inlet duct and the vacuum hose from the air bypass valve (see Section 18).

4   Remove the intercooler mounting bolts.

5   Loosen the hose clamp that secures the duct between the turbocharger and the intercooler and loosen the hose clamps that secure the duct between the intercooler and the throttle body. Lift up the intercooler and disconnect the turbocharger duct and the throttle body duct from the intercooler, then remove the intercooler.

6   If you're simply removing the intercooler to access some other component, no disassembly is required.

7   If you're removing the intercooler to replace it, remove the air bypass valve (see Section 18).

8   Remove the intercooler duct from the intercooler.

9   If you want to replace any part of the intercooler duct, loosen the clamps and disassemble it.

10 Installation is the reverse of removal.

2005 AND 2006 LEGACY AND OUTBACK MODELS

▶ **Refer to illustrations 19.15a and 19.15b**

11 Remove the engine cover (see *Intake manifold - removal and installation* in Chapter 2A).

12 Loosen the hose clamp that secures the air bypass duct to the air bypass valve, then disconnect the bypass duct from the bypass valve (see illustration 18.6).

13 Loosen the hose clamp that secures the outlet duct of the intercooler to the throttle body.

14 Remove the bolts that secure the intake duct to the turbocharger.

15 Remove the intercooler mounting bolts (see illustrations) and remove the intercooler.

16 If you're simply removing the intercooler to access some other component, no disassembly is required.

17 If you're removing the intercooler to replace it, remove the air bypass valve and install it on the new intercooler.

18 Installation is the reverse of removal.

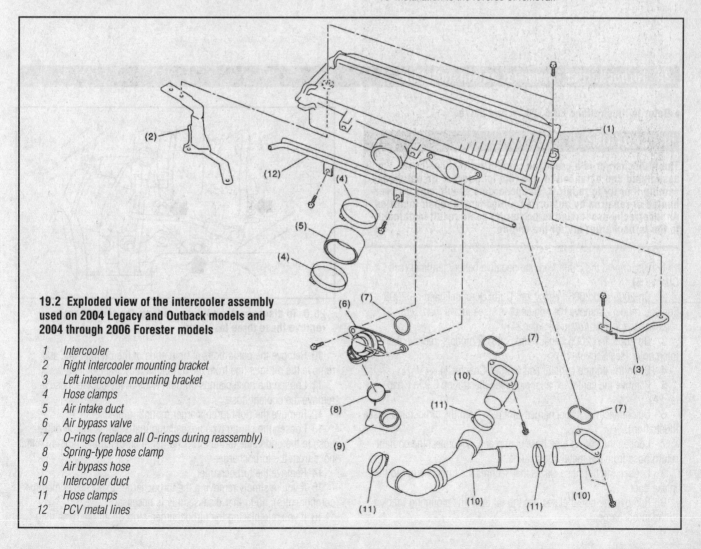

19.2 Exploded view of the intercooler assembly used on 2004 Legacy and Outback models and 2004 through 2006 Forester models

1   Intercooler
2   Right intercooler mounting bracket
3   Left intercooler mounting bracket
4   Hose clamps
5   Air intake duct
6   Air bypass valve
7   O-rings (replace all O-rings during reassembly)
8   Spring-type hose clamp
9   Air bypass hose
10 Intercooler duct
11 Hose clamps
12 PCV metal lines

19.15a To remove the intercooler, remove these mounting bolts from the right side (some models have a third mounting bolt on this side) . . .

19.15b . . . and this bolt from the left side (2005 and 2006 Legacy and Outback models)

20 Turbocharger - removal and installation

▶ **Refer to illustrations 20.6, 20.7a and 20.7b**

> ❋❋ **CAUTION:**
>
> **The turbocharger is a precision component that has been assembled and balanced to very fine tolerances. Do not disassemble it or try to repair it. Turbochargers should only be overhauled or repaired by authorized turbocharged repair facilities. An incorrectly assembled turbocharger could result in damage to the turbocharger and/or the engine.**

1 Disconnect the cable from the negative battery terminal (see Chapter 5).

2 On 2005 and 2006 Legacy and Outback models and on 2006 Forester models, remove the engine cover (see *Intake manifold - removal and installation* in Chapter 2A).

3 On 2005 and 2006 Legacy and Outback models, remove the intercooler (see Section 19).

4 Drain the engine coolant and oil (see Chapter 1).

5 Remove the center exhaust pipe (see illustration 6.9 in Chapter 2A).

6 Disconnect the turbocharger joint pipe from the turbocharger (see illustration).

7 Loosen the spring type hose clamp and disconnect the coolant return hose from the metal coolant line.

8 Loosen the big hose clamp that secures the turbocharger to the intake duct.

9 Remove the bolt that secures the oil inlet line mounting bracket to the turbocharger.

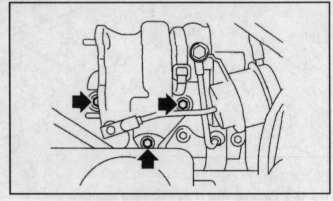

20.6 To disconnect the joint pipe from the turbocharger, remove these three fasteners

10 Remove the banjo bolts at both ends of the oil inlet line and remove the oil inlet line from the turbocharger.

11 Loosen the hose clamps on both ends of the coolant hose and remove the coolant hose.

12 Remove the right turbocharger mounting bracket.

13 Loosen the spring type hose clamp that secures the oil outlet hose to the underside of the turbocharger, then disconnect the oil outlet hose from the turbocharger.

14 Remove the turbocharger.

15 If you're simply removing the turbocharger to access some other component(s), no further disassembly is necessary.

16 If you're replacing the turbocharger, strip off all the remaining

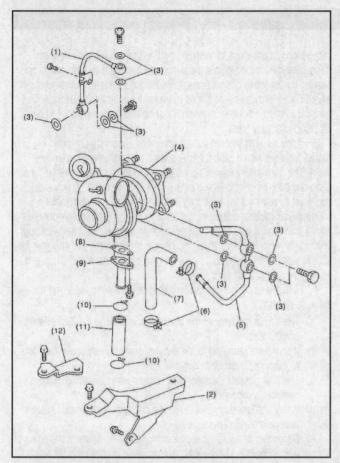

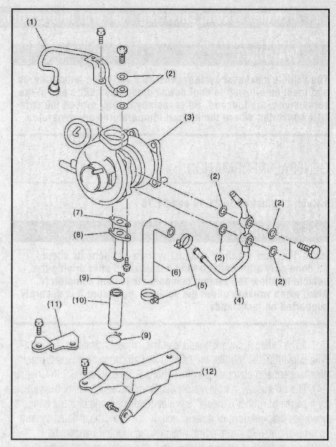

20.7a An exploded view of the turbocharger assembly used on 2004 Legacy and Outback models and on 2004 through 2006 Forester models:

1   Oil inlet line
2   Left turbocharger mounting bracket
3   Sealing washers (replace all sealing washers)
4   Turbocharger unit
5   Coolant line
6   Hose clamps
7   Coolant hose
8   Oil outlet pipe gasket (replace)
9   Oil outlet pipe
10 Spring type hose clamps
11 Oil outlet hose
12 Right turbocharger mounting bracket

20.7b An exploded view of the turbocharger assembly used on 2005 and 2006 Legacy and Outback models:

1   Oil inlet line
2   Sealing washers (replace all sealing washers)
3   Turbocharger unit
4   Coolant line
5   Hose clamps
6   Coolant hose
7   Oil outlet pipe gasket (replace)
8   Oil outlet pipe
9   Spring-type hose clamps
10 Oil outlet hose
11 Right turbocharger mounting bracket
12 Left turbocharger mounting bracket

parts and install them on the new turbocharger unit.

17 When installing the turbocharger, be sure to:

a) Use new sealing washers for the oil inlet pipe banjo fittings and, if removed, for the coolant pipe banjo fittings.

b) Tighten the oil inlet pipe banjo bolts and, if removed, the coolant pipe banjo bolts to the torque listed in this Chapter's Specifications.

c) Use a new gasket and nuts when reconnecting the joint pipe to the turbocharger. If you're reconnecting the joint pipe to the old

turbo unit, it's a good idea to clean the threads on the mounting studs with a thread chaser.

d) Apply anti-seize compound to the mounting studs and tighten the joint pipe nuts to the torque listed in this Chapter's Specifications.

18 Installation is otherwise the reverse of removal.

19 Refill the engine coolant and oil (see Chapter 1).

20 When you're done, start the engine and check for coolant, oil and exhaust leaks.

21 Exhaust system servicing - general information

⁜ WARNING:

The vehicle's exhaust system generates very high temperatures and must be allowed to cool down completely before any of the components are touched. Be especially careful around the catalytic converter, where the highest temperatures are generated.

GENERAL INFORMATION

▶ **Refer to illustration 21.1a and 21.1b**

⁜ WARNING:

Inspection and repair of exhaust system components should be done only after enough time has elapsed after driving the vehicle to allow the system components to cool completely. Also, when working under the vehicle, make sure it is securely supported on jackstands.

1   The exhaust system consists of the exhaust manifolds, the catalytic converter, the muffler, the tailpipe and all connecting pipes, brackets, hangers and clamps (see illustrations 6.5a, 6.5b and 6.9 in Chapter 2A). The exhaust system is suspended from the underside of the vehicle by a series of rubber hangers (see illustrations). If one of these hangers becomes cracked, torn or deteriorated, it can allow the exhaust system to drop slightly. At some point, when enough rubber hangers have broken, the exhaust system either hits some component underneath the vehicle, such as the rear axle, which produces an annoying buzzing noise, first at certain rpm, then eventually all the time.

2   To keep the exhaust system safe and quiet, conduct regular inspections of the exhaust system anytime that you're servicing anything underneath the vehicle. Look for any damaged or bent parts, open seams, holes, loose connections, excessive corrosion or other defects which could allow exhaust fumes to enter the vehicle. Deteriorated exhaust system components should not be repaired; they should be replaced with new parts.

3   If the exhaust system components are extremely corroded or rusted together, you'll probably need welding equipment to remove them. The convenient way to accomplish this is to have a muffler repair shop remove the corroded sections with a cutting torch. If, however, you want to save money by doing it yourself (and you don't have a welding outfit with a cutting torch), simply cut off the old components with a hacksaw. If you have compressed air, special pneumatic cutting chisels can also be used. If you do decide to tackle the job at home, be sure to wear safety goggles to protect your eyes from metal chips and work gloves to protect your hands.

4   Here are some simple guidelines to follow when repairing the exhaust system:

a) *Work from the back to the front when removing exhaust system components.*

b) *Apply penetrating oil to the exhaust system component fasteners to make them easier to remove.*

c) *Use new gaskets, hangers and clamps when installing exhaust systems components.*

d) *Apply anti-seize compound to the threads of all exhaust system fasteners during reassembly.*

e) *Be sure to allow sufficient clearance between newly installed parts and all points on the underbody to avoid overheating the floor pan and possibly damaging the interior carpet and insulation. Pay particularly close attention to the catalytic converter and heat shield.*

21.1a Some exhaust system hangers are simply pushed onto locator pins at both ends. One pin is bolted or welded to the body and the other is welded to the exhaust system

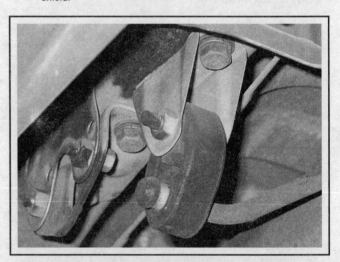

21.1b Other hangers are pushed onto a locator pin at the lower end, but secured to a mounting bracket by a bolt and nut at the upper end

Specifications

Fuel pressure (at idle)

Non-turbocharged engines
    Vacuum hose disconnected from fuel pressure regulator   41 to 46 psi
    Vacuum hose connected to fuel pressure regulator   30 to 34 psi
Turbocharged engines
    Vacuum hose disconnected from fuel pressure regulator   41 to 46 psi
    Vacuum hose connected to fuel pressure regulator   30 to 38 psi

Torque specifications   Ft-lbs (unless otherwise indicated)

Throttle body mounting bolts	
Conventional throttle body (non-turbocharged models)	191 in-lbs
Electronic throttle body (ULEV and turbocharged models)	71 in-lbs
Turbocharger assembly	
Joint pipe-to-turbocharger nuts	25.8
Oil inlet pipe banjo bolts	
Upper bolt	144 in-lbs
Lower bolt	21.7
Coolant pipe banjo bolts	24.6

Notes

Section

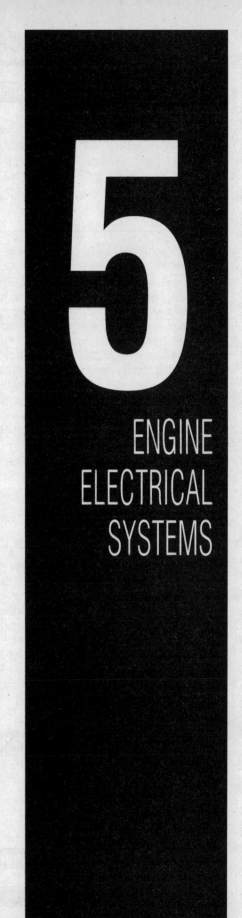

5

ENGINE
ELECTRICAL
SYSTEMS

1 General information, precautions and battery disconnection

The engine electrical systems include all ignition, charging and starting components. Because of their engine-related functions, these components are discussed separately from body electrical devices such as the lights, the instruments, etc. (all of which are included in Chapter 12).

PRECAUTIONS

Always observe the following precautions when working on the electrical system:

a) *Be extremely careful when servicing engine electrical components. They are easily damaged if checked, connected or handled improperly.*

b) *Never leave the ignition switched on for long periods of time when the engine is not running.*

c) *Never disconnect the battery cables while the engine is running.*

d) *Maintain correct polarity when connecting battery cables from another vehicle during jump starting - see the "Booster battery (jump) starting" section at the front of this manual.*

e) *Always disconnect the negative battery cable from the battery before working on the electrical system, but read the following battery disconnection procedure first.*

It's also a good idea to review the safety-related information regarding the engine electrical systems located in the "Safety first!" section at the front of this manual, before beginning any operation included in this Chapter.

BATTERY DISCONNECTION

Several systems on the vehicle require battery power to be available at all times, either to ensure their continued operation (radio, alarm system, power door locks, windows, etc.) or to maintain control unit memories (the Powertrain Control Module and other modules) that would be lost if the battery were to be disconnected. Therefore, whenever the battery is to be disconnected, first note the following to ensure that there are no unforeseen consequences of this action:

a) *The engine management system's PCM might lose some of the information stored in its memory when the battery is disconnected. This includes idling and operating values, any fault codes detected and system monitors required for emissions testing. Whenever the battery is disconnected, the computer might require a certain period of time to relearn these operating values (see Chapter 6 for more information about the engine management system and the PCM).*

b) *On any vehicle with power door locks, it is a wise precaution to remove the key from the ignition and to keep it with you, so that it does not get locked inside if the power door locks should engage accidentally when the battery is reconnected!*

Devices known as "memory-savers" can be used to avoid some of the above problems. Precise details vary according to the device used. Typically, you plug it into the cigarette lighter and connect it to a spare battery. Then you disconnect the vehicle battery from the electrical system. The memory-saver passes sufficient current to maintain audio unit security codes, PCM memory values, etc. and it also maintains always-hot circuits such as the clock and radio memory.

✳✳ WARNING 1:

Some of these devices allow a considerable amount of current to pass, which can mean that many of the vehicle's systems are still operational when the main battery is disconnected. If a "memory-saver" is used, ensure that the circuit concerned is actually "dead" before carrying out any work on it!

✳✳ WARNING 2:

If work is to be performed around any of the airbag system components, the battery must be disconnected. If a memory-saver device is used, power will be supplied to the airbag and personal injury may result if the airbag is accidentally deployed.

To disconnect the battery for service procedures requiring power to be cut from the vehicle, peel back the insulator (if equipped), loosen the negative cable clamp nut and detach the cable from the negative battery terminal (see Section 3). Isolate the cable end to prevent it from coming into accidental contact with the battery post.

2 Battery - emergency jump starting

Refer to the *Booster battery (jump) starting procedure* at the front of this manual.

3 Battery - check and replacement

✳✳ WARNING:

Hydrogen gas is produced by the battery, so keep open flames and lighted cigarettes away from it at all times. Always wear eye protection when working around a battery. Rinse off spilled electrolyte immediately with large amounts of water.

CHECK

▶ **Refer to illustrations 3.1a, 3.1b and 3.1c**

1 A battery cannot be accurately tested until it is at or near a fully charged state. Disconnect the negative battery cable from the battery

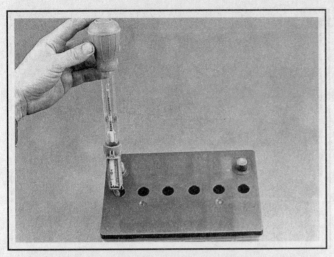

3.1a Use a battery hydrometer to draw electrolyte from the battery cell - this hydrometer is equipped with a thermometer to make temperature corrections

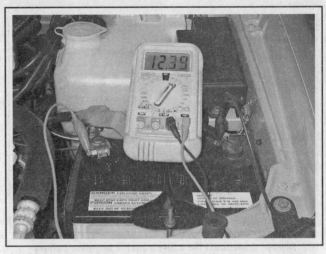

3.1b To test the open circuit voltage of the battery, connect the black probe of the voltmeter to the negative terminal and the red probe to the positive terminal of the battery. A fully charged battery should indicate about 12.5 volts

and perform the following tests:

a) ***Battery state of charge test*** *- Visually inspect the indicator eye (if equipped) on the top of the battery. If the indicator eye is dark in color, charge the battery as described in Chapter 1. If the battery is equipped with removable caps, check the battery electrolyte. The electrolyte level should be above the upper edge of the plates. If the level is low, add distilled water. DO NOT OVER-FILL. The excess electrolyte may spill over during periods of heavy charging. Test the specific gravity of the electrolyte using a hydrometer (see illustration). Remove the caps and extract a sample of the electrolyte and observe the float inside the barrel of the hydrometer. Follow the instructions from the tool manufacturer and determine the specific gravity of the electrolyte for each cell. A fully charged battery will indicate approximately 1.270 (green zone) at 68-degrees F (20-degrees C). If the specific gravity of the electrolyte is low (red zone), charge the battery as described in Chapter 1.*

b) ***Open circuit voltage test*** *- Using a digital voltmeter, perform an open circuit voltage test (see illustration). Connect the negative*

probe of the voltmeter to the negative battery post and the positive probe to the positive battery post. The battery voltage should be greater than 12.5 volts. If the battery is less than the specified voltage, charge the battery before proceeding to the next test. Do not proceed with the battery load test until the battery is fully charged.

c) ***Battery load test*** *- An accurate check of the battery condition can only be performed with a load tester (available at most auto parts stores). This test evaluates the ability of the battery to operate the starter and other accessories during periods of heavy amperage draw (load). Install a special battery load-testing tool onto the battery terminals (see illustration). Load test the battery according to the tool manufacturer's instructions. This tool utilizes a carbon pile to increase the load demand (amperage draw) on the battery. Maintain the load on the battery for 15 seconds and observe that the battery voltage does not drop below 9.6 volts. If the battery condition is weak or defective, the tool will indicate this condition immediately.*

➡**Note: Cold temperatures will cause the minimum voltage requirements to drop slightly. Follow the chart given in the tool manufacturer's instructions to compensate for cold climates. Minimum load voltage for freezing temperatures (32 degrees F/0-degrees C) should be approximately 9.1 volts.**

d) ***Battery drain test*** *- This test will indicate whether there's a constant drain on the vehicle's electrical system that can cause the battery to discharge. Make sure all accessories are turned off. If the vehicle has an underhood light, verify that it's working correctly, then disconnect it. Connect one lead of a digital ammeter to the disconnected negative battery cable clamp and the other lead to the negative battery post. A drain of approximately 100 milliamps or less is considered normal (due to the engine control compudigital clocks, digital radios and other components that normally cause a key-off battery drain). An excessive drain (approximately 500 milliamps or more) will cause the battery to discharge. The problem circuit or component can be located by removing the fuses, one at a time, until the excessive drain stops and normal drain is indicated on the meter.*

3.1c Some battery load testers are equipped with an ammeter which enables the battery load to be precisely dialed in, as shown - less expensive testers have a load switch and a voltmeter only

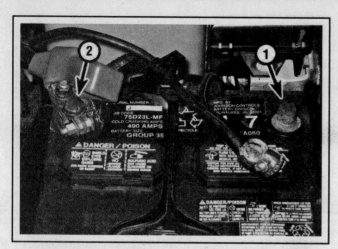

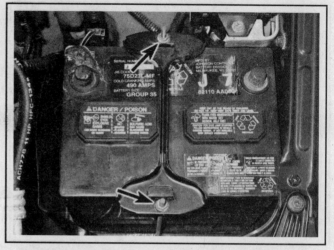

3.2 Always disconnect the cable from the negative battery terminal (1) first, before disconnecting the cable from the positive terminal (2)

3.4 To remove the battery hold-down strap, remove these two nuts

REPLACEMENT

♦ Refer to illustrations 3.2, 3.4 and 3.6

 CAUTION:

Always disconnect the negative cable first and hook it up last or you might accidentally short the battery with the tool that you're using to loosen the cable clamps.

2   Loosen the cable clamp nut and disconnect the battery cable from the negative battery post (see illustration). Isolate the cable end to prevent it from accidentally coming into contact with the battery post.

3   Loosen the cable clamp nut and disconnect the battery cable from the positive battery post (see illustration 3.2).

4   Remove the battery hold-down clamp nuts (see illustration) and remove the hold-down clamp.

5   Lift out the battery. Be careful - it's heavy. If the battery is too heavy for you, obtain a battery lifting strap to lift it out. Battery lifting straps are available at most auto parts stores for a reasonable price. They make removing and installing the battery both easier and safer.

6   While the battery is out, inspect the battery tray. The battery tray itself is plastic, so it won't corrode. But if any corrosion from the battery terminals has fallen onto the tray, remove it (see illustration) and rinse it off with water. Also inspect the area below the battery tray for any deposits of corrosion. If there's any sign of corrosion, clean the deposits with a mixture of baking soda and water to prevent further corrosion.

3.6 To remove the battery tray from the engine compartment, simply lift it out (note the directional arrow, on the floor of the tray, which points toward the front of the vehicle)

Flush the area with plenty of clean water and dry thoroughly.

7   If you are replacing the battery, make sure you replace it with a battery with identical dimensions, amperage rating, cold cranking rating, etc.

8   Installation is the reverse of removal.

9   After connecting the cables to the battery, apply a light coating of petroleum jelly or grease to the connections to help prevent corrosion.

4   Battery cables - check and replacement

♦ Refer to illustrations 4.5a, 4.5b, 4.6a and 4.6b

1   Periodically inspect the entire length of each battery cable for damage, cracked or burned insulation and corrosion. Poor battery cable connections can cause starting problems and decreased engine performance.

2   Check the cable-to-terminal connections at the ends of the cables for cracks, loose wire strands and corrosion. The presence of white, fluffy deposits under the insulation at the cable terminal connection is a sign that the cable is corroded and should be replaced. Check the terminals for distortion, missing mounting bolts and corrosion.

3   When removing the cables always disconnect the negative cable from the negative battery post first and hook it up last or you might accidentally short the battery with the tool that you're using to loosen

4.5a One battery ground cable is bolted to the left fender

4.5b Another ground cable is bolted to the top of the transaxle

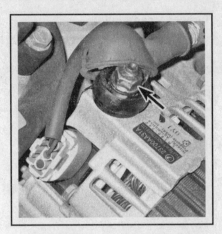

4.6a One battery positive cable is connected to the alternator

4.6b The other battery positive cable is connected to the starter solenoid terminal

the cable clamps. Even if only the positive cable is being replaced, be sure to disconnect the negative cable from the negative battery post first (see Chapter 1 for further information regarding battery cable maintenance).

4   Disconnect the old cables from the negative and positive battery terminals (see Section 3), then disconnect them at their opposite ends as follows.

5   Disconnect the ground cables from the left fender and from the transaxle (see illustrations).

6   Disconnect the positive cable from the alternator and the starter solenoid (see illustrations). (There's also a battery positive cable connected to the underside of the fuse box, but you have to disassemble the fuse box to replace this cable. This job is beyond the scope of the home mechanic.)

7   Note the routing of each cable to ensure correct installation, then detach any cable retaining clips or clamps and remove the cables.

8   If you are replacing either or both of the battery cables, take them with you when buying new cables. It is vitally important that you replace the cables with identical parts. Cables have characteristics that make them easy to identify. Positive cables are usually red and larger in cross-section; ground cables are usually black and smaller in cross-section.

9   Clean the threads of the starter solenoid or ground connection with a wire brush to remove rust and corrosion. Apply a light coat of battery terminal corrosion inhibitor or petroleum jelly to the threads to prevent future corrosion.

10   Attach the cable to the terminal and tighten the mounting nut/bolt securely.

11   Before connecting a new cable to the battery make sure that it reaches the battery post without having to be stretched.

12   After installing the cables connect the negative cable to the negative battery post.

5   Ignition system - general information and precautions

GENERAL INFORMATION

1   The ignition system is designed to ignite the fuel/air charge entering each cylinder at just the right moment. It does this by producing a high-voltage spark between the electrodes of each spark plug.

Non-turbocharged models

2   All non-turbocharged models are equipped with a single ignition coil assembly, which is located on the intake manifold, and four spark plug wires. On 2000 through 2004 models, the coil assembly is located on top of the intake manifold, right in the center of the manifold. On 2005 and 2006 models, the coil is located to the left of the throttle body, on the front left intake runner. On non-turbocharged models, the ignition coil is a waste spark design. The coil assembly actually consists of two separate coil units. Two cylinders are simultaneously fired by each coil. One cylinder is on its compression stroke and the other is on its exhaust stroke. The cylinder on its compression stroke consumes most of the secondary voltage supplied to the two spark plugs. When the plug in the companion cylinder (the one on its exhaust stroke) fires, it disperses any residual unburned air/fuel molecules, which lowers emissions.

Turbocharged models

3   Turbocharged models are equipped with four individual ignition coils. Each coil is bolted to the valve cover directly over a spark plug, and is connected directly to the plug. There are no spark plug wires.

PRECAUTIONS

4   When working on the ignition system, take the following precautions:

a) *Do not keep the ignition switch on for more than 10 seconds if the engine will not start.*
b) *Always connect a tachometer in accordance with the manufacturer's instructions. Some tachometers may be incompatible with these ignition systems. Consult the tool manufacturer's representative before buying a tachometer for use with this vehicle.*
c) *Never allow the ignition coil terminals to touch ground. Grounding the coil could result in damage to the igniter and/or the ignition coil.*
d) *Do not disconnect the battery when the engine is running.*

6   Ignition system - check

♦ **Refer to illustration 6.3**

✳✳ WARNING:

Because of the very high voltage generated by the ignition system, use extreme care when performing a procedure involving ignition components. This not only includes the coil and spark plugs, but related items connected to the system as well, such as the electrical connectors, tachometer and any test equipment.

➡**Note: The ignition system components on these models are expensive and difficult to diagnose. In the event of ignition system failure, if the checks do not clearly indicate the source of the ignition system problem, have the vehicle tested by a dealer service department or other qualified repair facility.**

1   If a malfunction occurs and the vehicle won't start, do not immediately assume that the ignition system is causing the problem. First, check the following items:

a) *Make sure the battery cable clamps, where they connect to the battery, are clean and tight.*
b) *Test the condition of the battery (see Section 3). If it does not pass all the tests, replace it with a new battery.*
c) *Check the ignition coil wiring and connections.*

2   If the engine turns over but won't start, make sure there is sufficient secondary ignition voltage to fire the spark plug.

3   To test the spark on a non-turbocharged model, obtain a calibrated ignition tester. (Such testers are available at most auto parts stores.) To use the tester, disconnect a spark plug wire from a spark plug, insert the tester into the spark plug wire boot and clip the other end to a good ground such as a valve cover bolt (see illustration). To test the spark on a turbocharged model, remove an ignition coil (see Section 7), insert the tester into the coil's boot.

4   Relieve the fuel pressure (see Chapter 4). The fuel system must be disabled while checking the ignition system.

5   Crank the engine and watch the tester.

6   If bright blue, well-defined sparks occur, the coil and, on non-turbocharged models, the spark plug wire are functioning normally. (A calibrated ignition tester doesn't tell you whether the spark plug itself is

6.3   To use a calibrated ignition tester, simply disconnect a spark plug wire (non-turbo models) or remove an ignition coil (turbo models) and connect it to the tester, clip the tester to a convenient ground and operate the starter. If there's enough power to fire the plug, sparks will be visible between the electrode tip and the tester body

functioning correctly because you are bypassing the plug.)

7   If no sparks occur or if the spark is weak or intermittent, check for battery voltage to the primary terminal of the ignition coil. If there is no battery voltage at the coil primary terminal, have the ignition system checked out by a dealer service department or other qualified repair shop.

8   Repeat this test between each spark plug wire (or ignition coil) and ground. Keep in mind that even if the coil is functioning normally and is firing the tester, one or more of the plugs themselves might be fouled, so remove, inspect and, if necessary, clean or replace the plugs (see Chapter 1).

9   If the ignition coil(s), spark plug wires and spark plugs test out okay, the Camshaft Position (CMP) sensor or Powertrain Control Module (PCM) might be defective. More advanced testing of the ignition system should be left to a dealer service department or other qualified repair shop.

7   Ignition coil - check and replacement

CHECK

➡Note: The only coils that you can check are those used on non-turbocharged models. On 2000 through 2004 models, you can check the primary, secondary and insulation resistance. On 2005 and 2006 models, there is no primary resistance specification; you can, however, check the secondary resistance on these models. There are no resistance specifications published for the individual coil units used on turbocharged models.

Non-turbocharged models

♦ Refer to illustrations 7.1 and 7.2

1   Check the primary resistance. With the ignition off, disconnect the four-terminal connector from the coil. Connect an ohmmeter across terminals 1 and 2 (see illustration). Next, connect the ohmmeter across terminals 2 and 4. Compare your measurements to the primary resis-

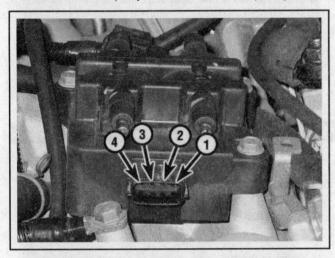

7.1 To check the ignition coil primary resistance, measure the resistance between terminals 1 and 2, then measure the resistance between terminals 2 and 4 (non-turbocharged models)

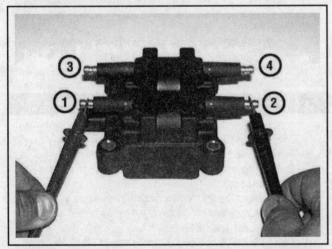

7.2 To check the ignition coil secondary resistance, measure the resistance between the paired coil towers of each coil unit (1 and 2, 3 and 4)

tance listed in this Chapter's Specifications. If the measured primary resistance is not within the specified range, replace the coil.

2   Check the secondary resistance. Connect an ohmmeter between the companion cylinder coil towers. First test cylinder numbers 1 and 2, then cylinders 3 and 4 (see illustration). The resistance should be as listed in this Chapter's Specifications for the secondary resistance. If not, replace the coil.

Turbocharged models

3   You cannot check the primary or secondary resistance of the individual coil-over-plug units used on DOHC models. If you have checked for spark with a calibrated ignition tester and have determined that there is no spark or poor spark on one of these coil units, the coil is probably bad (assuming that it's getting a primary voltage signal).

REPLACEMENT

Non-turbocharged models

♦ Refer to illustrations 7.6 and 7.7

➡Note: The ignition coil assembly is located on the top of the intake manifold on 2000 through 2005 models. 2006 models use a similar coil unit, but it's mounted vertically and is located on the left front intake runner instead of the top of the manifold. However, it's removed and installed exactly the same way as the earlier unit.

4   Disconnect the cable from the negative battery terminal (see Section 3).

5   Disconnect the spark plug wires from the ignition coil (see Chapter 1).

6   Disconnect the electrical connector from the ignition coil (see illustration).

7   Remove the ignition coil mounting bolts (see illustration) and remove the coil assembly.

8   Installation is the reverse of removal.

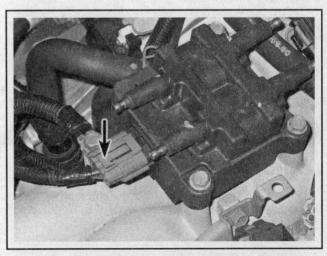

7.6 To disconnect the electrical connector from the ignition coil on a non-turbocharged model, depress this release tab and pull off the connector (2000 through 2005 unit shown; later units similar, though located on the left front intake runner, where it's mounted vertically)

Turbocharged models

➡Note: These ignition coils are mounted directly on top of each spark plug. There are no spark plug wires. Once you have removed the components that are in the way, replacing one of these coils is simply a matter of disconnecting the electrical connector and removing a mounting bolt.

Left-side coils

9 Disconnect the cable from the negative battery terminal (see Section 3).

10 Disconnect the electrical connector from the windshield washer motor.

11 Disconnect the rear window washer hose from the washer motor, then plug the connection to prevent washer fluid from leaking out.

12 Remove the two windshield washer fluid reservoir mounting bolts, then lift up the washer fluid reservoir and set it aside.

13 Disconnect the electrical connector from the ignition coil unit.

14 Remove the ignition coil retaining bolt, then detach the coil unit from the spark plug by pulling it straight out to the side.

15 Installation is the reverse of removal.

Right-side coils

16 Disconnect the cable from the negative battery terminal (see Section 3).

17 Remove the air filter housing (see Chapter 4).

18 Disconnect the electrical connector from the ignition coil unit.

7.7 To detach the ignition coil from the intake manifold on a non-turbocharged model, remove these three bolts (2000 through 2005 unit shown; later units similar, though located on the left front intake runner, where it's mounted vertically)

19 Remove the ignition coil retaining bolt, then detach the coil unit from the spark plug by pulling it straight out to the side.

20 Installation is the reverse of removal.

8 Charging system - general information and precautions

The charging system includes the alternator, a voltage regulator, a charge indicator or warning light, the battery, three fusible links and the wiring between all the components. The charging system supplies electrical power for the ignition system, the lights, the radio, etc. The alternator is driven by a drivebelt at the front of the engine.

The voltage regulator is located inside the alternator and is not separately serviceable. The voltage regulator limits the alternator's voltage to a preset value. This prevents power surges, circuit overloads, etc., during peak voltage output.

The charging system doesn't require much maintenance. However, you should inspect the drivebelt and battery at the intervals outlined in Chapter 1.

The charging system is protected by three large fusible links. In the event of charging system problems, check these fusible links for damage or broken contacts.

To protect the alternator and the charging system circuit, be very careful when making electrical connections:

a) *When reconnecting wires to the alternator from the battery, be sure to note the polarity.*

b) *Before using arc welding equipment to repair any part of the vehicle, disconnect the wiring from the alternator and the cables from the battery.*

c) *Never start the engine with a battery charger connected.*

d) *Always disconnect both battery cables before using a battery charger.*

e) *The alternator is turned by an engine drivebelt that could cause serious injury if your hands, hair or clothes become entangled in it with the engine running.*

f) *Because the alternator is connected directly to the battery, it could arc or cause a fire if overloaded or shorted out.*

9 Charging system - check

▶ **Refer to illustration 9.3**

1 If a malfunction occurs in the charging circuit, do not immediately assume that the alternator is causing the problem. First, check the following items:

a) *Make sure the battery cable clamps, where they connect to the battery, are clean and tight.*

b) *Test the condition of the battery (see Section 3). If it does not pass all the tests, replace it with a new battery.*

c) *Inspect the external alternator wiring and connections.*

d) *Check the drivebelt tension and inspect the condition of the*

drivebelt (see Chapter 1).

e) *Make sure that the alternator mounting bolts are tight.*

f) *Run the engine and verify that the alternator isn't making any abnormal noises.*

g) *Check the fusible links in the charging system (see the wiring diagrams at the end of Chapter 12). If they're burned, determine the cause and repair the circuit.*

h) *Check the charge light on the dash. It should illuminate when the ignition key is turned ON (engine not running). If it does not, check the circuit from the alternator to the charge light on the dash.*

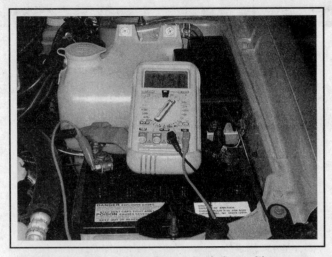

9.3 To measure charging voltage, attach the positive voltmeter lead to the battery's positive terminal and the negative lead to the negative battery terminal, then start the engine and record the voltage reading at idle

2   With the ignition key off, check the battery voltage with no accessories operating (see illustration 3.1b). It should be about 12.5 volts. (It might be slightly higher if the engine has been operating within the last hour.)

3   Start the engine and check the battery voltage again (see illustration). It should now be greater than the voltage indicated in Step 2, but not more than 15 volts. Turn on all the vehicle accessories (air conditioning, rear window defogger, blower motor, etc.) and increase the engine speed to 2,000 rpm - the voltage should not drop below the voltage indicated in Step 2.

4   If the indicated voltage is greater than the specified charging voltage, replace the voltage regulator.

➡**Note: On these models, it is recommended that the alternator and voltage regulator be replaced as a complete unit, using either a rebuilt or new alternator.**

5   If the indicated voltage reading is less than the specified charging voltage, the alternator is probably defective. Have the charging system checked at a dealer service department or other properly equipped repair facility.

➡**Note: Many auto parts stores will bench test an alternator off the vehicle. Refer to your local auto parts store regarding their policy, many will perform this service free of charge.**

10 Alternator - removal and installation

▶ **Refer to illustrations 10.4 and 10.5**

1   Disconnect the cable from the negative battery terminal (see Section 3).

2   Remove the drivebelt cover and remove the alternator drivebelt (see Chapter 1).

3   If the vehicle is equipped with cruise control, and if the cruise control cable is clipped to the small bracket that's located right behind the alternator electrical connector, detach the clip and set the cable

aside to give yourself more room to work.

4   Disconnect the battery cable and the electrical connector from the alternator (see illustration).

5   Remove the adjustment and pivot bolts and separate the alternator from the engine (see illustration).

6   Installation is the reverse of removal.

7   After the alternator is installed, adjust the drivebelt tension (see Drivebelt check, adjustment and replacement in Chapter 1).

10.4 Remove this nut (1) and disconnect the battery cable from the B+ terminal, then depress this release tab (2) and disconnect the electrical connector from the alternator

10.5 To detach the alternator from the engine, remove the adjustment bolt (A) and the pivot bolt (B), then lift the alternator out of the engine compartment

11 Starting system - general information and precautions

The starting system consists of the battery, the ignition switch fuse, the ignition switch, the starter relay, the clutch start switch (manual transaxles), the Transaxle Range (TR) sensor (automatic transaxles), the starter motor/solenoid assembly and the wiring connecting all of these components. The ignition switch fuse and starter relay are located in the fuse and relay box located behind the right kick panel inside the vehicle.

When the ignition key is turned to the START position, battery voltage is directed through the ignition switch fuse to the starter relay. The starter relay closes the starter control circuit, which runs through either the clutch start switch (manual transaxle) or the TR sensor (automatic transaxle). If the clutch pedal is depressed or the transaxle is in Neutral (manual transaxle), or if the shift lever is in PARK or NEUTRAL (automatic transaxle), battery voltage is sent to the starter solenoid, which engages the starter motor pinion gear with the flywheel/driveplate and the starter motor cranks the engine.

The starter motor on a vehicle equipped with a manual transaxle can be operated only when the clutch pedal is depressed. The starter on a vehicle equipped with an automatic transaxle can be operated only when the transaxle selector lever is in PARK or NEUTRAL.

Always observe the following precautions when working on the starting system:

a) *Excessive cranking of the starter motor can overheat it and cause serious damage. Never operate the starter motor for more than 15 seconds at a time without pausing for at least two minutes to allow it to cool.*

b) *The starter is connected directly to the battery and could arc or cause a fire if mishandled, overloaded or short-circuited.*

c) *Always detach the negative battery cable from the negative battery terminal before working on the starting system.*

12 Starter motor and circuit - in-vehicle check

▶ **Refer to illustrations 12.5 and 12.6**

1 If a malfunction occurs in the starting circuit, do not immediately assume that the starter is causing the problem. First, check the following items:

a) *Make sure that the battery cable clamps, where they connect to the battery terminals, are clean and tight.*

b) *Inspect the condition of the battery cables (see Section 4). Always replace defective battery cables with new ones.*

c) *Test the condition of the battery (see Section 3). If it does not pass all the tests, replace it with a new battery.*

d) *Inspect the condition of the starter wiring and connections. Refer to the wiring diagrams at the end of Chapter 12.*

e) *Make sure that the starter mounting bolts are tight.*

f) *Inspect any fusible links (if equipped) in the starter circuit (see the wiring diagrams at the end of Chapter 12). If they're burned, determine the cause and repair the circuit. Also inspect the ignition switch circuit (see the wiring diagrams at the end of Chapter 12).*

g) *Check the operation of the Transaxle Range (TR) sensor (automatic transaxle) or clutch start switch (manual transaxle). Make sure that the shift lever is in PARK or NEUTRAL. (automatic transaxle) or the clutch pedal is pressed (manual transaxle). The TR sensor or clutch start switch must operate correctly to provide battery voltage to the ignition switch. To replace and/or adjust the TR sensor, refer to Chapter 6. To replace and/or adjust the clutch start switch, refer to Chapter 8.*

2 If the starter does not actuate when the ignition switch is turned to the START position, check for battery voltage to the solenoid. Connect a test light or voltmeter to the starter solenoid positive terminal and have an assistant turn the ignition switch to the START position.

3 If there's no voltage at the solenoid, check the ignition switch fuse and the starter relay.

4 If there is voltage at the solenoid, but the starter motor does not operate, remove the starter (see Section 13) and bench test it (see Step 6).

5 If the starter turns over slowly, check the starter cranking voltage and the current draw from the battery. This test must be performed with the starter on the engine. Crank the engine over (for 10 seconds or less) and observe the battery voltage. It should not drop below 8.0 volts on manual transaxle models or 8.5 volts on automatic transaxle models. Also, observe the current draw using an ammeter (see illustration). It should not exceed 400 amps or drop below 250 amps.

12.5 To measure starter current draw with an inductive ammeter, simply hold the ammeter over the positive or negative cable (whichever cable has better clearance), then have an assistant crank over the engine

❋❋ CAUTION:

The battery cables may be excessively heated because of the large amount of amperage being drawn from the battery. Discontinue the testing until the starting system has cooled down. If the starter motor cranking amp values are not within the correct range, replace it with a new unit. There are several conditions that may affect the starter cranking potential. The battery must be in good condition and the battery cold-cranking rating must not be under-rated for the particular application. Be sure to check the battery specifications carefully. The battery terminals and cables must be clean and not corroded. Also, in cases of extreme cold temperatures, make sure the battery and/or engine block is warmed before performing the tests.

6   If the starter is getting voltage but doesn't operate, remove the starter motor (see Section 13) and test it on the bench (see illustration). Most likely the solenoid is defective. In some rare cases, the engine might be seized, so be sure to try and rotate the crankshaft pulley (see Chapter 2A) before proceeding. With the starter/solenoid assembly mounted in a vise on the bench, install one jumper cable from the negative battery terminal to the body of the starter. Install the other jumper cable from the positive battery terminal to the B+ terminal on the starter. Install a starter switch and apply battery voltage to the solenoid S terminal (for 10 seconds or less) and see if the solenoid plunger, shift lever and overrunning clutch extends and rotates the pinion drive. If the pinion drive extends but does not rotate, the solenoid is operating but

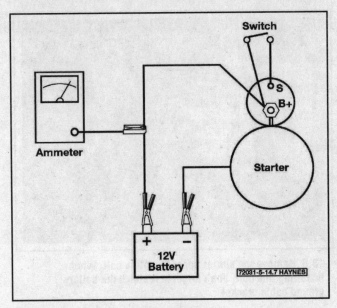

12.6 Starter motor bench testing details

the starter motor is defective. If there is no movement but the solenoid clicks, the solenoid and/or the starter motor is defective. If the solenoid plunger extends and rotates the pinion drive, the starter/solenoid assembly is working properly.

13 Starter motor - removal and installation

▶ **Refer to illustration 13.3, 13.4, 13.5 and 13.7**

1   Disconnect the cable from the negative battery terminal (see Section 3).
2   On non-turbo models, remove the air filter housing (see Chapter 4). On turbo models, remove the intercooler (see Chapter 4).
3   On non-turbo models, remove the air filter housing support bracket (see illustration).
4   Disconnect the wire and the large cable from the terminals on the starter solenoid (see illustration).

13.3 To detach the air filter housing support bracket, remove these two bolts (automatic transaxle shown manual transaxle is similar)

13.4 Remove this nut (1) and disconnect the starter cable from the B+ terminal on the starter solenoid, then depress this release tab (2) and disconnect the electrical connector from the solenoid

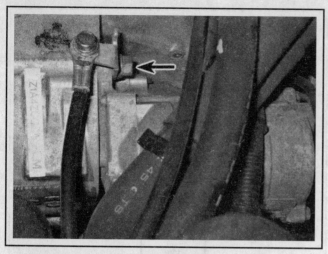

13.5 Remove the starter upper mounting bolt. When installing this bolt, don't forget to reattach the battery ground cable bracket

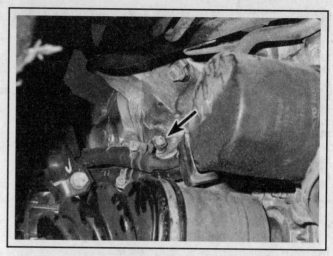

13.7 Remove the starter motor lower mounting bolt

5   Remove the upper starter motor mounting bolt (see illustration).
6   Raise the vehicle and place it securely on jackstands.
7   Remove the lower starter motor mounting bolt and detach the

starter from the engine (see illustration).
8   Installation is the reverse of removal.

Specifications

Firing order	1-3-2-4
Charging voltage	13.5 to 15 volts

Ignition coil

2000 through 2004 non-turbocharged models and 2004 ULEV models	
Primary resistance	0.657 to 1.387 ohms
Secondary resistance	10.88 to 14.72 k-ohms
Insulation resistance	More than 100 M-ohms
2005 non-turbocharged models	
Secondary resistance only	
Non-ULEV models	9.52 to 12.88 k-ohms
ULEV models	10.88 to 14.72 k-ohms
2006 non-turbocharged models (non-ULEV and ULEV models)	
Secondary resistance only	9.52 to 12.88 k-ohms
2004 through 2006 turbocharged models	N/A

6

EMISSIONS
AND ENGINE
CONTROL
SYSTEMS

Section

1 General information

▶ **Refer to illustration 1.6**

To minimize emission of tailpipe emissions into the atmosphere, both from incompletely burned and from evaporating gases, and to maintain good driveability and fuel economy, various emission control systems are used on these vehicles. They include the:

Evaporative Emission Control (EVAP) system
Exhaust Gas Recirculation (EGR) system
Multipoint Fuel Injection (MFI) system
Positive Crankcase Ventilation (PCV) system
Catalytic converters
Variable Valve Lift system
Variable Valve Timing system

The Sections in this Chapter include general descriptions, general inspection procedures within the scope of the home mechanic and component replacement procedures, where possible, for the compo-

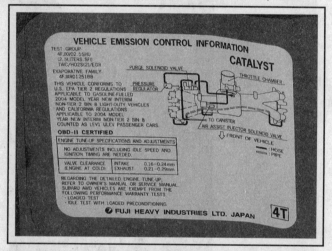

1.6 The Vehicle Emission Control Information (VECI) label is located in the engine compartment, usually on the underside of the hood, and specifies the emission systems used on your vehicle, tune-up specifications, if applicable, and vacuum hose routing

nents used in each of the systems listed above. You'll also find a general description of each information sensor and output actuator used in the engine management system, including its function and location, and a brief description of how it works (see Section 2). We have also included replacement procedures for all sensors and actuators.

Before assuming that an emissions control system is malfunctioning, check the fuel and ignition systems carefully. The diagnosis of some emission control devices requires specialized tools, equipment and training. If checking and servicing become too difficult or if a procedure is beyond your ability, consult a dealer service department or other repair shop. Remember, the most frequent cause of emissions problems is simply a loose or broken wire or vacuum hose, so always check the hose and wiring connections first.

This doesn't mean, however, that emissions control systems are particularly difficult to maintain and repair. You can quickly and easily perform many checks and do most of the regular maintenance at home with common tune-up and hand tools.

➡**Note: Because of a Federally mandated warranty which covers the emissions control system components, check with your dealer about warranty coverage before working on any emissions-related systems.**

Once the warranty has expired, you may wish to perform some of the component checks and/or replacement procedures in this Chapter to save money.

Pay close attention to any special precautions outlined in this Chapter. It should be noted that the illustrations of the various systems may not exactly match the system installed on your vehicle because of changes made by the manufacturer during production or from year-to-year.

A Vehicle Emissions Control Information (VECI) label (see illustration) is attached to the underside of the hood. This label contains important emissions specifications and adjustment information. Part of this label, the vacuum hose routing diagram, provides a vacuum hose schematic with emissions components identified. When servicing the engine or emissions systems, always refer to the VECI label and the vacuum hose routing diagram on your vehicle for up-to-date information.

2 On-Board Diagnostic (OBD) system and trouble codes

SCAN TOOL INFORMATION

▶ **Refer to illustration 2.2**

1 Hand-held scanners are the most powerful and versatile tools for analyzing engine management systems used on later model vehicles. Early model scanners handle codes and some diagnostics for many systems. Each brand of scan tool must be examined carefully to match the year, make and model of the vehicle you are working on. Some scan tools can use interchangeable cartridges, which are configured to

access the engine management systems of a specific automotive manufacturer. Some scan tool manufacturers offer cartridges compatible with vehicles manufactured on different continents (Asia, North America, Europe).

2 With the arrival of the Federally mandated emission control system (OBD-II), specially designed aftermarket scanners have been developed. Several tool manufacturers have released OBD-II scan tools for the home mechanic (see illustration). Aftermarket generic scanners should work with any model covered by this manual. Before purchasing a generic scan tool, contact the manufacturer of the scanner you're

planning to buy and verify that it will work properly with the OBD-II system that you want to scan. If necessary, of course, you can always have the codes extracted by a dealer service department or an independent repair shop with a professional scan tool.

OBD SYSTEM GENERAL DESCRIPTION

3   All models are equipped with the second generation On-Board Diagnostic (OBD-II) system. The OBD-II system includes a computer known as the Powertrain Control Module (PCM), information sensors that monitor various functions of the engine and send data to the PCM, and output actuators that carry out the PCM's various control commands. The OBD-II system also incorporates a series of diagnostic monitors that detect and identify fuel injection and emission control system faults and store the information in the computer memory. The system also tests sensors and output actuators, diagnoses drive cycles, freezes data and clears codes.

4   This powerful diagnostic computer must be accessed with an OBD-II scan tool and the 16 pin Data Link Connector (DLC) located under the driver's dash area. The PCM is the brain of the electronically controlled fuel and emissions system. It receives data from a number of sensors and other electronic components (switches, relays, etc.). Based on the information it receives, the PCM generates output signals to control various relays, solenoids (i.e. fuel injectors) and other actuators. The PCM is specifically calibrated to optimize the emissions, fuel economy and driveability of the vehicle.

5   It isn't a good idea to attempt diagnosis or replacement of the PCM or emission control components at home while the vehicle is under warranty. Because of a Federally mandated warranty which covers the emissions system components and because any owner-induced damage to the PCM, the sensors and/or the control devices may void this warranty, take the vehicle to a dealer service department if the PCM or a system component malfunctions.

INFORMATION SENSORS

➡Note: The following list provides a brief description of the function, operation and location of each of the important information sensors. We use the standard sensor terminology recommended by the Society of Automotive Engineers (SAE). Where Subaru uses other names for some sensors we provide the Subaru name as well.

6   **Accelerator Pedal Position (APP) sensor** - All turbocharged models and Ultra-Low Emission Vehicles (ULEVs) covered by this manual are equipped with an electronic control throttle system. The electronic control throttle system dispenses with a conventional accelerator cable by using an electronic throttle body instead of a conventional cable-operated throttle body. The Powertrain Control Module (PCM) controls the position of the throttle plate with a solenoid that's located in the throttle body. The PCM's commands are based on the inputs that it receives from the APP sensor, which is located at the top of the accelerator pedal assembly. Its electrical output signal, which is proportional to the angle of the accelerator pedal, is used by the electronic control throttle system to determine the corresponding opening angle of the throttle plate inside the throttle body.

7   **Barometric Pressure (BARO) senso**r or atmospheric pressure sensor or - The BARO sensor is used on 2000 Legacy and Outback models and on 2000 through 2002 Forester models. It's mounted on a small bracket, which is located on the right side of the engine compartment, usually on the right strut tower. The BARO sensor is a small barometer that measures atmospheric pressure, which is one of

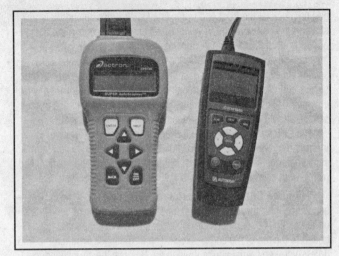

2.2 Scanners like these from Actron and AutoXray are powerful and (compared to the proprietary scan tools used at dealerships) relatively inexpensive. They can access all the generic (PO) codes, display definitions of codes, detect freeze frame information and have a lot of other features that were once found only on expensive professional scanners

the inputs needed by the PCM to calculate the pulse width (on-time) of the fuel injectors. (Subaru refers to the BARO sensor as an *atmospheric pressure sensor.*)

8   **Camshaft Position (CMP) sensor** - The CMP sensor monitors the position of the camshaft(s) and tells the Powertrain Control Module (PCM) when the piston in the No. 1 cylinder is on its compression stroke. The PCM uses the CMP sensor signal to synchronize the sequential firing of the fuel injectors.

On non-turbocharged engines, the CMP sensor is a *variable reluctance* type sensor that generates an analog (sine wave) signal pulse each time that a boss on the *tone wheel* passes by the sensor. The tone wheel is a ring that is mounted on the backside of the camshaft sprocket. The PCM counts the number of pulses and calculates the angular position of the camshaft. On non-turbocharged engines the CMP sensor is located on the left camshaft support, which is mounted between the backside of the timing belt cover and the front end of the left cylinder head.

On 2004 ULEV models, the CMP sensor is in the same location on the engine and works the same way as the CMP sensors on other non-turbocharged engines. On ULEV models, the CMP sensor is identical in location, design and operation to the CMP sensor described above for non-turbocharged engines.

On turbocharged models, there are two CMP sensors, one for each cylinder head. The CMP sensors are Hall Effect type sensors. The CMP sensor generates a pulse when one of the slots in the tone wheel passes by the sensor. The PCM measures the pulse and uses this calculation to determine when the piston in the No. 1 cylinder is on its compression stroke. On turbocharged engines, the CMP sensor is located on the cylinder head.

9   **Clutch Pedal Position (CPP) switch** - The CPP switch is used on 2004 and later Ultra Low Emission Vehicles (ULEVs). The CPP switch is basically a clutch start switch that's wired into the Powertrain Control Module (PCM). If you need to replace the CPP switch, refer to *Clutch start switch - replacement* in Chapter 8.

10   **Crankshaft Position (CKP) sensor** - The CKP sensor is mounted on top of the oil pump, which is located at the front of the

engine block, at the front end of the crankshaft, right behind the crankshaft timing belt sprocket. A *pulse wheel* or *tone wheel* is mounted on the front of the crankshaft right behind the timing belt sprocket. As the crankshaft rotates, each tooth on the tone wheel moves past the sensor. As each tooth moves past the sensor, the magnetic flux in the sensor coil changes because the air gap between the sensor tone wheel changes. This change in magnetic flux induces a voltage pulse in the sensor, and this pulse is sent to the PCM as an output signal.

The CKP sensor is the primary sensor that provides ignition information to the PCM. The PCM uses the CKP sensor to determine crankshaft position (which piston will be at TDC next) and crank speed (rpm), both of which it needs to synchronize the ignition system.

11 Engine Coolant Temperature (ECT) sensor - The ECT sensor, which measures the temperature of the engine coolant, is located on the engine coolant passage, which is the cast external passage bolted to the top of the engine block. The ECT sensor is difficult to find unless you know what you're looking for. Remove the air intake duct and look for the ECT sensor, which is located below the right rear intake manifold runner. The ECT sensor is screwed into the backside of the engine coolant pipe (the external coolant passage casting bolted to the top of the engine block). The wire to the connector is light gray on virtually all models, although Subaru does refer to the wire color for some ECT sensors as "non-colored" (white or natural).

The ECT sensor is a thermistor, i.e. its resistance decreases as the temperature increases, and its resistance increases as the temperature decreases. This type of thermistor is also referred to as a Negative Temperature Coefficient (NTC) thermistor. This variable resistance produces an analogous voltage drop across the sensor terminals, thus providing an electrical signal to the PCM that accurately reflects the engine coolant temperature.

The ECT sensor is a critical sensor because it tells the PCM when the engine is warmed up sufficiently to go into closed loop operation. And once the engine is in closed loop, the PCM also uses the ECT sensor to control fuel injector pulse width and ignition timing, and it uses the ECT sensor signal to determine when to purge the EVAP system.

12 Exhaust gas temperature sensor - The exhaust gas temperature sensor, which is used on turbocharged models, is located in the exhaust pipe that connects and is welded to the upstream and downstream catalytic converters. The exhaust gas temperature sensor measures the temperature of the exhaust gases exiting the upstream catalyst. The PCM uses this information to trim the pulse width of the fuel injectors so that the upstream catalyst doesn't overheat.

13 Fuel tank pressure sensor - The fuel tank pressure sensor is a component of the Evaporative Emission Control (EVAP) system. It's located at the fuel tank, in the line between the fuel tank sensor control valve and the fuel tank. The fuel tank pressure sensor monitors the pressure of fuel vapors inside the tank. When the vapor pressure exceeds the upper threshold, the fuel tank pressure sensor signals the PCM, which opens the pressure control solenoid valve, allowing the fuel vapors to migrate to the EVAP canister, where they are stored until they're purged.

14 Fuel temperature sensor - The fuel temperature sensor is an integral part of the fuel level sending unit, which is a component of the fuel pump/fuel level sending unit assembly, which is located in the fuel tank. The fuel temperature sensor cannot be serviced separately from the fuel level sending unit. If you need to replace the fuel temperature sensor, replace the fuel level sending unit.

15 Intake Air Temperature (IAT) sensor - The IAT sensor is used by the PCM to calculate air density, which is one of the variables that it must know in order to calculate injector pulse width and adjust

ignition timing (to prevent spark knock when air intake temperature is high). Like the ECT sensor, the IAT sensor is a Negative Temperature Coefficient (NTC) type thermistor, whose resistance decreases as the temperature increases. The IAT sensor is an integral component of the Manifold Absolute Pressure (MAP) sensor on some models (see paragraph 18), and an integral component of the Mass Air Flow (MAF) sensor on other models (see paragraph 19).

The IAT sensor is located on the air filter housing on 2000 and 2001 and 2003 and 2004 Legacy and Outback models, and on 2003 Forester models.

16 Intake Air Temperature/Manifold Absolute Pressure (IAT/MAP) sensor - The functions of the MAP and IAT sensors are combined into one assembly on 2000 and 2001 Legacy and Outback models with an automatic transaxle, on 2002 Legacy and Outback models and on all 2000 through 2002 Forester models. The IAT/MAP sensor is located on top of the throttle body on all of these models. If either the MAP or the IAT function of this sensor fails, you must replace the IAT/MAP sensor assembly.

17 Knock sensor - The knock sensor monitors engine vibration caused by detonation. Basically, a knock sensor converts engine vibration to an electrical signal. When the knock sensor detects a knock in one of the cylinders, it signals the PCM so that the PCM can retard ignition timing accordingly. The knock sensor contains a piezoelectric material, a certain type of piezoresistive crystal, that has the ability to produce a voltage when subjected to a mechanical stress. The piezoelectric crystal in the knock sensor vibrates constantly and produces an output signal that's proportional to the intensity of the vibration. As the intensity of the vibration increases, so does the voltage of the output signal. When the intensity of the crystal's vibration reaches a specified threshold, the PCM stores that value in its memory and retards ignition timing in all cylinders (the PCM does not selectively retard timing only at the affected cylinder). The PCM doesn't respond to the knock sensor's input when the engine is idling; it only responds when the engine reaches a specified speed.

The knock sensor is located under the left rear intake manifold runner (for cylinder No. 4), on top of the engine block, to the left of the centerline of the cases, near the back of the engine. You can access it without removing the intake manifold.

18 Manifold Absolute Pressure (MAP) sensor - The MAP sensor measures the intake manifold vacuum that draws the air/fuel mixture into the combustion chambers. The PCM uses this information to help it calculate injector pulse width and spark advance. Like the knock sensor, the MAP sensor contains a piezoresistive crystal (see *Knock sensor).* The PCM provides a "5-volt" (4.8 to 5.1 volts) reference to the MAP sensor and the MAP sensor returns a voltage signal that represents manifold pressure. A 0.5-volt output equals zero pressure; a 4.5-volt output equals ambient air pressure (14.7 psi at sea level, lower at altitude). The MAP sensor is also grounded through the PCM.

The MAP sensor is the single most important information sensor for determining the pulse width (on time) of the fuel injectors because it is, in effect, a barometer. The PCM needs to know the barometric pressure because air density changes with altitude. As the altitude increases the barometric pressure decreases, i.e. the amount of oxygen in the air decreases. Besides pulse-width and barometric pressure, the PCM also uses the MAP sensor to help it calculate engine load, manifold pressure, spark advance, idle speed, deceleration fuel shut-off and shift point strategies on automatic transaxles.

When you start the engine, the first thing that the PCM does after powering up is to look at the MAP sensor's output signal so that it knows the barometric pressure. (At sea level on a nice day - no stormy weather - barometric pressure equals 29.92 in-Hg. It drops 0.10 in-Hg for every 100 feet of altitude.) After the engine has been started the PCM looks at the MAP sensor signal every 12 milliseconds and compares each reading to the level of voltage right before the engine was started. The difference equals intake manifold vacuum. The MAP sensor is located on the intake manifold on all models.

The MAP sensor is located on the throttle body on 2000 and 2001 Legacy and Outback models with a manual transaxle and on all 2003 through 2006 non-turbocharged models. On all 2004 turbocharged models, the MAP sensor is located on top of the throttle body. On all 2005 and 2006 turbocharged models, the MAP sensor is located on the intake manifold. On some models, the MAP sensor and the IAT sensor are integrated into one unit (see next paragraph).

19 **Mass Air Flow/Intake Air Temperature (MAF/IAT) sensor** - The MAF sensor is the principal means by which the PCM monitors intake airflow. It uses a hot-wire sensing element to measure the amount of air entering the engine. Air passing over the hot wire causes it to cool down. The hot wire's temperature is maintained at 392 degrees F. above the ambient temperature by electrical current supplied to the wire and controlled by the PCM. A constantly "cold" wire located right next to the hot wire measures the ambient air temperature.) As intake air passes through the MAF sensor and over the hot wire, it cools the wire, and the control system immediately corrects the temperature back to its constant value. The current required to maintain the specified constant temperature value is used by the PCM as an indicator of airflow.

The functions of the MAF and the IAT sensors are combined into one assembly on 2005 and 2006 non-turbocharged models and on 2004 through 2006 turbocharged models. The MAF/IAT sensor is located on top of the air filter housing.

20 **Oil temperature sensor** - The oil temperature sensor is an information sensor for PCM control of the Variable Valve Lift system employed on all 2006 non-turbocharged models. It's located on the front upper left corner of the left cylinder head. For more information about the oil temperature sensor and the Variable Valve Lift system, refer to Section 29.

21 **Oxygen sensors** - Oxygen sensors generate a voltage signal that varies in accordance with the amount of oxygen in the exhaust stream. The PCM uses the data from the upstream oxygen sensor to calculate the injector pulse width. The downstream oxygen sensor monitors the oxygen content of the exhaust gases as they exit the catalytic converters. This information is used by the PCM to predict catalyst deterioration and/or failure. One job of the catalytic converter is to store excess oxygen. As long as the catalyst is functioning correctly, the downstream sensor should show little activity because there should be little oxygen exiting the catalyst. But as the catalyst deteriorates its ability to store oxygen is compromised. When the output signal from the downstream sensor starts to look like the output signal from the upstream sensor, the PCM stores a DTC and turns on the MIL to let you know that it's time to replace the catalyst.

There are two oxygen sensors. The upstream oxygen sensor is located just ahead of the upstream catalytic converter. The downstream sensor is located on the downstream catalyst. (Don't confuse either oxygen sensor with the exhaust gas temperature sensor, which is used only on turbocharged models. The exhaust gas temperature sensor is located in the joint pipe that connects the right exhaust manifold to the turbocharger.)

22 **Power Steering Pressure (PSP) sensor** - The PSP sensor monitors the hydraulic pressure of the power steering fluid in the power steering system. The PSP sensor provides a voltage input to the PCM that varies in accordance with changes in the hydraulic pressure.

The PCM uses the input signal from the PSP sensor to elevate the idle speed when the engine is already under some other load, such as the air conditioning compressor, while maneuvering the vehicle at low speed, such as parking or stop-and-go driving. The PSP sensor also signals the PCM to adjust the air assist injector solenoid valve during high-load situations such as parking. The PSP sensor is located on the power steering pump.

23 **Throttle Position (TP) sensor** - The TP sensor, which is located on the throttle body, is a rotary potentiometer, which is a type of variable resistor, that produces a variable voltage signal in proportion to the opening angle of the throttle plate. The PCM sends 5 volts to the TP sensor. As the plate opens and closes, the resistance of the TP sensor changes with it, altering the signal back to the PCM. The output voltage of the TP sensor is about 0.6 volt at idle (closed throttle plate) to 4.5 volts at wide-open throttle. This variable signal enables the PCM to calculate the position (opening angle) of the throttle plate. The PCM uses the TP sensor input, along with other sensor inputs, to adjust fuel injector pulse-width and ignition timing.

A TP sensor is used on all 2000 through 2004 non-turbocharged models. On these models you can replace the TP sensors. 2005 and 2006 non-turbocharged models and all turbocharged models are equipped with an electronic control throttle system. On models with the electronic control throttle system, the TP sensor is an integral part of the electronic throttle body and is not serviceable separately from the throttle body.

24 **Transmission Range (TR) sensor** - Like the Park/Neutral Position (PNP) switch that it replaces (or, as Subaru calls it, *the inhibitor switch)*, the TR sensor prevents you from starting the engine unless the automatic transaxle is in Park or Neutral, and it activates the back-up lights when you put the shift lever in Reverse. Unlike a PNP or inhibitor switch, however, the TR sensor also tells the PCM what gear the transaxle is in. The PCM uses this information to determine what gear the transaxle *should* be in based on the load, engine speed, etc. and to determine when to upshift and downshift the transaxle. The TR sensor is mounted on the right side of the transmission.

25 **Transmission speed sensors** - On vehicles with an automatic transmission, there are two speed sensors: the **Turbine Shaft Speed (TSS) sensor** and the **Output Shaft Speed (OSS) sensor**. Both sensors are located on the right side of the transmission. The TSS sensor provides the PCM with turbine shaft speed information, which the PCM uses to determine. The OSS sensor provides the PCM with output shaft speed information, which the PCM uses to determine transmission shift scheduling, Torque Converter Clutch (TCC) engagement scheduling and Electronic Pressure Control (EPC) pressure.

26 **Vehicle Speed Sensor (VSS)** - The VSS provides information to the PCM to indicate vehicle speed. It's also the sending unit for the speedometer on the instrument cluster. The VSS is a Hall-Effect sensor that generates a square waveform pattern with a frequency that's proportional to the speed of the vehicle. If the vehicle is moving at a relatively low speed, the VSS generates a signal with a lower frequency. As the vehicle speed increases, the VSS generates a signal with a higher frequency.

On vehicles with a manual transaxle, the VSS generates a four-pulse waveform signal for every rotation of the differential. This information is sent directly to the PCM on vehicles with a manual transaxle. The VSS is located on the top of the transaxle on vehicles with a manual transaxle.

On vehicles with an automatic transaxle, the VSS generates a 16-pulse waveform signal for every rotation of the differential. This information is sent first to the Transaxle Control Module (TCM), where it's converted to a four-pulse signal before being sent to the PCM. The PCM uses this information to determine when acceleration or deceleration occurs, so that it can alter parameters such as fuel injector pulse-width and ignition advance or retard. On automatics, there are actually two speed sensors. Both of them are located on the left side of the transaxle. The second sensor allows the TCM and PCM to monitor the various operational parameters of the transaxle. Both sensors are difficult to replace, because their wiring disappears into the transaxle housing. To disconnect the wiring harness for either sensor you have to remove the oil pan, drain the transaxle fluid and remove the valve body. We therefore don't recommend attempting to replace either sensor at home because servicing the valve body requires special skills. If either speed sensor must be replaced, have it done by a dealer or by a qualified transmission shop.

POWERTRAIN CONTROL MODULE (PCM)

27 Based on the information that it receives from the information sensors described above, the PCM adjusts fuel injector pulse width, idle speed, ignition spark advance, ignition coil dwell, EVAP canister purge operation and a lot of other things. It does so by controlling the *output actuators*. The following list provides a brief description of the function, location and operation of each of the important output actuators.

OUTPUT ACTUATORS

28 **Air assist injector solenoid valve** - When a load is imposed on the engine while it's idling or operating at low rpm, the PCM-controlled air assist injector solenoid valve directs additional air from the IAC valve (on the throttle body) into a small air passage connecting the intake manifold runners. The passage is located right at the injectors. Think of the air assist injector solenoid valve as an adjunct to the idle air control system. The air assist injector solenoid valve is used on 2000 through 2004 non-turbocharged models. It's bolted to a small mounting bracket that's located on the right front intake manifold runner (for the No. 1 cylinder).

29 **Electronic Throttle Body** - 2004 and 2005 ULEV models, 2005 and 2006 non-turbocharged vehicles and all turbocharged vehicles are equipped with Subaru's Electronic Control Throttle System. These vehicles do not have a conventional accelerator cable-actuated throttle body. Instead, they use a PCM-controlled electronic throttle body. The throttle plate inside this throttle body opened and closed by an integral throttle motor that is controlled by the PCM. There is also no cruise control cable and no Idle Air Control (IAC) motor. Cruise control and idling are handled electronically by the Powertrain Control Module (PCM). The electronic throttle body has a Throttle Position (TP) sensor, but it's an integral part of the throttle body and cannot be replaced separately from the throttle body assembly. The PCM determines the correct throttle plate angle by processing the input signal from the Accelerator Pedal Position (APP) sensor, which is located at the upper end of the accelerator pedal (see *Accelerator Pedal Position sensor* in paragraph 6).

30 **Evaporative Emission Control (EVAP) canister purge control solenoid valve** - When the engine is cold or still warming up, no captive fuel vapors are allowed to escape from the EVAP canister. After the engine is warmed up, the PCM energizes the canister purge control solenoid valve, which regulates the flow of these vapors from the canister to the intake manifold. The rate of vapor flow is regulated by the purge valve in response to commands from the PCM,

which controls the duty cycle of the valve. The EVAP canister purge valve is located in the engine compartment, on the underside of the intake manifold. For more information about the EVAP system, see Section 24.

31 **Evaporative Emission Control (EVAP) pressure control solenoid valve** - Gasoline inside the fuel tank is constantly emitting hydrocarbon vapors. As these vapors build up inside the tank the pressure goes up. When the pressure inside the tank exceeds atmospheric pressure, the PCM-controlled pressure control solenoid valve opens, allowing the fuel vapors to migrate to the EVAP canister, where they are stored until they're purged. The pressure control solenoid is located on the EVAP line between the fuel tank and the EVAP canister.

32 **Exhaust Gas Recirculation (EGR) valve** - When you pull a trailer, pass another vehicle or go up a steep hill, the temperature inside the combustion chambers heats up. When the temperature inside the combustion chambers reaches 2500-degrees F., the engine begins to produce oxides of nitrogen (NOx), which is an odorless, colorless and toxic gas that causes health problems for children, seniors, people with respiratory problems and people exercising outside on a smoggy day. The PCM-controlled EGR valve reduces NOx by introducing a controlled amount of spent exhaust gases into the intake manifold, which dilutes the air/fuel mixture, lowers combustion chamber temperatures and reduces the creation of NOx.

2003 through 2006 non-turbocharged Legacy and Outback models and 2004 through 2006 non-turbocharged Forester models are equipped with an EGR system. The typical EGR system consists of the EGR valve, the pipes connecting the left exhaust manifold to the EGR valve, the pipe connecting the EGR valve to the intake manifold and the Powertrain Control Module (PCM). The EGR valve is located on the backside of the intake manifold.

33 **Fuel injectors** - The PCM opens the fuel injectors sequentially (in firing order sequence). The PCM also controls the injector *pulse width*, which is the interval of time during which each injector is open. The pulse width of an injector (measured in milliseconds) determines the amount of fuel delivered. For more information on the fuel system and the fuel injectors, including injector replacement, refer to Chapter 4.

34 **Fuel pump relay** - When grounded by the PCM, the fuel pump relay provides battery voltage to the fuel pump. On 2000 through 2004 Legacy and Outback models, the fuel pump relay is located on the right end of the passenger compartment fuse and relay box. This fuse and relay box is located at the left end of the dash, ahead of the coin tray (2000 through 2003 models) or ahead of the fuse panel cover (2004 models). It's not actually necessary to remove the knee bolster to disconnect the electrical connector from the fuel pump relay. Instead, using a flashlight, locate the connector on the back of the relay (see illustration) and disconnect it. On 2005 and 2006 Legacy and Outback models, the fuel pump relay is located behind the right kick panel. Remove the right kick panel (see Chapter 11), then pull out the fuel pump relay. On 2000 through 2002 Forester models, the fuel pump relay is located on a small bracket mounted under the left end of the dash. On 2003 through 2006 Forester models, the fuel pump relay is located behind the right kick panel. Remove the right kick panel (see Chapter 11), then disconnect the electrical connector from the fuel pump relay.

35 **Idle Air Control (IAC) valve** - The PCM-controlled IAC valve, which is located on the throttle body, regulates the flow of air that bypasses the throttle plate when the engine is idling. The PCM opens and closes the IAC valve in response to loads - air conditioning and power steering loads, for example - to keep the engine idle speed at

its target rpm. The IAC valve also increases the idle speed during the early stages of the warm-up period and functions as a dashpot when the throttle plate is abruptly closed during sudden deceleration conditions. Vehicles equipped with an IAC valve are also equipped with an air assist injector solenoid valve, which also regulates the airflow rate in response to loads during idle conditions (see *Air assist injector solenoid valve*).

The IAC valve is used on all 2000 through 2003 models and on 2004 non-turbocharged models. 2005 and 2006 non-turbocharged models and all turbocharged models, all of which use an electronic control throttle system, dispense with the IAC valve because the PCM simply controls the opening angle of the throttle plate at all times, even during idle.

36 **Ignition coil(s)** - All ignition coil used by the vehicles covered in this manual are triggered by the PCM. All non-turbocharged models are equipped with a single ignition coil assembly, which is located on the intake manifold, and four spark plug wires. On 2000 through 2004 models, the coil assembly is located on top of the intake manifold, right in the center of the manifold. On 2005 and 2006 models, the coil is located to the left of the throttle body, on the front left intake runner. On non-turbocharged models, the ignition coil is a *waste spark* design. The coil assembly actually consists of two separate coil units Two cylinders are simultaneously fired by each coil. One cylinder is on its compression stroke and the other is on its exhaust stroke. The cylinder on its compression stroke consumes most of the secondary voltage supplied to the two spark plugs. When the plug in the companion cylinder (the one on its exhaust stroke) fires, it disperses any residual unburned air/fuel molecules, which lowers emissions. The firing order is 1-3-2-4. Refer to Chapter 1 for the cylinder locations.

Turbocharged models are equipped with four individual ignition coils. Each coil is bolted to the valve cover directly over a spark plug, and is connected directly to the plug. There are no spark plug wires. On these models, the firing order is also 1-3-2-4. Refer to Chapter 5 for more information on the ignition coils.

37 **Oil flow control solenoid valve** - The oil flow control solenoid valves (there are two of them) are PCM-controlled components in the variable valve timing system used on 2004 through 2006 turbocharged models. The variable valve timing system optimizes the opening and closing timing of the intake valves by continuously adjusting the phase angle of the intake camshaft sprockets in relation to the intake camshafts. There are two oil flow control solenoid valves, one for each intake camshaft. The valves are located on top of and at the front end of the valve covers.

Here's how it works: The PCM uses engine speed, vehicle speed, throttle opening angle inside the throttle body and other relevant data, then commands the oil flow control solenoid valve to move a spool inside the valve, which directs engine oil in or out of chambers inside the intake camshaft sprocket. One of these chambers, when filled with oil, advances the sprocket. The other chamber, when filled with oil, retards the sprocket. For more information about the oil flow control solenoid and the variable valve timing system, refer to Section 30.

38 **Oil switching valve (OSV)** - The oil switching valve is a component of the variable valve lift system, which is used on 2006 non-turbocharged models to improve engine power and fuel efficiency. The system alters the intake valve lift in accordance with driving conditions, improving combustion efficiency at medium-low speeds and improving intake air efficiency at high speeds. The intake valve rocker assembly is equipped with a special variable valve lift mechanism that can change the amount of lift in response to engine speed and load. The variable valve lift mechanism is operated by engine oil pressure, which is controlled by the PCM-controlled oil switching valve (OSV). For more information about the oil switching valve and the variable valve lift system, refer to Section 29.

39 **Secondary air combination valve** - The secondary air combination valves (there are two of them) are PCM-controlled components in the secondary air system used on 2006 turbocharged Forester models. When the PCM energizes the relays for the secondary air combination valves, they open the left and right secondary air combination valves and the secondary air pump, and air is pumped into the exhaust manifolds. The *left* secondary air combination valve is located on the front of the *right* cylinder head, and the right valve is located on top of the right part of the engine block. For more information about the secondary air combination valve, refer to Section 27.

40 **Tumble generator valve actuator** - The tumble generator valves reduce emissions during start-ups. A tumble generator valve *swirls* the air entering the combustion chamber. Swirl is the orderly rotation of the air/fuel mixture in the combustion chamber, which improves the dispersion (mixing) of the air/fuel mixture. There are two types of tumble generator valve systems used on the vehicles covered in this manual. The principal differences between the two systems is the location of the tumble generator valves. Regardless of the system, however, an PCM-controlled actuator controls the system. For more information about the tumble generator system, refer to Section 28.

OBD-II DIAGNOSTIC TROUBLE CODES (DTCS) AND THE MALFUNCTION INDICATOR LIGHT (MIL)

41 To test the critical emission control components, circuit and systems on an OBD-II vehicle, the PCM runs a series of *monitors* during each vehicle *trip*. The monitors are a series of testing protocols used by the PCM to determine whether each monitored component, circuit or system is functioning satisfactorily. The monitors must be run in a certain order. For example, the oxygen sensor monitor cannot run until the engine, the catalytic converter and the oxygen sensors are all warmed up. Another example, the misfire monitor cannot run until the engine is in closed-loop operation. And so on. An OBD-II trip consists of operating the vehicle (after an engine-off period) and driving it in such a manner that the PCM's monitors test all of the monitored components, circuits and systems at least once.

42 If the PCM recognizes a fault in some component, circuit or system while it's running the monitors, it stores a Diagnostic Trouble Code (DTC) and turns on the Malfunction Indicator Light (MIL) on the instrument cluster. A DTC can self-erase, but only after the MIL has been extinguished. For example, the MIL might be extinguished for a misfire or fuel system malfunction if the fault doesn't recur when monitored during the next three subsequent sequential driving cycles in which the conditions are similar to those under which the malfunction was first identified. (For other types of malfunctions, the criteria for extinguishing the MIL can vary.)

43 Once the MIL has been extinguished, the PCM must pass the diagnostic test for the most recent DTC for 40 *warm-up cycles* (80 warm-up cycles for the fuel system monitor and the misfire monitor). A typical warm-up cycle consists of the following components:

The engine has been started and is running
The engine temperature rises by at least 40-degrees above its
temperature when it was started
The engine coolant temperature crosses the 160-degree F mark
The engine is turned off after meeting the above criteria

OBTAINING DTCS

▸ **Refer to illustration 2.44**

44 Of course, if the MIL does NOT go out after several driving cycles, it's probably an indication that something must be repaired or replaced before the DTC can be erased and the MIL extinguished. This means that you will need to extract the DTC(s) from the PCM, make the necessary repair or replace a component, then erase the DTC yourself. You can extract the DTCs from the PCM by plugging a generic OBD-II scan tool (see illustration 2.2) into the PCM's data link connector (see illustration), which is located under the left side of the dash. Plug the scan tool into the 16-pin data link connector (DLC), then follow the instructions included with the scan tool to extract all the diagnostic codes.

ERASE THE DTC(S), TURN OFF THE MIL AND VERIFY THE REPAIR

45 Once you've completed the repair or replaced the component, use your code reader or scan tool to erase the DTC(s) and turn off the MIL. On most tools, you simply press a button to erase DTCs and turn off

the MIL, but on some tools you'll have to locate this function by using the menu on the tool's display. If it isn't obvious, follow the instructions that come with your tool.

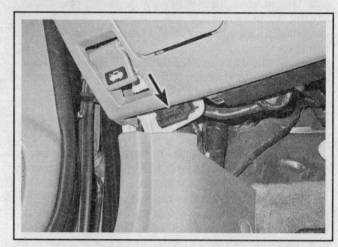

2.44 The 16-pin Data Link Connector (DLC) is located under the left side of the dash

OBD-II TROUBLE CODES

➥**Note: Not all trouble codes apply to all models.**

Code	Probable cause
P0011	Camshaft position/timing over-advanced or system performance problem (Bank 1)
P0021	Camshaft position/timing over-advanced or system performance problem (Bank 2)
P0030	Upstream oxygen sensor heater circuit malfunction
P0031	Upstream oxygen sensor heater circuit, low input
P0032	Upstream oxygen sensor heater circuit, high input
P0037	Downstream oxygen sensor heater circuit malfunction or low input
P0038	Downstream oxygen sensor heater circuit, high input
P0065	Air assist injector solenoid valve malfunction or circuit range or performance problem
P0066	Air assist injector solenoid valve circuit, low input
P0067	Air assist injector solenoid valve circuit, high input
P0068	Manifold Absolute Pressure (MAP) sensor range or performance problem
P0101	Mass Air Flow (MAF) sensor circuit, range or performance problem
P0102	Mass Air Flow (MAF) sensor circuit, low voltage input
P0103	Mass Air Flow (MAF) sensor circuit, high voltage input
P0106	Manifold Absolute Pressure (MAP) sensor circuit, range or performance problem
P0107	Manifold Absolute Pressure (MAP) sensor/Barometric Pressure (BARO) sensor circuit, low voltage input
P0108	Manifold Absolute Pressure (MAP) sensor/Barometric Pressure (BARO) sensor circuit, high voltage input
P0111	Intake Air Temperature (IAT) sensor circuit, range or performance problem

Code	Probable cause
P0112	Intake Air Temperature (IAT) sensor circuit, low input
P0113	Intake Air Temperature (IAT) sensor circuit, high input
P0116	Engine Coolant Temperature (ECT) sensor circuit, low voltage input
P0117	Engine Coolant Temperature (ECT) sensor circuit, high voltage input
P0117	Engine Coolant Temperature (ECT) sensor circuit, low voltage input
P0118	Engine Coolant Temperature (ECT) sensor circuit, high voltage input
P0121	Throttle Position (TP) sensor circuit, range or performance problem
P0121	Accelerator Pedal Position (APP) sensor circuit, range or performance problem
P0122	Throttle Position (TP) sensor circuit, low voltage input
P0122	Accelerator Pedal Position (APP) sensor circuit, low voltage input
P0123	Throttle Position (TP) sensor circuit, high voltage input
P0123	Accelerator Pedal Position (APP) sensor circuit, high voltage input
P0125	Insufficient coolant temperature for closed loop fuel control
P0128	Coolant thermostat malfunction or coolant temperature below thermostat regulating temperature
P0129	Barometric Pressure (BARO) sensor circuit, range or performance problem
P0130	Upstream oxygen sensor circuit, range or performance problem
P0131	Upstream oxygen sensor circuit, range or performance problem (low voltage input or open circuit)
P0132	Upstream oxygen sensor circuit, range or performance problem (high voltage input or circuit malfunction)
P0133	Upstream oxygen sensor circuit, slow response
P0134	Upstream oxygen sensor circuit, no activity detected
P0136	Downstream oxygen sensor circuit malfunction
P0137	Downstream oxygen sensor circuit, low voltage
P0138	Downstream oxygen sensor circuit, high voltage
P0139	Downstream oxygen sensor circuit, slow response
P0141	Downstream oxygen sensor heater circuit, low input
P0170	Fuel trim malfunction (automatic transaxle)
P0171	Fuel trim malfunction (air/fuel ratio too lean)
P0172	Fuel trim malfunction (air/fuel ratio too rich)
P0181	Fuel temperature sensor circuit, range or performance problem
P0182	Fuel temperature sensor circuit, low voltage input
P0183	Fuel temperature sensor circuit, high voltage input
P0222	Throttle Position (TP) sensor circuit, low voltage input
P0222	Accelerator Pedal Position (APP) sensor circuit, low voltage input
P0223	Throttle Position (TP) sensor circuit, high voltage input
P0223	Accelerator Pedal Position (APP) sensor circuit, high voltage input

OBD-II TROUBLE CODES (CONTINUED)

➡**Note: Not all trouble codes apply to all models.**

Code	Probable cause
P0230	Fuel pump primary circuit
P0244	Turbocharger wastegate solenoid circuit, range or performance problem
P0245	Turbocharger wastegate solenoid circuit, low voltage
P0246	Turbocharger wastegate solenoid circuit, high voltage
P0301	Cylinder number 1 misfire detected
P0302	Cylinder number 2 misfire detected
P0303	Cylinder number 3 misfire detected
P0304	Cylinder number 4 misfire detected
P0325	Knock sensor circuit malfunction
P0327	Knock sensor circuit, low voltage input
P0328	Knock sensor circuit, high voltage input
P0335	Crankshaft Position (CKP) sensor circuit malfunction
P0336	Crankshaft Position (CKP) sensor circuit, range or performance problem
P0340	Camshaft Position (CMP) sensor circuit malfunction (Bank 1 or single sensor)
P0341	Camshaft Position (CMP) sensor circuit, range or performance problem
P0345	Camshaft Position (CMP) sensor circuit malfunction (Bank 2)
P0400	Exhaust Gas Recirculation (EGR) system, flow problem
P0420	Catalyst system efficiency below threshold
P0440	Evaporative Emission Control (EVAP) system malfunction
P0442	Evaporative Emission Control (EVAP) system malfunction or small leak detected
P0443	Evaporative Emission Control (EVAP) system purge control valve circuit, low voltage input (manual transaxle)
P0444	Evaporative Emission Control (EVAP) system purge control valve circuit, low voltage input (automatic transaxle)
P0445	Evaporative Emission Control (EVAP) system purge control valve circuit, high voltage input (automatic transaxle)
P0446	Evaporative Emission Control (EVAP) system vent control circuit, low voltage input (manual transaxle)
P0447	Evaporative Emission Control (EVAP) system vent control circuit, low voltage input or open circuit
P0448	Evaporative Emission Control (EVAP) system vent control, high voltage input or short circuit
P0451	Evaporative Emission Control (EVAP) system pressure sensor, range or performance problem
P0452	Evaporative Emission Control (EVAP) system pressure sensor circuit, low voltage input
P0453	Evaporative Emission Control (EVAP) system pressure sensor circuit, high voltage input
P0456	Evaporative Emission Control (EVAP) system malfunction or very small leak detected
P0457	Evaporative Emission Control (EVAP) system leak detected (fuel filler neck cap loose or not installed)
P0458	Evaporative Emission Control (EVAP) system purge control valve circuit, low voltage

Code	Probable cause
P0459	Evaporative Emission Control (EVAP) system purge control valve circuit, high voltage
P0461	Fuel level sensor circuit, range or performance problem
P0462	Fuel level sensor circuit, low voltage input
P0463	Fuel level sensor circuit, high voltage input
P0464	Fuel level sensor circuit, intermittent input
P0480	Cooling fan relay circuit, low input
P0483	Cooling fan function problem
P0500	Vehicle Speed Sensor (VSS) malfunction
P0502	Vehicle Speed Sensor (VSS) circuit, low voltage input
P0503	Vehicle Speed Sensor (VSS) circuit, high voltage input or intermittent/erratic input
P0505	Idle Air Control (IAC) system circuit, low input
P0506	Idle Air Control (IAC) system rpm lower than expected
P0507	Idle Air Control (IAC) system rpm high higher than expected
P0512	Starter switch circuit, circuit malfunction or high voltage input
P0513	Incorrect immobilizer key
P0519	Idle control system malfunction
P0545	Exhaust Gas Temperature (EGT) sensor circuit, low voltage
P0546	Exhaust Gas Temperature (EGT) sensor circuit, high voltage
P0565	Cruise control ON signal
P0600	Incorrect Controller Area Network (CAN) communication
P0601	Powertrain Control Module (PCM) memory check sum error (manual transaxle)
P0604	Powertrain Control Module (PCM) memory check sum error or Random Access Memory (RAM) error
P0605	Powertrain Control Module (PCM) Read-Only Memory (ROM) error
P0607	powertrain Control Module (PCM) performance
P0638	Throttle actuator control range or performance problem
P0691	Cooling fan control circuit, low voltage
P0692	Cooling fan control circuit, high voltage
P0700	Request AT Malfunction Indicator Light (MIL) light ON
P0703	Torque converter or brake switch input malfunction
P0705	Transmission Range (TR) sensor circuit malfunction
P0710	Transmission fluid temperature sensor circuit malfunction
P0715	Torque converter turbine speed sensor circuit malfunction
P0716	Input/turbine speed sensor circuit, range or performance problem
P0720	Output speed sensor (VSS sensor No. 2) circuit malfunction
P0725	Engine speed input circuit malfunction

Code	Probable cause
P0726	Engine speed input circuit, range or performance problem
P0731	Incorrect 1st gear ratio
P0732	Incorrect 2nd gear ratio
P0733	Incorrect 3rd gear ratio
P0734	Incorrect 4th gear ratio
P0740 or P0741	Torque converter clutch system malfunction
P0743	Torque converter clutch system (lock-up duty solenoid) circuit malfunction
P0748	Pressure control solenoid (line pressure duty solenoid) circuit malfunction
P0753	Shift solenoid A (shift solenoid 1) electrical problem
P0758	Shift solenoid B (shift solenoid 2) electrical problem
P0771	Shift solenoid, performance problem or stuck in OFF position
P0778	Pressure control solenoid valve circuit malfunction
P0785	Shift/timing control solenoid valve circuit malfunction
P0851	Neutral switch input circuit, low voltage
P0852	Neutral switch input circuit, high voltage
P0864	Transaxle Control Module (TCM) communication circuit, range or performance problem
P0865	Transaxle Control Module (TCM) communication circuit, low voltage
P0866	Transaxle Control Module (TCM) communication circuit, high voltage

*Not all codes apply to all models

3 Accelerator Pedal Position (APP) sensor - replacement

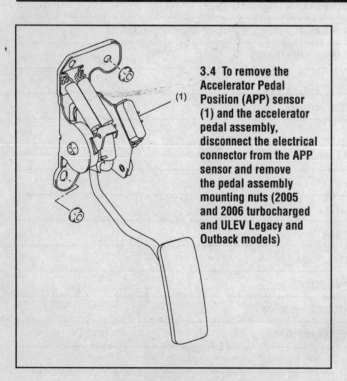

3.4 To remove the Accelerator Pedal Position (APP) sensor (1) and the accelerator pedal assembly, disconnect the electrical connector from the APP sensor and remove the pedal assembly mounting nuts (2005 and 2006 turbocharged and ULEV Legacy and Outback models)

▶ **Refer to illustration 3.4**

➡**Note:** The following section applies to turbocharged models and to Ultra Low Emission Vehicles (ULEVs). The APP sensor is at the upper end of the accelerator pedal assembly. If you need to replace the APP sensor you must replace the APP sensor and the accelerator pedal as a single assembly. The APP sensor is not removable.

1 Disconnect the cable from the negative battery terminal (see Chapter 5).

2 Remove the driver's side knee bolster (see Chapter 11).

3 Using a flashlight, disconnect the electrical connector from the APP sensor.

4 Remove the accelerator pedal assembly mounting nuts (see illustration) and remove the pedal assembly.

5 Installation is the reverse of removal.

4 Barometric Pressure (BARO) sensor - replacement

▶ Refer to illustration 4.2

➡Note: The BARO sensor is used on 2000 and 2001 Legacy and Outback models with an automatic transaxle and 2000 through 2002 Forester models. The BARO sensor is located on the front part of the right strut tower.

1 Disconnect the cable from the negative battery terminal (see Chapter 5).
2 Disconnect the electrical connector from the BARO sensor (see illustration).
3 Remove the BARO sensor mounting nut and remove the sensor.
4 Installation is the reverse of removal.

4.2 To remove the BARO sensor, depress the release tab (1) and disconnect the electrical connector, then remove the sensor mounting nut (2)

5 Camshaft Position (CMP) sensor - replacement

NON-TURBOCHARGED MODELS

▶ Refer to illustration 5.2

➡Note: The CMP sensor is located on the left cylinder head, between the backside of the timing belt cover and the front end of the valve cover, where it's mounted on a support that's bolted to the head.

1 Disconnect the cable from the negative battery terminal (see Chapter 5).
2 Disconnect the electrical connector from the CMP sensor (see illustration).
3 Remove the CMP sensor support mounting bolts and remove the support and the CMP sensor as a single assembly. (You can't remove the CMP sensor from the support without first removing the support because there isn't enough clearance between the CMP sensor mounting bolt and the valve cover to remove sensor mounting bolt.)
4 Unbolt the CMP sensor from the sensor support.
5 Installation is the reverse of removal.

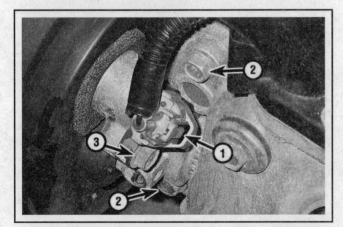

5.2 To remove the CMP sensor, depress the release tab (1) and pull off the connector, unscrew the support bolts (2) and remove the sensor/support assembly. The sensor can then be removed from the support by removing the mounting bolt (3) (non-turbocharged models)

TURBOCHARGED MODELS

▶ Refer to illustration 5.9

➡Note: There are two CMP sensors on turbocharged models. The CMP sensors are located on the back end of the cylinder heads, at the outer rear corner of each head.

6 On 2005 and 2006 models Legacy and Outback models and on 2006 Forester models, remove the engine cover (see *Intake manifold removal and installation* in Chapter 2A).
7 Disconnect the cable from the negative battery terminal (see Chapter 5).
8 If you're replacing the left CMP sensor, remove the intercooler assembly (see *Intercooler - removal and installation* in Chapter 4). If you're removing the right CMP sensor, you should be able to access the CMP sensor after pushing aside the electrical wiring and hoses in the area.
9 Disconnect the electrical connector from the CMP sensor (see illustration).
10 Remove the CMP sensor mounting bolt and remove the CMP sensor.
11 Installation is the reverse of removal.

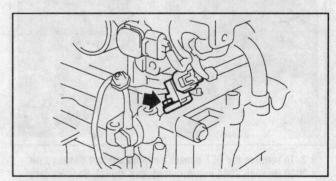

5.9 To remove the CMP sensor from the cylinder head, disconnect the electrical connector and remove the sensor mounting bolt (CMP sensor for right cylinder head shown, CMP sensor for left cylinder head identical) (2004 turbocharged model shown, others similar)

6 Clutch Pedal Position (CPP) switch - replacement

The CPP switch is used on 2004 and later Ultra-Low Emission Vehicles (ULEVs). The CPP switch is really just a clutch start switch that's wired into the Powertrain Control Module (PCM). If you need to replace the CPP switch, refer to *Clutch start switch- check and replacement* in Chapter 8.

7 Crankshaft Position (CKP) sensor - replacement

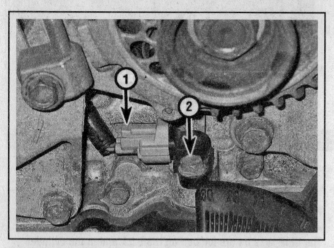

7.4 To detach the CKP sensor from the engine block, depress this release tab (1) and disconnect the electrical connector, then remove the sensor mounting bolt (2) and remove the sensor from the block

▶ **Refer to illustration 7.4**

➡**Note: The CKP sensor is located on top of and at the front of the engine block, right below the alternator and right above the timing belt cover.**

1 Disconnect the cable from the negative battery terminal (see Chapter 5).

2 On 2005 and 2006 turbocharged Legacy and Outback models and on 2006 turbocharged Forester models, remove the engine cover (see *Intake manifold - removal and installation* in Chapter 2A).

3 Remove the accessory drivebelt (see Chapter 1).

4 Disconnect the electrical connector from the CKP sensor (see illustration).

5 Remove the CKP sensor mounting bolt.

6 Installation is the reverse of removal.

8 Engine Coolant Temperature (ECT) sensor - replacement

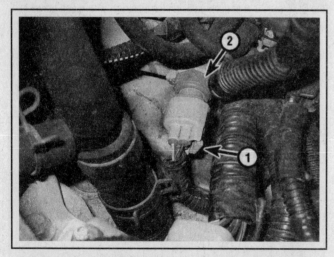

8.3 To remove the ECT sensor from the coolant passage on a 2000 through 2004 non-turbocharged model, depress this release tab (1) and disconnect the electrical connector, then unscrew the ECT sensor (2) from the coolant passage with a large box wrench or with a deep socket

❊❊ **WARNING:**

Wait until the engine is completely cool before beginning this procedure.

2000 THROUGH 2004 NON-TURBOCHARGED MODELS

▶ **Refer to illustrations 8.3 and 8.5**

➡**Note: The ECT sensor is located under the right rear intake manifold runner (for cylinder No. 3), on top of the right rear part of the engine block. It's screwed into the backside of the coolant passage that's bolted to the top of the block.**

1 Disconnect the cable from the negative battery terminal (see Chapter 5). Partially drain the engine coolant (so it's below the level of the sensor - see Chapter 1).

2 Remove the air intake duct and the air filter housing (see *Air filter housing - removal and installation* in Chapter 4).

3 Disconnect the electrical connector from the ECT sensor (see illustration).

4 Unscrew the ECT sensor from the coolant passage.

8.5 Wrap the threads of the ECT sensor with Teflon™ tape to prevent coolant from leaking past the threads

5   Wrap the threads of the ECT sensor with Teflon tape (see illustration).

6   Installation is the reverse of removal. Refill the cooling system (see Chapter 1).

TURBOCHARGED MODELS AND 2005 AND 2006 NON-TURBOCHARGED MODELS

♦ **Refer to illustration 8.10**

➡**Note: The ECT sensor is located on top of the engine block, under the right side of the alternator.**

7   Disconnect the cable from the negative battery terminal (see Chapter 5). Partially drain the engine coolant (so it's below the level of the sensor - see Chapter 1).

8.10 To remove the ECT sensor on turbocharged models and on 2005 and 2006 non-turbocharged models, disconnect the electrical connector (1), then unscrew the ECT sensor (2)

8   On 2005 and 2006 turbocharged Legacy and Outback models and on 2006 turbocharged Forester models, remove the engine cover (see *Intake manifold - removal and installation* in Chapter 2A).

9   Remove the alternator (see Chapter 5).

10 Disconnect the electrical connector from the ECT sensor (see illustration).

11 Unscrew and remove the ECT sensor.

12 Wrap the threads of the ECT sensor with Teflon tape (see illustration 8.5).

13 Installation is the reverse of removal. Refill the cooling system (see Chapter 1).

9   Exhaust temperature sensor - replacement

♦ **Refer to illustrations 9.3 and 9.5**

❊❊ WARNING:

Wait until the engine is completely cool before beginning this procedure.

➡**Note: The exhaust temperature sensor, which is used only on turbocharged models, is located in the joint pipe, which connects the right exhaust manifold to the turbocharger assembly.**

1   On 2005 and 2006 Baja, Legacy and Outback models and on 2006 Forester models, remove the engine cover (see *Intake manifold - removal and installation* in Chapter 2A).

2   Disconnect the cable from the negative battery terminal (see Chapter 5).

3   Disconnect the exhaust temperature sensor electrical connector (2004 Baja models and 2004 and 2005 Forester models, see illustration; 2005 and 2006 Legacy and Outback models, see illustration 15.15).

4   Remove the joint pipe/pre-catalyst (see Section 23).

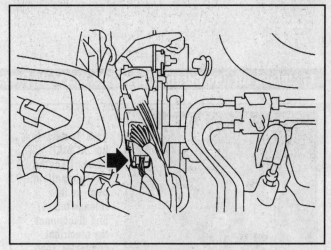

9.3 The exhaust temperature sensor electrical connector is located near the firewall (2004 turbocharged Baja models and 2004 and 2005 turbocharged Forester models)

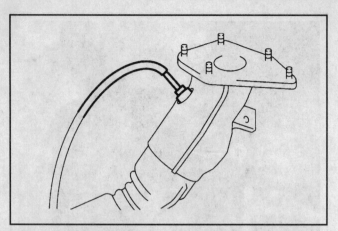

9.5 The exhaust temperature sensor is located in joint pipe/ pre-catalyst, which connects the right exhaust manifold to the turbocharger. The threads of the sensor will likely be difficult to loosen from the joint pipe/pre-catalyst, so have some penetrant handy to loosen them up

5   Unscrew the exhaust temperature sensor from the joint pipe/pre-catalyst (see illustration).

➡**Note: If the sensor is difficult to loosen, spray the base of the sensor with some penetrant and give it some time to soak into the threads, then try again.**

6   If you're going to install the old exhaust temperature sensor, apply anti-seize compound to the threads of the sensor to facilitate future removal. If you're installing a new exhaust temperature sensor, it's not necessary to apply anti-seize compound to the threads; the threads on new sensors already have anti-seize compound on them.

7   Installation is otherwise the reverse of removal. Be sure to tighten the exhaust temperature sensor to the torque listed in this Chapter's Specifications.

10 Intake Air Temperature (IAT) sensor - replacement

▶ **Refer to illustration 10.3**

➡**Note: The IAT sensor is used on 2000 and 2001 Legacy and Outback models with a manual transaxle and on 2003 and 2004 Legacy, Outback and Forester models. It's located on the front of the air filter housing.**

1   Disconnect the cable from the negative battery terminal (see Chapter 5).

2   Disconnect the electrical connector from the IAT sensor.

3   Pull the IAT sensor out of the air filter housing (see illustration).

4   Inspect the condition of the mounting grommet in the air filter housing. Make sure that it's in good condition to prevent air leaks.

5   Installation is the reverse of removal.

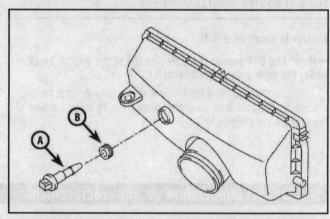

10.3 After removing the IAT sensor (1) from the front of the air filter housing, inspect the condition of the sensor mounting grommet (2). If it's cracked, torn or deteriorated, replace it to prevent an air leak

11 Intake Air Temperature/Manifold Absolute Pressure (IAT/MAP) sensor - replacement

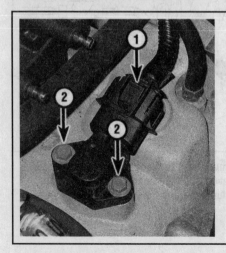

11.3 To detach the IAT/MAP sensor from the intake manifold, depress this release tab (1) and disconnect the electrical connector, then remove the sensor mounting bolts (2) and remove the sensor

▶ **Refer to illustrations 11.3 and 11.5**

➡**Note: The IAT/MAP sensor is used on 2000 and 2001 Legacy and Outback models with an automatic transaxle, on 2002 Legacy and Outback models and on 2000 through 2002 Forester models. The IAT/MA sensor is located on top of the intake manifold, near the ignition coil.**

1   Disconnect the cable from the negative battery terminal (see Chapter 5).

2   Disconnect the spark plug wires from the coil high tension terminals for the Nos. 2 and 4 cylinders (see Chapter 1).

3   Disconnect the electrical connector from the IAT/MAP sensor (see illustration).

4   Remove the IAT/MAP sensor mounting bolts and remove the sensor.

5   Remove and discard the old IAT/MAP sensor O-ring (see illustration). To prevent air leaks, always use a new O-ring when installing the IAT/MAP sensor whether you're installing the old sensor or a new unit.

6   Installation is the reverse of removal.

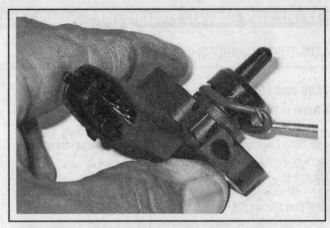

11.5 Be sure to remove the old O-ring from the sensor and discard it. Use a new O-ring when installing the sensor whether you're installing a new one or the old unit

12 Knock sensor - replacement

▶ **Refer to illustrations 12.4 and 12.5**

➡Note: The knock sensor is located under the intake manifold, on top of the engine block, to the left of the centerline of the cases and near the back.

1   On 2005 and 2006 turbocharged Legacy and Outback models and on 2006 turbocharged Forester models, remove the engine cover (see *Intake manifold - removal and installation* in Chapter 2A).

2   Disconnect the cable from the negative battery terminal (see Chapter 5).

3   On turbocharged models, remove the intercooler (see Chapter 4).

4   Disconnect the knock sensor electrical connector (see illustration).

➡Note: On 2000 through 2002 models, there are two knock sensor connectors, one right at the sensor and the other at the

end of a short pigtail harness. But the one at the sensor is very difficult, if not impossible, to disconnect until you have removed the knock sensor from the engine. So if you're removing or replacing the knock sensor on one of these models, disconnect the pigtail harness connector first, then disconnect the other connector after you have removed the knock sensor. The knock sensors used on 2003 and later models are not equipped with this extra connector.

5   Before removing the sensor, note how it is oriented (the pigtail harness should be at approximately a 60-degree angle to the back of the engine). If necessary, use a marking pen to make a mark on the engine block where the sensor's pigtail is. Next, remove the knock sensor retaining bolt (see illustration) and remove the knock sensor.

6   Installation is otherwise the reverse of removal. Be sure to tighten the knock sensor retaining bolt to the torque listed in this Chapter's Specifications.

12.4 To disconnect the knock sensor electrical connector, depress this release tab and separate the two halves of the connector

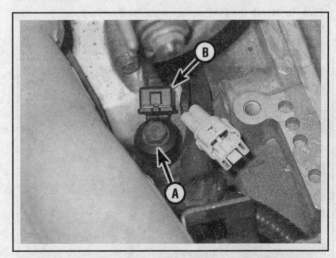

12.5 To detach the knock sensor from the engine block, remove this retaining bolt (A). Note the extra knock sensor connector (B), which is used on 2000 through 2002 models. This connector can only be disconnected after removing the knock sensor

13 Manifold Absolute Pressure (MAP) sensor - replacement

NON-TURBOCHARGED MODELS

2000 and 2001 models

▶ **Refer to illustration 13.4**

➡**Note: The MAP sensor is located on the throttle body on 2000 and 2001 Legacy and Outback models with a manual transaxle.**

1   Disconnect the cable from the negative battery terminal (see Chapter 5).

2   Remove the Idle Air Control (IAC) solenoid valve from the throttle body (see Section 22).

3   Disconnect the electrical connector from the MAP sensor.

4   Remove the MAP sensor mounting screws (see illustration) and remove the MAP sensor from the throttle body.

5   Remove and discard the old MAP sensor gasket.

6   Installation is the reverse of removal. Be sure to use new gaskets when installing the MAP sensor and the IAC valve.

2003 through 2006 models

▶ **Refer to illustration 13.8**

➡**Note: The MAP sensor is located on the throttle body on 2003 through 2006 models.**

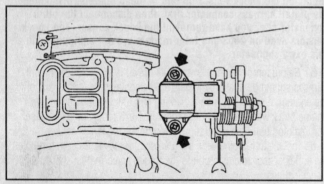

13.4 To detach the MAP sensor from the throttle body, remove these two mounting screws (2000 and 2001 Legacy and Outback models with a manual transaxle)

13.8 To detach the MAP sensor from the throttle body, depress the tab and disconnect the electrical connector (1), then remove the sensor mounting screws (2) (2003 through 2006 non-turbo models)

7   Disconnect the cable from the negative battery terminal (see Chapter 5).

8   Disconnect the electrical connector from the MAP sensor (see illustration).

9   Remove the MAP sensor mounting screws and remove the MAP sensor.

10 Remove and discard the old MAP sensor O-ring (see illustration 11.5).

11 Installation is the reverse of removal. Be sure to use a new O-ring.

TURBOCHARGED MODELS

2004 Legacy and Outback models and 2004 through 2006 Forester models

▶ **Refer to illustration 13.13**

➡**Note: On 2004 turbocharged Legacy and Outback models and on 2004 through 2006 turbocharged Forester models, the MAP sensor is located on top of the throttle body.**

12 Disconnect the cable from the negative battery terminal (see Chapter 5).

13 Disconnect the electrical connector from the MAP sensor (see illustration).

14 Remove the MAP sensor mounting screws and remove the sensor.

15 Remove and discard the old O-ring from the MAP sensor (see illustration 11.5).

16 Installation is the reverse of removal. Be sure to use a new O-ring.

2005 and 2006 Legacy and Outback models

▶ **Refer to illustration 13.18**

➡**Note: On 2005 and 2006 turbocharged Legacy and Outback models, the MAP sensor is located on a small solenoid valve bracket in front of the intake manifold runner for the No. 1 cylinder.**

17 Disconnect the cable from the negative battery terminal (see Chapter 5).

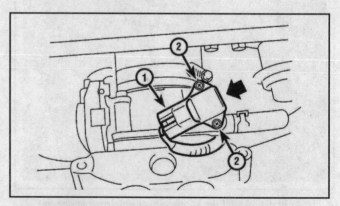

13.13 To detach the MAP sensor from the throttle body on a 2004 turbocharged Legacy or Outback model, or on a 2004 through 2006 turbocharged Forester model, disconnect the electrical connector (1), then remove the MAP sensor mounting screws (2)

18 Locate the MAP sensor (see illustration) on the small bracket in front of the intake manifold runner for the No. 1 cylinder.

19 Disconnect the electrical connector from the MAP sensor.

20 Disconnect the vacuum hose and filter from the intake manifold.

21 Remove the MAP sensor mounting nut and remove the MAP sensor.

22 Disconnect the vacuum hose from the MAP sensor.

23 Inspect the condition of the vacuum hose. If it's cracked, torn or deteriorated, replace it.

24 Installation is the reverse of removal.

13.18 The MAP sensor on 2005 and 2006 turbocharged Legacy and Outback models is located on a small bracket in front of the intake manifold runner for the No. 1 cylinder

14 Mass Air Flow/Intake Air Temperature (MAF/IAT) sensor - replacement

▶ **Refer to illustration 14.2**

➡**Note: The MAF/IAT sensor is used on 2005 and 2006 non-turbocharged models and on 2004 through 2006 turbocharged models. The MAF/IAT sensor is located on top of the air filter housing.**

1 Disconnect the cable from the negative battery terminal (see Chapter 5).

2 Disconnect the electrical connector from the MAF/IAT sensor (see illustration).

3 Remove the MAF/IAT sensor mounting screws.

4 Installation is the reverse of removal.

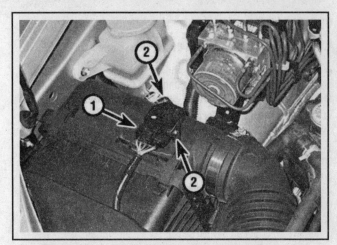

14.2 To detach the MAF/IAT sensor from the air filter housing, disconnect the electrical connector (1) and remove the sensor mounting screws (2) (2004 through 2006 turbocharged model shown, 2005 and 2006 non-turbocharged models similar)

15 Oxygen sensors - general information and replacement

GENERAL INFORMATION

1 Use special care when servicing an oxygen sensor:

Oxygen sensors have a permanently attached pigtail and electrical connector that can't be removed from the sensor. Damage to or removal of the pigtail or the electrical connector will ruin the sensor.

Keep grease, dirt and other contaminants away from the electrical connector and the oxygen sensor.

Do not use cleaning solvents of any kind on an oxygen sensor.

Do not drop or roughly handle an oxygen sensor.

REPLACEMENT

➡**Note: Because it is installed in the exhaust manifold or catalytic converter, both of which contract when cool, an oxygen sensor might be very difficult to loosen when the engine is cold. Rather than risk damage to the sensor, start and run the engine for a minute or two, then shut it off. Be careful not to burn yourself during the following procedure.**

Non-turbocharged models

2 Disconnect the cable from the negative terminal of the battery (see Chapter 5).

3 Raise the vehicle and place it securely on jackstands.

15.4a Oxygen sensor location on non-turbocharged models. Normally we would recommend using an oxygen sensor socket to remove oxygen sensors, but on many of these models you won't have room to put an oxygen sensor socket on the sensor, so you'll have to use a big wrench to remove the sensor instead

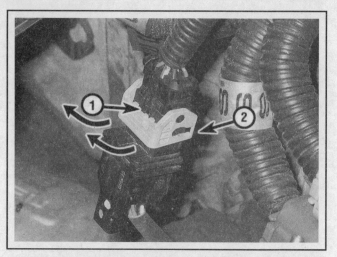

15.4b A typical electrical connector for the upstream oxygen sensor on a non-turbocharged model. To disconnect it, depress the lug (1), push open the lock (2) and swing it open, then unplug the connector. Most upstream sensor connectors have a similar locking mechanism on them

Upstream oxygen sensor

▶ Refer to illustrations 15.4a and 15.4b

➡Note: On non-turbocharged models, the upstream oxygen sensor is located just behind the flange between the two exhaust manifolds and the front end of the catalytic converter.

4   Locate the upstream oxygen sensor (see illustration), then trace the sensor's electrical harness up to its connector. On most models, you'll find the connector for the upstream sensor in the rear of the engine compartment (see illustration). Disconnect the connector, then go back under the vehicle and unscrew the sensor. We recommend using an oxygen sensor socket where possible, because it protects the sensor from damage during removal and installation. However, on many of these models you will have to use a large wrench because there isn't enough room to put an oxygen sensor socket on the sensor.

5   After removing the old upstream oxygen sensor, clean the threads of the sensor bore in the exhaust manifold.

6   If you're going to install the old sensor, apply anti-seize compound to the threads of the sensor to facilitate future removal. If you're going to install a new oxygen sensor, it's not necessary to apply anti-

seize compound to the threads. The threads on new sensors already have anti-seize compound on them.

7   Installation is otherwise the reverse of removal. Be sure to tighten the sensor to the torque listed in this Chapter's Specifications.

Downstream oxygen sensor

▶ Refer to illustrations 15.8 and 15.9

➡Note: The downstream oxygen sensor is located on the catalytic converter.

8   Trace the electrical lead from the downstream oxygen sensor to the electrical connector and disconnect it (see illustration).

9   Unscrew and remove the downstream oxygen sensor with a large wrench (see illustrations).

10   After removing the old downstream oxygen sensor, clean the threads of the sensor bore in the catalytic converter.

11   If you're going to install the old sensor, apply anti-seize compound to the threads of the sensor to facilitate future removal.

12   If you're going to install a new oxygen sensor, it's not necessary to apply anti-seize compound to the threads. The threads on new sensors already have anti-seize compound on them.

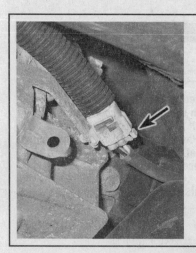

15.8 A typical downstream oxygen sensor electrical connector. To disconnect this particular type, depress the release tab and pull the two halves of the connector apart. Expect to find - and look for - some sort of locking mechanism on the downstream sensor connector before trying to unplug it

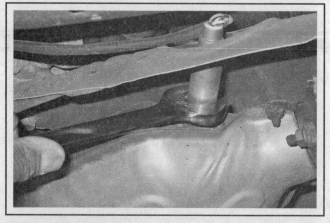

15.9 A typical downstream oxygen sensor on a non-turbocharged model. Use a large wrench to unscrew it

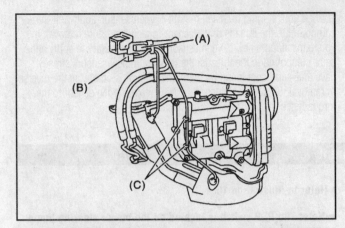

15.15 On 2005 and 2006 turbo Legacy and Outback models, the connector (A) for the upstream oxygen sensor is located right above the connector (B) for the exhaust temperature sensor. Be sure to detach the two sensor harness clips on the right valve cover (C) before removing the sensor (the Baja and Forester similar)

13 Installation is otherwise the reverse of removal. Be sure to tighten the sensor to the torque listed in this Chapter's Specifications.

Turbocharged models

14 Disconnect the cable from the negative terminal of the battery (see Chapter 5).

Upstream oxygen sensor

♦ **Refer to illustrations 15.15, 15.18 and 15.19**

➡**Note: The upstream oxygen sensor is located on the right exhaust manifold.**

15 Disconnect the upstream oxygen sensor electrical connector (see illustration).

16 Detach the clips for the upstream oxygen sensor harness (see illustration 15.15).

17 Loosen the lug nuts for the right front wheel. Raise the front of the vehicle and place it securely on jackstands. Remove the right front wheel.

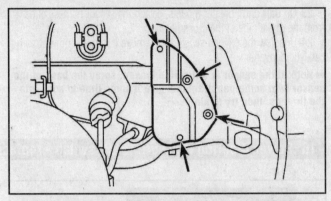

15.18 To access the upstream oxygen sensor, remove these fasteners, then remove this service hole cover from the wheelwell inner splash shield

18 Remove the service hole cover in the wheel housing splash shield (see illustration).

19 Unscrew the oxygen sensor (see illustration) and remove it from the right exhaust manifold.

➡**Note: If the sensor is difficult to loosen, spray the base of the sensor with some penetrant and give it some time to soak into the threads, then try again.**

20 If you're going to install the old oxygen sensor, apply anti-seize compound to the threads of the sensor to facilitate future removal. If you're installing a new oxygen sensor, it's not necessary to apply anti-seize compound to the threads; the threads on new sensors already have anti-seize compound on them. Installation is otherwise the reverse of removal. Be sure to tighten the downstream oxygen sensor to the torque listed in this Chapter's Specifications.

Downstream oxygen sensor

♦ **Refer to illustration 15.22**

➡**Note: The downstream oxygen sensor is located on the downstream catalytic converter.**

21 Raise the vehicle and place it securely on jackstands.

22 Locate the oxygen sensor (see illustration), trace the sensor electrical harness to its connector and disconnect the connector.

15.19 A typical upstream oxygen sensor location on a turbocharged model. On one of these models, you could easily fit an oxygen sensor socket on the sensor, so if you have access to this special tool, use it instead of a wrench, to protect the sensor

15.22 A typical downstream oxygen sensor on a turbocharged model. To find the sensor electrical connector, trace the sensor harness to the connector. (On turbocharged Baja and Forester models, also detach the oxygen sensor harness clips from the upper side of the crossmember)

23 On Baja and Forester models, detach the sensor harness clips from the upper side of the crossmember.

24 Unscrew the oxygen sensor and remove it from the downstream catalytic converter.

→Note: If the sensor is difficult to loosen, spray the base of the sensor with some penetrant and give it some time to soak into the threads, then try again.

25 If you're going to install the old oxygen sensor, apply anti-seize compound to the threads of the sensor to facilitate future removal. If you're installing a new oxygen sensor, it's not necessary to apply anti-seize compound to the threads; the threads on new sensors already have anti-seize compound on them. Installation is otherwise the reverse of removal. Be sure to tighten the downstream oxygen sensor to the torque listed in this Chapter's Specifications.

16 Power Steering Pressure (PSP) switch - replacement

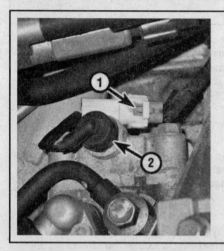

16.2 Depress the release tab and disconnect the PSP switch electrical connector (1), then peel back the rubber cover (2) and unscrew the switch

♦ Refer to illustration 16.2

→Note: The PSP switch is located on the power steering pump on most models.

1 Disconnect the cable from the negative terminal of the battery (see Chapter 5).

2 Disconnect the PSP switch electrical connector (see illustration).

3 Unscrew the PSP switch.

4 Installation is the reverse of removal. Be sure to tighten the PSP switch securely.

5 Check the power steering fluid level, adding as necessary (see Chapter 1).

17 Throttle Position (TP) sensor - replacement

♦ Refer to illustrations 17.2, 17.4, 17.5a and 17.5b

→Note: The TP sensor is located on the throttle body. This procedure does not apply to the electronic throttle bodies used on ULEV models, 2005 and 2006 non-turbocharged models and on all turbocharged models.

1 Disconnect the cable from the negative terminal of the battery (see Chapter 5).

2 Disconnect the electrical connector from the TP sensor (see illustration).

3 Remove the TP sensor mounting screws (see illustration 17.2) and remove the TP sensor.

4 When installing the TP sensor, make sure that the tang on the movable part of the TP sensor is positioned on the correct side of the pin on the throttle plate shaft (see illustration).

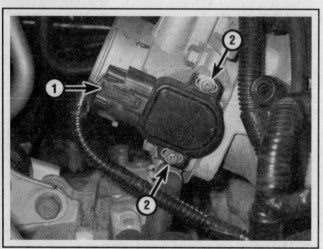

17.2 To detach the TP sensor from the throttle body, depress this release tab (1) and detach the electrical connector, remove the sensor mounting screws (2) and remove the sensor from the throttle body

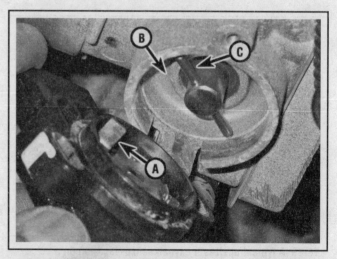

17.4 When installing the TP sensor, make sure that the tang (A) on the rotating part of the sensor is on the correct side (B) of the pin (C) on the throttle plate shaft

17.5a Install the TP sensor mounting screws loosely, plug in the sensor electrical connector, backprobe the signal return and ground wires of the sensor connector, turn the ignition to ON (don't start it) . . .

5   Install the TP sensor mounting screws loosely, plug in the sensor electrical connector, then backprobe the signal return and ground wires (on our vehicle these were the black and white wires) of the sensor connector (see illustration) Turn the engine to ON (don't start it), then rotate the TP sensor slightly until the voltmeter indicates between 0.45 and 0.55 volt (see illustration) with the throttle plate closed. When the indicated voltage is within the specified range, tighten the TP sensor screws securely, but don't overtighten them.

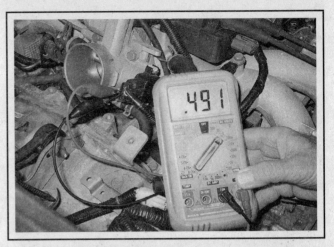

17.5b . . . then verify that, with the throttle plate closed, the voltmeter indicates between 0.45 and 0.55 volt. If the indicated voltage is outside this range, rotate the TP sensor slightly until the reading is within the specified range. When the indicated voltage is within specification, tighten the TP sensor screws securely (but don't overtighten them)

➡Note: On some models, the wire colors may be different. Backprobing between one of the wires you need and the other wires will not give you a reading that's even close to what you're looking for. When you backprobe the two correct wires you will get a reading close to or within the specified range.

18   Transmission Range (TR) sensor - replacement

◆ Refer to illustrations 18.5, 18.6, 18.7, 18.8 and 18.9

➡Note: The TR sensor is located on the right side of the transaxle. This procedure applies to all TR sensors except those used on 2005 and 2006 turbocharged Legacy and Outback models with the 5AT automatic transaxle. On these models, the TR sensor is mounted on the valve body and cannot be serviced at home. If the TR sensor on one of these models must be replaced, have it replaced by the dealer or a transmission shop.

1   Disconnect the cable from the negative terminal of the battery (see Chapter 5).
2   Put the shift lever in Neutral.
3   Raise the vehicle and place it securely on jackstands.
4   Remove the center exhaust pipe section (see Chapter 4). On later models you might also have to remove the front part of the exhaust system (see Chapter 4).
5   Disconnect the electrical connector from the TR sensor (see illustration).
6   Disconnect the shift cable from the manual lever and from the

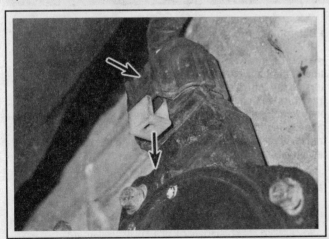

18.5 To disconnect the electrical connector from the TR sensor, pull the lock straight down and remove it (lower arrow), then depress the release tab (upper arrow) and unplug the connector from the sensor

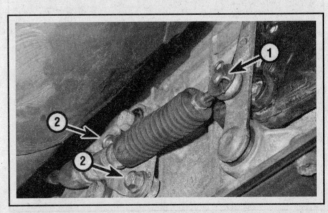

18.6 To detach the shift cable from the transaxle, remove the cotter pin (1) (and washer) that secures the cable to the manual lever, remove the two cable bracket mounting bolts (2), then slide the end of the cable off the pin on the manual lever

18.7 To detach the TR sensor from the transaxle, remove these three mounting bolts

18.8 To remove the TR sensor from the transaxle, shift the manual lever to the PARK position (all the way to the left), then remove the sensor

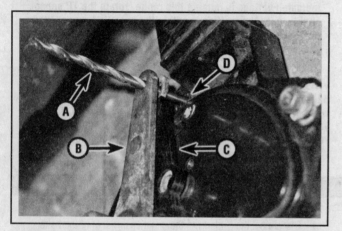

18.9 To adjust the TR sensor, insert a 5/32-inch drill bit (A) through the holes in the end of the manual lever (B) and the sensor lever (C) and into the alignment hole (D) in the sensor body, then tighten the TR sensor mounting bolts securely

transaxle (see illustration) and set it aside.

7   Remove the TR sensor mounting bolts (see illustration).

8   Shift the manual lever to the PARK position, which is all the way to the left (see illustration) and remove the TR sensor.

9   To adjust the TR sensor, place the sensor in position, install the TR sensor bolts loosely, then insert a 5/32-inch drill bit through the alignment holes in the ends of the manual lever and the sensor lever and into the alignment hole in the sensor body (see illustration). Then tighten the sensor bolts securely.

10 Installation is otherwise the reverse of removal.

19   Vehicle Speed Sensor (VSS) - replacement

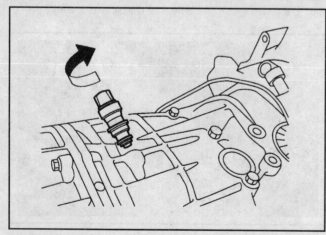

19.4 To remove the VSS from the transaxle, simply unscrew it

▶ **Refer to illustration 19.4**

➡ **Note: On manual transaxles, the VSS is located on the right side of the transaxle. On automatics, there are two speed sensors on the left side of the transaxle, but you have to drain the transmission fluid, remove the oil pan and remove the valve body to disconnect the electrical connectors, so we don't recommend trying this at home. If a speed sensor on an automatic transaxle must be replaced, have it done by a qualified service technician.**

1   Disconnect the cable from the negative terminal of the battery (see Chapter 5).

2   Raise the vehicle and support it securely on jackstands.

3   Disconnect the electrical connector from the VSS.

4   Unscrew the VSS (see illustration) from the transaxle.

5   Installation is the reverse of removal.

20 Powertrain Control Module (PCM) - replacement

▶ **Refer to illustrations 20.3, 20.4 and 20.5**

➡**Note: The PCM is located inside the vehicle, on the lower part of the right (passenger) side firewall, under the carpet and a protective cover.**

1   Disconnect the cable from the negative battery terminal (see Chapter 5).

2   Remove the sill plate and pull back the passenger side carpet to expose the PCM protective access cover (see Chapter 11).

3   Remove the protective cover retaining bolts (see illustration) and remove the cover.

4   Remove the PCM mounting nuts (see illustration) and rotate the PCM 90 degrees so that the electrical connectors are facing toward you.

5   Disconnect the electrical connectors from the PCM (see illustration).

6   Disengage the harness tie from the mounting bracket on the PCM and remove the PCM.

✴✴ CAUTION:

Be sure to use a special computer anti-static device to eliminate the chance of PCM damage when handling the PCM.

7   Installation is the reverse of removal.

20.3 A typical PCM protective cover. To remove it, simply remove the retaining bolts (the exact shape of these covers varies somewhat among different models but they're all quite similar)

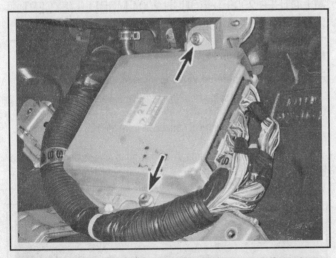

20.4 To detach the PCM from the firewall, remove these two nuts

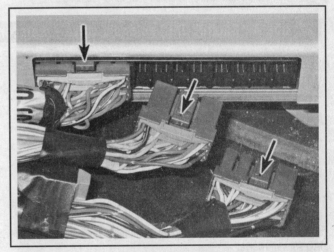

20.5 To disconnect the electrical connectors from the PCM, depress the release tab on each connector and carefully pull it out of the PCM

21 Air assist injector solenoid valve - replacement

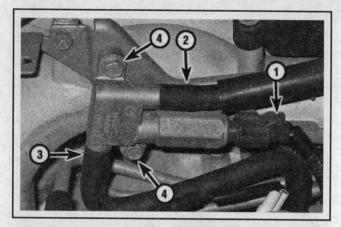

21.2 A typical air assist injector solenoid valve. To remove it from the intake manifold:

1   *Depress this release tab and disconnect the electrical connector*
2   *Disconnect the hose coming from the Idle Air Control (IAC) valve*
3   *Disconnect the hose that connects the valve to the air passages in the intake manifold*
4   *Remove the air assist injector solenoid valve mounting bolts*

▶ **Refer to illustration 21.2**

➡**Note: The air assist injector solenoid valve is used on 2000 through 2004 non-turbocharged models. It's located on the front of the right front intake manifold runner (for the No. 1 cylinder).**

1   Disconnect the cable from the negative battery terminal (see Chapter 5).
2   Disconnect the electrical connector from the air assist injector solenoid valve (see illustration).
3   Disconnect the hose coming from the Idle Air Control (IAC) valve and the hose going to the air passages in the intake manifold (see illustration 21.2).
4   Remove the air assist injector solenoid valve mounting bolts.
5   Installation is the reverse of removal.

22 Idle Air Control (IAC) solenoid valve - replacement

2000 AND 2001 LEGACY AND OUTBACK MODELS WITH A MANUAL TRANSAXLE

▶ **Refer to illustration 22.3**

➡**Note: The IAC solenoid valve is located on the throttle body.**

1   Disconnect the cable from the negative battery terminal (see Chapter 5).
2   Disconnect the electrical connector from the IAC solenoid valve.
3   Disconnect the air bypass hose from the IAC solenoid valve (see illustration).
4   Remove the IAC solenoid valve mounting screws and remove the IAC solenoid valve.
5   Installation is the reverse of removal.

22.3 Unplug the electrical connector from the IAC solenoid valve, then disconnect the air bypass hose (2000 and 2001 Legacy and Outback models with a manual transaxle)

ALL OTHER 2000 THROUGH 2004 MODELS (EXCEPT 2004 TURBOCHARGED MODELS)

▶ **Refer to illustration 22.7**

➡**Note: The IAC solenoid valve is located on the throttle body.**

6   Disconnect the cable from the negative battery terminal (see Chapter 5).
7   Disconnect the electrical connector from the IAC solenoid valve (see illustration).
8   Remove the IAC solenoid valve mounting screws and remove the IAC solenoid valve.
9   Installation is the reverse of removal.

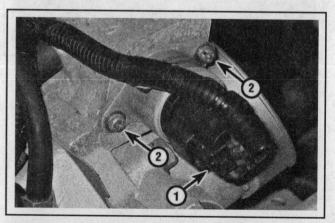

22.7 To detach the IAC solenoid valve from the throttle body, depress this release (1) and disconnect the electrical connector, then remove the mounting screws (2) and remove the valve (all models except 2000 and 2001 Legacy and Outback models with a manual transaxle, or turbo models)

2004 TURBOCHARGED MODELS AND ALL 2005 AND 2006 MODELS

10 These models are equipped with an electronic control throttle system. The electronic throttle body used on these models does not have an IAC solenoid valve. This function is handled by a PCM-controlled motor inside the throttle body that maintains the appropriate throttle plate angle in response to inputs from a number of information sensors.

23 Catalytic converters - description and component replacement

GENERAL DESCRIPTION

1 The catalytic converter is an emission control device installed in the exhaust system that reduces pollutants from the exhaust gas stream. There are two types of converters: The oxidation catalyst reduces the levels of hydrocarbon (HC) and carbon monoxide (CO) by adding oxygen to the exhaust stream to produce water vapor (H_2O) and carbon dioxide (CO_2). The reduction catalyst lowers the levels of oxides of nitrogen (NOx) by removing oxygen from the exhaust gases to produce nitrogen (N) and oxygen. These two types of catalysts are combined into a three-way catalyst that reduces all three pollutants.

2 The amount of oxygen entering the catalyst is critical to its operation because without oxygen it cannot convert harmful pollutants into harmless compounds. The catalyst is most efficient at capturing and storing oxygen when it converts the exhaust gases of an intake charge that's mixed at the ideal (stoichiometric) air/fuel ratio of 14.7:1. If the air/fuel ratio is leaner than stoichiometric for an extended period of time, the catalyst will store even more oxygen. But if the air/fuel ratio is richer than stoichiometric for any length of time, the oxygen content in the catalyst can become totally depleted. If this condition occurs, the catalyst will not convert anything!

3 Because the catalyst's ability to store oxygen is such an important factor in its operation, it can also be considered a factor in the catalyst's eventual inability to do its job. The PCM monitors the oxygen content going into and coming out of the catalyst by comparing the voltage signals from the upstream and downstream oxygen sensors. When the catalyst is functioning correctly, there is very little oxygen to monitor at the outlet end of the catalyst because it's capturing, storing and releasing oxygen as needed to convert HC, CO and NOx into more benign substances. But as the catalyst ages, it slowly loses its ability to store oxygen, and the downstream oxygen sensor tells the PCM that the oxygen content in the catalyzed exhaust gases is going up. When the amount of oxygen exiting the catalyst reaches a specified threshold, the PCM stores a Diagnostic Trouble Code (DTC) and turns on the Malfunction Indicator Light (MIL).

COMPONENT REPLACEMENT

4 Disconnect the cable from the negative battery terminal (see Chapter 5).

5 Raise the vehicle and place it securely on jackstands.

6 Remove the upstream and downstream oxygen sensors (see Section 15).

Non-turbocharged models

▶ Refer to illustrations 23.7 and 23.8

➡**Note: On these models the upstream and downstream catalysts, and the exhaust pipe that connects them, are welded together into a single assembly. So if you have to replace either catalyst, you must replace the entire catalyst assembly.**

7 Remove the front mounting flange bolts and nuts (see illustration).

8 Remove the rear mounting flange bolts and nuts (see illustration) and remove the catalyst assembly.

9 Installation is the reverse of removal.

Turbocharged models

➡**Note: On these models there are three catalysts: the pre-catalytic converter, the upstream catalyst and the downstream catalyst.**

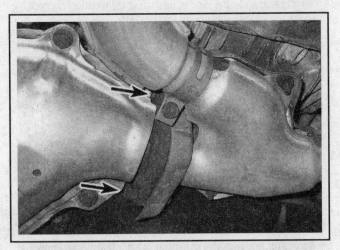

23.7 To detach the front end of the catalyst assembly from the exhaust manifold assembly, remove these bolts and nuts (non-turbocharged models)

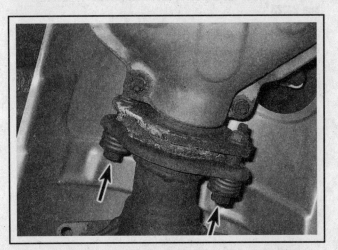

23.8 To detach the rear end of the catalyst assembly from the rest of the exhaust system, remove these bolts and nuts (non-turbocharged models)

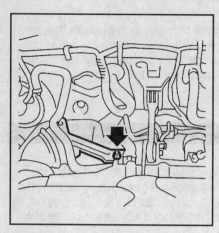

23.12 To detach the intercooler mounting bracket, remove this nut

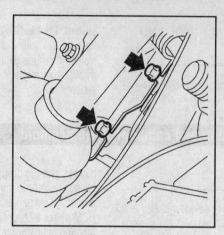

23.15 To detach the lower edge of the turbocharger lower cover, remove these two bolts

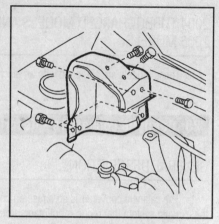

23.16 To remove the turbocharger upper cover, remove these bolts

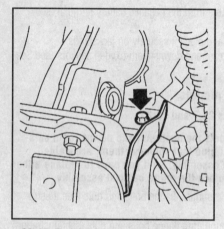

23.17 To remove the turbocharger lower cover, remove this bolt

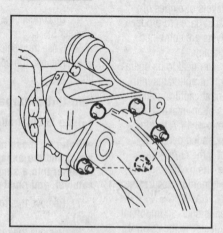

23.18 To disconnect the center exhaust pipe from the turbocharger, remove these nuts and bolts

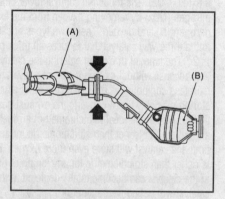

23.23 To disconnect the upstream catalytic converter (A) from the downstream catalytic converter (B), remove the nuts and bolts at this flange. When reconnecting the two converters, be sure to use a new flange gasket

Upstream and downstream catalytic converters

♦ **Refer to illustrations 23.12, 23.15, 23.16, 23.17, 23.18 and 23.23**

➥**Note: The upstream and downstream catalysts are both part of the center exhaust pipe. To replace either of these catalysts, you must first remove the center exhaust pipe, then unbolt the catalyst that you want to replace.**

10 Remove the engine cover, if equipped (see *Intake manifold - removal and installation* in Chapter 2A).

11 Disconnect the cable from the negative battery terminal (see Chapter 5).

12 Remove the intercooler (see Chapter 4) and the intercooler mounting bracket (see illustration).

13 Raise the vehicle and place it securely on jackstands.

14 Remove the engine under cover (see *Exhaust manifold - removal and installation* in Chapter 2A).

15 Working under the vehicle, remove the bolts that secure the lower edge of the turbocharger lower cover (see illustration).

16 Remove the turbocharger upper cover (see illustration).

17 Remove the bolts that secure the turbocharger lower cover and the center exhaust pipe (see illustration).

18 Unbolt the center exhaust pipe from the turbocharger (see illustration).

19 Working under the vehicle, disconnect the electrical connector from the rear oxygen sensor (see Section 15).

20 Unbolt the center exhaust pipe from the rear exhaust pipe (see illustration 23.8).

21 Remove the bolt that secures the small bracket on the center exhaust pipe to the transaxle.

22 Remove the bolt that secures the small bracket on the center exhaust pipe to the hanger bracket and remove the center exhaust pipe.

23 Unbolt the front catalytic converter from the rear catalytic converter (see illustration).

24 When bolting the two catalytic converters back together again, be sure to use a new gasket at the flange.

25 Installation is otherwise the reverse of removal.

Pre-catalytic converter/joint pipe

♦ **Refer to illustrations 23.30 and 23.31**

➥**Note: The pre-catalytic converter is an integral component of the joint pipe (the pipe that connects the right exhaust manifold to the turbocharger), so to replace the pre-catalyst you'll have to replace the joint pipe.**

23.30 To detach the exhaust manifold heat shield, remove these bolts (the bolt pattern might be slightly different on some heat shields)

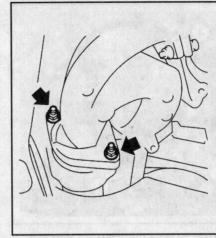

23.31 To disconnect the right exhaust manifold from the joint pipe, remove these nuts

26 Remove the engine cover, if equipped (see *Intake manifold - removal and installation* in Chapter 2A).

27 Disconnect the cable from the negative battery terminal (see Chapter 5).

28 Disconnect the exhaust temperature sensor (2004 Baja models and 2004 and 2005 Forester models, see illustration 9.3; 2005 and 2006 Legacy and Outback models, see illustration 15.15).

29 Remove the upstream oxygen sensor (see Section 15).

30 Remove the right exhaust manifold heat shield (see illustration).

31 Remove the nuts that secure the front exhaust manifold to the joint pipe (see illustration).

32 Remove the center exhaust pipe (see Steps 12 through 22).

33 Remove the turbocharger (see Chapter 4).

34 Remove the pre-catalytic converter/joint pipe.

35 Installation is the reverse of removal. Be sure to use new gaskets at the upper and lower mounting flanges of the pre-catalytic converter/joint pipe and be sure to tighten the nuts and bolts to the torque listed in this Chapter's Specifications.

24 Evaporative Emission Control (EVAP) system - description and component replacement

DESCRIPTION

1 The Evaporative Emissions Control (EVAP) system absorbs fuel vapors (unburned hydrocarbons) and, during engine operation, releases them into the intake manifold from which they're drawn into the intake ports where they mix with the incoming air-fuel mixture.

2 The EVAP system consists of the fuel tank filler neck cap, the fuel cut valve, the EVAP canister, the drain filter, the drain valve, the fuel tank pressure sensor, the pressure control solenoid valve, the shut-off valve, the vent valve and the purge control solenoid valve. Everything except the purge control solenoid valve is located underneath the vehicle, tucked between the right rear wheelwell and the right inside corner of the rear bumper cover. The EVAP canister purge valve is located in the engine compartment, under the right side of the intake manifold.

3 Modern EVAP systems are quite complex. But basically, here's how it works: The gasoline inside the fuel tank evaporates constantly and produces fuel vapors. The **pressure control solenoid valve** monitors the pressure inside the tank and keeps the Powertrain Control Module (PCM) informed. When the PCM senses that the pressure has exceeded the specified threshold, it energizes the pressure control solenoid valve, which opens, allowing the vapors to migrate to the **EVAP canister**. The canister stores these vapors until the PCM energizes the **purge control solenoid valve**, which opens and *purges* the EVAP system, i.e. allows intake manifold vacuum to pull the vapors from the canisters into the intake manifold.

4 When the EVAP system is being purged and stored vapors inside the canister are being pulled out of the canister by intake manifold vacuum, a vacuum condition would quickly result inside the canister if it were not vented to atmospheric pressure. So during purging, atmospheric air is drawn into the EVAP canister through the **drain filter**, where any impurities are removed. From the drain filter, air is drawn through the **drain valve**, then into the canister.

5 The EVAP system *diagnostic monitor* is an OBD-II test that the PCM runs to check the EVAP system and the fuel tank for leaks. When the PCM runs the OBD-II EVAP system monitor, it energizes the **atmospheric pressure switching solenoid**, which closes off the passage between the fuel filler neck pipe (atmospheric pressure) and the fuel tank. The PCM also closes the drain valve during OBD-II system monitoring.

6 During refueling, three different valves play a role in protecting the EVAP system from being contaminated by raw gasoline. The **shut-off valve**, which is located at the top of the fuel filler neck pipe, closes the EVAP line to prevent the fuel nozzle from accidentally pumping fuel into the EVAP system. Down at the fuel tank, the **fuel cut valve**, which is an integral component of the fuel tank - it's built into the top of the tank - prevents fuel from entering the EVAP system during refueling. As the fuel level in the tank rises, a float in the fuel cut valve moves up and closes the hole in the bottom of the fuel cut valve so that no fuel can enter the EVAP system. As the level of fuel inside the fuel tank rises during refueling, fuel vapors are produced in the space between the rising fuel level and the roof of the tank. The **vent valve**, which is also located on the fuel tank, allows these vapors to migrate to the EVAP canister. When the pressure inside the fuel tank exceeds atmospheric pressure, a spring-loaded diaphragm opens and allows the excessive pressure to push the vapors into the canister. The EVAP system's ability to vent vapors to the canister during refueling is the principal feature

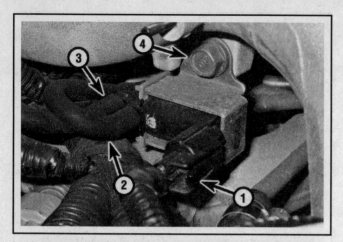

24.9a Purge control solenoid valve (2000 through 2004 unit shown; units on other models similar)

1 To disconnect the electrical connector, depress this release tab and pull off the connector
2 Disconnect the EVAP hose from the valve (this hose is coming from the EVAP canister)
3 Disconnect the EVAP hose from the valve (this hose goes to the intake manifold)
4 Remove the purge control solenoid valve mounting bolt and remove the valve

of the vehicle's **On-Board Refueling Vapor Recovery (ORVR)** system. The vent valve also has a float inside it that blocks the vapor passage through the valve once the tank is full.

7   In the event that an EVAP line becomes kinked or pinched, the **fuel tank filler neck cap** has a relief valve that prevents the formation of a vacuum inside the tank. When the EVAP system is functioning normally, the fuel tank filler neck cap is sealed by a sealing ring that's compressed when you screw on the cap. If a vacuum develops inside the fuel tank, atmospheric pressure forces a spring inside the filler cap to open a valve in the bottom of the cap, which open the fuel tank to the atmosphere. Air at atmospheric pressure is drawn into the relative vacuum of the fuel tank, keeping the air inside the tank (above the fuel) equalized with the outside atmospheric pressure.

COMPONENT REPLACEMENT

Purge control solenoid valve

Non-turbocharged models

♦ **Refer to illustrations 24.9a, 24.9b and 24.9c**

➡**Note: The purge control solenoid valve is located on the engine, under the right intake manifold runners (Nos. 1 and 3 cylinders).**

8   Disconnect the cable from the negative battery terminal (see Chapter 5).
9   Disconnect the electrical connector from the purge control solenoid valve (see illustrations).
10 Clearly mark the two EVAP hoses, then disconnect them from the purge control solenoid valve.
11 Remove the purge control solenoid valve mounting bolt and remove the valve.
12 Installation is the reverse of removal. Make sure that you reconnect the EVAP hoses to their correct ports on the purge control solenoid valve.

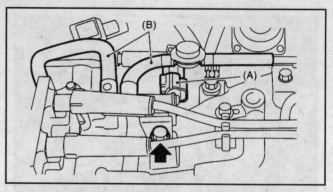

24.9b Purge control solenoid valve (2005 ULEV models)

A   Electrical connector   B   EVAP hoses

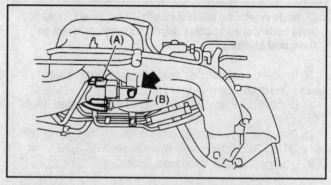

24.9c Purge control solenoid valve (2005 and 2006 non-ULEV models)

A   Electrical connector   B   EVAP hoses

Turbocharged models

2004 Baja and 2004 through 2006 Forester models

♦ **Refer to illustration 24.15**

➡**Note: The purge control solenoid valve is located on a small bracket in front of the intake manifold, behind and to the right of the alternator.**

13 Remove the engine cover, if equipped (see *Intake manifold - removal and installation* in Chapter 2A).
14 Disconnect the cable from the negative battery terminal (see Chapter 5).
15 Disconnect the electrical connector from the purge control solenoid valve (see illustration).

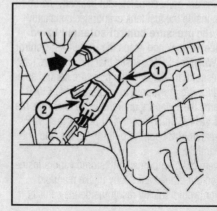

24.15 To remove the purge control solenoid valve (1), disconnect the electrical connector (2), then remove the mounting bolt (2004 turbocharged Baja models and 2004 through 2006 turbocharged Forester models)

24.21 Purge control solenoid valve (2005 and 2006 turbocharged Legacy and Outback models)

1 *Disconnect the electrical connector from the purge control solenoid valve*
2 *Remove the solenoid mounting bracket bolts and detach the bracket and solenoids as a single assembly*
3 *Remove the purge control solenoid valve from the mounting bracket*

16 Remove the purge control solenoid valve mounting bolt and pull out the valve far enough to access the two EVAP hoses.

17 Clearly mark the two EVAP hoses, then disconnect them from the purge control solenoid valve and remove the valve.

18 Installation is the reverse of removal. Make sure that you reconnect the EVAP hoses to their correct ports on the purge control solenoid valve.

2005 and 2006 Legacy and Outback models

♦ Refer to illustration 24.21

➡Note: The purge control solenoid valve is located next to the wastegate control solenoid valve on a small mounting bracket on the front of the intake manifold.

19 Remove the engine cover (see *Intake manifold - removal and installation* in Chapter 2A).

20 Disconnect the cable from the negative battery terminal (see Chapter 5).

21 Disconnect the electrical connector from the purge control solenoid valve (see illustration).

22 Remove the purge control solenoid valve mounting bracket mounting bolts (see illustration 24.21) and detach the bracket and solenoids as a single assembly from the intake manifold. (It's not necessary to disconnect the electrical connector from the solenoid next to the purge control solenoid valve, which is the wastegate control solenoid valve for the turbocharger wastegate.)

23 Clearly label, then disconnect the two EVAP hoses from the purge control solenoid valve.

24 Remove the purge control solenoid valve mounting bolt.

25 Installation is the reverse of removal. Make sure that you reconnect the EVAP hoses to their correct ports on the purge control solenoid valve.

EVAP canister

26 Disconnect the cable from the negative battery terminal (see Chapter 5).

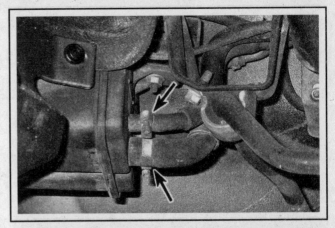

24.28 On 2000 through 2004 models, loosen these two hose clamps and disconnect the two EVAP hoses from the EVAP canister (Forester shown, Legacy and Outback similar)

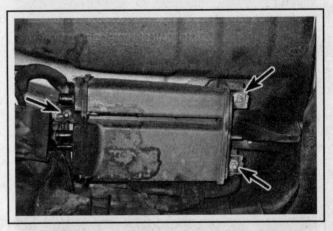

24.29 On 2000 through 2004 models, remove these three fasteners to detach and remove the EVAP canister (Legacy shown, Outback and Forester similar)

27 Raise the rear of the vehicle and place it securely on jackstands. On 2005 and 2006 Legacy and Outback models, loosen the lug nuts for the left rear wheel before raising the vehicle.

2000 through 2004 models

♦ Refer to illustrations 24.28 and 24.29

➡Note: On 2000 through 2004 models, the EVAP canister assembly is located underneath the vehicle, at the right rear corner, behind the right rear wheel and ahead of the rear bumper cover.

28 Disconnect the EVAP hoses from the EVAP canister assembly (see illustration).

29 Remove the canister mounting bolts/nuts (see illustration) and remove the canister.

30 Installation is the reverse of removal.

2005 and 2006 Forester models

31 On the front end of the EVAP canister, disconnect the electrical connector from the drain valve and disconnect the EVAP hoses from the EVAP canister assembly.

32 Disconnect the quick-connect fitting from the rear end of the EVAP canister. If you're unfamiliar with quick-connect fittings, refer to Section 4 in Chapter 4.

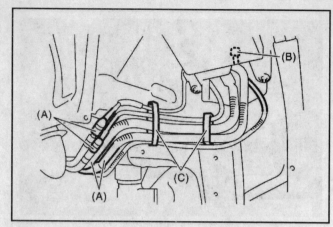

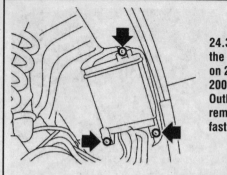

24.39 To detach the EVAP canister on 2005 and 2006 Legacy and Outback models, remove these three fasteners

24.38 On 2005 and 2006 Legacy and Outback models, disconnect the EVAP hose quick-connect fittings (A) and the drain valve electrical connector (B), then remove the hose clips (C)

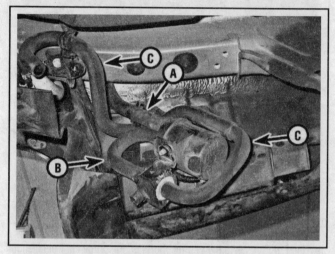

24.46 Before removing the drain filter or drain valve, make sure that you clearly label all of the EVAP hoses to ensure that they're correctly installed during reassembly (2000 through 2004 models)

A   This hose admits fresh outside air to the drain filter
B   This hose connects the drain filter to the drain valve
C   This hose connects the drain valve to the EVAP canister

24.45 To detach the drain filter from its mounting bracket, remove this nut (1). To detach the drain filter/drain valve mounting bracket, remove these two bolts (2) (2000 through 2004 models)

33 Disconnect the vent hose.
34 Remove the three EVAP canister mounting nuts (see illustration 24.29) and remove the canister assembly.
35 Installation is the reverse of removal.

2005 and 2006 Legacy and Outback models

▸ Refer to illustrations 24.38 and 24.39

➡Note: The EVAP canister is located behind the left rear wheel-well.

36 Remove the left rear wheel.
37 Remove the splash shield from the left rear wheelwell (see Chapter 11).
38 Disconnect the EVAP hose quick-connect fittings and the drain valve electrical connector and remove the EVAP hose clips (see illustration).
39 Remove the EVAP canister mounting fasteners (see illustration) and remove the canister.
40 Installation is the reverse of removal.

Drain filter and drain valve

2000 through 2004 models

▸ Refer to illustrations 24.45 and 24.46

➡Note: The drain filter and drain valve are located above the EVAP canister.

41 Disconnect the cable from the negative battery terminal (see Chapter 5).
42 Raise the rear of the vehicle and place it securely on jackstands.
43 Remove the EVAP canister (see Steps 28 and 29).
44 Disconnect the electrical connector from the drain valve.
45 Remove the nut that secures the drain filter to its mounting bracket (it's easier to loosen it now while everything is still bolted to the vehicle), then remove the mounting bracket bolts (see illustration).
46 Carefully lower the drain filter/drain valve assembly to access the EVAP hoses, clearly label the EVAP hoses (see illustration), then disconnect them from the drain filter and drain valve.
47 Remove the mounting bracket nut and separate the drain filter from the drain valve/mounting bracket.
48 Installation is the reverse of removal.

24.52 To detach the fuel tank pressure sensor mounting bracket, remove this bolt, then pull the sensor down to access the electrical connector and EVAP hoses (2000 and 2001 Legacy and Outback models)

2005 and 2006 models

49 On these models the drain valve and drain filter are integral components of the EVAP canister. They cannot be serviced separately.

Fuel tank pressure sensor

2000 and 2001 models Legacy and Outback models

▶ Refer to illustrations 24.52 and 24.53

➡Note: The fuel tank pressure sensor is located underneath the vehicle, above the inner CV joint boot for the right rear driveaxle.

50 Disconnect the cable from the negative battery terminal (see Chapter 5).

51 Raise the rear of the vehicle and place it securely on jackstands.

52 Remove the fuel tank pressure sensor mounting bracket bolt (see illustration), then pull down the sensor so that you can access the electrical connector and the EVAP hoses.

53 Disconnect the electrical connector from the fuel tank pressure sensor (see illustration).

54 Disconnect the EVAP hoses from the fuel tank pressure sensor and remove the sensor.

55 Installation is the reverse of removal.

2002 through 2004 models Baja, Legacy, Outback

▶ Refer to illustrations 24.60 and 24.62

➡Note: The fuel tank pressure sensor is located underneath the vehicle, above the inner CV joint boot for the right rear driveaxle. On these models, the fuel tank pressure sensor shares its mounting bracket with the atmospheric pressure solenoid valve (2002 models) or the fuel tank pressure sensor control valve (2004 and 2004 models). Either of these valves can be removed from the mounting bracket once the assembly has been removed from the vehicle, but the fuel tank pressure sensor cannot because it's permanently attached to the bracket. So if you're replacing the fuel tank pressure sensor you must remove the atmosphere pressure solenoid valve or the fuel tank pressure sensor control valve from the bracket and swap it over to the new fuel tank pressure sensor.

56 Disconnect the cable from the negative battery terminal (see Chapter 5).

57 Remove the fuel filler neck cap to equalize the pressure inside the fuel tank with the atmosphere.

58 Raise the rear of the vehicle and place it securely on jackstands.

59 Disconnect the electrical connectors from the fuel tank pressure sensor and from the atmospheric pressure solenoid valve (2002

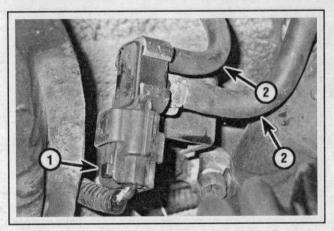

24.53 Depress this release tab (1) to disconnect the electrical connector from the fuel tank pressure sensor, then label and disconnect the EVAP hoses (2) (2000 and 2001 Legacy and Outback models)

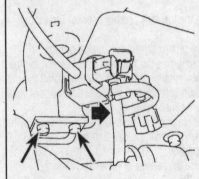

24.60 Disconnect the fuel tank pressure hose from the fuel tank pressure sensor, then remove the mounting bolts (2002 through 2004 Legacy and Outback models)

models) or the fuel tank pressure sensor control valve (2003 and 2004 models).

60 Disconnect the fuel tank pressure hose from the fuel tank pressure sensor (see illustration).

61 Remove the fuel tank pressure sensor mounting bracket bolts, then carefully pull down and remove the fuel tank pressure sensor and atmospheric pressure solenoid valve or fuel tank pressure sensor control valve as a single assembly.

62 Remove the atmospheric pressure solenoid valve or fuel tank

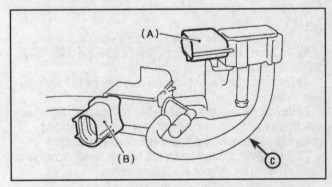

24.62 The fuel tank pressure sensor (A) is not removable from its mounting bracket. The atmospheric pressure solenoid valve/fuel tank pressure control valve (B) is removable and must be swapped to the new mounting bracket. You'll also have to disconnect the hose (C) between the valve and the sensor (2002 through Legacy and Outback models)

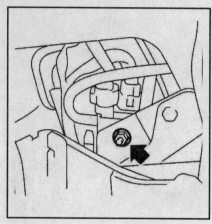

24.71 To detach the mounting bracket for the fuel tank pressure sensor and the fuel tank sensor control valve, remove this nut (2005 and 2006 Legacy and Outback models)

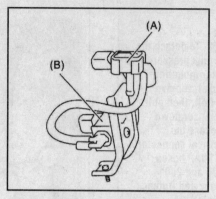

24.72 On 2005 and 2006 Legacy and Outback models, the fuel tank pressure sensor (A) and the fuel tank sensor control valve (B) are mounted on the same mounting bracket and must be replaced as single assembly. Neither component can be replaced separately

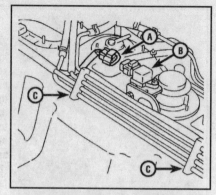

24.76 Disconnect the electrical connector (A) from the fuel tank pressure sensor (B), then disengage the clips (C) that secure the fuel lines to the fuel tank (2000 through 2002 Forester model shown, 2003 through 2006 models similar)

pressure control valve from the fuel tank pressure sensor mounting bracket (see illustration).

63 The fuel tank pressure sensor cannot be separated from its mounting bracket. If you're replacing the fuel tank pressure sensor, the new unit will come with a new mounting bracket. Simply install the old atmospheric pressure solenoid valve or fuel tank pressure control valve on the new fuel tank pressure sensor mounting bracket.

64 If you're replacing the atmospheric pressure solenoid valve or the fuel tank pressure control valve, install the new unit on the old fuel tank pressure sensor mounting bracket.

65 Installation is otherwise the reverse of removal.

2005 and 2006 Baja, Legacy and Outback models

▶ Refer to illustrations 24.71 and 24.72

➡Note: **The fuel tank pressure sensor is located underneath the vehicle, above the inner CV joint boot for the right rear driveaxle. On these models, the fuel tank pressure sensor and the fuel tank sensor control valve are a single assembly. So if you're replacing either component you must replace the entire assembly.**

66 Disconnect the cable from the negative battery terminal (see Chapter 5).

67 Remove the fuel filler neck cap to equalize the pressure inside the fuel tank with the atmosphere.

68 Raise the rear of the vehicle and place it securely on jackstands.

69 Disconnect the electrical connectors from the fuel tank pressure sensor and the fuel tank sensor control valve.

70 Disconnect the fuel tank pressure hose from the fuel tank pressure sensor.

71 Remove the nut that secures the fuel tank pressure sensor/fuel tank sensor control valve mounting bracket (see illustration) and remove the sensor, valve and bracket as a single assembly.

72 The fuel tank pressure sensor and fuel tank sensor control valve (see illustration) are replaced as a single assembly.

73 Installation is the reverse of removal.

Forester models

▶ Refer to illustration 24.76

➡Note: **The fuel tank pressure sensor is located on top of the fuel tank.**

74 Remove the fuel tank (see Chapter 4).

75 Remove the fuel line protector.

76 Disconnect the electrical connector from the fuel tank pressure sensor (see illustration).

77 Disengage the clips that secure the fuel lines to the fuel tank.

78 Two of the fuel lines are blocking access to the fuel tank pressure sensor mounting bracket bolt. Carefully move these two lines up so that you can access the bolt, then remove the bolt or nut and bolt and remove the fuel tank pressure sensor.

79 Disconnect the fuel tank pressure hose from the fuel tank pressure sensor.

80 Installation is the reverse of removal.

Atmospheric pressure solenoid valve/fuel tank pressure sensor control valve (2002 through 2004 Legacy and Outback models).

➡Note: **The atmospheric pressure solenoid valve (2002 models) and the fuel tank pressure sensor control valve (2003 and 2004 models) are located underneath the vehicle, above the inner CV joint boot for the right rear driveaxle. They're on the same mounting bracket as the fuel tank pressure sensor.**

81 Remove the fuel tank pressure sensor and its mounting bracket (see Steps 56 through 61).

82 Remove the atmospheric pressure solenoid valve (2002 models) or the fuel tank pressure sensor control valve (2003 and 2004 models) from the fuel tank pressure sensor mounting bracket (see illustration 24.62).

83 Installation is the reverse of removal.

Fuel tank sensor control valve (2005 and 2006 Legacy and Outback models)

➡Note: **The fuel tank sensor control valve is located underneath the vehicle, above the inner CV joint boot for the right rear driveaxle.**

84 On these models, the fuel tank sensor control valve and the fuel tank pressure sensor are a single assembly. So if you're replacing either component you must replace the entire assembly (see Steps 66 through 72).

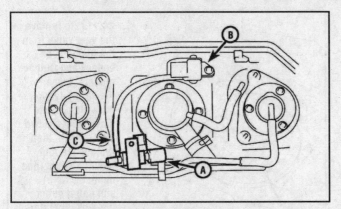

24.88 On Forester models, the fuel tank control valve (A) is located opposite the fuel tank pressure sensor (B). Before removing the fuel tank control valve, disconnect the hose (C) that connects it to the fuel tank pressure sensor

Fuel tank sensor control valve (Forester models)

♦ Refer to illustration 24.88

➡Note: The fuel tank sensor control valve is located on top of the fuel tank.

85 Remove the fuel tank (see Chapter 4).
86 Remove the fuel line protector.
87 Disconnect the electrical connector from the fuel tank sensor control valve.
88 Disconnect the hose (see illustration) from the fuel tank sensor control valve.
89 Remove the fuel tank sensor control valve.
90 Installation is the reverse of removal.

Pressure control solenoid valve

91 Disconnect the cable from the negative battery terminal (see Chapter 5).
92 Raise the rear of the vehicle and place it securely on jackstands.

Baja, Legacy and Outback models

♦ Refer to illustrations 24.93

➡Note: The pressure control solenoid is located underneath the vehicle, above the rear axle differential.

93 Locate the pressure control solenoid valve above the rear axle differential (see illustration) and disconnect the electrical connector from the solenoid valve.
94 Clearly label the EVAP hoses connected to the pressure control solenoid valve, then disconnect them from the valve.
95 On 2000 through 2004 models, disengage the two pressure control solenoid valve mounting tabs from the valve mounting bracket and remove the valve. On 2005 and 2006 models, remove the pressure control solenoid mounting bracket bolt, remove the pressure control solenoid and bracket as a single assembly, then detach the valve from the bracket.
96 Installation is the reverse of removal.

2000 through 2003 Forester models

♦ Refer to illustration 24.99

➡Note: The pressure control solenoid valve is located above the EVAP canister.

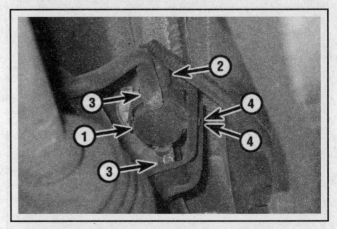

24.93 To remove the pressure control solenoid valve on 2000 through 2004 Baja, Legacy and Outback models (later models similar):

1   *Pressure control solenoid valve assembly*
2   *Disconnect the electrical connector*
3   *Disconnect the EVAP hoses*
4   *Disengage these two mounting tabs from the mounting bracket and remove the pressure control solenoid valve*

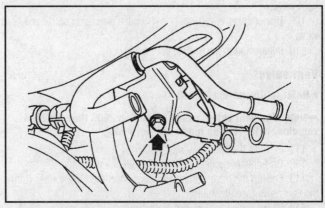

24.99 Disconnect the EVAP hoses, then remove the bolt that secures the pressure control solenoid mounting bracket to the vehicle body (2000 through 2003 Forester models)

97 Remove the EVAP canister (see Steps 27 through 35).
98 Disconnect the EVAP hoses from the metal EVAP lines.
99 Remove the bolt that secures the pressure control solenoid mounting bracket to the vehicle body (see illustration).
100 Disconnect the electrical connector from the pressure control solenoid valve.
101 Disconnect the two EVAP hoses from the pressure control solenoid valve, then remove the solenoid valve and bracket.
102 Detach the pressure control solenoid valve from its mounting bracket.
103 Disconnect the vacuum hose from the pressure control solenoid valve.
104 Installation is the reverse of removal.

2004 through 2006 Forester models

♦ Refer to illustration 24.105

➡Note: The pressure control solenoid valve is located above the EVAP canister.

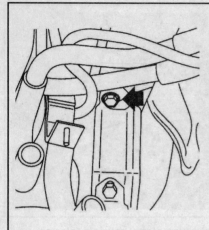

24.105 To detach the pressure control solenoid mounting bracket from the vehicle body, remove this bolt (2004 through 2006 Forester models)

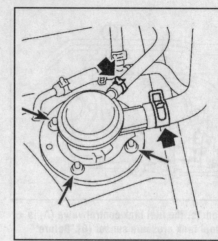

24.113 To remove the vent valve from the fuel tank on Legacy and Outback models, loosen the spring-type hose clamps and disconnect the two EVAP hoses, then remove the four mounting nuts (one nut not visible) and pull it out of the tank (Forester models similar)

105 Remove the bolt that secures the pressure control solenoid valve mounting bracket to the vehicle body (see illustration).

106 Disconnect the electrical connector from the pressure control solenoid valve.

107 Detach the pressure control solenoid valve from its mounting bracket.

108 Disconnect the two EVAP hoses from the pressure control solenoid valve.

109 Disconnect the vacuum hose from the pressure control solenoid valve.

110 Installation is the reverse of removal.

Vent valve

▶ Refer to illustration 24.113

➡Note: The vent valve, which is used on 2000 through 2004 vehicles, is located on top of the fuel tank.

111 Remove the fuel tank (see Chapter 4).

112 On Forester models, remove the fuel line protector.

113 Loosen the hose clamps and disconnect the EVAP hoses from the vent valve (see illustrations).

114 Remove the vent valve mounting nuts.

115 Remove and discard the old rubber gasket.

116 Installation is the reverse of removal.

Shut valve

▶ Refer to illustrations 24.118, 24.121 and 24.122

➡Note: The shut valve is located near the top of the fuel filler neck pipe. To replace the shut valve you'll have to remove the fuel filler neck pipe.

117 Disconnect the cable from the negative battery terminal (see Chapter 5).

118 Open the fuel filler cap door, unscrew the cap and remove the screws that secure the filler ring (see illustration).

119 Loosen the lug nuts for the right rear wheel. Raise the vehicle and place it securely on jackstands. Remove the right rear wheel.

120 Remove the splash shield from the right rear wheelwell (see Chapter 11).

121 Disconnect the EVAP hoses from the pipes on the fuel filler neck pipe (see illustration).

122 Remove any fasteners that secure the fuel filler neck pipe to the vehicle body (see illustration).

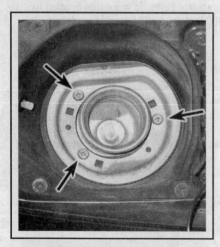

24.118 To detach the upper end of the fuel filler neck assembly from the vehicle body, remove the screws that secure the filler ring to the body

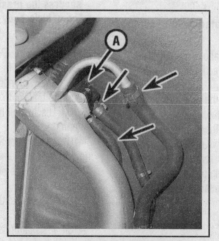

24.121 Disconnect any EVAP hoses connected to the fuel filler neck pipe and to the shut valve (A)

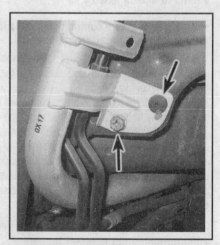

24.122 To detach the fuel filler neck pipe from the vehicle body, remove these fasteners

123 Trace the fuel filler neck pipe to its lower end, loosen the hose clamp that secures the filler hose to the filler neck pipe and disconnect the hose from the pipe. (If you're unable to work the hose off the filler neck pipe, wait until after you have unbolted the lower end of the pipe in the next step, then pull the pipe out of the hose.)

124 Remove the filler neck pipe lower mounting bolt and remove the filler neck assembly.

125 Remove the two shut valve mounting nuts and remove the shut valve from the fuel filler neck pipe.

126 Installation is the reverse of removal.

25 Exhaust Gas Recirculation (EGR) system - description and component replacement

DESCRIPTION

1 2003 through 2006 non-turbocharged Legacy and Outback models and 2004 through 2006 non-turbocharged Forester models are equipped with an Exhaust Gas Recirculation (EGR) system. When you pull a trailer, pass another vehicle or go up a steep hill, the temperature inside the combustion chambers heats up. When the temperature inside the combustion chambers reaches 2500 degrees F., the engine begins to produce oxides of nitrogen (NOx), which is an odorless, colorless and toxic gas that causes health problems for children, seniors, people with respiratory problems and people exercising outside on a smoggy day. The EGR system reduces NOx by introducing a controlled amount of spent exhaust gases into the intake manifold, which dilutes the air/fuel mixture, lowers combustion chamber temperatures and reduces the creation of NOx.

COMPONENT REPLACEMENT

EGR valve

▶ Refer to illustration 25.4

➥Note: The EGR is located on the intake manifold.

2 Disconnect the cable from the negative battery terminal (see Chapter 5).

3 Disconnect the electrical connector from the EGR valve.

4 Remove the EGR mounting bolts (see illustration) and remove the EGR valve from the intake manifold.

5 Remove and discard the old EGR valve gasket.

6 Remove all exhaust deposits from the EGR valve mounting surface on the manifold and, if you plan to use the same valve, the mount-

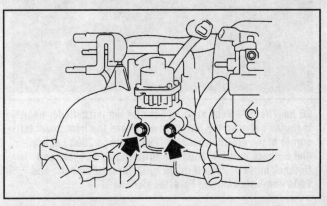

25.4 To detach the EGR valve from the intake manifold, remove these two bolts

ing surface of the valve itself. Look for exhaust deposits in the valve outlet. Remove deposit build-up with a scraper or screwdriver.

❊❊ CAUTION:

Don't wash the EGR valve in solvents or degreaser, either of which will permanently damage the diaphragm inside the valve.

7 If the EGR passage contains an excessive build-up of deposits, clean it out with a wire wheel. Make sure that all loose particles are completely removed to prevent them from clogging the EGR valve or from being ingested into the engine.

8 Installation is the reverse of removal. Be sure to use a new gasket and tighten the EGR valve mounting bolts to the torque listed in this Chapter's Specifications.

26 Positive Crankcase Ventilation (PCV) system - description and component replacement

DESCRIPTION

1 The Positive Crankcase Ventilation (PCV) system reduces hydrocarbon emissions by directing blow-by gases and crankcase vapors into the intake manifold, where they're mixed with intake air before drawn into the combustion chambers where they're consumed along with the air/fuel mixture. The PCV system does this by circulating fresh air from the air filter housing through a series of hoses into the crankcase, where the fresh air mixes with blow-by gases before being drawn from the crankcase by intake vacuum, through the PCV valve and then into the intake manifold.

2 During idle and part-throttle conditions, intake manifold vacuum is high. Blow-by gases and crankcase vapors flow from the crankcase

into the intake manifold through the PCV valve and the crankcase ventilation hose (also known as the PCV hose) into the intake manifold. The strong intake manifold vacuum also pulls fresh air from the air intake duct or the air filter housing through the fresh air inlet hoses into the crankcase.

3 During wide-open throttle conditions, intake manifold vacuum is not high enough to pull fresh air into the crankcase or to pull blow-by gases or crankcase vapors out of the crankcase. Instead, other hoses allow some of the blow-by gases and crankcase vapors to flow out of the crankcase and into the air intake duct or air filter housing, from which they're pulled into the intake manifold along with intake air.

4 There is no scheduled maintenance interval for the PCV valve or the PCV system hoses. But over time the PCV system might become

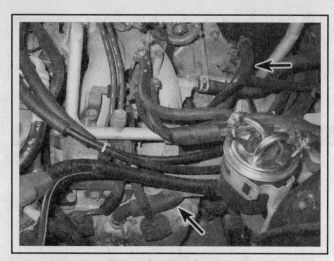

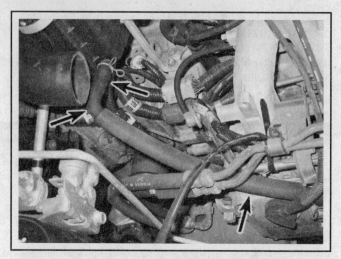

26.5a The PCV fresh air inlet hose for the left cylinder head is routed between the left valve cover and the front lower left corner of the air filter housing (2000 through 2003 Legacy and Outback models; 2004 non-turbocharged Legacy and Outback models; 2000 through 2003 Forester models; and 2004 non-turbocharged Forester models)

26.5b The PCV fresh air inlet hose for the right cylinder head is routed between the right valve cover and the front lower right corner of the air filter housing (2000 through 2003 Legacy and Outback models; 2004 non-turbocharged Legacy and Outback models; 2000 through 2003 Forester models; and 2004 non-turbocharged Forester models)

less efficient as an oily residue of sludge builds up inside the PCV valve and the hoses. One symptom of a clogged PCV system is leaking seals. When crankcase vapors can't escape, pressure builds inside the bottom end and eventually causes crankshaft seals to leak. So anytime that you're changing the oil filter, air filter, fuel filter, spark plugs, etc. it's a good idea to pull off the PCV hoses and inspect them. If the hoses are clogged, remove them and clean them out. If they're cracked, torn or deteriorated, replace them.

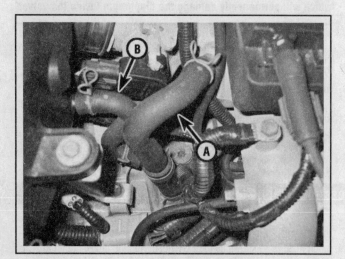

26.9 The typical crankcase ventilation hose (A), or PCV hose, connects the crankcase to the intake manifold. The other hose (B) connecting the PCV hose to the air filter housing allows blow-by gases and crankcase vapors to migrate to the air filter housing during part-throttle conditions (2000 through 2003 Legacy and Outback models; 2004 non-turbocharged Legacy and Outback models; 2000 through 2003 Forester models; and 2004 non-turbocharged Forester models)

COMPONENT REPLACEMENT

Fresh air inlet hoses

▶ **Refer to illustrations 26.5a and 26.5b**

5   There are two fresh air inlet hoses (see illustrations). To disconnect either hose, simply loosen the hose clamps and pull off the hose at each end.

6   Inspect the hoses for cracks, tears and deterioration. If either hose is damaged or worn, replace it.

7   Installation is the reverse of removal.

Crankcase ventilation hose (PCV hose)

▶ **Refer to illustration 26.9**

8   Remove the air intake duct assembly (see *Air filter housing - removal and installation* in Chapter 4).

9   The crankcase ventilation hose, or PCV hose (see illustration) connects the crankcase to the intake manifold. On 2000 through 2003 Legacy and Outback models, 2004 non-turbocharged Legacy and Outback models, 2000 through 2003 Forester models and 2004 non-turbocharged Forester models, you'll also note a short hose connecting the PCV hose to the air filter housing. This is the hose that allows blow-by gases and crankcase vapors to migrate into the intake manifold during part-throttle conditions. To disconnect the PCV hose, simply loosen the hose clamps and pull off the hose at each end.

10   Inspect the hose for cracks, tears and deterioration. If the hose is damaged or worn, replace it.

11   Installation is the reverse of removal.

PCV valve

▶ **Refer to illustration 26.13**

➡**Note: The PCV valve is located on the right rear corner of the crankcase, at the lower end of the crankcase ventilation hose.**

12 Disconnect the crankcase ventilation hose (see Steps 8 and 9).

13 Unscrew the PCV valve (see illustration).

14 Installation is the reverse of removal. Be sure to tighten the PCV valve securely.

26.13 To remove the PCV valve, simply unscrew it with a large wrench

27 Secondary air injection system - description and component replacement

DESCRIPTION

1 The secondary air injection system, which is used only on 2006 turbocharged Forester models, is a PCM-controlled system that pumps extra air into the exhaust system during open-loop operation, i.e. cold starts, to help oxidize unburned hydrocarbons until the oxygen sensors and the catalytic converters are warmed up. The system consists of a PCM-controlled electric air pump and two secondary air combination valves, one for each exhaust manifold. When the PCM energizes the relays for the secondary air combination valves, they open the left and right secondary air combination valves and the secondary air pump, and air is pumped into the exhaust manifolds. The *left* secondary air combination valve is located on the front of the *right* cylinder head, and the right valve is located on top of the right part of the engine block.

COMPONENT REPLACEMENT

Secondary air pump

◆ Refer to illustration 27.3

➡Note: The secondary air pump is located at the left front corner of the engine compartment, near the fuse box.

2 Disconnect the cable from the negative battery terminal (see Chapter 5).

3 Disconnect the electrical connector from the secondary air pump (see illustration).

4 Disconnect the hose from the secondary air pump (see illustration 27.3).

5 Remove the secondary air pump mounting bracket bolts (see illustration 27.3).

6 Installation is the reverse of removal.

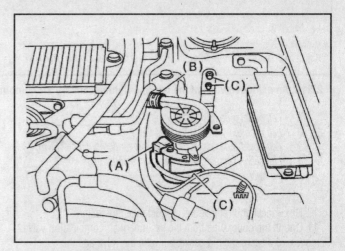

27.3 To remove the secondary air pump, disconnect the electrical connector (A), loosen the hose clamp (B) and disconnect the hose, then remove the three mounting bracket bolts (C) and remove the pump assembly

SECONDARY AIR COMBINATION VALVES

7 Disconnect the cable from the negative battery terminal (see Chapter 5).

8 Remove the intercooler (see Chapter 4).

Left secondary air combination valve

◆ Refer to illustration 27.10

9 Disconnect the electrical connector from the left secondary air combination valve.

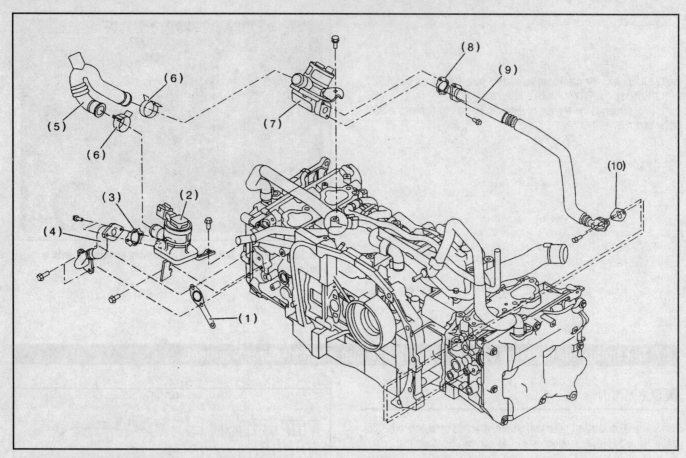

27.10 An exploded view of the left and right secondary air combination valve

1 Left outlet pipe gasket (at cylinder head)	6 Air duct hose clamps
2 Left secondary air combination valve	7 Right secondary air combination valve
3 Left outlet pipe gasket (at secondary air combination valve)	8 Right outlet pipe gasket (at secondary air combination valve)
4 Left secondary air combination valve outlet pipe	9 Right secondary air combination valve outlet pipe
5 Air duct	10 Right outlet pipe gasket (at cylinder head)

10 Disconnect and remove the air duct (see illustration).

11 Unbolt the outlet pipe from the secondary air combination valve. Remove and discard the old gasket between the valve and the outlet pipe.

12 Unbolt the left secondary air combination valve.

13 Installation is the reverse of removal. Be sure to use a new gasket when reconnecting the outlet pipe to the secondary air combination valve.

Right secondary air combination valve

14 Remove the left secondary air combination valve (see Steps 9

through 12).

15 Remove the intake manifold (see Chapter 2A).

16 Disconnect the electrical connector from the right secondary air combination valve.

17 Unbolt the outlet pipe from the right secondary air combination valve outlet pipe. Remove and discard the old gasket between the valve and the outlet pipe.

18 Unbolt the right secondary air combination valve.

19 Installation is the reverse of removal. Be sure to use a new gasket when reconnecting the outlet pipe to the secondary air combination valve.

28 Tumble generator - description and component replacement

DESCRIPTION

1 The tumble generator system is used on 2004 and 2005 ULEV models and on some 2005 and 2006 non-ULEV, non-turbocharged models and on 2004 through 2006 turbocharged models. The tumble

generator valves reduce emissions during start-ups. A tumble generator valve *swirls* the air entering the combustion chamber. Swirl is the orderly rotation of the air/fuel mixture in the combustion chamber, which improves the dispersion (mixing) of the air/fuel mixture. There are two types of tumble generator valve systems used on the vehicles covered in this manual. The principal differences between the two sys-

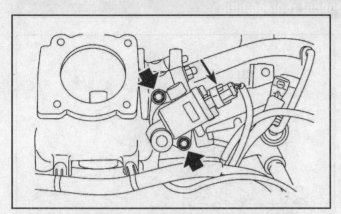

28.7 To remove the tumble generator valve actuator from the intake manifold plenum on 2004 and 2005 ULEV models, and on some 2005 and 2006 non-ULEV, non-turbocharged models, disconnect the electrical connector and remove the two actuator mounting bolts

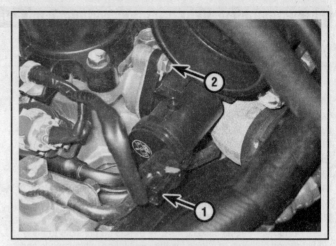

28.13 A typical tumble generator valve actuator (right actuator on 2006 turbocharged Outback shown, other actuators identical or similar). To detach the actuator from the tumble generator assembly, depress the release tab and disconnect the electrical connector (1), then remove the mounting bolt (2) and remove the actuator

tems is the location of the tumble generator valves.

2   On 2004 and 2005 ULEV models and on some 2005 and 2006 non-ULEV, non-turbocharged models, the system consists of four butterfly valves housed in the intake manifold plenum. In this system, each pair of valves is fitted on a single shaft and controls the airflow through the intake runners for one cylinder head. One pair of valves controls the intake runners for cylinder nos. 1 and 3 and another pair of valves control the runners for cylinder nos. 2 and 4. On these models, the tumble generator valve actuator is located at the right rear corner of the intake manifold plenum.

3   On 2004 through 2006 turbocharged models, the tumble generator valves (butterfly valves) are housed in the lower intake manifolds (Subaru refers to the lower intake manifolds as *tumble generator housings*). There is one valve for each intake runner, and each pair of valves is fitted to a common shaft. There are two actuators. The actuator for the left cylinder head is located at the rear end of the lower intake manifold and the actuator for the right cylinder head is located at the front end of the lower intake manifold.

4   Both systems work the same way: When you start a cold engine, the PCM determines that the engine coolant is cold, turns on a timer and energizes the tumble generator valve actuator, which (almost, but not quite) closes the butterfly valves. When the valves are closed, air entering the combustion chambers is forced to go through a very small cross-sectional area, which means that it moves through this bottleneck at very high speed, which creates a *tumbling* motion (swirl), which enables the mixture to be burned more completely. The timer turns off the tumble generator valve actuator once the engine is warmed up. The system only operates during cold start-ups.

5   If you want to remove or replace a tumble generator actuator, the procedure for doing so is located below. If you want to replace the tumble generator housing (the intake manifold plenum or the lower intake manifold), see *Intake manifold - removal and installation* in Chapter 2A.

COMPONENT REPLACEMENT

Tumble generator valve actuator (2004 and 2005 ULEV models and some 2005 and 2006 non-ULEV, non-turbocharged models)

◆ Refer to illustration 28.7

➡Note: The tumble generator valve actuator is located at the right rear corner of the intake manifold plenum, to the right of the throttle body (see illustration 5.22 in Chapter 2A).

6   Disconnect the cable from the negative battery terminal (see Chapter 5).

7   Disconnect the electrical connector from the tumble generator valve actuator (see illustration).

8   Remove the tumble generator valve actuator mounting bolts and remove the actuator.

9   Installation is the reverse of removal. Be sure to tighten the actuator mounting bolts securely.

Tumble generator valve actuators (2004 through 2006 turbocharged models)

◆ Refer to illustration 28.13

➡Note: The tumble generator valve actuators are located on the ends of the tumble generator assemblies. The left tumble generator valve actuator is located at the rear of the left tumble generator assembly. The right tumble generator valve actuator is located at the front of the right tumble generator assembly (see illustration 5.30a or 5.30b in Chapter 2A).

10 Disconnect the cable from the negative battery terminal (see Chapter 5).

11 If you're going to remove or replace the tumble valve actuator, remove the intercooler (see Chapter 4).

12 If you're going to remove or replace the tumble valve actuator, remove the air intake duct (see *Air filter housing - removal and installation* in Chapter 4).

13 Disconnect the electrical connector from the tumble generator valve actuator (see illustration).

14 Remove the tumble generator valve actuator mounting bolts and remove the tumble generator valve actuator.

15 Installation is the reverse of removal. Be sure to tighten the tumble generator valve actuator mounting bolts securely.

29 Variable Valve Lift system - description and component replacement

DESCRIPTION

1   The Variable Valve Lift system, which is used on 2006 non-turbocharged models, improves fuel economy and power and lowers exhaust emissions by changing the lift of the intake valves in accordance with engine speed and load. The system consists of a special camshaft, a variable valve lift mechanism and an Oil Switching Valve (OSV) for each cylinder head. There are three intake cam lobes on each camshaft: a normal lift cam lobe, a variable high-lift cam lobe and a variable low-lift cam lobe. The variable valve lift mechanism consists of a low-lift arm, a high-lift arm, a torsion spring and a small oil chamber that houses two locking pins and a spring.

2   During low engine speeds, the OSV directs oil pressure to the side of the oil chamber that locks up the low-lift arm, which opens and closes the intake valves at a lower lift ratio. The lower lift ratio produces more speed through the intake port, which promotes better swirl inside the combustion chamber, which produces more complete combustion, more torque and better efficiency.

3   As the engine speed increases so does the oil pressure, and the OSV reroutes engine oil to the other end of the oil chamber, unlocking the low-lift arm and locking the high-lift arm, which opens and closes the intake valves at a higher lift ratio. The higher lift ratio allows more air to enter the combustion chamber, which produces more power.

4   The oil temperature sensor is an information sensor for PCM control of the OSV. It's located on the rear upper right corner of the right cylinder head, near the OSV for the right head.

5   The variable valve lift diagnosis oil pressure switch is another PCM information sensor for the system. It's located on the front upper left corner of the left cylinder head, near the OSV for the left head.

COMPONENT REPLACEMENT

Oil switching solenoid valves (OSV) and OSV holders

Right OSV and OSV holder

◆ Refer to illustration 29.10

➡Note: There are two oil switching solenoid valves. They're located on the cylinder heads.

6   Disconnect the cable from the negative battery cable (see Chapter 5).

7   Remove the air filter housing (see Chapter 4).

8   Detach the engine harness electrical connector from its bracket.

9   Disconnect the electrical connector from the OSV.

10 Remove the OSV retaining bolt and remove the OSV (see illustration).

11 Remove the oil temperature sensor (see illustration 29.10).

12 Remove the variable valve lift diagnosis oil pressure switch (see illustration 29.10).

13 Remove the OSV holder mounting bolts and remove the holder (see illustration 29.10).

14 Remove and discard the old switching valve holder gasket.

15 Installation is the reverse of removal. Be sure to use a new switching valve holder gasket and tighten all bolts securely.

Left OSV and OSV holder

16 Disconnect the cable from the negative battery cable (see Chapter 5).

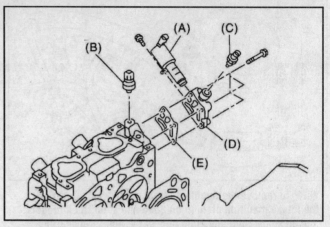

29.10 An exploded view of the right oil switching solenoid valve (OSV) and OSV holder assembly (left OSV similar):

  A   *Right oil switching solenoid valve (OSV)*
  B   *Right variable valve lift diagnosis oil pressure switch*
  C   *Oil temperature sensor*
  D   *OSV holder*
  E   *Gasket*

17 Remove the accessory drivebelts (see Chapter 1).

18 Remove the crankshaft pulley (see Chapter 2A).

19 Remove the timing belt cover and the timing belt (see Chapter 2A).

20 Remove the left camshaft sprocket (see Chapter 2A).

21 Remove the rear timing belt cover (see Chapter 2A).

22 Disconnect the electrical connector from the OSV.

23 Remove the OSV retaining bolt and remove the OSV.

24 Remove the variable valve lift diagnosis oil pressure switch.

25 Remove the OSV holder mounting bolts and remove the holder.

26 Remove and discard the old switching valve holder gasket.

27 Installation is the reverse of removal. Be sure to use a new switching valve holder gasket and tighten all bolts securely.

Variable valve lift diagnosis oil pressure switch

➡Note: There are two variable valve lift diagnosis pressure switches, one for each cylinder head. The left variable valve lift diagnosis oil pressure switch is located on the upper front end of the left cylinder head, right behind the left oil switching valve (OSV). The right variable valve lift diagnosis oil pressure switch is located on the on the upper rear end of the of the right cylinder head, just ahead of the right OSV.

28 Disconnect the cable from the negative battery cable (see Chapter 5).

29 Remove the air filter housing (see Chapter 4).

30 Detach the engine harness electrical connector from its bracket.

31 Unscrew and remove the variable valve lift diagnosis oil pressure switch (see illustration 29.10).

32 Installation is the reverse of removal. Be sure to tighten the variable valve lift diagnosis oil pressure switch securely.

Oil temperature sensor

➡Note: The oil temperature sensor is located on the holder for the right oil switching valve (OSV), which is located on the upper rear end of the right cylinder head.

33 Disconnect the cable from the negative battery cable (see Chapter 5).

34 Remove the air filter housing (see Chapter 4).

35 Detach the engine harness electrical connector from its bracket.

36 Unscrew and remove the oil temperature sensor (see illustration 29.10).

37 Installation is the reverse of removal. Be sure to tighten the oil temperature sensor securely.

30 Variable Valve Timing system - description and component replacement

DESCRIPTION

1 The variable valve timing system, which is used on 2004 through 2006 turbocharged models, adjusts the opening and closing timing of the intake valves by altering the phase angle of the camshaft sprockets relative to the camshafts. The Powertrain Control Module (PCM) continuously monitors the angle (position) of the crankshaft, engine speed, vehicle speed, throttle opening and other inputs, then determines the optimal phase angle of the camshaft sprockets.

2 Inside each intake camshaft sprocket are hydraulic chambers that can either advance or retard the cam sprocket in relation to the position of the camshaft. The flow of engine oil into and out of these two chambers is controlled by the oil flow control solenoid valves (there are two of them, one for each intake camshaft sprocket). The PCM continuously commands the oil flow control solenoid valve to move a spool inside the oil flow control solenoid valves, which directs engine oil in or out of chambers inside the intake camshaft sprockets. One of these chambers, when filled with oil, advances the sprocket. The other chamber, when filled with oil, retards the sprocket. The oil flow control solenoid valves are located on top of and at the front end of the valve covers.

COMPONENT REPLACEMENT

Variable valve timing solenoid valves/oil flow control solenoid valves

▶ Refer to illustrations 30.6a and 30.6b

➡Note: The variable valve timing solenoid valves (2004 models) or the oil flow control solenoid valves (2005 and 2006 models) are located on top of the cylinder heads, right behind the timing belt cover.

3 Remove the engine cover, if equipped (see *Intake manifold - removal and installation* in Chapter 2A).

4 Disconnect the cable from the negative battery terminal (see Chapter 5).

5 If you're going to remove the right variable valve timing solenoid valve/oil flow control solenoid valve, remove the air intake duct (see *Air filter housing - removal and installation* in Chapter 4).

6 Disconnect the electrical connector from the variable valve timing solenoid valve/oil flow control solenoid valve (see illustrations).

7 Remove the variable valve timing solenoid valve/oil flow control solenoid valve retaining bolt (see illustration 30.6a or 30.6b) and remove the solenoid valve.

8 Installation is the reverse of removal. Be sure to tighten the retaining bolt securely.

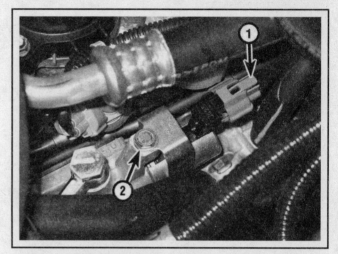

30.6a Left variable valve timing solenoid valve/oil flow control solenoid valve. Depress this release tab (1), remove the retaining bolt (2) and pull out the valve

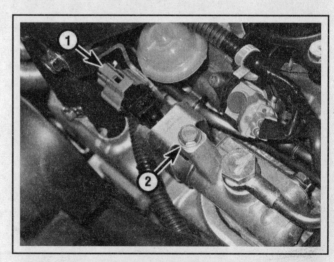

30.6b Right variable valve timing solenoid valve/oil flow control solenoid valve. Depress this release tab (1), remove the retaining bolt (2) and pull out the valve

Specifications

Torque specifications

Exhaust Gas Recirculation (EGR) valve mounting bolts	168 in-lbs
Exhaust temperature sensor	182 in-lbs
Knock sensor retaining bolt	209 in-lbs
Oxygen sensors	182 in-lbs
Pre-catalytic converter/joint pipe mounting flange nuts and bolts	26 ft-lbs

Section

Reference to other Chapters

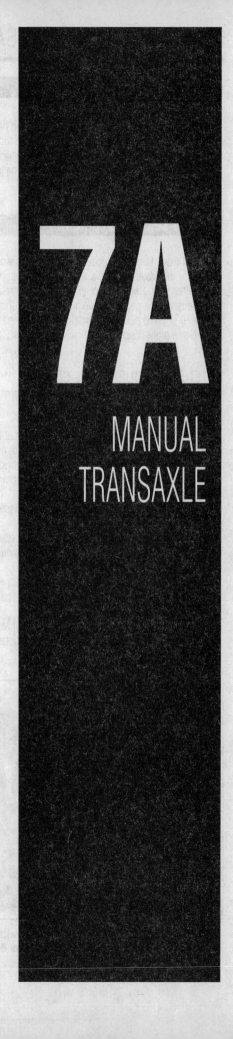

7A

MANUAL TRANSAXLE

1 General information

The manual transaxle is a fully-synchronized five-speed unit. The transaxle is actually several components bolted together into a single assembly: the clutch housing; the main case, which houses the differential and transmission; and the rear case. The transaxle is removed and installed as a single assembly; do not try to separate any of these components from the transaxle. If the transaxle must be replaced, obtain a complete new, rebuilt or used assembly.

2 Oil seal replacement

1   Oil leaks frequently occur as a result of a worn extension housing oil seal or driveaxle oil seal, a vehicle speed sensor seal or back-up light switch seal. Replacement of these seals is relatively easy, since the repairs can be performed without removing the transaxle from the vehicle. If you see puddles of lubricant under the transaxle, raise the vehicle and place it securely on jackstands. First, try to determine the source of the leak.

EXTENSION HOUSING OIL SEAL

▶ **Refer to illustrations 2.5 and 2.7**

2   The extension housing oil seal is located at the extreme rear end of the transaxle, where the driveshaft is attached. If the extension housing seal is leaking, there will be a buildup of lubricant on the front end of the driveshaft, and lubricant may even be dripping from the rear of the transaxle.

3   Remove the driveshaft from the transaxle (see Chapter 8).

4   Remove the heat shield (see Chapter 7B).

5   Using a seal removal tool or screwdriver (see illustration), carefully pry the oil seal out of the rear of the transaxle. Do not damage the splines on the output shaft.

6   If the oil seal cannot be removed with a screwdriver or prybar, a special oil seal removal tool (available at auto parts stores) will be required.

7   Using a seal driver or a large deep socket as a drift, install the new oil seal (see illustration). Drive it into the bore squarely and make sure it's completely seated.

8   Lubricate the splines of the output shaft and the outside of the driveshaft sleeve yoke with lightweight grease, then install the driveshaft. Be careful not to damage the lip of the new seal.

9   Installation is the reverse of the removal.

10   Remove the jackstands and lower the vehicle.

DRIVEAXLE OIL SEALS

11   Remove the exhaust manifold (see Chapter 2A) and the center exhaust pipe (see Chapter 4).

12   Place a drain pan under the transaxle.

13   Remove the driveaxle(s) from the transaxle (see Chapter 8).

14   Use a special seal removal tool and pry the driveaxle oil seal from the transaxle. If necessary, remove the oil seal using a blunt screwdriver. Be careful not to damage the transaxle while removing the oil seal.

15   Using a large section of pipe or a large deep socket as a drift, install the new oil seal into the transaxle. Drive it into the bore squarely and make sure it's completely seated.

16   Lightly oil the driveaxle seal then install the driveaxles (see Chapter 8).

17   Installation is the reverse of removal.

18   Remove the jackstands and lower the vehicle.

19   Check the transaxle lubricant level (manual transaxle) or differential lubricant level (automatic transaxle), adding as necessary to bring it to the appropriate level (see Chapter 1).

2.5 Remove the extension housing seal with a seal removal tool or a large screwdriver; make sure you don't damage the splines on the output shaft

2.7 Make sure the seal is square to the bore, then use a hammer and seal driver or large socket to tap the new extension housing seal into place; make sure the outside diameter of the socket is slightly smaller than the outside diameter of the new seal

3 Shift lever - removal and installation

▶ **Refer to illustrations 3.2, 3.10, 3.11, 3.12 and 3.13**

1   Disconnect the cable from the negative terminal of the battery (see Chapter 5).
2   Unscrew the shift lever knob from the shift lever (see illustration).
3   Remove the center console and the shift lever boot (see Chapter 11).

4   Remove the clamps from the boot and insulator assembly (see illustration 3.2).
5   Remove the boot and insulator assembly from the plate assembly.
6   Separate the plate assembly from the center console.
7   Raise the vehicle and place it securely on jackstands.

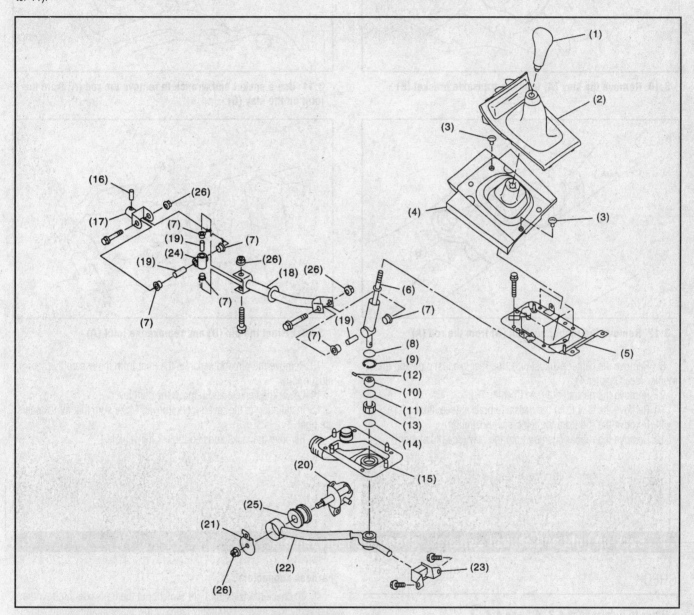

3.2 An exploded view of a typical shift lever assembly (2006 Legacy shown)

1	Gear shift knob	10	Bushing	19	Spacer
2	Front cover assembly	11	O-ring	20	Bracket
3	Clamp	12	Spring pin	21	Washer
4	Boot and insulator assembly	13	Bushing B	22	Stay
5	Plate assembly	14	O-ring	23	Rubber cushion
6	Lever	15	Boot	24	Boss
7	Bushing	16	Spring pin	25	Bushing
8	Lock wire	17	Joint	26	Self locking nut
9	Snap ring	18	Rod		

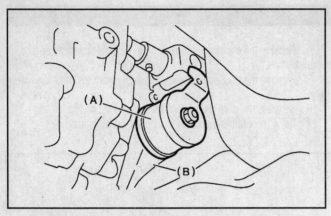

3.10 Remove the stay (A) from the transaxle bracket (B)

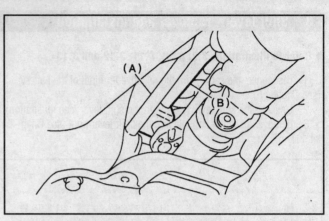

3.11 Use a socket and wrench to remove the rod (A) from the joint on the stay (B)

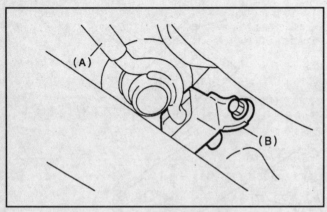

3.12 Remove the rubber cushion (B) from the rod (A)

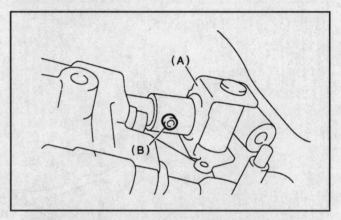

3.13 Extract the pin (B) and remove the joint (A)

8   Remove the center exhaust pipe, the rear exhaust pipe and the muffler (see Chapter 4).
9   Remove the heat shield (see Chapter 7B).
10 Remove the stay from the transaxle bracket (see illustration).
11 Remove the rod from the joint (see illustration).
12 Remove the rubber cushion from the stay (see illustration).

13 Remove the pin and separate the joint from the assembly (see illustration).
14 Lower the vehicle and remove the shift lever.
15 Installation is the reverse of removal. Make sure that all fasteners are tight.
16 Remove the jackstands and lower the vehicle.

4   Back-up light and neutral switches - check and replacement

CHECK

▶ **Refer to illustrations 4.2, 4.3 and 4.4**

1   Raise the vehicle and place it securely on jackstands.
2   The back-up light switch and the neutral switch (see illustration) are located on the left side of the transaxle.
3   To check either switch, trace the electrical lead back to its connector (see illustration) and hook up an ohmmeter.

➡**Note: On turbocharged models, remove the intercooler (see Chapter 4) to access the back-up light switch and neutral switch**

harness connectors.

4   To check the back-up light switch, put the transaxle into reverse and verify that there's continuity (zero or low resistance) (see illustration). Then put the transaxle in any other gear and verify that there's no continuity (high or infinite resistance).
5   To check the neutral switch, put the transaxle in Neutral and verify that there's continuity (zero or low resistance). Then put the transaxle in any other gear and verify that there's no continuity (high or infinite resistance).
6   If either switch fails to operate as described, replace it.

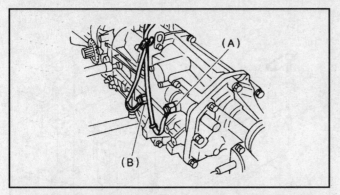

4.2 The back-up light switch (B) is located on the left side of the rear case; the neutral switch (A) is located right behind the back-up light switch

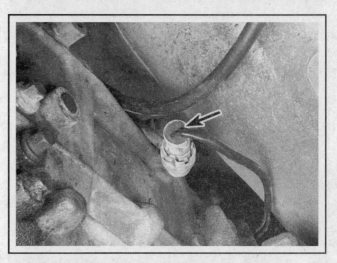

4.3 To check either switch, trace the electrical lead back to its connector, unplug the connector and hook up an ohmmeter to the connector terminals

REPLACEMENT

7 Simply unscrew the old switch, install the new switch (make sure the washer is installed) and tighten it to the torque listed in this Chapter's Specifications.

8 Verify that the new switch works properly (see above), then plug in the electrical connector.

9 Remove the jackstands and lower the vehicle.

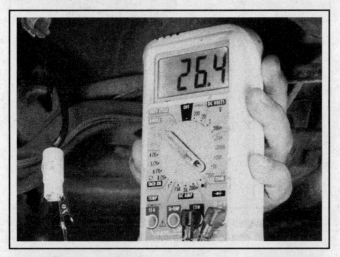

4.4 The back-up light switch should have continuity only in Reverse; the neutral switch should have continuity only in Neutral

5 Transaxle mount - check and replacement

▶ **Refer to illustrations 5.2, 5.3a and 5.3b**

1 Raise the vehicle and place it securely on jackstands.

2 Insert a large screwdriver or prybar into the space between the transaxle and the crossmember and try to pry the transaxle up slightly (see illustration). The transaxle should move very little. If it moves a lot, inspect the rubber portions of the two mounts. If either mount is damaged, replace the transaxle mount assembly.

3 To replace a mount, remove the bolts attaching the mount to the crossmember and to the transaxle (see illustrations).

4 Raise the transaxle slightly with a jack and remove the mount.

5 Installation is the reverse of the removal procedure. Be sure to tighten the bolts securely.

6 Remove the jackstands and lower the vehicle.

5.2 To check the transaxle mount, insert a large prybar between the rubber portion of the mount and the crossmember, then try to lever the transaxle up slightly; if it moves easily and excessively, replace the mount

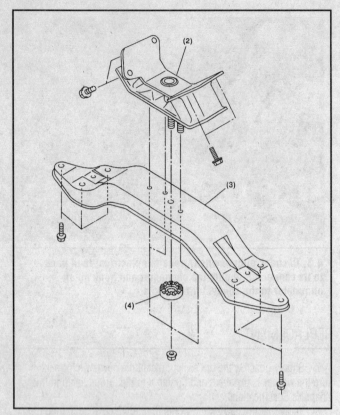

5.3a An exploded view of a typical transaxle mount and crossmember arrangement on an automatic transaxle

2   Transaxle mount
3   Transaxle rear crossmember
4   Stopper

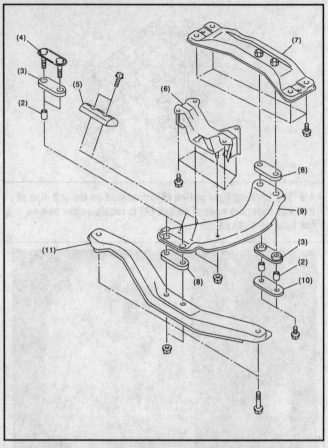

5.3b An exploded view of a typical transaxle mount and crossmember arrangement on a manual transaxle

2	Spacer	7	Rear crossmember
3	Cushion C	8	Cushion D
4	Front plate	9	Center crossmember
5	Damper - turbocharged	10	Rear plate
	models	11	Front crossmember
6	Transaxle mount		

6   Manual transaxle - removal and installation

REMOVAL

▶ **Refer to illustrations 6.9 and 6.17**

1   Open the hood and prop it open with the hood stay.

2   Disconnect the cable from the negative terminal of the battery (see Chapter 5).

3   Remove the air intake duct, the resonator and the air filter housing (see Chapter 4).

4   On turbocharged models, remove the intercooler (see Chapter 4).

5   Remove the air filter housing support brackets.

6   Clearly label, then unplug, all electrical connectors accessible from above that would interfere with transaxle removal.

7   Unbolt the battery ground cable at the transaxle.

8   Remove the starter (see Chapter 5).

9   Remove the clutch release cylinder (see Chapter 8). On 2004 turbocharged models, it will be necessary to remove the release fork shaft from the transaxle. Unscrew the cover plug located below the release cylinder, install a 6 mm diameter bolt into the release fork shaft and remove the shaft from the transaxle (see illustration).

10 Support the rear of the engine with an engine hoist or support fixture (see Chapter 2B, illustration 7.27a). Remove the upper engine mount brace (see illustration).

11 Remove the upper transaxle-to-engine bolts.

12 Raise the vehicle and support it securely on jackstands.

13 Remove the engine splash shield (see Chapter 2A).

14 Remove the exhaust manifold (see Chapter 2A), the center exhaust pipe, the rear exhaust pipe (turbocharged models) and the muffler (see Chapter 4).

15 Remove the driveshaft (see Chapter 8).

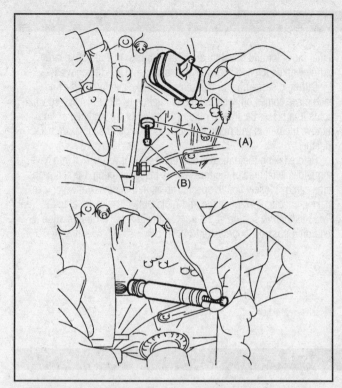

6.9 Install a 6 mm diameter bolt (B) into the clutch release fork shaft (A) and withdraw the shaft from the transaxle (2004 turbo models)

16 Remove the heat shield (see Chapter 2A).

17 Remove the hanger bracket from the right side of the transaxle (see illustration).

18 Remove the gear shift rod and the stay from the transaxle (see illustration 3.11).

19 Remove the stay from the transaxle.

20 Detach the stabilizer bar links from the lower control arms (see Chapter 10).

21 Separate the lower balljoints from the steering knuckles (see Chapter 10).

22 Remove the front driveaxles (see Chapter 8).

23 Place a transaxle jack or a floor jack equipped with a transmission adapter head under the transaxle. As a safety measure, secure the transaxle to the jack head with a tie-down, or a piece of chain or rope.

24 Remove the lower transaxle-to-engine nuts/bolts.

25 Remove the rear crossmember (see illustration 5.3b).

26 Move the transaxle jack to the rear slightly to disengage the input shaft from the splines on the clutch disc, then slowly lower the transaxle assembly. Keep a hand on the transaxle while lowering the assembly.

INSTALLATION

27 Apply a little multi-purpose grease to the input shaft splines.

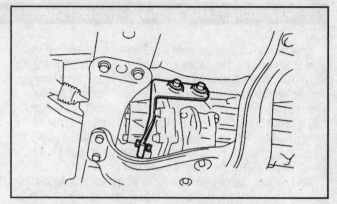

6.17 Remove the hanger bracket from the transaxle

Support the transaxle on the jack then raise it into alignment with the engine.

28 Slowly and carefully slide the transaxle forward and insert the input shaft into the clutch hub. If the input shaft hangs up, rotate the crankshaft or the transaxle output shaft until the input shaft splines are aligned with the clutch hub splines. Guide the transaxle forward until the transaxle and engine are fully engaged, then install the lower transaxle-to-engine fasteners and tighten them to the torque listed in this Chapter's Specifications.

29 Install the crossmember. Tighten all crossmember and mount nuts and bolts securely.

30 Remove the jack supporting the transaxle.

31 Install the driveaxles (see Chapter 8).

32 Install the shift linkage and tighten all fasteners securely (see Section 3).

33 Install the driveshaft (see Chapter 8).

34 Install the exhaust manifold (see Chapter 2A) and the exhaust pipe assembly (see Chapter 4).

35 Plug in the oxygen sensor connectors and the connectors for the back-up light switch and the neutral start switch.

36 Install the clutch release cylinder (see Chapter 8). Bleed the air from the clutch hydraulic lines if necessary.

37 Reattach the stabilizer bar link bolts (see Chapter 10).

38 Install the balljoints to the control arms (see Chapter 10).

39 Remove the jackstands and lower the vehicle.

40 Install the upper transaxle-to-engine bolts and tighten them to the torque listed in this Chapter's Specifications.

41 Install the starter motor (see Chapter 5).

42 Install the upper engine mount brace. Tighten the nuts and bolts securely.

43 Plug in any remaining unplugged electrical connectors. Reattach all ground wires.

44 Connect the battery ground cable to the battery.

45 Add lubricant to the transaxle by referring to the appropriate Section in Chapter 1.

46 Start the engine and check the exhaust system for any leaks or noise.

47 Check the shift linkage for smooth operation.

7 Manual transaxle overhaul - general information

Overhauling a manual transaxle is a difficult job for the do-it-your-selfer. It involves the disassembly and reassembly of many small parts. Numerous clearances must be precisely measured and, if necessary, changed with select fit spacers and snap-rings. If transaxle problems arise, you can remove and install the transaxle yourself, but overhaul should be left to a transaxle repair shop. Rebuilt transaxles may be available - check with your dealer parts department and auto parts stores. At any rate, the time and money involved in an overhaul are almost sure to exceed the cost of a rebuilt unit.

Nevertheless, it's not impossible for an inexperienced mechanic to rebuild a transaxle if the special tools are available and the job is done in a deliberate step-by-step manner so nothing is overlooked.

The tools necessary for an overhaul include internal and external snap-ring pliers, a bearing puller, a slide hammer, a set of pin punches, a dial indicator and possibly a hydraulic press. In addition, a large, sturdy workbench and a vise or transaxle stand will be required.

During disassembly of the transaxle, make careful notes of how each piece comes off, where it fits in relation to other pieces and what holds it in place. Be sure to note how the parts are installed as you remove them; this will make it much easier to get the transaxle back together.

Before taking the transaxle apart for repair, it will help if you have some idea what area of the transaxle is malfunctioning. Certain problems can be closely tied to specific areas in the transaxle, which can make component examination and replacement easier. Refer to the *Troubleshooting* section at the front of this manual for information regarding possible sources of trouble.

Specifications

Torque specifications	Ft-lbs	Nm
Back-up light switch/neutral switch		
2000 through 2004	18	25
2005 and later	24	32
Transaxle-to-engine fasteners		
Lower nuts	36	50
Upper bolts	36	50

Section

7B

AUTOMATIC TRANSAXLE

1 General information

All vehicles covered in this manual are equipped with either a five-speed manual transaxle or a four-speed (4AT) or a five-speed (5AT) automatic transaxle. All information on the automatic transaxle is included in this Part of Chapter 7. Information for the manual transaxle can be found in Part A.

The automatic transaxle shift lever can move through seven positions (early models) or four positions (later models). There are two types of shift levers; standard shift type and sport model type. The sport model can be operated in standard mode and sport mode. Sport mode is selected by moving the shift lever laterally from DRIVE (move to the right [early models] or left [late models]) where sport shifting can be selected by moving the shift lever forward for upshifts or back for downshifts.

Special tools and equipment are needed to service automatic transaxles because of their complexity. This Chapter is restricted to routine maintenance, general diagnosis and transaxle removal and installation.

If the transaxle requires major repair work, it should be left to a dealer service department or other qualified repair shop. Once properly diagnosed, however, you can remove and install the transaxle yourself and save the expense, and have the repair work done by a transmission shop.

2 Diagnosis - general

→Note: Automatic transaxle malfunctions may be caused by five general conditions: poor engine performance, improper adjustments, hydraulic malfunctions, mechanical malfunctions or malfunctions in the Powertrain Control Module or its signal network. Diagnosis of these problems should always begin with a check of the easily repaired items: fluid level and condition (see Chapter 1), and shift cable adjustment (see Section 3). Next, perform a road test to determine if the problem has been corrected or if more diagnosis is necessary. Because the transaxle relies on many sensors in the engine control system, and since the transmission shift points are controlled by the Powertrain Control Module, you'll also want to check to see if any trouble codes have been stored in the PCM (see Chapter 6 for a list of trouble codes and how to extract them). If the problem persists after the preliminary tests and corrections are completed, additional diagnosis should be done by a dealer service department or transmission repair shop. Refer to the Troubleshooting section at the front of this manual for transaxle problem diagnosis.

PRELIMINARY CHECKS

1 Drive the vehicle to warm the transaxle to normal operating temperature.

2 Check the fluid level as described in Chapter 1:

a) *If the fluid level is unusually low, add enough fluid to bring the level within the designated area of the dipstick, then check for external leaks.*

b) *If the fluid level is abnormally high, drain off the excess, then check the drained fluid for contamination by coolant. The presence of engine coolant in the automatic transaxle fluid indicates that a failure has occurred in the internal radiator walls that separate the coolant from the transaxle fluid (see Chapter 3).*

c) *If the fluid is foaming, drain it and refill the transaxle, then check for coolant in the fluid or a high fluid level.*

3 Check the engine idle speed.

→Note: If the engine is malfunctioning, do not proceed with the preliminary checks until it has been repaired and runs normally.

4 Inspect the shift cable (see Section 3). Make sure that it's properly adjusted and that it operates smoothly.

5 Check the transaxle range (TR) sensor adjustment (see Chapter 6).

FLUID LEAK DIAGNOSIS

6 Most fluid leaks are easy to locate visually. Repair usually consists of replacing a seal or gasket. If a leak is difficult to find, the following procedure may help.

7 Identify the fluid. Make sure it's transmission fluid and not engine oil or brake fluid (automatic transmission fluid is a deep red color).

8 Try to pinpoint the source of the leak. Drive the vehicle several miles, then park it over a large sheet of cardboard. After a minute or two, you should be able to locate the leak by determining the source of the fluid dripping onto the cardboard.

9 Make a careful visual inspection of the suspected component and the area immediately around it. Pay particular attention to gasket mating surfaces. A mirror is often helpful for finding leaks in areas that are hard to see.

10 If the leak still cannot be found, clean the suspected area thoroughly with a degreaser or solvent, then dry it.

11 Drive the vehicle for several miles at normal operating temperature and varying speeds. After driving the vehicle, visually inspect the suspected component again.

12 Once the leak has been located, the cause must be determined before it can be properly repaired. If a gasket is replaced but the sealing flange is bent, the new gasket will not stop the leak. The bent flange must be straightened.

13 Before attempting to repair a leak, check to make sure that the following conditions are corrected or they may cause another leak.

→Note: Some of the following conditions cannot be fixed without highly specialized tools and expertise. Such problems must be referred to a transmission shop or a dealer service department.

Gasket leaks

14 Check the pan periodically. Make sure the bolts are tight, no bolts are missing, the gasket is in good condition and the pan is flat (dents in the pan may indicate damage to the valve body inside).

15 If the pan gasket is leaking, the fluid level or the fluid pressure may be too high, the vent may be plugged, the pan bolts may be too tight, the pan sealing flange may be warped, the sealing surface of the transaxle housing may be damaged, the gasket may be damaged or the transaxle casting may be cracked or porous. If sealant instead of gasket

material has been used to form a seal between the pan and the transaxle housing, it may be the wrong sealant.

Seal leaks

16 If a transaxle seal is leaking, the fluid level or pressure may be too high, the vent may be plugged, the seal bore may be damaged, the seal itself may be damaged or improperly installed, the surface of the shaft protruding through the seal may be damaged or a loose bearing may be causing excessive shaft movement.

17 Make sure the dipstick tube seal is in good condition and the tube is properly seated. Periodically check the area around the speedometer gear or vehicle speed sensor for leakage. If transaxle fluid is evident, check the O-ring for damage. Also inspect the driveshaft oil seal for leakage.

Case leaks

18 If the case itself appears to be leaking, the casting is porous and will have to be repaired or replaced.

19 Make sure the oil cooler hose fittings are tight and in good condition. The transaxle oil cooler lines on these models are equipped with quick connect fittings - always inspect the O-rings if a leak is suspected.

Fluid comes out vent pipe or fill tube

20 If this condition occurs, the transaxle is overfilled, there is coolant in the fluid, the case is porous, the dipstick is incorrect, the vent is plugged or the drain back holes are plugged.

---

3 Shift cable - check, replacement and adjustment

✳✳ WARNING:

The models covered by this manual are equipped with a Supplemental Restraint System (SRS), more commonly known as airbags. Always disable the airbag system before working in the vicinity of any airbag system component to avoid the possibility of accidental deployment of the airbag(s), which could cause personal injury (see Chapter 12). Do not use a memory saving device to preserve the PCM or radio memory when working on or near airbag system components

CHECK

1 Firmly apply the parking brake and try to momentarily operate the starter in each shift lever position. The starter should only operate when the shift lever is in the PARK or NEUTRAL positions. If the starter operates in any position other than PARK or NEUTRAL, adjust the shift cable (see below). If, after adjustment, the starter still operates in positions other than PARK or NEUTRAL, the transmission range (TR) sensor is defective (see Chapter 6).

REPLACEMENT

♦ **Refer to illustrations 3.7, 3.8, 3.9, 3.10 and 3.11**

2 Disconnect the cable from the negative terminal of the battery (see Chapter 5).

3 Make sure the shift lever is in the NEUTRAL position.

4 Raise the vehicle and place it securely on jackstands.

5 Remove the engine splash shield (see Chapter 2A).

6 Remove the exhaust manifold (see Chapter 2A), the exhaust pipe and the muffler (see Chapter 4).

7 Remove the heat shield (see illustration).

8 Remove the locking clip from the shift lever on the transaxle (see illustration).

9 Remove the shift cable bracket from the shift cable plate assembly (see illustration).

10 Working under the vehicle on the shift lever linkage, remove the shift cable end (see illustration).

11 Separate the shift cable from the shift cable mount bracket (see illustration).

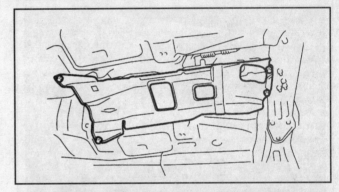

3.7 Remove the heat shield to access the shift cable

➡**Note: Later models are equipped with a clamp that must be expanded to remove the shift cable from the mount bracket (see illustration 3.19).**

12 Remove the shift cable from the vehicle.

13 Installation is the reverse of removal. Tighten the shift cable plate assembly bolts to the torque listed in this Chapter's Specifications. When you're done, adjust the cable (see below).

3.8 Remove the locking clip from the shift lever on the transaxle

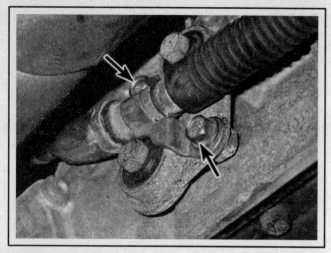

3.9 Remove the bolts and separate the shift cable and shift cable plate from the transaxle

3.10 Use a back-up wrench to hold the shift cable when removing adjusting nut A from the cable end

| A | Adjusting nut A | C | Hold with a wrench to |
| B | Adjusting nut B | | prevent turning |

3.11 On early models, loosen the shift cable lock nut to release the cable from the shift cable bracket

ADJUSTMENT

14 Make sure the shift lever is in the NEUTRAL position.

15 Raise the vehicle and place it securely on jackstands.

16 Remove the engine splash shield (see Chapter 2A).

17 Remove the center exhaust pipe and the muffler (see Chapter 4).

18 Working under the vehicle, remove the heat shield (see illustration 3.7).

19 Working under the vehicle below the console linkage, loosen Adjusting nut A and Adjusting nut B on both sides of the cable end (see illustration).

20 Turn Adjusting nut B until it contacts the linkage arm.

21 Install a back-up wrench onto Adjusting nut B to keep it from rotating and tighten Adjusting nut A to the torque listed in this Chap-

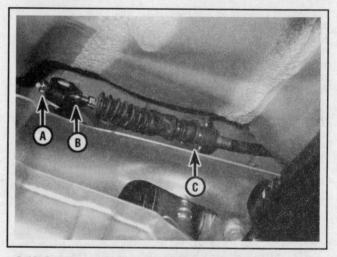

3.19 Details of the shift cable adjustment

| A | Adjusting nut A | C | Late model cable bracket |
| B | Adjusting nut B | | clamp |

ter's Specifications.

22 Remove the jackstands and lower the vehicle.

23 Move the shift lever through all gear positions and verify that the indicated positions correspond with the actual gear positions at the shift lever console. Also verify that the engine will start only in PARK and NEUTRAL, and that the back-up lights come on when the shift lever is placed in REVERSE. If necessary, readjust the cable until these conditions are met. It may also be necessary to adjust the transmission range sensor (see Chapter 6).

4   Shift lever - replacement

▶ **Refer to illustrations 4.6, 4.6b, 4.6c, 4.6d, 4.6e, 4.7 and 4.8**

1   Disconnect the cable from the negative terminal of the battery (see Chapter 5).

2   Make sure the shift lever is in the NEUTRAL position.

3   Raise the vehicle and place it securely on jackstands.

4   Disconnect the shift cable from the shift lever on the transaxle (see Section 3).

5   Lower the vehicle and remove the center console (see Chapter 11).

6   Remove the shift lever grip (see illustrations). On some models the grip is secured by one or two screws. On other models, the grip simply unscrews from the shaft.

➡**Note: On some models it is not necessary to remove the shift lever grip to access the various components of the shift lever system.**

7   Unplug the electrical connectors for the shift-lock solenoid and the park position switch (see illustration).

8   Remove the shift lever base mounting bolts (see illustration) and remove the shift lever assembly.

9   Installation is the reverse of removal. Adjust the shift cable as described in Section 3.

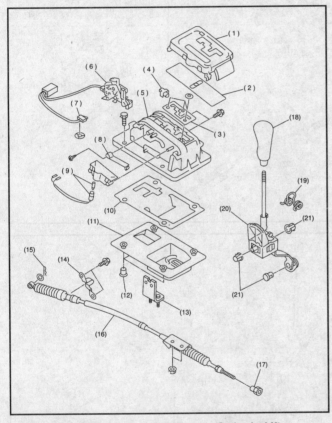

4.6a Typical 2000 through 2004 Legacy/Outback shift lever assembly

1	Indicator cover	12	Washer
2	Slider	13	Cable bracket
3	Pattern plate	14	Cable clamp
4	Stopper	15	Snap pin
5	Frame	16	Outer cable
6	Solenoid assembly	17	Nut
7	Park position switch	18	Grip
8	Detent spring	19	Spring
9	Illumination bulb	20	Select lever assembly
10	Plate	21	Bushing
11	Rubber boot		

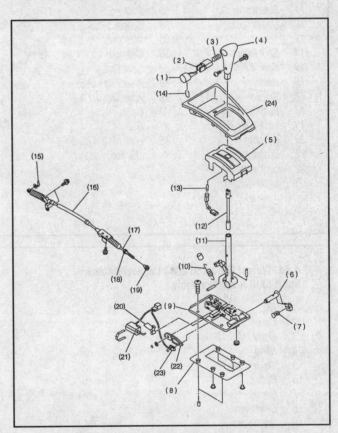

4.6b 2000 through 2002 Forester shift lever assembly

1	Button A	13	Indicator light bulb
2	Button B	14	Clip
3	Spring	15	Snap pin
4	Grip	16	Shift cable cover
5	Indicator cover	17	Shift cable
6	Lower select lever	18	Nut (front)
7	Pin	19	Nut (rear)
8	Packing	20	Lock plate
9	Plate	21	Shift lock solenoid
10	Detent spring	22	Lock arm
11	Upper select lever	23	Park position switch
12	Rod	24	Front cover

4.6c 2003 and later Forester shift lever assembly

1	Grip	23	Bushing
2	Indicator cover	24	Lock plate C
3	Cover	25	Shift lock solenoid
4	Blind	26	Clamp
5	Cushion	27	Indicator light bulb
6	Button	28	Clip
7	Clip	29	Lower shift lever
8	Park position switch	30	Bushing
9	Spring	31	Base plate
10	Guide plate	32	Grommet
11	Detent arm	33	Packing
12	Detent spring	34	Spacer
13	Tube	35	Washer
14	Shift lever	36	Snap pin
15	Spring pin	37	Select cable
16	Bushing	38	Adjusting nut B
17	Bracket	39	Adjusting nut A
18	Bushing	40	Cover
19	Lock plate B	41	Clip
20	Bushing	42	Lock plate A (turbo-charged models)
21	Bushing		
22	Lock plate A (non-turbocharged models)		

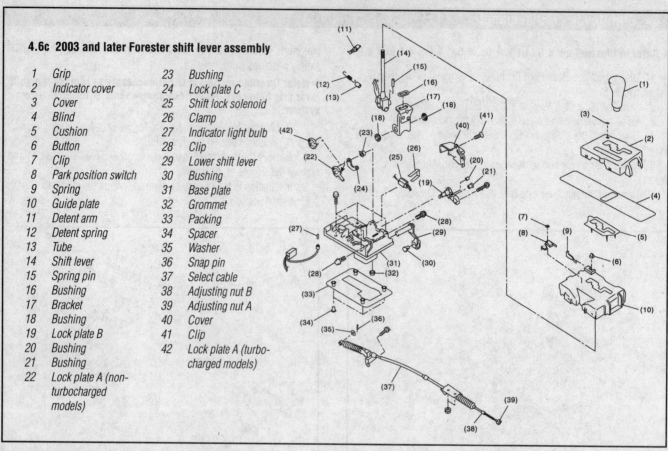

4.6d Typical 2003 and 2004 Legacy/Outback Sport Shift lever assembly

1	Grip	27	Base plate
2	Cover	28	Grommet
3	Cover	29	Bracket plate
4	Blind	30	Spacer
5	Guide plate	31	Bulb
6	Button	32	Rod
7	Spring	33	Spring
8	Detent arm	34	Bushing
9	Spring pin	35	Clip
10	Lever	36	Packing
11	Detent spring	37	Spacer
12	Tube	38	Washer
13	Arm bracket	39	Snap pin
14	Cushion	40	Shift cable
15	Adjusting nut A		
16	Bushing		
17	Bushing		
18	Lock plate B		
19	Clamp		
20	Shift lock solenoid		
21	Bushing		
22	Lock plate A		
23	Spacer		
24	Clip		
25	Linkage arm		
26	Bushing		

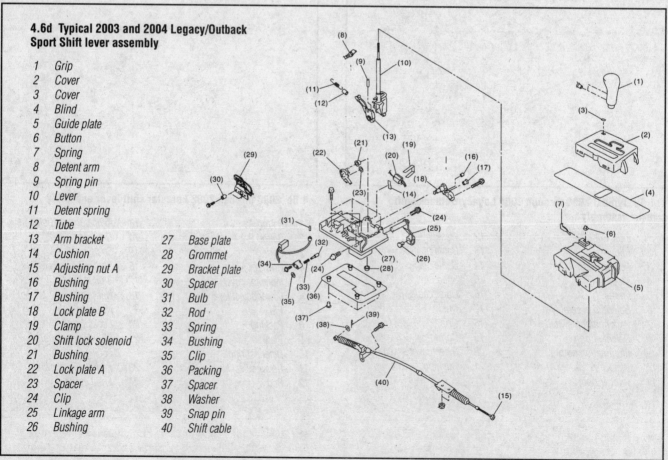

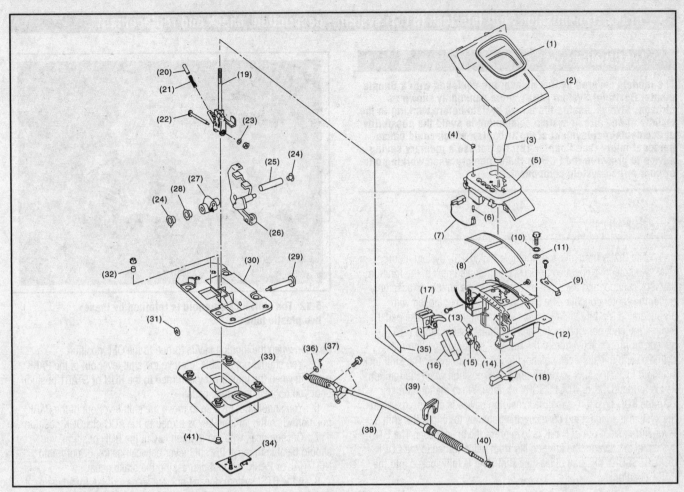

4.6e Typical 2005 and 2006 Legacy/Outback shift lever assembly

1	Ring indicator	9	Detent spring	17	Shift lock	23	Washer	32	Collar
2	Front cover	10	Spring washer		solenoid	24	Bushing A	33	Packing
3	Grip	11	Washer		assembly	25	Collar	34	Cable bracket
4	Release cover	12	Upper guide plate	18	Check plate	26	Arm assembly	35	Sheet
5	Indicator	13	Up switch	19	Shift lever	27	Bushing plate	36	Washer
	assembly	14	Down switch		assembly	28	Bushing B	37	Retaining clip
6	Indicator valve	15	Sport Mode	20	Sheet check ball	29	Shaft	38	Shift cable
7	Valve harness		switch	21	Return spring	30	Lower plate	39	Clamp
8	Blind	16	Switch cover	22	Shaft	31	Clamp	40	Adjusting nut A
								41	Bushing

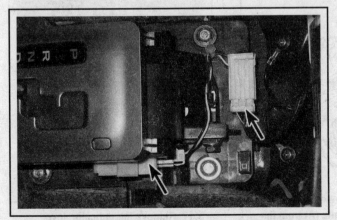

4.7 Unplug the shift lock solenoid and park position switch electrical connectors

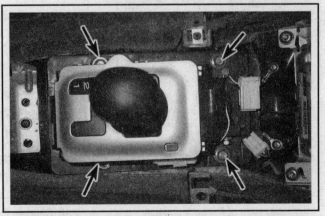

4.8 Remove the mounting bolts from the base of the shift lever assembly (2001 Legacy shown, other models similar)

5 Brake Transmission Shift Interlock (BTSI) system - description, check and replacement

> **❊❊ WARNING:**
>
> The models covered by this manual are equipped with a Supplemental Restraint System (SRS), more commonly known as airbags. Always disable the airbag system before working in the vicinity of any airbag system component to avoid the possibility of accidental deployment of the airbag(s), which could cause personal injury (see Chapter 12). Do not use a memory saving device to preserve the PCM or radio memory when working on or near airbag system components.

DESCRIPTION

1   The Brake Transmission Shift Interlock (BTSI) system incorporates two solenoid-operated devices; one mounted next to the ignition key lock cylinder and the other mounted onto the shift lever assembly under the center console. The BTSI system is also equipped with an Integrated Module that receives information from the brake pedal switch, the park position switch and the transmission range (TR) sensor for proper activation of the key lock solenoid (ignition lock cylinder) and the shift lock solenoid (console shift lever). The shift lock solenoid locks the shift lever into the PARK position when the ignition key is in the LOCK or ACCESSORY position. When the ignition key is in the RUN position, a magnetic holding device is energized. When the system is functioning correctly, the only way to unlock the shift lever and move it out of PARK is to depress the brake pedal. The BTSI system also prevents the ignition key from being turned to the LOCK or ACCESSORY position unless the shift lever is fully locked into the PARK position.

CHECK

2   Verify that the ignition key can be removed only in the PARK position.

3   When the shift lever is in the PARK position, you should be able to rotate the ignition key from OFF to LOCK. But when the shift lever is in any gear position other than PARK (including NEUTRAL), you should not be able to rotate the ignition key to the LOCK position.

4   You should not be able to move the shift lever out of the PARK

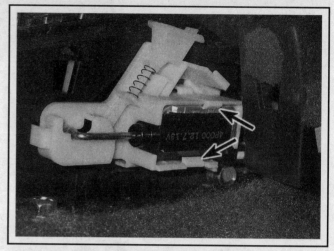

5.12 The shift lock solenoid is retained by these two plastic tabs

position when the ignition key is turned to the OFF position.

5   You should not be able to move the shift lever out of the PARK position when the ignition key is turned to the RUN or START position until you depress the brake pedal.

6   You should not be able to move the shift lever out of the PARK position when the ignition key is turned to the ACC or LOCK position.

7   Once in gear, with the ignition key in the RUN position, you should be able to move the shift lever between gears, or put it into NEUTRAL or PARK, without depressing the brake pedal.

8   If the BTSI system doesn't operate as described, try adjusting it as follows.

REPLACEMENT

9   Disconnect the cable from the negative terminal of the battery (see Chapter 5, Section 1).

Key lock solenoid

10   The key lock solenoid must be replaced as a single unit along with the ignition lock cylinder. Refer to Chapter 12 for replacement.

5.13 Location of the park position switch (it's retained by a press-on nut from underneath)

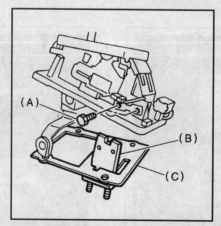

5.15 Remove the bolts (A) from the cable bracket (B) and separate the frame from the plate (C)

5.17 Remove the indicator cover

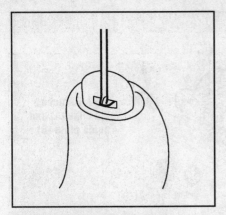

5.21a Remove the clip from the underside of the shift lever button and pull the button out of the handle grip

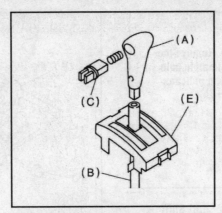

5.21b After removing the set screws from the handle grip, press the button (C) and lift the handle grip (A) from the shift lever (B), followed by the indicator cover (E)

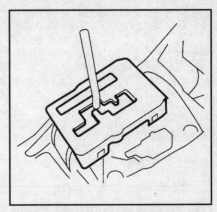

5.22 Remove the indicator light and the indicator cover - 2003 and later models shown

Shift lock solenoid and park position switch

11 Remove the center console (see Chapter 11).

2000 through 2004 Legacy/Outback models with standard shift

▶ **Refer to illustrations 5.12, 5.13, 5.15 and 5.17**

12 If you're just removing the shift lock solenoid, spread the retaining tangs and slide the solenoid out of its holder (see illustration), then unplug its electrical connector.

13 If you have to remove the park position switch (see illustration), remove the shift lever assembly (see Section 3).

14 Remove the four mounting bolts for the rubber boot (see illustration 4.6a).

15 Remove the bolts and separate the cable bracket and plate from the frame (see illustration).

16 Unscrew the shift lever grip.

17 Remove the indicator cover (see illustration).

▶ **Note: On some later models, it may be necessary to remove the cushion and the blind from the frame to access the park position switch.**

18 Disconnect the shift lock solenoid connector.

19 Remove park position switch retainer.

20 Installation is the reverse of removal.

Forester models

▶ **Refer to illustrations 5.21a, 5.21b, 5.22, 5.24, 5.25 and 5.26**

21 On 2000 through 2002 Forester models, pry the clip out from the underside of the shift lever button A and remove the button (see illustration). Remove the screws from the shift lever grip (see illustration 4.6b). While pressing button B, lift the handle grip off the lever stalk, then remove the indicator cover from the frame (see illustration).

22 Remove the indicator light and the indicator cover (see illustration).

23 On 2003 and later models, unscrew the shift lever grip, then remove the slider and the cushion (see illustration 4.6c).

24 Remove the cover (see illustration).

▶ **Note: The cover on 2000 through 2002 models is lifted from the top of the frame (see illustration 4.6b).**

25 Remove the clip and separate the park position switch from the frame (see illustration).

26 Remove the shift lock solenoid mounting clamp (see illustration).

27 Installation is the reverse of removal.

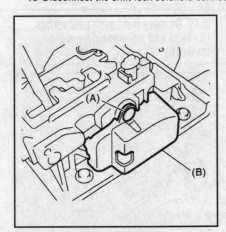

5.24 Remove the clip (A) and pull off the cover (B) to access the shift lock solenoid - 2003 and later models shown

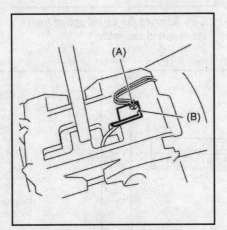

5.25 Remove the clip (A) and separate the park position switch (B) from the frame - 2003 and later models shown

5.26 Remove the mounting clamp (A) and the connector (B) from the shift lock solenoid - 2003 and later models shown

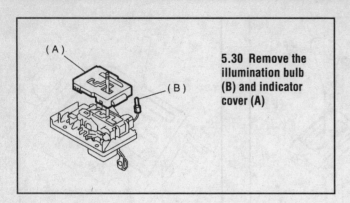

5.30 Remove the illumination bulb (B) and indicator cover (A)

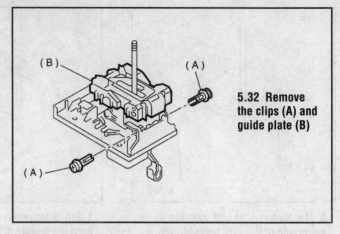

5.32 Remove the clips (A) and guide plate (B)

2003 and 2004 Legacy/Outback models with Sport Shift

♦ Refer to illustrations 5.30 and 5.32

28 Remove the shift lever assembly (see Section 3).

29 Remove the plugs and mounting screws and lift the handle grip from the shift lever (see illustration 4.6d).

30 Remove the illumination bulb and indicator cover (see illustration).

31 Remove the blind (see illustration 4.6d).

32 Remove the clips and guide plate (see illustration).

33 Remove the shift lock solenoid clamp (see illustration 5.26).

34 Remove shift lock solenoid along with the cushion (see illustration 4.6d).

35 Installation is the reverse of removal.

2005 and 2006 Legacy/Outback models

♦ Refer to illustrations 5.38, 5.39, 5.41 and 5.42

36 Unscrew the shift lever grip (see illustration 4.6e).

37 Remove the illumination bulb and the indicator cover from the shift lever assembly (see illustration 4.6e).

38 Working at the shift lever assembly on the center console, disconnect the shift lock solenoid connector at the guide plate (see illustration).

39 Position the shift lever in NEUTRAL and remove the detent spring from the solenoid assembly (see illustration).

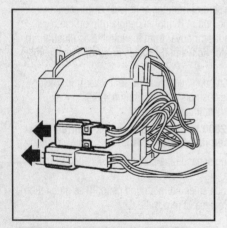

5.38 Disconnect the shift lock solenoid connectors at the guide plate

5.39 Remove the detent spring from the solenoid assembly

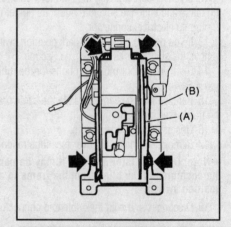

5.41 Remove the upper guide plate (A) bolts and separate it from the frame (B)

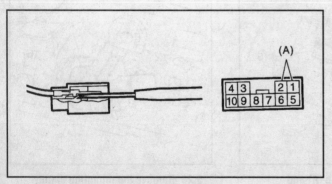

5.42 Use a screwdriver to release the spring clip inside the connector block at terminals A

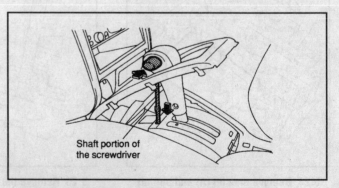

5.45a On 2000 through 2002 Forester models, remove the trim cover and insert a screwdriver into the hole and depress the BTSI override button

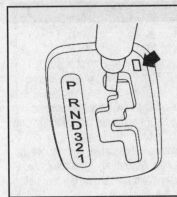

5.45b Location of the BTSI override button hole on 2000 through 2004 models (includes 2005 and 2006 Forester)

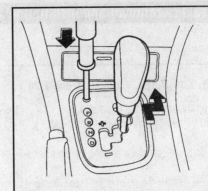

5.45c Location of the BTSI override button hole on 2005 and later Legacy/Outback models

40 Remove the mounting bolt from the shift lock solenoid and switch assembly and separate the assembly from the shift lever frame.

41 Remove the upper guide plate (see illustration).

42 Use a small screwdriver to disconnect the park position switch from the P terminal in the connector block (see illustration).

43 Remove the park position switch from the frame.

44 Installation is the reverse of removal.

SHIFT LOCK OVERRIDE FEATURE

♦ Refer to illustrations 5.45a, 5.45b and 5.45c

45 In the event the Brake Transmission Shift Interlock (BTSI) system

fails and the shift lever cannot be moved out of gear, the system is equipped with an override feature. The BTSI system can be bypassed and the shift lever can be used in manual operation with the parking brake ON and the engine OFF.

a) *On 2000 through 2002 Foresters, lift the center console trim panel (see Chapter 11). Press the override button with a screwdriver (see illustration) and shift the select lever into NEUTRAL.*

b) *On all other models, locate the override button alongside the shift lever (see illustrations) on the center console, carefully pry the protective cover off, press the override button and shift the select lever into NEUTRAL.*

6 Transmission Control Module (TCM) - removal and installation

✳✳ WARNING:

The models covered by this manual are equipped with a Supplemental Restraint System (SRS), more commonly known as airbags. Always disable the airbag system before working in the vicinity of any airbag system component to avoid the possibility of accidental deployment of the airbag(s), which could cause personal injury (see Chapter 12). Do not use a memory saving device to preserve the PCM or radio memory when working on or near airbag system components

6.3 Location of the transmission control module on a non-turbocharged model - turbocharged models slightly different

REMOVAL

♦ Refer to illustration 6.3

1 Disconnect the cable from the negative terminal of the battery (see Chapter 5).

2 Remove the knee bolster from the left side of the lower instrument panel (see Chapter 11).

3 Disconnect the transmission control module connector (see illustration).

4 Unscrew the mounting nuts from the TCM bracket and remove the TCM.

INSTALLATION

5 Installation is the reverse of removal.

6 On 2004 and later Legacy/Outback and 2005 and later Forester, the TCM must relearn the operating parameters before the vehicle can be driven. Have the TCM programmed by a dealer service department or other qualified automotive repair facility.

7   Automatic transaxle - removal and installation

REMOVAL

▶ **Refer to illustrations 7.5, 7.10, 7.12a, 7.12b, 7.20 and 7.28**

1   Open the hood and prop it open with the hood stay.

2   Disconnect the cable from the negative terminal of the battery (see Chapter 5).

3   Remove the air intake duct, the resonator and the air filter housing (see Chapter 4).

4   On turbocharged models, remove the intercooler (see Chapter 4).

5   Remove the air filter housing support brackets (see illustration).

6   Disconnect the transmission harness connectors.

7   Clearly label, then unplug, any other electrical connectors that would interfere with removal.

8   Remove the bolt and detach the battery ground cable at the transaxle.

9   Remove the starter (see Chapter 5).

10   Support the rear of the engine with an engine hoist or support fixture (see Chapter 2B, illustration 7.27a). Remove the upper engine mount brace (see illustration).

11   Install a wrench onto the crankshaft pulley for the purpose of rotating the engine for access to the torque converter bolts. Remove the drivebelt cover plate, if necessary, for access.

12   Remove the rubber service plug (see illustration) and remove the torque converter-to-driveplate bolts (see illustration). Mark the relationship of the torque converter to the driveplate and remove the four bolts which attach the torque converter to the driveplate

13   Remove the upper transaxle-to-engine bolts.

14   Raise the vehicle and support it securely on jackstands.

15   Remove the automatic transaxle fluid dipstick tube.

16   Remove the engine splash shield (see Chapter 2A).

17   Remove the exhaust manifold (see Chapter 2A), the center exhaust pipe, the rear exhaust pipe (turbocharged models) and the muffler (see Chapter 4).

18   Remove the driveshaft (see Chapter 8).

19   Drain the fluid from the transaxle (see Chapter 1).

7.5 Engine compartment details on a typical early model Legacy

A   *Air filter housing support brackets*
B   *Upper engine mount*
C   *Torque converter bolt access hole*

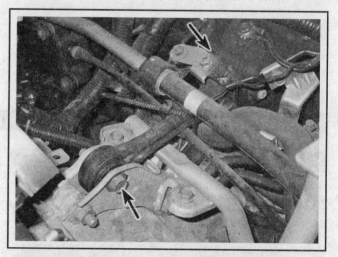

7.10 Location of the upper engine mount brace bolts

7.12a Pull out the rubber plug that covers the torque converter bolt access hole

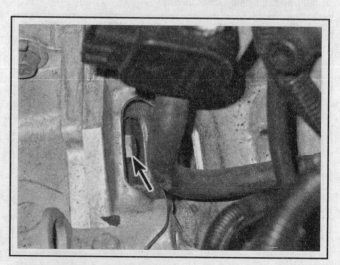

7.12b Torque converter bolt

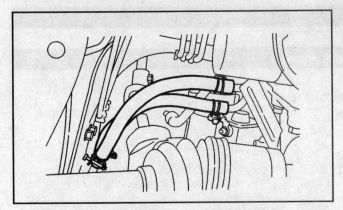

7.20 Disconnect the automatic transaxle fluid lines from the metal pipes at the transaxle

20 Disconnect the transaxle fluid cooler hoses from the metal lines (see illustrations).

21 Remove the heat shield (see illustra-tion 3.7).

22 Disconnect the shift cable from the lever on the transaxle and detach the cable bracket and shift cable from the transaxle (see Section 3).

23 Detach the stabilizer bar links from the lower control arms (see Chapter 10).

24 Separate the lower balljoints from the steering knuckles (see Chapter 10).

25 Remove the front driveaxles (see Chapter 10).

26 Place a transaxle jack or a floor jack equipped with a transmission adapter head under the transaxle. As a safety measure, secure the transaxle to the jack head with a tie-down, or a piece of chain or rope.

27 Remove the lower transaxle-to-engine nuts/bolts.

28 Remove the rear crossmember (see illustration).

29 Move the jack to the rear slightly to disengage the torque converter from the engine, then slowly lower the transaxle and torque converter assembly. Keep a hand on the torque converter, which can fall out once the transaxle is detached from the engine.

INSTALLATION

30 Replace the driveaxle oil seals, if necessary (see Chapter 7A).

31 Support the transaxle on the jack and raise it into alignment with the engine. Slowly and carefully slide the transaxle forward until the engine and transaxle are fully engaged.

32 Install the rear crossmember. Tighten the crossmember bolts and nuts securely.

33 Install the lower transaxle-to-engine mounting nuts and tighten them to the torque listed in this Chapter's Specifications. In the engine

7.28 Location of the transaxle crossmember mounting bolts

compartment, install the upper transaxle-to-engine bolts and tighten them to the torque listed in this Chapter's Specifications.

34 Line up the marks you made on the torque converter and driveplate, install the torque converter-to-driveplate bolts and tighten them to the torque listed in this Chapter's Specifications.

35 Remove the jack supporting the transaxle.

36 Install the driveaxles (see Chapter 8).

37 Reattach the stabilizer bar links (see Chapter 10).

38 Attach the shift cable and the cable bracket to the transaxle (see Section 3). Make sure the cable is correctly adjusted (see Section 4).

39 Install the driveshaft (see Chapter 8).

40 Reattach the automatic transaxle fluid cooler lines and install the dipstick tube.

41 Install the rear exhaust pipe heat shield.

42 Install the exhaust system (see Chapter 2A and Chapter 4).

43 Reconnect any electrical connectors that were unplugged from underneath.

44 Remove the jackstands and lower the vehicle.

45 Install the upper engine mount and tighten the bolts and nuts securely.

46 Install the starter motor (see Chapter 5).

47 Plug in the electrical connectors that are accessible from above.

48 Add the recommended automatic transmission fluid to the transaxle by referring to the appropriate Section in Chapter 1. Install the dipstick.

49 Connect the negative battery cable.

50 Start the engine and check the exhaust system for any leaks or noise.

51 Check the shift cable for smooth operation.

9 Automatic transaxle overhaul - general information

In the event of a problem occurring, it will be necessary to establish whether the fault is electrical, mechanical or hydraulic in nature, before repair work can be contemplated. Diagnosis requires detailed knowledge of the transaxle's operation and construction, as well as access to specialized test equipment, and so is deemed to be beyond the scope of this manual. It is therefore essential that problems with the automatic transaxle are referred to a dealer service department or other qualified repair facility for assessment.

Note that a faulty transaxle should not be removed before the vehicle has been diagnosed by a knowledgeable technician equipped with the proper tools, as troubleshooting must be performed with the transaxle installed in the vehicle.

Specifications

Torque specifications	Ft-lbs(unless otherwise indicated)	Nm
Shift cable plate bolts	18	25
Shift cable adjusting nut A	66 in-lbs	8
Torque converter bolts	18	25
Transaxle-to-engine nuts/bolts		
Lower transaxle-to-engine nuts/bolts	37	50
Upper bolts	37	50

Section

8

CLUTCH AND DRIVELINE

1 General information

The Sections in this Chapter deal with the components from the rear of the engine to the rear wheels (except for the transaxle, which is covered in Chapter 7) and to the front wheels. In this Chapter, the components are grouped into three categories: clutch, driveshaft and driveaxles. Separate Sections in this Chapter cover checks and repair procedures for components in each group.

Since nearly all these procedures involve working under the vehicle, make sure it's safely supported on sturdy jackstands or a hoist where the vehicle can be safely raised and lowered.

2 Clutch - description and check

▶ **Refer to illustrations 2.1a, 2.1b and 2.2**

1   All vehicles with a manual transmission have a single dry plate, diaphragm spring-type clutch. The clutch disc has a splined hub which allows it to slide along the splines of the transmission input shaft. The clutch and pressure plate are held in contact by spring pressure exerted by the diaphragm in the pressure plate (see illustrations).

2   The clutch release system is operated by hydraulic pressure. The hydraulic release system consists of the clutch pedal, a master cylinder and reservoir, a release (or slave) cylinder and the hydraulic line connecting the two components (see illustration).

3   When the clutch pedal is depressed, a pushrod pushes against brake fluid inside the master cylinder, applying hydraulic pressure to the release cylinder, which pushes the release bearing against the diaphragm fingers of the clutch pressure plate.

4   Terminology can be a problem when discussing the clutch components because common names are in some cases different from those used by the manufacturer. For example, the driven plate is also called the clutch plate or disc, the clutch release bearing is sometimes called a throwout bearing, the release cylinder is sometimes called the slave cylinder.

5   Unless you're replacing components with obvious damage, do these preliminary checks to diagnose clutch problems:

a) *The first check should be of the fluid level in the master cylinder. If the fluid level is low, add fluid as necessary and inspect the hydraulic system for leaks. If the master cylinder reservoir is dry, bleed the system as described in Section 5 and recheck the clutch operation.*

b) *To check "clutch spin-down time," run the engine at normal idle speed with the transmission in Neutral (clutch pedal up - engaged). Disengage the clutch (pedal down), wait several seconds and shift the transmission into Reverse. No grinding noise should be heard. A grinding noise would most likely indicate a bad pressure plate or clutch disc.*

c) *To check for complete clutch release, run the engine (with the parking brake applied to prevent vehicle movement) and hold the clutch pedal approximately 1/2-inch from the floor. Shift the transmission between 1st gear and Reverse several times. If the shift is rough, component failure is indicated.*

d) *Visually inspect the pivot bushing at the top of the clutch pedal to make sure there's no binding or excessive play.*

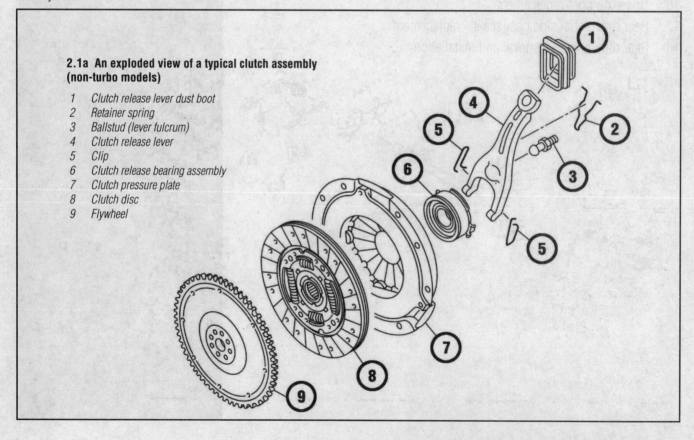

2.1a An exploded view of a typical clutch assembly (non-turbo models)

1   *Clutch release lever dust boot*
2   *Retainer spring*
3   *Ballstud (lever fulcrum)*
4   *Clutch release lever*
5   *Clip*
6   *Clutch release bearing assembly*
7   *Clutch pressure plate*
8   *Clutch disc*
9   *Flywheel*

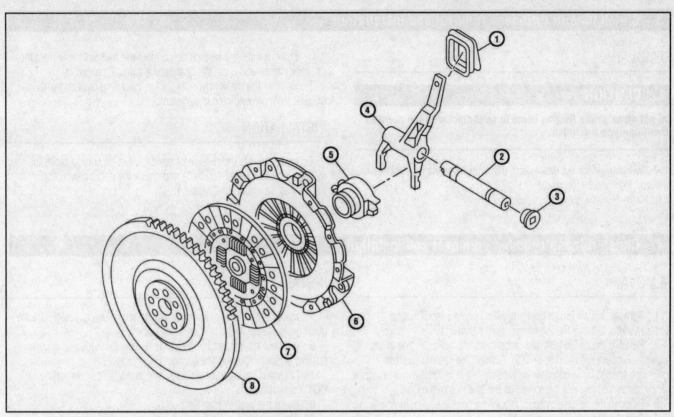

2.1b An exploded view of a typical clutch assembly (some turbo models)

1   Release lever dust boot
2   Release lever shaft
3   Plug

4   Release lever
5   Release bearing
6   Clutch pressure plate

7   Clutch disc
8   Flywheel

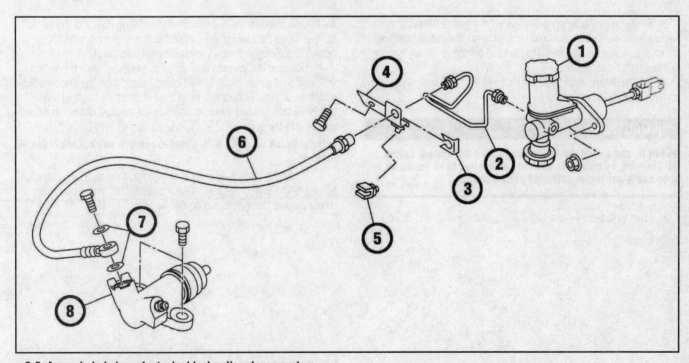

2.2 An exploded view of a typical hydraulic release system

1   Master cylinder assembly
2   Pipe
3   Clip

4   Bracket
5   Clip
6   Clutch hose

7   Washer
8   Release cylinder

3 Clutch master cylinder - removal and installation

REMOVAL

✳✳ CAUTION:

Do not allow brake fluid to come in to contact with the paint as it will damage the finish.

1 Working under the dashboard, disconnect the master cylinder pushrod from the clutch pedal.

2 Using a flare-nut wrench disconnect the hydraulic line from the master cylinder and drain the fluid into a suitable container.
3 Remove the master cylinder flange mounting nuts and withdraw the unit from the engine compartment.

INSTALLATION

4 Installation is the reverse of removal, but be sure to bleed the hydraulic system (see Section 5) and check the pedal height and freeplay as described in Chapter 1.

4 Clutch release cylinder - removal and installation

REMOVAL

1 Remove the air intake duct and filter housing (see Chapter 4). On Turbo models, remove the intercooler (see Chapter 4).
2 Remove the banjo bolt and disconnect the hydraulic line at the release cylinder (see illustration 2.2). Discard the sealing washers - new ones should be used upon installation. Have a small can and rags handy, as some fluid will be spilled as the line is removed.
3 Remove the release cylinder mounting bolts (see illustration 2.2).
4 Remove the release cylinder.

INSTALLATION

5 Install the release cylinder on the clutch housing. Make sure the pushrod is seated in the release lever pocket.
6 Connect the hydraulic line to the release cylinder, using new sealing washers. Tighten the connection.
7 Fill the clutch master cylinder with brake fluid (conforming to DOT 3 specifications).
8 Bleed the system (see Section 5).
9 The remainder of installation is the reverse of removal.

5 Clutch hydraulic system - bleeding

1 Bleed the hydraulic system whenever any part of the system has been removed or the fluid level has fallen so low that air has been drawn into the master cylinder. The bleeding procedure is very similar to bleeding a brake system.
2 Fill the clutch master cylinder reservoir with new brake fluid conforming to DOT 3 specifications.

✳✳ CAUTION:

Do not re-use any of the fluid coming from the system during the bleeding operation or use fluid which has been inside an open container for an extended period of time.

3 Have an assistant depress the clutch pedal and hold it. Open the bleeder valve on the release cylinder, allowing fluid and any air to escape. Close the bleeder valve when the flow of fluid (and bubbles) ceases. Once closed, have your assistant release the pedal.
4 Continue this process until all air is evacuated from the system, indicated by a solid stream of fluid being ejected from the bleeder valve each time with no air bubbles. Keep a close watch on the fluid level inside the brake master cylinder reservoir - if the level drops too far, air will get into the system and you'll have to start all over again.
➡**Note: Wash the area with water to remove any excess brake fluid.**
5 Check the brake fluid level again, and add some, if necessary, to bring it to the appropriate level. Check carefully for proper operation before placing the vehicle into normal service.

6 Clutch components - removal, inspection and installation

✳✳ WARNING:

Dust produced by clutch wear is hazardous to your health. DO NOT blow it out with compressed air and DO NOT inhale it. DO NOT use gasoline or petroleum-based solvents to remove the dust. Brake system cleaner should be used to flush the dust into a drain pan. After the clutch components are wiped clean with a rag, dispose of the contaminated rags and cleaner in a covered, marked container.

REMOVAL

▸ Refer to illustration 6.5

1   Access to the clutch components is normally accomplished by removing the transaxle, leaving the engine in the vehicle. If the engine is being removed for major overhaul, check the clutch for wear and replace worn components as necessary. However, the relatively low cost of the clutch components compared to the time and trouble spent gaining access to them warrants their replacement anytime the engine or transaxle is removed, unless they are new or in near-perfect condition. The following procedures are based on the assumption the engine will stay in place.

2   Remove the transaxle from the vehicle (see Chapter 7, Part A). Support the engine while the transaxle is out. Preferably, an engine support fixture or a hoist should be used to support it from above.

3   The clutch fork and release bearing can remain attached to the transaxle housing for the time being.

4   To support the clutch disc during removal, install a clutch alignment tool through the clutch disc hub.

5   Carefully inspect the flywheel and pressure plate for indexing marks. The marks are usually an X, an O or a white letter. If they cannot be found, scribe or paint marks yourself so the pressure plate and the flywheel will be in the same alignment during installation (see illustration).

6   Turning each bolt a little at a time, loosen the pressure plate-to-flywheel bolts. Work in a criss-cross pattern until all spring pressure is relieved. Then hold the pressure plate securely and completely remove the bolts, followed by the pressure plate and clutch disc.

INSPECTION

▸ Refer to illustrations 6.9, 6.11a and 6.11b

7   Ordinarily, when a problem occurs in the clutch, it can be attributed to wear of the clutch driven plate assembly (clutch disc). However, all components should be inspected at this time.

8   Inspect the flywheel for cracks, heat checking, grooves and other obvious defects. If the imperfections are slight, a machine shop can machine the surface flat and smooth, which is highly recommended regardless of the surface appearance. Refer to Chapter 2 for the flywheel removal and installation procedure.

9   Inspect the lining on the clutch disc. There should be at least 1/16-inch of lining above the rivet heads. Check for loose rivets, distortion, cracks, broken springs and other obvious damage (see illustration). As mentioned above, ordinarily the clutch disc is routinely replaced, so if in doubt about the condition, replace it with a new one.

10 The release bearing should also be replaced along with the clutch

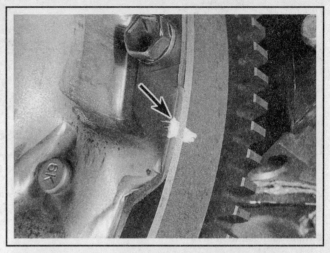

6.5 Mark the relationship of the pressure plate to the flywheel (if you're planning to re-use the old pressure plate)

disc (see Section 7).

11 Check the machined surfaces and the diaphragm spring fingers of the pressure plate (see illustrations). If the surface is grooved or otherwise damaged, replace the pressure plate. Also check for obvious damage, distortion, cracking, etc. Light glazing can be removed with emery cloth or sandpaper. If a new pressure plate is required, new and re-manufactured units are available.

12 Check the pilot bearing in the end of the crankshaft for excessive wear, scoring, dryness, roughness and any other obvious damage. If any of these conditions are noted, replace the bearing (see Section 8).

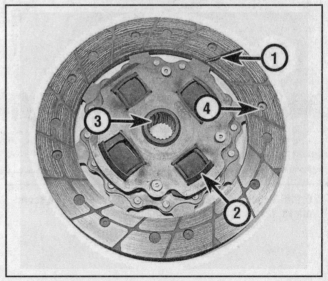

6.9 The clutch disc

1   **Lining** - *this will wear down in use*
2   **Springs or dampers** - *check for cracking and deformation*
3   **Splined hub** - *the splines must not be worn and should slide smoothly on the transmission input shaft splines*
4   **Rivets** - *these secure the lining and will damage the flywheel or pressure plate if allowed to contact the surfaces*

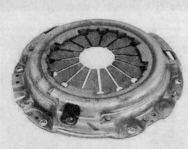
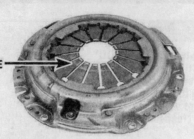

EXCESSIVE WEAR

NORMAL FINGER WEAR   **EXCESSIVE FINGER WEAR**   **BROKEN OR BENT FINGERS**

6.11a Replace the pressure plate if excessive wear or damage are noted

INSTALLATION

▶ **Refer to illustration 6.14**

13 Before installation, clean the flywheel and pressure plate machined surfaces with brake cleaner, lacquer thinner or acetone. It's important that no oil or grease is on these surfaces or the lining of the clutch disc. Handle the parts only with clean hands.

14 Position the clutch disc and pressure plate against the flywheel with the clutch held in place with an alignment tool (see illustration). Make sure the disc is installed properly (most replacement clutch discs will be marked "flywheel side" or something similar - if not marked, install the clutch disc with the damper springs toward the transaxle).

15 Tighten the pressure plate-to-flywheel bolts only finger tight, working around the pressure plate.

16 Center the clutch disc by ensuring the alignment tool extends through the splined hub and into the pilot bearing in the crankshaft. Wiggle the tool up, down or side-to-side as needed to center the disc. Tighten the pressure plate-to-flywheel bolts a little at a time, working in a criss-cross pattern to prevent distorting the cover. After all of the bolts are snug, tighten them to the torque listed in this Chapter's Specifications. Remove the alignment tool.

17 Using high-temperature grease, lubricate the inner groove of the release bearing (see Section 7). Also place a small amount of grease on the release lever contact areas and the transaxle input shaft bearing retainer.

18 Install the clutch release bearing (see Section 7).

19 Install the transaxle and all components removed previously.

6.11b Inspect the pressure plate surface for excessive score marks, cracks and signs of overheating

6.14 Center the clutch disc in the pressure plate with the clutch alignment tool

7 Clutch release bearing - removal, inspection and installation

REMOVAL

▶ **Refer to illustrations 7.2a, 7.2b, 7.3a and 7.3b**

1 Remove the transaxle (see Chapter 7A).
2 Remove the release bearing retaining clips (or springs) from the bearing and remove the bearing from the input shaft (see illustrations).
3 If the release lever pivots on a ballstud, pry off the release lever from the ballstud and remove the lever and the rubber sealing boot from the transaxle (see illustrations). If it is necessary to remove the lever of the type that pivots on a cross shaft, remove the plug (see illustration 2.1b) and knock out the release lever shaft.

INSPECTION

▶ **Refer to illustration 7.4**

4 Hold the bearing and rotate the outer portion while applying pressure (see illustration). If the bearing doesn't turn smoothly or if it's noisy, replace it. Wipe the bearing with a clean shop rag and inspect

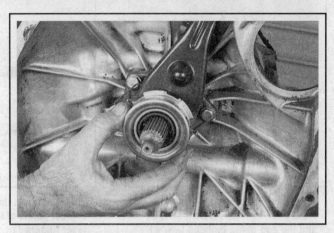

7.2a Disengage the retaining clips from the release bearing . . .

it for cracks, wear and other damage. Do NOT immerse the bearing in solvent; it's a sealed unit, so putting it into solvent will ruin it.

7.2b . . . and slide the release bearing off the input shaft; note which end of the bearing faces toward the clutch pressure plate diaphragm fingers - this is the bearing surface, and the bearing must be installed this way

7.3a The release lever is secured to the ballstud by a wire retainer spring on the backside of the lever; to disengage the lever from the ballstud, insert a screwdriver behind the lever and carefully but firmly pry it off . . .

7.3b . . . then pull the release lever and the old rubber dust boot out through the hole in the bellhousing

7.4 To check the release bearing, turn it while pushing on it at the same time; the bearing should rotate smoothly and quietly; if it's rough or noisy, replace it

7.6a Lubricate the sleeve of the input shaft bearing retainer (arrow) and the end of the ballstud (arrow) with high-temperature grease

7.6b Lubricate the lever-to-bearing contact points of the two release lever fingers . . .

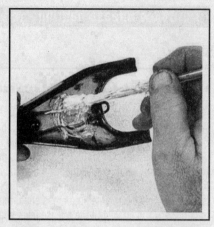

7.6c . . . then turn over the lever and lubricate the pocket for the ballstud and the retainer spring

INSTALLATION

◆ Refer to illustrations 7.6a, 7.6b and 7.6c

5   Replace the release bearing retaining clips, or the release bearing/ballstud retainer spring, if they're deformed or weak

6   Apply a light coat of grease to the sleeve of the input shaft bearing retainer and the input shaft splines (see illustration), and to the contact surfaces of the release lever (see illustrations).

7   Installation is essentially the reverse of removal. Make sure the release lever is properly positioned on the ballstud, then push it firmly until the ballstud pops into place between the two sides of the retainer spring.

8   Install the release bearing and secure it with the retaining clips.

9   Install the transaxle (see Chapter 7A).

8   Pilot bearing - inspection and replacement

◆ Refer to illustrations 8.5 and 8.6

1   The clutch pilot bearing is a needle roller type bearing which is pressed into the rear of the crankshaft. It's greased at the factory and does not require additional lubrication. Its primary purpose is to support the front of the transaxle input shaft. The pilot bearing should be inspected whenever the clutch components are removed from the engine, and replaced, if you have any doubt about its condition.

➡Note: If the engine has been removed from the vehicle, disregard the following steps which don't apply.

2   Remove the transaxle (see Chapter 7A).

3   Remove the clutch components (see Section 6).

4   Using a flashlight, inspect the bearing for excessive wear, scoring, dryness, roughness and any other obvious damage. If any of these conditions are noted, replace the bearing.

5   Removal can be accomplished with a special puller available at most auto parts stores (see illustration), or with a slide hammer and an internal puller attachment.

6   To install the new bearing, lightly lubricate the outside surface with grease, then drive it into the recess with a soft-face hammer (see illustration). Some bearings have an O-ring seal, which must face out.

7   Install the clutch components, transaxle and all other components removed previously. Tighten all fasteners to the recommended torque values.

8.5 A slide hammer with an internal puller attachment is handy for removing a pilot bearing

8.6 Tap the bearing into place with a bearing driver or a socket that is slightly smaller than the outside diameter of the bearing

9 Clutch start switch - check and replacement

CHECK

1 Verify that the engine will not start when the clutch pedal is released.

2 Verify that the engine will start when the clutch pedal is depressed all the way.

3 If the engine won't start with the pedal depressed, or starts with the pedal released, unplug the electrical connector to the switch. The clutch start switch is located near the top of the clutch pedal. Check continuity between the connector terminals with the clutch pedal depressed.

4 If there's continuity between the terminals with the pedal depressed, the switch is okay; if there's no continuity between the ter-minals with the pedal depressed, replace the switch. If there's continuity between the terminals when the clutch pedal is released, replace the switch.

REPLACEMENT

5 Unplug the switch electrical connector, if you haven't already done so.

6 Loosen the locknut and unscrew the switch from the clutch pedal bracket.

7 Installation is the reverse of removal. To adjust the switch, loosen the locknut and turn the switch in or out, as necessary, to provide con-tinuity through the switch when the clutch pedal is depressed.

10 Driveshafts, universal joints and driveaxles - general information

DRIVESHAFTS AND UNIVERSAL JOINTS

▶ **Refer to illustration 10.1**

1 The driveshaft (see illustration) transmits power between the transaxle and the rear differential. Universal joints are located at either end of the driveshaft; a third U-joint is installed right behind the center bearing.

2 The driveshaft employs a splined sleeve yoke at the front end, which slips into the extension housing. This arrangement allows the driveshaft to slide back-and-forth within the extension housing during vehicle operation. An oil seal prevents fluid from leaking out of the extension housing and keeps dirt from entering the transaxle. If leakage is evident at the front of the driveshaft, replace the oil seal (see Chap-ter 7A).

3 The rear end of the driveshaft is bolted to the differential pinion flange.

4 A center bearing supports the connection between the front and

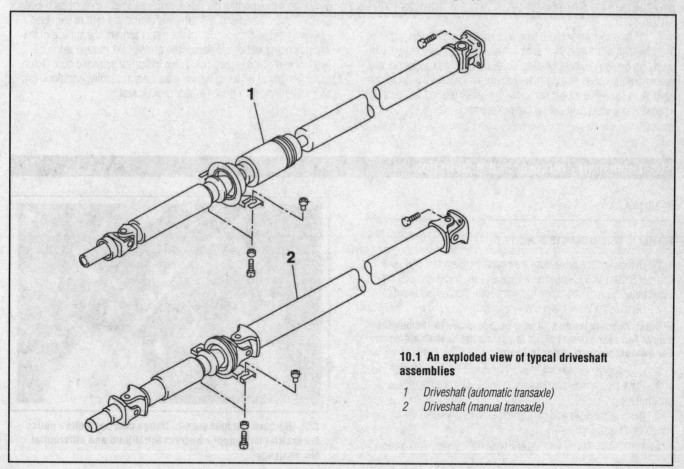

10.1 An exploded view of typcal driveshaft assemblies

1   Driveshaft (automatic transaxle)
2   Driveshaft (manual transaxle)

rear tubes of the driveshaft. The center bearing is a ball-type bearing mounted in a rubber cushion attached to the vehicle floorpan. The bearing is pre-lubricated and sealed at the factory.

5 The driveshaft assembly requires very little service. The universal joints are lubricated for life, and cannot be rebuilt; if a U-joint on one of these models is worn or damaged, replace the driveshaft.

6 Since the driveshaft is a balanced unit, it's important that no undercoating, mud, etc. be allowed to stay on it. When the vehicle is raised for service it's a good idea to clean the driveshaft and inspect it for any obvious damage. Also, make sure the small weights used to originally balance the driveshaft are in place and securely attached. Whenever the driveshaft is removed it must be reinstalled in the same relative position to preserve the balance.

7 Problems with the driveshaft are usually indicated by a noise or vibration while driving the vehicle. A road test should verify if the problem is the driveshaft or another vehicle component. Refer to the *Troubleshooting* section at the front of this manual. If you suspect trouble, inspect the driveline (see the next Section).

DRIVEAXLES

8 All models are equipped with a pair of front driveaxles and two rear driveaxles. The front and rear driveaxle assemblies are identical in design. Some driveaxles consist of an inner and outer ball-and-cage type CV joint connected by an axleshaft; others have a "tri-pot" inner joint and a ball-and-cage outer joint. The inner CV joint can be disassembled; the axleshaft and outer CV joint are a single assembly and cannot be disassembled; they can, however, be cleaned and inspected, and the boots can be replaced.

11 Driveline inspection

1 Raise the rear of the vehicle and support it securely on jackstands. Block the front wheels to keep the vehicle from rolling off the stands.

2 Crawl under the vehicle and visually inspect the driveshaft. Look for any dents or cracks in the tubing. If any are found, the driveshaft must be replaced.

3 Check for oil leakage at the front and rear of the driveshaft. Leakage where the driveshaft enters the transaxle indicates a defective transaxle/transfer case seal (see Chapter 7A). Leakage where the driveshaft joins the differential indicates a defective pinion seal (see Section 14).

4 While under the vehicle, have an assistant rotate a rear wheel so the driveshaft will rotate. As it does, make sure the universal joints are operating properly without binding, noise or looseness. Listen for any noise from the center bearing (if equipped), indicating it's worn or damaged. Also check the rubber portion of the center bearing for cracking or separation, which will necessitate replacement.

5 The universal joint can also be checked with the driveshaft motionless, by gripping your hands on either side of the joint and attempting to twist the joint. Any movement at all in the joint is a sign of considerable wear. Lifting up on the shaft will also indicate movement in the universal joints.

6 Check all driveshaft U-joint mounting bolts; make sure they're tight.

7 Finally, check for looseness in the CV joints of the front and rear driveaxles. Also check for grease or oil leakage from around the driveaxles by inspecting the rubber boots and both ends of each axle. Leakage at the wheel end of a driveaxle indicates a torn or damaged rubber boot (see Section 16). (If the tear is serious, the surface of the wheel housing will be splattered with grease.) Oil leakage at the differential end of a driveaxle could also indicate a damaged boot (again, look for signs of oil being thrown onto the surrounding components), or it could indicate a defective side gear oil seal.

12 Driveshaft - removal and installation

REMOVAL

▶ **Refer to illustrations 12.5 and 12.6**

1 Disconnect the cable from the negative battery terminal (see Chapter 5, Section 1). Raise the vehicle and support it securely on jackstands. Place the transaxle in Neutral with the parking brake off.

2 Remove the heat shield cover.

➡**Note: On some models, it may be necessary to remove the center and rear exhaust pipes to access the heat shield cover. For exhaust removal, refer to Chapter 4.**

3 If equipped, remove the differential mount front cover.

4 Place match marks on the rear U-joint yoke and the differential pinion flange.

5 Remove the bolts and nuts which attach the yoke to the pinion flange (see illustration).

6 Remove the center bearing retaining bolts (see illustration).

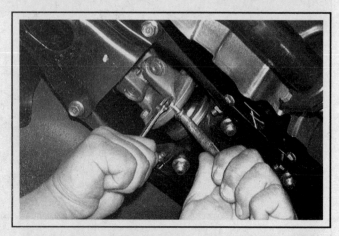

12.5 Remove the four yoke-to-flange nuts and bolts - notice the match marks applied across the U-joint and differential pinion flange

12.6 Remove the center bearing retaining bolts

7   Pull the sleeve yoke out of the extension housing and remove the driveshaft. Plug the extension housing to prevent transaxle lubricant from leaking out.

8   If you're replacing the center bearing, refer to Section 13.

INSTALLATION

9   Lubricate the sleeve yoke splines, then remove the extension housing plug and carefully insert the sleeve yoke into the extension housing. Make sure you don't damage the extension housing seal or the splines of the transaxle output shaft.

10 Raise the center bearing into place, install the center bearing retaining bolts and tighten them to the torque listed in this Chapter's Specifications.

11 Align the match marks you made on the rear U-joint yoke and the pinion flange, connect the yoke to the flange with the nuts and bolts and tighten them to the torque listed in this Chapter's Specifications.

12 The remainder of installation is the reverse of removal.

13 Center bearing - replacement

▶ **Refer to illustrations 13.3, 13.4, 13.5, 13.6 and 13.7**

1   Remove the driveshaft assembly (see Section 13).

2   Put the driveshaft assembly in a bench vise.

3   Mark the relationship of the center U-joint to the front driveshaft flange, then unbolt the U-joint from the flange (see illustration) and remove the rear driveshaft.

4   Mark the relationship of the flange to the front driveshaft, then unstake the nut (see illustration) and remove it.

5   Remove the flange with a puller (see illustration), or have it pressed off at an automotive machine shop.

6   To separate the front driveshaft from the center bearing, lightly tap the threaded nose with a brass hammer (see illustration). Remove the flange and the washer.

7   Inspect the center bearing. Make sure it rotates smoothly and quietly (see illustration). If you detect any sign of roughness, noise or excessive play, replace the center bearing.

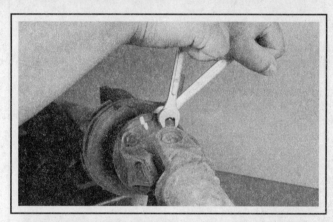

13.3 Mark the relationship of the center U-joint to the front driveshaft flange, then remove the nuts and bolts that attach the U-joint to the flange

13.4 Mark the relationship of the flange to the front driveshaft, then unstake the nut and remove it

13.5 Remove the flange with a puller (if you don't have a suitable puller, have it pressed off at an automotive machine shop)

13.6 Carefully tap the driveshaft through the center bearing with a brass hammer (be sure to hold the driveshaft with one hand while striking it so that it doesn't fall on the floor when it breaks free)

8   Install the center bearing on the front driveshaft. If you have trouble getting the center bearing onto the front driveshaft, take the front driveshaft and center bearing to an automotive machine shop and have the center bearing installed.

9   Coat both sides of the large washer and the driveshaft splines with grease, then install the washer and the flange. Make sure the marks you made on the flange and the front driveshaft are aligned. Tighten the flange nut to the torque listed in this Chapter's Specifica-

tions, then stake it with a hammer and punch. Again, if the flange is difficult to install, take the front driveshaft and flange to an automotive machine shop and have the flange installed.

10 Make sure the marks you made on the flange and the U-joint are aligned, then attach the rear driveshaft. Tighten the U-joint-to-flange bolts and nuts to the torque listed in this Chapter's Specifications.

11 Install the driveshaft assembly (see Section 12).

14 Rear differential pinion seal - replacement

▶ **Refer to illustrations 14.3, 14.4, 14.5, 14.6 and 14.7**

1   Raise the vehicle and support it securely on jackstands. Place the transaxle in Neutral with the parking brake off.

2   Remove the driveshaft (see Section 12).

3   Using an inch-pound torque wrench, measure the turning torque of the pinion flange (see illustration). Jot down this figure and save it

for reassembly.

4   Holding the flange with a suitable tool, remove the retaining nut (see illustration).

5   Remove the pinion flange; use a puller if necessary (see illustration).

6   Remove the old seal (see illustration).

7   Install a new seal (see illustration).

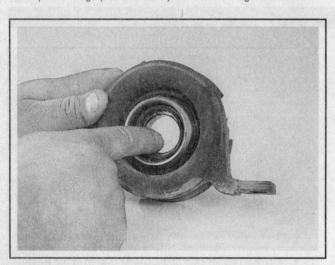

13.7 Make sure the center bearing rotates smoothly and quietly; if it doesn't, replace it

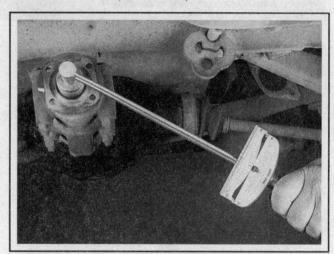

14.3 Using an inch-pound torque wrench, measure the turning torque of the pinion flange, jot down this number and save it for reassembly

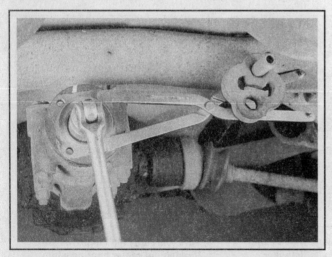

14.4 Holding the flange with a suitable tool (such as this pin spanner braced by an exhaust hanger bracket), remove the retaining nut (if you don't have a pin spanner, try a pair of large water pump pliers or a plumber's wrench)

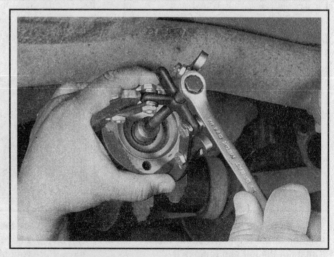

14.5 Sometimes you can remove the pinion flange by simply pulling it off; if not, use a small puller

14.6 Remove the old seal with a seal removal tool (shown) or with a large screwdriver

8   Installation is the reverse of removal. Gradually tighten the pinion flange retaining nut to the minimum torque listed in this Chapter's Specifications; as you're tightening the nut, use the figure you recorded prior to disassembly to periodically check the pinion flange turning torque. By the time the retaining nut's minimum specified torque is reached, the turning torque of the pinion flange should be the same as

14.7 Install the new seal with a large socket; make sure the seal is square to the bore, then carefully tap it into place until it's fully seated

it was before disassembly. When this figure is attained, tighten the nut to increase the turning torque by five inch-pounds.
9   Install the driveshaft (see Section 12).
10 Lower the vehicle.

15 Driveaxles - removal and installation

FRONT DRIVEAXLE

▶ **Refer to illustrations 15.1a, 15.1b, 15.5a, 15.5b, 15.6a, 15.6b and 15.7**

1   Remove the wheel cover. Unstake, then loosen, the driveaxle nut (see illustrations).

✳✳ CAUTION:

Just break the nut loose at this time. If it is loosened very much or removed with the wheel on the ground (supporting the weight of the vehicle) the front hub bearings can be damaged.

2   Loosen the wheel lug nuts, raise the vehicle and place it securely on jackstands.

15.1a Before you can remove the driveaxle nut, "unstake" it: Using a small punch, restore the inner edge of the nut where it's been peened over to lock the nut onto the driveaxle

15.1b With the vehicle on the ground, have an assistant put the transaxle in gear and apply the brakes while you break the driveaxle nut loose with a breaker bar

15.5a Disengage the driveaxle from the steering knuckle

15.5b If the splines on the stub shaft hang up on the splines in the hub, knock them loose with a hammer and punch

3   Remove the wheel.

4   Disconnect the control arm from the steering knuckle (see Chapter 10).

5   Remove the driveaxle nut, then pull the driveaxle assembly out of the steering knuckle (see illustration). Make sure you don't damage the lip of the inner steering knuckle seal. If the outer CV joint splines are stuck in the hub, knock the driveaxle loose with a hammer and punch (see illustration). If that doesn't break the splines loose, remove the brake disc (see Chapter 9) and push the driveaxle from the hub using a two-jaw puller.

6   Some models have a spring pin that locks the inner end of the driveaxle assembly to the differential side gear shaft, locate the spring pin and remove pin (see illustration), then disengage the inner end of the driveaxle from the differential (see illustration).

7   On models that do not use a spring pin, pry the inner CV joint out of the differential (see illustration).

8   If you're planning to replace a CV joint boot or overhaul an inner CV joint, proceed to the next section. This is also a good time to inspect the inner and outer bearings in the knuckle and decide whether to reuse them or install new ones (see Chapter 10).

9   Installation is the reverse of removal. If you damaged the lip of the inner steering knuckle seal, be sure to replace the seal before installing the driveaxle assembly (see Chapter 10). Be sure to use a new

spring pin to lock the inner CV joint to the differential stub shaft. Make sure you install the spring pin from the chamfered side of the hole. Tighten the driveaxle nut as securely as you can with the vehicle raised, then install the wheel and lug nuts and lower the vehicle to the ground. Tighten the driveaxle nut to the torque listed in this Chapter's Specifications, and the wheel lug nuts to the torque listed in the Chapter 1 Specifications.

10   Check the transaxle lubricant level (manual transaxle) or differential lubricant level (automatic transaxle), adding as necessary (see Chapter 1).

REAR DRIVEAXLE

11   Unstake, then loosen, the driveaxle nut (see illustrations 15.1a and 15.1b).

> ✳✳ **CAUTION:**
>
> **Just break the nut loose at this time. If it is loosened very much or removed with the wheel on the ground (supporting the weight of the vehicle) the hub bearings can be damaged.**

15.6a To disconnect the front driveaxle from the differential, knock out the spring pin with a hammer and punch (early models)

15.6b Disengage the front driveaxle from the front differential

15.7 Using a prybar, carefully pry the inner end of the driveaxle from the transaxle (later models)

12 Loosen the rear wheel lug nuts, raise the vehicle and place it securely on jackstands. Remove the rear wheels.

13 Remove the rear differential (see Section 18).

14 Remove the driveaxle nut, then pull the driveaxle assembly out of the rear knuckle. Make sure you don't damage the lip of the inner rear knuckle seal. If the splines on the outer CV joint spindle hang up on the splines in the hub, knock them loose with a hammer and punch (see illustration 15.5b).

15 If you're planning to replace a CV joint boot, proceed to the next section. This is also a good time to inspect the inner and outer bearings in the rear knuckle and decide whether to reuse them or install new ones (see Chapter 10).

16 Installation is the reverse of removal. Tighten the driveaxle nut as securely as you can with the vehicle raised, then install the wheel and lug nuts and lower the vehicle to the ground. Tighten the driveaxle nut to the torque listed in this Chapter's Specifications, and the wheel lug nuts to the torque listed in the Chapter 1 Specifications.

16 Driveaxle boot replacement

→**Note: If the CV joints exhibit signs of wear indicating need for an overhaul (usually due to torn boots), explore all options before beginning the job. Complete rebuilt driveaxles are available on an exchange basis, which eliminates much time and work. Whichever route you choose to take, check on the cost and availability of parts before disassembling the vehicle.**

1 Remove the driveaxle (see Section 15).

2 Mount the driveaxle in a vise. The jaws of the vise should be lined with wood or rags to prevent damage to the axleshaft.

INNER CV JOINT

Ball-and-cage type

Disassembly

▶ **Refer to illustrations 16.3a, 16.6b, 16.4, 16.5, 16.7, 16.9, 16.10 and 16.11**

3 Pry open the locking tabs on the boot clamps, remove the clamps from the boot and discard them (see illustrations).

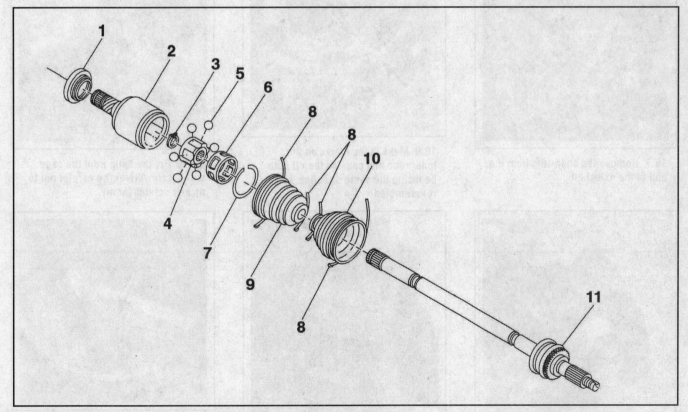

16.3a An exploded view of the ball-and-cage type rear driveaxle assembly

1	Baffle plate	4	Inner race	7	Circlip or wire retainer	9	Inner CV joint boot
2	Outer race	5	Ball bearings		ring	10	Outer CV joint boot
3	Snap-ring	6	Cage	8	Boot clamps	11	Outer CV joint

16.3b To remove the boot clamps, pry open the locking tabs

16.4 Pry the wire retainer ring from the CV joint housing with a small screwdriver

16.5 With the retainer removed, the outer race can be pulled off the bearing assembly

4   Slide the boot back on the axleshaft and pry the wire ring ball retainer from the outer race (see illustration).

5   Pull the outer race off the inner bearing assembly (see illustration).

6   Wipe as much grease as possible off the inner bearing.

7   Remove the snap-ring from the end of the axleshaft (see illustration).

8   Slide the inner bearing assembly off the axleshaft.

9   Mark the inner race and cage to ensure that they are reassembled with the correct sides facing out (see illustration).

16.7 Remove the snap-ring from the end of the axleshaft

16.9 Make index marks on the inner race and cage so they'll both be facing the same direction when reassembled

16.10 Pry the balls from the cage with a screwdriver (be careful not to nick or scratch them)

16.11 Tilt the inner race 90-degrees and rotate it out of the cage

16.12a Inspect the inner race lands and grooves for pitting and score marks

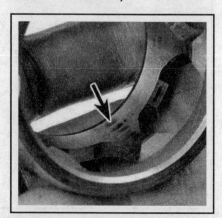

16.12b Inspect the cage for cracks, pitting and score marks (shiny spots are normal and don't affect operation)

16.14 Press the balls into the cage through the windows

16.15 Wrap the splined area of the axle with tape to prevent damage to the boot

10 Using a screwdriver or piece of wood, pry the balls from the cage (see illustration). Be careful not to scratch the inner race, the balls or the cage.

11 Rotate the inner race 90-degrees, align the inner race lands with the cage windows and rotate the race out of the cage (see illustration).

Inspection

▶ **Refer to illustrations 16.12a and 16.12b**

12 Clean the components with solvent to remove all traces of grease. Inspect the cage and races for pitting, score marks, cracks and other signs of wear and damage. Shiny, polished spots are normal and will not adversely affect CV joint performance (see illustrations). If the outer CV joint boot is torn or damaged, now is the time to set aside the inner CV joint parts, remove the outer boot, and clean and inspect the outer CV joint.

Reassembly

▶ **Refer to illustrations 16.14, 16.15, 16.16, 16.20, 16.23, 16.24a, 16.24b, 16.24c and 16.24d**

13 Insert the inner race into the cage. Verify that the matchmarks are on the same side. However, it's not necessary for them to be in direct alignment with each other.

14 Press the balls into the cage windows with your thumbs (see illustration).

15 Wrap the axleshaft splines with tape to avoid damaging the boot (see illustration).

16 Slide the small boot clamp and boot onto the axleshaft, then remove the tape.

17 Install the inner race and cage assembly on the axleshaft with the larger diameter side or "bulge" of the cage facing the axleshaft end (see illustration).

18 Install the snap-ring (see illustration 16.7).

19 Fill the boot with CV joint grease (normally included with the new boot kit).

20 Pack the inner race and cage assembly with grease, by hand, until grease is worked completely into the assembly (see illustration).

21 Slide the outer race down onto the inner race and install the wire ring retainer.

22 Wipe any excess grease from the axle boot groove on the outer race. Seat the small diameter of the boot in the recessed area on the axleshaft and install the clamp. Push the other end of the boot onto the outer CV joint housing and seat it into the recessed area on the housing.

23 Position the CV joint mid-way through its travel, then equalize the pressure in the boot by inserting a dull screwdriver between the boot and the outer race (see illustration). Don't damage the boot with the tool.

16.17 Install the inner race and cage assembly with the large diameter end toward the splined end of the axleshaft

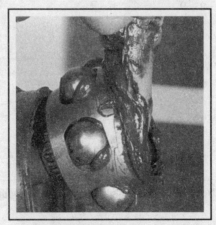

16.20 Pack grease into the bearing until it's completely full

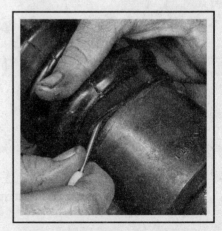

16.23 Equalize the pressure inside the boot by inserting a small screwdriver between the boot and the outer race

24 Install the boot clamps (see illustrations). A special clamp installation tool is needed. The tool is available at most auto parts stores.

25 Install the driveaxle assembly (see Section 15).

Tri-pot type

Disassembly

▶ **Refer to illustrations 16.27a, 16.27b, 16.28 and 16.29**

26 Pry open the locking tabs on the boot clamps (see illustration 16.3b), remove the boot clamps from the boot and discard them (see illustrations).

27 Remove the wire retainer ring (see illustration 16.4), then slide the outer race off the tri-pot bearing assembly (see illustration). Before removing the race, wipe the grease off the tri-pot bearing assembly and scribe or paint alignment marks on the outer race and the tri-pot bearing assembly (see illustration) so they can be returned to their original position.

28 Remove the snap-ring from the end of the axleshaft, then mark the relationship of the tri-pot bearing assembly to the axleshaft (see illustration).

16.24a Secure the boot clamps with a special banding tool such as the one shown here (available at most auto parts stores): install the clamp, thread it onto the tool, pull the clamp tight . . .

16.24b . . . peen over the locking tabs . . .

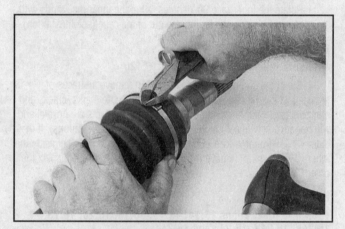

16.24c . . . and cut off the excess

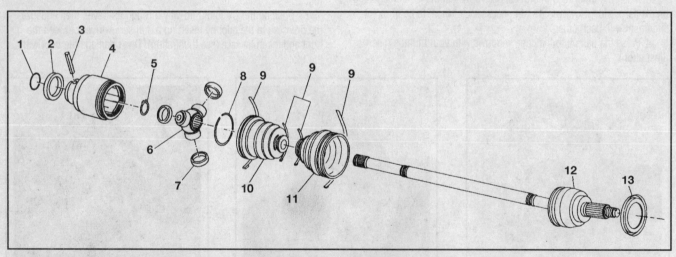

16.27a An exploded view of the tri-pot type front driveaxle assembly used on early models

1	O-ring	6	Tri-pot assembly (or "spider")	10	Inner CV joint boot
2	Baffle plate	7	Bearings	11	Outer CV joint boot
3	Spring pin	8	Wire retainer ring	12	Outer CV joint
4	Outer race	9	Boot clamps	13	Baffle plate
5	Snap-ring				

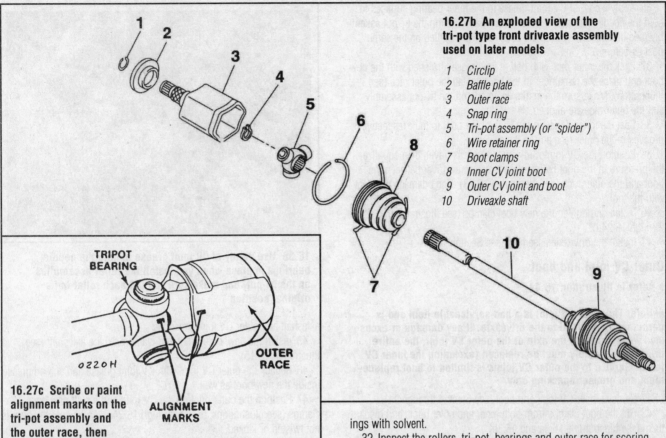

16.27b An exploded view of the tri-pot type front driveaxle assembly used on later models

1 Circlip
2 Baffle plate
3 Outer race
4 Snap ring
5 Tri-pot assembly (or "spider")
6 Wire retainer ring
7 Boot clamps
8 Inner CV joint boot
9 Outer CV joint and boot
10 Driveaxle shaft

16.27c Scribe or paint alignment marks on the tri-pot assembly and the outer race, then slide the outer race off

ings with solvent.

32 Inspect the rollers, tri-pot, bearings and outer race for scoring, pitting or other signs of abnormal wear, which will warrant the replacement of the inner CV joint.

Reassembly

▶ **Refer to illustrations 16.35, 16.36 and 16.37**

33 Wrap the splines of the axleshaft with tape to avoid damaging the new boot, then slide the boot onto the axleshaft (see illustration 16.15). Remove the tape.

34 Align the match marks you made before disassembly and tap the tri-pot assembly onto the axleshaft with a hammer and brass drift.

35 Install the outer snap-ring (see illustration).

29 Secure the bearing rollers with tape, then remove the tri-pot bearing assembly from the axleshaft with a brass drift and a hammer (see illustration). Remove the tape, but don't let the rollers fall off and get mixed up.

30 Remove the old boot and discard it.

Inspection

31 Clean the old grease from the outer race and the tri-pot bearing assembly. Carefully disassemble each section of the tri-pot assembly, one at a time so as not to mix up the parts, and clean the needle bear-

16.28 Remove the snap-ring from the end of the axleshaft, then mark the relationship of the tri-pot bearing assembly to the axleshaft

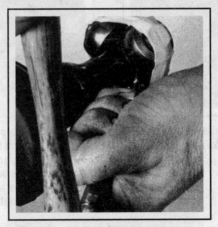

16.29 Secure the bearing rollers with tape and drive the tri-pot off the shaft with a hammer and brass drift

16.35 Install the tri-pot assembly on the axleshaft, making sure the punch marks are lined up, then install the snap-ring

36 Apply a coat of CV joint grease to the inner bearing surfaces to hold the needle bearings in place when reassembling the tri-pot assembly (see illustration). Make sure each roller is installed on the same post as before.

37 Pack the outer race with half of the grease furnished with the new boot and place the remainder in the boot. Install the outer race (see illustration). Make sure the marks you made on the tri-pot assembly and the outer race are aligned.

38 Seat the inner ridges in the ends of the boot in their respective grooves in the outer race and in the axleshaft.

39 Position the CV joint mid-way through its travel, then equalize the pressure in the boot by inserting a dull screwdriver between the boot and the outer race (see illustration 16.23). Don't damage the boot with the tool.

40 Install and tighten the new boot clamps (see illustrations 16.24a through 16.24d).

41 Install the driveaxle assembly (see Section 15).

Outer CV joint and boot

▶ Refer to illustration 16.44

➡ Note: The outer CV joint is a non-serviceable item and is permanently retained to the driveaxle. If any damage or excessive wear occurs to the axle or the outer CV joint, the entire driveaxle assembly must be replaced (excluding the inner CV joint). Service to the outer CV joints is limited to boot replacement and grease repacking only.

42 Remove inner CV joint and boot (see Steps 4 through 11).

43 Cut the boot clamps from both inner and outer boots and discard them (see illustrations 16.3a and 16.3b).

44 Remove the outer CV joint boot. Wash the outer CV joint assembly in solvent and inspect it (see illustration) as described in Step 12. If any outer CV joint components are excessively worn, replace the

16.36 Use plenty of CV joint grease to hold the needle bearings in place when you install the roller assemblies on the tri-pot, and make sure you put each roller in its original position

axleshaft and outer CV joint assembly.

45 Install the new, outer boot and clamp onto the axleshaft (see illustration 16.15).

46 Repack the outer CV joint with CV joint grease and spread grease inside the new boot as well.

47 Position the outer boot on the CV joint and install new boot clamps (see illustrations 16.24a through 16.24d). Make sure the boot is not twisted or kinked.

48 Reassemble the inner CV joint and boot (see Steps 13 through 24 or Steps 33 through 40).

49 Install the driveaxle (see Section 15).

16.37 Pack the outer race with grease and slide it over the tri-pot assembly - make sure the match marks on the outer race and tri-pot line up

16.44 After the old grease has been rinsed away and the cleaning solvent has been blown out with compressed air, rotate the outer joint housing through its full range of motion and inspect the bearing surfaces for wear or damage - if any of the balls, the race or cage look damaged, replace the driveaxle and outer joint

17 Rear differential side gear seals - replacement

▶ **Refer to illustration 17.1**

1   The rear differential side gear seals can become worn and leak gear lubricant onto the differential housing and inner CV joint (see illustration). If your differential is covered with gear lube, replace the seals.

2   Loosen the rear wheel lug nuts, block the front wheels, raise the rear of the vehicle and support it securely on jackstands. Remove the rear wheel(s).

3   Drain the gear lubricant from the differential (see Chapter 1).

4   Remove the rear differential (see Section 18).

5   Carefully pry out the driveaxle oil seal with a seal removal tool or a large screwdriver. Be careful not to damage or scratch the seal bore.

6   Using a seal installer or a large deep socket as a drift, install the new oil seal. Drive it into the bore squarely and make sure it's completely seated.

7   Installation is the reverse of removal. Lubricate the lip of the new seal with multi-purpose grease, before installing the driveaxles. Be careful not to damage the lip of the new seal.

8   Fill the rear differential with the type and quantity of lubricant specified in Chapter 1.

9   Install the wheel and lug nuts, then lower the vehicle. Tighten the lug nuts to the torque listed in the Chapter 1 Specifications.

17.1 If your rear differetial looks like this, it's time to change the side gear seals

10 Drive the vehicle, then inspect for leaks around the seal and retainer.

18 Rear differential - removal and installation

REMOVAL

▶ **Refer to illustrations 18.4, 18.6, 18.7, 18.8a and 18.8b**

1   Loosen the rear wheel lug nuts, block the front wheels and raise the rear of the vehicle. Support it securely on jackstands. Remove the rear wheels.

2   Drain the lubricant from the differential (see Chapter 1).

3   Disconnect the driveshaft from the rear differential (see Section 12). Remove the rear exhaust pipe and muffler (see Chapter 4).

4   Pry the inner CV joint out of the differential just far enough to release the snap ring (see illustration).

➡**Note: The driveaxles can not be removed from the differential until the differential has been lowered from the vehicle.**

5   Support the rear of the differential with a floor jack.

6   Remove the mounting fasteners that attach the differential to the rear crossmember (see illustration).

7   Remove the four front mounting fasteners and bracket (see illustration).

18.4 Pry the inner CV joint out of the differential just far enough to release the snap ring; use one of the bearing retainer bolts as a fulcrum for the lever - do NOT use the bearing retainer itself or you may crack it

18.6 Remove these fasteners that attach the differential to the rear crossmember

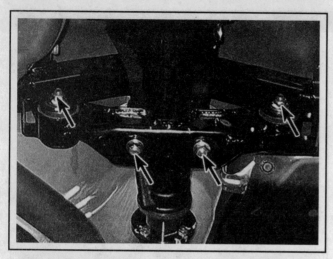

18.7 To detach the front end of the differential, remove these fasteners

8   Carefully lower the differential enough to separate the driveaxles from the differential (see illustrations).

9   Carefully lower the differential and remove it from under the vehicle.

10 With the differential removed from the vehicle, now would be a good time to check or replace the rubber mounts for the differential mounting brackets and/or the rear crossmember.

INSTALLATION

11 Place the differential on the jack head and position it directly underneath the mounting bracket and crossmember.

12 Raise the differential enough to install the driveaxles into the differential.

13 Raise the differential into position and install the rear mounting nuts loosely. Then install the front mounting nuts. Tighten all mounting fasteners securely.

14 Install the driveshaft (see Section 12).

15 If it was drained, fill the differential with the type and amount of

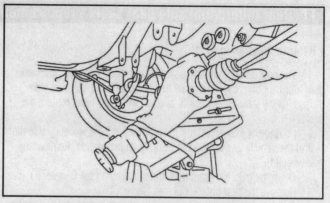

18.8a Lower the differential enough to separate the driveaxles from the differential. If the driveaxles are difficult to remove from the differential, use the pry bar to remove them

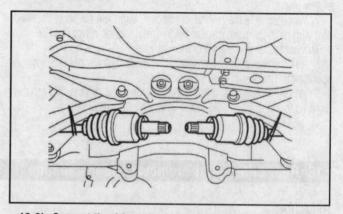

18.8b Support the driveaxles buy securing the driveaxles to the lateral links using a piece of wire

lubricant specified in Chapter 1.

16 Install the wheels, remove the jack and lower the vehicle to the ground. Tighten the wheel lug nuts to the torque listed in the Chapter 1 Specifications.

Specifications

Torque specifications	Ft-lbs	Nm
Center bearing retaining bolts	38.3	52
Clutch pressure plate bolts	11.6	16
Driveshaft-to-pinion flange nuts/bolts	23.1	31
Front driveaxle nut		
Legacy and Outback		
2004 and earlier models	159	216
2005 and later models	162	220
Forester		
2002 and earlier models	137	186
2003 and 2004 models	140	190
2005 and later models	162	220
Rear driveaxle nut		
Legacy and Outback		
2004 and earlier models	174	235
2005 models	140	190
2006 models	177	240
Forester		
2002 and earlier models	137	186
2003 and later models	140	190
Rear differential pinion flange nut	134	181

Notes

Section

Reference to other Chapters

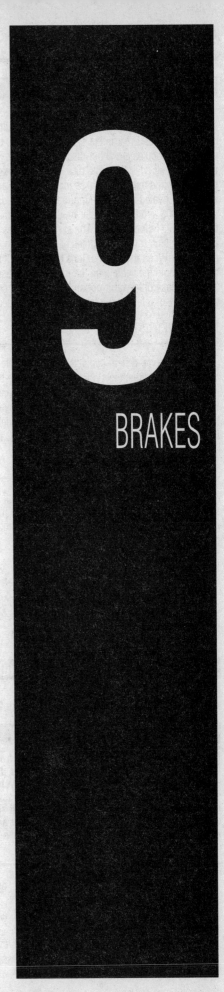

9

BRAKES

1 General information

The vehicles covered by this manual are equipped with hydraulically operated front and rear brake systems. The front brakes are disc type and the rear brakes are either disc or drum type. Both the front and rear brakes are self adjusting. The disc brakes automatically compensate for pad wear, while the drum brakes incorporate an adjustment mechanism which is activated as the parking brake is applied.

The 2003 and later Forester models, with a manual transaxle, may feature a hill-holder system. The system engages when the vehicle is on an incline (of three degrees or greater) and the clutch pedal is depressed. When these conditions occur, the hill holder actuates the brakes to hold the vehicle on the incline. This results in less clutch wear and ease of forward motion when stopped on a hill. The hill-holder system releases the brake as the clutch pedal is released.

HYDRAULIC SYSTEM

The hydraulic system consists of two separate circuits. The master cylinder has separate reservoir chambers for the two circuits, and, in the event of a leak or failure in one hydraulic circuit, the other circuit will remain operative. A proportioning valve provides brake balance between the front and rear brakes on earlier models while the Anti-lock Brake System (ABS) performs this operation on later models.

POWER BRAKE BOOSTER

The power brake booster - which utilizes engine manifold vacuum and atmospheric pressure to provide assistance to the hydraulically operated brakes - is mounted on the firewall in the engine compartment.

PARKING BRAKE

The parking brake operates the rear brakes only, through cable actuation. It's activated by a lever mounted in the center console.

SERVICE

After completing any operation involving disassembly of any part of the brake system, always test drive the vehicle to check for proper braking performance before resuming normal driving. When testing the brakes, perform the tests on a clean, dry, flat surface. Conditions other than these can lead to inaccurate test results.

Test the brakes at various speeds with both light and heavy pedal pressure. The vehicle should stop evenly without pulling to one side or the other. Avoid locking the brakes, because this slides the tires and diminishes braking efficiency and control of the vehicle.

Tires, vehicle load and wheel alignment are factors which also affect braking performance.

PRECAUTIONS

There are some general cautions and warnings involving the brake system on this vehicle:

a) *Use only brake fluid conforming to DOT 3 specifications.*
b) *The brake pads and linings contain fibers which are hazardous to your health if inhaled. Whenever you work on brake system components, clean all parts with brake system cleaner. Do not allow the fine dust to become airborne. Also, wear an approved filtering mask.*
c) *Safety should be paramount whenever any servicing of the brake components is performed. Do not use parts or fasteners which are not in perfect condition, and be sure that all clearances and torque specifications are adhered to. If you are at all unsure about a certain procedure, seek professional advice. Upon completion of any brake system work, test the brakes carefully in a controlled area before putting the vehicle into normal service. If a problem is suspected in the brake system, don't drive the vehicle until it's fixed.*

2 Disc brake pads - replacement

♦ **Refer to illustrations 2.4 and 2.5a through 2.5s**

❋❋ WARNING:

Disc brake pads must be replaced on both front or both rear wheels at the same time; never replace the pads on only one side. Also, the dust created by the brake system is harmful to your health. Never blow it out with compressed air and don't inhale any of it. An approved filtering mask should be worn when working on the brakes. Do not, under any circumstances, use petroleum-based solvents to clean brake parts. Use brake system cleaner only!

1 Loosen the wheel lug nuts, raise the front, or rear, of the vehicle and support it securely on jackstands.

2 Remove the wheels. Release the parking brake lever if you're working on the rear brakes.

3 Remove about two-thirds of the fluid from the master cylinder reservoir. Position a drain pan under the brake assembly.

2.4 Wash the brake assembly with brake system cleaner; do NOT use compressed air to blow off the brake dust

4   Before beginning, wash down the entire brake assembly with brake system cleaner (see illustration).

5   To replace the front brake pads, follow the accompanying illustrations, beginning with illustration 2.5a. Be sure to stay in order and read the caption under each illustration. Work on one brake assembly at a time so that you'll have something to refer to if you get in trouble. To replace the rear brake pads, follow the same photos (the rear brake pad and caliper are slightly smaller than the front setup but are otherwise virtually identical; refer to illustration 2.5s if necessary.

6   While the pads are removed, inspect the caliper for brake fluid leaks and ruptures in the piston boot. Replace the caliper if necessary (see Section 3). Also inspect the brake disc carefully (see Section 4). If machining is necessary, follow the information in that Section to remove the disc. If you're replacing the rear pads, this would be a good time to remove the caliper and disc and inspect the parking brake shoes (see Section 13).

7   Before installing the caliper guide and lock pins, make sure you clean them and inspect them for corrosion, scoring and other damage. If they're damaged or worn, replace them. Be sure to tighten the caliper bolts to the torque listed in this Chapter's Specifications.

8   Install the brake pads on the opposite wheel, then install the wheels and lower the vehicle. Tighten the wheel lug nuts to the torque listed in the Chapter 1 Specifications.

9   Add brake fluid to the reservoir until it's full (see Chapter 1).

2.5a Depress the piston(s) into the caliper with a C-clamp to make room for the new brake pads

Pump the brakes several times to seat the pads against the discs, then check the fluid level again.

10 Check the operation of the brakes before driving the vehicle in traffic. Try to avoid heavy brake applications until the brakes have been applied lightly several times to seat the pads.

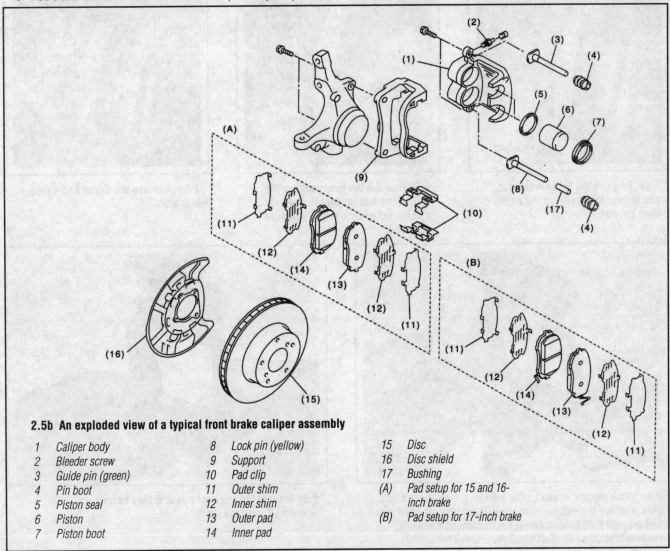

2.5b An exploded view of a typical front brake caliper assembly

1	Caliper body	8	Lock pin (yellow)	15	Disc
2	Bleeder screw	9	Support	16	Disc shield
3	Guide pin (green)	10	Pad clip	17	Bushing
4	Pin boot	11	Outer shim	(A)	Pad setup for 15 and 16-inch brake
5	Piston seal	12	Inner shim	(B)	Pad setup for 17-inch brake
6	Piston	13	Outer pad		
7	Piston boot	14	Inner pad		

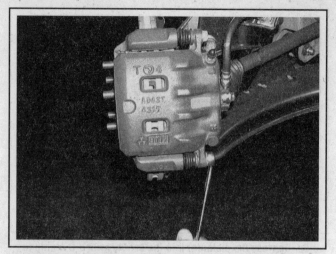

2.5c Remove the lower caliper bolt (on the lower pin), swing the caliper up for access to the brake pads. To detach the caliper completely, remove both caliper bolts but do not let the caliper hang by the brake hose

2.5d Remove the outer brake pad and shims, then remove the shim(s) from the pad (if a shim is damaged, replace it)

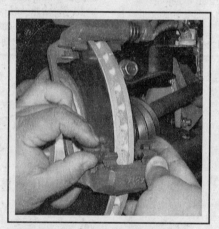

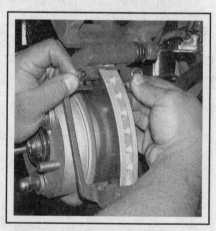

2.5e Remove the inner brake pad and shims, then remove the shims from the pad

2.5f Remove the lower anti-rattle clip, clean and inspect it, then set it aside for re-use; if it is damaged, replace it

2.5g Remove the upper anti-rattle clip also

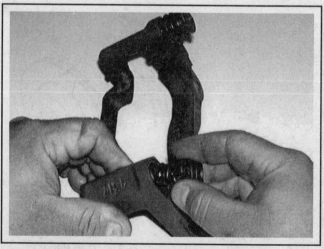

2.5h If the caliper doesn't slide well on the guide and lock pins, remove the caliper from the caliper support, then clean and inspect both pins; if either pin is damaged or worn, replace it (caliper support bracket removed for clarity)

2.5i Inspect the pin dust boots; if they're torn or cracked, replace them

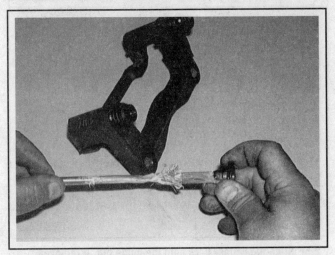

2.5j Lubricate the pin(s) with high-temperature grease

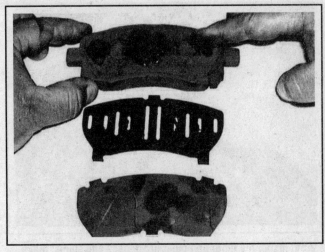

2.5k The brake pads may have either one or two shims; apply anti-squeal compound to the backing plates of the new pads . . .

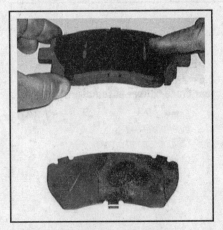

2.5l . . . install the inner shim on the pad . . .

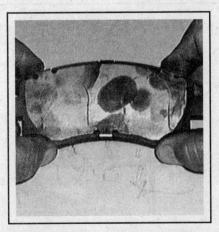

2.5m . . . followed by the outer shim (if applicable)

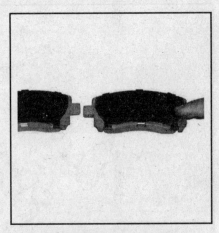

2.5n Assemble the other pad and shim(s), then apply anti-squeal compound to the outer shims of both pads

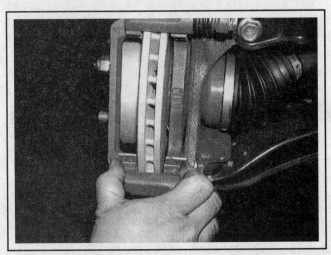

2.5o Install the lower anti-rattle clip on the caliper support bracket . . .

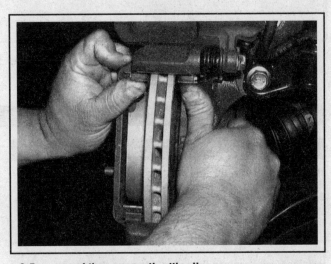

2.5p . . . and the upper anti-rattle clip

2.5q Install the inner and outer brake pads and shims; make sure the pads are correctly seated in the caliper support

2.5r Slide the caliper back onto the guide pin, if removed, then pivot it down over the new pads, install the caliper bolt and tighten it to the torque listed in this Chapter's Specifications

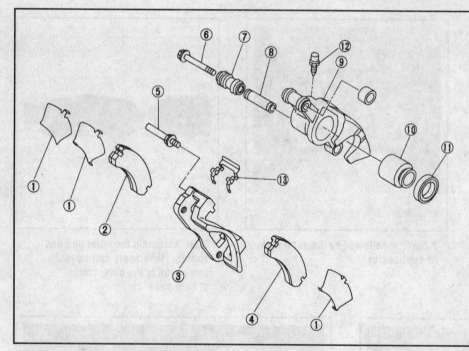

2.5s An exploded view of a typical rear brake caliper assembly

1 Shims
2 Inner brake pad
3 Caliper support bracket
4 Outer brake pad
5 Caliper guide pin
6 Caliper lock pin
7 Lock pin boot
8 Lock pin sleeve (bushing)
9 Caliper body
10 Piston
11 Piston dust boot
12 Bleeder screw
13 Pad anti-rattle clip

3 Brake caliper - removal and installation

✳✳ WARNING:

The dust created by the brake system is harmful to your health. Never blow it out with compressed air and don't inhale any of it. An approved filtering mask should be worn when working on the brakes. Do not, under any circumstances, use petroleum-based solvents to clean brake parts. Use brake system cleaner only!

➥Note: Always replace the calipers in pairs (front/front, rear/ rear) - never replace just one of them.

REMOVAL

▸ Refer to illustration 3.2

1 Loosen the wheel lug nuts, raise the front, or rear, of the vehicle and support it securely on jackstands. Release the parking brake lever if you're working on the rear brakes. Initially follow the instructions in the previous Section and remove the disc brake pads.

2 Place a container under the caliper and have some rags handy to catch any spilled brake fluid. Remove the brake hose-to-caliper banjo

3.2 If you're replacing the caliper, remove the banjo bolt that attaches the brake hose to the caliper; discard the old sealing washers and install new ones when you reattach the brake hose to the caliper

bolt (see illustration). Plug the hose to prevent contaminants from entering the brake hydraulic system and to prevent fluid from leaking out the hose.

➡**Note: If you're simply removing the caliper for access to other components, don't disconnect the hose from the caliper.**

3   Unbolt and remove the caliper from the caliper support bracket (see Section 2).

INSTALLATION

4   Install the brake pads (see Section 2).

5   Before installing the caliper assembly on the caliper support, clean the caliper lock pin and guide pin, then apply high-temperature grease to them (see illustrations 2.5h through 2.5j).

6   Install the caliper assembly and, if necessary, reconnect the brake line to the caliper. Use new sealing washers and tighten the banjo bolt and the caliper bolts to the torque listed in this Chapter's Specifications.

7   Bleed the brake system (see Section 10).

4   Brake disc - inspection, removal and installation

✳✳ WARNING:

The dust created by the brake system is harmful to your health. Never blow it out with compressed air and don't inhale any of it. An approved filtering mask should be worn when working on the brakes. Do not, under any circumstances, use petroleum-based solvents to clean brake parts. Use brake system cleaner only!

INSPECTION

▶ **Refer to illustrations 4.3, 4.4a, 4.4b, 4.5a and 4.5b**

1   Loosen the wheel lug nuts, raise the vehicle and support it securely on jackstands. Remove the wheel and install the lug nuts to

hold the disc in place against the hub flange.

➡**Note: If the lug nuts don't contact the disc when screwed on all the way, install washers under them. If you're checking the rear disc, release the parking brake.**

2   Remove the brake caliper as outlined in Section 3. It isn't necessary to disconnect the brake hose. After removing the caliper bolts, suspend the caliper out of the way with a piece of wire. Don't let the caliper hang by the hose and don't stretch or twist the hose.

3   Visually inspect the disc surface for score marks and other damage. Light scratches and shallow grooves are normal after use and may not always be detrimental to brake operation, but deep scoring requires disc removal and refinishing by an automotive machine shop. Be sure to check both sides of the disc (see illustration). If pulsating has been noticed during application of the brakes, suspect disc runout.

4.3 The brake pads on this vehicle were obviously neglected, as they wore down completely and cut deep grooves into the disc - wear this severe means the disc must be replaced

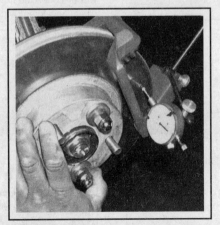

4.4a Check brake disc runout with a dial indicator; check both sides of the disc

4.4b Using a swirling motion, remove the glaze from the disc with sandpaper or emery cloth

4.5a The minimum thickness of this disc is cast into the hub area (typical), look for the minimum thickness for your disc in this area

4.5b Measure the thickness of the disc with a micrometer and compare it to the specified minimum thickness

4.6a Front caliper support bracket mounting bolts

4 To check disc runout, place a dial indicator at a point about 1/2-inch from the outer edge of the disc (see illustration). Set the indicator to zero and turn the disc. The indicator reading should not exceed the specified allowable runout limit. If it does, the disc should be refinished by an automotive machine shop.

➡ **Note: The discs should be resurfaced regardless of the dial indicator reading, as this will impart a smooth finish and ensure a perfectly flat surface, eliminating any brake pedal pulsation or other undesirable symptoms related to questionable discs. At the very least, if you elect not to have the discs resurfaced, remove the glaze from the surface with emery cloth or sandpaper, using a swirling motion (see illustration).**

5 It's absolutely critical that the disc not be machined to a thickness under the specified minimum thickness. The minimum (or discard) thickness is cast or stamped into the disc. The disc thickness can be checked with a micrometer (see illustrations).

REMOVAL

♦ **Refer to illustrations 4.6a, 4.6b and 4.7**

6 Remove the caliper support bracket bolts (see illustrations) and remove the support bracket.

7 Slide the disc off the hub. If the disc is stuck to the hub and won't come off, thread two bolts into the holes provided and tighten them (see illustration).

➡ **Note: If you're removing a rear disc and it won't come off (but isn't stuck to the hub flange), refer to Section 13 and back-off the parking brake adjuster.**

8 If you're removing a rear disc, inspect the parking brake shoes (see Section 13).

INSTALLATION

8 Thoroughly clean all parts. Install the disc.

9 Install the caliper support bracket and tighten the bracket bolts to the torque listed in this Chapter's Specifications.

10 Install the brake pads and caliper (see Sections 2 and 3) and tighten the caliper bolts to the torque listed in this Chapter's Specifications.

11 Install the wheel, then lower the vehicle to the ground. Tighten the lug nuts to the torque listed in the Chapter 1 Specifications. Depress the brake pedal a few times to bring the brake pads into contact with the disc. Bleeding won't be necessary unless the brake hose was disconnected from the caliper. Check the operation of the brakes carefully before driving the vehicle.

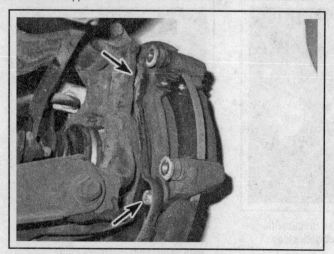

4.6b The rear caliper support bracket mounting bolts can be accessed through the rear arm of the suspension

4.7 If the disc is stuck, thread two 8 mm bolts into the threaded holes in the disc and tighten them to force the disc off the hub

5 Drum brake shoes - replacement

▶ Refer to illustrations 5.3a, 5.3b and 5.13

✳✳ WARNING:

Drum brake shoes must be replaced on both wheels at the same time - never replace the shoes on only one wheel. Also, the dust created by the brake system is harmful to your health. Never blow it out with compressed air and don't inhale any of it. An approved filtering mask should be worn when working on the brakes. Do not, under any circumstances, use petroleum-based solvents to clean brake parts. Use brake system cleaner only!

✳✳ CAUTION:

Whenever the brake shoes are replaced, the return and hold-down springs should also be replaced. Due to the continuous heating/cooling cycle the springs are subjected to, they can lose tension over a period of time and may allow the shoes to drag on the drum and wear at a much faster rate than normal.

1 Loosen the wheel lug nuts, raise the rear of the vehicle and support it securely on jackstands. Block the front wheels to keep the vehicle from rolling off the stands.

2 Remove the rear wheels. Release the parking brake.

3 Pull off the brake drums (see illustration). The brake drums may be difficult or impossible to remove if the shoes have worn the drums excessively. If you can't pull off the drums, remove the access hole plug for the adjuster from the backing plate and, using a brake adjuster tool and a narrow screwdriver (or two screwdrivers), push the adjuster lever off the star wheel and turn the star wheel to retract the shoes (see illustration).

4 Wash the brake assembly thoroughly with brake system cleaner before beginning work. Do NOT use compressed air to blow off the brake assembly.

5 Clean the brake drums and check them for score marks, deep grooves, hard spots (which will appear as small discolored areas) and cracks. If the drums are worn, scored or out-of-round, they can be resurfaced by an automotive machine shop.

➡Note: Professionals recommend resurfacing the drums whenever a brake job is done. Resurfacing will eliminate the possibility of out-of-round drums. If the drums are worn so much they can't be resurfaced without exceeding the maximum allowable diameter (stamped or cast on the drum), new ones will be

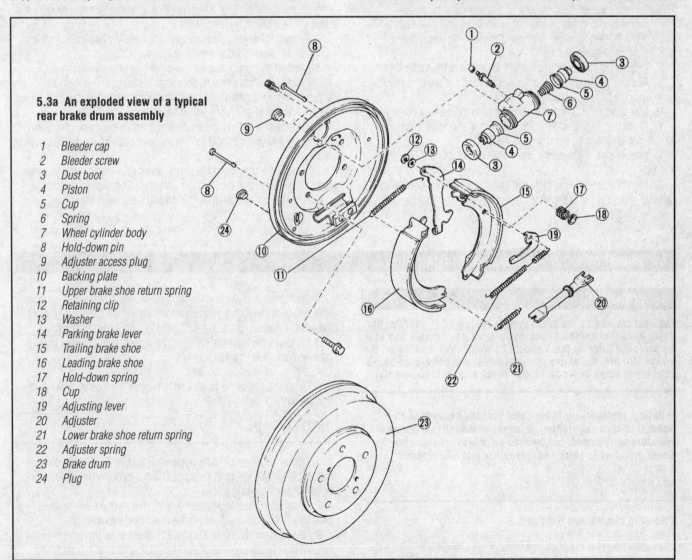

5.3a An exploded view of a typical rear brake drum assembly

1   Bleeder cap
2   Bleeder screw
3   Dust boot
4   Piston
5   Cup
6   Spring
7   Wheel cylinder body
8   Hold-down pin
9   Adjuster access plug
10 Backing plate
11 Upper brake shoe return spring
12 Retaining clip
13 Washer
14 Parking brake lever
15 Trailing brake shoe
16 Leading brake shoe
17 Hold-down spring
18 Cup
19 Adjusting lever
20 Adjuster
21 Lower brake shoe return spring
22 Adjuster spring
23 Brake drum
24 Plug

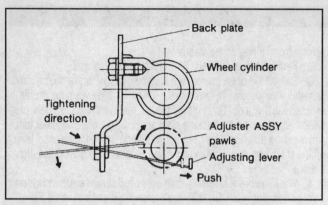

5.3b To back off the brake shoes, insert a screwdriver through the access hole in the backing plate, push the adjusting lever off the adjuster wheel and turn the wheel with another screwdriver

required. At the very least, if you elect not to have the drums resurfaced, remove the glazing from the surface with sandpaper or emery cloth using a swirling motion.

6   Work on only one drum brake assembly at a time. Do not begin disassembling the other brake until you have reassembled the first one. That way, you can use the other one as a reference, if necessary.

7   Using a hold-down spring tool, push down and give each hold-down cup a 90-degree twist, disconnect the hold-down cups and remove the hold-down springs.

8   Disconnect the lower shoe return spring from the brake shoes.

9   Remove the leading and trailing shoes and the adjuster mechanism from the backing plate.

10 Disconnect the parking brake cable from the parking brake lever.

11 Place the leading and trailing brake shoe and adjuster assembly on a bench and remove the rest of the parts.

12 Inspect and, if necessary, replace the wheel cylinder (see Section 6).

13 Clean off the backing plate and apply brake grease or high-temperature grease to the brake shoe contact areas on the backing plate (see illustration).

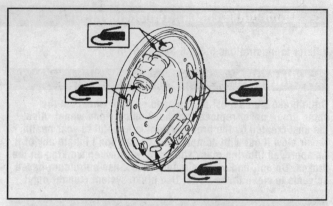

5.13 Before reassembling the brake assembly, lubricate the raised pads, the slots in the wheel cylinder pistons and the ends of the lower shoe retaining plate with high-temperature grease

14 Apply brake grease to the threaded portion of the adjuster and to the tips of the adjuster, where it engages the brake shoes. Engage the slots in the brake shoes with the ends of the adjuster. Attach the upper return spring to both shoes to hold them in place.

15 Position the shoes and adjuster on the brake backing plate and engage the upper ends of the shoes, one at a time, with the slots on the ends of the wheel cylinder pistons.

16 Attach the lower return spring to the leading and trailing shoes.

17 Install the hold-down pins, springs and cups.

18 Repeat this procedure for the other rear brake assembly.

19 Install the brake drums. To adjust the brake shoes, turn the adjuster (see illustration 5.3b) until the wheel stops turning, then back off the adjuster slightly. The wheel should now turn freely and you shouldn't be able to hear the shoes dragging on the drum; if it doesn't turn freely and you can hear the shoes drag, back off the adjuster a little more.

20 Install the wheels and lug nuts, lower the vehicle and tighten the lug nuts to the torque listed in the Chapter 1 Specifications. Test the brakes for proper operation before driving the vehicle in traffic.

6   Wheel cylinder - removal and installation

✳✳ WARNING:

The dust created by the brake system is harmful to your health. Never blow it out with compressed air and don't inhale any of it. An approved filtering mask should be worn when working on the brakes. Do not, under any circumstances, use petroleum-based solvents to clean brake parts. Use brake system cleaner only!

➡ Note: If replacement is indicated (usually because of fluid leakage or sticky operation), it is recommended that the wheel cylinders be replaced, not overhauled. Always replace the wheel cylinders in pairs - never replace just one of them.

REMOVAL

▶ **Refer to illustrations 6.2 and 6.3**

1   Remove the brake drum and brake shoes (see Section 5).

2   Remove the brake line fitting from the rear of the wheel cylinder with a flare-nut wrench (see illustration). Don't pull the metal line out of the wheel cylinder - it could bend, making installation difficult.

3   Remove the two nuts securing the wheel cylinder to the brake backing plate (see illustration).

4   Remove the wheel cylinder.

5   Plug the end of the brake line to prevent the loss of brake fluid and the entry of dirt.

INSTALLATION

6   Place the wheel cylinder in position and, while it's still loose, connect the brake line to it, being careful not to cross thread the fitting. Don't tighten the fitting yet.

7   Install the bolts and tighten them to the torque listed in this Chapter's Specifications. Tighten the line fitting securely.

8   Bleed the brakes (see Section 10). Don't drive the vehicle in traffic until the operation of the brakes has been thoroughly tested.

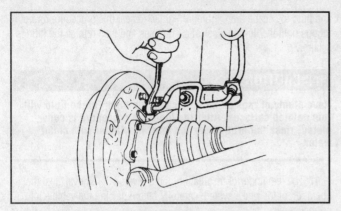

6.2 Disconnect the brake line fitting with a flare-nut wrench (to protect the corners of the nut)

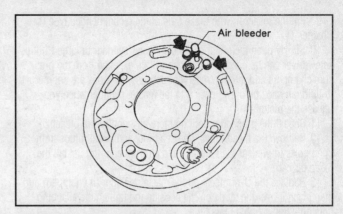

6.3 To detach the wheel cylinder from the backing plate, remove these two retaining bolts

7 Master cylinder - removal and installation

REMOVAL

▶ **Refer to illustration 7.2**

1 Place some shop rags underneath the master cylinder to catch any spilled brake fluid, then remove the brake fluid from the reservoir.

☀☀ CAUTION:

Brake fluid will damage paint. Cover all body parts and be careful not to spill fluid during this procedure. Clean any spilled fluid immediately and wash the area thoroughly with water.

➡**Note: A large syringe or poultry baster works well for removing the brake fluid from the reservoir but cannot be used for anything else afterwards.**

2 Unplug the electrical connector for the brake fluid level indicator (see illustration).
3 Place some rags or newspapers under the brake line fittings.

Using a flare-nut wrench, unscrew the brake line tube nuts and allow any residual fluid to drain onto the rags.
4 Remove the nuts that attach the master cylinder to the power brake booster.
5 Remove the master cylinder from the engine compartment, being careful not to spill any fluid.

INSTALLATION

▶ **Refer to illustration 7.8**

6 If a new master cylinder is being installed, the booster pushrod length must be checked and adjusted. Refer to Section 15 of this chapter for check and adjustment procedures.
7 Bench bleed the new master cylinder before installing it. Mount the master cylinder in a vise, with the jaws of the vise clamping on the mounting flange.
8 Attach a pair of master cylinder bleeder tubes to the outlet ports of the master cylinder (see illustration).

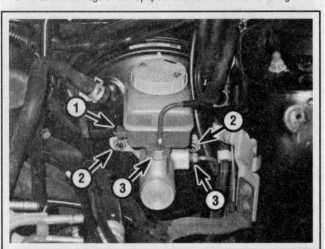

7.2 Master cylinder details:

1   *Electrical connector*   3   *Brake line fittings*
2   *Mounting nuts*

7.8 The best way to bleed air from the master cylinder before installing it on the vehicle is with a pair of bleeder tubes that direct brake fluid back into the reservoir during bleeding

9   Fill the reservoir with brake fluid of the recommended type (see Chapter 1).

10   Slowly push the pistons into the master cylinder (a large Phillips screwdriver can be used for this) - air will be expelled from the pressure chambers and into the reservoir. Because the tubes are submerged in fluid, air can't be drawn back into the master cylinder when you release the pistons.

11   Repeat the procedure until no more air bubbles are present.

12   Remove the bleed tubes, one at a time, and install plugs in the open ports to prevent fluid leakage and air from entering. Install the reservoir cap.

13   Replace the O-ring seal on the master cylinder (if equipped) and then place it over the studs on the booster and tighten the attaching nuts only finger tight at this time.

14   Thread the brake line fittings into the master cylinder. Since the master cylinder is still a bit loose, it can be moved slightly in order for the fittings to thread in easily. Be careful not to cross-thread or strip the fittings as they are installed.

15   Fully tighten the mounting nuts, then the brake line fittings. Tighten the nuts to the torque listed in this Chapter's Specifications.

16   Fill the master cylinder reservoir with fluid, then bleed the master cylinder and the brake system as described in Section 10. To bleed the cylinder on the vehicle, have an assistant depress the brake pedal and hold the pedal to the floor. Loosen the fitting just enough to allow air and fluid to escape then tighten it lightly. Repeat this procedure on both fittings until the fluid is clear of air bubbles and then tighten the fittings securely.

✳✳ CAUTION:

Have plenty of rags on hand to catch the fluid - brake fluid will ruin painted surfaces. After the bleeding procedure is completed, rinse the area under the master cylinder with clean water.

17   The remainder of installation is the reverse of removal. Test the operation of the brake system carefully before placing the vehicle into normal service.

✳✳ WARNING:

Do not operate the vehicle if you are in doubt about the effectiveness of the brake system. On models equipped with ABS, it is possible for air to become trapped in the anti-lock brake system hydraulic control unit, so, if the pedal continues to feel spongy after repeated bleedings or the BRAKE or ANTI-LOCK light stays on, have the vehicle towed to a dealer service department or other qualified shop to be bled with the aid of a scan tool.

8   Brake hoses and lines - check and replacement

1   About every six months, with the vehicle raised and placed securely on jackstands, the flexible hoses which connect the steel brake lines with the front and rear brake assemblies should be inspected for cracks, chafing of the outer cover, leaks, blisters and other damage. These are important and vulnerable parts of the brake system and inspection should be complete. A light and mirror will be needed for a thorough check. If a hose exhibits any of the above defects, replace it with a new one.

FLEXIBLE HOSES

▸ **Refer to illustration 8.3**

2   Clean all dirt away from the ends of the hose.

3   Unscrew the metal tube nut with a flare nut wrench, pull the retaining clip straight out from the hose fitting at the frame bracket and remove the hose from the bracket. On front hoses, remove the hose mounting bolt from the bracket on the strut (see illustration).

4   Disconnect the hose from the caliper and discard the sealing washers.

5   Attach the new brake hose to the caliper using new sealing washers. Tighten the brake hose banjo bolt to the torque listed in this Chapter's Specifications.

6   Installation is the reverse of removal. Make sure that the hose is routed correctly and not twisted.

7   Bleed the brake system (see Section 10).

METAL BRAKE LINES

8   When replacing brake lines, be sure to use the correct parts. Don't use copper tubing for any brake system components. Purchase

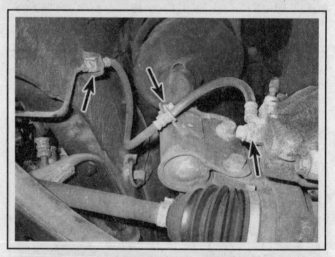

8.3   Remove the brake hose from these three points

steel brake lines from a dealer parts department or auto parts store.

9   Prefabricated brake line, with the tube ends already flared and fittings installed, is available at auto parts stores and dealer parts departments. These lines can be bent to the proper shapes using a tubing bender.

10   When installing a new line, make sure it's supported in the original brackets and has plenty of clearance between moving or hot components.

11   After installation, check the master cylinder fluid level and add fluid as necessary. Bleed the brake system as outlined in Section 10 and test the brakes carefully before placing the vehicle into normal operation.

9   Proportioning valve - replacement

▶ Refer to illustration 9.1

➡Note: The 2005 and later Legacy models are not equipped with a proportioning valve.

1   Unscrew all four brake line tube nuts with a flare nut wrench (see illustration).

2   Remove the mounting bolt for the proportioning valve.

3   Installation is the reverse of removal. Bleed the brake system as outlined in Section 10 and test the brakes carefully before placing the vehicle into normal operation.

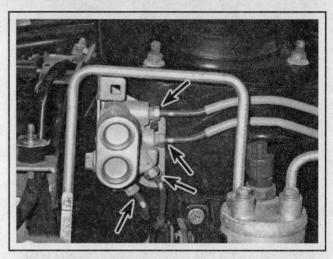

9.1 To replace the proportioning valve, carefully unscrew all line fittings with a flare-nut wrench and remove the mounting bracket bolt from the strut tower

10   Brake hydraulic system - bleeding

▶ Refer to illustrations 10.1 and 10.8

※※ WARNING 1:

If air has found its way into the hydraulic control unit on models with ABS, the system must be bled with the use of a scan tool. If the brake pedal feels spongy even after bleeding the brakes, or the ABS light on the instrument panel does not go off, or if you have any doubts whatsoever about the effectiveness of the brake system, have the vehicle towed to a dealer service department or other repair shop equipped with the necessary tools for bleeding the system.

※※ WARNING 2:

Wear eye protection when bleeding the brake system. If the fluid comes in contact with your eyes, immediately rinse them with water and seek medical attention.

➡Note: Bleeding the brake system is necessary to remove any air that's trapped in the system when it's opened during removal and installation of a hose, line, caliper, wheel cylinder or master cylinder.

1   It will probably be necessary to bleed the system at all four brakes if air has entered the system due to low fluid level, or if the brake lines have been disconnected at the master cylinder.

➡Note: If the master cylinder has run dry (due to a leak in the system) or the master cylinder has been replaced, begin by bleeding the master cylinder (see illustration).

2   If a brake line was disconnected only at a wheel, then only that caliper or wheel cylinder must be bled.

3   If a brake line is disconnected at a fitting located between the master cylinder and any of the brakes, that part of the system served by the disconnected line must be bled.

4   Remove any residual vacuum (or hydraulic pressure) from the

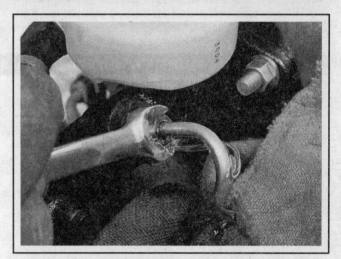

10.1 Have an assistant depress the brake pedal and hold it down. Briefly loosen the line fitting to allow air and fluid to escape. Repeat this procedure on both line fittings until the fluid is clear of air bubbles

brake power booster by applying the brake several times with the engine off.

5   Remove the master cylinder reservoir cap and fill the reservoir with brake fluid. Reinstall the cap.

➡Note: Check the fluid level often during the bleeding operation and add fluid as necessary to prevent the fluid level from falling low enough to allow air bubbles into the master cylinder.

6   Have an assistant on hand, as well as a supply of new brake fluid, an empty clear plastic container, a length of plastic, rubber or vinyl tubing to fit over the bleeder valve and a wrench to open and close the bleeder valve.

7   Beginning at the right rear wheel, loosen the bleeder screw

10.8 When bleeding the brakes, a hose is connected to the bleeder screw at the caliper or wheel cylinder and then submerged in brake fluid - air will be seen as bubbles in the tube and container (all air must be expelled before moving to the next wheel)

slightly, then tighten it to a point where it's snug but can still be loosened quickly and easily.

8   Place one end of the tubing over the bleeder screw fitting and submerge the other end in brake fluid in a container (see illustration).

9   Have the assistant slowly depress the brake pedal and hold it in the depressed position.

10   While the pedal is held depressed, open the bleeder screw just enough to allow a flow of fluid to leave the valve. Watch for air bubbles to exit the submerged end of the tube. When the fluid flow slows after a couple of seconds, tighten the screw and have your assistant release the pedal.

11   Repeat Steps 9 and 10 until no more air is seen leaving the tube, then tighten the bleeder screw and proceed to the left rear wheel, the right front wheel and the left front wheel, in that order, and perform the same procedure. Be sure to check the fluid in the master cylinder reservoir frequently.

12   Always use fresh brake fluid when bleeding the brake system. Old brake fluid contains moisture which can boil and disable the brake system.

13   Refill the master cylinder with fluid at the end of the operation.

14   Check the operation of the brakes. The pedal should feel solid when depressed, with no sponginess. If necessary, repeat the entire process.

> ### ☆☆ WARNING:
>
> **Do not operate the vehicle if you are in doubt about the effectiveness of the brake system. On models equipped with ABS, it's possible for air to become trapped in the anti-lock brake system hydraulic control unit, so, if the pedal continues to feel spongy after repeated bleedings or the BRAKE or ANTI-LOCK light stays on, have the vehicle towed to a dealer service department or other qualified shop to be bled with the aid of a scan tool.**

11   Parking brake cable(s) - adjustment, removal and installation

ADJUSTMENT

♦ **Refer to illustration 11.5**

1   Before adjusting the parking brake, make sure that the brake hydraulic system is free of all air (see Section 10) and that the rear brakes have been adjusted properly (rear drum brake models, see Section 5) or the parking brake shoes have been adjusted properly (rear disc brake models, see Section 13).

2   Firmly apply the parking brake lever three to five times.

3   Count how many clicks the brake lever travels before it becomes fully engaged. The correct number is five to six clicks. If the parking brake lever needs more than this number of clicks before it's fully applied, the cable is stretched. If it applies the brakes in less than this number, the cable is too tight. Adjust the parking brake as follows.

4   Remove the center console cover (see Chapter 11).

5   Back off the locknut (see illustration), then turn the adjuster nut clockwise to tighten the cable or counterclockwise to loosen it.

6   Pull up on the parking brake lever again and count how many clicks it takes to fully apply the parking brake. Repeat the adjustment procedure if necessary.

7   After the adjustment is made, tighten the locknut against the adjuster nut.

➡**Note: If the correct adjustment cannot be achieved, it's possible the cables may be stretched beyond the point of adjustment and in need of replacement; but this condition would be considered rare.**

8   Install the center console cover (see Chapter 11).

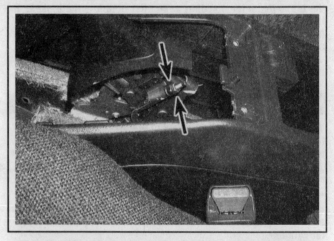

11.5 To adjust the parking brake cable, loosen the locknut, then tighten or loosen the adjuster nut. The adjustment is correct when the parking brake is fully applied when the lever clicks five to six times

REMOVAL AND INSTALLATION

♦ **Refer to illustrations 11.13a, 11.13b, 11.14, 11.16a and 11.16b**

9   Remove the center console (see Chapter 11).

10   Loosen the cable locknut and adjuster nut (see illustration 11.5).

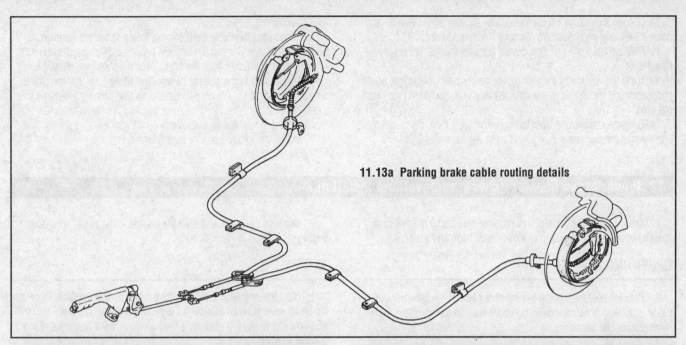

11.13a Parking brake cable routing details

11.13b Remove the cable from the clips and brackets that secure it

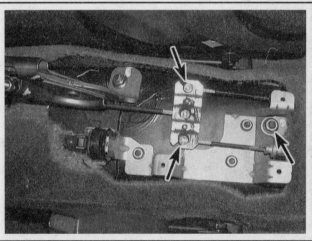

11.14 Disengage the parking brake cables from the equalizer, peel back the carpet and remove the two cable clamp nuts right behind the equalizer (one clamp nut not visible)

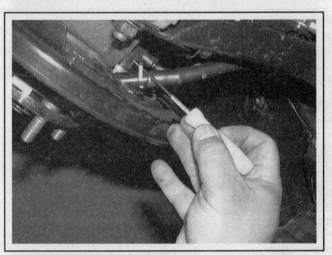

11.16a To detach the parking brake cable from the brake backing plate, remove this retainer clip . . .

11.16b . . . then pull the cable through the backing plate

11 Loosen the rear wheel lug nuts, raise the rear of the vehicle and place it securely on jackstands. Remove the rear wheels.

12 Remove the front fuel tank covers (Legacy models only) (see Chapter 4).

13 Trace the routing of the rear cables and remove all clamps and/or clips attaching the cables to the vehicle body or suspension (see illustrations).

14 Disengage the cable from the equalizer, peel back the carpet and remove the two cable clamp nuts right behind the equalizer

(see illustration).

15 Disengage the cable from the rear brake assembly (rear drum brake models, see Section 5; rear disc brake models, see Section 13).

16 Detach the cable from the brake backing plate (see illustrations).

17 Installation is the reverse of removal. Make sure that the cables are routed so that they're not kinked and so that nothing interferes with them.

18 Adjust the cables (see above).

19 Install the center console (see Chapter 11).

---

12 Power brake booster - check, removal and installation

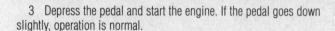

1 The power brake booster unit requires no special maintenance apart from periodic inspection of the vacuum hose and the case.

OPERATING CHECK

2 Depress the brake pedal several times with the engine off and make sure there is no change in the pedal reserve distance (the minimum distance to the floor).

12.7 Disconnect the vacuum hose from the power brake booster

3 Depress the pedal and start the engine. If the pedal goes down slightly, operation is normal.

AIRTIGHTNESS CHECK

4 Start the engine and turn it off after one or two minutes. Depress the pedal several times slowly. If the pedal goes down farther the first time but gradually rises after the second or third depression, the booster is airtight.

5 Depress the brake pedal while the engine is running, then stop the engine with the brake pedal depressed. If there is no change in the pedal reserve travel after holding the pedal for 30 seconds, the booster is airtight.

REMOVAL

▶ **Refer to illustrations 12.7, 12.9, and 12.10**

6 If the booster is defective, replace it with a new or rebuilt unit. The booster cannot be overhauled.

7 Disconnect the vacuum hose from the booster unit (see illustration).

8 Remove the master cylinder (see Section 7).

9 Working on the inside of the vehicle, remove the cotter pin and the pushrod clevis pin, and disconnect the booster pushrod clevis from the brake pedal (see illustration).

10 Remove the four booster-to-firewall nuts (see illustration), then remove the booster from the vehicle.

12.9 To disconnect the power brake booster pushrod from the brake pedal, remove the retaining clip and pull out the clevis pin

12.10 To detach the power brake booster from the firewall, remove the mounting nuts (one hidden in this photo)

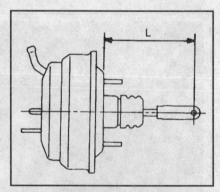

12.12 Measure the length (L) of the booster pushrod and compare your measurement to the length listed in this Chapter's Specifications; if the pushrod is out of specification, loosen the locknut and screw the pushrod in or out

INSTALLATION

♦ **Refer to illustration 12.12**

11 Installation is the reverse of removal. Tighten the booster-to-firewall nuts to the torque listed in this Chapter's Specifications.

12 If you're installing a new power brake booster, adjust the pushrod length to the length listed in this Chapter's Specifications. Loosen the locknut and turn the pushrod until it's at the specified length (see illustration).

13 Bleed the brake system (see Section 10).

---

13 Parking brake shoes (rear disc brakes only) - inspection and replacement

♦ Refer to illustrations 13.3, 13.4, 13.5 and 13.6a through 13.6o

❋❋ WARNING:

Parking brake shoes must be replaced on both wheels at the same time - never replace the shoes on only one wheel. Also, the dust created by the brake system is harmful to your health. Never blow it out with compressed air and don't inhale any of it. An approved filtering mask should be worn when working on the brakes. Do not, under any circumstances, use petroleum-based solvents to clean brake parts. Use brake system cleaner only!

1 Loosen the wheel lug nuts, raise the rear of the vehicle and support it securely on jackstands. Block the front wheels to keep the vehicle from rolling off the stands.

2 Remove the rear wheels. Release the parking brake.

3 Remove the brake discs (see Section 4). It's not necessary to disconnect the brake hoses from the brake calipers. Make sure you support the calipers with coat hangers or pieces of wire. It may be difficult or impossible to remove the discs if the parking brake shoes have worn them excessively. If you can't pull off the discs, remove the access hole plug for the parking brake shoe adjuster from the backing plate and, using a brake adjuster tool or a narrow screwdriver, back off the brake shoes by turning the star wheel on the adjuster (see illustration).

4 Wash the parking brake assemblies with brake system cleaner before beginning work (see illustration). Do not use compressed air to blow off the brake assembly.

5 Wash the disc brakes and check the parking brake drums for score marks, deep grooves, hard spots (which will appear as small discolored areas) and cracks. If the parking brake drums are worn, scored

13.3 If a rear disc proves difficult or impossible to remove, pull out the adjuster hole access plug from the backing plate and back off the parking brake shoes by turning the star wheel on the adjuster with an adjuster tool or a screwdriver

or out-of-round, they can be resurfaced by an automotive machine shop.

➡**Note: Professionals recommend resurfacing drums whenever a brake job is done. Resurfacing will eliminate the possibility of out-of-round drums. If the drums are worn so much they can't**

13.4 Wash the parking brake assembly with brake system cleaner before disassembling anything

13.5 Don't be confused by the two specifications cast into the drum area of the disc: The spec on the left is the minimum thickness for the brake disc; the spec on the right is the maximum diameter for the drum (typical)

13.6a Exploded view of the parking brake shoes (disc brake models)

1 Backing plate
2 C-clip
3 Spring washer
4 Parking brake lever
5 Primary parking brake shoe
6 Secondary parking brake shoe
7 Strut spring
8 Strut
9 Shoe guide plate
10 Primary shoe return spring
11 Secondary shoe return spring
12 Adjusting spring
13 Adjuster
14 Shoe hold-down cup
15 Shoe hold-down spring
16 Shoe hold-down pin
17 Adjusting hole plug

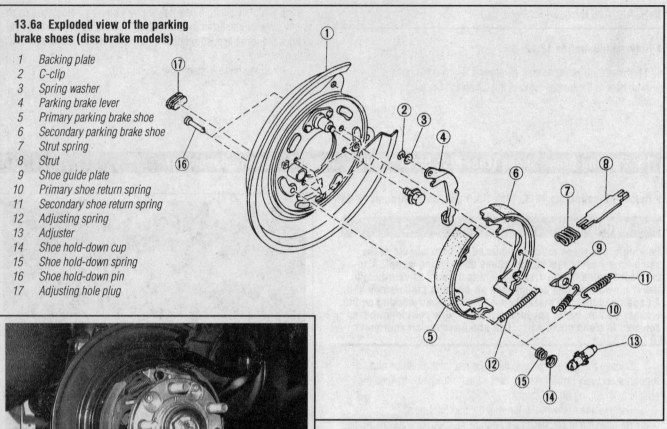

13.6b Using a hold-down spring tool (or screwdriver if the hold-down cup has a slot), push down and give the hold-down cup a 90-degree twist, disconnect the hold-down cup and remove the hold-down spring

be resurfaced without exceeding the maximum allowable diameter - which is stamped into the drum portion of the disc (see illustration) - new ones will be required. At the very least, if you elect not to have the drums resurfaced, remove the glazing from the surface with sandpaper or emery cloth using a swirling motion. This is also a good time to inspect the discs themselves for wear (see Section 4).

6 To replace the parking brake shoes, follow the accompanying photos, beginning with illustration 13.6a. Be sure to stay in order and read the caption under each illustration. Work on only one parking brake assembly at a time. Do not begin disassembling the second parking brake assembly until you have reassembled the first. That way, you will have one assembled parking brake to use as a reference, if necessary.

13.6c Remove the secondary (rear) shoe hold-down spring the same way

13.6d Unhook the secondary shoe return spring from the anchor pin with a brake spring tool, then unhook the spring from the secondary shoe

13.6e Remove the strut and strut spring

13.6f Unhook the primary shoe return spring from the anchor pin with a brake spring tool, then unhook the spring from the shoe

13.6g Remove the brake shoes, lower return spring and adjuster as a single unit, remove the adjuster and spring, then detach the parking brake cable from the lever

13.6h Clean off the backing plate, then lubricate the brake shoe contact areas with high-temperature grease

13.6i Transfer the parking brake lever to the new secondary shoe, then connect the cable to the lever and position the shoe on the backing plate

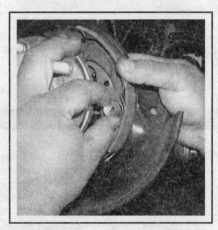

13.6j Install the hold-down pin, spring and cup, then lock down the spring by pushing in on the cup and turning it 90-degrees

13.6k Install the strut and strut spring; make sure that the slot in the rear end of the strut is correctly engaged with the slot in the secondary shoe

13.6l Hook the lower return spring to the bottom of each shoe and install the adjuster between them

13.6m Place the primary shoe and shoe guide plate in position . . .

13.6n . . . then install the hold-down pin, spring and retainer

13.6o Hook the upper return springs to each shoe and, using a brake spring tool, hook them over the anchor pin

7   Repeat this procedure for the other parking brake assembly.

8   Install the brake discs (see Section 4). To adjust the parking brake shoes, turn the adjuster (see illustration 13.3) until the shoes rub on the drum, then back off the adjuster until they don't.

9   Install the caliper support brackets, the brake pads and the calipers (see Sections 2 and 3).

10 Install the rear wheels and lug nuts, lower the vehicle and tighten the lug nuts to the torque listed in the Chapter 1 Specifications. Adjust the parking brake (see Section 11). Test the brakes for proper operation before driving the vehicle in traffic.

14 Hill-holder system - adjustment and component replacement

➡**Note: The hill-holder system is a feature on 2003 and later Forester models with manual transmissions.**

ADJUSTMENT

◆ **Refer to illustrations 14.3a and 14.3b**

1   The hill-holder system uses the vehicles braking system to work. It consists of a valve assembly that is hydraulically linked to the brake master cylinder and a cable that is mechanically linked to the clutch pedal.

2   Find a hill with at least three degrees of incline (the system will not engage with less than three degrees of incline).

3   Drive the vehicle up the hill and then stop. With the clutch pedal depressed, take your foot off the brake. If the vehicle starts to roll backward, the cable is too loose and needs adjusting. Loosen the locknut for the cable adjusting nut (near the valve assembly) and tighten the cable adjusting nut a small amount (see illustrations).

➡**Note: When turning the adjusting nut, make sure that the cable does not move or twist.**

4   Repeat the test and note whether the vehicle remains in place or rolls backward. If it still rolls, tighten the adjusting nut a little more.

5   Follow this procedure until the hill-holder system holds the vehicle in position on the hill.

⁕⁕ **CAUTION:**

Be careful not to tighten the cable any more than necessary. Tightening the cable adjusting nut too much will keep the brakes engaged and prevent the vehicle from rolling freely when the clutch pedal is released.

6   To confirm that the cable is not adjusted too tightly, place the vehicle in neutral and release the clutch pedal while on the hill. Briefly remove your foot from the brake to see how the vehicle responds. The vehicle should roll freely. If it does not, the cable may be adjusted too tightly.

7   Repeat the adjustment procedure until the hill-holder system operates properly. Once the adjustment is made, tighten the locknut securely making sure not to change the position of the adjusting nut.

8   If the brakes are continually engaged, check the hill-holder return spring. If it is broken, replace the hill-holder mechanism immediately. Release the brakes by removing the hill-holder cable locknut and adjusting nut, removing the cable from the valve assembly and manually retracting the hill-holder valve lever.

COMPONENT REPLACEMENT

Hill-holder cable

➡**Note: Break in the new cable by operating the clutch at least 30 times before adjusting it.**

9   Remove the locknut and adjuster nut from the end of the hill-holder cable and then remove the cable from the hill-holder valve.

10 Remove the clip holding the cable to the hill-holder valve.

11 Remove the cable end from the clutch lever.

12 Remove any clamps holding the cable in place along its length, then remove the cable.

13 Installation is the reverse of removal. Make sure that the cable is installed correctly at both ends. Do not tighten the adjusting nut until the cable has been adjusted.

14 Adjust the hill-holder cable (see above).

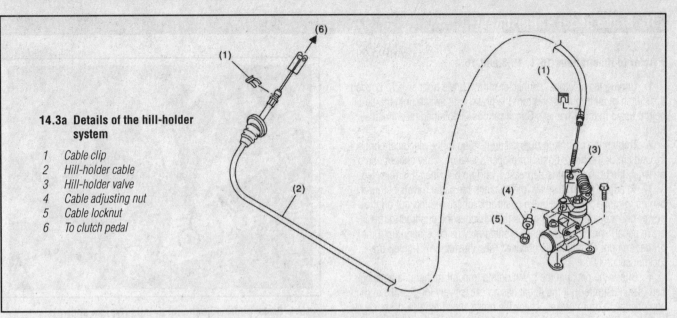

14.3a Details of the hill-holder system

1 Cable clip
2 Hill-holder cable
3 Hill-holder valve
4 Cable adjusting nut
5 Cable locknut
6 To clutch pedal

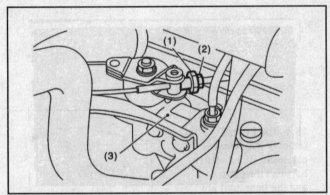

14.3b Turn the adjusting nut to tighten or loosen the hill-holder cable

1 Adjusting nut   3 Hill holder valve
2 Locknut

Hill-holder valve

15 Place shop rags underneath the master cylinder and the hill-holder valve to catch any spilled brake fluid. Drain the fluid from the master cylinder reservoir.

16 Remove the hill-holder cable from the hill-holder valve (see above).

17 Disconnect the brake line fittings from the valve.

18 Remove the hill-holder valve mounting bolts and remove the valve.

19 Inspect the return spring. If it's worn or damaged, replace it.

20 To inspect the valve, rotate it back and forth in your hands. If the sound of a rolling ball is heard, then the valve is probably still good.

21 Apply a lithium-based grease to all of the moving parts of the valve mechanism. Work the lever a few times to make sure it is working correctly and to loosen it up.

22 Installation is the reverse of removal. Make sure to adjust the cable (see above).

23 Bleed the brakes (see Section 10).

15 Brake light switch - replacement

▶ **Refer to illustration 15.1**

➡ **Note: Replacing the brake light switch will affect the brake pedal adjustment.**

1 Disconnect the electrical connector from the brake light switch (see illustration).

2 Remove the switch by removing the nut that is closest to the brake pedal stop (see illustration 16.1).

3 Install the new switch by rotating it until the plunger (on the switch) is completely compressed and the threaded end of the switch is just against the brake pedal stop.

4 Check and adjust the brake pedal height and freeplay (see Section 16).

5 Tighten the switch mounting nuts securely.

6 Connect the electrical connector to the switch and then check the rear brake lights for proper operation.

15.1 The brake light switch is located near the top of the brake pedal

16 Brake pedal - adjustment

▶ **Refer to illustrations 16.1, 16.3 and 16.4**

1   Unplug the electrical connector for the brake light switch. Loosen the switch mounting nuts and turn the brake light switch until the pedal height listed in this Chapter's Specifications is obtained (see illustration).

2   Tighten the mounting nuts securely, plug in the electrical connector and check the brake lights for proper operation. They should come on when the brake pedal is depressed, and go out when it is released.

3   To adjust pedal freeplay (the distance the pedal travels before it begins to move the power brake pushrod), loosen the locknut on the power brake pushrod (at the clevis that attaches the pushrod to the brake pedal) and turn the pushrod (pliers may be necessary) until the proper amount of freeplay is obtained (see illustration). Tighten the locknut securely.

4   Check the pedal at the given points to confirm that it is as specified (see illustration). If the pedal has an excessively long stroke and is equipped with drum brakes, check the brake shoe lining-to-drum clearance (see Chapter 1).

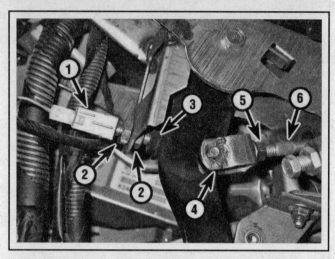

16.1 Brake pedal adjustment details (typical shown):

1   Brake light switch and connector
2   Brake light switch mounting nuts
3   Brake pedal stop
4   Clevis
5   Clevis locknut
6   Power brake booster input (push) rod

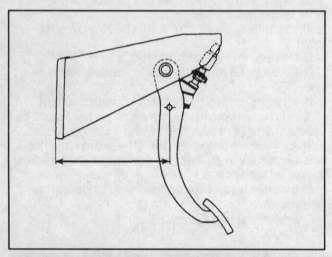

16.3 Brake pedal height is measured from the pedal to the firewall

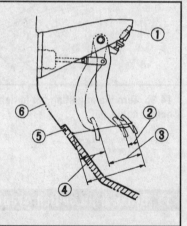

16.4 Brake pedal freeplay and reserve clearance (the distance between the pedal and the floor mat) are measured between the indicated points

1   Brake light switch
2   Brake pedal freeplay
3   Brake pedal stroke
4   Reserve clearance
5   Floor mat
6   Firewall

17 Anti-lock Brake System (ABS) - general information

GENERAL INFORMATION

▶ **Refer to illustration 17.2**

1   The anti-lock brake system is designed to maintain vehicle steerability, directional stability and optimum deceleration under severe braking conditions on most road surfaces. It does so by monitoring the rotational speed of each wheel and controlling the brake line pressure to each wheel during braking. This prevents the wheels from locking up.

2   The ABS system has three main components - the wheel speed sensors, the electronic control unit (ECU) and the hydraulic unit (see illustration). Four wheel speed sensors - one at each wheel - send a variable voltage signal to the control unit, which monitors these signals, compares them to its program and determines whether a wheel is about to lock up. When a wheel is about to lock up, the control unit signals the hydraulic unit to reduce hydraulic pressure (or not increase it further) at that wheel's brake caliper. Pressure modulation is handled by electrically-operated solenoid valves.

3   If a problem develops within the system, an ABS warning light

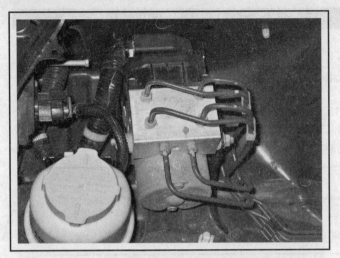

17.2 The ABS control module and hydraulic control unit

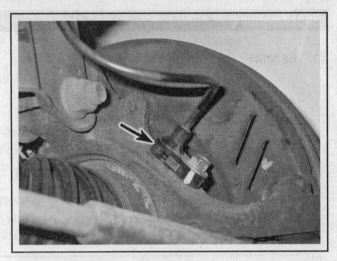

17.9a ABS front wheel speed sensor

will glow on the dashboard. Sometimes, a visual inspection of the ABS system can help you locate the problem. Carefully inspect the ABS wiring harness. Pay particularly close attention to the harness and connections near each wheel. Look for signs of chafing and other damage caused by incorrectly routed wires. If a wheel sensor harness is damaged, the sensor must be replaced.

✻✻ WARNING:

Do NOT try to repair an ABS wiring harness. The ABS system is sensitive to even the smallest changes in resistance. Repairing the harness could alter resistance values and cause the system to malfunction. If the ABS wiring harness is damaged in any way, it must be replaced.

✻✻ CAUTION:

Make sure the ignition is turned off before unplugging or reattaching any electrical connections.

17.9b ABS rear wheel speed sensor

DIAGNOSIS AND REPAIR

4   If a dashboard warning light comes on and stays on while the vehicle is in operation, the ABS system requires attention. Although special electronic ABS diagnostic testing tools are necessary to properly diagnose the system, you can perform a few preliminary checks before taking the vehicle to a dealer service department.

   a) *Check the brake fluid level in the reservoir.*
   b) *Verify that the computer electrical connectors are securely connected.*
   c) *Check the electrical connectors at the hydraulic control unit.*
   d) *Check the fuses.*
   e) *Follow the wiring harness to each wheel and verify that all connections are secure and that the wiring is undamaged.*

5   If the above preliminary checks do not rectify the problem, the vehicle should be diagnosed by a dealer service department or other qualified repair shop. Due to the complex nature of this system, all actual repair work must be done by a qualified automotive technician.

WHEEL SPEED SENSOR - REMOVAL AND INSTALLATION

▸ **Refer to illustrations 17.9a and 17.9b**

6   Loosen the wheel lug nuts, raise the vehicle and support it securely on jackstands. Remove the wheel.

7   Make sure the ignition key is turned to the Off position.

8   Trace the wiring back from the sensor, detaching all brackets and clips while noting its correct routing, then disconnect the electrical connector.

9   Remove the mounting bolt and carefully pull the sensor out from the knuckle (see illustrations).

10   Installation is the reverse of the removal procedure. Tighten the mounting bolt to the torque listed in this Chapter's Specifications.

11   Install the wheel and lug nuts, tightening them securely. Lower the vehicle and tighten the lug nuts to the torque listed in the Chapter 1 Specifications.

Specifications

General

Brake fluid type	See Chapter 1
Brake pedal adjustments	
Pedal freeplay	3/64 to 1/8 inch (1.2 to 3.2 mm)
Pedal height	5 inches (127 mm)
Power brake booster pushrod length	5-23/32 inches (145.25 mm)

Disc brakes (front and rear)

Minimum brake pad thickness	See Chapter 1
Disc minimum thickness	Refer to the dimension marked on the disc
Disc runout limit	0.003 inch (0.076 mm)

Rear drum brake

Minimum brake shoe lining thickness	See Chapter 1
Brake drum maximum diameter	Refer to the dimension marked on the drum

Torque specifications	Ft-lbs (unless otherwise indicated)	Nm
Brake hose-to-caliper banjo bolt	156 in-lbs	17.6
Caliper support bracket bolts		
Front support bracket	59	80
Rear support bracket	39	53
Front caliper bolt		
2004 and earlier models	27	36.6
2005 and later models	20	27
Master cylinder mounting nut	120 in-lbs	13.5
Proportioning valve mounting fasteners	156 in-lbs	17.6
Rear caliper bolt		
Forester	28	40
Legacy		
2004 and earlier models	28	40
2005 and later models		
Vented style rotor	28	40
Solid style rotor	19	25.7
Wheel cylinder mounting bolts	72 in-lbs	8.1

Section

Reference to other Chapters

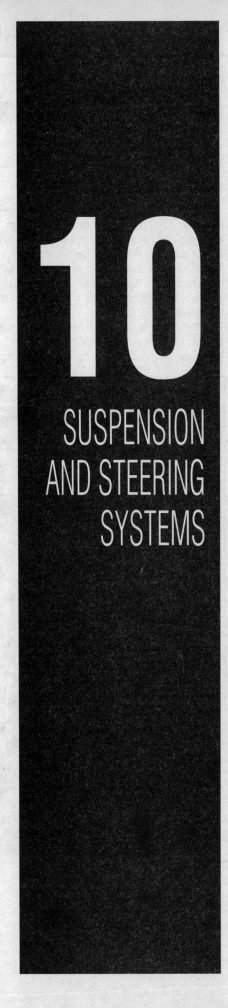

10

SUSPENSION AND STEERING SYSTEMS

1 General information

SUSPENSION

▶ **Refer to illustrations 1.1 1.2a and 1.2b**

The front suspension is fully independent (see illustration). It consists of strut/coil spring assemblies, control arms, steering knuckles and a stabilizer bar. The upper end of each strut is attached to the body and the lower end is bolted to the steering knuckle. The lower end of the knuckle is attached to the control arm by a balljoint. The inner end of the control arm is bolted to a crossmember. The stabilizer bar is attached to the crossmember by a pair of clamps and is connected to the control arms by links.

The rear suspension is also fully independent (see illustration). It consists of strut/coil spring assemblies (Forester), or shock/coil spring assemblies (Legacy/Outback), trailing arms, control arms, knuckles and a stabilizer bar. The upper end of each strut or shock is attached to the body and the lower end is bolted to the knuckle. The knuckle is positioned by the links and the trailing arm. The inner ends of the links are bolted to the crossmember; the outer ends of the links are bolted to the knuckle. The front ends of the trailing arms are bolted to the body; the rear ends of the trailing arms are bolted to the knuckles. The stabilizer bar is attached to the crossmember by a pair of clamps and is connected to the control arms by links.

STEERING

All models use a power-assisted rack-and-pinion type steering gear. The steering gear is connected to the steering knuckles by a pair of tie-rods.

1.1 Typical front suspension components

1	Stabilizer bar	5	Steering knuckles	8	Control arm bushing clamps
2	Stabilizer bar bushing clamps	6	Balljoints	9	Steering gear boots
3	Tie-rods	7	Control arms	10	Steering gear clamp bolts
4	Tie-rod ends				

1.2a Rear Forester suspension components

1 Stabilizer bar
2 Stabilizer bar bushing clamps
3 Stabilizer bar links
4 Rear links
5 Front links
6 Trailing arms
7 Rear knuckles

1.2b Rear Legacy suspension components

1 Trailing arm/rear knuckles
2 Rear struts
3 Front links
4 Stabilizer bar links
5 Rear links
6 Stabilizer bar bushing clamps
7 Stabilizer bar

2 Strut/coil spring assembly (front) - removal and installation

⁂ WARNING:

Struts and/or coil springs must be replaced in pairs - never replace just one of them.

REMOVAL

▶ **Refer to illustrations 2.4a, 2.4b and 2.5**

1 Loosen the front wheel lug nuts, block the rear wheels, raise the front of the vehicle and place it securely on jackstands. Remove the front wheels.

2 Detach the brake hose from the its bracket on the strut (see illustration 2.4a).

3 Remove ABS sensor from the steering knuckle, if equipped (see Chapter 9).

4 Detach the ABS sensor lead from the strut (see Chapter 9), mark the relationship of the upper camber adjustment bolt to the strut flange, then remove the strut-to-knuckle nuts and bolts (see illustrations).

➡ **Note: If a new strut is being installed, it is still important to mark the bolt position; there is an indexing mark on the strut flange, and the proper alignment mark on the bolt must line up with it when installed to preserve the camber setting.**

5 In the engine compartment, remove the mounting nuts that attach the top of the strut to the strut tower (see illustration). Support the strut with one hand (or have an assistant hold it) while doing this.

6 Remove the strut assembly. If you're planning to replace either the strut or the coil spring, refer to Section 3.

INSTALLATION

➡ **Note: The manufacturer recommends using new self-locking mounting nuts when installing the strut assembly to the strut tower.**

7 Place the strut assembly in position and install, but don't tighten, the upper mounting nuts.

8 Insert the steering knuckle into the strut flange, install the strut-to-knuckle bolts and align the mark you made on the upper bolt with the mark on the strut flange. Tighten the bolts and nuts to the torque listed in this Chapter's Specifications.

9 Install the ABS sensor, if equipped.

10 Reattach the brake hose bracket to the strut.

11 Install the wheels and lug nuts.

12 Lower the vehicle and tighten the lug nuts to the torque listed in the Chapter 1 Specifications. Tighten the upper strut mounting nuts to the torque listed in this Chapter's Specifications.

13 Have the front end alignment checked and, if necessary, adjusted.

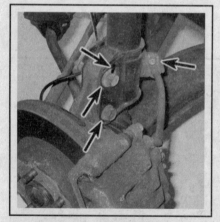

2.4a Mark the relationship of the upper strut-to-knuckle bolt to the strut and note how the brake line is attached

2.4b Remove the strut-to-knuckle nuts and bolts and the ABS harness bracket from the strut

2.5 Mounting nuts for the strut/coil spring assembly with marks on one stud and the strut tower for installation

3 Strut/coil spring - replacement

⁂ WARNING:

Struts and/or coil springs must be replaced in pairs - never replace just one of them.

➡ **Note: You'll need a spring compressor for this procedure. Spring compressors are available on a daily rental basis at most auto parts stores or equipment yards.**

1 If the struts or coil springs exhibit the telltale signs of wear (leaking fluid, loss of damping capability, chipped, sagging or cracked coil springs) explore all options before beginning any work. The strut/shock absorber assemblies are not serviceable and must be replaced if a problem develops. However, strut assemblies complete with springs may be available on an exchange basis, which eliminates much time and work. Whichever route you choose to take, check on the cost and availability of parts before disassembling your vehicle.

✳✳ WARNING:

Disassembling a strut is potentially dangerous and utmost attention must be directed to the job, or serious injury may result. Use only a high quality spring compressor and carefully follow the manufacturer's instructions furnished with the tool. After removing the coil spring from the strut assembly, set it aside in a safe, isolated area.

DISASSEMBLY

◆ **Refer to illustrations 3.3, 3.4a, 3.4b, 3.5, 3.6 and 3.7**

2   Remove the strut and spring assembly (see Section 2).

3   Mount the strut assembly in a vise. Line the vise jaws with wood or rags to prevent damage to the unit and don't tighten the vise excessively. Following the tool manufacturer's instructions, install the spring compressor (which can be obtained at most auto parts stores or equipment yards on a daily rental basis) on the spring and compress it sufficiently to relieve all pressure from the upper spring seat (see illustration). This can be verified by wiggling the spring.

4   Loosen the damper shaft nut with a socket wrench (see illustrations).

5   Remove the nut and lift off the upper strut mount (see illustration). Remove the spacer. Inspect the bearing in the strut mount for smooth operation. If it doesn't turn smoothly, replace the strut mount. Check the rubber portion of the strut mount for cracking and general deterioration. If there is any separation of the rubber, replace it.

6   Remove the upper spring seat (see illustration), the rubber seat and the dust cover. Inspect the upper seat, the rubber seat and the dust cover for cracking and hardness. Replace all damaged parts.

3.3 Install the spring compressor in accordance with the tool manufacturer's instructions and compress the spring until all pressure is relieved from the upper spring seat

7   Carefully lift the compressed spring from the assembly (see illustration) and set it in a safe place.

✳✳ WARNING:

Never place your head near the end of the spring!

8   Slide the rubber bumper off the damper shaft. Inspect it for cracking and hardness. If it's worn or damaged, replace it.

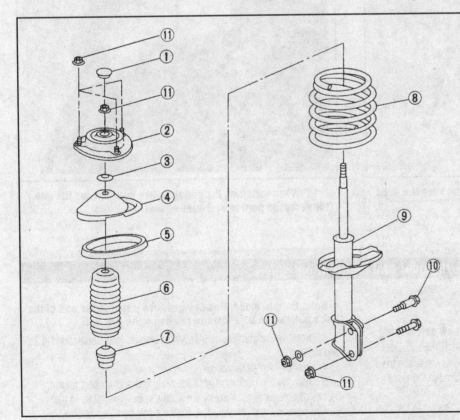

3.4a An exploded view of the front strut/coil spring assembly

1   Dust cover
2   Strut mount
3   Spacer
4   Upper spring seat
5   Rubber seat
6   Dust boot
7   Rubber bumper
8   Coil spring
9   Strut
10   Camber adjusting bolt
11   Self-locking nuts

3.4b Remove the damper shaft nut

3.5 Remove the upper mount from the damper shaft

3.6 Remove the upper spring seat from the damper shaft

REASSEMBLY

▶ **Refer to illustration 3.10**

➡**Note: The manufacturer recommends using a new self-locking nut when assembling the strut.**

9   Fully compress and retract the damper rod at least four times to purge air that may be in the strut.

10   Extend the damper rod to its full length and install the rubber bumper.

11   Carefully place the coil spring onto the lower insulator, with the end of the spring resting in the lowest part of the insulator (see illustration).

12   Install the dust cover, the rubber seat and the upper spring seat.

13   Install the spacer and the upper strut mount. Install a new self-locking nut and tighten it to the torque listed in this Chapter's Specifications.

14   Install the strut/coil spring assembly (see Section 2).

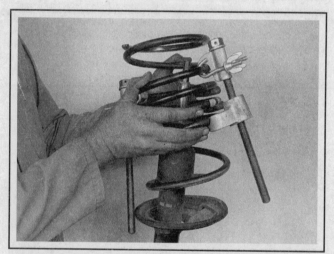

3.7 Remove the compressed spring assembly; keep the ends of the spring pointed away from your body

3.10 When installing the spring, make sure the end fits into the recessed portion of the lower seat

4   Stabilizer bar and links (front) - removal and installation

▶ **Refer to illustrations 4.2a and 4.2b**

➡**Note: The manufacturer recommends using new self-locking mounting nuts when installing the stabilizer bar links.**

1   Loosen the wheel lug nuts. Block the rear wheels, raise the front of the vehicle and place it securely on jackstands. Remove the front wheels.

2   Unbolt the stabilizer bar from the links that connect it to the control arms (see illustrations).

➡**Note: On late model link designs, use a tool in the end of the link's ballstud to hold it while removing the link nut.**

3   Remove the stabilizer bar bushing clamps (see illustrations 4.2a and 4.2b).

4   Remove the stabilizer bar.

5   Remove the bushings from the stabilizer and inspect them for cracks or deterioration. Inspect the stabilizer bar for cracks in the curved portions and deformation. Replace any parts, as necessary.

4.2a Remove the link nuts (A) to remove the link and then remove the stabilizer bar bushing clamp fasteners (B) to remove the bar (early model design shown)

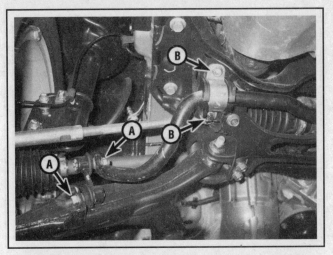

4.2b Remove the link nuts (A) to remove the link and then remove the stabilizer bar bushing clamp fasteners (B) to remove the bar (late model design shown)

6   Installation is the reverse of removal. Tighten the fasteners to the torque listed in this Chapter's Specifications.

7   Install the wheels and lug nuts and lower the vehicle.

8   Tighten the lug nuts to the torque listed in the Chapter 1 Specifications.

5   Control arm (front) - removal and installation

▶ Refer to illustrations 5.4a, 5.4b, 5.5a and 5.5b

➡ Note: The manufacturer recommends using new self-locking mounting nuts when installing the control arm.

1   Loosen the wheel lug nuts, block the rear wheels, raise the front of the vehicle and place it securely on jackstands. Remove the front wheel.

2   On 2003 and later Forester models, remove the subframe (see below).

3   Disconnect the stabilizer bar from the control arm (see Section 4).

4   Remove the balljoint pinch bolt from the steering knuckle, then separate the balljoint from the steering knuckle (see illustrations).

5   Remove the front pivot bolt and nut and the rear bushing clamp bolts (see illustration) and then remove the control arm. On 2005 and later Legacy models, remove the support plate mounting bolts and the mounting nut from the stud at the rear of the control arm (see illustration).

6   Inspect the control arm bushings for cracks or deterioration. Inspect the control arm for cracks and deformations. Replace any damaged parts. To separate the balljoint from the control arm, refer to Section 6.

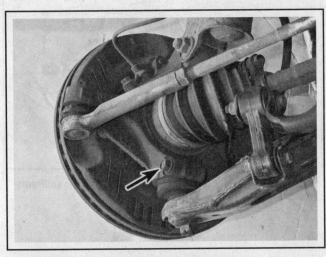

5.4a Remove the balljoint pinch bolt from the steering knuckle . . .

5.4b . . . insert a large prybar between the control arm and the steering knuckle and lever the balljoint out of the knuckle

5.5a The control arm mounting bracket and pivot bolt (typical design)

5.5b The control arm mounting nut, support plate fasteners and pivot bolt (2005 and later Legacy model shown)

7   Installation is the reverse of removal. Tighten the balljoint pinch bolt to the torque listed in this Chapter's Specifications. Before tightening the control arm pivot bolt and bracket bolts, raise the outer end of the control arm with a floor jack to simulate normal ride height, then tighten the fasteners to the torque listed in this Chapter's Specifications.

8   Install the wheel and lug nuts, then lower the vehicle.

9   Tighten the wheel lug nuts to the torque listed in the Chapter 1 Specifications.

SUBFRAME REMOVAL AND INSTALLATION (2003 AND LATER FORESTER MODELS)

▶ **Refer to illustrations 5.12a and 5.12b**

➡**Note: The manufacturer recommends using new bolts when installing the subframe.**

10   Remove the front engine splash shield (see Chapter 2)

11   Loosen the rear-most mounting bolt but leave it installed enough to help support the weight of the subframe.

12   Remove the remaining mounting bolts working from the rear of the vehicle to the front (see illustrations).

> ❋❋ **CAUTION:**
>
> **Make sure to secure the subframe as the mounting bolts are removed. The rear-most bolt can assist in supporting the subframe but it's best to work with an assistant for this procedure.**

13   Installation if the reverse of removal. Tighten the mounting bolts to the torque listed in this Chapter's Specifications. Work in the reverse order of removal by tightening the bolts from front to rear for installation.

5.12a Subframe mounting bolt locations (some bolts are hidden and the design may vary slightly)

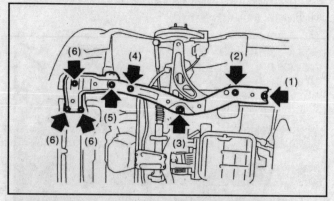

5.12b Use the order illustrated when removing the subframe mounting bolts (the design may vary slightly)

6   Balljoints - check and replacement

CHECK

1   Inspect the control arm balljoints for looseness anytime either of them is separated from the control arm. See if you can turn the ballstud in its socket with your fingers. If the balljoint is loose, or if the ballstud can be turned, replace the balljoint. You can also check the balljoints with the suspension assembled as follows.

2   Raise the front of the vehicle and support it securely on jackstands.

3   Wipe each balljoint clean and inspect the seal for cuts and tears. If the seal is damaged it can be replaced, but it's a good idea to go ahead and replace the balljoint.

4   Place a large prybar under the balljoint and resting on the wheel, then try to pry the balljoint up while feeling for movement between the balljoint and steering knuckle. Now, pry between the control arm and the steering knuckle and try to lever the down while feeling for movement between the balljoint and steering knuckle. If any movement is evident in either check, the balljoint is worn and should be replaced.

5   Have an assistant grasp the tire at the top and bottom and move the top of the tire in-and-out. Check for looseness in the balljoint stud castellated nut. If any looseness is felt, suspect a worn balljoint stud or a widened hole in the control arm. If the latter problem exists, the control arm should be replaced as well as the balljoint.

REPLACEMENT

▶ **Refer to illustrations 6.8 and 6.9**

6   Loosen the wheel lug nuts. Block the rear wheels, raise the front of the vehicle and place it on jackstands. Remove the front wheel.

7   Remove the cotter pin and loosen, but don't remove, the castle nut on the ballstud.

8   Separate the control arm from the balljoint with a two-jaw puller, balljoint separator or picklefork tool. (see illustration).

➡**Note: The use of a picklefork tool will most likely damage the balljoint boot, but it doesn't matter since the balljoint is being replaced. For all other operations requiring the control arm to be separated from the steering knuckle, the balljoint can easily be detached from the steering knuckle (see Section 5).**

9   Remove the balljoint pinch bolt from the steering knuckle (see illustration 5.4a). Use a large screwdriver to pry open the slot in the steering knuckle, then install the castle nut onto the end of the ballstud and use it as a handle to pull the balljoint out of the knuckle (see illustration).

6.8 Separate the balljoint from the control arm with a puller or balljoint separator

6.9 Use a screwdriver to pry open the slot in the steering knuckle to facilitate removal of the balljoint from the knuckle

10   Install the balljoint into the knuckle and tighten the pinch bolt to the torque listed in this Chapter's Specifications.

11   Reattach the control arm to the to the balljoint (steering knuckle) and tighten the castle nut to the torque listed in this Chapter's Specifications. Install a new cotter pin.

7   Steering knuckle/hub assembly (front) - removal and installation

✳✳ WARNING:

Dust created by the brake system is harmful to your health. Never blow it out with compressed air and don't inhale any of it. Do not, under any circumstances, use petroleum-based solvents to clean brake parts. Use brake system cleaner only.

➡**Note: The manufacturer recommends using new self-locking mounting nuts when installing the strut assembly to the steering knuckle.**

1   Unstake and loosen the driveaxle nut (see Chapter 8).

2   Loosen the wheel lug nuts, block the rear wheels, raise the front of the vehicle and place it securely on jackstands. Remove the front wheel.

3   Remove the brake caliper, the caliper support bracket and the brake disc. On models with ABS, remove the front wheel speed sensor and carefully secure it aside (see Chapter 9).

4   Disconnect the tie-rod end from the steering knuckle (see Section 17).

5   Loosen, but do not remove, the strut-to-steering knuckle nuts

(see illustrations 2.4a and 2.4b).

➡**Note: Be sure to mark the relationship of the upper bolt to the strut flange to preserve the camber angle on reassembly.**

6   Separate the control arm from the steering knuckle (see Section 5).

7   Remove the strut-to-knuckle nuts and bolts.

8   Remove the driveaxle nut and pull the steering knuckle off the outer CV joint. If the hub sticks to the CV joint splines, push the stub shaft out of the hub with a two-jaw puller (see Chapter 8).

✳✳ **CAUTION:**

Be careful not to overextend the inner CV joint.

9   While the steering knuckle is removed, the front wheel bearings can be replaced by a qualified repair facility if necessary. If either CV joint boot is damaged, it should be replaced at this time also (see Chapter 8).

10 While the suspension is disassembled, inspect and, if necessary, replace the control arm balljoint (see Section 6).

11 Installation is the reverse of removal. Be sure to align the mark on the upper strut-to-knuckle bolt with the mark on the strut flange, and tighten all fasteners to the torque listed in this Chapter's Specifications.

12 Install the wheel and lug nuts, then lower the vehicle.

13 Tighten the lug nuts to the torque listed in the Chapter 1 Specifications.

14 Have the front end alignment checked and, if necessary, adjusted.

8   Hub and wheel bearing (front) - replacement

2005 AND LATER LEGACY MODELS

◆ **Refer to illustration 8.3**

1   Apply the parking brake. Loosen the wheel lug nuts and the driveaxle/hub nut (see Chapter 8). Raise the front of the vehicle and support it securely on jackstands. Remove the wheel.

2   Remove the brake caliper and brake disc. Also remove the wheel speed sensor from the steering knuckle (see Chapter 9).

3   Remove the hub mounting bolts from the back of the steering knuckle (see illustration).

4   Remove the driveaxle/hub nut and push the driveaxle through the hub splines as the hub and bearing assembly is removed. If the driveaxle sticks in the hub, you'll have to push it out with a puller (see Chapter 8).

✳✳ **CAUTION:**

Be careful not to overextend the inner CV joint. Once the hub has been removed, support the outer end of the driveaxle with a length of wire or rope.

5   Installation is the reverse of removal, noting the following points:

a) *Tighten the hub mounting bolts to the torque listed in this Chapter's Specifications.*

b) *Tighten the brake caliper mounting bracket bolts, caliper mounting bolts and the wheel speed sensor bolt to the torque listed in the Chapter 9 Specifications.*

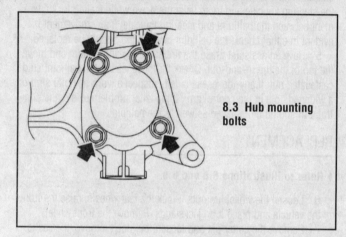

8.3 Hub mounting bolts

c) *Tighten the driveaxle/hub nut to the torque listed in the Chapter 8 Specifications.*

d) *Tighten the wheel lug nuts to the torque listed in the Chapter 1 Specifications.*

ALL OTHER MODELS

6   Due to the special tools and expertise required to press the hub and bearing from the steering knuckle, this job should be left to a professional mechanic. However, the steering knuckle and hub may be removed as an assembly and taken to an automotive machine shop or qualified repair facility for service. See Section 7 for the steering knuckle and hub removal procedure.

9   Strut/coil spring assembly (rear) (Forester) - removal and installation

◆ **Refer to illustrations 9.1, 9.5 and 9.6**

➡**Note 1: Only Forester models are equipped with rear strut/coil spring assemblies. All other models are equipped with shock/coil spring assemblies, see Section 10.**

➡**Note 2: The manufacturer recommends using new self-locking mounting nuts when installing the strut assembly.**

1   Remove the trim piece covering the strut upper mounting nuts (see illustration).

2   Loosen the rear wheel lug nuts, block the front wheels, raise the rear of the vehicle and support it securely on jackstands. Remove the rear wheels.

3   On 2002 and earlier Forester models with rear disc brakes, remove the brake hose banjo bolt from the caliper and detach the hose from the bracket on the strut (see Chapter 9). On 2002 and earlier Forester models with rear drum brakes, unscrew the metal brake line from the flexible brake hose at the bracket on the strut, remove the U-clip and detach the hose and line from the bracket (see Chapter 9).

9.1 Remove the trim covers to get to the upper mounts for the rear strut assemblies

9.5 To detach the strut from the rear knuckle, remove these fasteners

9.6 To detach the strut from the body, remove these nuts

4   Place a floor jack under the rear knuckle and raise it till it just contacts the knuckle.

5   Remove the strut-to-knuckle nuts and bolts (see illustration). If the bolts are difficult to remove, raise the jack slightly until the bolts come out easily.

6   Have an assistant support the strut, then remove the strut upper mounting nuts (see illustration).

7   Installation is the reverse of removal. Use the jack to raise or lower the knuckle to align the holes in the strut bracket with the holes

in the knuckle. Make sure that all fasteners are tightened to the torque listed in this Chapter's Specifications.

8   On 2002 and earlier Forester models, bleed the brakes (see Chapter 9).

9   If you need to disassemble the strut/coil spring assembly in order to replace either the strut or the coil spring, refer to Section 3.

10   Install the wheels and lug nuts, then lower the vehicle.

11   Tighten the wheel lug nuts to the torque listed in the Chapter 1 Specifications.

10 Shock/coil spring assembly (rear) (Legacy/Outback) - removal and installation

▶ Refer to illustrations 10.1 and 10.4

➡ Note 1: Forester models are not equipped with rear shock/coil spring assemblies. They are equipped with strut/coil spring assemblies (see Section 9.)

➡ Note 2: The manufacturer recommends using new self-locking mounting nuts when installing the shock assembly.

1   On Sedan models, move the carpet in the trunk to access the shock upper mounting nuts (see illustration). On Wagon models, move the carpet near the wheel wells aside to access the shock upper mount-

ing nuts.

2   Loosen the rear wheel lug nuts, block the front wheels, raise the rear of the vehicle and support it securely on jackstands. Remove the rear wheels.

3   Place a floor jack under the rear knuckle and raise it till it just contacts the knuckle.

4   Remove the shock-to-knuckle fasteners (see illustration). If the bolt is difficult to remove, raise the knuckle slightly with the jack until the bolt comes out easily.

5   Have an assistant support the shock, then remove the shock

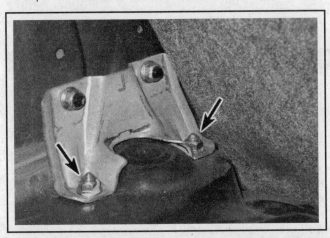

10.1 The rear upper shock mounting bracket and fasteners are located in the trunk (sedan model shown)

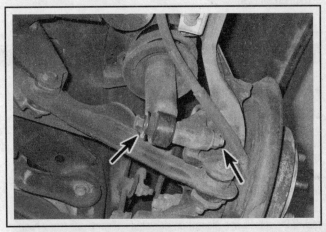

10.4 The shock lower mounting fasteners (sedan model shown)

upper mounting nuts (see illustration 10.1).

6   Installation is the reverse of removal. Use the jack to raise or lower the knuckle to align the hole in the shock with the hole in the knuckle. Make sure that all fasteners are tightened to the torque listed in this Chapter's Specifications.

7   If you need to disassemble the shock/coil spring assembly in order to replace either the shock or the coil spring, refer to Section 3.

8   Install the wheels and lug nuts, then lower the vehicle.

9   Tighten the wheel lug nuts to the torque listed in the Chapter 1 Specifications.

11 Stabilizer bar, bushings and links (rear) - removal and installation

♦ **Refer to illustrations 11.2a, 11.2b and 11.3**

➡**Note: The manufacturer recommends using new self-locking mounting nuts when installing the stabilizer bar links.**

1   Raise the rear of the vehicle and support it securely on jackstands. Block the front wheels to prevent the vehicle from rolling.

➡**Note: On 2005 and later Legacy models, remove the rear wheels.**

2   Detach the link from the stabilizer bar by holding the ballstud with an Allen wrench and removing the nut (see illustration).

➡**Note 1: On 2002 and earlier Forester models, the links do not utilize ballstuds. Simply remove the fasteners to detach the**

links (see illustration).

➡**Note 2: It's only necessary to remove the link's upper fastener to remove the stabilizer bar. However, you can detach the lower fastener in order to remove the link itself.**

3   Unbolt the retainer from each side of the stabilizer bar and then remove the bar (see illustration).

4   Pull the bushings off the bar and inspect them for cracks or other damage. If the bushings are damaged, replace them. Also, check the stabilizer bar links for loose balljoints (or worn link bushings for 2002 and earlier Forester models) and replace them as necessary.

5   Installation is the reverse of removal. Be sure to tighten all fasteners to the torque listed in this Chapter's Specifications.

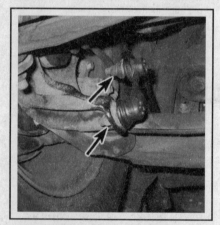

11.2a Remove the link's upper mounting nut from the ballstud to detach it from the stabilizer bar (typical shown)

11.2b Remove the link's upper mounting fasteners

11.3 Remove the fasteners for the stabilizer bar retainers to remove the bar

12 Trailing arm - removal and installation

♦ **Refer to illustrations 12.2 and 12.3**

➡**Note 1: The following procedure applies to Forester models only. All Legacy models have a trailing arm that is integrated with the rear knuckle and hub assembly. See Section 15 for trailing arm/rear knuckle removal on all Legacy models.**

➡**Note 2: The manufacturer recommends using new self-locking mounting nuts when installing the trailing arm.**

1   Loosen the rear wheel lug nuts, block the front wheels, raise the rear of the vehicle and place it on jackstands. Remove the rear wheel.

2   Detach the parking brake cable from the trailing arm (see illustration).

3   Remove the nut and pivot bolt that attach the forward end of the trailing arm to the trailing arm bracket (see illustration).

4   Remove the nut and bolt that attaches the trailing arm to the rear knuckle (see illustration 12.3).

5   Remove the trailing arm.

6   Inspect the trailing arm bushings. If they're cracked, hardened or otherwise worn, have them pressed out and new ones pressed in at an automotive machine shop.

7   Installation is the reverse of removal. After the bolts and nuts have been installed, raise the rear knuckle with a floor jack to simulate normal ride height, then tighten the trailing arm bolts to the torque listed in this Chapter's Specifications.

12.2 Remove the parking brake cable brackets on the trailing arm

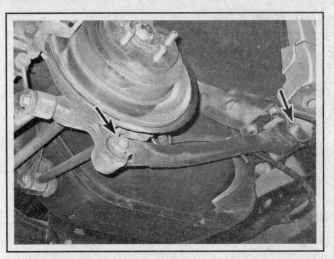

12.3 Trailing arm mounting fasteners

13 Rear suspension links - removal and installation

FORESTER MODELS

♦ Refer to illustrations 13.2 and 13.4

➡**Note: The manufacturer recommends using new self-locking mounting nuts when installing the suspension links.**

1   Loosen the rear wheel lug nuts, block the front wheels, raise the rear of the vehicle and place it on jackstands. Remove the rear wheel.

2   Scribe or paint alignment marks on the rear link adjusting bolt and the rear crossmember (see illustration).

3   Disconnect the rear stabilizer link from the rear link (see Section 11).

4   Remove the fasteners that attach the links to the rear knuckle (see illustration).

5   Remove the fasteners which attach the inner ends of the links to the rear crossmember (see illustration 13.4).

➡**Note: Remove the protector cap that covers one of the link fasteners, if applicable.**

6   Inspect the link bushings. If they're cracked or dried out or otherwise worn, have them pressed out and new ones pressed in at an automotive machine shop.

7   Installation is the reverse of removal. Be sure to align the match-marks on the inner rear link fastener and the crossmember. After all fasteners have been installed, raise the rear knuckle with a floor jack to simulate normal ride height, then tighten the link fasteners to the torque listed in this Chapter's Specifications.

8   Have the rear wheel alignment checked and, if necessary, adjusted.

13.2 To ensure that the correct toe-in is maintained, scribe or paint alignment marks on the adjuster bolt and crossmember before removing the bolt (Forester model)

13.4 Rear suspension link mounting fasteners (Forester model)

LEGACY MODELS

9 Loosen the rear wheel lug nuts, block the front wheels, raise the rear of the vehicle and place it on jackstands. Remove the rear wheel.

Front link

▶ **Refer to illustration 13.10**

10 Remove the fasteners that attach the front link to the rear knuckle and the subframe (see illustration).

11 Inspect the link bushings. If they're cracked or dried out or otherwise worn, have them pressed out and new ones pressed in at an automotive machine shop.

Rear link

▶ **Refer to illustrations 13.12 and 13.13**

12 Scribe or paint alignment marks on the rear link adjusting bolt and the subframe (see illustration).

13 Remove the fasteners that attach the rear link to the rear knuckle and the subframe (see illustration 13.10).

➡**Note: On 2002 and earlier models, remove the right-hand subframe support in order to remove the right-rear link (see illustration).**

14 Inspect the link bushings. If they're cracked or dried out or otherwise worn, have them pressed out and new ones pressed in at an automotive machine shop.

Upper link

▶ **Refer to illustration 13.15**

15 Remove the fasteners that attach the upper link to the rear knuckle and the subframe (see illustration).

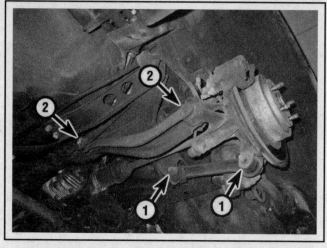

13.10 Rear suspension link details (Legacy model):

1 *Front link mounting fastener*
2 *Rear link mounting fastener*

16 Inspect the link bushings. If they're cracked or dried out or otherwise worn, have them pressed out and new ones pressed in at an automotive machine shop.

All links

17 Installation is the reverse of removal. Be sure to align the matchmarks on the inner rear link fastener and the crossmember, if applicable. After all fasteners have been installed, raise the rear knuckle with a floor jack to simulate normal ride height, then tighten the link fasteners to the torque listed in this Chapter's Specifications.

18 Have the rear wheel alignment checked and, if necessary, adjusted.

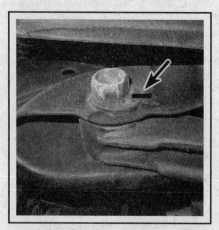

13.12 To ensure that the correct toe-in is maintained, scribe or paint alignment marks on the adjuster bolt and subframe before removing the bolt (Legacy model)

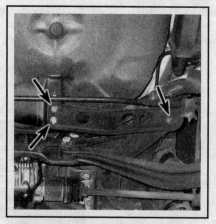

13.13 Right-hand subframe support and mounting fasteners

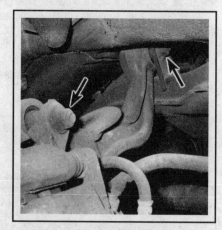

13.15 Rear suspension upper link mounting fasteners

14 Hub and wheel bearings (rear) - replacement

LEGACY MODELS

▶ **Refer to illustration 14.5**

1   Loosen the rear driveaxle nut (see Chapter 8).

2   Loosen the rear wheel lug nuts, block the front wheels, raise the rear of the vehicle and place it on jackstands. Remove the rear wheel.

3   On models with rear drum brakes, remove the brake drum (see Chapter 9).

4   On models with rear disc brakes, remove the caliper and hang it out of the way with a piece of wire, remove the caliper support bracket and the brake disc (see Chapter 9).

5   Remove the hub mounting bolts from the back of the knuckle (see illustration). Suspend the backing plate safely aside.

6   Remove the driveaxle/hub nut and push the driveaxle through the hub splines as the hub and bearing assembly is removed. If the driveaxle sticks in the hub, you'll have to push it out with a puller (see Chapter 8).

❋❋ CAUTION:

Be careful not to overextend the inner CV joint. Once the hub has been removed, support the outer end of the driveaxle with a length of wire or rope.

7   Installation is the reverse of removal, noting the following points:

a) *Tighten the hub mounting bolts to the torque listed in this Chapter's Specifications.*

b) *Tighten the brake caliper mounting bracket bolts, caliper mounting bolts and the wheel speed sensor bolt to the torque listed in the Chapter 9 Specifications.*

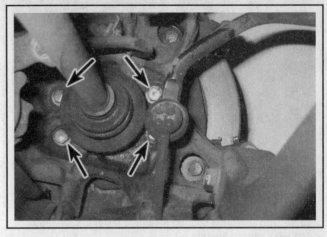

14.5 Rear hub mounting bolts

c) *Tighten the driveaxle/hub nut to the torque listed in the Chapter 8 Specifications.*

d) *Tighten the wheel lug nuts to the torque listed in the Chapter 1 Specifications.*

FORESTER MODELS

8   Due to the special tools and expertise required to press the hub and bearings from the rear knuckle, this job should be left to a professional mechanic. However, the knuckle and hub may be removed as an assembly and taken to an automotive machine shop or qualified repair facility for service. See Section 15 for the rear knuckle and hub removal procedure.

15 Rear knuckle/hub assembly - removal and installation

1   Loosen the rear driveaxle nut (see Chapter 8).

2   Loosen the rear wheel lug nuts, block the front wheels, raise the rear of the vehicle and place it on jackstands. Remove the rear wheel.

3   Loosen the parking brake cable adjustment so that the cable is loose (see Chapter 9).

FORESTER MODELS

4   On models with rear drum brakes, remove the brake shoe assembly and the remove the wheel cylinder (see Chapter 9).

5   On models with rear disc brakes, remove the brake disc and the parking brake assembly (see Chapter 9).

6   Detach the parking brake cable from the backing plate (see Chapter 9).

7   Remove the rear wheel speed sensor, if equipped (see Chapter 9).

8   Disconnect the trailing arm from the rear knuckle (see Section 12).

9   Disconnect the control arms from the rear knuckle (see Section 13).

10 Remove the strut-to-knuckle nuts and bolts (see Section 9).

11 Remove the driveaxle nut and pull the knuckle off the outer CV joint. If the hub sticks to the CV joint splines, push the stub shaft out of the hub with a two-jaw puller (see Chapter 8).

❋❋ CAUTION:

Be careful not to overextend the inner CV joint.

12 While the knuckle is removed, the wheel bearings can be replaced by a qualified repair facility if necessary. If either CV joint boot is damaged, it should be replaced at this time also (see Chapter 8).

13 Remove the brake backing plate fasteners and then remove the backing plate.

14 If you need to remove the hub or wheel bearings from the rear knuckle, refer to Section 14.

15.15 The subframe support mounting fasteners for 2005 and later Legacy models

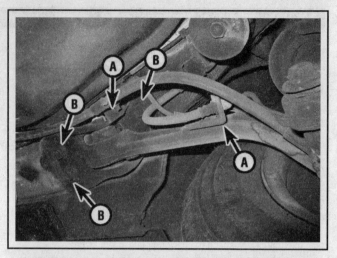

15.18 Remove the brackets (A) that are attached to the arm portion of the knuckle. Remove the knuckle bracket fasteners (B) to remove the knuckle (2001 models shown, other models similar)

LEGACY MODELS

♦ **Refer to illustrations 15.15 and 15.18**

➡**Note: The rear knuckle and trailing arm are integrated on Legacy models.**

15 On 2005 and later models, support the subframe securely and then remove the subframe support (see illustration).

16 On models with rear drum brakes, remove the brake shoe assembly and the wheel cylinder (see Chapter 9).

17 On models with rear disc brakes, remove the brake disc and the parking brake assembly (see Chapter 9).

18 Remove any brackets that are attached to the arm portion of the knuckle (see illustration).

19 Remove the stabilizer bar link from the knuckle (see Section 11).

20 Remove the rear wheel speed sensor, if equipped (see Chapter 9).

21 Remove the hub and wheel bearing assembly and suspend the backing plate safely aside (see Section 14).

22 Detach the shock absorber from the knuckle (see Section 10).

23 Support the rear knuckle with a floor jack and then disconnect the suspension links from the knuckle (see Section 13).

24 Remove the bracket that holds the arm portion of the knuckle to the body (see illustration 15.18). Carefully remove the knuckle and then

inspect the bushing for wear. If bushing replacement is necessary, have a qualified automotive shop perform the work.

25 Check the condition of the CV boots while the knuckle is removed and replace if necessary (see Chapter 8).

ALL MODELS

26 Installation is the reverse of removal, noting the following points:

a) *Raise the rear knuckle with a floor jack to simulate normal ride height, then tighten the various link, support and trailing arm fasteners to the torque values listed in this Chapter's Specifications.*

b) *Tighten the brake component fasteners to the torque values listed in the Chapter 9 Specifications.*

c) *Tighten the driveaxle/hub nut to the torque listed in the Chapter 8 Specifications.*

d) *Tighten the wheel lug nuts to the torque listed in the Chapter 1 Specifications.*

e) *On vehicles equipped with drum brakes, bleed the brake system (see Chapter 9).*

f) *Readjust the parking brake cable (see Chapter 9).*

16 Steering wheel - removal and installation

❉❉ WARNING 1:

These vehicles are equipped with a Supplemental Restraint System (SRS), more commonly known as airbags. Always disable the airbag system before working in the vicinity of any airbag system component to avoid the possibility of accidental deployment of the airbag(s), which could cause personal injury (see Chapter 12).

❉❉ WARNING 2:

Do not use a memory saving device to preserve the PCM or radio memory when working on or near airbag system components.

REMOVAL

♦ **Refer to illustrations 16.3, 16.4, 16.7a, 16.7b and 16.9**

1 Park the vehicle with the wheels pointing straight ahead. Disconnect the cable from the negative terminal of the battery (see Chapter 5, Section 1).

2 Disable the airbag system (see Chapter 12).

3 Remove the airbag module from the steering wheel (see illustration).

4 Carefully lift the airbag module away from the steering wheel and then disconnect the electrical connectors (see illustration).

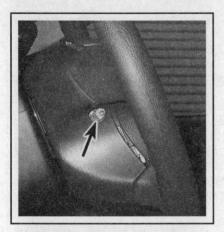

16.3 Remove the airbag module mounting fasteners from the side of the steering wheel

16.4 Separate the air bag module from the steering wheel and disconnect the electrical connector

16.7a Install a steering wheel puller to release the steering wheel from the steering shaft

➡Note: These connectors (like most) have release tabs or some kind of release mechanism that must be moved in order to separate them.

5　Remove the airbag module and store it in a safe location.

❇❇ WARNING:

Carry the airbag module with the trim side facing away from you, and set the airbag module down with the trim side facing up. Don't place anything on top of the airbag module.

6　Loosen the steering wheel retaining nut until it meets the end of the steering shaft; but leave it on.

7　Release the steering wheel from the steering shaft using a steering wheel puller (see illustrations). The puller screw must be in contact with the steering shaft.

❇❇ CAUTION:

Don't thread the bolts of the puller into the steering wheel more than five turns, as they could contact the airbag clockspring and damage it. Once the steering wheel is released, remove

the puller and the retaining nut and then mark the relationship of the steering wheel hub to the steering shaft. The index mark will help ensure that the steering wheel is installed in its original position on the steering shaft.

8　Disconnect any remaining electrical connectors and lift the steering wheel off the shaft, feeding the wiring harness through the hole in the wheel.

❇❇ CAUTION:

Do not turn the clockspring, steering shaft or front wheels while the steering wheel is removed. The airbag clockspring could be damaged if the steering wheel is reinstalled with these components misaligned. If one of the components is turned, perform the alignment procedures found later in this section.

9　If it is necessary to remove the clockspring, remove the steering column covers (see Chapter 11), unplug its electrical connectors and then detach it from the combination switch (see illustration).

➡Note: The electrical connector can be found by following the wires on the clockspring down the steering column.

16.7b Mark the relationship of the steering wheel to the steering shaft

16.9 Clockspring mounting fasteners and alignment marks

INSTALLATION

10 With the wheels pointing straight ahead, make absolutely sure that the airbag clockspring is centered. This shouldn't be a problem as long as you have not turned the steering shaft while the wheel was removed. If for some reason the shaft was turned, center the clockspring as follows:

a) *Rotate the clockspring clockwise until it stops (don't apply too much force, though).*

b) *Rotate the clockspring counterclockwise about 2-3/4 turns until the small arrows on the clockspring align at the bottom (see illustration 16.9).*

11 Installation is the reverse of removal, noting the following points:

a) *Make sure the airbag clockspring is centered before installing the steering wheel.*

b) *When installing the steering wheel, engage the pins on the clockspring with the slots on the steering wheel hub while also noting the alignment marks on the steering shaft and the steering wheel hub.*

c) *Tighten the steering wheel nut to the torque listed in this Chapter's Specifications.*

d) *Carefully install the airbag module on the steering wheel tightening the mounting bolts to the torque values listed in this Chapter's Specifications and making certain all electrical connectors are properly connected beforehand.*

e) *Enable the airbag system (see Chapter 12).*

17 Tie-rod ends - removal and installation

▶ **Refer to illustrations 17.2a, 17.2b, 17.4 and 17.6**

1 Loosen the wheel lug nuts. Block the rear wheels. Raise the front of the vehicle and support it securely. Remove the front wheel.

17.2a Loosen and back off the jam nut from the tie-rod end . . .

2 Loosen the jam nut enough to mark the position of the tie-rod end in relation to the threads (see illustrations).

3 Remove the cotter pin and loosen - but don't remove - the nut on the tie-rod end stud.

4 Disconnect the tie-rod end from the steering knuckle with a puller (see illustration). Remove the nut and separate the tie-rod end from the steering knuckle.

5 Unscrew the tie-rod end from the tie-rod.

6 If you're planning to install the old tie-rod end, you should inspect the tie-rod end boot for cracks or tears. If it's damaged, simply remove the boot ring, slide off the old boot, wipe off the balljoint with a clean rag, lubricate it with chassis grease, slide on a new boot and install the boot ring (see illustration).

7 Thread the tie-rod end on to the marked position and insert the tie-rod end stud into the steering knuckle. Tighten the jam nut securely.

8 Install the nut on the stud and tighten it to the torque listed in this Chapter's Specifications. Install a new cotter pin.

9 Install the wheel and lug nuts. Lower the vehicle and tighten the wheel lug nuts to the torque listed in the Chapter 1 Specifications.

10 Have the alignment checked and, if necessary, adjusted.

17.2b . . . and mark the position of the tie-rod end on the tie-rod

17.4 Install a suitable small puller or tie-rod removal tool such as the one shown to force the tie-rod end ballstud out of the steering knuckle

17.6 To replace the old boot on the tie-rod end, remove the boot retaining ring

18 Steering gear boots - replacement

▶ **Refer to illustration 18.3**

1   Loosen the front wheel lug nuts, raise the vehicle and support it securely on jackstands. Remove the wheel.

2   Remove the tie-rod end (see Section 17).

3   Remove the steering gear boot clamps and slide off the boot (see illustration).

4   Before installing the new boot, wrap the threads on the end of the tie-rod with a layer of tape so the small end of the new boot isn't damaged.

5   Slide the new boot into position until it seats in the groove on the steering gear and then install new clamps.

6   Remove the tape from the tie-rod and install the tie-rod end (see Section 17).

7   Install the wheel and lug nuts. Lower the vehicle and tighten the lug nuts to the torque listed in the Chapter 1 Specifications.

8   Have the alignment checked and, if necessary, adjusted.

18.3 Remove the small clamp and large wire to remove the steering gear boot

19 Steering gear - removal and installation

▶ **Refer to illustrations 19.8, 19.9, 19.11 and 19.12**

✳✳ WARNING:

Make sure the steering shaft is not turned while the steering gear is removed or you could damage the airbag clockspring. To prevent the shaft from turning, place the ignition key in he lock position or thread the seatbelt through the steering wheel and clip it into place.

1   Disconnect the cable from the negative terminal of the battery (see Chapter 5, Section 1).

2   Loosen the wheel lug nuts. Block the rear wheels, raise the front of the vehicle and place it securely on jackstands. Remove the front wheels.

3   On 2001 and earlier Legacy models, remove the air duct that leads to the throttle body (see Chapter 4).

4   Disconnect the tie-rod ends from the steering knuckles (see Section 17).

5   Remove the bottom engine cover, if equipped (see Chapter 2).

6   On 2003 and later Forester models, remove the subframe (see Section 5)

7   Remove the front exhaust pipes, if necessary (see Chapter 4).

8   Remove the jacking plate, if equipped (see illustration).

9   On 2005 and later Legacy models, remove the crossmember support plate (see illustration).

10 Remove the stabilizer bar (see Section 4).

11 Disconnect the power steering fluid lines from the steering gear (see illustration).

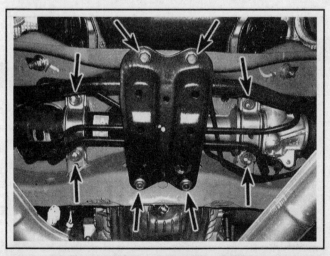

19.8 Jacking plate and steering gear mounting fasteners (2001 Legacy model shown, other models similar)

19.9 The crossmember support plate mounting fasteners (2005 and later Legacy models only)

19.11 Disconnect the power steering lines from the steering gear lines at the right (passenger's) side of the steering gear

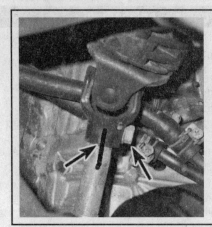

19.12 Mark the relationship of the steering shaft U-joint to the steering gear input shaft and then remove the pinch bolt

→Note: On some models, access can be made from underneath the vehicle.

12 Mark the relationship of the U-joint that connects the steering shaft to the steering gear input shaft (see illustration).

13 Remove the steering shaft U-joint pinch bolt (see illustration 19.12).

14 Remove the steering gear mounting bolts (see illustration 19.8) and remove the steering gear from the passenger's side of the vehicle.

15 Installation is the reverse of removal, noting the following points:

a) Be sure to align the mark on the U-joint with the mark on the shaft, and tighten the steering gear mounting bolts, the U-joint

pinch bolt, and the tie-rod end-to-steering knuckle nuts to the torque values listed in this Chapter's Specifications.

b) Tighten the exhaust pipe fasteners to the torque listed in the Chapter 4 Specifications

c) Install the wheels and lug nuts. Lower the vehicle and tighten the lug nuts to the torque listed in this Chapter's Specifications.

d) Fill the steering system with the recommended fluid and then check for leaks (see Chapter 1). Bleed the system (see Section 22).

e) Have the wheel alignment checked and, if necessary, adjusted.

20 Power steering pump - removal and installation

REMOVAL

2002 and earlier Forester models

♦ Refer to illustrations 20.2, 20.3, 20.6, 20.7 and 20.8

1 Using a syringe, remove the power steering fluid from the power steering pump reservoir.

2 Remove the drivebelt pulley cover (see illustration).

3 Loosen the power steering pump pulley retaining nut (see illustration).

4 Remove the drivebelt (see Chapter 1).

5 Remove the power steering pump pulley nut and pulley.

6 Detach the power steering fluid line clamps (see illustration).

7 Disconnect the fluid lines from the power steering pump and the reservoir (see illustration).

8 Remove the bolts from the front of the power steering pump and then remove the pump (see illustration).

20.2 Drivebelt pulley cover mounting fasteners

20.3 Hold the pulley with a pin spanner tool to loosen the retaining nut (similar model shown)

20.6 Line clamp mounting bolts (similar model shown)

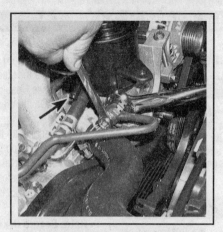

20.7 Disconnect the power steering fluid lines from the power steering pump and from the reservoir (similar model shown)

20.8 Power steering pump mounting bolts (similar model shown)

9   The reservoir can be separated from the pump by opening up the reservoir and removing the mounting bolts on the inside. Place the pump in a vice and protect the pump by placing wood or plastic jaw liners between the vise and the pump. Don't over tighten the vise! The pump can be easily damaged.

All other models

▶ **Refer to illustrations 20.13 and 20.16**

10   Remove the drivebelt pulley cover or engine cover.

11   On turbo charged models, remove the air intake duct (see Chapter 4).

12   Remove the drivebelt (see Chapter 1).

13   Disconnect the electrical connector for the pump switch (see illustration).

14   Detach the power steering fluid line clamps (see illustration 20.6).

15   Disconnect the fluid line couplings from the power steering pump (see illustration 20.13).

16   Remove the pump bracket mounting bolts and then remove the pump and bracket as a unit (see illustration 20.13 and accompanying illustration).

17   Carefully mount the pump and bracket in a vice.

18   Remove the two front pump-to-mounting bracket bolts through the pulley (see illustration 20.16)

19   Remove the single rear pump-to-bracket mounting bolt and then separate the pump from the bracket by prying it away from the bottom of the bracket.

INSTALLATION

20   Installation is the reverse of removal. Tighten the pump mounting fasteners and the pulley nut (2002 and earlier Forester models only) to the torque listed in this Chapter's Specifications. Tighten all other fasteners securely. Refer to Chapter 1 for drivebelt installation.

21   Add new power steering fluid and check for any leaks in the system (see Chapter 1). Bleed the power steering system (see Section 22).

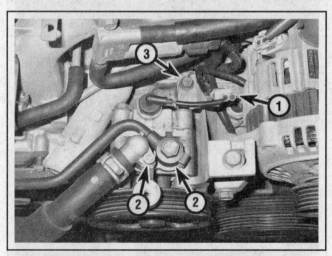

20.12 Power steering pump details (2001 Legacy model shown, other models are similar):

1	Electrical connector	3	Bracket mounting bolt
2	Fluid line couplings		

20.16 Power steering pump mounting details (2001 Legacy model shown, other models are similar):

1	Bracket mounting bolts	4	Pump to bracket mounting
2	Drivebelt adjusting bolt		bolts
3	Mounting and lock bolt		

21 Steering column - removal and installation

▶ Refer to illustrations 21.2, 21.4, 21.5 and 21.6

※※ WARNING 1:

These vehicles are equipped with a Supplemental Restraint System (SRS), more commonly known as airbags. Always disable the airbag system before working in the vicinity of any airbag system component to avoid the possibility of accidental deployment of the airbag(s), which could cause personal injury (see Chapter 12).

※※ WARNING 2:

Do not use a memory saving device to preserve the PCM or radio memory when working on or near airbag system components.

1   Remove the steering wheel (see Section 16).
2   Mark the relationship of the universal joint to the steering shaft and then remove the pinch bolt that holds the steering shaft to the U-joint (see illustration).
3   Remove the steering column covers and the lower instrument trim panel (see Chapter 11).
4   Remove the plate mounted in front of the steering column (see illustration).
5   Disconnect all the electrical connectors, remove any harnesses and electrical components attached to the steering column that would interfere with removal (see illustration).
6   Remove the steering column mounting bolts and then carefully guide the steering column out from the instrument panel (see illustration).

➡Note: Secure the steering shaft to keep it from turning. If it is turned, the clockspring will have to be re-centered.

7   Installation is the reverse of removal, noting the following points:

  a) Be sure to align the mark on the U-joint with the mark on the steering shaft and tighten the steering column mounting bolts and the U-joint pinch bolt to the torque values listed in this Chapter's Specifications.

  b) If the steering shaft was turned while the steering column was removed, re-center the clockspring (see Section 16).

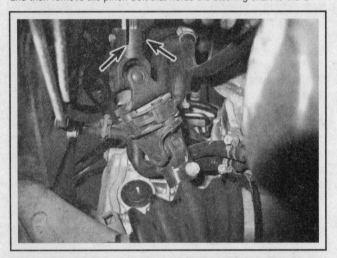

21.2 Mark the universal joint and steering shaft before removing the pinch bolt (2001 Legacy model shown, other models similar)

21.4 Plate mounting fasteners

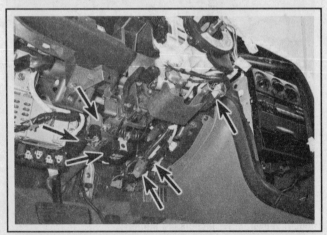

21.5 Remove the various connectors, harnesses and components from the steering column (2001 Legacy model shown, other models similar)

21.6 Steering column mounting bolts

22 Power steering system - bleeding

1   The power steering system must be bled whenever a line is disconnected. Bubbles can be seen in power steering fluid that has air in it and the fluid will often have a tan or milky appearance. Low fluid level can cause air to mix with the fluid, resulting in a noisy pump as well as foaming of the fluid.

2   Open the hood and check the fluid level in the reservoir, adding the specified fluid necessary to bring it up to the proper level (see Chapter 1).

3   Start the engine and slowly turn the steering wheel several times from left-to-right and back again. Do not turn the wheel completely from lock-to-lock. Check the fluid level, topping it up as necessary until it remains steady and no more bubbles are visible.

23 Wheels and tires - general information

◆ **Refer to illustration 23.1**

All models covered by this manual are equipped with metric-sized radial tires (see illustration). Use of other size or type of tires may affect the ride and handling of the vehicle. Don't mix different types of tires, such as radials and bias belted, on the same vehicle as handling may be seriously affected. It's recommended that tires be replaced in pairs on the same axle, but if only one tire is being replaced, be sure it's the same size, structure and tread design as the other.

Because tire pressure has a substantial effect on handling and wear, the pressure on all tires should be checked at least once a month or before any extended trips (see Chapter 1).

Wheels must be replaced if they are bent, dented, leak air, have elongated bolt holes, are heavily rusted, out of vertical symmetry or if the lug nuts won't stay tight. Wheel repairs that use welding or peening are not recommended.

Tire and wheel balance is important to the overall handling, braking and performance of the vehicle. Unbalanced wheels can adversely affect handling and ride characteristics as well as tire life. Whenever a tire is installed on a wheel, the tire and wheel should be balanced by a shop with the proper equipment.

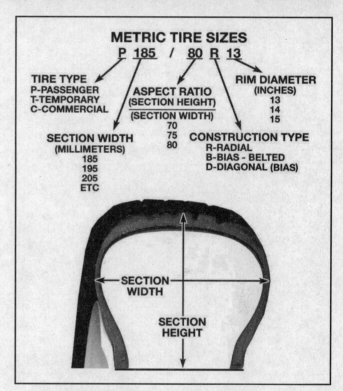

23.1 Metric tire size code

24 Wheel alignment - general information

◆ **Refer to illustration 24.1**

A wheel alignment refers to the adjustments made to the wheels so they are in proper angular relationship to the suspension and the ground. Wheels that are out of proper alignment not only affect vehicle control, but also increase tire wear. The alignment angles normally measured are camber, caster and toe-in (see illustration). Toe-in and camber on the front, and toe-in on the rear are the only adjustable angles on these vehicles. The other angles should be measured to check for bent or worn suspension parts.

Wheel alignment is a very exacting process, one in which complicated and expensive machines are necessary to perform the job properly. You should have a technician with the proper equipment perform these tasks. We will, however, use this space to give you a basic idea of what is involved with a wheel alignment so you can better understand the process and deal intelligently with the shop that does the work.

Toe-in is the turning in of the wheels. The purpose of a toe specification is to ensure parallel rolling of the wheels. In a vehicle with zero toe-in, the distance between the front edges of the wheels will be the same as the distance between the rear edges of the wheels. The actual amount of toe-in is normally only a fraction of an inch. On the front end, toe-in is controlled by the tie-rod end position on the tie-rod. On the rear end, it's controlled by a cam bolt on the inner end of the rearmost control arm or link. Incorrect toe-in will cause the tires to wear improperly by making them scrub against the road surface.

Camber is the tilting of the wheels from vertical when viewed from one end of the vehicle. When the wheels tilt out at the top, the camber is said to be positive (+). When the wheels tilt in at the top the camber is negative (-). The amount of tilt is measured in degrees from vertical and this measurement is called the camber angle. This angle affects the amount of tire tread which contacts the road and compensates for changes in the suspension geometry when the vehicle is cornering or traveling over an undulating surface. On the front end, camber is adjusted by a cam bolt (the upper strut-to-knuckle bolt). Rear camber is not adjustable.

Caster is the tilting of the front steering axis from the vertical. A tilt toward the rear is positive caster and a tilt toward the front is negative caster.

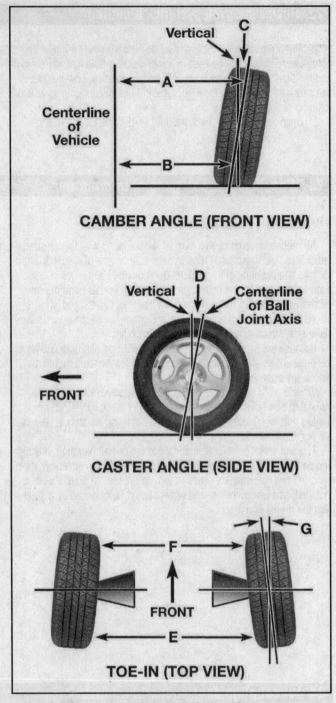

24.1 Camber, caster and toe-in angles

A minus B = C (degrees camber)
D = caster (expressed in degrees)
E minus F = toe-in (measured in inches)
G = toe-in (expressed in degrees)

Specifications

Torque specifications	Ft-lbs	Nm
Front suspension (Legacy)		
Balljoint-to-control arm nut	29	39
Control arm		
2004 and earlier		
Front pivot bolt/nut*	74	100
Rear pivot stud nut*	137	186
Rear bushing bolts*	181	245
2005 and later		
Front pivot bolt/nut*	70	95
Rear support plate		
Mounting bolt*	111	150
Mounting nuts*	81	110
Stabilizer bar		
Stabilizer bar bushing retainer bolts	18	25
Stabilizer link bolts/nuts*		
2004 and earlier	22	30
2005 and later	33	45
Steering knuckle-to-balljoint pinch bolt	37	50
Strut/coil spring assembly		
Damper rod-to-mount nut*	41	55
Strut-to-steering knuckle bolts/nuts	112	152
Strut upper mounting nuts*	15	20
Front suspension (Forester)		
Balljoint-to-control arm nut	30	40
Control arm		
Front pivot bolt/nut*	74	100
Rear pivot stud nut	140	190
Rear bushing bracket bolts*	184	250
Stabilizer bar		
Stabilizer bar bushing retainer bolts	18	25
Stabilizer link bolts/nuts*		
2002 and earlier	33	45
2003 and later	41	55
Steering knuckle-to-balljoint pinch bolt	37	50
Strut/coil spring assembly		
Damper rod-to-mount nut*	41	55
Strut-to-steering knuckle bolts/nuts	129	175
Strut upper mounting nuts*	15	20
Subframe		
Front (3) and rear (2) mounting bolts*	52	71
Middle (3) mounting bolts*	41	55

Torque specifications	Ft-lbs	Nm
Rear suspension (Legacy)		
Rear links (front, rear and upper) bolts/nuts*	89	120
Rear hub assembly bolts	48	65
Rear knuckle/trailing arm bracket bolts	92	125
Stabilizer bar		
Stabilizer bar bushing retainer bolts	30	40
Stabilizer-to-link bolts/nuts*	33	45
Strut assembly		
Damper rod-to-mount nut*	23	30
Strut-to-knuckle bolts/nuts	118	160
Strut upper mounting nuts*	23	30
Subframe support		
2003 and later		
Support-to-knuckle bracket bolt	92	125
Support-to-subframe bolt	129	175
2002 and earlier (right-hand side)		
Support-to-subframe bolt	129	176
Support-to-chassis bolts	48	65
Rear suspension (Forester)		
Front and rear links		
Link-to-rear crossmember bolt/nut*	74	100
Link-to-rear knuckle bolt/nut*	103	140
Trailing Arm		
Trailing arm bracket-to-body bolts*	74	100
Trailing arm-to-rear knuckle bolt/nut*	67	90
Stabilizer bar		
Stabilizer bar bushing retainer bolts	18	25
Stabilizer-to-link bolts/nuts*	33	45
Strut assembly		
Damper rod-to-mount nut*	23	30
Strut-to-knuckle bolts/nuts	148	200
Strut upper mounting nuts*	23	30
Steering		
Jacking plate	14	20
Crossmember support plate	44	60
Power steering pump pulley nut (2002 and earlier Forester models)	58	78
Power steering pump mounting bolts		
Pump-to-bracket mounting bolts	144 in-lbs	16
Bracket-to-engine mounting bolts		
Front mounting bolts	16	22
Rear mounting bolt	28	38
Tie-rod end-to-steering knuckle nut	29	39
Steering gear mounting bolts	44	60
Steering shaft U-joint pinch bolt	17	24
Steering wheel nut	33	45

The manufacturer states that these fastener(s) must be replaced whenever removed

Section

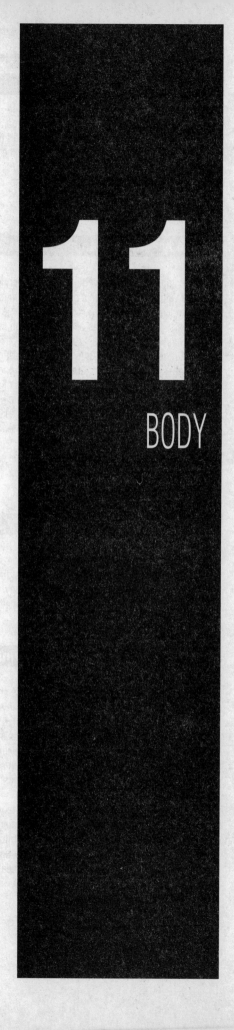

11

BODY

1 General information

These models feature a 'unibody' construction, using a floor pan with front and rear frame side rails which support the body components, front and rear suspension systems and other mechanical components. Certain components are particularly vulnerable to accident damage and can be unbolted and repaired or replaced. Among these parts are the body moldings, front fenders, bumpers, hood, doors, trunk lid and all glass.

Only general body maintenance practices and body panel repair procedures within the scope of the do-it-yourselfer are included in this Chapter.

2 Body - maintenance

1 The condition of your vehicle's body is very important, because the resale value depends a great deal on it. It's much more difficult to repair a neglected or damaged body than it is to repair mechanical components. The hidden areas of the body, such as the wheel wells, the frame and the engine compartment, are equally important, although they don't require as frequent attention as the rest of the body.

2 Once a year, or every 12,000 miles, it's a good idea to have the underside of the body steam cleaned. All traces of dirt and oil will be removed and the area can then be inspected carefully for rust, damaged brake lines, frayed electrical wires, damaged cables and other problems. The front suspension components should be greased after completion of this job.

3 At the same time, clean the engine and the engine compartment with a steam cleaner or water-soluble degreaser.

4 The wheel wells should be given close attention, since undercoating can peel away and stones and dirt thrown up by the tires can cause the paint to chip and flake, allowing rust to set in. If rust is found, clean down to the bare metal and apply an anti-rust paint.

5 The body should be washed about once a week. Wet the vehicle thoroughly to soften the dirt, then wash it down with a soft sponge and plenty of clean soapy water. If the surplus dirt is not washed off very carefully, it can wear down the paint.

6 Spots of tar or asphalt thrown up from the road should be removed with a cloth soaked in solvent.

7 Once every six months, wax the body and chrome trim. If a chrome cleaner is used to remove rust from any of the vehicle's plated parts, remember that the cleaner also removes part of the chrome, so use it sparingly.

3 Vinyl trim - maintenance

Don't clean vinyl trim with detergents, caustic soap or petroleum-based cleaners. Plain soap and water works just fine, with a soft brush to clean dirt that may be ingrained. Wash the vinyl as frequently as the rest of the vehicle. After cleaning, application of a high-quality rubber and vinyl protectant will help prevent oxidation and cracks. The protectant can also be applied to weatherstripping, vacuum lines and rubber hoses, which often fail as a result of chemical degradation, and to the tires.

4 Upholstery and carpets - maintenance

1 Every three months remove the floor mats and clean the interior of the vehicle (more frequently if necessary). Use a stiff whisk broom to brush the carpeting and loosen dirt and dust, then vacuum the upholstery and carpets thoroughly, especially along seams and crevices.

2 Dirt and stains can be removed from carpeting with basic household or automotive carpet shampoos available in spray cans. Follow the directions and vacuum again, then use a stiff brush to bring back the 'nap' of the carpet.

3 Most interiors have cloth or vinyl upholstery, either of which can be cleaned and maintained with a number of material-specific cleaners or shampoos available in auto supply stores. Follow the directions on the product for usage, and always spot-test any upholstery cleaner on an inconspicuous area (bottom edge of a back seat cushion) to ensure that it doesn't cause a color shift in the material.

4 After cleaning, vinyl upholstery should be treated with a protectant.

➡**Note: Make sure the protectant container indicates the product can be used on seats - some products may make a seat too slippery. Caution: Do not use protectant on vinyl-covered steering wheels.**

5 Leather upholstery requires special care. It should be cleaned regularly with saddlesoap or leather cleaner. Never use alcohol, gasoline, nail polish remover or thinner to clean leather upholstery.

6 After cleaning, regularly treat leather upholstery with a leather conditioner, rubbed in with a soft cotton cloth. Never use car wax on leather upholstery.

7 In areas where the interior of the vehicle is subject to bright sunlight, cover leather seating areas of the seats with a sheet if the vehicle is to be left out for any length of time.

5 Body repair - minor damage

REPAIR OF SCRATCHES

1 If the scratch is superficial and does not penetrate to the metal of the body, repair is very simple. Lightly rub the scratched area with a fine rubbing compound to remove loose paint and built-up wax. Rinse the area with clean water.

2 Apply touch-up paint to the scratch, using a small brush. Continue to apply thin layers of paint until the surface of the paint in the scratch is level with the surrounding paint. Allow the new paint at least two weeks to harden, then blend it into the surrounding paint by rubbing with a very fine rubbing compound. Finally, apply a coat of wax to the scratch area.

3 If the scratch has penetrated the paint and exposed the metal of the body, causing the metal to rust, a different repair technique is required. Remove all loose rust from the bottom of the scratch with a pocket knife, then apply rust inhibiting paint to prevent the formation of rust in the future. Using a rubber or nylon applicator, coat the scratched area with glaze-type filler. If required, the filler can be mixed with thinner to provide a very thin paste, which is ideal for filling narrow scratches. Before the glaze filler in the scratch hardens, wrap a piece of smooth cotton cloth around the tip of a finger. Dip the cloth in thinner and then quickly wipe it along the surface of the scratch. This will ensure that the surface of the filler is slightly hollow. The scratch can now be painted over as described earlier in this Section.

REPAIR OF DENTS

▶ **See photo sequence**

4 When repairing dents, the first job is to pull the dent out until the affected area is as close as possible to its original shape. There is no point in trying to restore the original shape completely as the metal in the damaged area will have stretched on impact and cannot be restored to its original contours. It is better to bring the level of the dent up to a point which is about 1/8-inch below the level of the surrounding metal. In cases where the dent is very shallow, it is not worth trying to pull it out at all.

5 If the back side of the dent is accessible, it can be hammered out gently from behind using a soft-face hammer. While doing this, hold a block of wood firmly against the opposite side of the metal to absorb the hammer blows and prevent the metal from being stretched.

6 If the dent is in a section of the body which has double layers, or some other factor makes it inaccessible from behind, a different technique is required. Drill several small holes through the metal inside the damaged area, particularly in the deeper sections. Screw long, self tapping screws into the holes just enough for them to get a good grip in the metal. Now the dent can be pulled out by pulling on the protruding heads of the screws with locking pliers.

7 The next stage of repair is the removal of paint from the damaged area and from an inch or so of the surrounding metal. This is easily done with a wire brush or sanding disk in a drill motor, although it can be done just as effectively by hand with sandpaper. To complete the preparation for filling, score the surface of the bare metal with a screwdriver or the tang of a file or drill small holes in the affected area. This will provide a good grip for the filler material. To complete the repair, see the Section on filling and painting.

REPAIR OF RUST HOLES OR GASHES

8 Remove all paint from the affected area and from an inch or so of the surrounding metal using a sanding disk or wire brush mounted in a drill motor. If these are not available, a few sheets of sandpaper will do the job just as effectively.

9 With the paint removed, you will be able to determine the severity of the corrosion and decide whether to replace the whole panel, if possible, or repair the affected area. New body panels are not as expensive as most people think and it is often quicker to install a new panel than to repair large areas of rust.

10 Remove all trim pieces from the affected area except those which will act as a guide to the original shape of the damaged body, such as headlight shells, etc. Using metal snips or a hacksaw blade, remove all loose metal and any other metal that is badly affected by rust. Hammer the edges of the hole on the inside to create a slight depression for the filler material.

11 Wire brush the affected area to remove the powdery rust from the surface of the metal. If the back of the rusted area is accessible, treat it with rust inhibiting paint.

12 Before filling is done, block the hole in some way. This can be done with sheet metal riveted or screwed into place, or by stuffing the hole with wire mesh.

13 Once the hole is blocked off, the affected area can be filled and painted. See the following subsection on filling and painting.

FILLING AND PAINTING

14 Many types of body fillers are available, but generally speaking, body repair kits which contain filler paste and a tube of resin hardener are best for this type of repair work. A wide, flexible plastic or nylon applicator will be necessary for imparting a smooth and contoured finish to the surface of the filler material. Mix up a small amount of filler on a clean piece of wood or cardboard (use the hardener sparingly). Follow the manufacturer's instructions on the package, otherwise the filler will set incorrectly.

15 Using the applicator, apply the filler paste to the prepared area. Draw the applicator across the surface of the filler to achieve the desired contour and to level the filler surface. As soon as a contour that approximates the original one is achieved, stop working the paste. If you continue, the paste will begin to stick to the applicator. Continue to add thin layers of paste at 20-minute intervals until the level of the filler is just above the surrounding metal.

16 Once the filler has hardened, the excess can be removed with a body file. From then on, progressively finer grades of sandpaper should be used, starting with a 180-grit paper and finishing with 600-grit wet-or-dry paper. Always wrap the sandpaper around a flat rubber or wooden block, otherwise the surface of the filler will not be completely flat. During the sanding of the filler surface, the wet-or-dry paper should be periodically rinsed in water. This will ensure that a very smooth finish is produced in the final stage.

17 At this point, the repair area should be surrounded by a ring of bare metal, which in turn should be encircled by the finely feathered edge of good paint. Rinse the repair area with clean water until all of the dust produced by the sanding operation is gone.

18 Spray the entire area with a light coat of primer. This will reveal

These photos illustrate a method of repairing simple dents. They are intended to supplement Body repair - minor damage in this Chapter and should not be used as the sole instructions for body repair on these vehicles.

1   If you can't access the backside of the body panel to hammer out the dent, pull it out with a slide-hammer-type dent puller. In the deepest portion of the dent or along the crease line, drill or punch hole(s) at least one inch apart . . .

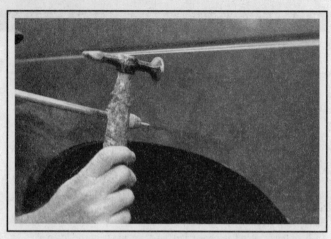

2   . . . then screw the slide-hammer into the hole and operate it. Tap with a hammer near the edge of the dent to help 'pop' the metal back to its original shape. When you're finished, the dent area should be close to its original contour and about 1/8-inch below the surface of the surrounding metal

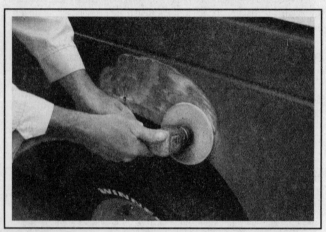

3   Using coarse-grit sandpaper, remove the paint down to the bare metal. Hand sanding works fine, but the disc sander shown here makes the job faster. Use finer (about 320-grit) sandpaper to feather-edge the paint at least one inch around the dent area

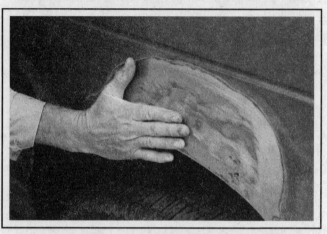

4   When the paint is removed, touch will probably be more helpful than sight for telling if the metal is straight. Hammer down the high spots or raise the low spots as necessary. Clean the repair area with wax/silicone remover

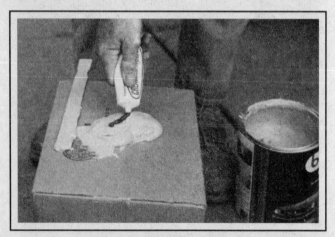

5   Following label instructions, mix up a batch of plastic filler and hardener. The ratio of filler to hardener is critical, and, if you mix it incorrectly, it will either not cure properly or cure too quickly (you won't have time to file and sand it into shape)

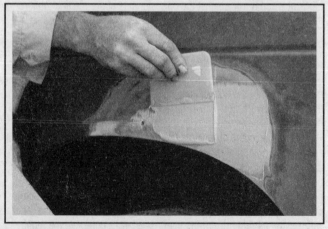

6   Working quickly so the filler doesn't harden, use a plastic applicator to press the body filler firmly into the metal, assuring it bonds completely. Work the filler until it matches the original contour and is slightly above the surrounding metal

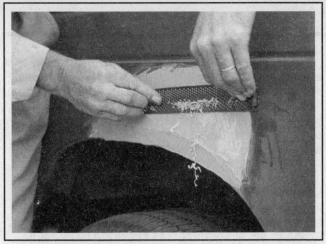

7   Let the filler harden until you can just dent it with your fingernail. Use a body file or Surform tool (shown here) to rough-shape the filler

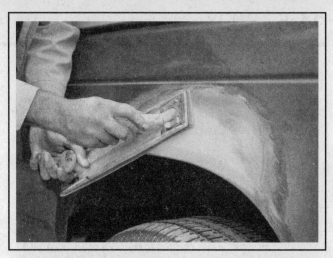

8   Use coarse-grit sandpaper and a sanding board or block to work the filler down until it's smooth and even. Work down to finer grits of sandpaper - always using a board or block - ending up with 360 or 400 grit

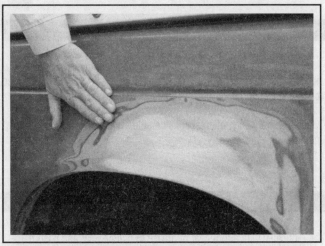

9   You shouldn't be able to feel any ridge at the transition from the filler to the bare metal or from the bare metal to the old paint. As soon as the repair is flat and uniform, remove the dust and mask off the adjacent panels or trim pieces

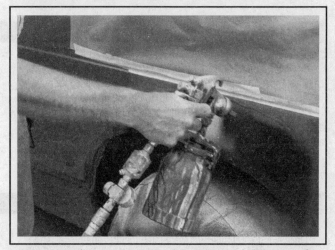

10   Apply several layers of primer to the area. Don't spray the primer on too heavy, so it sags or runs, and make sure each coat is dry before you spray on the next one. A professional-type spray gun is being used here, but aerosol spray primer is available inexpensively from auto parts stores

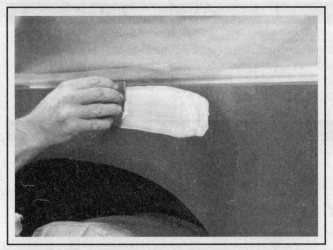

11   The primer will help reveal imperfections or scratches. Fill these with glazing compound. Follow the label instructions and sand it with 360 or 400-grit sandpaper until it's smooth. Repeat the glazing, sanding and respraying until the primer reveals a perfectly smooth surface

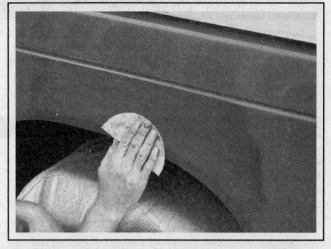

12   Finish sand the primer with very fine sandpaper (400 or 600-grit) to remove the primer overspray. Clean the area with water and allow it to dry. Use a tack rag to remove any dust, then apply the finish coat. Don't attempt to rub out or wax the repair area until the paint has dried completely (at least two weeks)

any imperfections in the surface of the filler. Repair the imperfections with fresh filler paste or glaze filler and once more smooth the surface with sandpaper. Repeat this spray-and-repair procedure until you are satisfied that the surface of the filler and the feathered edge of the paint are perfect. Rinse the area with clean water and allow it to dry completely.

19 The repair area is now ready for painting. Spray painting must be carried out in a warm, dry, windless and dust free atmosphere. These conditions can be created if you have access to a large indoor work area, but if you are forced to work in the open, you will have to pick the day very carefully. If you are working indoors, dousing the floor in the work area with water will help settle the dust which would otherwise be in the air. If the repair area is confined to one body panel, mask off the surrounding panels. This will help minimize the effects of a slight mismatch in paint color. Trim pieces such as chrome strips, door handles, etc., will also need to be masked off or removed. Use masking tape and several thickness of newspaper for the masking operations.

20 Before spraying, shake the paint can thoroughly, then spray a test area until the spray painting technique is mastered. Cover the repair area with a thick coat of primer. The thickness should be built up using several thin layers of primer rather than one thick one. Using 600-grit wet-or-dry sandpaper, rub down the surface of the primer until it is very smooth. While doing this, the work area should be thoroughly rinsed with water and the wet-or-dry sandpaper periodically rinsed as well. Allow the primer to dry before spraying additional coats.

21 Spray on the top coat, again building up the thickness by using several thin layers of paint. Begin spraying in the center of the repair area and then, using a circular motion, work out until the whole repair area and about two inches of the surrounding original paint is covered. Remove all masking material 10 to 15 minutes after spraying on the final coat of paint. Allow the new paint at least two weeks to harden, then use a very fine rubbing compound to blend the edges of the new paint into the existing paint. Finally, apply a coat of wax.

6 Body repair - major damage

1 Major damage must be repaired by an auto body shop specifically equipped to perform body and frame repairs. These shops have the specialized equipment required to do the job properly.

2 If the damage is extensive, the body must be checked for proper alignment or the vehicle's handling characteristics may be adversely affected and other components may wear at an accelerated rate.

3 Due to the fact that all of the major body components (hood, fenders, etc.) are separate and replaceable units, any seriously damaged components should be replaced rather than repaired. Sometimes the components can be found in a wrecking yard that specializes in used vehicle components, often at considerable savings over the cost of new parts.

7 Hinges and locks - maintenance

Once every 3000 miles, or every three months, the hinges and latch assemblies on the doors, hood and trunk should be given a few drops of light oil or lock lubricant. The door latch strikers should also

be lubricated with a thin coat of grease to reduce wear and ensure free movement. Lubricate the door and trunk locks with spray-on graphite lubricant.

8 Windshield and fixed glass - replacement

Replacement of the windshield and fixed glass requires the use of special fast-setting adhesive/caulk materials and some specialized tools

and techniques. These operations should be left to a dealer service department or a shop specializing in glass work.

9 Hood - removal, installation and adjustment

➡**Note: The hood is heavy and somewhat awkward to remove and install - at least two people should perform this procedure.**

REMOVAL AND INSTALLATION

1 Use blankets or pads to cover the cowl area of the body and fenders. This will protect the body and paint as the hood is lifted off.

2 Make marks or scribe a line around the hood hinge to ensure proper alignment during installation (see illustration).

3 Disconnect any wires that will interfere with removal.

4 With an assistant helping you support the hood, remove the hinge-to-hood bolts.

5 Lift off the hood.

6 Installation is the reverse of removal.

ADJUSTMENT

▶ **Refer to illustrations 9.10 and 9.11**

7 Fore-and-aft and side-to-side adjustment of the hood is done by moving the hinge plate slot after loosening the bolts or nuts.

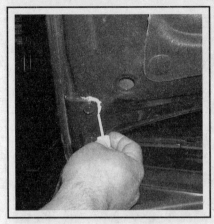

9.2 Before removing the hood, draw a line around the hinge plate

9.10 To adjust the position of the hood, mark the relationship of the striker to the hood, then loosen the striker bolts and slide the striker fore-and-aft or side-to-side as necessary

9.11 Screw the hood bumpers in or out to adjust the hood flush with the fenders

8   Scribe a line around the entire hinge plate so you can determine the amount of movement (see illustration 9.2).

9   Loosen the bolts or nuts and move the hood into correct alignment. Move it only a little at a time. Tighten the hinge bolts and carefully lower the hood to check the position.

10 After installing the hood, adjust the striker, if necessary. The striker can be adjusted fore-and-aft as well as from side-to-side so that the hood closes securely and flush with the fenders. To make the adjustment, scribe a line or mark around the striker mounting flange to provide a reference point, then loosen the striker bolts and reposition the striker as necessary (see illustration). Be sure to tighten the striker mounting bolts securely.

11 Also, if necessary, adjust the hood bumpers (see illustration) so that the hood is flush with the fenders when it's closed.

12 The hood latch assembly, as well as the hinges, should be periodically lubricated with lithium-base grease to prevent binding and wear.

10 Hood release latch and cable - removal and installation

LATCH

▶ **Refer to illustrations 10.2 and 10.3**

1   Remove the radiator grille (see Section 11).
2   Scribe a line around the latch to aid alignment when installing, then detach the latch retaining bolts from the radiator support (see illustration) and remove the latch.

3   Disengage the hood release cable from the latch assembly (see illustration).

4   Installation is the reverse of the removal procedure.

10.2 To detach the hood latch, remove these three retaining bolts

10.3 Flip the hood latch over and disengage the hood release cable from the latch mechanism (make sure to remember how the cable is routed before you disconnect it)

CABLE

▶ **Refer to illustration 10.8**

5　Disconnect the hood release cable from the latch assembly as described above.

6　Attach a piece of stiff wire to the end of the cable, trace the cable back to the firewall and detach all cable retaining clips.

7　Working in the passenger compartment, remove the knee bolster (see Section 27).

8　Detach the screws securing the hood release lever (see illustration).

9　Disengage the cable from the hood release lever (see illustration).

10　Pull the old cable into the passenger compartment until you can see the stiff wire that you attached to the cable. A grommet insulates the cable hole in the firewall from the elements. The new cable should have a new grommet, so you can remove and discard the old cable grommet. Make sure the new grommet is already on the new cable (if not, slip the old grommet onto the new cable), then detach the old cable from the wire and attach the new cable to the wire.

11　Working from the engine compartment side of the firewall, pull the wire through the cable hole in the firewall.

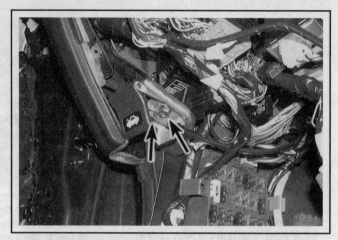

10.8 After removing the driver's side panel lower cover, detach the hood release lever retaining screws and pull the cable rearward into the passenger compartment

12　Installation is otherwise the reverse of the removal. Working from the passenger compartment side, push the grommet into place with your fingers. Make sure it's fully seated in the hole in the firewall.

11 Radiator grille - removal and installation

▶ **Refer to illustrations 11.1 and 11.3**

1　The radiator grille is held in place by either clips or fasteners depending on what model you're working on (see illustration)

2　If you're working on a radiator grille secured by fasteners, remove the fasteners, then remove the grille.

3　On models with clips, once the four upper clips are released, pull the upper part of the grille forward and disengage it from the lower hooks (see illustration).

4　Installation is the reverse of removal.

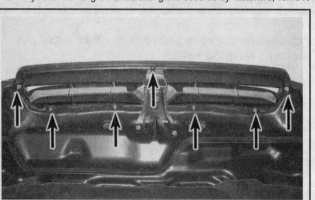

11.1 Typical radiator grille fastener locations for 2004 and earlier Legacy and Outback models (other models with fasteners similar)

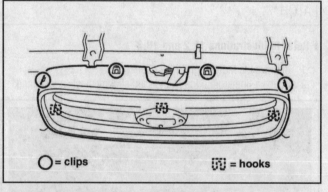

11.3 Typical radiator clip locations (2004 Forester shown, other models with clips similar)

12 Bumper covers - removal and installation

FRONT

▶ **Refer to illustrations 12.2, 12.3a, 12.3b, 12.3c and 12.3d**

1　Raise the vehicle and support it securely on jackstands.

2　Working behind and below the bumper assembly, remove the front part of the wheel housing mud guard and the small splash shield ahead of it (see illustration).

3　Remove the bumper cover retaining fasteners (see illustrations).

4　Installation is the reverse of removal.

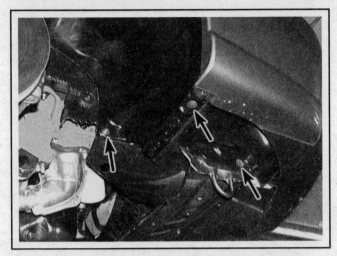

12.2 To gain access to the fasteners that attach the ends of the bumper cover, detach the front part of the mud guard and the small splash shield in front of it by removing the fasteners (Outback model shown, other models similar)

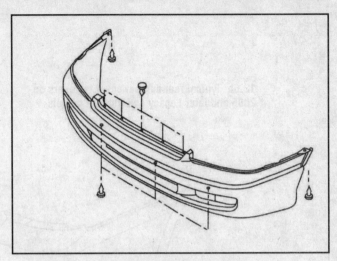

12.3a Front bumper cover fasteners on 2004 and earlier Legacy and Outback models

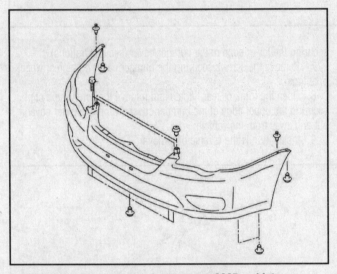

12.3b Front bumper cover fasteners on 2005 and later Legacy and Outback models

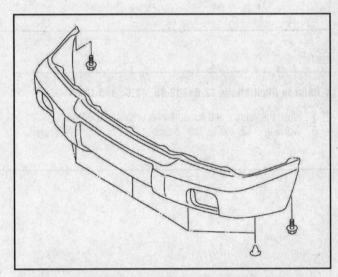

12.3c Front bumper cover fasteners on 2002 and earlier Forester models

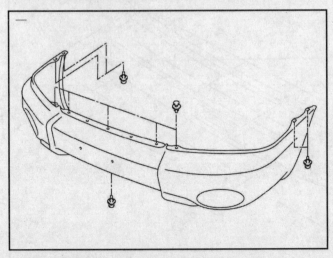

12.3d Front bumper cover fasteners on 2003 and later Forester models

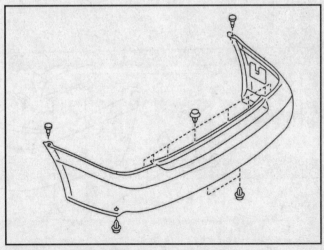

12.6a Typical rear bumper cover fasteners on 2004 and earlier Legacy and Outback models

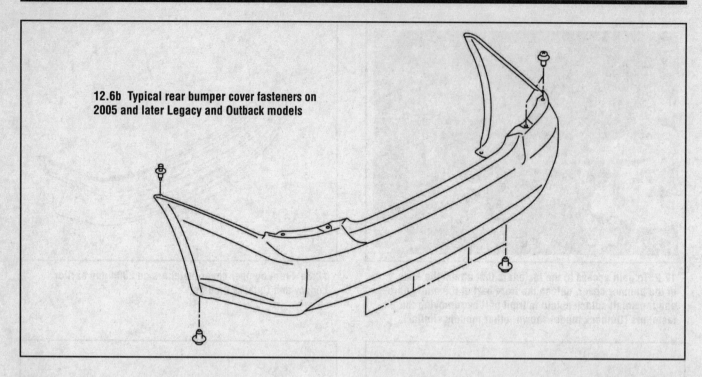

12.6b Typical rear bumper cover fasteners on 2005 and later Legacy and Outback models

REAR

▶ **Refer to illustrations 12.6a, 12.6b, 12.6c and 12.6d**

5   Raise the vehicle and support it securely on jackstands.
6   Working under the vehicle, detach the plastic clips and screws securing the lower edge of the bumper cover (see illustrations).
7   Remove the screws securing the bumper cover in the rear wheel openings.
8   Open the trunk or rear liftgate and remove the screws and clips securing the upper edge of the bumper cover. Pull the bumper cover out and away from the vehicle.
9   Installation is the reverse of removal.

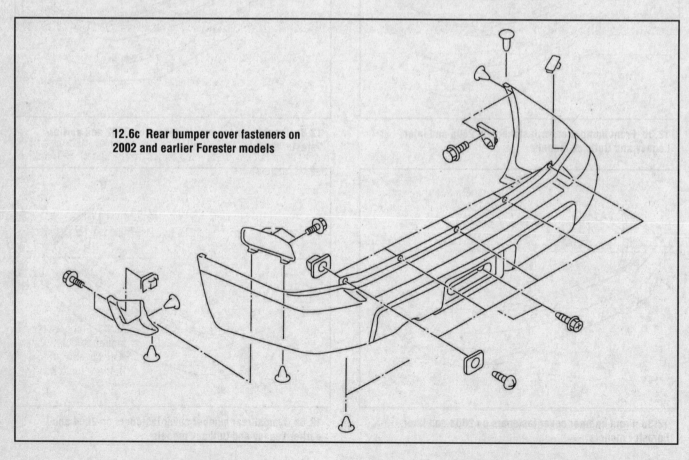

12.6c Rear bumper cover fasteners on 2002 and earlier Forester models

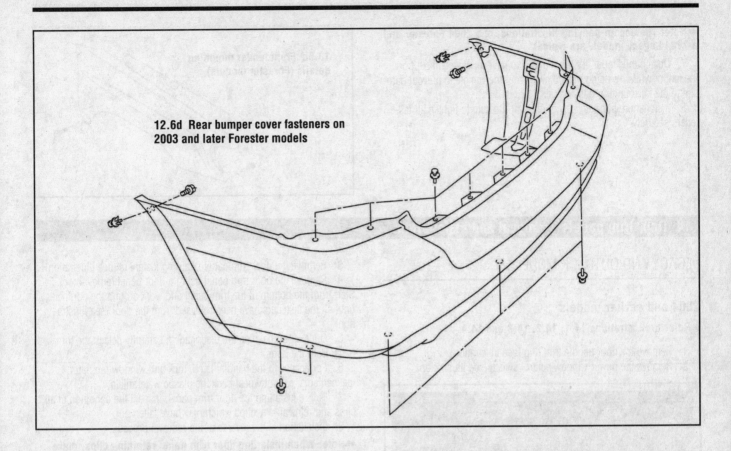

12.6d Rear bumper cover fasteners on 2003 and later Forester models

13 Front fender - removal and installation

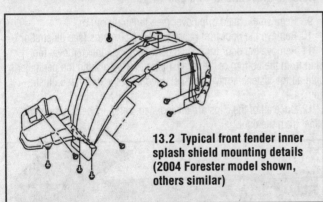

13.2 Typical front fender inner splash shield mounting details (2004 Forester model shown, others similar)

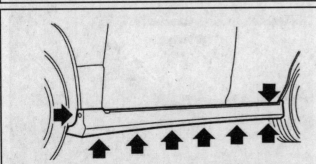

13.4 Side sill spoiler mounting locations (2004 Forester model shown, other models similar)

▶ **Refer to illustrations 13.2, 13.4, 13.6a and 13.6b**

1   Loosen the front wheel lug nuts, raise the vehicle and support it securely on jackstands. Remove the wheel.

2   Remove the inner fender splash shield from the wheel housings (see illustration).

➡**Note: The accompanying illustration is typical. Various combinations of fasteners are used to secure the splash shield on various models.**

3   Remove the front bumper cover (see Section 12).

4   Remove the side sill spoiler (see illustration).

5   Remove the headlight housings (see Chapter 12).

6   Remove the fender mounting bolts and nuts (see illustrations).

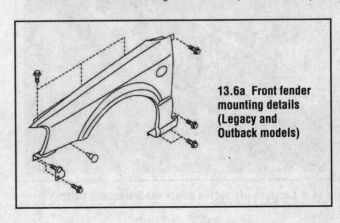

13.6a Front fender mounting details (Legacy and Outback models)

➡Note: The accom-panying illustrations, of a 2004 Forester and a 2004 Legacy model, are typical.

7 Detach the fender. It's a good idea to have an assistant support the fender while it's being moved away from the vehicle to prevent damage to the surrounding body panels.

8 Installation is the reverse of removal. Be sure to tighten all fasteners securely.

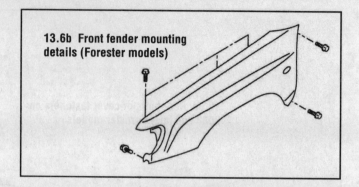

13.6b Front fender mounting details (Forester models)

---

14 Door trim panels - removal and installation

LEGACY AND OUTBACK MODELS

2004 and earlier models

▸ **Refer to illustrations 14.1, 14.2, 14.3 and 14.4**

1 Remove the door handle trim ring (see illustration).
2 Remove the power window control switch (see illustration).

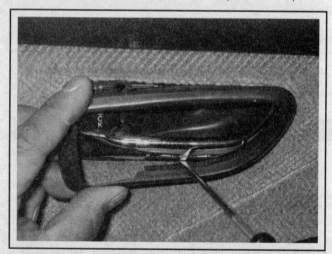

14.1 Carefully pry out the door handle trim ring

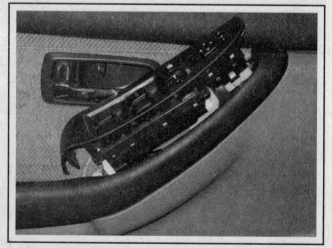

14.2 Carefully pry out the power window control switch

3 Remove the door trim panel retaining fasteners (see illustration).
4 Remove the door trim panel using a door panel removal tool. Start from the bottom of the trim panel and work around the perimeter until all the fasteners have been released from the door (see illustration).
5 Once all of the clips are disengaged, carefully detach the trim panel from the door.
6 For access to the handle, latch, lock and window regulator mechanisms, carefully peel back the plastic watershield.
7 Before installing the door trim panel, inspect the condition of all clips and reinstall any clips which may have fallen out.
8 Installation is the reverse of the removal procedure.

➡Note: When installing door trim panel retaining clips, make sure the clips are lined up with their mating holes first, then gently tap the clips in with the palm of your hand.

2005 and later models

▸ **Refer to illustrations 14.9 and 14.10**

9 Remove the hand grip cover (see illustration).
10 Remove the door trim panel retaining fasteners (see illustration).
11 Remove the door trim panel using a door panel removal tool. Start from the bottom of the trim panel and work around the perimeter until all the fasteners have been released from the door (see illustration 14.4).
12 Once all of the clips are disengaged, carefully detach the trim panel from the door.

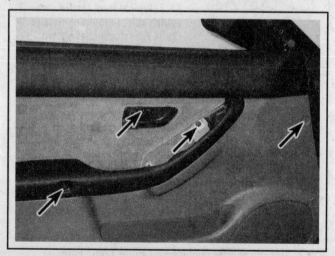

14.3 Door trim panel retaining fastener locations

14.4 Carefully pry the clips free so the door trim panel can be removed

14.9 Push the top of the hand grip upward, then remove the hand grip cover by twisting it towards the front of the vehicle

14.10 Remove the door trim panel retaining fasteners

13 For access to the handle, latch, lock and window regulator mechanisms, carefully peel back the plastic watershield.

14 Before installing the door trim panel, inspect the condition of all clips and reinstall any clips which may have fallen out.

15 Installation is the reverse of the removal procedure.

➡**Note: When installing door trim panel retaining clips, make sure the clips are lined up with their mating holes first, then gently tap the clips in with the palm of your hand.**

FORESTER MODELS

16 Remove the door handle trim ring (see illustration 14.1).

17 Remove the power window control switch (see illustration 14.2).

18 Remove the door trim panel using a door panel removal tool. Start from the bottom of the trim panel and work around the perimeter until all the fasteners have been released from the door (see illustration 14.4).

19 For access to the handle, latch, lock and window regulator mechanisms, carefully peel back the plastic watershield.

20 Before installing the door trim panel, inspect the condition of all clips and reinstall any clips which may have fallen out.

21 Installation is the reverse of the removal procedure.

➡**Note: When installing door trim panel retaining clips, make sure the clips are lined up with their mating holes first, then gently tap the clips in with the palm of your hand.**

15 Door - removal, installation and adjustment

➡**Note: The door is heavy and somewhat awkward to remove and install - at least two people should perform this procedure.**

REMOVAL AND INSTALLATION

▸ **Refer to illustration 15.2, 15.4 and 15.6**

1 Open the door all the way and support it on jacks or blocks covered with rags to prevent damaging the paint.

2 Remove the front pillar lower trim and disconnect the door's electrical connector from the body harness (see illustration).

3 Detach the rubber conduit between the body and the door. Then pull the wiring harness through the conduit.

4 Remove the door stop strut (see illustration).

5 Mark around the door hinges with a pen or a scribe to facilitate realignment during reassembly.

6 With an assistant holding the door, remove the hinge to door bolts and lift off the door (see illustration).

7 Installation is the reverse of removal.

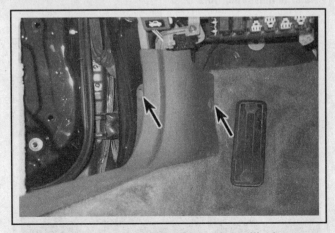

15.2 Remove the fasteners securing the front pillar lower trim panel

15.4 Remove the door stop strut retaining bolt

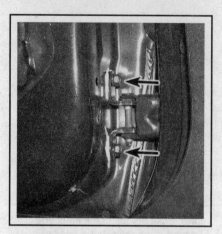

15.6 Remove the door hinge bolts

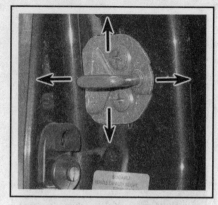

15.10 Adjust the door lock striker by loosening the mounting screws and gently tapping the striker in the desired direction

ADJUSTMENT

▶ **Refer to illustration 15.10**

8   Having proper door to body alignment is a critical part of a well functioning door assembly. First check the door hinge pins for excessive play. Fully open the door and lift up and down on the door without lifting the body. If a door has 1/16-inch or more excessive play, the hinges should be replaced.

9   Door-to-body alignment adjustments are made by loosening the hinge-to-body bolts or hinge-to-door bolts and moving the door. Proper body alignment is achieved when the top of the doors are parallel with the roof section, the front door is flush with the fender, the rear door is flush with the rear quarter panel and the bottom of the doors are aligned with the lower rocker panel. If these goals can't be reached by adjusting the hinge-to-body or hinge-to-door bolts, body alignment shims may have to be purchased and inserted behind the hinges to achieve correct alignment.

10 To adjust the door closed position, scribe a line or mark around the striker plate to provide a reference point, then verify that the door latch is contacting the center of the latch striker. If it isn't, adjust the vertical position of the striker (see illustration).

11 If necessary, adjust the horizontal position of the striker, so that the door panel is flush with the center pillar or rear quarter panel and provides positive engagement with the latch mechanism.

16 Door handles, key lock cylinder and latch - removal and installation

1   Raise the window, then remove the door trim panel and peel away the watershield (see Section 14).

INSIDE HANDLE

▶ **Refer to illustration 16.2**

2   Detach the actuating rods or cables between the inside door handle and the latch assembly, then remove the door handle retaining screw(s) (see illustration).

3   Pull the handle free from the door and remove it from the vehicle.

4   Installation is the reverse of removal.

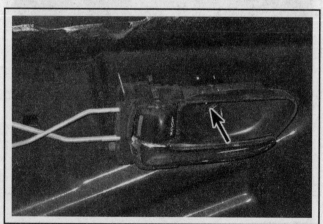

16.2 Remove the inside door handle screw

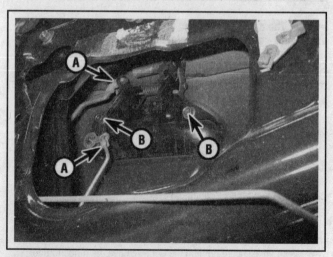

16.5 Disengage the actuating rods from the handle (A) then remove the handle mounting fasteners (B)

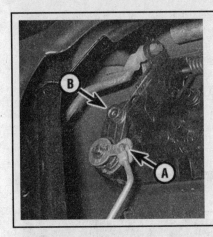

16.8 Unclip the actuating rod (A), then remove the key lock cylinder mounting fastener (B)

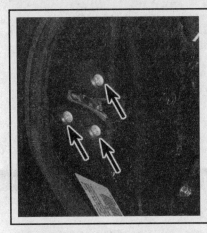

16.13 Remove the latch screws from the end of the door

OUTSIDE HANDLE

▶ **Refer to illustration 16.5**

5   Working through the access hole, disengage the actuating rods from the outside door handle and from the key lock cylinder (see illustration).

6   Detach the outside handle retaining nuts, then remove the handle from the door.

7   Installation is the reverse of removal.

KEY LOCK CYLINDER

▶ **Refer to illustration 16.8**

8   Unclip the actuating rod from the key lock cylinder (see illustration).

9   Remove the key lock cylinder mounting bolt, and remove the cylinder from the handle.

10   Installation is the reverse of removal.

DOOR LATCH

▶ **Refer to illustration 16.13**

11   Disengage the inside handle-to-latch actuating rods from the latch.

12   Working through the access hole, disengage the outside handle-to-latch rods and the lock cylinder-to-latch rod from the latch assembly.

13   Remove the three screws securing the latch to the door (see illustration), then remove the latch assembly from the door.

14   Installation is the reverse of removal.

17 Door window glass - removal and installation

▶ **Refer to illustrations 17.3 and 17.4**

1   Remove the door trim panel and the plastic watershield (see Section 14).

2   Unplug the electrical connector for the power mirror and remove the mirror from the door (see Section 19).

3   Remove the inner stabilizer (see illustration).

4   Operate the power window switch and lower the window glass to gain access to the window glass retainer bolts (see illustration). Remove the window glass retainer bolts.

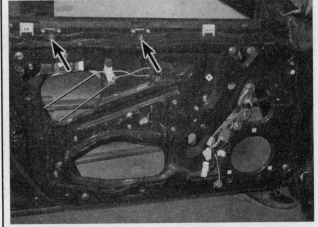

17.3 Inner stabilizer mounting fasteners

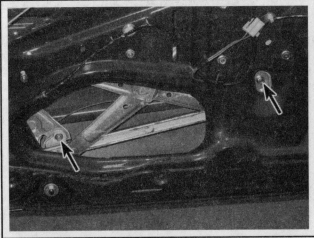

17.4 Window glass retainer bolts

5   Remove the glass by carefully pulling it up and out.

6   Installation is the reverse of removal. If it is necessary to adjust the glass, loosen the adjustment bolts on the stabilizers, sashes and up-stops, carefully raise the window and position the glass in the window opening so it is level and contacting the weatherstrip evenly all the way around. Have an assistant press in slightly on the window to give it a bit of preload on the weatherstrip, then tighten the adjustment bolts. To fine-tune the adjustment, loosen the necessary adjustment bolts and move the up-stops, sashes or stabilizers as required, then tighten them securely. Verify that the window goes up and down smoothly, and that the door opens and closes easily. If the door 'pops' when you open it or is hard to close, there is too much preload on the glass

18 Door window glass regulator and motor - removal and installation

▶ **Refer to illustration 18.4**

1   Remove the door trim panel and the plastic watershield (see Section 14).

2   Remove the door window glass assembly (see Section 17).

3   Unplug the electrical connector from the window regulator motor.

4   Remove the regulator mounting bolts (see illustration).

5   Pull the regulator assembly through the service hole in the door frame to remove it.

6   To remove the motor from the regulator assembly, simply remove the three fasteners securing it to the regulator assembly.

7   Installation is the reverse of removal.

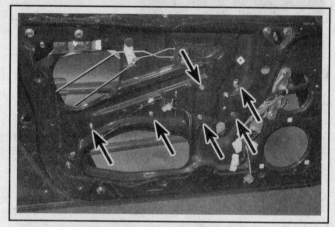

18.4 Window regulator mounting fasteners

19 Outside mirrors - removal and installation

▶ **Refer to illustrations 19.2 and 19.3**

1   Remove the door trim panel (see Section 14).

2   Unplug the mirror electrical connector (see illustration).

3   Remove the mirror retaining screws (see illustration) and detach the mirror from the vehicle.

4   Installation is the reverse of removal.

19.2 Disconnect the electrical connector for the outside mirror

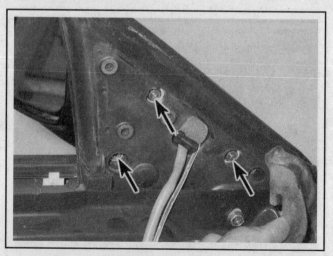

19.3 Outside mirror mounting fasteners

20 Trunk lid - removal and installation

▶ Refer to illustration 20.3

➡ Note: The trunk lid is heavy and somewhat awkward to remove and install - at least two people should perform this procedure.

1   Open the trunk lid and cover the edges of the trunk compartment with pads or cloths to protect the painted surfaces when the lid is removed.

2   Disconnect any cables or wire harness connectors attached to the trunk lid that would interfere with removal.

3   Make alignment marks around the hinge mounting bolts with a marking pen (see illustration).

4   While an assistant supports the trunk lid, remove the lid-to-hinge bolts on both sides and lift it off.

5   Installation is the reverse of removal.

➡ Note: When reinstalling the trunk lid, align the lid-to-hinge bolts with the marks made during removal.

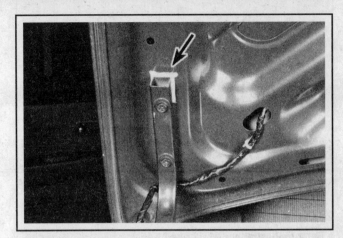

20.3 Draw around the hinge with a marking pen before loosening the bolts to ensure proper alignment of the trunk lid when it's reinstalled

21 Trunk lid latch and lock cylinder - removal and installation

LATCH

2004 and earlier models

▶ Refer to illustration 21.2

1   Open the trunk and remove any trunk lid trim panels around the latch. Scribe or paint a line around the latch assembly for a reference point to ensure that the latch is correctly aligned when installed again.

2   Disengage the rod connecting the lock cylinder to the latch (see illustration).

3   The trunk lid latch is retained by two nuts or bolts. Detach these bolts, then remove the latch.

4   Installation is the reverse of removal. Make sure the latch is aligned with the marks you made prior to removal.

2005 and later models

5   Open the trunk and remove any trunk lid trim panels around the latch.

6   The trunk lid latch is retained by two fasteners. Detach these bolts, then disconnect the electrical connector and cable from the back of the latch. Remove the latch.

7   Installation is the reverse of removal. Make sure the latch is aligned with the marks you made prior to removal.

TRUNK LOCK CYLINDER

2004 and earlier models

▶ Refer to illustration 21.9

8   Open the trunk and remove the trunk lid trim panels.

9   Detach the latch to lock cylinder rod from the lock cylinder, then using a pair of pliers remove the lock cylinder retaining clip (see illustration).

10 Working from the outside of the trunk lid, grasp the lock cylinder and pull it outward to remove it.

11 Installation is the reverse of removal.

21.2 Disengage this rod from the latch

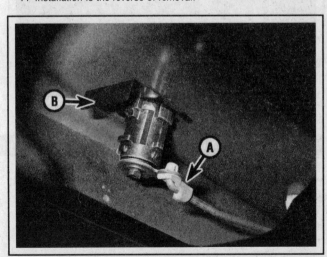

21.9 Disengage this rod from the lock cylinder (A), then remove the lock cylinder retaining clip (B)

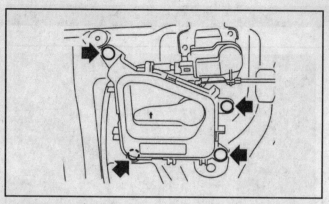

21.13 Trunk lid release handle mounting fasteners

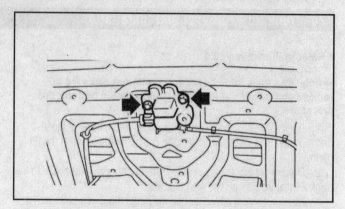

21.15 Trunk lock mounting fasteners

2005 and later models

▶ **Refer to illustrations 21.13 and 21.15**

12 Open the trunk and remove the trunk lid trim panels.

13 Remove the trunk lid release handle (see illustration).
14 Disconnect the connectors and the trunk opener cable.
15 Remove the two fasteners, then remove the lock assembly (see illustration).

22 Liftgate support struts - removal and installation

▶ **Refer to illustrations 22.2a and 22.2b**

➡**Note: The liftgate is heavy and somewhat awkward to hold - at least two people should perform this procedure.**

1 Open the rear liftgate and support it securely.

2 Remove the retaining bolts at both ends of the support strut and detach it from the vehicle (see illustrations).
3 Installation is the reverse of removal.

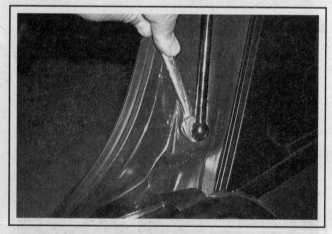

22.2a Unscrew the lower end of the liftgate strut from the body as shown . . .

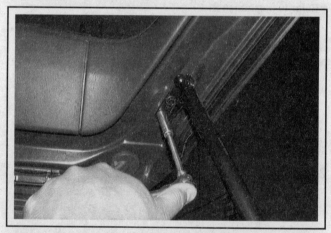

22.2b . . . then detach the upper end of the strut from the liftgate (don't try to pry the spherical bearings loose on these struts - they can't be removed that way)

23 Liftgate - removal, installation and adjustment

➡**Note: The liftgate is heavy and somewhat awkward to hold - at least two people should perform this procedure.**

REMOVAL AND INSTALLATION

▶ **Refer to illustration 23.4**

1 Open the liftgate and support it securely.

2 Remove the liftgate trim panels and disconnect the rear washer hose and all wiring harness connectors leading to the liftgate.
3 While an assistant supports the liftgate, detach the support struts from the liftgate (see Section 22).
4 Draw a line around the liftgate hinges for a reference point to aid the installation procedure. Then detach the hinge-to-liftgate bolts (see illustration) and remove the liftgate from the vehicle.
5 Installation is the reverse of removal.

23.4 Before loosening the liftgate retaining bolts, draw a line around the hinge plate for a reinstallation reference

ADJUSTMENT

6   Adjustments are made by loosening the hinge-to liftgate bolts and moving the liftgate. Proper alignment is achieved when the edges of the liftgate are parallel with the rear quarter panel and the top of the tailgate.
7   To provide positive engagement with the latch mechanism, the latch striker may need to be adjusted. To get to the striker, remove the trim piece between the bumper cover and the carpeting. Then mark the relationship of the striker to the body, loosen the striker bolts and move the striker fore-and-aft and/or side-to-side as necessary to achieve positive engagement.

24 Liftgate latch and outside handle - removal and installation

▶ **Refer to illustration 24.2**

1   Open the liftgate and support it securely.
2   To gain access to most of the following components, the interior trim panels on the liftgate must be removed. Using a trim panel removal tool or a small screwdriver, carefully pry out the trim panel retaining clips (see illustration) and detach the trim panel from the liftgate.

LATCH

3   Remove the bolts from the latch assembly, then disconnect the electrical connector and the outer handle cable.
4   Remove the latch.
5   Installation is the reverse of removal.

OUTSIDE HANDLE

6   Remove the rear wiper motor assembly (see Chapter 12).
7   Disconnect the outer handle cable, then remove the handle

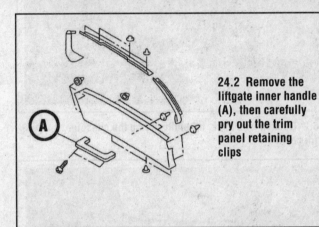

24.2 Remove the liftgate inner handle (A), then carefully pry out the trim panel retaining clips

mounting fasteners.
8   Remove the handle.
9   Installation is the reverse of removal.

25 Steering column covers - removal and installation

▶ **Refer to illustration 25.3**

❄ WARNING:

Models covered by this manual are equipped with a Supplemental Restraint System (SRS), more commonly known as airbags. Always disable the airbag system before working in the vicinity of any airbag system component to avoid the possibility of accidental deployment of the airbag, which could cause personal injury (see Chapter 12).

1   Disconnect the cable from the negative terminal of the battery, see Chapter 5, Section 1.
2   Remove the steering wheel (see Chapter 10).
3   If you need to remove the upper half of the steering column cover, remove the instrument cluster trim bezel (see Section 27). (It's not necessary to remove the cluster trim bezel to remove the lower half of the steering column cover.)
4   Remove the steering column cover screw (see illustration).

25.3 Steering column cover retaining screw (Legacy model shown, other models similar)

5   Separate the cover halves and detach them from the steering column.
6   Installation is the reverse of removal.

26 Center console - removal and installation

✳✳ WARNING:

Models covered by this manual are equipped with a Supplemental Restraint System (SRS), more commonly known as airbags. Always disable the airbag system before working in the vicinity of any airbag system component to avoid the possibility of accidental deployment of the airbag, which could cause personal injury (see Chapter 12).

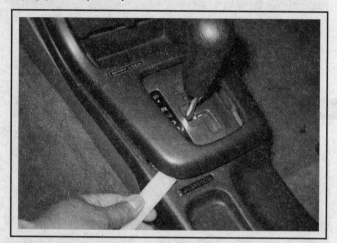

26.2 Using a trim stick, carefully pry up the console trim cover

1 On manual transaxle models, remove the shift lever knob (see Chapter 7B).

LEGACY AND OUTBACK MODELS

2004 and earlier models

▶ **Refer to illustrations 26.2, 26.3 and 26.4**

2 Remove the center console front trim cover (see illustration).
3 Remove the console cover and tray (see illustration).
4 Remove the remaining center console fasteners and remove the center console (see illustration).
5 Installation is the reverse of removal.

2005 and later models

▶ **Refer to illustrations 26.6, 26.10a, 26.10b and 26.10c**

6 Remove the center console box (see illustration).
7 Using a trim stick, carefully pry up the trim piece around the shift lever and remove it from the console.
8 Remove the knee bolster (see Section 27).
9 Remove the glove box lower cover (see Section 27).
10 Remove the center console side panels (see illustrations).
11 Remove the radio (see Chapter 12). Remove the center console.
12 Installation is the reverse of removal.

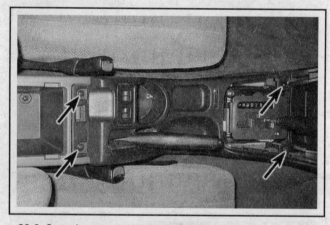

26.3 Console cover and tray mounting fasteners

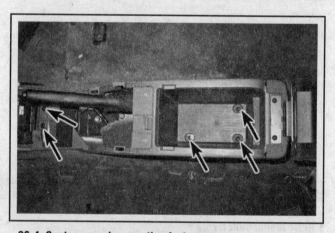

26.4 Center console mounting fasteners

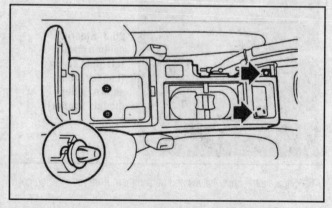

26.6 Center console box mounting fastener locations

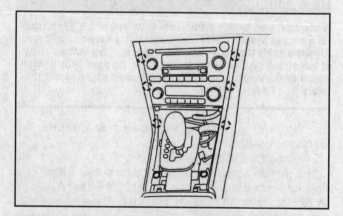

26.10a Carefully unclip the center console side panels . . .

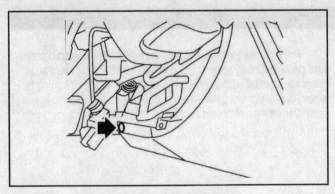

26.10b ... then remove the clip at the front of the side panel ...

FORESTER MODELS

2002 and earlier models

▶ **Refer to illustrations 26.13 and 26.14**

13 Remove the console cover and, on manual transaxle models, the shift lever boot (see illustration).

14 Remove the console retaining screws (see illustration).

15 Unplug any electrical connectors, then remove the center console.

16 Installation is the reverse of removal.

2003 and later models

▶ **Refer to illustrations 26.18 and 26.19**

17 Using a trim stick, carefully pry up the trim piece around the shift

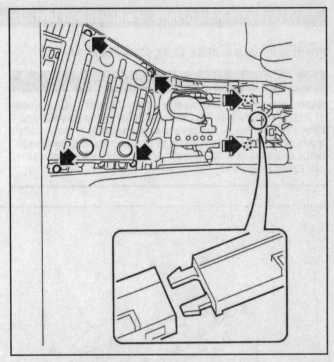

26.10c ... and the six mounting fasteners

lever and remove it from the console.

18 Remove the console cover (see illustration).

19 Remove the remaining center console fasteners (see illustration).

20 Detach the console side panels and remove the center console

21 Installation is the reverse of removal.

26.13 Remove the console cover and shift lever boot

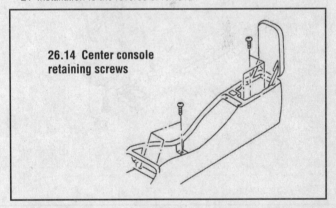

26.14 Center console retaining screws

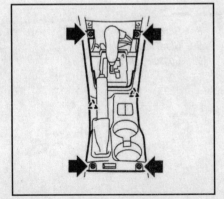

26.18 Remove the fasteners for the console cover

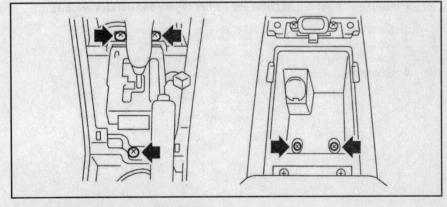

26.19 Center console mounting fasteners

27 Dashboard trim panels - removal and installation

♦ Refer to illustration 27.1a, 27.1b, 27.1c and 27.1d

❊❊ **WARNING:**

Models covered by this manual are equipped with a Supplemental Restraint System (SRS), more commonly known as airbags. Always disable the airbag system before working in the vicinity of any airbag system component to avoid the possibility of accidental deployment of the airbag, which could cause personal injury (see Chapter 12).

1 These panels (see illustrations) provide access to various instrument panel mounting screws. Some of the covers use fasteners and others are pried off with a screwdriver or trim stick. If you're going to remove the instrument panel, remove all of the covers. Refer to the illustrations for the removal procedure.

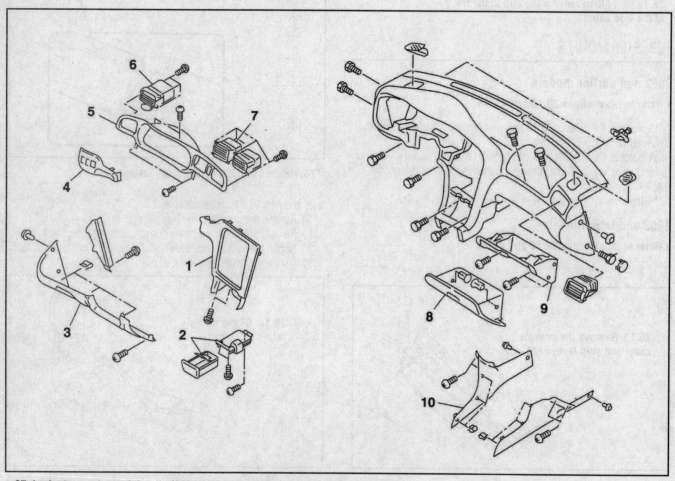

27.1a Instrument panel details (2004 and earlier Legacy and Outback models)

1	Center panel	5	Instrument cluster bezel	8	Glove box lid
2	Ash tray	6	Grille vent	9	Glove box panel
3	Knee bolster	7	Grille center	10	Console side covers
4	Switch panel				

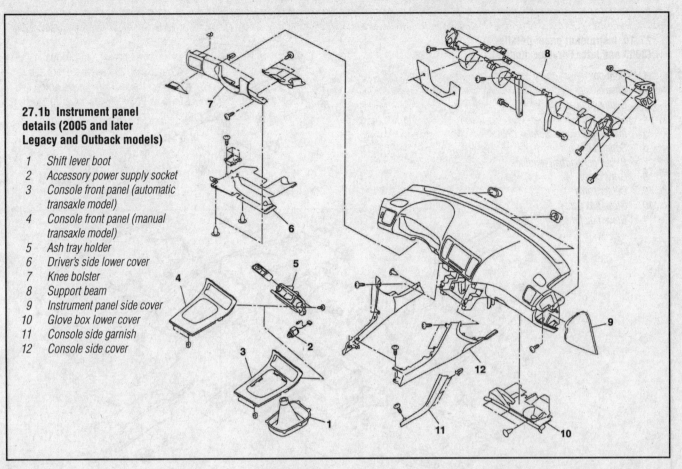

27.1b Instrument panel details (2005 and later Legacy and Outback models)

1   Shift lever boot
2   Accessory power supply socket
3   Console front panel (automatic transaxle model)
4   Console front panel (manual transaxle model)
5   Ash tray holder
6   Driver's side lower cover
7   Knee bolster
8   Support beam
9   Instrument panel side cover
10 Glove box lower cover
11 Console side garnish
12 Console side cover

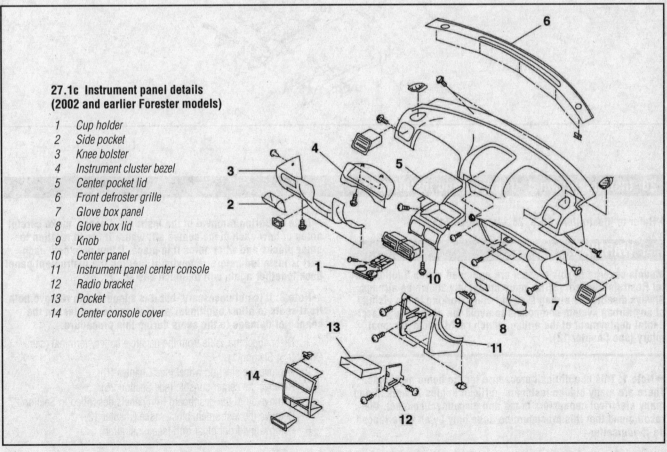

27.1c Instrument panel details (2002 and earlier Forester models)

1   Cup holder
2   Side pocket
3   Knee bolster
4   Instrument cluster bezel
5   Center pocket lid
6   Front defroster grille
7   Glove box panel
8   Glove box lid
9   Knob
10 Center panel
11 Instrument panel center console
12 Radio bracket
13 Pocket
14 Center console cover

27.1d Instrument panel details (2003 and later Forester models)

1. Coin box
2. Knee bolster
3. Center compartment
4. Grille cover
5. Instrument cluster bezel
6. Support beam
7. Passenger's airbag module
8. Grille cover
9. Center panel
10. Glove box panel
11. Glove box lid

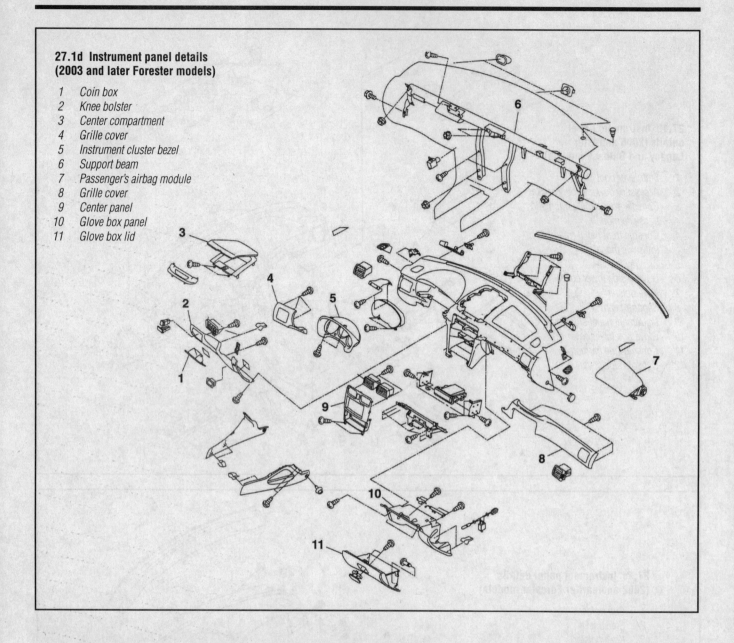

28 Instrument panel - removal and installation

▶ Refer to illustrations 28.6, 28.11a and 28.11b

✳✳ WARNING:

Models covered by this manual are equipped with a Supplemental Restraint System (SRS), more commonly known as airbags. Always disable the airbag system before working in the vicinity of any airbag system component to avoid the possibility of accidental deployment of the airbag, which could cause personal injury (see Chapter 12).

➡ **Note 1:** This is a difficult procedure for the home mechanic. There are many hidden fasteners, difficult angles to work in and many electrical connectors to tag and disconnect/connect. We recommend that this procedure be done only by an experienced do-it-yourselfer.

➡ **Note 2:** During removal of the instrument panel, make careful notes of how each piece comes off, where it fits in relation to other pieces and what holds it in place. If you note how each part is installed before removing it, getting the instrument panel back together again will be much easier.

➡ **Note 3:** It is not necessary, but it is suggested to remove both front seats to allow additional working space and lessen the chance of damage to the seats during this procedure.

1. Disconnect the cable from the negative battery terminal (see Chapter 5, Section 1).
2. Remove the steering wheel (see Chapter 10).
3. Remove the center console (see Section 26).
4. Remove all of the dashboard trim panels described in Section 27.
5. Remove the instrument cluster (see Chapter 12).
6. Remove the front pillar trim (see illustration).

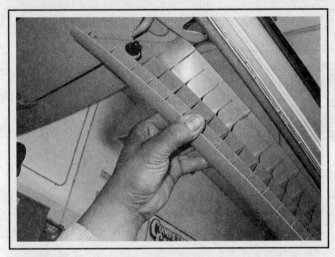

28.6 Remove the front pillar trim by carefully releasing the clips (typical)

7   Remove the fasteners and lower the steering column (see Chapter 10).

8   Remove the sill trim/kick panels from each side.

9   Remove the radio (see Chapter 12) and the heater control assembly (see Chapter 3).

10 Disconnect the instrument panel electrical connectors.

➡**Note: A number of electrical connectors must be disconnected in order to remove the instrument panel. Most are designed so that they will only fit on the matching connector (male or female), but if there is any doubt, mark the connectors with masking tape and a marking pen before disconnecting them.**

11 Remove the fasteners securing the instrument panel. Depending on which model you're working on, refer to illustrations 27.1b, 27.1d, 28.11a or 28.11b for instrument panel mounting details.

12 Pull the instrument panel away from the firewall and detach any electrical connectors interfering with removal.

13 Once all the electrical connectors are detached, lift the instrument panel then pull it away from the windshield and take it out through the door opening.

➡**Note: This is a two-person job.**

14 Installation is the reverse of removal.

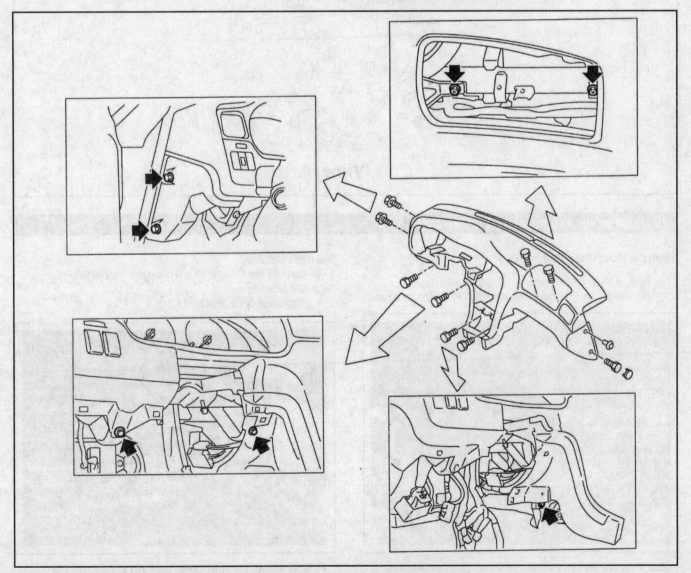

28.11a Instrument panel mounting details (2004 and earlier Legacy and Outback models)

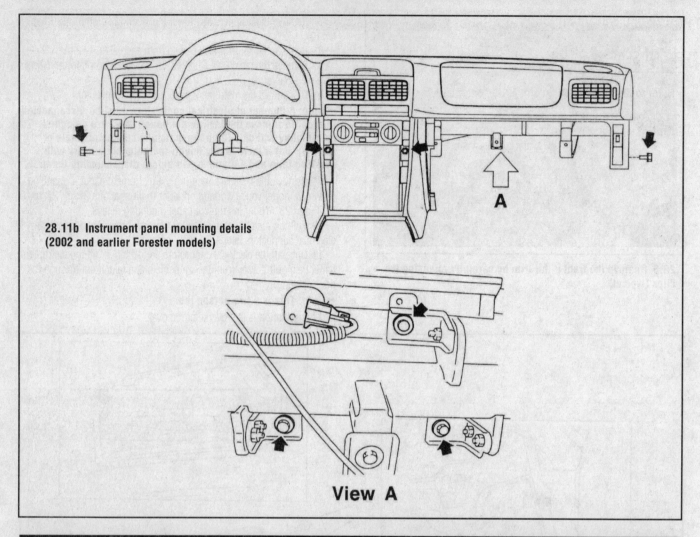

28.11b Instrument panel mounting details (2002 and earlier Forester models)

View A

29 Cowl cover - removal and installation

▶ **Refer to illustrations 29.2 and 29.3**

1　Remove the windshield wiper arms (see Chapter 12).
2　Remove the two push pins, then carefully peel off the front panel seal (see illustration).
3　Carefully pry off the cowl and disengage the plastic clips securing it (see illustration).
4　Installation is the reverse of removal.

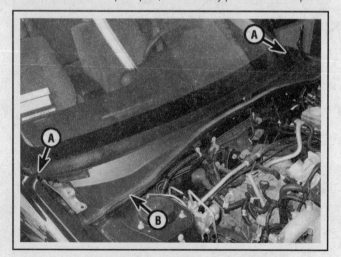

29.2　Remove the two push pin fasteners (A), then starting from the edge, carefully peel away the front panel seal (B)

29.3　To detach the cowl cover, carefully pry it loose (its perimeter is secured by a series of push-type clips)

30 Seats - removal and installation

FRONT SEAT

▶ **Refer to illustrations 30.2a and 30.2b**

1   Position the seat all the way forward or all the way to the rear to access the retaining bolts.
2   Detach any bolt trim covers and remove the retaining bolts (see illustrations).
3   Tilt the seat upward to access the underneath, then disconnect any electrical connectors and lift the seat from the vehicle.
4   Installation is the reverse of removal.

REAR SEAT

▶ **Refer to illustration 30.5**

5   Detach the bolt trim covers and remove the seat cushion retaining bolts (see illustration). Then lift up on the front edge and remove the cushion from the vehicle.
6   Detach the retaining bolts at the lower edge of the seat back.
7   Lift up on the lower edge of the seat back and remove it from the vehicle.
8   Installation is the reverse of removal.

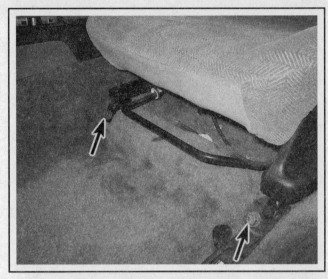

30.2a To detach a front seat from the floorpan, remove these two bolts from the front end of the seat rails . . .

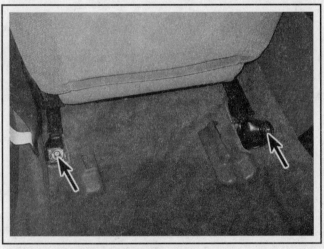

30.2b . . . and these bolts from the rear

30.5 Remove the seat cushion retaining bolts (Legacy model shown, other models similar)

Notes

Section

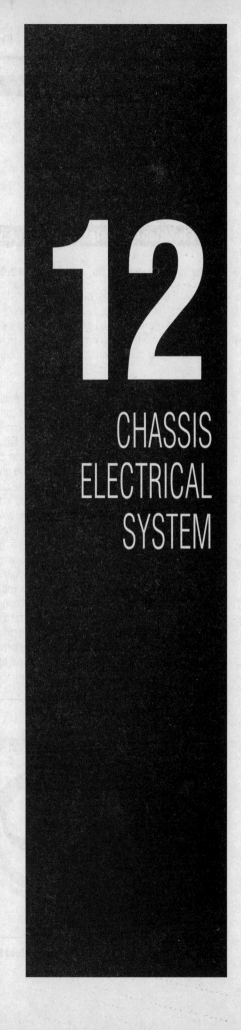

12

CHASSIS ELECTRICAL SYSTEM

1   General information

The electrical system is a 12-volt, negative ground type. Power for the lights and all electrical accessories is supplied by a lead/acid-type battery, which is charged by the alternator.

This Chapter covers repair and service procedures for the various electrical components not associated with the engine. Information on the battery, alternator and starter motor can be found in Chapter 5.

It should be noted that when portions of the electrical system are serviced, the cable should be disconnected from the negative terminal of the battery terminal to prevent electrical shorts and/or fires.

2   Electrical troubleshooting - general information

▶ **Refer to illustrations 2.5a, 2.5b, 2.6 and 2.9**

A typical electrical circuit consists of an electrical component, any switches, relays, motors, fuses, fusible links or circuit breakers related to that component and the wiring and connectors that link the component to both the battery and the chassis. To help you pinpoint an electrical circuit problem, wiring diagrams are included at the end of this Chapter.

Before tackling any troublesome electrical circuit, first study the appropriate wiring diagrams to get a complete understanding of what makes up that individual circuit. Noting if other components related to the circuit are operating properly, for instance, can often narrow down trouble spots. If several components or circuits fail at one time, chances are the problem is in a fuse or ground connection, because several circuits are often routed through the same fuse and ground connections.

Electrical problems usually stem from simple causes, such as loose or corroded connections, a blown fuse, a melted fusible link or a failed relay. Visually inspect the condition of all fuses, wires and connections in a problem circuit before troubleshooting the circuit.

If test equipment and instruments are going to be utilized, use the diagrams to plan ahead of time where you will make the necessary connections in order to accurately pinpoint the trouble spot.

For electrical troubleshooting, you'll need a voltmeter, a circuit tester or a 12-volt bulb with a set of test leads; a continuity tester, which includes a bulb, battery and set of test leads; and a jumper wire, with a circuit breaker, which can be used to bypass electrical components (see illustrations). Before attempting to locate a problem with test instruments, use the wiring diagram(s) to decide where to make the connections.

VOLTAGE CHECKS

Voltage checks should be performed if a circuit is not functioning properly. Connect one lead of a circuit tester to either the negative terminal of the battery terminal or a known good ground. Connect the other lead to a connector in the circuit being tested, preferably nearest

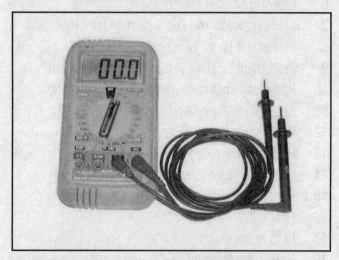

2.5a The most useful tool for electrical troubleshooting is a digital multimeter that can check volts, amps, and test continuity

2.6 To use a test light, clip the lead to a known good ground, then test connectors, wires or electrical sockets with the pointed probe. If the bulb lights, the circuit that you're testing has battery voltage

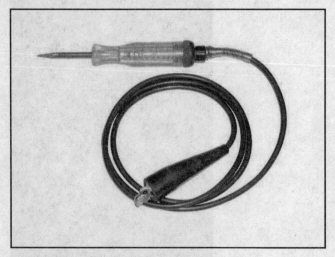

2.5b A simple test light is a very handy tool for testing voltage

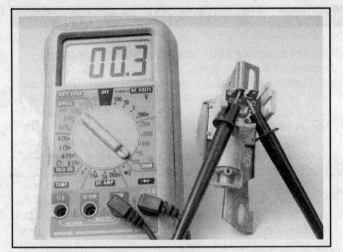

2.9 With a multimeter set to the ohm scale, you can check the resistance across two terminals. When checking for continuity, a low reading indicates continuity, a high reading or infinity indicates lack of continuity

to the battery or fuse (see illustration). If the bulb of the tester lights, voltage is present, which means that the part of the circuit between the connector and the battery is problem free. Continue checking the rest of the circuit in the same fashion. When you reach a point at which no voltage is present, the problem lies between that point and the last test point with voltage. Most of the time the problem can be traced to a loose connection.

➡**Note: Keep in mind that some circuits receive voltage only when the ignition key is in the ACC (accessory) or ON/RUN position.**

FINDING A SHORT

One method of finding shorts in a live circuit is to remove the fuse and connect a test light in place of the fuse terminals (fabricate two jumper wires with small spade terminals, plug the jumper wires into the fuse box and connect the test light). There should be voltage present in the circuit. Move the suspected wiring harness from side-to-side while watching the test light. If the bulb goes off, there is a short to ground somewhere in that area, probably where the insulation has rubbed through.

GROUND CHECK

Perform a ground test to check whether a component is properly grounded. Disconnect the battery and connect one lead of a continuity tester or multimeter (set to the ohm scale), to a known good ground. Connect the other lead to the wire or ground connection being tested. If the resistance is low (less than 5 ohms), the ground is good. If the bulb on a self-powered test light does not go on, the ground is not good.

CONTINUITY CHECK

A continuity check is done to determine if there are any breaks in a circuit - if it is passing electricity properly. With the circuit off (no power in the circuit), a self-powered continuity tester or multimeter can be used to check the circuit. Connect the test leads to both ends of the circuit (or to the power end and a good ground), and if the test light comes on the circuit is passing current properly (see illustration). If the resistance is low (less than 5 ohms), there is continuity; if the reading is 10,000 ohms or higher, there is a break somewhere in the circuit. The same procedure can be used to test a switch, by connecting the continuity tester to the switch terminals. With the switch turned on the test light should come on (or low resistance should be indicated on a meter).

FINDING AN OPEN CIRCUIT

When diagnosing for possible open circuits, it is often difficult to locate them by sight because the connectors hide oxidation or terminal misalignment. Merely wiggling a connector on a sensor or in the wiring harness may correct the open circuit condition. Remember this when an open circuit is indicated when troubleshooting a circuit. Intermittent problems may also be caused by oxidized or loose connections.

Electrical troubleshooting is simple if you keep in mind that all electrical circuits are basically electricity running from the battery, through the wires, switches, relays, fuses and fusible links to each electrical component (light bulb, motor, etc.) and to ground, from which it is passed back to the battery. Any electrical problem is an interruption in the flow of electricity to and from the battery.

CONNECTORS

Most electrical connections on these vehicles are made with multi-wire plastic connectors. The mating halves of many connectors are secured with locking clips molded into the plastic connector shells. The mating halves of large connectors, such as some of those under the instrument panel, are held together by a bolt through the center of the connector.

To separate a connector with locking clips, use a small screwdriver to pry the clips apart carefully, then separate the connector halves. Pull only on the shell, never pull on the wiring harness as you may damage the individual wires and terminals inside the connectors. Look at the connector closely before trying to separate the halves. Often the locking clips are engaged in a way that is not immediately clear. Additionally, many connectors have more than one set of clips.

Each pair of connector terminals has a male half and a female half. When you look at the end view of a connector in a diagram, be sure to understand whether the view shows the harness side or the component side of the connector. Connector halves are mirror images of each other, i.e. a terminal shown on the right side end-view of one half will be on the left side end view of the other half.

3   Fuses, fusible links and circuit breakers - general information

FUSES

▶ **Refer to illustrations 3.1a, 3.1b and 3.3**

The electrical circuits of the vehicle are protected by a combination of fuses, circuit breakers and fusible links. There are two fuse boxes: the engine compartment fuse box and the passenger compartment fuse box. The engine compartment fuse box (see illustration) is located on the left side of the engine compartment on all models. The passenger compartment fuse box is located at the left end of the instrument panel, ahead of the coin tray (see illustration) on all Forester models and on all 2000 through 2004 Baja, Legacy and Outback models. On 2005 and 2006 Baja, Legacy and Outback models, it's located in the same spot, except that the coin tray is gone, replaced by the fuse panel cover. To access the passenger compartment fuse box, pull out the coin tray or remove the fuse panel cover.

Each of the fuses is designed to protect a specific circuit, as identi-

3.1a The engine compartment fuse box is located on the left side of the engine compartment. It includes a fuse and relay guide on the underside of the fuse box cover

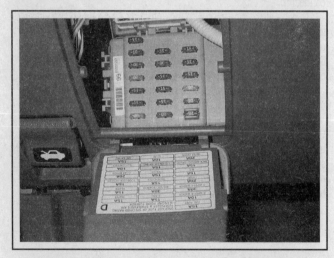

3.1b All passenger compartment fuse boxes are located at the left end of the instrument panel, ahead of the coin tray (2000 through 2004 models) or the fuse panel cover (2005 and 2006 models). When you pull out the coin tray or the fuse panel cover, you'll find a handy fuse guide on the backside

fied on the fuse cover. Spare fuses and a special removal tool are included in the fuse box cover.

Miniaturized fuses are employed in the fuse blocks. These compact fuses, with blade terminal design, allow fingertip removal and replacement. If an electrical component fails, always check the fuse first. The best way to check the fuses is with a test light. Check for power at the exposed terminal tips of each fuse. If power is present at one side of the fuse but not the other, the fuse is blown. A blown fuse can also be identified by visually inspecting it (see illustration).

To replace a fuse, simply pull out the bad fuse and push in a new fuse. Always replace blown a blown fuse with a replacement unit of the same type and amperage rating. Fuses of different amperage ratings are physically interchangeable, but don't replace a blown fuse with one rating with a replacement fuse with a different rating. Always replace bad fuses with new units with the exact same amperage rating. Replacing a fuse with one of a higher or lower value than specified is not recommended. Each electrical circuit needs a specific amount of protection. The amperage rating of every fuse is molded into the fuse body.

If the replacement fuse immediately fails, don't replace it again until the cause of the problem is isolated and corrected. In most cases, this will be a short circuit in the wiring caused by a broken or deteriorated wire.

FUSIBLE LINKS

Some circuits, such as the part of the starter circuit that connects the starter motor to the alternator, are protected by fusible links. Fusible links are used in circuits that carry high current or are not ordinarily fused. Cartridge type fusible links (also referred to as "maxi-fuses") are located in the engine compartment fuse and relay box and are similar to a large fuse. After disconnecting the negative terminal of the battery cable, simply unplug and replace a fusible link with a new unit of the same amperage.

CIRCUIT BREAKERS

Circuit breakers protect certain circuits, such as the power windows or heated seats. Depending on the vehicle's accessories, there might be one or two circuit breakers, and they're usually located inside the vehicle, where they're scattered throughout the area under the instrument panel.

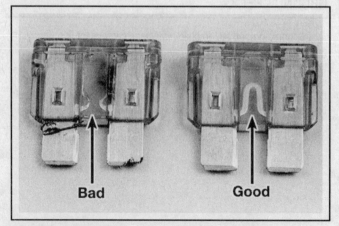

3.3 When a fuse blows, the element between the terminals melts

Because circuit breakers reset automatically, an electrical overload in a circuit-breaker-protected system will cause the circuit to fail momentarily, then come back on. If the circuit does not come back on, check it immediately.

For a basic check, pull the circuit breaker up out of its socket on the fuse panel, but just far enough to probe with a voltmeter. The breaker should still contact the sockets.

With the voltmeter negative lead on a good chassis ground, touch each end prong of the circuit breaker with the positive meter probe. There should be battery voltage at each end. If there is battery voltage only at one end, the circuit breaker must be replaced.

Some circuit breakers must be reset manually.

4 Turn signal/hazard flasher - check and replacement

✳✳ WARNING:

The models covered by this manual are equipped with a Supplemental Restraint System (SRS), more commonly known as airbags. Always disarm the airbag system before working in the vicinity of any airbag system component to avoid the possibility of accidental deployment of the airbag, which could cause personal injury (see Section 24).

CHECK

◆ **Refer to illustration 4.1**

1 When the turn signal switch is actuated, the flasher unit flashes the turn signal lights; when the hazard flasher switch is actuated, the flasher unit flashes all four turn signal lights simultaneously. The turn signal/hazard flasher under the driver's side of the instrument panel (see illustration).

2 When the flasher unit is functioning properly, an audible click can be heard during its operation. If the turn signals fail on one side or the other and the flasher unit does not make its characteristic clicking sound, or if it flashes much more rapidly than normal, a faulty turn signal bulb is indicated.

3 If both turn signals fail to blink, the problem may be due to a blown fuse, a faulty flasher unit, a broken switch or a loose or open

4.1 Location of the turn signal/hazard flasher unit (2001 Legacy shown, others similar)

connection. If a quick check of the fuse box indicates that the turn signal fuse has blown, check the wiring for a short before installing a new fuse.

REPLACEMENT

4 To remove the flasher, remove the knee bolster and reinforcement panel behind it (see Chapter 11, Section 27), unplug the electrical connector from the flasher unit, then remove the mounting bolt (see illustration 4.1). Installation is the reverse of removal.

5 Relays - general information and testing

GENERAL INFORMATION

1 Several electrical accessories in the vehicle, such as the fuel injection system, horns, starter, and fog lamps use relays to transmit the electrical signal to the component. Relays use a low-current circuit (the control circuit) to open and close a high-current circuit (the power circuit). If the relay is defective, that component will not operate properly. Most relays are mounted in the engine compartment fuse and relay box. (There are also some relays mounted on or near the passenger compartment fuse box, but they're not visible until you remove the knee bolster.) If you suspect a faulty relay, simply remove it and test it using the procedure below. Or have it tested by a dealer service department. Defective relays cannot be repaired; they must be replaced with a new unit.

TESTING

◆ **Refer to illustration 5.2**

2 Most of the relays used in these vehicles are normally open relays (see illustration).

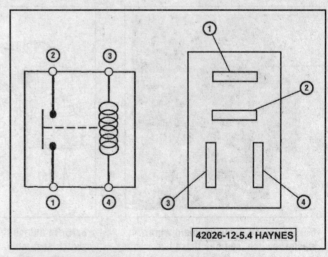

42026-12-5.4 HAYNES

5.2 Typical normally open relay (see text for testing procedure)

3   Refer to the wiring diagram for the circuit to determine the proper connections for the relay you're testing. If you can't determine the correct connection from the wiring diagrams, however, you may be able to determine the test connections from the information that follows.

4   Two of the terminals are the relay control circuit and connect to the relay coil. The other relay terminals are the power circuit. When the relay is energized, the coil creates a magnetic field that closes the larger contacts of the power circuit to provide power to the circuit loads.

5   To test a normally-open relay, use an ohmmeter to verify that there is no continuity between terminal No. 1 and No. 2 when the power is disconnected. Then verify that there is continuity between terminal No. 1 and No. 2 when the No. 3 and No. 4 terminals are connected to power and ground.

6   If the relay fails the above test, replace it.

6   Steering column switches - replacement

✳✳ WARNING:

The models covered by this manual are equipped with a Supplemental Restraint System (SRS), more commonly known as airbags. Always disarm the airbag system before working in the vicinity of any airbag system component to avoid the possibility of accidental deployment of the airbag, which could cause personal injury (see Section 24).

HEADLIGHT/TURN SIGNAL SWITCH

▶ Refer to illustrations 6.3 and 6.4

1   Disconnect the cable from the negative terminal of the battery (see Chapter 5).
2   Remove the instrument panel lower cover and the upper and

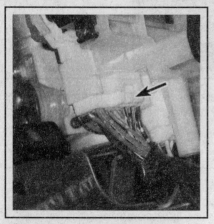

6.3 To disconnect the electrical connector from the headlight/turn signal switch, depress this release tab and pull the connector straight down

6.4 To detach the headlight/turn signal switch, remove these two mounting screws

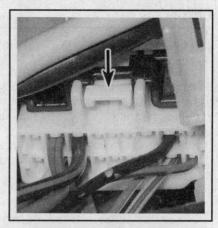

6.8 To disconnect the electrical connector from the windshield wiper/washer switch, depress this release tab and pull out the connector (all models except 2005 and 2006 Baja, Legacy and Outback models)

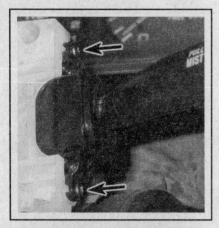

6.9 To detach the windshield wiper/washer switch, remove these two mounting screws (all models except 2005 and 2006 Baja, Legacy and Outback models)

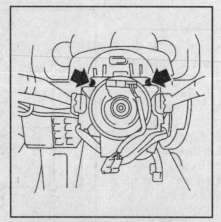

6.15 To detach the combination switch assembly, remove these two mounting screws (2005 and 2006 Baja, Legacy and Outback models)

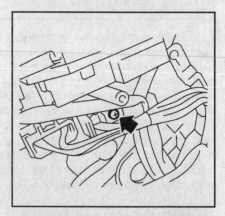

6.16 To detach the windshield wiper/washer switch from the combination switch assembly, remove this mounting screw (2005 and 2006 Baja, Legacy and Outback models)

lower steering column covers (see Chapter 11).

3 Disconnect the electrical connector from the headlight/turn signal switch (see illustration).

4 Remove the headlight/turn signal switch mounting screws (see illustration) and remove the switch.

5 Installation is the reverse of removal.

WINDSHIELD WIPER/WASHER SWITCH

All models except 2005 and 2006 Baja, Legacy and Outback models

▶ **Refer to illustrations 6.8 and 6.9**

6 Disconnect the cable from the negative terminal of the battery (see Chapter 5).

7 Remove the instrument panel lower cover and the upper and lower steering column covers (see Chapter 11).

8 Disconnect the electrical connector from the windshield wiper/washer switch (see illustration).

9 Remove the windshield wiper/washer switch mounting screws (see illustration) and remove the switch.

10 Installation is the reverse of removal.

2005 and 2006 Baja, Legacy and Outback models

▶ **Refer to illustrations 6.15 and 6.16**

11 Disconnect the cable from the negative terminal of the battery (see Chapter 5).

12 Remove the steering wheel (see Chapter 10).

13 Remove the upper and lower steering column covers (see Chapter 11).

14 Disconnect the electrical connector from the windshield wiper/washer switch.

15 Remove the three combination switch mounting screws (see illustration) and pull out the combination switch.

16 Remove the windshield wiper/washer switch mounting screw (see illustration) and remove the switch.

17 Installation is the reverse of removal.

7   Ignition switch and key lock cylinder - check and replacement

▶ **Refer to illustrations 7.3, 7.4 and 7.7**

❉❉ WARNING:

The models covered by this manual are equipped with a Supplemental Restraint System (SRS), more commonly known as airbags. Always disarm the airbag system before working in the vicinity of any airbag system component to avoid the possibility of accidental deployment of the airbag, which could cause personal injury (see Section 24).

1 Disconnect the cable from the negative terminal of the battery (see Chapter 5).

2 Remove the instrument panel lower cover, the upper and lower steering column covers and the instrument cluster trim panel (see Chapter 11).

3 Disconnect the ignition switch electrical connector (see illustration).

4 Remove the plate, if equipped, underneath the steering column assembly (see illustration).

5 On models with a tilt steering column, move the tilt lever down far enough to clear the ignition switch.

6 If you're just replacing the ignition switch, remove the switch retaining screw (see illustration 7.4) and remove the switch. If you're not replacing the ignition switch, it's not necessary to remove it now in order to remove the key lock cylinder. However, if you're replacing the key lock cylinder, you'll have to remove the ignition switch after you remove the key lock cylinder and install it in the new key lock cylinder unit.

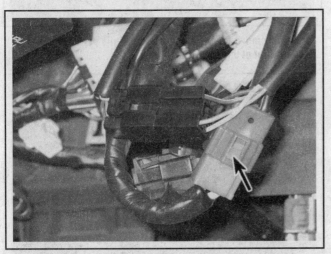

7.3 To disconnect the ignition switch electrical connector, depress this release tab and pull the two halves of the connector apart. Trace the wires from the ignition switch down to the connector to make sure that you're unplugging the right connector

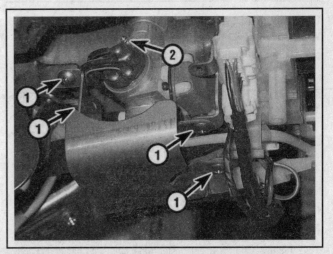

7.4 To remove the plate, if equipped, from underneath the steering column, remove these four fasteners (1) (one fastener not visible), then remove the ignition switch retaining screw (2) and pull the switch out of the key lock cylinder housing

7   If you're replacing the key lock cylinder, use a hammer and punch to unscrew the two breakaway bolts (see illustration).

➡**Note: If the bolts can't be unscrewed using this method, you'll have to drill a hole down the center of each bolt and unscrew them with a screw extractor, or use a larger drill bit and drill out the entire bolt head.**

8   Remove the ignition switch and key lock cylinder assembly.

9   If you're replacing the key lock cylinder, remove the ignition switch from the key lock cylinder assembly (see illustration 7.4).

10 Installation is the reverse of removal. When installing the lock cylinder bolts, tighten them until their heads twist off.

7.7 Using a hammer and punch, knock these breakaway bolts in a counterclockwise direction to unscrew them, remove the upper clamp and detach the key lock cylinder/ ignition switch assembly from the steering column assembly by pulling it straight down

8   Instrument panel switches - replacement

✷✷ WARNING:

The models covered by this manual are equipped with a Supplemental Restraint System (SRS), more commonly known as airbags. Always disarm the airbag system before working in the vicinity of any airbag system component to avoid the possibility of accidental deployment of the airbag, which could cause personal injury (see Section 24).

➡**Note: The procedure for removing and installing the heater and air conditioning control assembly is in Chapter 3.**

2000 THROUGH 2004 BAJA, LEGACY AND OUTBACK MODELS

Cruise control switch, fog light switch and windshield wiper de-icer switch

◗ **Refer to illustrations 8.1a, 8.1b and 8.2**

1   Carefully pry the switch panel out of the instrument panel (see illustration), pull out the panel and disconnect the electrical connectors from the switch(es) (see illustration).

2   Remove the cruise control switch, fog light switch and/or windshield wiper de-icer switch from the switch panel (see illustration).

3   When installing a switch, push it into the switch panel from the front side of the panel until it snaps into place.

4   Installation is otherwise the reverse of removal.

Hazard flasher switch

◗ **Refer to illustrations 8.5, 8.6 and 8.7**

5   Remove the instrument cluster trim panel (see Chapter 11) and disconnect the electrical connector from the hazard flasher switch (see illustration).

6   Remove the hazard flasher switch retaining screws (see illustration) and remove the switch from the instrument cluster trim panel.

8.1a To remove the switch panel, carefully pry it loose from the instrument panel . . .

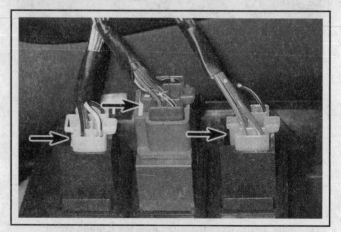

8.1b . . . then push in the release tab on each of the three electrical connectors and disconnect them

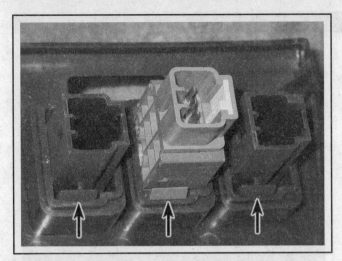

8.2 To remove a switch from the switch panel, push the locking tab toward the switch housing and push out the switch towards the front of the panel

7   Disengage the hazard flasher switch from its mounting bracket (see illustration).

8   When installing the hazard flasher switch, push it into its mounting bracket until it snaps into place.

9   Installation is otherwise the reverse of removal.

2005 AND 2006 BAJA, LEGACY AND OUTBACK MODELS

Illumination brightness control switch, remote control mirror switch, windshield wiper de-icer switch and/or Vehicle Dynamics Control OFF switch

10   All of these switches are located at the left end of the instrument panel, in the instrument panel lower cover, which must be removed (see Chapter 11) to access the switch connectors and the switch release tabs. Once the instrument panel lower cover is removed, these switches are removed in a similar fashion to the switches on earlier models.

Hazard flasher switch

11   The hazard flasher switch is located on the radio/heater and air conditioning control assembly, at the upper right corner of the assembly. Remove the console box, the console front panel and the console side garnish (see Chapter 11), then remove the radio (see Section 10).

12   Remove the hazard flasher switch from the radio trim panel.

13   Installation is the reverse of removal.

FORESTER MODELS

Fog light switch and rear window de-icer switch

14   These switches are located at the left end of the instrument panel, in the instrument panel lower cover, which must be removed (see Chapter 11) to access the switch connectors and the switch release tabs. Once the instrument panel lower cover is removed, these switches are removed in a similar fashion to the switches on 2000 through 2004 Baja, Legacy and Outback models (see illustration 8.2).

Hazard flasher switch and rear window defogger switch

2000 through 2002 models

15   The hazard flasher switch and rear window defogger switch are located in the center of the dash, right below the center vent. To replace one of these switches, remove the center panel (see Chapter 11), then remove the switch from the center panel.

2003 through 2006 models (hazard flasher switch only)

16   The hazard flasher switch is located in the center of the instrument panel, in the center vent. To replace the hazard flasher switch, remove the center panel (see Chapter 11), then remove the switch from the panel.

8.5 After detaching the instrument cluster trim panel from the instrument panel, depress this release tab and disconnect the electrical connector from the hazard flasher switch

8.6 To detach the hazard flasher switch assembly from the instrument cluster trim panel, remove these screws

8.7 To detach the hazard flasher switch from its mounting bracket, depress this release tab and push the switch out of the bracket

9 Instrument cluster - removal and installation

▶ Refer to illustrations 9.4 and 9.5

✳✳ WARNING:

The models covered by this manual are equipped with a Supplemental Restraint System (SRS), more commonly known as airbags. Always disarm the airbag system before working in the vicinity of any airbag system component to avoid the possibility of accidental deployment of the airbag, which could cause personal injury (see Section 24).

1 Disconnect the cable from the negative terminal of the battery terminal (see Chapter 5).
2 If the vehicle is equipped with a tilt steering column, lower the column to its lowest position.
3 Remove the instrument cluster trim bezel (see Chapter 11).
4 Remove the instrument cluster mounting screws (see illustration) and pull the instrument cluster out of the instrument panel.
5 Disconnect the electrical connectors from the backside of the instrument cluster (see illustration), then carefully remove the cluster.
6 Installation is the reverse of removal.

9.4 To detach the instrument cluster assembly, remove the cluster mounting screws (the number and location of the screws is slightly different on various models)

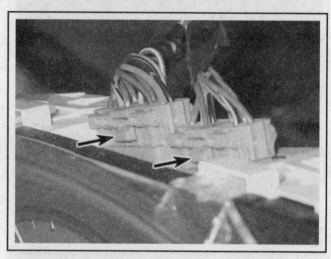

9.5 To disconnect the electrical connectors from the instrument cluster, find the release tabs, depress them and unplug the connectors from the cluster (not all release tabs are the same type or in the same location on all cluster connectors)

10 Radio and speakers - removal and installation

✳✳ WARNING:

The models covered by this manual are equipped with a Supplemental Restraint System (SRS), more commonly known as airbags. Always disarm the airbag system before working in the vicinity of any airbag system component to avoid the possibility of accidental deployment of the airbag, which could cause personal injury (see Section 24).

RADIO

2000 through 2004 Baja, Legacy and Outback models

▶ Refer to illustrations 10.3, 10.4 and 10.5

1 Disconnect the cable from the negative terminal of the battery (see Chapter 5).
2 Remove the front cover and the center panel (see Chapter 11).
3 Remove the radio mounting bracket screws (see illustration).

10.3 To detach the radio from the instrument panel, remove these four screws (2000 through 2004 Baja, Legacy and Outback models)

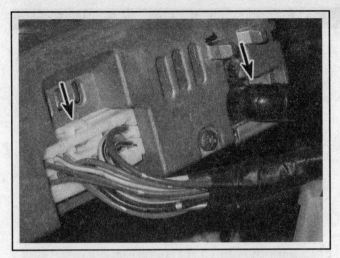

10.4 Pull out the radio assembly far enough to depress the release tab and disconnect the electrical connector, then disconnect the antenna cable and remove the radio (2000 through 2004 Baja, Legacy and Outback models)

4   Pull out the radio and mounting bracket assembly far enough to disconnect the antenna lead and electrical connectors from the backside of the radio (see illustration) and remove the radio.
5   Remove the radio from its mounting bracket (see illustration).
6   Installation is the reverse of removal.

2005 and 2006 Baja, Legacy and Outback models

▶ **Refer to illustration 10.9**

7   Disconnect the cable from the negative terminal of the battery terminal (see Chapter 5).
8   Remove the console box, the console front panel and the console side garnish (see Chapter 11).
9   Remove the radio mounting screws (see illustration).
10 Pull out the radio far enough to disconnect the antenna lead and electrical connectors from the backside of the radio and remove the radio.
11 Remove the radio from its mounting bracket (see illustration 10.5).
12 Installation is the reverse of removal.

Forester models

13 Disconnect the cable from the negative terminal of the battery terminal (see Chapter 5).
14 Remove the front cover and the center console panel (see Chapter 11).
15 Remove the radio mounting screws.
16 Pull out the radio far enough to disconnect the antenna lead and electrical connectors from the backside of the radio and remove the radio.
17 Installation is the reverse of removal.

SPEAKERS

Front door speakers

▶ **Refer to illustration 10.19**

18 Remove the front door trim panel (see Chapter 11).
19 Remove the front door speaker mounting screws (see illustration).
20 Pull out the speaker, disconnect the electrical connector and remove the speaker.
21 Installation is the reverse of removal.

Rear door speakers

22 Remove the rear door trim panel (see Chapter 11).
23 Remove the front door speaker mounting screws (see illustration 10.19).
24 Pull out the speaker, disconnect the electrical connector and remove the speaker.
25 Installation is the reverse of removal.

10.5 To detach the radio unit from its mounting bracket, remove the screws from each side (2000 through 2004 Baja, Legacy and Outback models)

10.9 To detach the radio from the instrument panel, remove these six screws (2005 and 2006 Baja, Legacy and Outback models)

10.19 To detach a front door speaker from the door, remove the speaker mounting screws

11 Antenna - removal and installation

❊❊ WARNING:

The models covered by this manual are equipped with a Supplemental Restraint System (SRS), more commonly known as airbags. Always disarm the airbag system before working in the vicinity of any airbag system component to avoid the possibility of accidental deployment of the airbag, which could cause personal injury (see Section 24).

ANTENNA MAST AND CABLE

▸ Refer to illustrations 11.1 and 11.3

➡Note: 2000 and 2001 models have a conventional antenna mast, which is mounted at the left front corner of the roof. The cable for the antenna mast is routed through the left A-pillar, down behind the left kick panel area, then under the driver's side carpet and up into the console area, where it's connected to a much shorter cable that is plugged into the backside of the radio.

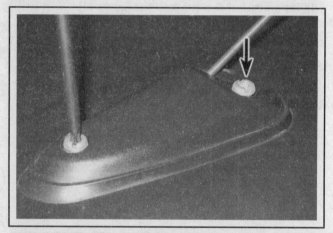

11.1 To detach the antenna base, remove these two mounting screws (2000 and 2001 models)

1 Remove the antenna base mounting screws (see illustration).
2 Remove the driver side carpeting and remove the center console left side panel (see *Center console - removal and installation* in Chapter 11).
3 Trace the antenna cable down from the A-pillar, down through the kick panel area, across the floorpan and up the left side of the center console area, where it's connected to the cable that goes to the back of the radio (see illustration). Disconnect the two cables.
4 Attach a wire to the old antenna cable, then pull the cable up through the A-pillar. Attach the wire to the new antenna cable and run it back through the A-pillar. Once the cable has been correctly routed back to the radio cable, reconnect the two cables.
5 Installation is otherwise the reverse of removal.

REAR WINDOW GRID-TYPE ANTENNA

6 2002 and later models are equipped with a rear window grid-type antenna. It's not removable. But if the antenna is damaged, you can repair it the same way that you would repair the rear window defogger (see Section 13).

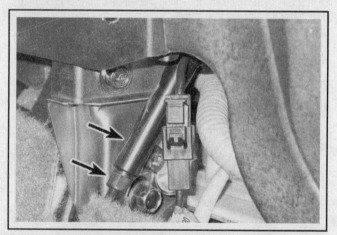

11.3 To disconnect the antenna mast cable from the antenna cable going up to the radio, simply pull the two halves of the connector apart (2000 and 2001 models)

12 Wiper motors - replacement

FRONT WIPER MOTOR AND LINKAGE

▸ Refer to illustrations 12.2, 12.3, 12.4, 12.7, 12.8 and 12.9

1 Disconnect the cable from the negative terminal of the battery terminal (see Chapter 5).
2 Remove the protective cap from each windshield wiper arm (see illustration).
3 Remove the nut that secures each wiper arm to its shaft (see illustration).
4 Mark the relationship of each wiper arm to its shaft (see illustration).
5 Remove the wiper arms.
6 Remove the cowl cover (see Chapter 11).

12.2 Carefully pry off the protective cap from each windshield wiper arm

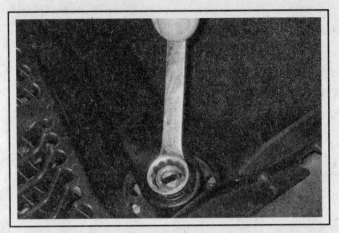

12.3 Remove the nut that secures each wiper arm to its shaft

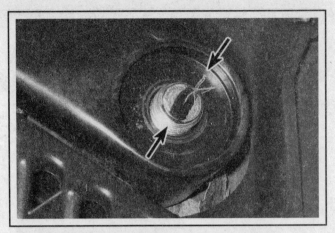

12.4 Before removing each wiper arm, mark the relationship of the arm to its shaft to ensure correct alignment when it's reinstalled

7   Disconnect the electrical connector from the wiper motor (see illustration).

8   Remove the wiper motor and linkage assembly retaining bolts and nut (see illustration) and remove the wiper motor and linkage assembly from the cowl.

9   Separate the wiper motor from the linkage assembly (see illustration).

10   Installation is the reverse of removal.

REAR WIPER MOTOR (WAGON MODELS)

♦ Refer to illustrations 12.15a and 12.15b

11   Disconnect the cable from the negative terminal of the battery terminal (see Chapter 5).

12   Flip up the wiper arm cover.

13   Remove the nut that secures the wiper arm to the motor shaft.

14   Mark the relationship of the wiper arm to its shaft (see illustration 12.4).

15   Remove the wiper arm (see illustrations). Note the installation sequence of the spacers and cushion used on Forester models and on 2000 through 2004 Legacy and Outback models. These parts must be installed in the correct sequence when installing the rear wiper arm.

16   Remove the liftgate trim panel (see Chapter 11).

17   Disconnect the electrical connector from the wiper motor.

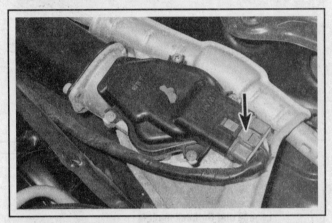

12.7 To disconnect the electrical connector from the windshield wiper motor, depress the release tab and pull off the connector

18   Remove the wiper motor mounting bolts and remove the motor from the liftgate.

19   Installation is the reverse of removal.

12.8 To detach the windshield wiper motor and linkage assembly, remove the nut from the firewall and the two mounting bolts from the left end of the assembly

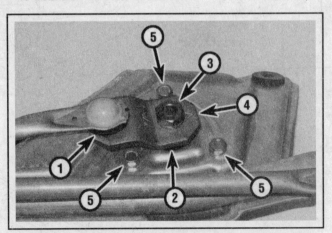

12.9 To detach the motor from the linkage assembly, pry off the linkage arm (1) from the crank arm (2), remove the crank arm nut (3), mark the relationship of the arrow (4) on the crank arm with the mounting bracket, remove the crank arm, then remove the motor mounting bolts (5)

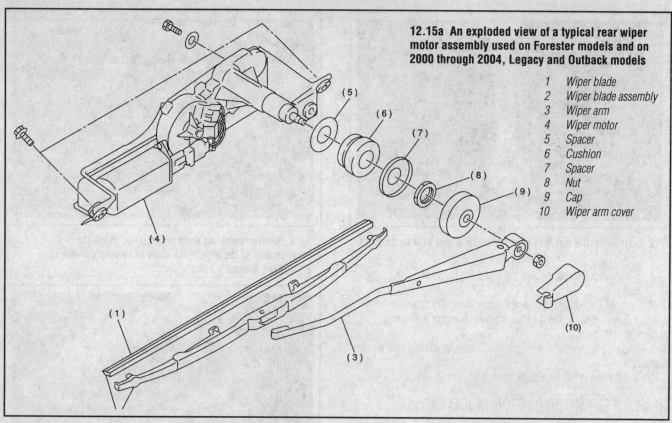

12.15a An exploded view of a typical rear wiper motor assembly used on Forester models and on 2000 through 2004, Legacy and Outback models

1. Wiper blade
2. Wiper blade assembly
3. Wiper arm
4. Wiper motor
5. Spacer
6. Cushion
7. Spacer
8. Nut
9. Cap
10. Wiper arm cover

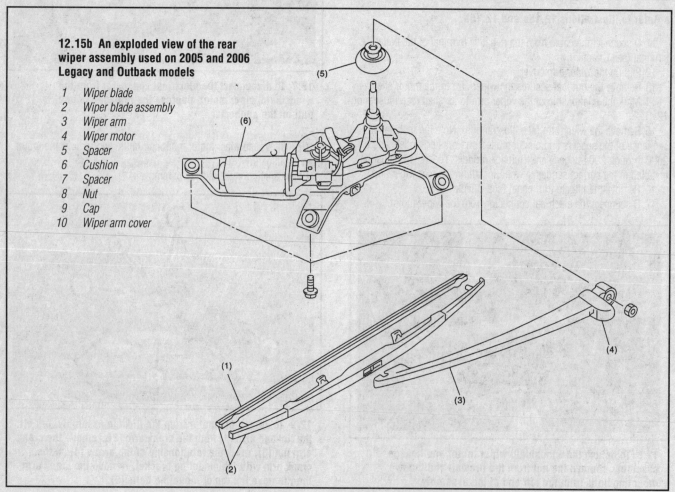

12.15b An exploded view of the rear wiper assembly used on 2005 and 2006 Legacy and Outback models

1. Wiper blade
2. Wiper blade assembly
3. Wiper arm
4. Wiper motor
5. Spacer
6. Cushion
7. Spacer
8. Nut
9. Cap
10. Wiper arm cover

13 Rear window defogger - check and repair

1   The rear window defogger consists of a number of horizontal elements baked onto the glass surface.

2   Small breaks in the element can be repaired without removing the rear window.

CHECK

▶ **Refer to illustrations 13.4, 13.5 and 13.7**

3   Turn the ignition switch and defogger system switches to the ON position. Using a voltmeter, place the positive probe against the defogger grid positive terminal and the negative probe against the ground terminal. If battery voltage is not indicated, check the fuse, defogger switch and related wiring. If voltage is indicated, but all or part of the defogger doesn't heat, proceed with the following tests.

4   When measuring voltage during these tests, wrap a piece of aluminum foil around the tip of the voltmeter positive probe and press the foil against the heating element with your finger (see illustration). Place the negative probe on the defogger grid ground terminal.

5   Check the voltage at the center of each heating element (see illustration). If the voltage is 5 or 6-volts, the element is okay (there is no break). If there is not voltage, the element is broken between the center of the element and the positive end. If the voltage is 10 to 12 volts the element is broken between the center of the element and ground. Check each heating element.

6   Connect the negative lead to a good body ground. The reading should stay the same. If it doesn't, the ground connection is bad.

7   To find the break, place the voltmeter negative probe against the defogger ground terminal. Place the voltmeter positive probe with the foil strip against the heating element at the positive terminal end and slide it toward the negative terminal end. The point at which the voltmeter deflects from several volts to zero is the point at which the heating element is broken (see illustration).

REPAIR

▶ **Refer to illustration 13.13**

8   Repair the break in the element using a repair kit specifically

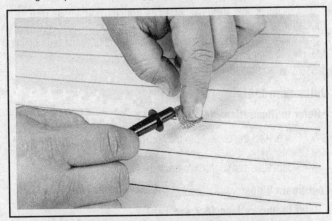

13.4 When measuring the voltage at the rear window defogger grid, wrap a piece of aluminum foil around the positive probe of the voltmeter and press the foil against the wire with your finger

13.5 To determine if a heating element has broken, check the voltage at the center of each element; if the voltage is 5 or 6-volts, the element is unbroken, but if the voltage is 10 or 12-volts, the element is broken between the center and the ground side. If there is no voltage, the element is broken between the center and the positive side

13.7 To find the break, place the voltmeter negative lead against the defogger ground terminal, place the voltmeter positive lead with the foil strip against the heating element at the positive terminal end and slide it toward the negative terminal end. The point at which the voltmeter reading changes abruptly is the point at which the element is broken

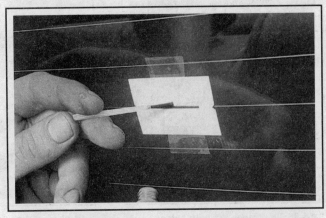

13.13 To use a defogger repair kit, apply masking tape to the inside of the window at the damaged area, then brush on the special conductive coating

recommended for this purpose, available at most auto parts stores. Included in this kit is plastic conductive epoxy.

9 Prior to repairing a break, turn off the system and allow it to cool off for a few minutes.

10 Lightly buff the element area with fine steel wool, then clean it thoroughly with rubbing alcohol.

11 Use masking tape to mask off the area being repaired.

12 Thoroughly mix the epoxy, following the instructions provided with the repair kit.

13 Apply the epoxy material to the slit in the masking tape, overlapping the undamaged area about 3/4-inch on either end (see illustration).

14 Allow the repair to cure for 24 hours before removing the tape and using the system.

14 Headlight bulbs - replacement

✵✵ WARNING:

Halogen gas-filled bulbs are under pressure and may shatter if the surface is scratched or the bulb is dropped. Wear eye protection and handle the bulbs carefully, grasping only the base whenever possible. Do not touch the surface of the bulb with your fingers because the oil from your skin could cause it to overheat and fail prematurely. If you do touch the bulb surface, clean it with rubbing alcohol.

14.2 To disconnect the electrical connector from the headlight bulb holder, depress the release tab and pull off the connector (2000 through 2003 Legacy models)

2000 THROUGH 2004 LEGACY AND OUTBACK MODELS

Legacy models

⬧ **Refer to illustrations 14.2, 14.3a and 14.3b**

1 Disconnect the cable from the negative terminal of the battery (see Chapter 5).

2 Disconnect the electrical connector from the bulb holder (see illustration).

3 Rotate the lock ring counterclockwise and remove the bulb holder from the headlight housing (see illustrations).

4 Installation is the reverse of removal.

Outback models

⬧ **Refer to illustrations 14.6a and 14.6b**

5 Disconnect the cable from the negative terminal of the battery (see Chapter 5).

6 Remove the headlight bulb cover (see illustrations).

Low-beam bulbs

⬧ **Refer to illustrations 14.7 and 14.8**

7 Disconnect the electrical connector with the black wire (see illustration).

8 Remove the retainer spring (see illustration).

9 Replace the low beam bulb.

10 Installation is the reverse of removal.

14.3a To remove the bulb holder, rotate the lock ring counterclockwise . . .

14.3b . . . then pull the bulb holder out of the headlight housing (2000 through 2003 Legacy models)

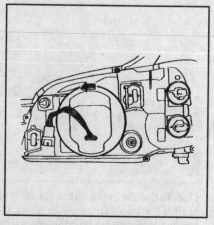

14.6a To remove the headlight cover, turn it counterclockwise . . .

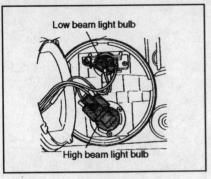

14.6b . . . and pull it off to access the high beam and low beam bulbs

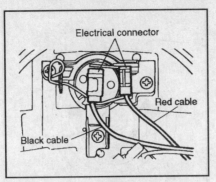

14.7 There are two connectors, one with a black wire and the other with a red wire. Disconnect the connector with the black wire

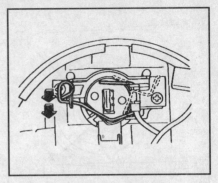

14.8 To disengage the retainer spring, push down the left end

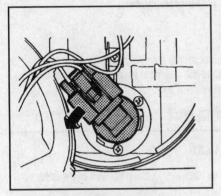

14.12 To remove the bulb holder from the headlight housing, turn it counterclockwise

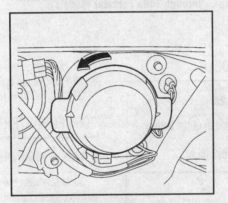

14.17 To remove the bulb cover, rotate it counterclockwise (2005 and 2006 Baja, Legacy and Outback models)

14.18 To replace a low beam bulb, disconnect the electrical connector and disengage the retainer spring (2005 and 2006 Baja, Legacy and Outback models)

High-beam bulbs

▶ Refer to illustration 14.12

11 Disconnect the electrical connector from the bulb holder.

12 Remove the bulb holder from the headlight housing by turning it counterclockwise (see illustration).

13 Carefully insert the new bulb into the housing. Make sure that you don't touch the bulb with your fingers.

14 Turn the bulb holder clockwise to lock it in place.

15 Reconnect the electrical connector.

2005 AND 2006 LEGACY AND OUTBACK MODELS

16 Disconnect the cable from the negative terminal of the battery (see Chapter 5).

Low-beam bulbs

▶ Refer to illustrations 14.17 and 14.18

17 Remove the bulb cover (see illustration).

18 Disconnect the electrical connector and disengage the retainer spring (see illustration).

19 Remove the old bulb and install a new one.

20 Installation is the reverse of removal.

High-beam bulbs

▶ Refer to illustration 14.21

21 Disconnect the electrical connector from the bulb (see illustration).

22 Remove the bulb from the headlight housing by turning it counterclockwise.

23 Install a new bulb. Make sure that you don't touch the glass with your fingers.

24 Installation is the reverse of removal.

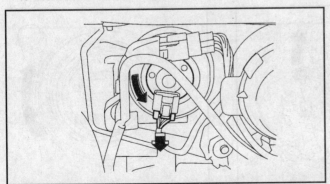

14.21 To replace a high beam bulb, disconnect the electrical connector, then rotate the bulb counterclockwise and remove it from the headlight housing (2005 and 2006 Baja, Legacy and Outback models)

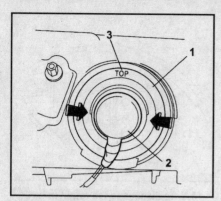

14.26 Remove the rubber cover (1) and disconnect the electrical connector (2). When installing the rubber cover, make sure that the TOP mark (3) is at 12 o'clock (2000 through 2005 Forester models)

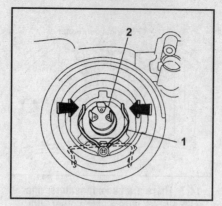

14.27 Disengage the retainer spring (1) to release the bulb (2) (2000 through 2005 Forester models)

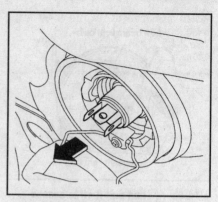

14.28 To remove the bulb from the headlight housing, pull it straight back (2000 through 2005 Forester models)

2000 THROUGH 2005 FORESTER MODELS

♦ Refer to illustrations 14.26, 14.27 and 14.28

25 Disconnect the cable from the negative terminal of the battery (see Chapter 5).

26 Disconnect the electrical connector (see illustration).

14.31 If you're replacing the low- or high-beam bulb on the left side headlight housing, remove the screw that retains the windshield washer nozzle, then set the windshield washer nozzle aside (2006 Forester models)

27 Disengage the retainer spring (see illustration).

28 Remove the bulb from the headlight assembly (see illustration).

29 Installation is the reverse of removal.

2006 FORESTER MODELS

♦ Refer to illustration 14.31

30 Disconnect the cable from the negative terminal of the battery terminal (see Chapter 5).

31 If you're replacing the low- or high-beam bulb on the left side headlight housing, remove the screw (see illustration) that retains the windshield washer fluid reservoir, then set the fluid reservoir aside.

Low-beam bulbs

♦ Refer to illustrations 14.32 and 14.33

✳✳ WARNING:

Canadian-spec XT models use high-intensity-discharge (HID) bulbs for the low beam bulbs. HID bulbs use an extremely high voltage. To avoid the risk of an electric shock and serious injury, do not attempt to replace these bulbs at home. Do not try to replace the high-beam bulbs either. And don't try to remove and

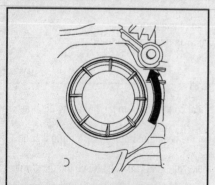

14.32 To remove the bulb cover, rotate it counterclockwise (2006 Forester models)

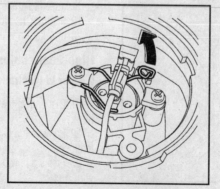

14.33 Disengage the bulb retainer spring, then pull out the bulb and the electrical connector unit (2006 Forester models)

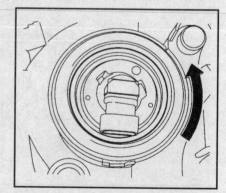

14.38 To remove the high-beam bulb from the headlight housing, turn it counterclockwise

install the headlight housing on these models. Instead, if the headlight housing, high-beam bulb or low-beam bulb needs service, have it done by a Subaru dealer or other qualified repair shop.

32 Remove the bulb cover (see illustration).

33 Disengage the bulb retainer spring (see illustration), then pull out the bulb and the electrical connector unit.

34 Disconnect the electrical connector from the bulb.

35 Install the new bulb in the electrical connector by pushing it straight into the connector.

36 Installation is otherwise the reverse of removal

High-beam bulbs

▶ **Refer to illustration 14.38**

37 Disconnect the electrical connector from the bulb.

38 Remove the bulb from the headlight housing (see illustration).

39 Installation is the reverse of removal.

15 Headlight housings - removal and installation

✳✳ WARNING 1:

Canadian-spec XT models use high-intensity-discharge (HID) bulbs for the low beam bulbs. HID bulbs use an extremely high voltage. To avoid the risk of an electric shock and serious injury, do not attempt to replace these bulbs at home. Do not try to replace the high-beam bulbs either. And don't try to remove and install the headlight housing on these models. Instead, if the headlight housing, high-beam bulb or low-beam bulb needs service, have it done by a Subaru dealer.

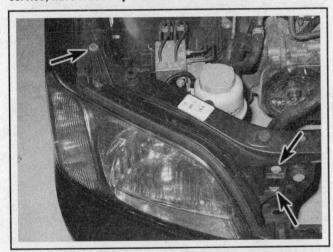

15.4a To detach the headlight housing from a 2000 through 2004 Baja, Legacy or Outback model, remove these bolts . . .

15.4b . . . then pull out the headlight housing and disconnect all electrical connectors

✳✳ WARNING 2:

Many of these vehicles are equipped with halogen gas-filled headlight bulbs, which are under pressure and may shatter if the surface is damaged or the bulb is dropped. Wear eye protection and handle the bulbs carefully, grasping only the base whenever possible. Do not touch the surface of the bulb with your fingers because the oil from your skin could cause it to overheat and fail prematurely. If you do touch the bulb surface, clean it with rubbing alcohol.

2000 THROUGH 2004 BAJA, LEGACY AND OUTBACK MODELS

▶ **Refer to illustrations 15.4a and 15.4b**

1 Disconnect the cable from the negative terminal of the battery terminal (see Chapter 5).

2 If you're removing the right headlight housing, remove the air intake duct (see *Air filter housing - removal and installation* in Chapter 4).

3 Disconnect the electrical connector(s) from the headlight bulb(s) (see Section 14) and from the parking, turn signal and sidemarker light bulbs. (If you can't reach all of the connectors at this time, you can disconnect the rest of the connectors after pulling out the headlight housing.)

4 Remove the three headlight housing mounting bolts (see illustration), pull out the housing and disconnect any other electrical connectors from the housing (see illustration).

5 Installation is the reverse of removal. Adjust the headlight when you're done (see Section 16).

2005 AND 2005 BAJA, LEGACY AND OUTBACK MODELS

▶ **Refer to illustration 15.10**

6 Disconnect the cable from the negative terminal of the battery terminal (see Chapter 5).

7 If you're removing the right headlight housing, remove the air intake duct (see *Air filter housing - removal and installation* in Chapter 4).

8 Remove the front grille and the front bumper cover (see Chapter 11).

9 Disconnect the electrical connectors from the headlight bulbs (see Section 14) and from the parking, turn signal and sidemarker light

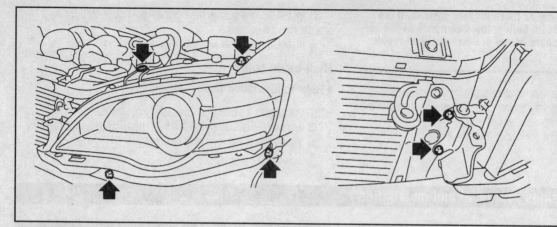

15.10 To detach the headlight housing on 2005 and 2006 Baja, Legacy and Outback models, remove these five bolts and the single clip

bulbs. (If you can't reach all of the connectors at this time, you can disconnect the rest of the connectors after pulling out the headlight housing.)

10 Remove the five headlight housing mounting bolts and disengage the single clip (see illustration), then pull out the headlight housing and, if you haven't already done so, disconnect all electrical connectors.

11 Installation is the reverse of removal.

2000 THROUGH 2005 FORESTER MODELS

▶ **Refer to illustration 15.16**

12 Disconnect the cable from the negative terminal of the battery terminal (see Chapter 5).

13 If you're removing the right headlight housing, remove the air intake duct (see *Air filter housing - removal and installation* in Chapter 4).

14 Remove the front grille and the headlight side cover (see Chapter 11).

15 Disconnect the electrical connectors from the headlight bulb (see Section 14) and from the parking, turn signal and sidemarker light bulbs. (If you can't reach all of the connectors at this time, you can disconnect the rest of the connectors after pulling out the headlight housing.)

16 Remove the three headlight housing mounting bolts (see illustration), then pull out the headlight housing and disconnect all electrical connectors.

17 Installation is the reverse of removal.

2006 FORESTER MODELS

▶ **Refer to illustrations 15.21**

18 Disconnect the cable from the negative terminal of the battery terminal (see Chapter 5).

19 If you're removing the right headlight housing, remove the air intake duct (see *Air filter housing - removal and installation* in Chapter 4).

20 Remove the front bumper cover (see Chapter 11).

21 Remove the four headlight housing mounting bolts (see illustration), then pull out the headlight housing and disconnect all electrical connectors.

22 Installation is the reverse of removal.

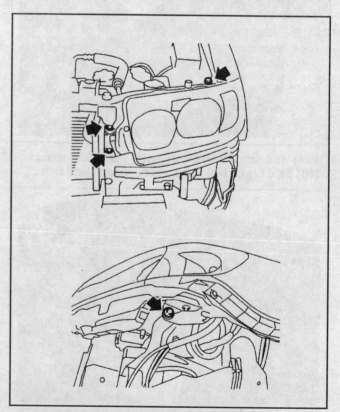

15.21 To detach the headlight housing on 2006 Forester models, remove these four bolts

15.16 To detach the headlight housing on 2000 through 2005 Forester models, remove these three bolts

16 Headlights - adjustment

▶ Refer to illustrations 16.1a, 16.1b and 16.3

→Note: The headlights must be aimed correctly. If adjusted incorrectly they could blind the driver of an oncoming vehicle and cause a serious accident or seriously reduce your ability to see the road. The headlights should be checked for proper aim every 12 months and any time a new headlight is installed or front end bodywork is performed. It should be emphasized that the following procedure is only an interim step that will provide temporary adjustment until a properly equipped shop can adjust the headlights.

1   Each headlight has a single adjusting screw for adjusting up-and-down movement (see illustrations).

2   There are several methods for adjusting the headlights. The simplest method requires a blank wall 25 feet in front of the vehicle and a level floor.

3   Position masking tape vertically on the wall in reference to the vehicle centerline and the centerlines of both headlights (see illustration).

4   Position a horizontal tape line in reference to the centerline of all the headlights.

→Note: It might be easier to position the tape on the wall with the vehicle parked only a few inches away.

5   Adjustment should be made with the vehicle sitting level, the gas tank half-full and no unusually heavy load in the vehicle.

6   Starting with the low beam adjustment, position the high intensity zone so it is two inches below the horizontal line and two inches to the right of the headlight vertical line. Adjustment is made by turning the adjusting screw to raise or lower the beam.

7   With the high beams on, the high intensity zone should be vertically centered with the exact center just below the horizontal line.

→Note: It might not be possible to position the headlight aim exactly for both high and low beams. If a compromise must be made, keep in mind that the low beams are the most used and have the greatest effect on driver safety.

8   Have the headlights adjusted by a dealer service department or service station at the earliest opportunity.

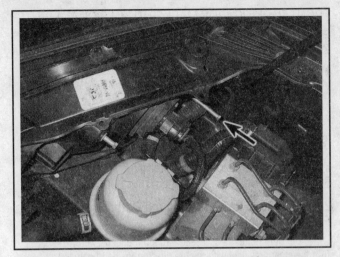

16.1a Headlight adjustment screw location - 2000 through 2004 Baja, Legacy and Outback models (2000 through 2005 Forester models similar)

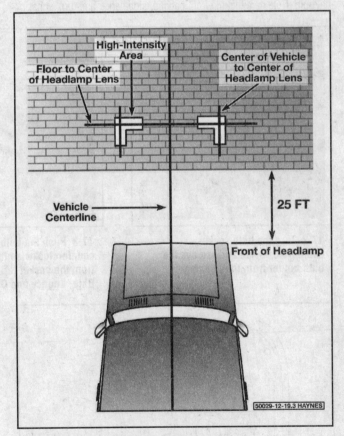

16.3 Headlight adjustment details

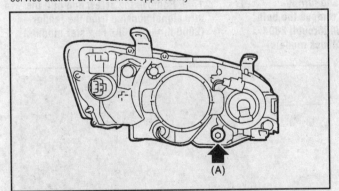

16.1b Headlight adjustment screw location - 2005 and 2006 Baja, Legacy and Outback models and 2006 Forester models

17 Bulb replacement

FRONT PARKING/SIDE MARKER/TURN SIGNAL LIGHTS

2000 through 2004 Baja, Legacy and Outback models

▶ **Refer to illustrations 17.2 and 17.3**

1 Remove the headlight housing (see Section 15).
2 Turn the bulb socket counterclockwise (see illustration).
3 Push the bulb and turn it counterclockwise to remove the bulb from the socket (see illustration).
4 Installation is the reverse of removal. Be sure to check the headlight adjustment after the headlight housing has been installed (see Section 16).

2005 and 2006 Baja, Legacy and Outback and 2006 Forester models

5 The bulb holder is accessed through the fenderwell. Turn the steering wheel with the tire directed inside to gain access to the front of the fenderwell.
6 Partially remove the inner fenderwell to access the bulb holder.
7 Turn the socket counterclockwise and remove the front turn signal bulb. Note here that the front parking, sidemarker and turn signal

bulb is the same.
8 Installation is the reverse of removal.

2000 through 2002 Forester models

▶ **Refer to illustration 17.9**

9 Remove the screw and pull the turn signal housing from the fender (see illustration).
10 Turn the bulb holder counterclockwise and remove it from the housing.
11 Remove the bulb from the bulb holder socket.
12 Installation is the reverse of the removal.

2003 through 2005 Forester models

▶ **Refer to illustration 17.14**

13 Remove the front headlight housing (see Section 15).
14 Turn the bulb and remove the bulb from the socket (see illustration).
15 Installation is the reverse of removal. Be sure to check the headlight adjustment after the headlight housing has been installed (see Section 16).

17.2 Turn the bulb socket counterclockwise and remove the bulb holder from the housing

17.3 Push the bulb and turn it counterclockwise to remove the bulb from the socket (2000 through 2004 Baja, Legacy and Outback models)

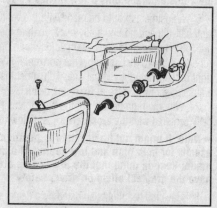

17.9 Remove the screw and pull the turn signal housing from the fender (2000 through 2002 Forester models)

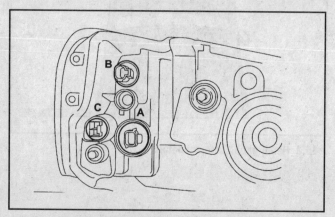

17.14 Location of the front turn signal light (A), the parking light (B) and the front side marker light (C) bulbs (2003 through 2005 Forester models)

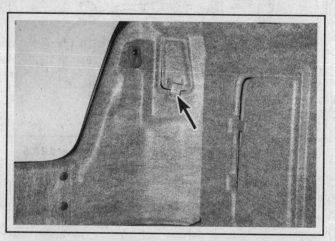

17.16 Lift the cover up for bulb access (2000 through 2004 Baja, Legacy and Outback models)

17.17 Location of the rear turn signal light bulb (A) and the brake/tail light bulb (B) (2000 through 2004 Baja, Legacy and Outback models)

17.18 Push the turn signal bulb and turn it counterclockwise to remove it

17.19 Pull the rear turn brake/tail light bulb out of the socket

REAR SIDE MARKER/BRAKE/TURN SIGNAL LIGHTS

2000 through 2004 Baja, Legacy and Outback models

Sedan models

▶ Refer to illustrations 17.16, 17.17, 17.18 and 17.19

16 Open the trunk lid and remove the rear combination light cover (see illustration).

17 Turn the bulb holder counterclockwise and remove it from the housing (see illustration).

18 To remove the turn signal bulb, push the bulb and turn it counterclockwise (see illustration).

19 To remove the brake light bulb, pull the bulb out of the socket (see illustration).

20 Installation is the reverse of the removal.

Station wagon models

▶ Refer to illustrations 17.21, 17.22 and 17.24

21 Use a flat-bladed screwdriver and pry the service hole covers open (see illustration).

22 Remove the upper and lower mounting nuts, slide the combination light assembly to the rear and remove it from the vehicle (see illustration).

23 Remove the screws that retain the cover to the light assembly,

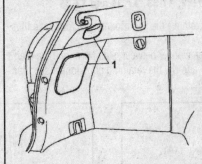

17.21 Location of the service hole covers for the rear turn signal and brake light bulbs on a station wagon

then remove the cover.

24 Turn the bulb holder counterclockwise and remove it from the housing (see illustration).

25 To remove the turn signal bulb, pull the bulb out of the socket.

26 To remove the brake light bulb, push the bulb and turn it counterclockwise.

27 Installation is the reverse of the removal.

2005 and 2006 Baja, Legacy and Outback

Sedan models

▶ Refer to illustration 17.29

28 Push the knobs to remove the tail light cover.

29 Turn the bulb holder counterclockwise and remove it from the housing (see illustration).

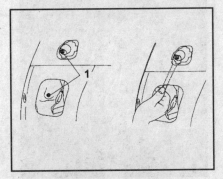

17.22 Remove the upper and lower nuts (1) and slide the rear combination light assembly to the rear of the body for removal

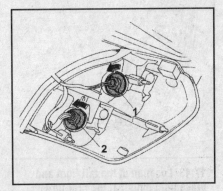

17.24 Location of the rear turn signal light bulb (1) and the brake light bulb (2)

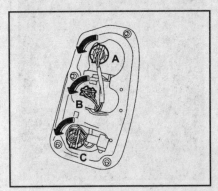

17.29 Location of the rear turn signal bulb (A), the back-up light bulb (B) and the brake/tail/side marker bulb (C)

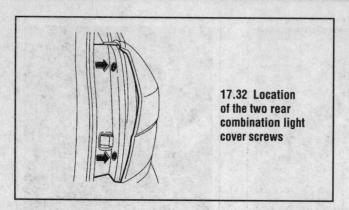

17.32 Location of the two rear combination light cover screws

30 To remove a bulb, push the bulb and turn it counterclockwise.
31 Installation is the reverse of removal.

Station wagons

▶ Refer to illustrations 17.32, 17.33, 17.34 and 17.35

32 Raise the liftgate and remove the two mounting screws (see illustration).

33 Insert a flat-bladed screwdriver between side cover and the rear combination light assembly and pry the retaining clips loose (see illustration).

34 Remove the upper and lower mounting screws and pull the assembly from the body to access the bulbs (see illustration).
35 Turn the bulb holder counterclockwise and remove it from the housing (see illustration).
36 To remove a bulb, push the bulb and turn it counterclockwise.
37 Installation is the reverse of removal.

2000 through 2002 Forester models

38 Working in the rear compartment, pull the knob to release the rear light cover.
39 Turn the bulb holder counterclockwise and remove it from the housing.
40 To remove a bulb, push the bulb and turn it counterclockwise.
41 Installation is the reverse of removal.

2003 through 2006 Forester

▶ Refer to illustrations 17.42 and 17.43

42 Remove the rear combination light assembly mounting screws (see illustration). Pull the assembly out to access the bulbs.
43 Turn the bulb holder counterclockwise and remove it from the housing (see illustration).
44 Pull the bulb from the holder.
45 Installation is the reverse of the removal.

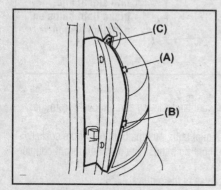

17.33 Insert a flat-bladed screwdriver between side cover and the rear combination light side cover at point A, then B, then C (in that order) (2005 and 2006 Legacy and Outback station wagon models)

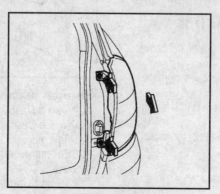

17.34 Location of the two rear combination light mounting screws (2005 and 2006 Legacy and Outback station wagon models)

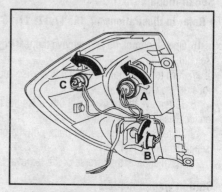

17.35 Location of the rear brake/tail light bulb (A), the turn signal bulb (B) and the rear side marker (C) (2005 and 2006 Legacy and Outback station wagon models)

17.42 Remove the two mounting screws (2003 through 2006 Forester)

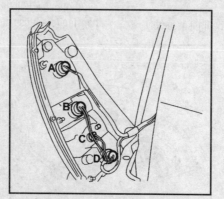

17.43 Location of the tail light and brake light bulb (A), the rear turn signal bulb (B), the back-up light bulb (C) and the tail light and brake light bulb (D)

17.46 Press the tab and pivot the cover down to release the hinges

17.47 Location of the back-up light bulb (A) and the brake/tail light bulb (B)

BRAKE/BACK-UP LIGHTS (IN TRUNK LID OR LIFTGATE)

2000 through 2004 Baja, Legacy and Outback models

▶ Refer to illustrations 17.46 and 17.47

46 Remove the light cover by pressing the tab and pivoting the cover down to release the hinges (see illustration).

➡Note: On station wagon models, move the knob up and open the cover.

47 Turn the bulb holder counterclockwise and remove it from the housing (see illustration).

48 To remove a bulb, push the bulb and turn it counterclockwise.

49 Installation is the reverse of removal.

2005 and 2006 Baja, Legacy and Outback station wagons

50 Use a flat-bladed screwdriver to remove the bulb cover from the top of the left side rear gate trim.

51 Turn the bulb holder counterclockwise and remove it from the housing.

52 Pull the bulb out of the socket.

53 Installation is the reverse of removal.

2000 through 2002 Forester models

54 Use a flat-bladed screwdriver to remove the light bulb cover located on the liftgate.

55 Turn the bulb holder counterclockwise and remove it from the housing.

56 Pull the bulb out of the socket.

57 Installation is the reverse of removal.

HIGH-MOUNT BRAKE LIGHTS

2000 through 2004 Baja/Legacy/Outback and all Forester models

Sedan models

▶ Refer to illustration 17.58

58 Pry the edge of the high mount brake light cover with a screwdriver (see illustration).

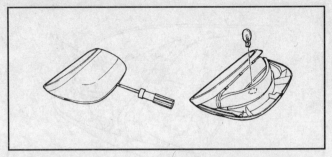

17.58 Pry the edge of the high-mount brake light cover with a screwdriver

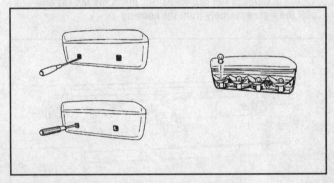

17.61 First remove the plastic screw covers to access the screws

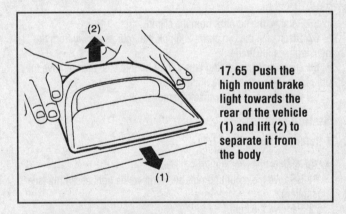

17.65 Push the high mount brake light towards the rear of the vehicle (1) and lift (2) to separate it from the body

59 Pull the bulb from the socket.

60 Installation is the reverse of the removal.

Station wagon and Forester models

▶ Refer to illustration 17.61

61 Pry the mounting screw plastic covers with a flat-bladed screwdriver (see illustration).

62 Remove the mounting screws using a Phillips screwdriver and remove the high mount brake light cover.

63 Pull the bulb from the socket.

64 Installation is the reverse of the removal.

2005 and 2006 Baja/Legacy and Outback models

Sedans

▶ Refer to illustrations 17.65, 17.67 and 17.68

65 Push the high mount brake light towards the rear of the vehicle, raise the rear of the assembly and remove the mounting clips (see illustration).

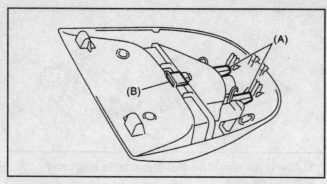

17.67 Disengage the two claws (A), press the tab (B) and pull the light assembly from the housing

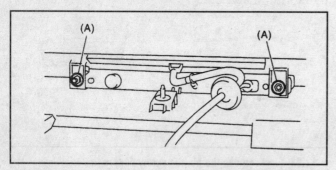

17.71 Location of the high-mount brake light mounting nuts

66 Remove the harness from the clamp.

67 Disengage the two claws and pull the light assembly from the housing (see illustration).

68 Disengage the locking tabs to pull off the lens, then remove the bulb from the housing (see illustration).

69 Installation is the reverse of removal.

Station wagons

◆ Refer to illustration 17.71

70 Remove the roof spoiler.

71 Remove the mounting nuts and remove the light assembly (see illustration).

72 Remove the bulb.

73 Installation is the reverse of removal.

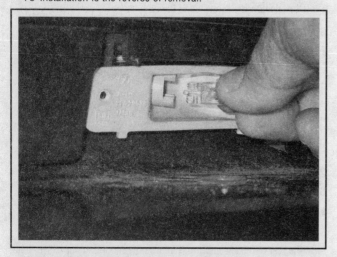

17.76 Pull the bulb straight out from the holder

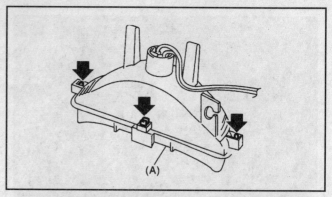

17.68 Disengage the locking tabs, take off the lens, then remove the bulb from the housing

17.74 Location of the license plate light lens screws

LICENSE PLATE LIGHT

◆ Refer to illustrations 17.74 and 17.76

74 Remove the license plate light retaining screws (see illustration).

75 Separate the lens from the housing.

76 Remove the bulb from its socket by pulling it straight out (see illustration).

77 Installation is the reverse of removal.

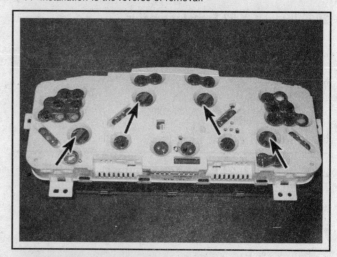

17.79 Location of the instrument cluster bulbs

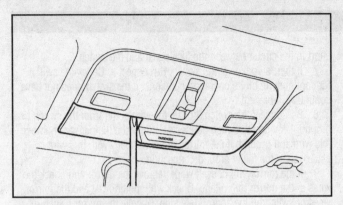

17.81 Pry the lens from the housing

17.82 It may be necessary to turn the bulb until the flat surfaces at the ends are aligned vertically. Pull the bulb straight out.

INSTRUMENT CLUSTER LIGHTS

▶ **Refer to illustration 17.79**

78 Remove the instrument cluster (see Section 9).
79 Rotate the bulb holder counterclockwise to remove it (see illustration).
80 Installation is the reverse of removal.

INTERIOR LIGHTS AND DOME LIGHTS

▶ **Refer to illustrations 17.81 and 17.82**

81 Pry the interior lens off the interior light housing (see illustration).
82 Detach the bulb from the terminals (see illustration). It may be necessary to turn the bulb until the flat surfaces at the ends are aligned vertically. Pull the bulb straight out.
83 Installation is the reverse of removal.

18 Horn - replacement

▶ **Refer to illustrations 18.1 and 18.2**

1   The horns are located in front of the radiator and, if equipped, the air conditioning condenser (see illustration).

2   To replace either horn, disconnect the electrical connector (see illustration) and remove the bracket bolt.
3   Detach the horn from its mounting bracket.
4   Installation is the reverse of removal.

18.1 Typically, the horns are located on small mounting brackets that are bolted to the vertical support in front of the radiator and condenser. To detach a horn, simply remove the mounting bracket bolt

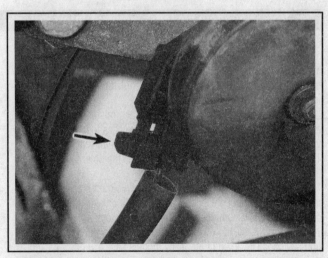

18.2 To disconnect the electrical connector from a horn, depress the release tab and pull off the connector

19 Electric side view mirrors - general information

1   Most electric rear view mirrors use two motors to move the glass; one for up and down adjustments and one for left-right adjustments.

2   The control switch has a selector portion that sends voltage to the left or right side mirror. With the ignition ON but the engine OFF, roll down the windows and operate the mirror control switch through all functions (left-right and up-down) for both the left and right side mirrors.

3   Listen carefully for the sound of the electric motors running in the mirrors.

4   If the motors can be heard but the mirror glass doesn't move, there's probably a problem with the drive mechanism inside the mirror.

5   If the mirrors don't operate and no sound comes from the mirrors, check the fuse.

6   If the fuse is OK, remove the mirror control switch from its mounting without disconnecting the wires attached to it. Turn the ignition ON and check for voltage at the switch. There should be voltage at one terminal. If there's no voltage at the switch, check for an open or short in the circuit between the fuse panel and the switch.

7   If there's voltage at the switch, disconnect it. Check the switch for continuity in all its operating positions. If the switch does not have continuity, replace it.

8   Re-connect the switch. Locate the wire going from the switch to ground. Leaving the switch connected, connect a jumper wire between this wire and ground. If the mirror works normally with this wire in place, repair the faulty ground connection.

9   If the mirror still doesn't work, remove the mirror and check the wires at the mirror for voltage. Check with ignition ON and the mirror selector switch on the appropriate side. Operate the mirror switch in all its positions. There should be voltage at one of the switch-to-mirror wires in each switch position (except the neutral "off" position).

10   If there's not voltage in each switch position, check the circuit between the mirror and control switch for opens and shorts.

11   If there's voltage, remove the mirror and test it off the vehicle with jumper wires. Replace the mirror if it fails this test.

20 Cruise control system - general information

1   On non-turbocharged and non-ULEV models, the cruise control system maintains vehicle speed with a PCM-controlled servo located in the engine compartment, which is connected to the throttle body by a cable. The system consists of the cruise control unit, brake switch, control switches, vacuum hose and vehicle speed sensor. Some features of the system require special testers and diagnostic procedures that are beyond the scope of this manual. Listed below are some general procedures that may be used to locate common problems. Turbocharged and ULEV models have an electronic throttle body and do not use a cruise control cable (the PCM is in direct control of the electronic throttle body).

2   Locate and check the fuses (see Section 3).

3   Check the brake light switch (see Chapter 9).

4   Visually inspect the control cable between the actuator assembly and throttle body for free movement, replace it if necessary.

5   Check for trouble codes (see Chapter 6).

6   Test drive the vehicle to determine if the cruise control is now working. If it isn't, take it to an automotive electrical specialist for further diagnosis.

21 Power window system - general information

1   The power window system operates electric motors, mounted in the doors, which lower and raise the windows. The system consists of the control switches, relays, the motors, regulators and associated wiring.

2   The power windows can be lowered and raised from the master control switch by the driver or by remote switches located at the individual windows. Each window has a separate motor that is reversible. The position of the control switch determines the polarity and therefore the direction of operation.

3   The circuit is protected by a fuse and a circuit breaker. Each motor is also equipped with an internal circuit breaker, this prevents one stuck window from disabling the whole system.

4   The power window system will only operate when the ignition switch is ON. In addition, many models have a window lockout switch at the master control switch which, when activated, disables the switches at the rear windows and, sometimes, the switch at the passenger's window also. Always check these items before troubleshooting a window problem.

5   These procedures are general in nature, so if you can't find the problem using them, take the vehicle to a dealer service department or other properly equipped repair facility.

6   If the power windows won't operate, always check the fuse and circuit breaker first.

7   If only the rear windows are inoperative, or if the windows only operate from the master control switch, check the rear window lockout switch for continuity in the unlocked position. Replace it if it doesn't have continuity.

8   Check the wiring between the switches and fuse panel for continuity. Repair the wiring, if necessary.

9   If only one window is inoperative from the master control switch, try the other control switch at the window.

➡**Note: This doesn't apply to the driver's door window.**

10   If the same window works from one switch, but not the other, check the switch for continuity. If the continuity is not as specified, replace the switch.

11   If the switch tests OK, check for a short or open in the circuit between the affected switch and the window motor.

12   If one window is inoperative from both switches, remove the trim panel from the affected door and check for voltage at the switch and at the motor while the switch is operated.

13 If voltage is reaching the motor, disconnect the glass from the regulator (see Chapter 11). Move the window up and down by hand while checking for binding and damage. Also check for binding and damage to the regulator. If the regulator is not damaged and the window moves up and down smoothly, replace the motor. If there's binding or damage, lubricate, repair or replace parts, as necessary.

14 If voltage isn't reaching the motor, check the wiring in the circuit for continuity between the switches and motors. You'll need to consult the wiring diagram for the vehicle. If the circuit is equipped with a relay, check that the relay is grounded properly and receiving voltage.

15 Test the windows after you are done to confirm proper repairs.

22 Power door lock system - general information

The power door lock system operates the door lock actuators mounted in each door. The system consists of the switches, actuators, a control unit and associated wiring. Diagnosis can usually be limited to simple checks of the wiring connections and actuators for minor faults that can be easily repaired. The system uses an electronic control unit; in-depth diagnosis should be left to a dealership service department. The door lock control unit is located behind the instrument panel, to the right of the fuse box.

Power door lock systems are operated by bi-directional solenoids located in the doors. The lock switches have two operating positions: Lock and Unlock. When activated, the switch sends a ground signal to the door lock control unit to lock or unlock the doors. Depending on which way the switch is activated, the control unit reverses polarity to the solenoids, allowing the two sides of the circuit to be used alternately as the feed (positive) and ground side.

Some vehicles may have an anti-theft systems incorporated into the power locks. If you are unable to locate the trouble using the following general Steps, consult a dealer service department.

1 Always check the circuit protection first. Some vehicles use a combination of circuit breakers and fuses.

2 Operate the door lock switches in both directions (Lock and Unlock) with the engine off. Listen for the click of the solenoids operating.

3 Test the switches for continuity. Replace the switch if there's not continuity in both switch positions.

4 Check the wiring between the switches, control unit and solenoids for continuity. Repair the wiring if there's no continuity.

5 Check for a bad ground at the switches or the control unit.

6 If all but one lock solenoids operate, remove the trim panel from the affected door (see Chapter 11) and check for voltage at the solenoid while the lock switch is operated. One of the wires should have voltage in the Lock position; the other should have voltage in the Unlock position.

7 If the inoperative solenoid is receiving voltage, replace the solenoid.

8 If the inoperative solenoid isn't receiving voltage, check the relay or for an open or short in the wire between the lock solenoid and the control unit.

➡**Note: It's common for wires to break in the portion of the harness between the body and door (opening and closing the door fatigues and eventually breaks the wires).**

23 Daytime Running Lights (DRL) - general information

The Daytime Running Lights (DRL) system, which is required on new Canadian models, illuminates the headlights when the engine is running. The DRL system supplies reduced power to the headlights so they won't be too bright for daytime use, which also prolongs headlight life.

24 Airbags - general information

1 All models are equipped with a Supplemental Restraint System (SRS), more commonly known as an airbag. This system is designed to protect the driver and front seat passenger from serious injury in the event of a head-on or frontal collision. It consists of an airbag module in the center of the steering wheel and, if equipped, another airbag inside the instrument panel, right above the glove compartment. Additionally, some models are equipped with side-impact airbags, side curtain airbags and seat belt pre-tensioners (which are pyrotechnic devices that reduce the slack in the front seat belts during an impact of sufficient force to trigger the airbags.

AIRBAGS

Driver's side

2 The airbag inflator module contains a housing incorporating the cushion (airbag) and inflator unit, mounted in the center of the steering wheel. The inflator assembly is mounted on the back of the housing over a hole through which gas is expelled, inflating the bag almost instantaneously when an electrical signal is sent from the system. The roll connector, generally referred to as the clockspring, on the steering column under the module carries this signal to the module. The clockspring can transmit an electrical signal regardless of steering wheel position.

Passenger's side, side impact and side curtain airbags

3 The passenger side airbag is mounted above the glove compartment and designated by the letters SRS (Supplemental Restraint System). It consists of an inflator containing an igniter, a bag assembly, a housing and a trim cover.

4 The passenger airbag is considerably larger than the steering wheel-mounted unit. The trim cover is textured and painted to match the instrument panel and has a molded seam that splits when the bag inflates.

5   Side impact airbags, on models so equipped, are located in the outer sides of the front seat backs.

6   Side curtain airbags, on models so equipped, are mounted along the outer edges of the headliner, right above the door opening.

AIRBAG CONTROL MODULE

7   The airbag control module supplies the current to the airbag system in the event of a collision, even if battery power is cut off. It checks this system every time the vehicle is started, causing the airbag warning light on the instrument cluster to go on then off, if the system is operating properly. If there is a fault in the system, the light will go on and stay on, flash, or the dash will make a beeping sound. If this happens, the vehicle should be taken to your dealer immediately for service.

PRECAUTIONS

Disabling the SRS system

⁕⁑ WARNING:

Failure to follow these precautions could result in accidental deployment of the airbag and personal injury.

8   Whenever working in the vicinity of the steering wheel, steering column or any of the other SRS system components, the system must be disarmed. To disarm the system:

a) *Point the wheels straight ahead and turn the ignition key to the LOCK position.*

b) *Disconnect the cable from the negative terminal of the battery terminal.*

c) *Wait at least two minutes for the back-up power supply capacitor to be depleted.*

9   Whenever handling an airbag module, always keep the airbag opening (the trim side) pointed away from your body. Never place the airbag module on a bench of other surface with the airbag opening facing the surface. Always place the airbag module on a flat surface in a safe location with the airbag opening facing up (don't set it in a corner or next to a wall). Never dispose of a live airbag module. Return it to your dealer service department for safe deployment, using special equipment, and disposal.

10 Never measure the resistance of any SRS component. An ohmmeter has a built-in battery supply that could accidentally deploy the airbag. When working around the instrument panel and console, you will see several large yellow connectors; they're the harness connectors for the airbag system. Generally speaking, it's a good idea to avoid unplugging these yellow connectors unless absolutely necessary.

11 Always disable the airbag system when working in the vicinity of the front grille or bumper. Use extreme caution when working around the front impact sensors. Do not remove or unplug them unless absolutely necessary.

12 Never use electrical welding equipment on a vehicle equipped with an airbag without first disconnecting the cables from the battery terminals (negative first, positive last) (see Chapter 5).

25 Wiring diagrams - general information

Since it isn't possible to include all wiring diagrams for every year covered by this manual, the following diagrams are those that are typical and most commonly needed.

Prior to troubleshooting any circuits, check the fuse and circuit breakers (if equipped) to make sure they're in good condition. Make sure the battery is properly charged and check the cable connections (see Chapter 1).

When checking a circuit, make sure that all connectors are clean, with no broken or loose terminals. When unplugging a connector, do not pull on the wires. Pull only on the connector housings themselves.

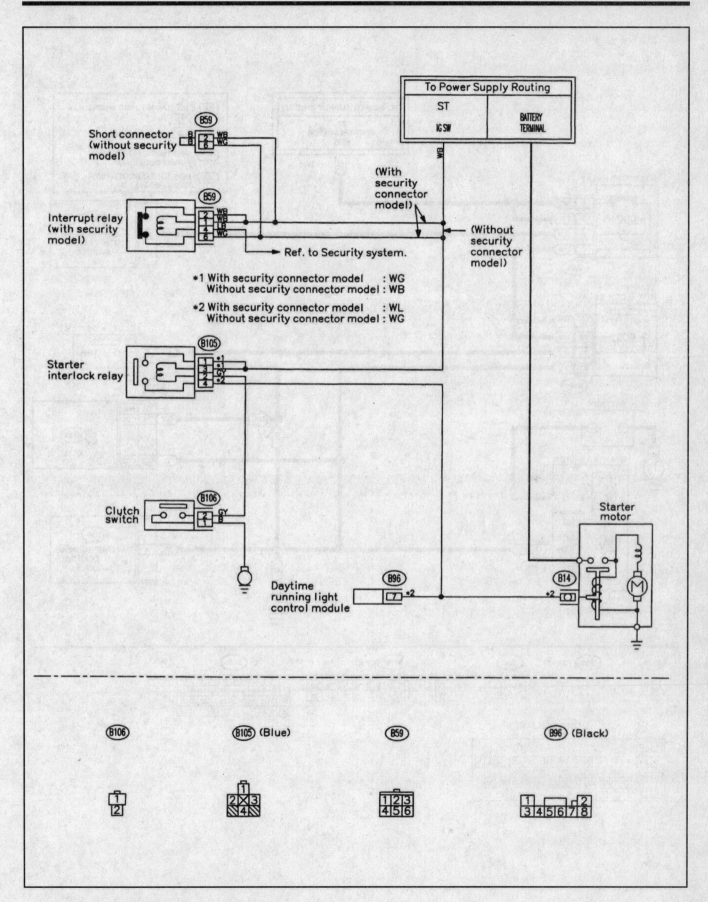

Typical earlier model starting system wiring diagram

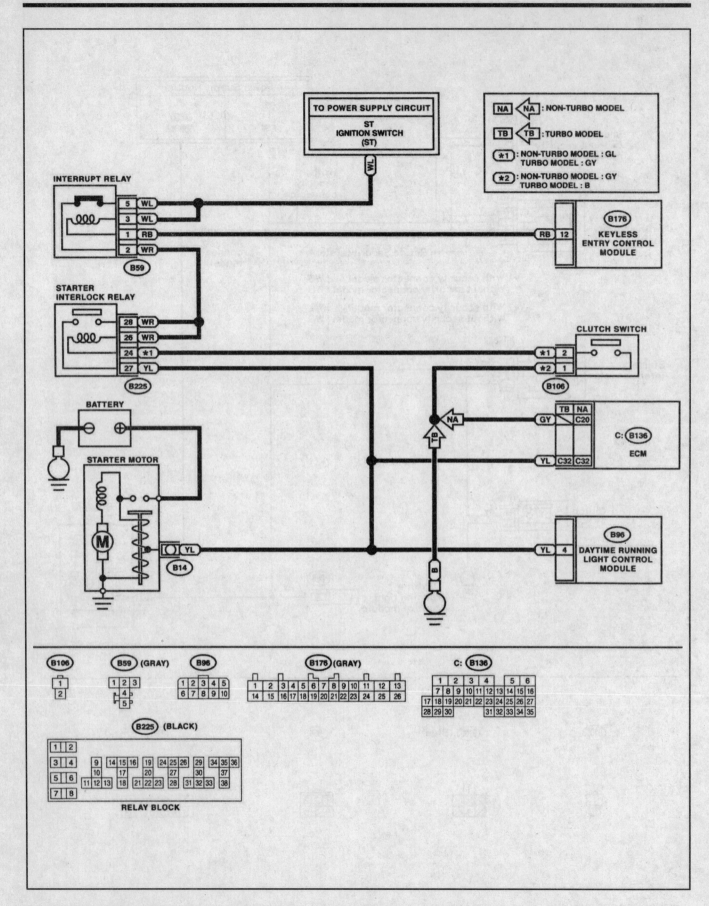

Typical later model starting system wiring diagram (manual transaxle)

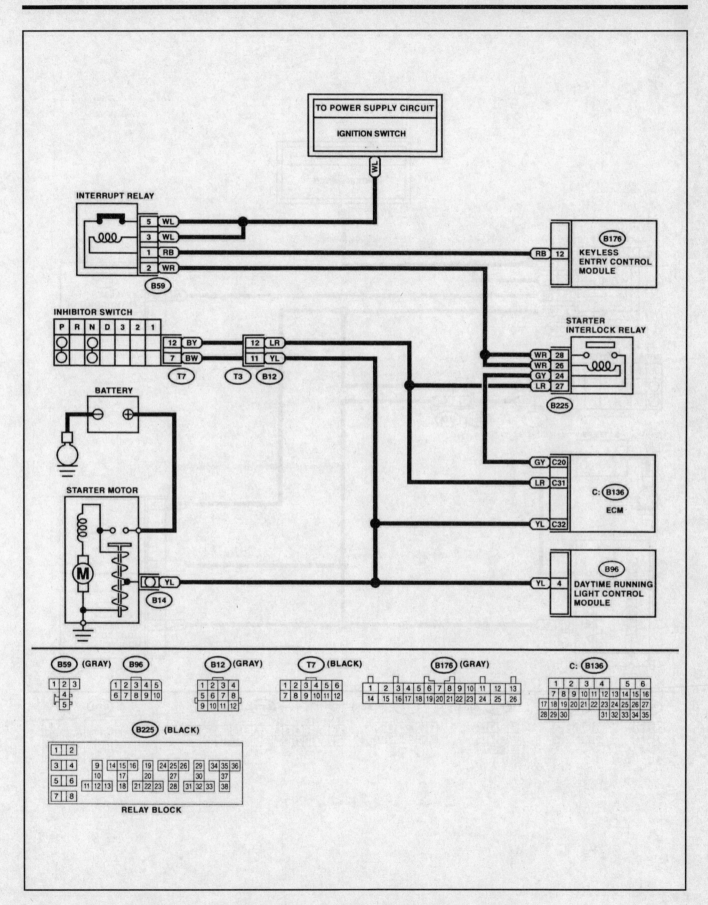

Typical later model starting system wiring diagram wiring diagram (automatic transaxle, non-turbo)

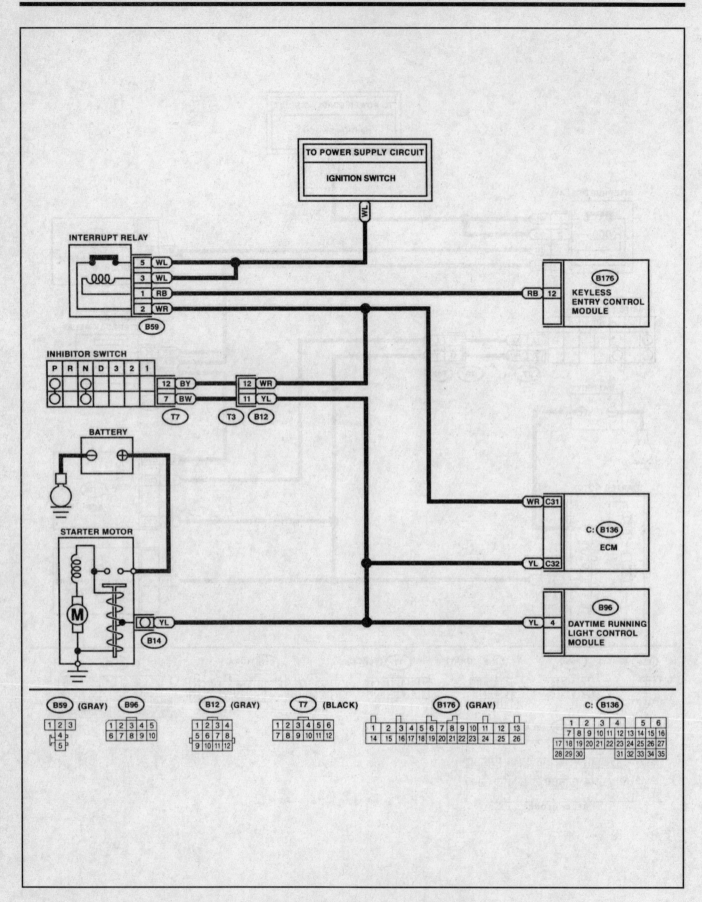

Typical later model starting system wiring diagram wiring diagram (automatic transaxle, turbo)

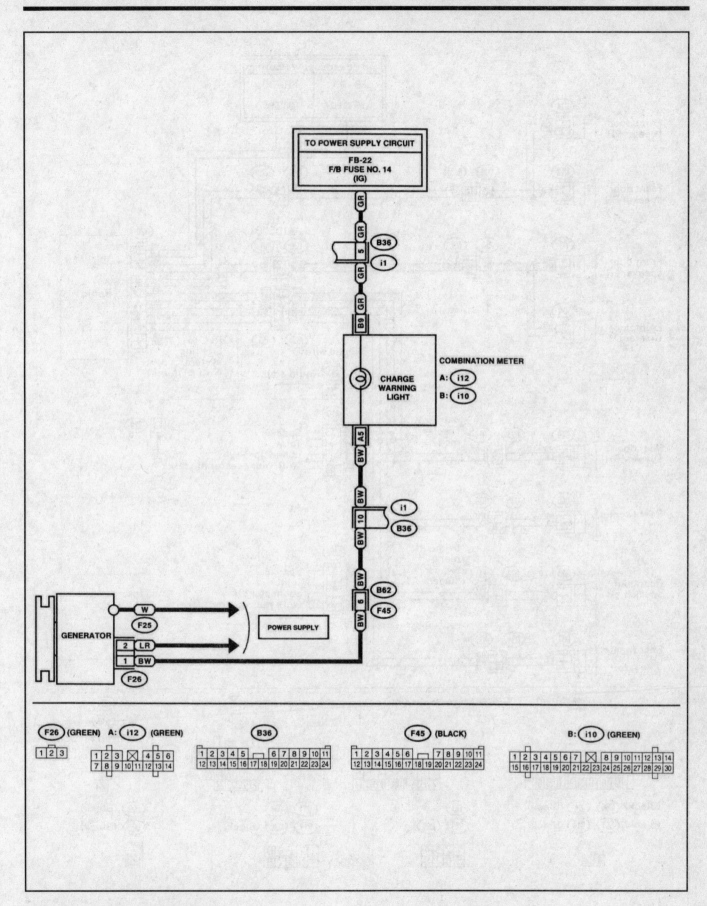

Typical charging system wiring diagram

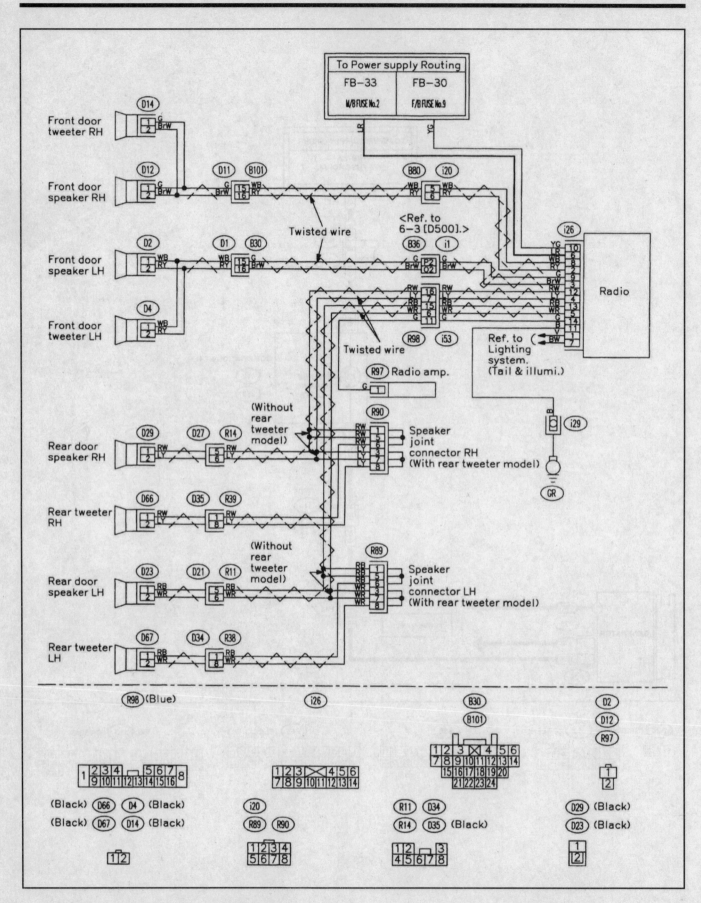

Typical earlier model audio system wiring diagram

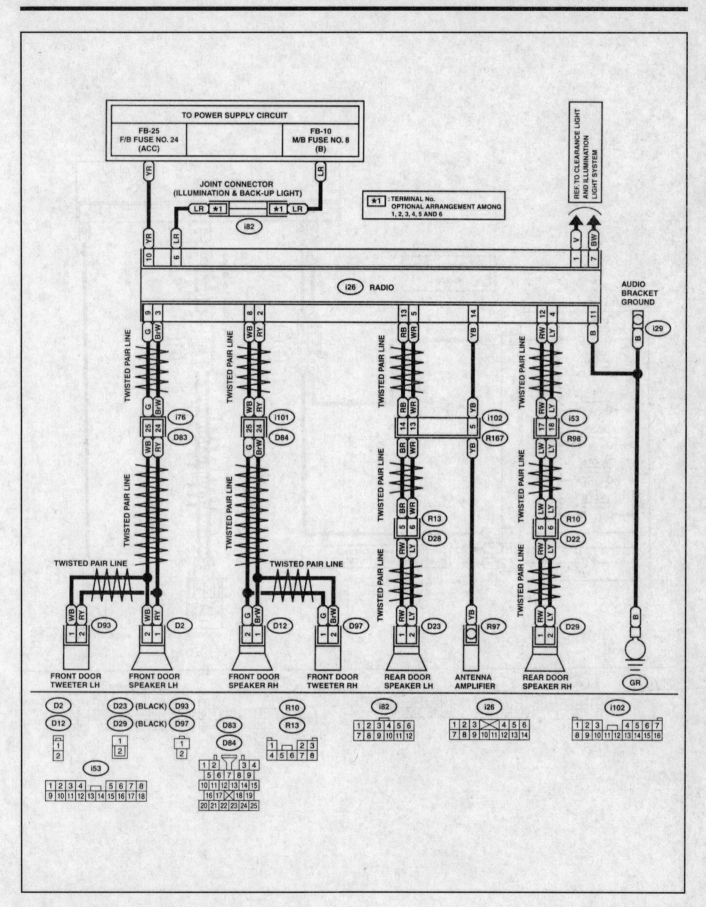

Typical later model audio system wiring diagram (1 of 2)

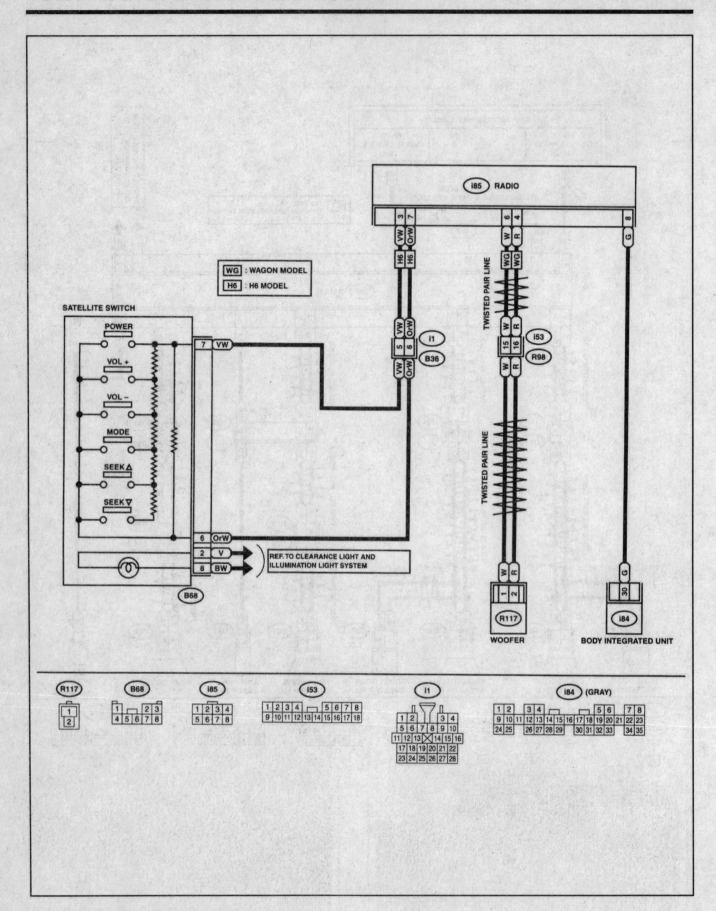

Typical later model audio system wiring diagram (2 of 2)

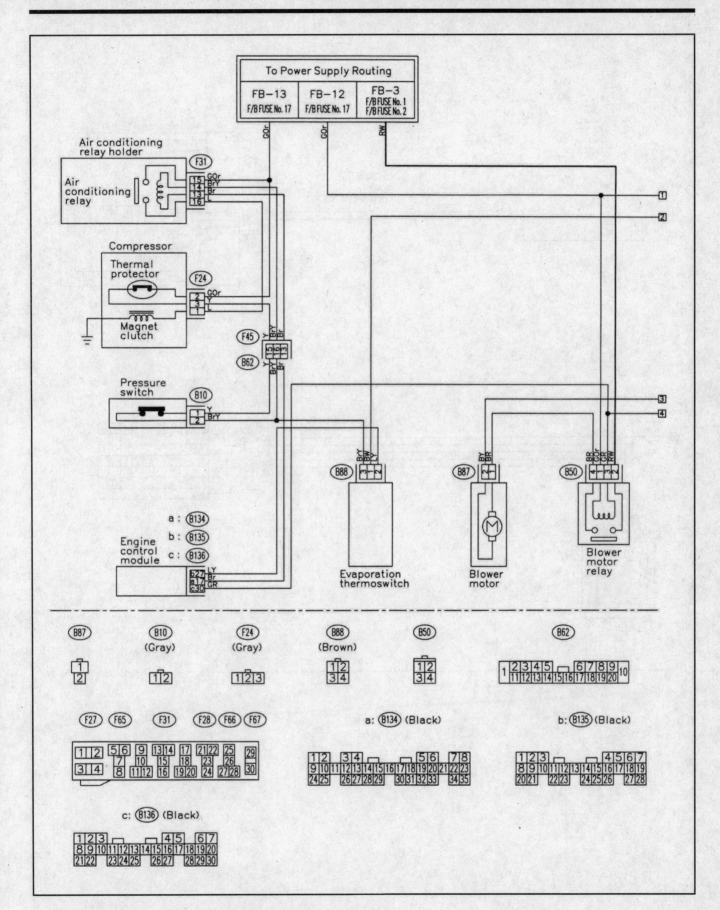

Typical earlier model air conditioning system wiring diagram (1 of 2)

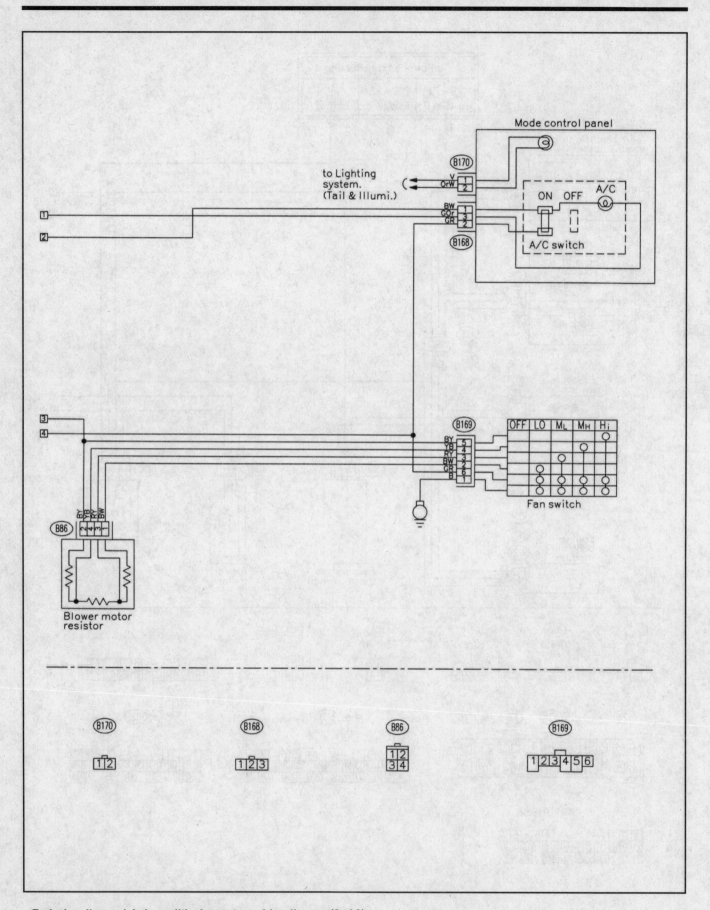

Typical earlier model air conditioning system wiring diagram (2 of 2)

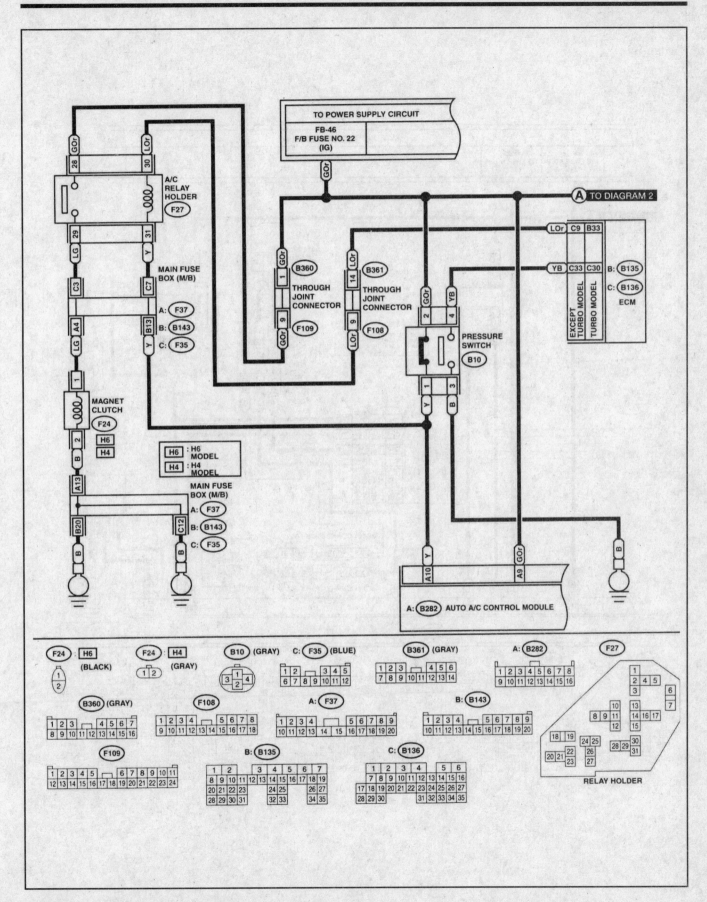

Typical later model air conditioning system wiring diagram (1 of 4)

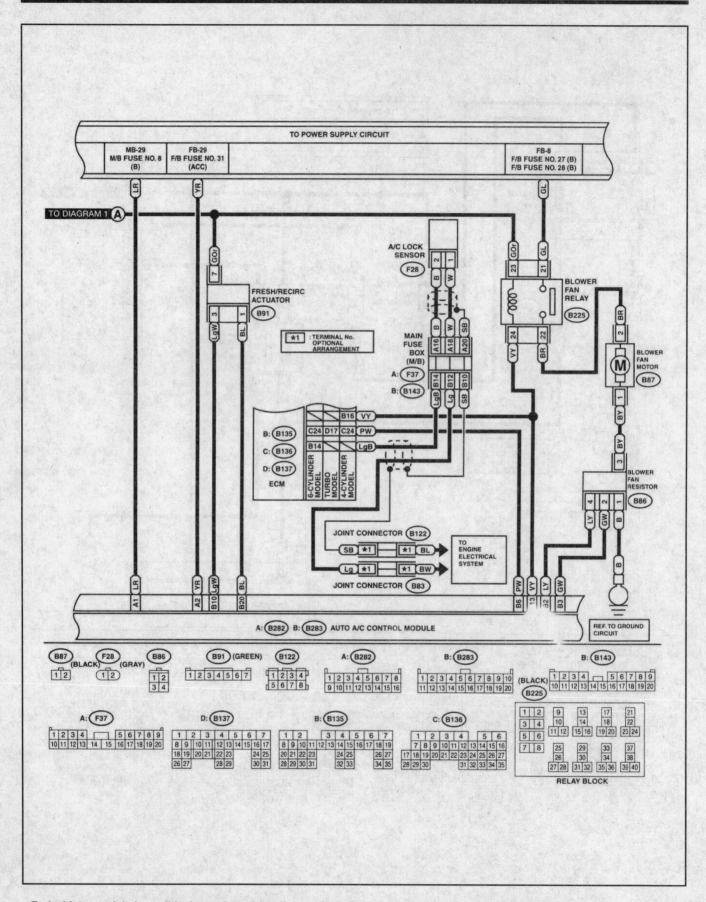

Typical later model air conditioning system wiring diagram (2 of 4)

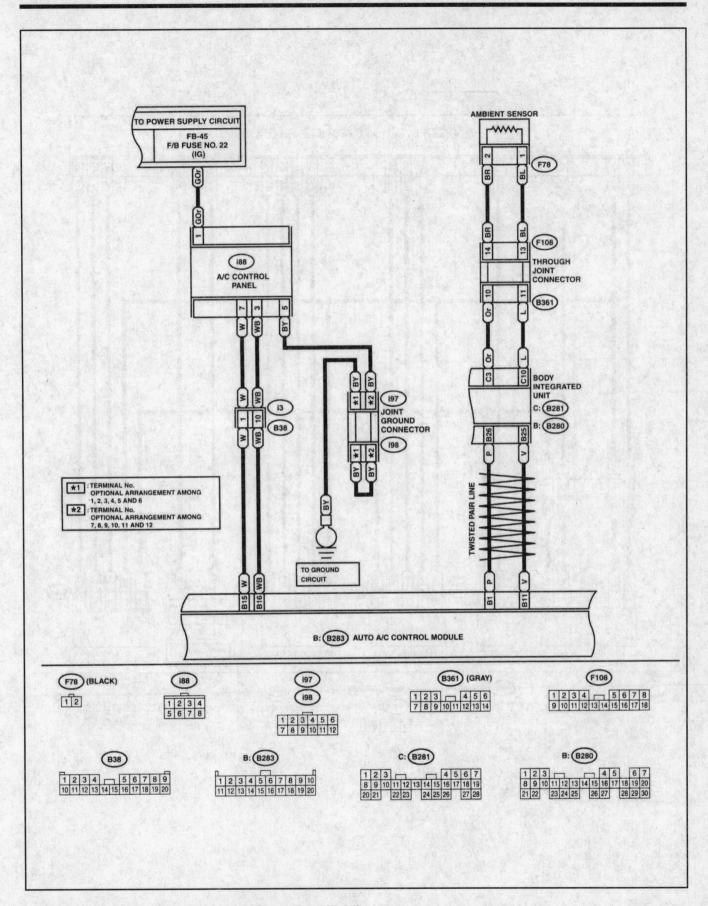

Typical later model air conditioning system wiring diagram (3 of 4)

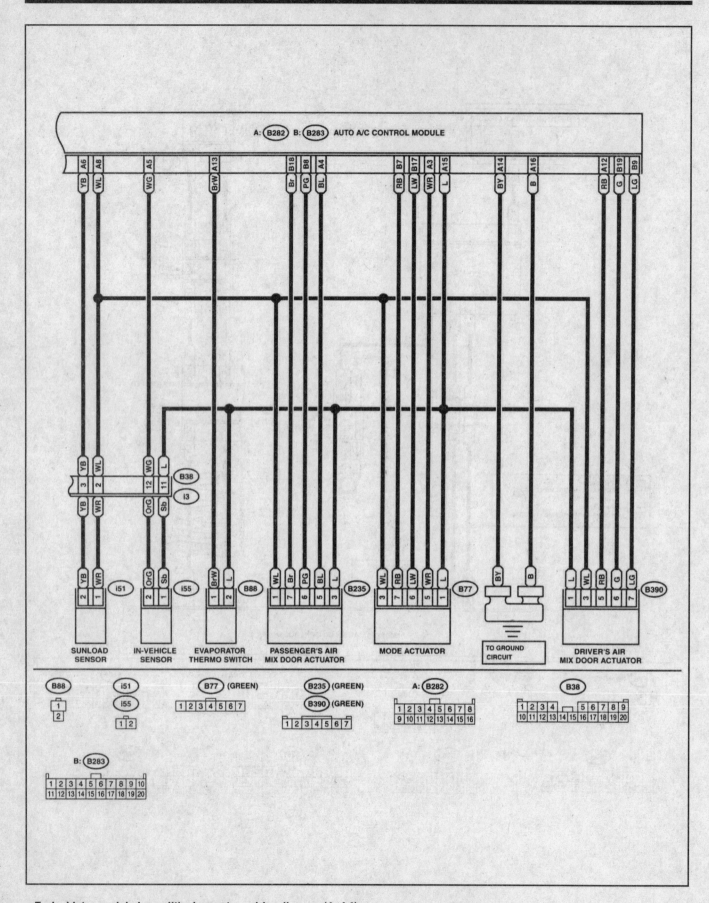

Typical later model air conditioning system wiring diagram (4 of 4)

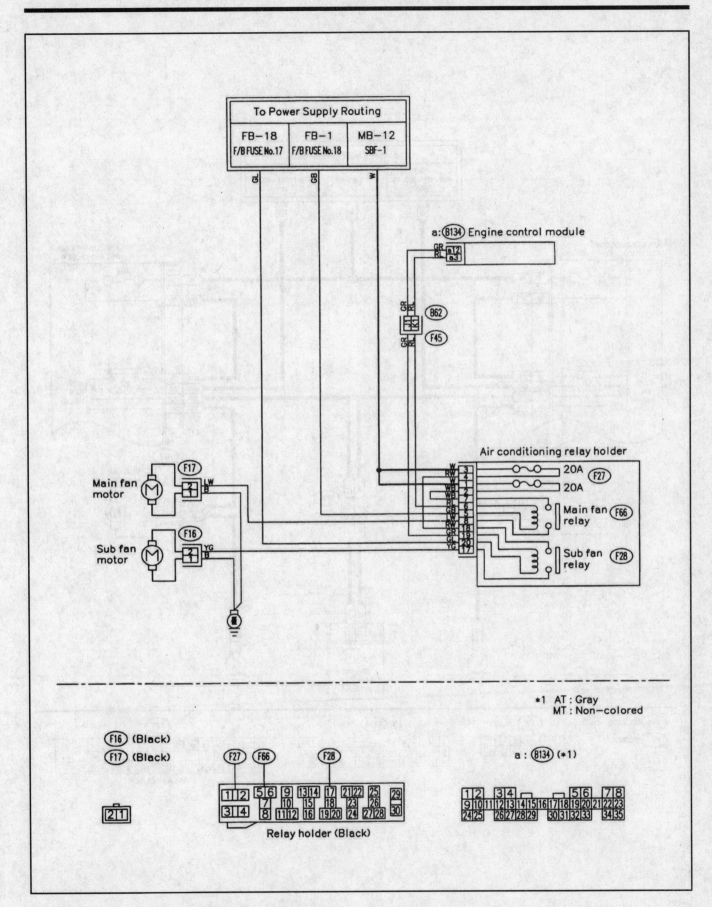

Typical earlier model radiator fan circuit wiring diagram

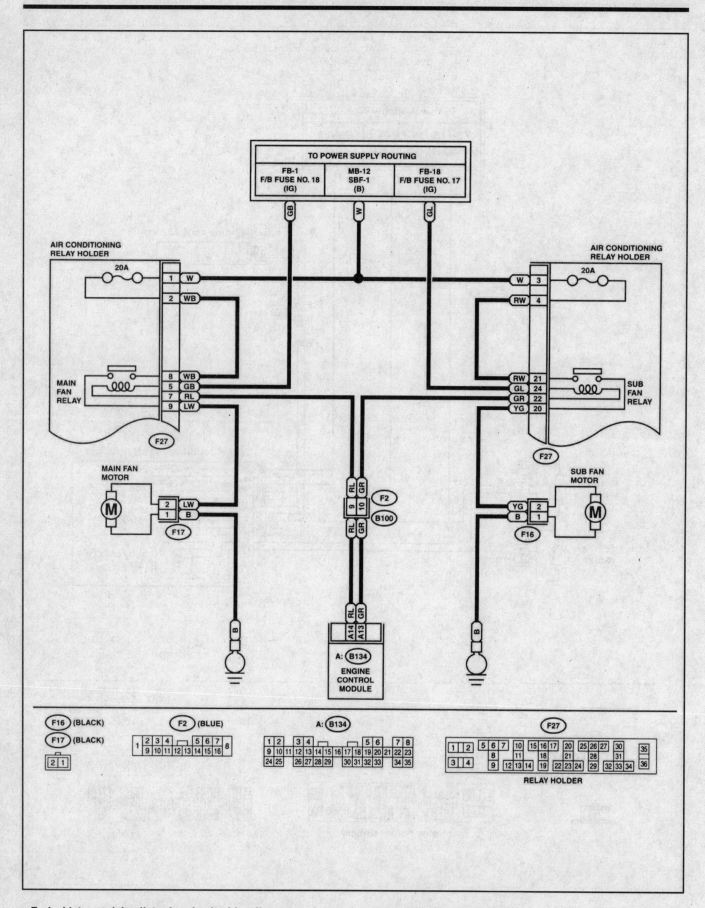

Typical later model radiator fan circuit wiring diagram

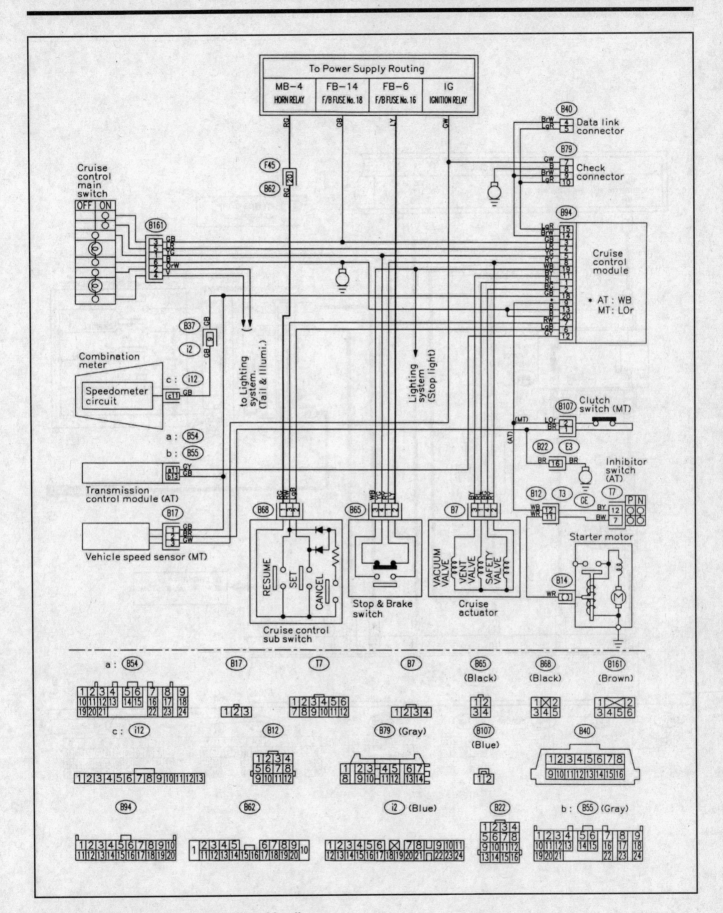

Typical earlier model cruise control system wiring diagram

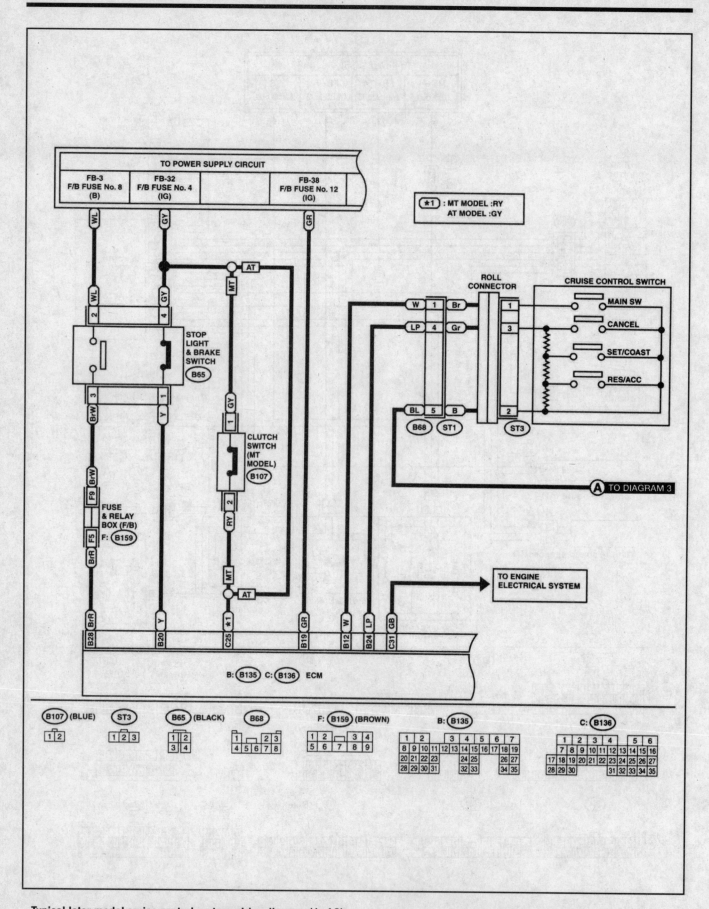

Typical later model cruise control system wiring diagram (1 of 3)

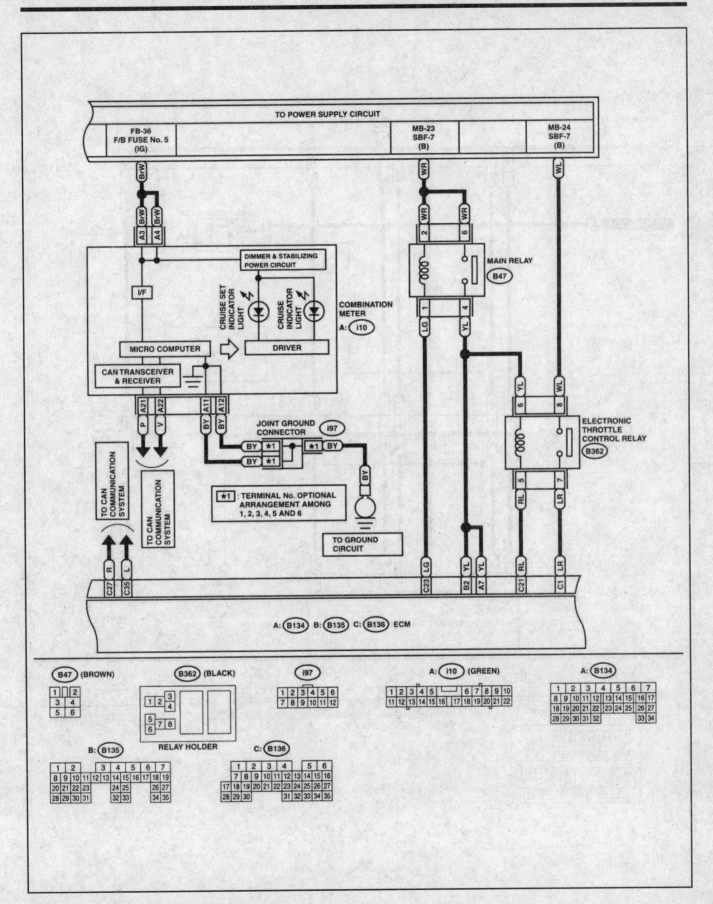

Typical later model cruise control system wiring diagram (2 of 3)

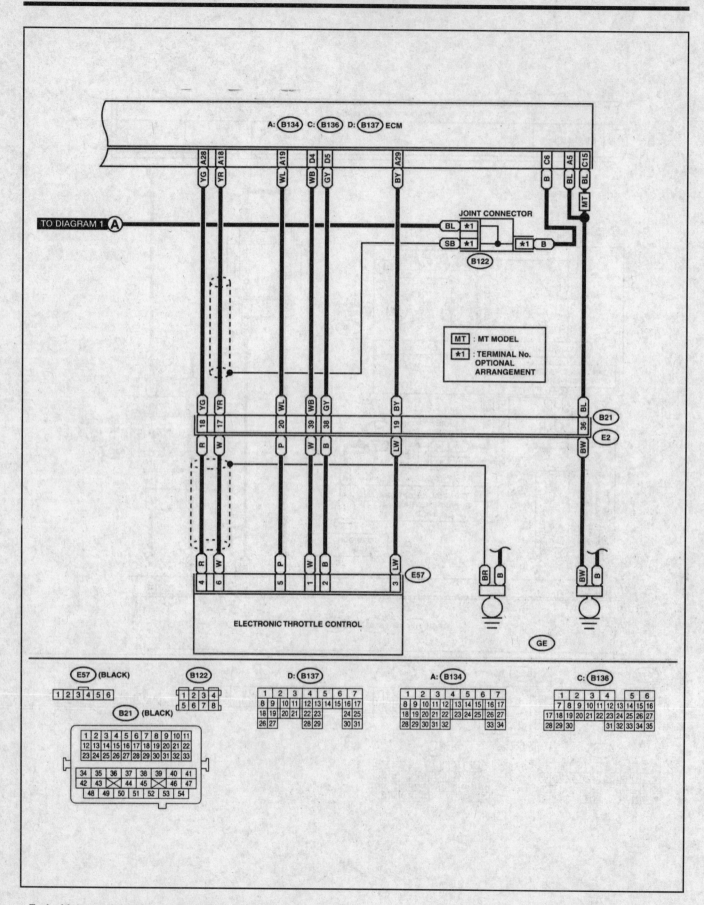

Typical later model cruise control system wiring diagram (3 of 3)

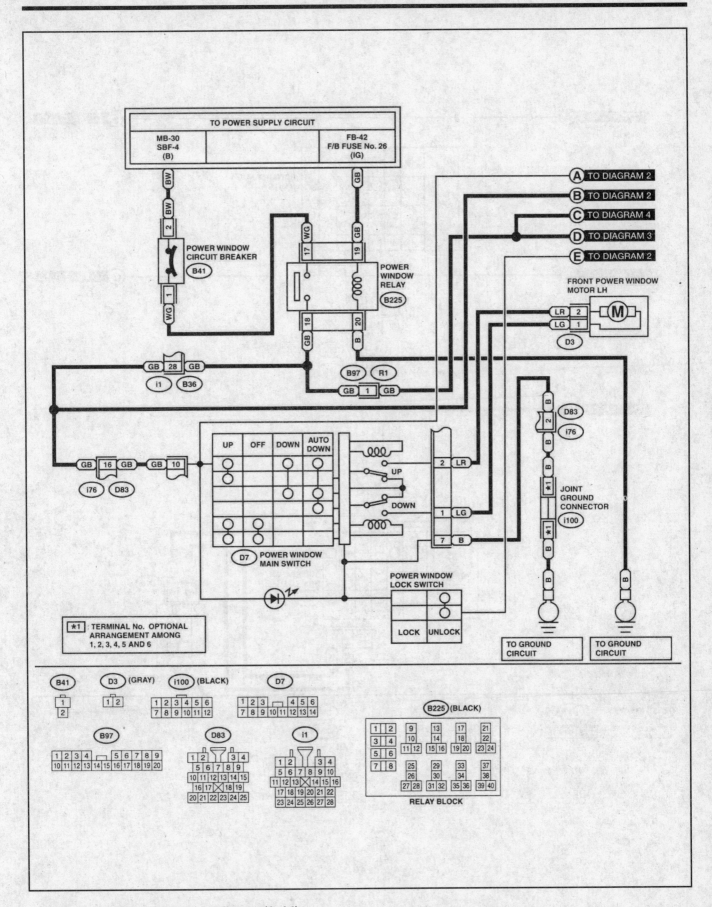

Typical power window system wiring diagram (1 of 4)

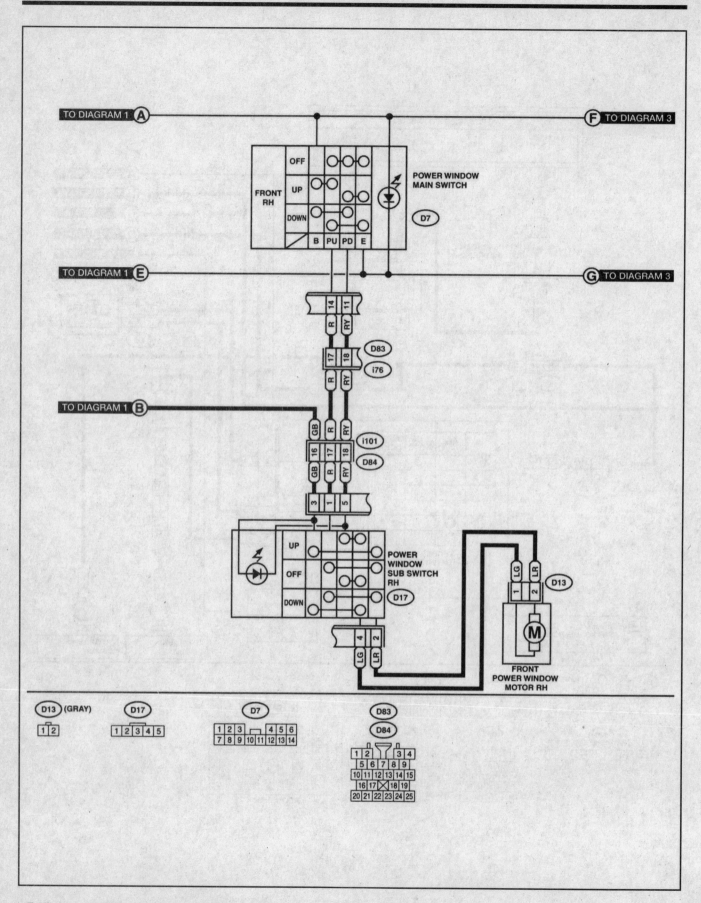

Typical power window system wiring diagram (2 of 4)

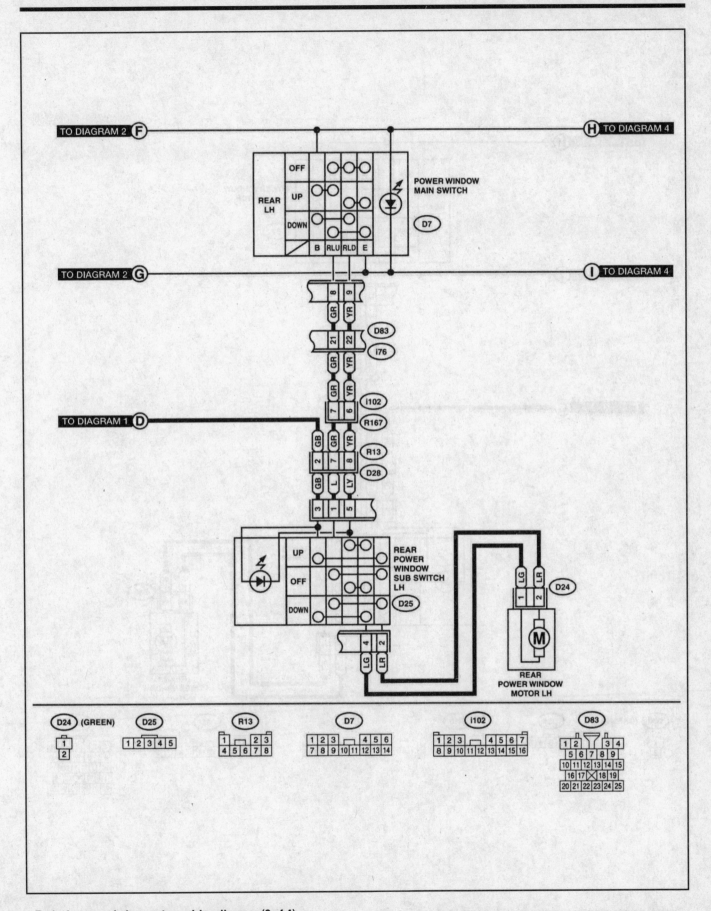

Typical power window system wiring diagram (3 of 4)

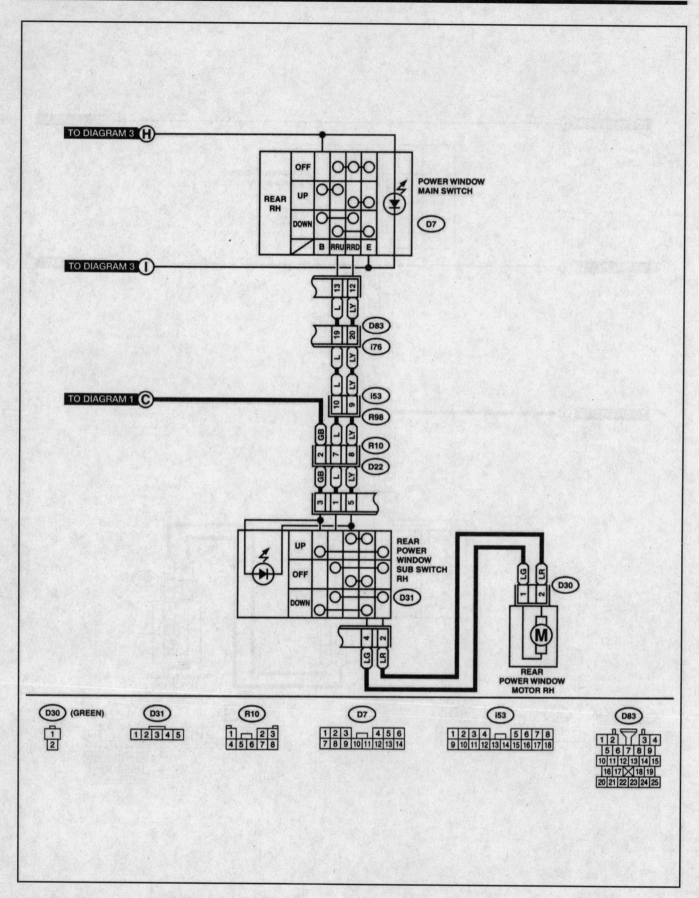

Typical power window system wiring diagram (4 of 4)

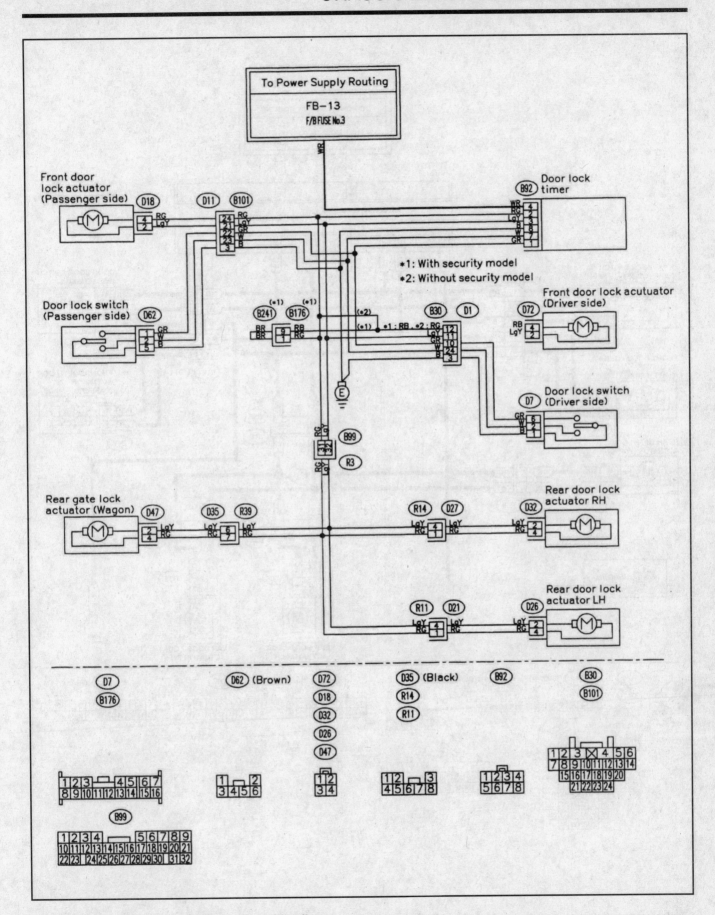

Typical earlier model power door lock system wiring diagram

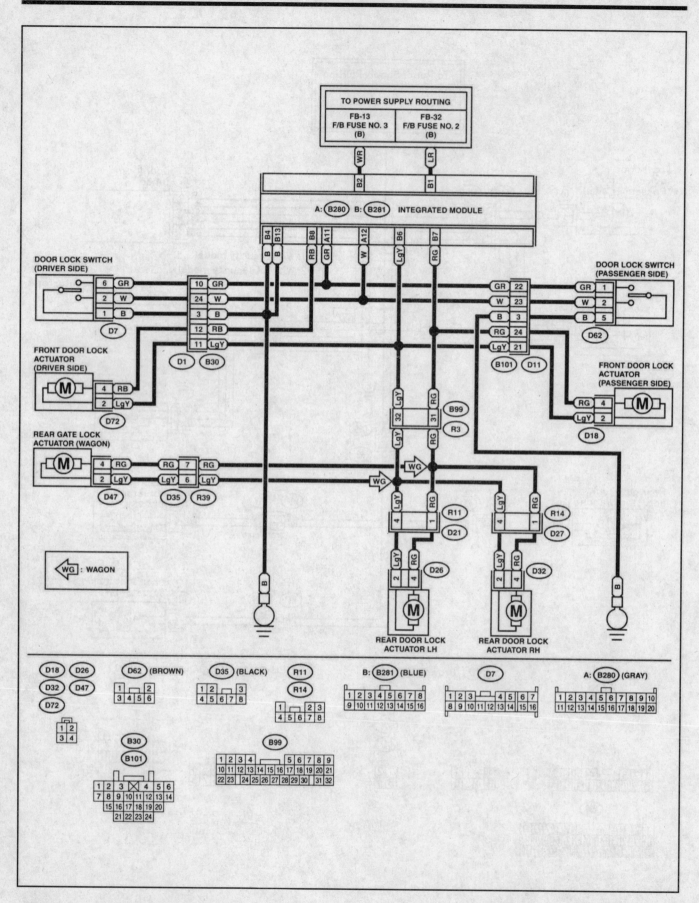

Typical later model power door lock system wiring diagram

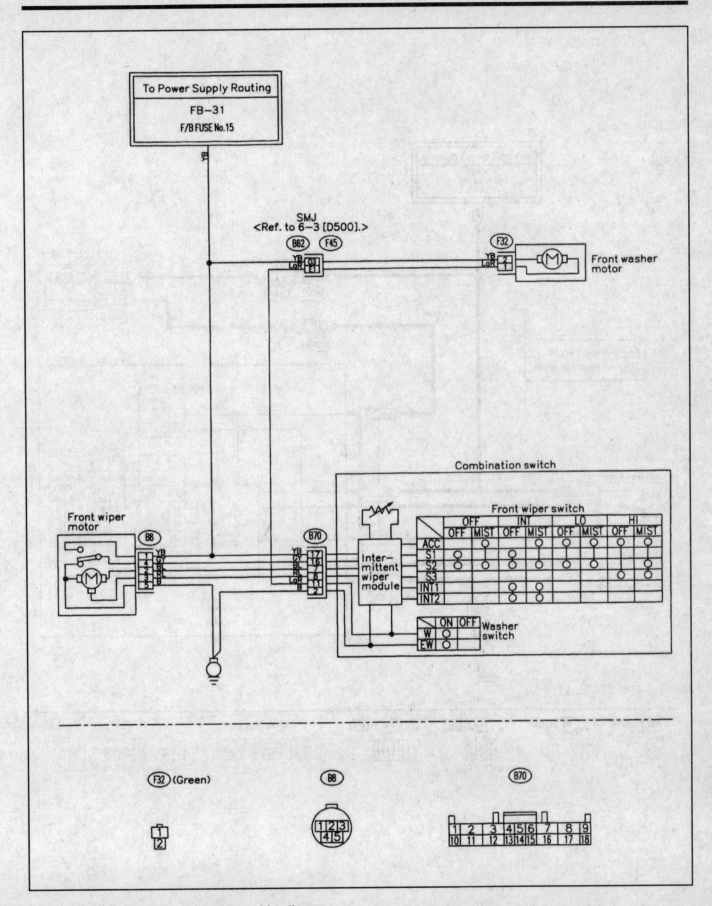

Typical earlier model wiper/washer system wiring diagram

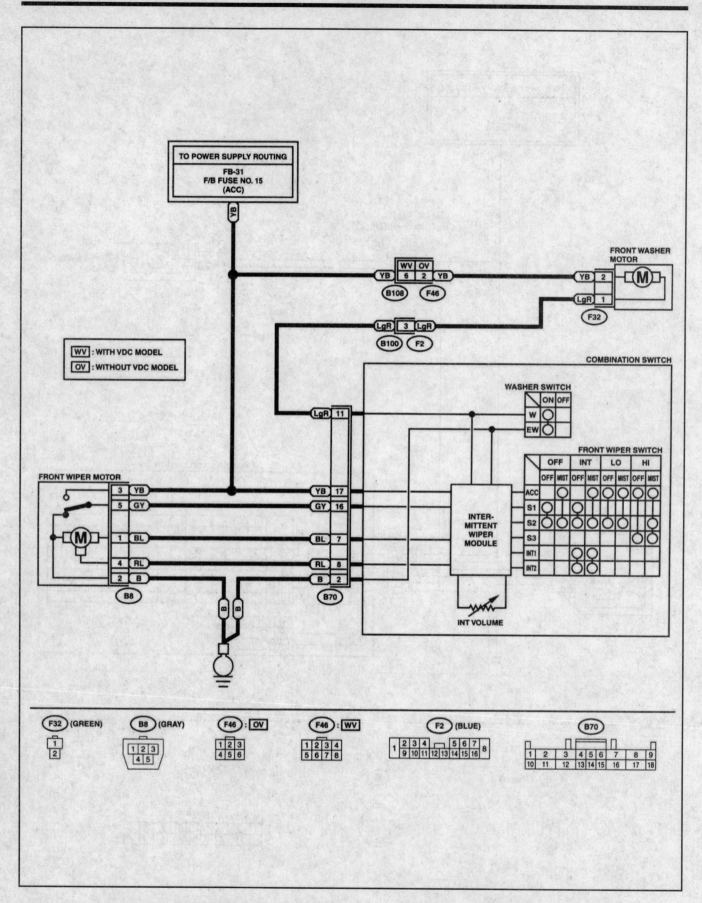

Typical later model front wiper/washer system wiring diagram

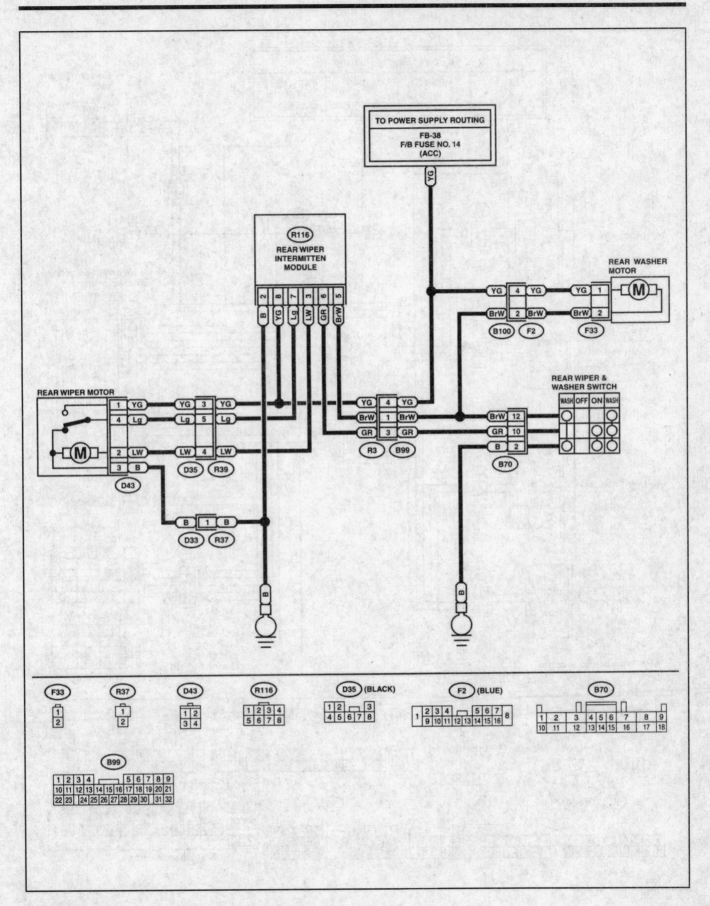

Typical later model rear wiper/washer system wiring diagram

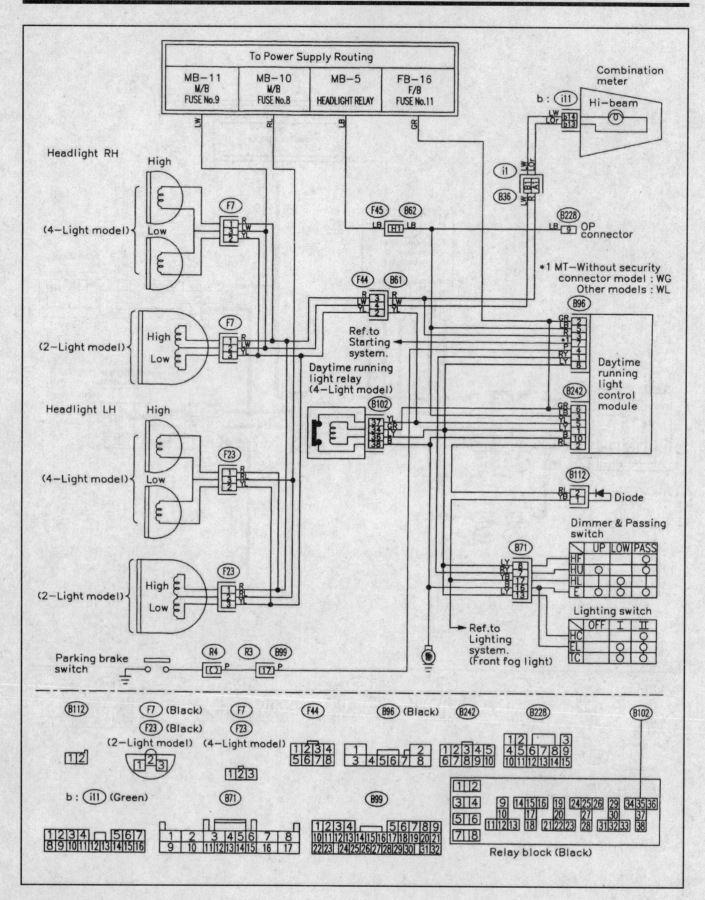

Typical earlier model headlight system wiring diagram

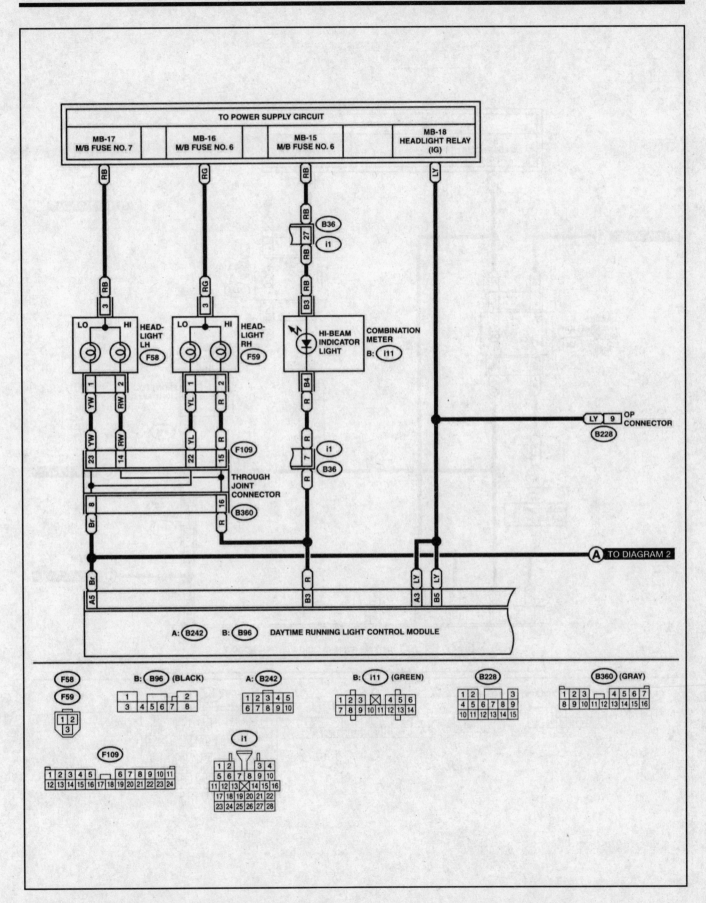

Typical later model headlight system wiring diagram (1 of 3)

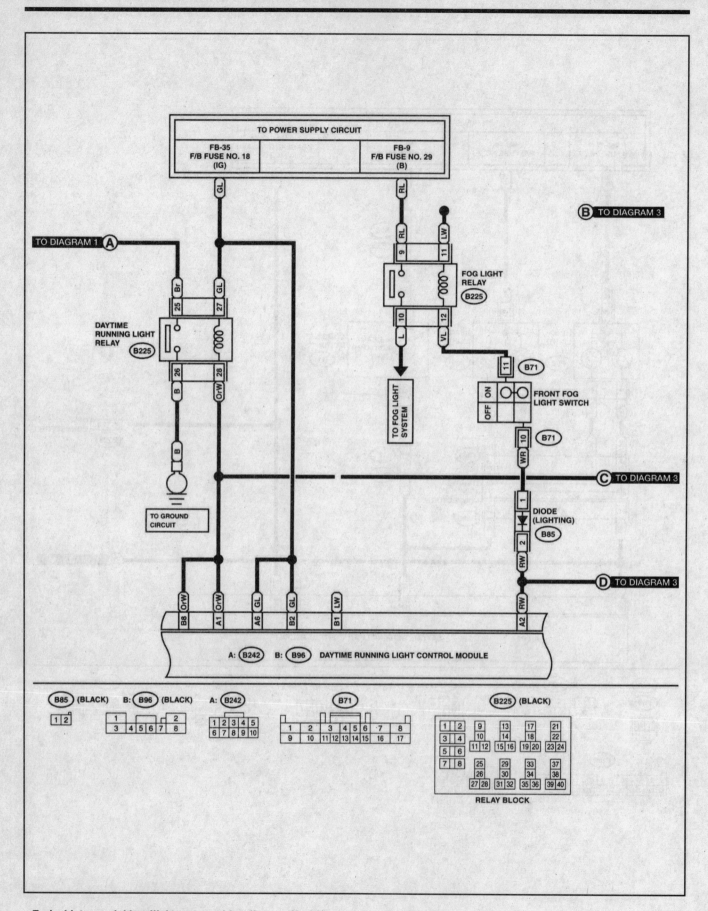

Typical later model headlight system wiring diagram (2 of 3)

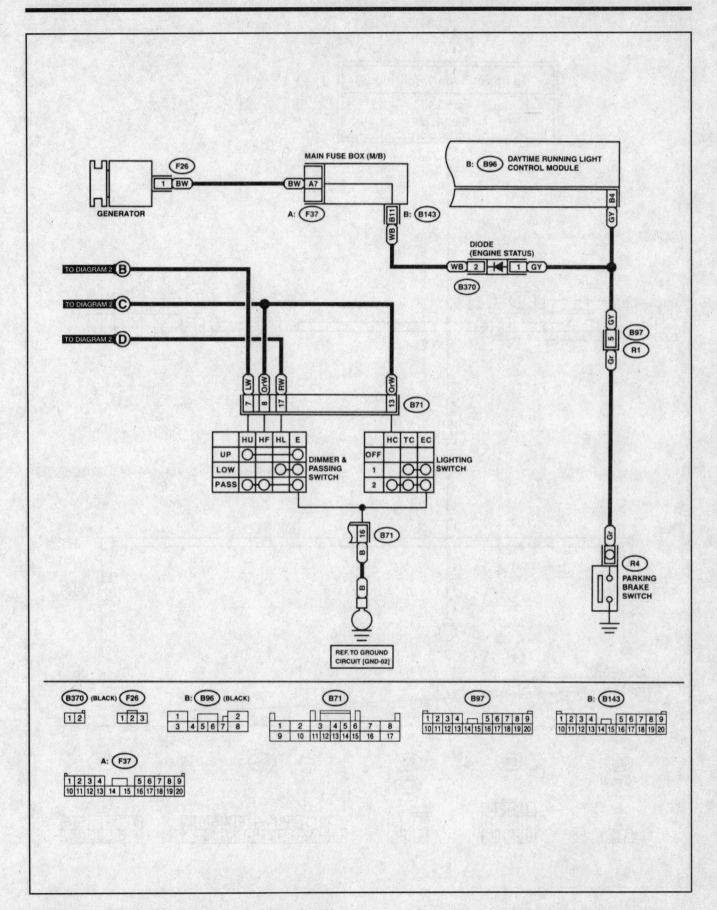

Typical later model headlight system wiring diagram (3 of 3)

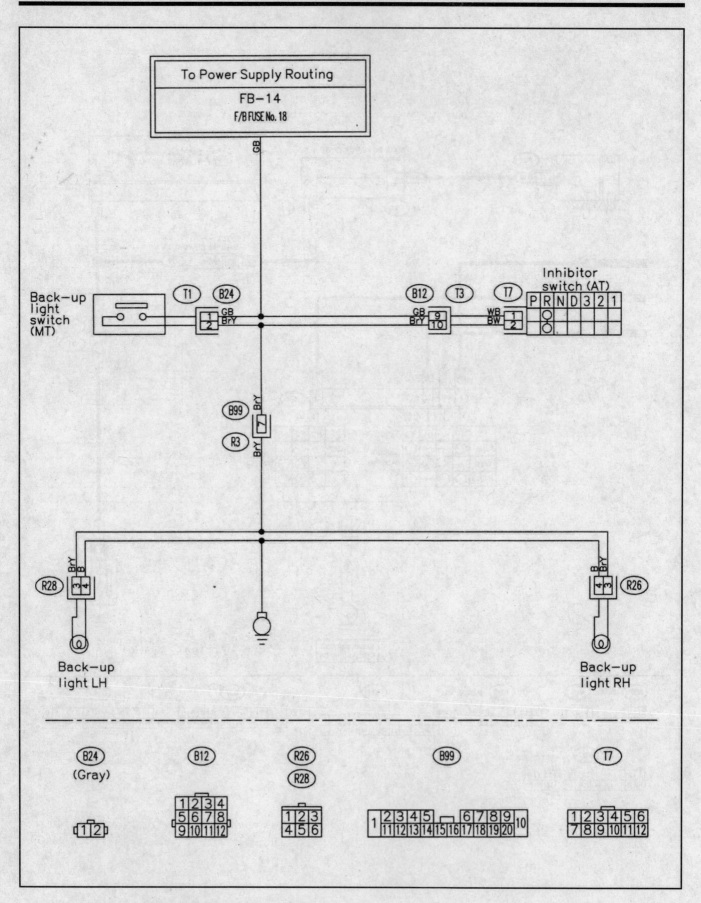

Typical earlier model back-up lighting system wiring diagram

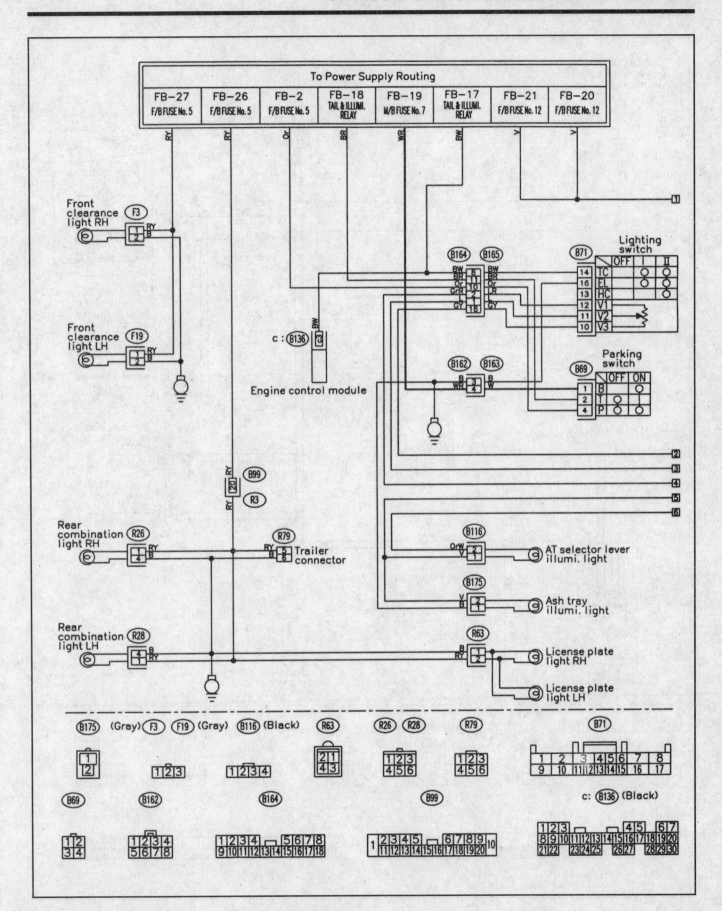

Typical earlier model clearance and illumination lighting (1 of 2)

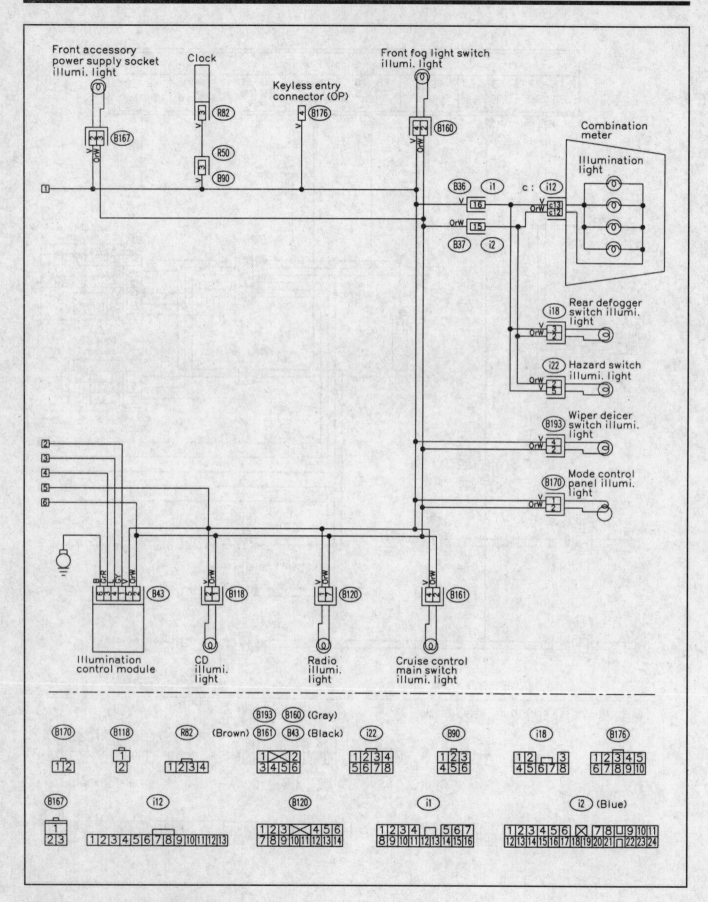

Typical earlier model clearance and illumination lighting (2 of 2)

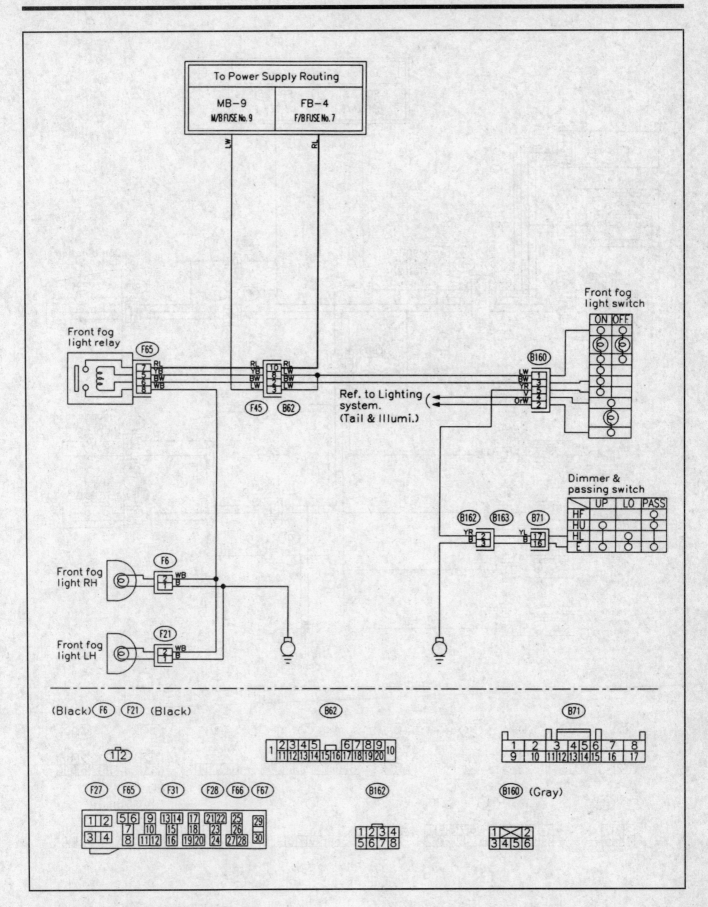

Typical earlier model fog light wiring diagram

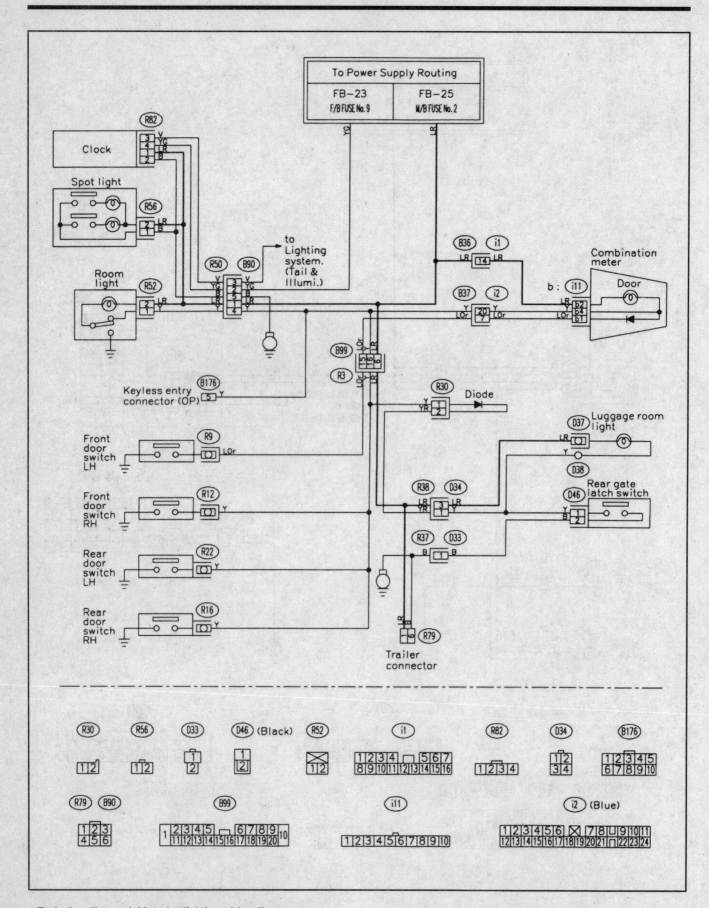

Typical earlier model interior lighting wiring diagram

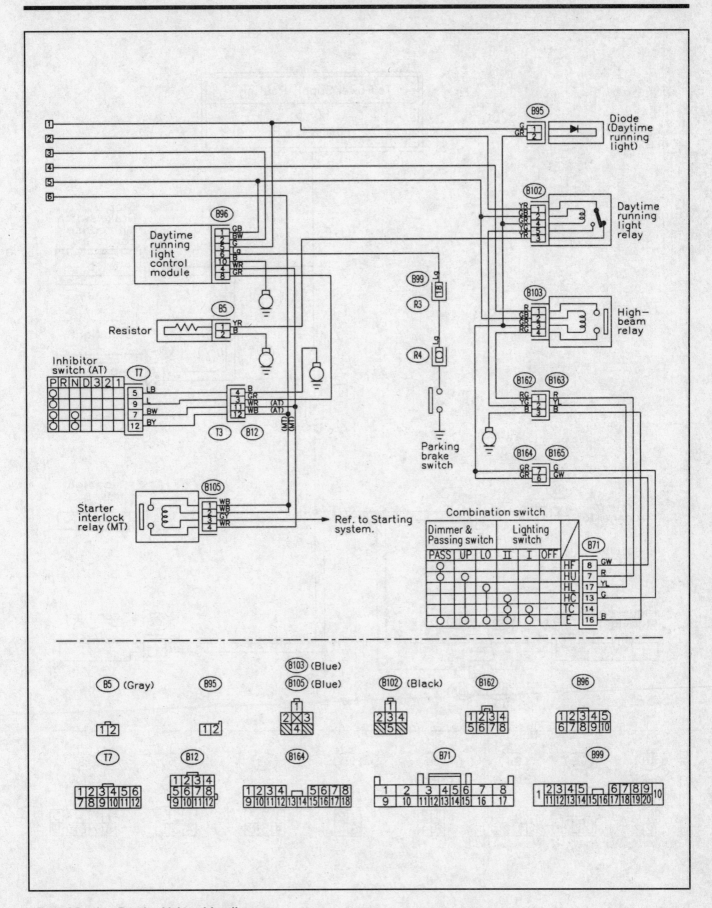

Typical Daytime Running Lights wiring diagram

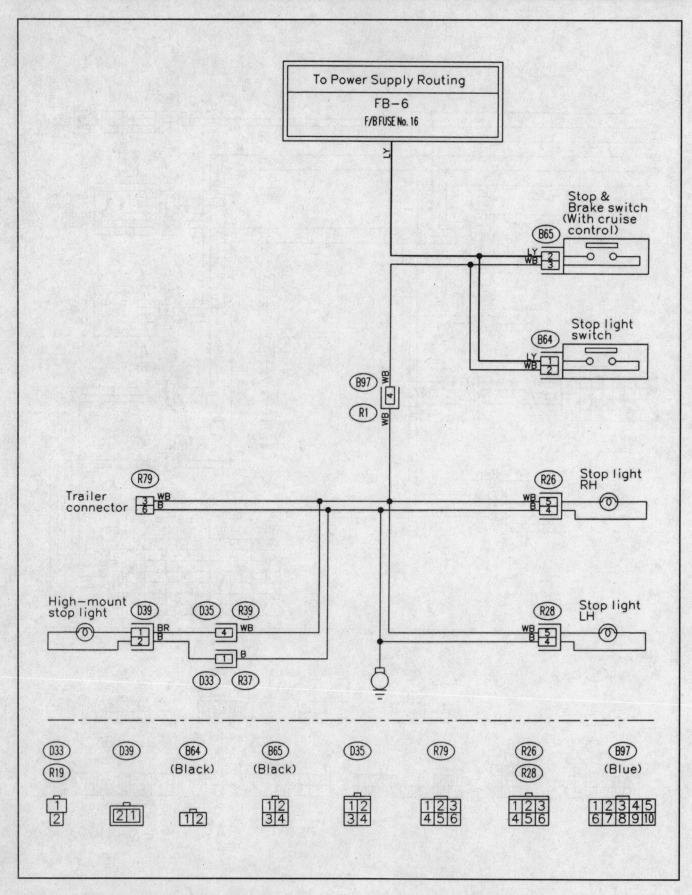

Typical earlier model brake light system wiring diagram

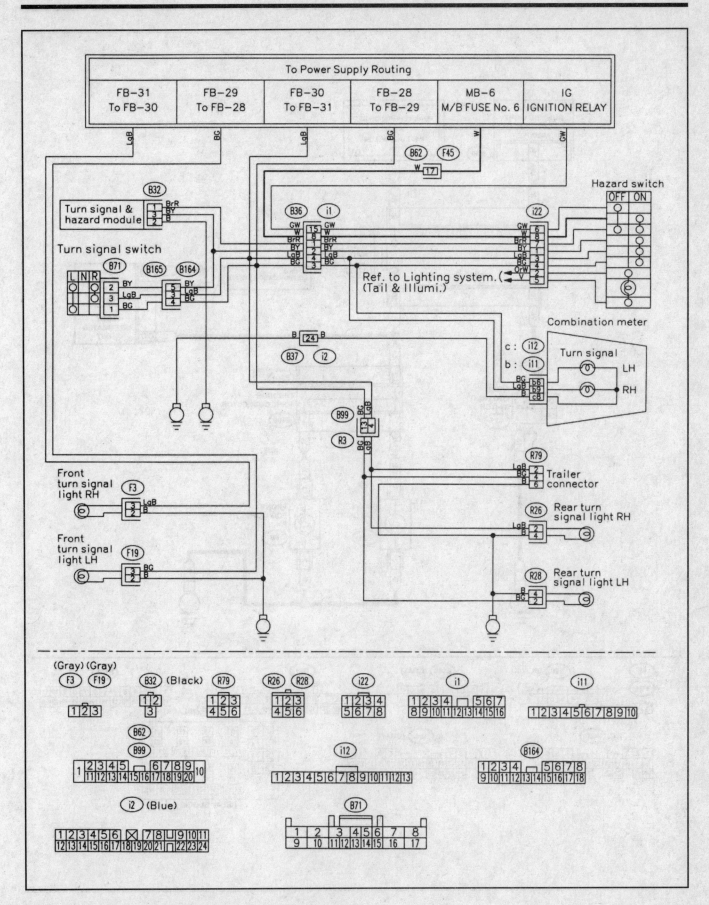

Typical earlier model turn signal and hazard light wiring diagram

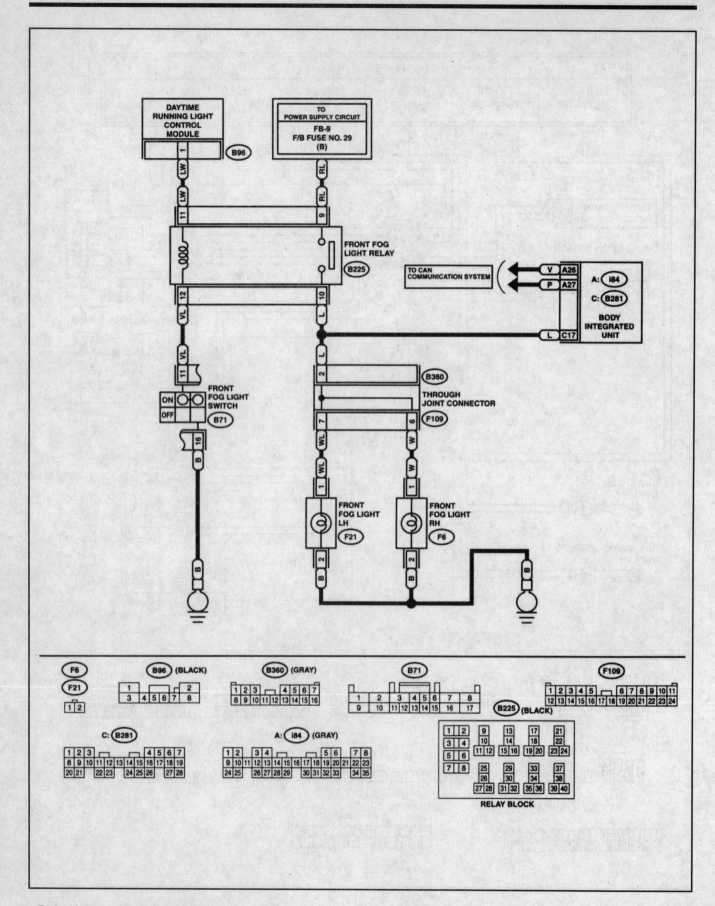

Typical later model fog light system wiring diagram

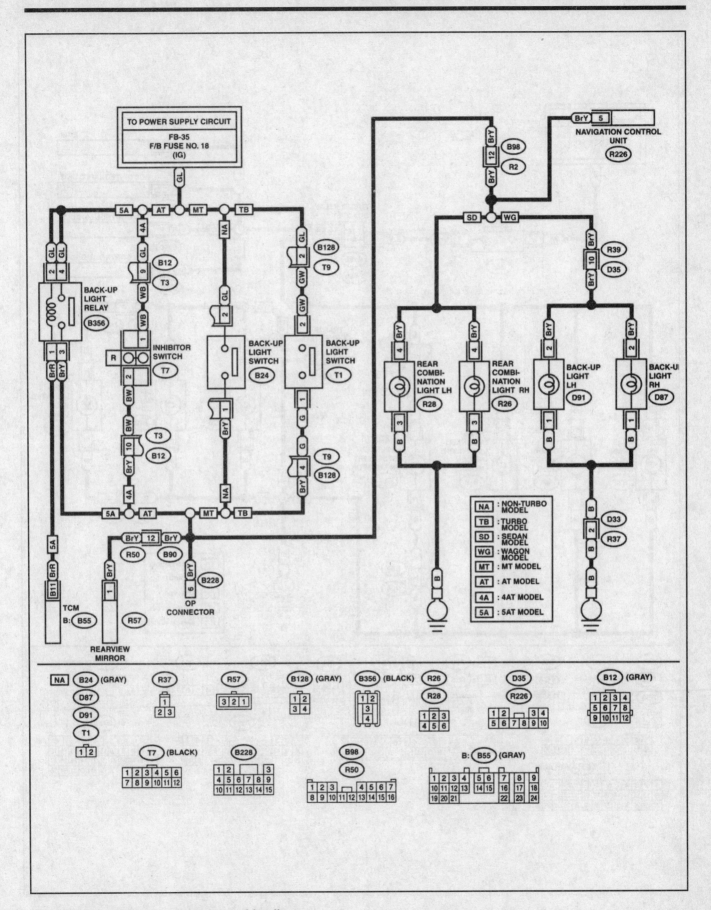

Typical later model back-up light system wiring diagram

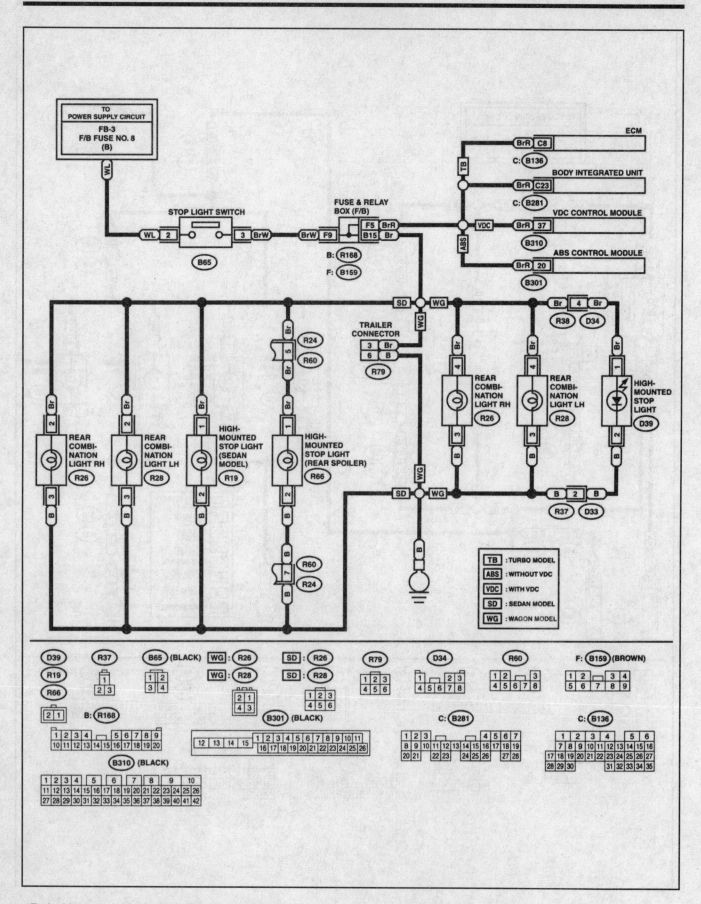

Typical later model brake light system wiring diagram

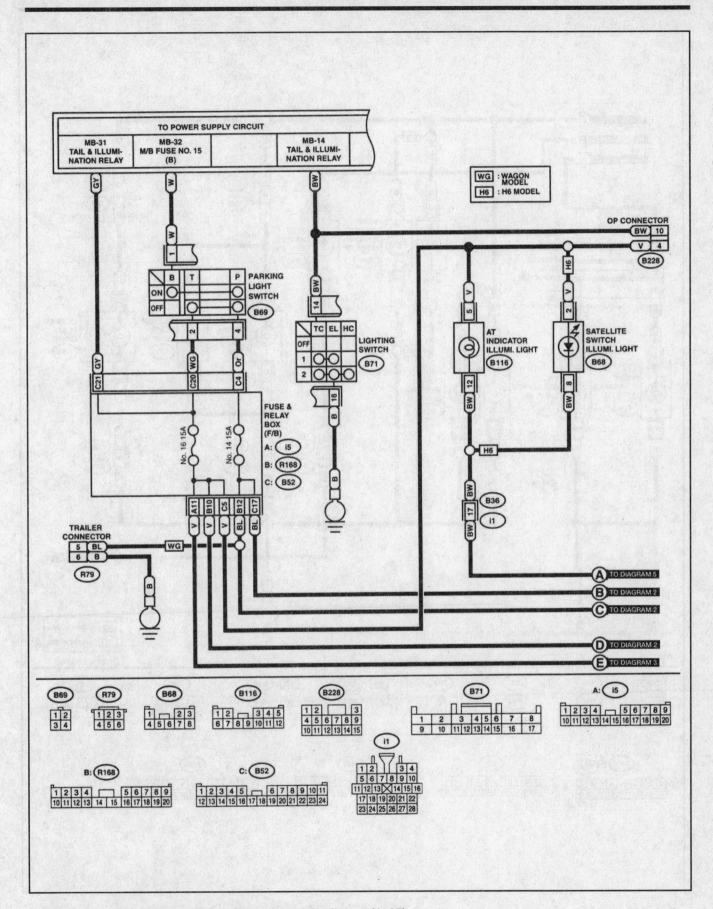

Typical later model clearance light and illumination wiring diagram (1 of 5)

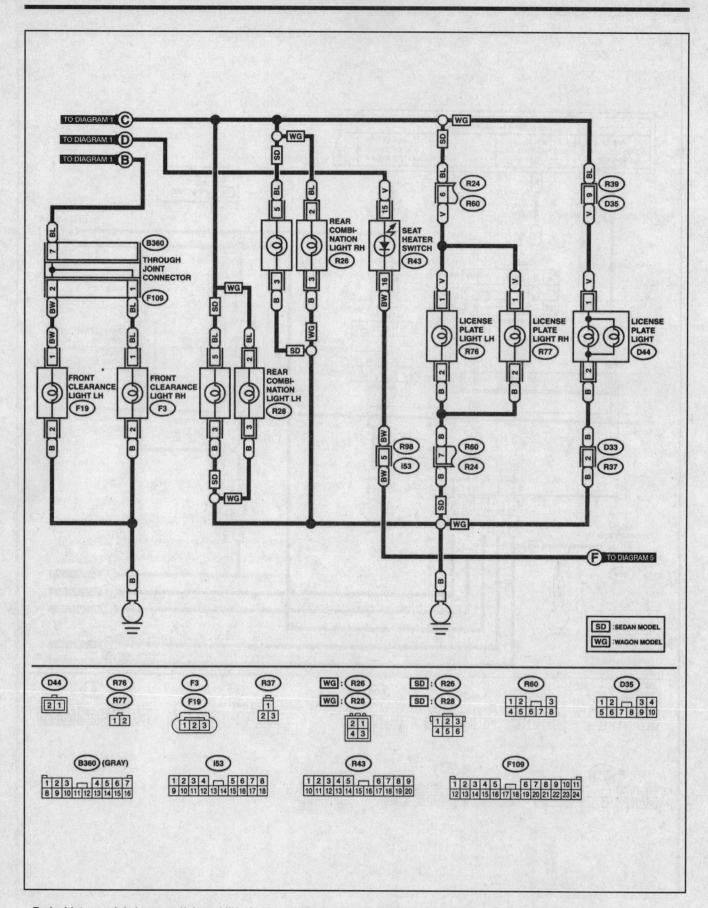

Typical later model clearance light and illumination wiring diagram (2 of 5)

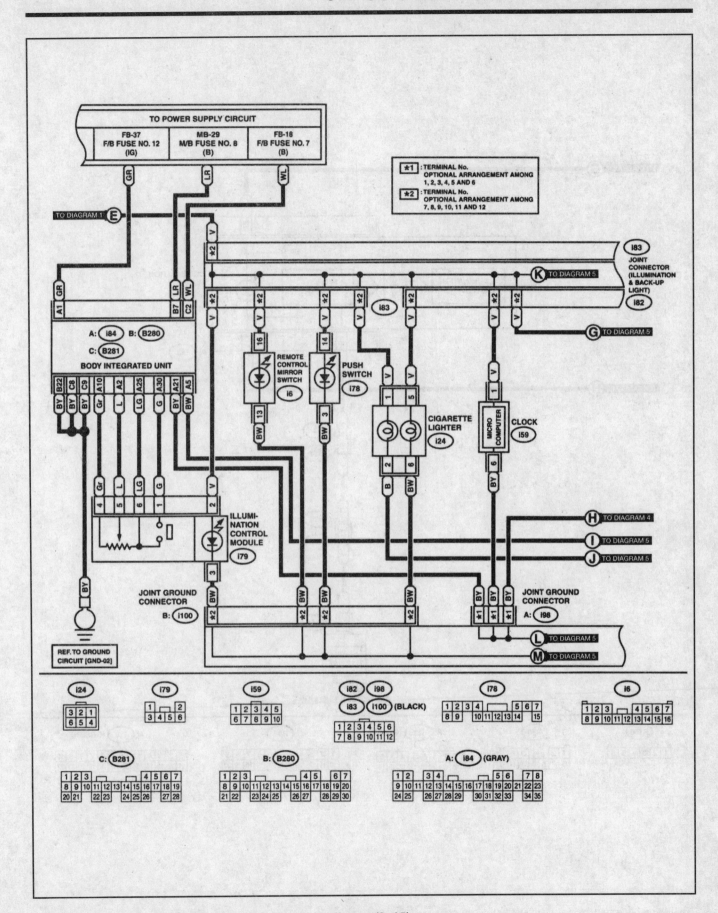

Typical later model clearance light and illumination wiring diagram (3 of 5)

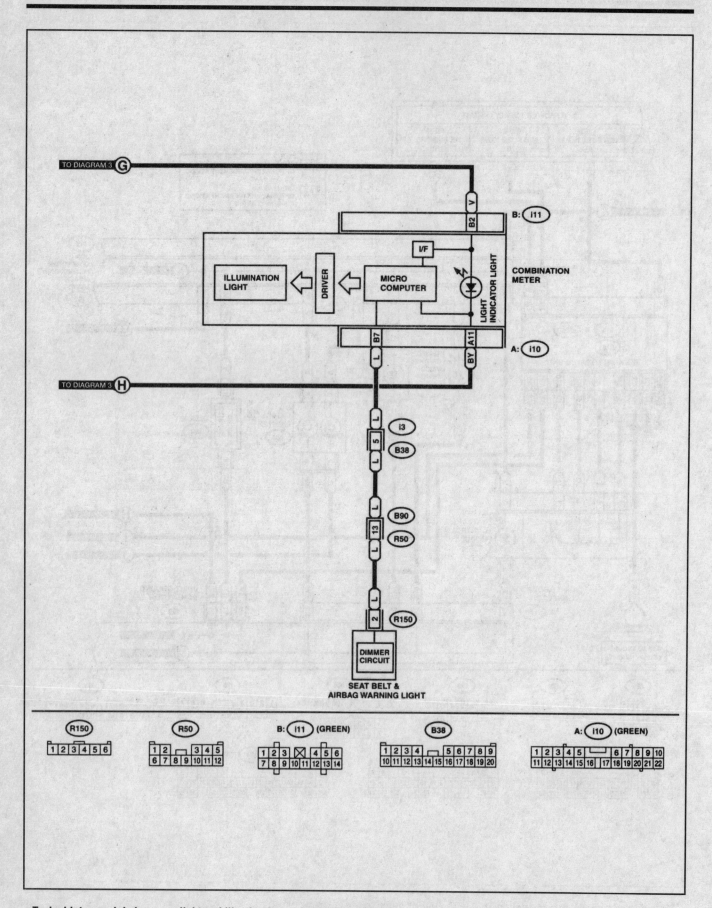

Typical later model clearance light and illumination wiring diagram (4 of 5)

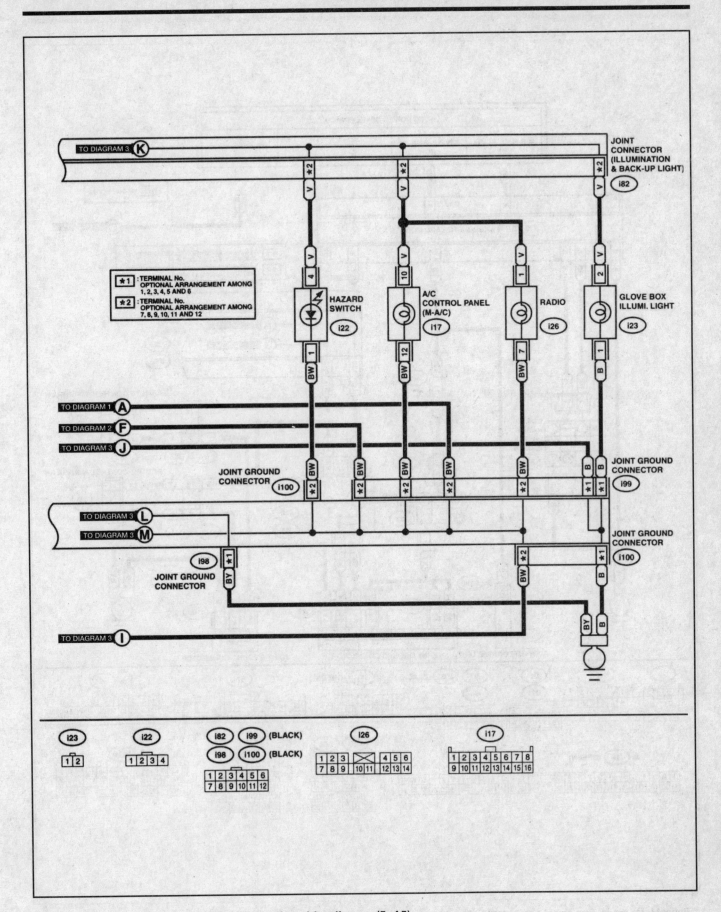

Typical later model clearance light and illumination wiring diagram (5 of 5)

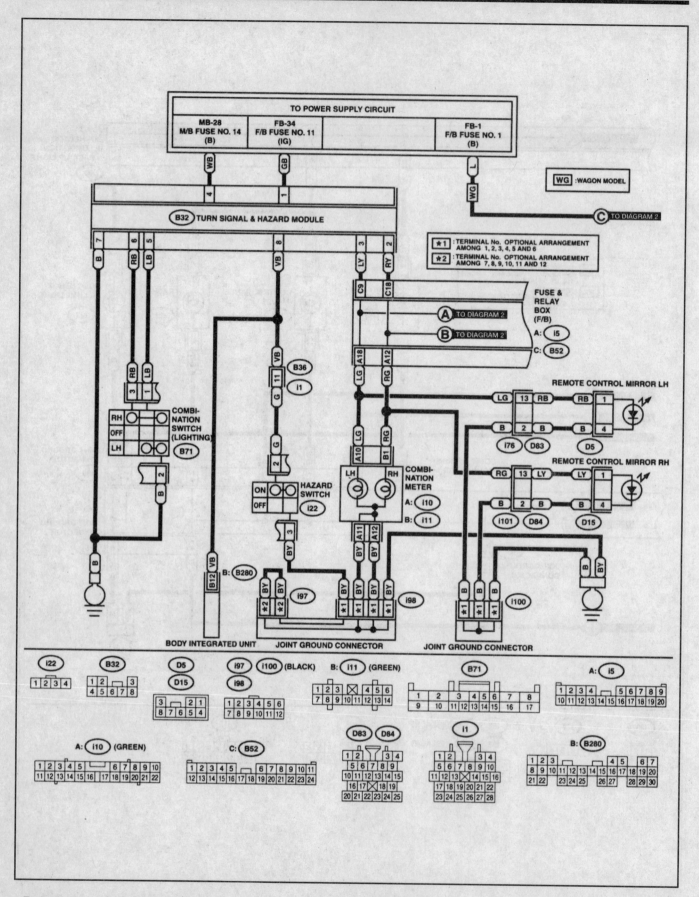

Typical later model turn signal and hazard light system wiring diagram (1 of 2)

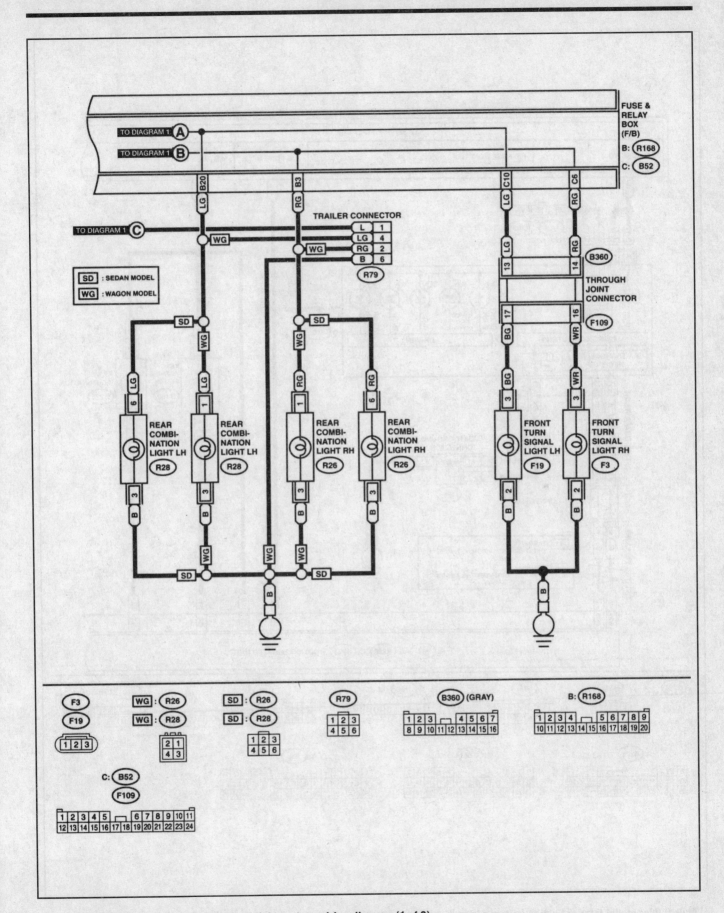

Typical later model turn signal and hazard light system wiring diagram (1 of 2)

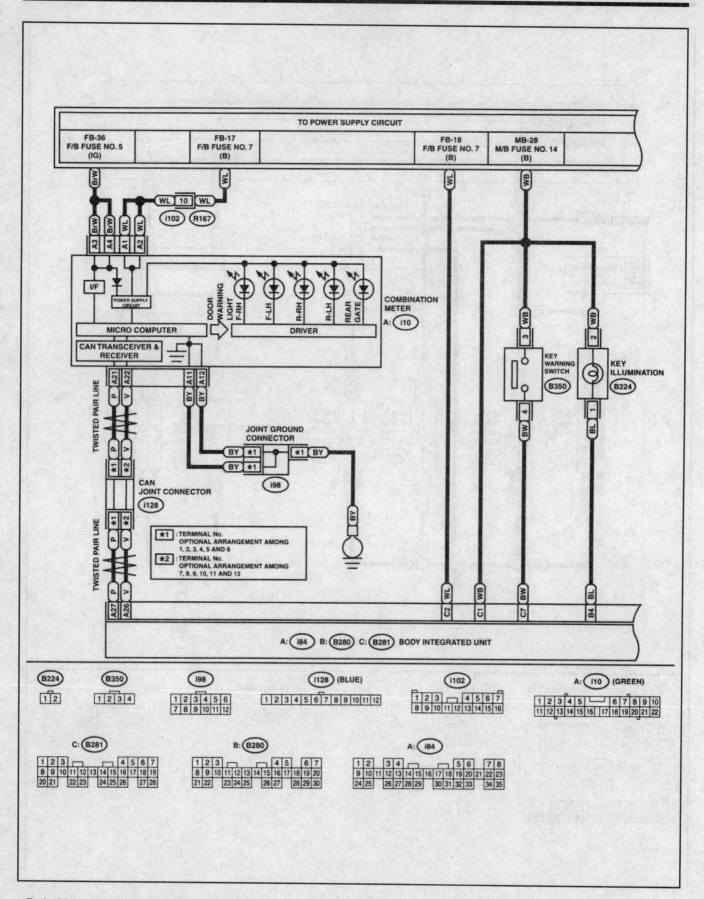

Typical later model interior lighting system wiring diagram (1 of 4)

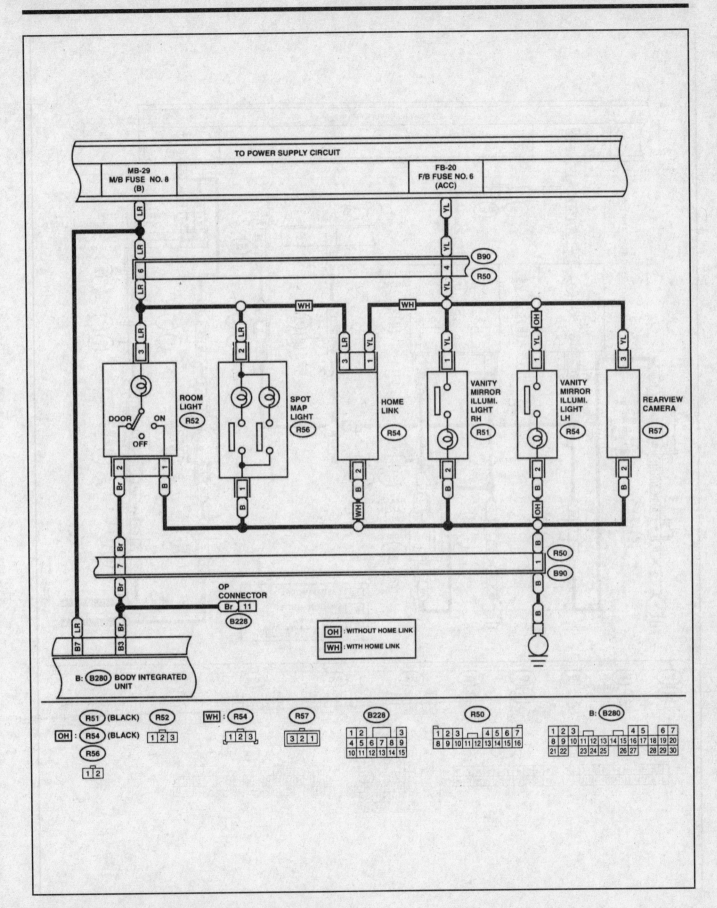

Typical later model interior lighting system wiring diagram (2 of 4)

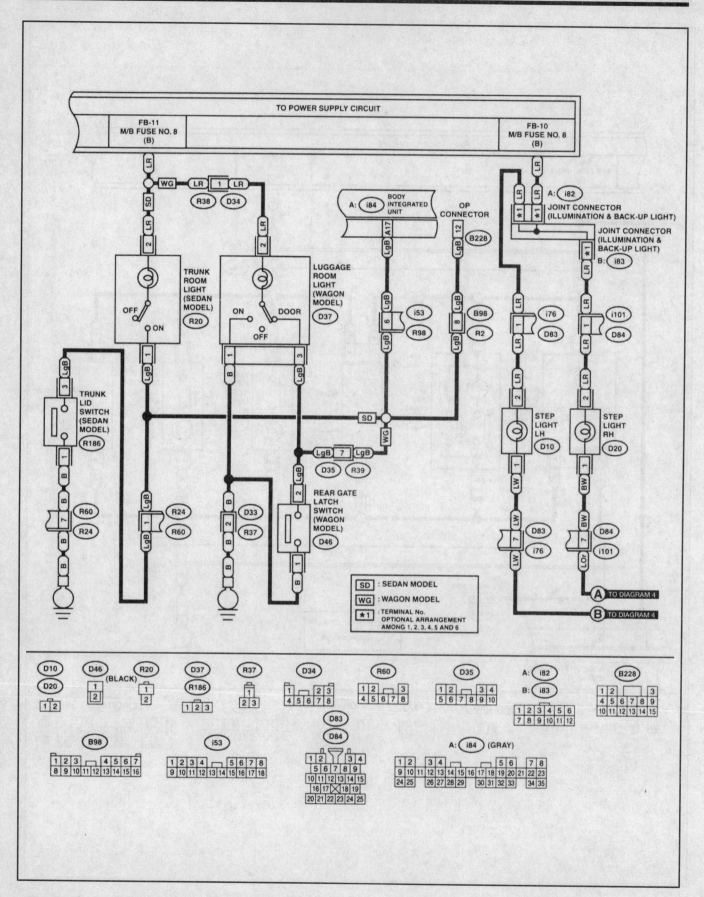

Typical later model interior lighting system wiring diagram (3 of 4)

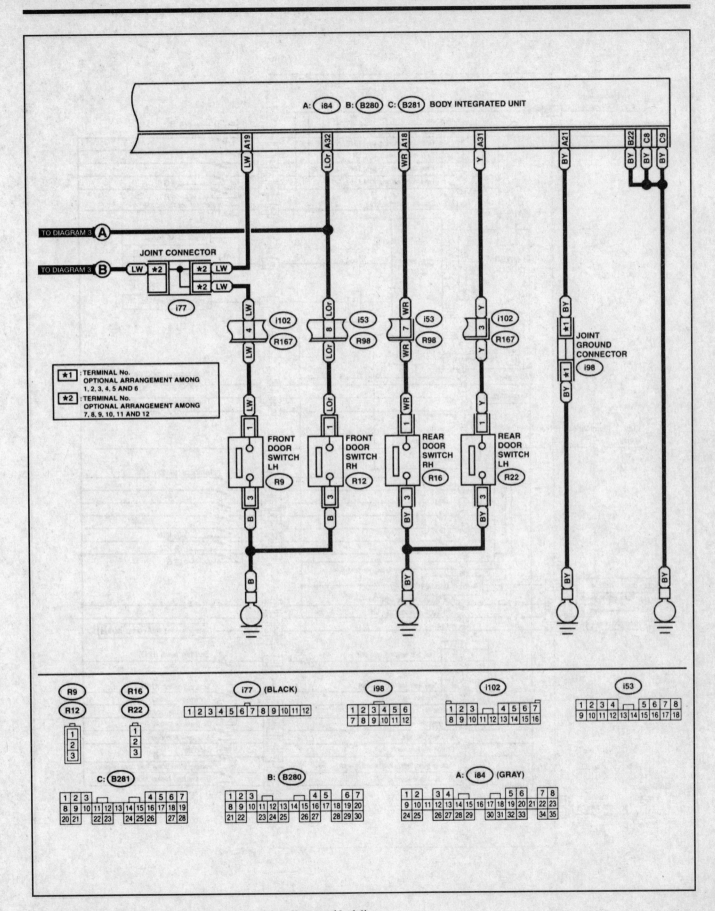

Typical later model interior lighting system wiring diagram (4 of 4)

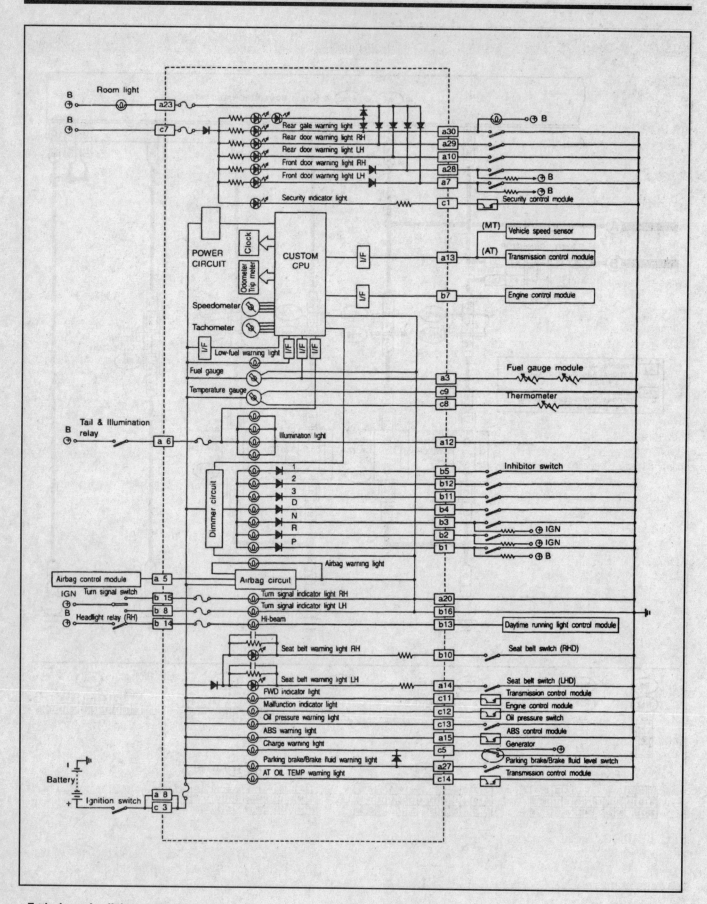

Typical warning light system wiring diagram

GLOSSARY

AIR/FUEL RATIO: The ratio of air-to-gasoline by weight in the fuel mixture drawn into the engine.

AIR INJECTION: One method of reducing harmful exhaust emissions by injecting air into each of the exhaust ports of an engine. The fresh air entering the hot exhaust manifold causes any remaining fuel to be burned before it can exit the tailpipe.

ALTERNATOR: A device used for converting mechanical energy into electrical energy.

AMMETER: An instrument, calibrated in amperes, used to measure the flow of an electrical current in a circuit. Ammeters are always connected in series with the circuit being tested.

AMPERE: The rate of flow of electrical current present when one volt of electrical pressure is applied against one ohm of electrical resistance.

ANALOG COMPUTER: Any microprocessor that uses similar (analogous) electrical signals to make its calculations.

ARMATURE: A laminated, soft iron core wrapped by a wire that converts electrical energy to mechanical energy as in a motor or relay. When rotated in a magnetic field, it changes mechanical energy into electrical energy as in a generator.

ATMOSPHERIC PRESSURE: The pressure on the Earth's surface caused by the weight of the air in the atmosphere. At sea level, this pressure is 14.7 psi at 32°F (101 kPa at 0°C).

ATOMIZATION: The breaking down of a liquid into a fine mist that can be suspended in air.

AXIAL PLAY: Movement parallel to a shaft or bearing bore.

BACKFIRE: The sudden combustion of gases in the intake or exhaust system that results in a loud explosion.

BACKLASH: The clearance or play between two parts, such as meshed gears.

BACKPRESSURE: Restrictions in the exhaust system that slow the exit of exhaust gases from the combustion chamber.

BAKELITE: A heat resistant, plastic insulator material commonly used in printed circuit boards and transistorized components.

BALL BEARING: A bearing made up of hardened inner and outer races between which hardened steel balls roll.

BALLAST RESISTOR: A resistor in the primary ignition circuit that lowers voltage after the engine is started to reduce wear on ignition components.

BEARING: A friction reducing, supportive device usually located between a stationary part and a moving part.

BIMETAL TEMPERATURE SENSOR: Any sensor or switch made of two dissimilar types of metal that bend when heated or cooled due to the different expansion rates of the alloys. These types of sensors usually function as an on/off switch.

BLOWBY: Combustion gases, composed of water vapor and unburned fuel, that leak past the piston rings into the crankcase during normal engine operation. These gases are removed by the PCV system to prevent the buildup of harmful acids in the crankcase.

BRAKE PAD: A brake shoe and lining assembly used with disc brakes.

BRAKE SHOE: The backing for the brake lining. The term is, however, usually applied to the assembly of the brake backing and lining.

BUSHING: A liner, usually removable, for a bearing; an anti-friction liner used in place of a bearing.

CALIPER: A hydraulically activated device in a disc brake system, which is mounted straddling the brake rotor (disc). The caliper contains at least one piston and two brake pads. Hydraulic pressure on the piston(s) forces the pads against the rotor.

CAMSHAFT: A shaft in the engine on which are the lobes (cams) which operate the valves. The camshaft is driven by the crankshaft, via a belt, chain or gears, at one half the crankshaft speed.

CAPACITOR: A device which stores an electrical charge.

CARBON MONOXIDE (CO): A colorless, odorless gas given off as a normal byproduct of combustion. It is poisonous and extremely dangerous in confined areas, building up slowly to toxic levels without warning if adequate ventilation is not available.

CARBURETOR: A device, usually mounted on the intake manifold of an engine, which mixes the air and fuel in the proper proportion to allow even combustion.

CATALYTIC CONVERTER: A device installed in the exhaust system, like a muffler, that converts harmful byproducts of combustion into carbon dioxide and water vapor by means of a heat-producing chemical reaction.

CENTRIFUGAL ADVANCE: A mechanical method of advancing the spark timing by using flyweights in the distributor that react to centrifugal force generated by the distributor shaft rotation.

CHECK VALVE: Any one-way valve installed to permit the flow of air, fuel or vacuum in one direction only.

CHOKE: A device, usually a moveable valve, placed in the intake path of a carburetor to restrict the flow of air.

CIRCUIT: Any unbroken path through which an electrical current can flow. Also used to describe fuel flow in some instances.

CIRCUIT BREAKER: A switch which protects an electrical circuit from overload by opening the circuit when the current flow exceeds a predetermined level. Some circuit breakers must be reset manually, while most reset automatically.

COIL (IGNITION): A transformer in the ignition circuit which steps up the voltage provided to the spark plugs.

COMBINATION MANIFOLD: An assembly which includes both the intake and exhaust manifolds in one casting.

COMBINATION VALVE: A device used in some fuel systems that routes fuel vapors to a charcoal storage canister instead of venting them into the atmosphere. The valve relieves fuel tank pressure and allows fresh air into the tank as the fuel level drops to prevent a vapor lock situation.

COMPRESSION RATIO: The comparison of the total volume of the cylinder and combustion chamber with the piston at BDC and the piston at TDC.

CONDENSER: 1. An electrical device which acts to store an electrical charge, preventing voltage surges. 2. A radiator-like device in the air conditioning system in which refrigerant gas condenses into a liquid, giving off heat.

CONDUCTOR: Any material through which an electrical current can be transmitted easily.

CONTINUITY: Continuous or complete circuit. Can be checked with an ohmmeter.

COUNTERSHAFT: An intermediate shaft which is rotated by a mainshaft and transmits, in turn, that rotation to a working part.

CRANKCASE: The lower part of an engine in which the crankshaft and related parts operate.

CRANKSHAFT: The main driving shaft of an engine which receives reciprocating motion from the pistons and converts it to rotary motion.

CYLINDER: In an engine, the round hole in the engine block in which the piston(s) ride.

CYLINDER BLOCK: The main structural member of an engine in which is found the cylinders, crankshaft and other principal parts.

CYLINDER HEAD: The detachable portion of the engine, usually fastened to the top of the cylinder block and containing all or most of the combustion chambers. On overhead valve engines, it contains the valves and their operating parts. On overhead cam engines, it contains the camshaft as well.

DEAD CENTER: The extreme top or bottom of the piston stroke.

DETONATION: An unwanted explosion of the air/fuel mixture in the combustion chamber caused by excess heat and compression, advanced timing, or an overly lean mixture. Also referred to as "ping".

DIAPHRAGM: A thin, flexible wall separating two cavities, such as in a vacuum advance unit.

DIESELING: A condition in which hot spots in the combustion chamber cause the engine to run on after the key is turned off.

DIFFERENTIAL: A geared assembly which allows the transmission of motion between drive axles, giving one axle the ability to turn faster than the other.

DIODE: An electrical device that will allow current to flow in one direction only.

DISC BRAKE: A hydraulic braking assembly consisting of a brake disc, or rotor, mounted on an axle, and a caliper assembly containing, usually two brake pads which are activated by hydraulic pressure. The pads are forced against the sides of the disc, creating friction which slows the vehicle.

DISTRIBUTOR: A mechanically driven device on an engine which is responsible for electrically firing the spark plug at a predetermined point of the piston stroke.

DOWEL PIN: A pin, inserted in mating holes in two different parts allowing those parts to maintain a fixed relationship.

DRUM BRAKE: A braking system which consists of two brake shoes and one or two wheel cylinders, mounted on a fixed backing plate, and a brake drum, mounted on an axle, which revolves around the assembly.

DWELL: The rate, measured in degrees of shaft rotation, at which an electrical circuit cycles on and off.

ELECTRONIC CONTROL UNIT (ECU): Ignition module, module, amplifier or igniter. See Module for definition.

ELECTRONIC IGNITION: A system in which the timing and firing of the spark plugs is controlled by an electronic control unit, usually called a module. These systems have no points or condenser.

END-PLAY: The measured amount of axial movement in a shaft.

ENGINE: A device that converts heat into mechanical energy.

EXHAUST MANIFOLD: A set of cast passages or pipes which conduct exhaust gases from the engine.

FEELER GAUGE: A blade, usually metal, or precisely predetermined thickness, used to measure the clearance between two parts.

FIRING ORDER: The order in which combustion occurs in the cylinders of an engine. Also the order in which spark is distributed to the plugs by the distributor.

FLOODING: The presence of too much fuel in the intake manifold and combustion chamber which prevents the air/fuel mixture from firing, thereby causing a no-start situation.

FLYWHEEL: A disc shaped part bolted to the rear end of the crankshaft. Around the outer perimeter is affixed the ring gear. The starter drive engages the ring gear, turning the flywheel, which rotates the crankshaft, imparting the initial starting motion to the engine.

FOOT POUND (ft. lbs. or sometimes, ft.lb.): The amount of energy or work needed to raise an item weighing one pound, a distance of one foot.

FUSE: A protective device in a circuit which prevents circuit overload by breaking the circuit when a specific amperage is present. The device is constructed around a strip or wire of a lower amperage rating than the circuit it is designed to protect. When an amperage higher than that stamped on the fuse is present in the circuit, the strip or wire melts, opening the circuit.

GEAR RATIO: The ratio between the number of teeth on meshing gears.

GENERATOR: A device which converts mechanical energy into electrical energy.

HEAT RANGE: The measure of a spark plug's ability to dissipate heat from its firing end. The higher the heat range, the hotter the plug fires.

HUB: The center part of a wheel or gear.

HYDROCARBON (HC): Any chemical compound made up of hydrogen and carbon. A major pollutant formed by the engine as a byproduct of combustion.

HYDROMETER: An instrument used to measure the specific gravity of a solution.

INCH POUND (inch lbs.; sometimes in.lb. or in. lbs.): One twelfth of a foot pound.

INDUCTION: A means of transferring electrical energy in the form of a magnetic field. Principle used in the ignition coil to increase voltage.

INJECTOR: A device which receives metered fuel under relatively low pressure and is activated to inject the fuel into the engine under relatively high pressure at a predetermined time.

INPUT SHAFT: The shaft to which torque is applied, usually carrying the driving gear or gears.

INTAKE MANIFOLD: A casting of passages or pipes used to conduct air or a fuel/air mixture to the cylinders.

JOURNAL: The bearing surface within which a shaft operates.

KEY: A small block usually fitted in a notch between a shaft and a hub to prevent slippage of the two parts.

MANIFOLD: A casting of passages or set of pipes which connect the cylinders to an inlet or outlet source.

MANIFOLD VACUUM: Low pressure in an engine intake manifold formed just below the throttle plates. Manifold vacuum is highest at idle and drops under acceleration.

MASTER CYLINDER: The primary fluid pressurizing device in a hydraulic system. In automotive use, it is found in brake and hydraulic clutch systems and is pedal activated, either directly or, in a power brake system, through the power booster.

MODULE: Electronic control unit, amplifier or igniter of solid state or integrated design which controls the current flow in the ignition primary circuit based on input from the pick-up coil. When the module opens the primary circuit, high secondary voltage is induced in the coil.

NEEDLE BEARING: A bearing which consists of a number (usually a large number) of long, thin rollers.

OHM: (Ω) The unit used to measure the resistance of conductor-to-electrical flow. One ohm is the amount of resistance that limits current flow to one ampere in a circuit with one volt of pressure.

OHMMETER: An instrument used for measuring the resistance, in ohms, in an electrical circuit.

OUTPUT SHAFT: The shaft which transmits torque from a device, such as a transmission.

OVERDRIVE: A gear assembly which produces more shaft revolutions than that transmitted to it.

OVERHEAD CAMSHAFT (OHC): An engine configuration in which the camshaft is mounted on top of the cylinder head and operates the valve either directly or by means of rocker arms.

OVERHEAD VALVE (OHV): An engine configuration in which all of the valves are located in the cylinder head and the camshaft is located in the cylinder block. The camshaft operates the valves via lifters and pushrods.

OXIDES OF NITROGEN (NOx): Chemical compounds of nitrogen produced as a byproduct of combustion. They combine with hydrocarbons to produce smog.

OXYGEN SENSOR: Use with the feedback system to sense the presence of oxygen in the exhaust gas and signal the computer which can reference the voltage signal to an air/fuel ratio.

PINION: The smaller of two meshing gears.

PISTON RING: An open-ended ring with fits into a groove on the outer diameter of the piston. Its chief function is to form a seal between the piston and cylinder wall. Most automotive pistons have three rings: two for compression sealing; one for oil sealing.

PRELOAD: A predetermined load placed on a bearing during assembly or by adjustment.

PRIMARY CIRCUIT: the low voltage side of the ignition system which consists of the ignition switch, ballast resistor or resistance wire, bypass, coil, electronic control unit and pick-up coil as well as the connecting wires and harnesses.

PRESS FIT: The mating of two parts under pressure, due to the inner diameter of one being smaller than the outer diameter of the other, or vice versa; an interference fit.

RACE: The surface on the inner or outer ring of a bearing on which the balls, needles or rollers move.

REGULATOR: A device which maintains the amperage and/or voltage levels of a circuit at predetermined values.

RELAY: A switch which automatically opens and/or closes a circuit.

RESISTANCE: The opposition to the flow of current through a circuit or electrical device, and is measured in ohms. Resistance is equal to the voltage divided by the amperage.

RESISTOR: A device, usually made of wire, which offers a preset amount of resistance in an electrical circuit.

RING GEAR: The name given to a ring-shaped gear attached to a differential case, or affixed to a flywheel or as part of a planetary gear set.

ROLLER BEARING: A bearing made up of hardened inner and outer races between which hardened steel rollers move.

ROTOR: 1. The disc-shaped part of a disc brake assembly, upon which the brake pads bear; also called, brake disc. 2. The device mounted atop the distributor shaft, which passes current to the distributor cap tower contacts.

SECONDARY CIRCUIT: The high voltage side of the ignition system, usually above 20,000 volts. The secondary includes the ignition coil, coil wire, distributor cap and rotor, spark plug wires and spark plugs.

SENDING UNIT: A mechanical, electrical, hydraulic or electromagnetic device which transmits information to a gauge.

SENSOR: Any device designed to measure engine operating conditions or ambient pressures and temperatures. Usually electronic in nature and designed to send a voltage signal to an on-board computer, some sensors may operate as a simple on/off switch or they may provide a variable voltage signal (like a potentiometer) as conditions or measured parameters change.

SHIM: Spacers of precise, predetermined thickness used between parts to establish a proper working relationship.

SLAVE CYLINDER: In automotive use, a device in the hydraulic clutch system which is activated by hydraulic force, disengaging the clutch.

SOLENOID: A coil used to produce a magnetic field, the effect of which is to produce work.

SPARK PLUG: A device screwed into the combustion chamber of a spark ignition engine. The basic construction is a conductive core inside of a ceramic insulator, mounted in an outer conductive base. An electrical charge from the spark plug wire travels along the conductive core and jumps a preset air gap to a grounding point or points at the end of the conductive base. The resultant spark ignites the fuel/air mixture in the combustion chamber.

SPLINES: Ridges machined or cast onto the outer diameter of a shaft or inner diameter of a bore to enable parts to mate without rotation.

TACHOMETER: A device used to measure the rotary speed of an engine, shaft, gear, etc., usually in rotations per minute.

THERMOSTAT: A valve, located in the cooling system of an engine, which is closed when cold and opens gradually in response to engine heating, controlling the temperature of the coolant and rate of coolant flow.

TOP DEAD CENTER (TDC): The point at which the piston reaches the top of its travel on the compression stroke.

TORQUE: The twisting force applied to an object.

TORQUE CONVERTER: A turbine used to transmit power from a driving member to a driven member via hydraulic action, providing changes in drive ratio and torque. In automotive use, it links the driveplate at the rear of the engine to the automatic transmission.

TRANSDUCER: A device used to change a force into an electrical signal.

TRANSISTOR: A semi-conductor component which can be actuated by a small voltage to perform an electrical switching function.

TUNE-UP: A regular maintenance function, usually associated with the replacement and adjustment of parts and components in the electrical and fuel systems of a vehicle for the purpose of attaining optimum performance.

TURBOCHARGER: An exhaust driven pump which compresses intake air and forces it into the combustion chambers at higher than atmospheric pressures. The increased air pressure allows more fuel to be burned and results in increased horsepower being produced.

VACUUM ADVANCE: A device which advances the ignition timing in response to increased engine vacuum.

VACUUM GAUGE: An instrument used to measure the presence of vacuum in a chamber.

VALVE: A device which control the pressure, direction of flow or rate of flow of a liquid or gas.

VALVE CLEARANCE: The measured gap between the end of the valve stem and the rocker arm, cam lobe or follower that activates the valve.

VISCOSITY: The rating of a liquid's internal resistance to flow.

VOLTMETER: An instrument used for measuring electrical force in units called volts. Voltmeters are always connected parallel with the circuit being tested.

WHEEL CYLINDER: Found in the automotive drum brake assembly, it is a device, actuated by hydraulic pressure, which, through internal pistons, pushes the brake shoes outward against the drums.

NOTES

MASTER INDEX

A

I

J

K

L

M

O

OIL PAN, REMOVAL AND INSTALLATION, 2A-28

OIL PRESSURE CHECK, 2B-4

OIL PUMP, REMOVAL, INSPECTION AND INSTALLATION, 2A-29

OIL, ENGINE, LEVEL CHECK, 1-8

ON-BOARD DIAGNOSTIC (OBD) SYSTEM AND TROUBLE CODES, 6-2

OUTSIDE MIRRORS, REMOVAL AND INSTALLATION, 11-16

OXYGEN SENSORS, GENERAL INFORMATION AND REPLACEMENT, 6-19

P

PADS, DISC BRAKE, REPLACEMENT, 9-2

PARKING BRAKE
cable(s), adjustment, removal and installation, 9-14
shoes (models with rear disc brakes), replacement, 9-17

PARTS, REPLACEMENT, BUYING, 0-10

PEDAL, BRAKE, ADJUSTMENT, 9-22

PILOT BEARING, INSPECTION AND REPLACEMENT, 8-8

PINION SEAL, REPLACEMENT, 8-12

PISTON RINGS, INSTALLATION, 2B-17

PISTONS
installation, 2B-20
removal, 2B-10

POSITIVE CRANKCASE VENTILATION (PCV) SYSTEM, DESCRIPTION AND COMPONENT REPLACEMENT, 6-37

POWER BRAKE BOOSTER, CHECK, REMOVAL AND INSTALLATION, 9-16

POWER DOOR LOCK SYSTEM, GENERAL INFORMATION, 12-29

POWER STEERING
fluid level check, 1-10
fluid type, 1-33
pump, removal and installation, 10-20
system, bleeding, 10-23

POWER STEERING PRESSURE (PSP) SWITCH, REPLACEMENT, 6-22

POWER WINDOW SYSTEM, GENERAL INFORMATION, 12-28

POWERTRAIN CONTROL MODULE (PCM), REPLACEMENT, 6-25

PROPORTIONING VALVE, REPLACEMENT, 9-13

R

RADIATOR GRILLE, REMOVAL AND INSTALLATION, 11-8

RADIATOR, COOLANT RESERVOIR AND COOLANT FILLER TANK, REMOVAL AND INSTALLATION, 3-6

RADIO AND SPEAKERS, REMOVAL AND INSTALLATION, 12-10

REAR DIFFERENTIAL
lubricant level check, 1-12
pinion seal, replacement, 8-12
side gear seals, replacement, 8-21
removal and installation, 8-21

REAR KNUCKLE/HUB ASSEMBLY, REMOVAL AND INSTALLATION, 10-15

REAR MAIN OIL SEAL, REPLACEMENT, 2A-31

REAR SUSPENSION LINKS, REMOVAL AND INSTALLATION, 10-13

REAR WINDOW DEFOGGER, CHECK AND REPAIR, 12-15

RECALL INFORMATION, 0-8

RECEIVER-DRIER, AIR CONDITIONING, REMOVAL AND INSTALLATION, 3-19

RECOMMENDED LUBRICANTS AND FLUIDS, 1-33

REGULATOR AND MOTOR, WINDOW, REMOVAL AND INSTALLATION, 11-16

RELAYS, GENERAL INFORMATION AND TESTING, 12-5

RELEASE BEARING, CLUTCH, REMOVAL, INSPECTION AND INSTALLATION, 8-7

RELEASE CYLINDER, CLUTCH, REMOVAL AND INSTALLATION, 8-4

REPAIR OPERATIONS POSSIBLE WITH THE ENGINE IN THE VEHICLE, 2A-2

REPLACEMENT PARTS, BUYING, 0-10

ROTOR, BRAKE, INSPECTION, REMOVAL AND INSTALLATION, 9-7

ROUTINE MAINTENANCE SCHEDULE, 1-6

ROUTINE MAINTENANCE, 1-1 THROUGH 1-36